Advances in Human-Computer Interaction

Edited by
Shane Pinder

Advances in Human-Computer Interaction
Edited by Shane Pinder

Republished by InTech
Janeza Trdine 9, 51000 Rijeka, Croatia

Additional hard copies can be obtained from orders@intechopen.com

Advances in Human-Computer Interaction, Edited by Shane Pinder
p. cm.
ISBN 978-953-7619-15-2

For EU product safety concerns:
IN TECH d.o.o., Prolaz Marije Krucifikse Kozulić 3, 51000 Rijeka, Croatia,
info@intechopen.com or visit our website at intechopen.com.

Meet the editor

Shane Pinder holds a BSc in Mechanical Engineering from the Royal Military College of Canada and an MSc in Aerospace Engineering from Carleton University. His doctoral studies involved the development of a GPSbased takeoff performance monitor at the University of Saskatchewan. He is a former Lieutenant in the Canadian Forces.

Preface

It is an impossible task to bring together, under a single cover, the many facets of human-computer interaction. After all, we have come a long way in the past several decades, to a point where we consider not only what may be intuitive to the designer, but rather the user, the environment, and the intent of our efforts. No single person can claim expertise across the entire field, which now brings together professions that formerly did not share the same vocabulary and still, in many cases, do not share the same philosophy. It is only appropriate that the study of human-machine interaction reveals a greater complexity within human-to-human interaction.

In these 34 chapters, we survey the broad disciplines that loosely inhabit the study and practice of human-computer interaction. Our authors are passionate advocates of innovative applications, novel approaches, and modern advances in this exciting and developing field. It is our wish that the reader consider not only what our authors have written and the experimentation they have described, but also the examples they have set. This book brings together the work of experts around the world who have used their expertise to overcome barriers in language, culture, and abilities, to name only a few challenges.

The editors would like to thank the authors, who have committed so much effort to the publication of this work.

Editor

Shane Pinder
Director of Research
Defiant Engineering
Canada
shane.pinder@defy.ca

Contents

Preface VII

1. Technology Enabled Learning Worlds 001
Ray Adams and Andrina Granić

2. Current Challenges and Applications for Adaptive User Interfaces 013
Victor Alvarez-Cortes, Víctor H. Zárate, Jorge A. Ramírez Uresti and Benjamin E. Zayas

3. Towards a Reference Architecture for Context-Aware Services 031
Axel Bürkle, Wilmuth Müller and Uwe Pfirrmann

4. A Robust Hand Recognition In Varying Illumination 053
Yoo-Joo Choi, Je-Sung Lee and We-Duke Cho

5. How Do Programmers Think? 071
Anthony Cox and Maryanne Fisher

6. Experiential Design: Findings from Designing Engaging Interactive Environments 085
Peter Dalsgaard

7. Evaluation of Human Cognitive Characteristics in Interaction with Computer 107
Nebojša Đorđević and Dejan Rančić

8. Audio Interfaces for Improved Accessibility 121
Carlos Duarte and Luís Carriço

9. Intelligent Interfaces for Technology-Enhanced Learning 143
Andrina Granić

10. Design of Text Comprehension Activities with RETUDISAuth 161
Grammatiki Tsaganou and Maria Grigoriadou

11. Computer-based Cognitive and Socio-emotional Training in Psychopathology 173
Ouriel Grynszpan

12. Facial Expression Recognition as an Implicit Customers' Feedback 189
Zolidah Kasiran, Saadiah Yahya (Dr) and Zaidah Ibrahim

13. Natural Interaction Framework for Navigation Systems on Mobile Devices 199
Ceren Kayalar and Selim Balcisoy

14. Review of Human-Computer Interaction Issues in Image Retrieval 215
Mohammed Lamine Kherfi

15. Smart SoftPhone Device for Networked Audio-Visual QoS/QoE Discovery & Measurement 241
Jinsul Kim

16. Sonification System of Maps for Blind 263
Gintautas Daunys and Vidas Lauruska

17. Advancing the Multidisciplinary Nature of HCI in an Undergraduate Course 273
Cynthia Y. Lester

18. Simple Guidelines for Testing VR Applications 289
Livatino Salvatore and Koeffel Christina

19. Mobile Device Interaction in Ubiquitous Computing 311
Thorsten Mahler and Michael Weber

20. Integrating Software Engineering and Usability Engineering 331
Karsten Nebe, Dirk Zimmermann and Volker Paelke

21. Automated Methods for Webpage Usability & Accessibility Evaluations 351
Hidehiko Okada and Ryosuke Fujioka

22. Emotion Recognition via Continuous Mandarin Speech 365
Tsang-Long Pao, Jun-Heng Yeh and Yu-Te Chen

23. Nomad Devices Adaptation for Offering Computer Accessible Services 385
L. Pastor-Sanz, M. F. Cabrera-Umpiérrez, J. L. Villalar, C. Vera-Munoz, M. T. Arredondo, A. Bekiaris andC. Hipp

24. Rewriting Context and Analysis: Bringing Anthropology into HCI Research 397
Minna Räsänen and James M. Nyce

25. Interface Design of Location-Based Services 415
Chris Kuo-Wei Su and Li-Kai Chen

26. Brain-CAVE Interface Based on Steady-State Visual Evoked Potential 437
Hideaki Touyama

27. Multimodal Accessibility of Documents 451
Georgios Kouroupetroglou and Dimitrios Tsonos

28. The Method of Interactive Reduction of Threat of Isolation in the Contemporary Human Environment 471
Teresa Musioł and Katarzyna Ujma-Wąsowicz

29. Physical Selection as Tangible User Interface 499
Pasi Välkkynen

30. Geometry Issues of Gaze Estimation 513
Arantxa Villanueva, Juan J. Cerrolaza and Rafael Cabeza

31. Investigation of a Distance Presentation Method using Speech Audio Navigation for the Blind or Visually Impaired 535
Chikamune Wada

32. The Three-Dimensional User Interface 543
Hou Wenjun

33. User Needs for Mobility Improvement for People with Functional Limitations 575
Marion Wiethoff, Sacha Sommer, Sari Valjakka, Karel van Isacker, Dionisis Kehagias and Dimitrios Tzovaras

34. Recognizing Facial Expressions Using Model-based Image Interpretation 587
Matthias Wimmer, Zahid Riaz, Christoph Mayer and Bernd Radig

1

Technology Enabled Learning Worlds

Ray Adams[1] and Andrina Granić[2]
[1]*CIRCUA, School of Computing Science, Middlesex University*
[2]*Faculty of Science, University of Split*
[1]*United Kingdom,* [2]*Croatia*

1. Introduction

We live in a dramatically evolving knowledge society that is founded on the assumption of equal access to relevant skills and technology-dispensed knowledge. If so, then effective inclusion in society requires powerful new learning resources. In this newer social context, organisations may increasingly become learning organisations and employees may increasingly become knowledge workers. At the same time, new levels of accessibility are equally important to motivate the identification and removal of new barriers to inclusion created inadvertently by new technologies. On this basis, our purpose here is to identify and evaluate some of the key issues that are essential to the new types of learning that will be needed by knowledge workers in learning organisations. To do so, we combine expertise in cognitive science and computing science.

First, we present and evaluate three different approaches to human learning supported by technology:

- *definition of learning resources;* learning resources are defined as information that is stored in a variety of media that supports learning, including materials for example in print, video and software formats,
- *definition of (technology-enhanced) learning environments;* learning environments, as places arranged to enhance the learning experience, are defined on an interdisciplinary basis comprising three essential components: pedagogical functions, appropriate technologies and social organization of education and
- *definition of learning worlds;* learning worlds are partially immersive, virtual milieu that deploy smart and adaptive teaching and learning technologies to create novel experiences based on sound pedagogical and psychological principles.

Second, we present and evaluate some key issues that include:

- The changing role of *digital libraries* to meet the increasing thirst for knowledge.
- How can *learning environments* be designed and evaluated for accessibility, usability and ambient smartness?
- The design and development of more effective, *technology-enhanced learning environments.*
- How can ubiquitous learning environments be developed?
- What new assessment methods must be developed to guide the design and development of such systems?

- How can new technologies such as virtual reality applications and brain computer interfaces be applied to effective human learning?

We show how a simple but innovative synthesis of key disciplines such as computing science and cognitive science, can be deployed in combination with such topics as ergonomics, e-learning, pedagogy, cognitive psychology, interactive system design, neuropsychology etc to create new learning worlds that boost human learning to meet the demands of the 21st century.

2. A framework for different approaches to human learning supported by technology

There are at least three different perspectives on human learning, namely learning resources, technology-enhanced learning environments and learning worlds as defined in turn below. As our primary focus is on *human* learning, our treatment of learning resources, technology-enhanced learning environments and learning worlds etc will also need to have a focus on the human. To do so, we introduce a simple and convenient structure that may help you to see the key issues and what needs to be done with them in the dual context of human learning and e-learning technologies. Only the relevant details will be presented here, but you may wish to follow up any issues of interest or where you need greater clarity, by referring to our reference list.

At a simple but effective level, a human technology system can be captured by a consideration of:

- A user model (a depiction of the requirements, preferences, strengths and weaknesses of the intended users / students)
- A technological model (a description of the key parameters of the technological platforms to be used, permanent, default or current)
- A context-of-use model (a model that captures the relevant aspects of the context or contexts for which the system is intended; namely software such as the operating system, the physical context such as at home or in a street, the psychological context such as working as part of a small or large team and the social / cultural context such as a Western European country or a South American location).
- A task model (a model that captures the nature and features of the task or tasks that the system is intended to support, such as a traveller dealing with emails or a tourist storing and displaying photographs). Here, of course, we are particularly looking at the subset of tasks that are to do with the human acquisition of new knowledge and skills. Also, in this sub-context, the user is more likely to be referred to as a student, learner etc.

To make the above structure a little more concrete, we now present a little more of a typical user model structure. To do so, we have chosen our own user model structure, not because it is the best, but because it is both typical and relatively simple.

As you will see from the diagram (see Fig. 1), Simplex Two is a theory that seeks to capture the key aspects of human information processing by identifying nine components of human cognition and related processes. These nine components have been validated in two recently published studies (Adams, 2007) that show that Simplex Two captures many, if not all, vital, global aspects of human psychology. Readers should consult this flagship paper if they want to consider the justification and natures of each component or module. The theory is set out below as a flow diagram in which the human is depicted, in part, as a processor of information. Information enters the system through the senses into a sensory / perceptual system or into a feedback system and then into the Executive Function. This Executive Function orchestrates all conscious activities of the system and the eight other modules. However, each module possesses both memory and the capacity to process and transform any information that it holds. The Executive Function creates the necessary coordination required between the different functions so that a specific task can be carried out.

Each module of Simplex Two captures an important aspect of the human learner's psychology. Each module has been selected for three reasons. First, it is an important overall aspect of human psychology, second it is reflected in the concerns of interactive system designers and third it is identified in the meta-analyses reported by Adams (2007). The nine modules are summarised as follows:

1. **Perception / input module.** This module deals with the initial registration and evaluation of incoming sensory information and, in conjunction with other modules, initial attempts at sense making.
2. **Feedback management**. Surprisingly, the human brain seems to have at least two perceptual systems (Milner & Goodale, 1995), including a second input system that deals with the feedback that arises as a consequence of our own actions (both physical and cognitive). This dichotomy is also found in the interests of system designers and current work on system design (Adams, 2007). This module processes the feedback provided to the learner from the environment and from e-learning resources.
3. **Working memory**. When we carry out any task, we often have to hold information in our head whilst doing so. For example, we hold a phone number, a password or sets of instructions. This is referred to as working memory (Baddeley and Hitch, 1974; Baddeley, 2000). Timescales vary, but many tasks would be impossible were it not for this function (Ericsson & Kintsch, 1995). Working memory is an important component of Broadbent's Maltese cross theory (Broadbent, 1984), a theory from which Simplex has developed. This module of Simplex keeps and processes the information that we need to hold in mind whilst carrying out our tasks.
4. **Emotions and drives**. When we are dealing with incoming information, it is often of some significance to us, rather than being neutral. It may be interesting, threatening, stressful, frustrating, relevant etc. The human mind is quick to determine if something in our environment is a threat or an attraction and to respond accordingly. This module deals with the emotional and motivational responses to events, imbuing them with significance and meaning. Even with e-learning, the student's emotions and motivations become engaged and exert a significant influence on learning and performance. For computer learning systems, the designer must take significant account of the intended learners' emotional and motivational responses. Do they enjoy using the system or is it irritating or frustrating? Do they find the system a source of motivation or discouragement?
5. **Output**. This module stores and selects the correct responses that a student needs to make in a given context to a given stimulus. To do so, it must set up and hold the required response in memory and to build up a long-term repertoire of possible responses associated with specific context and stimuli.
6. **Output sequences**. In many cases, the learner must construct a complex sequence of responses as an important aspect of new skill acquisition. For example, we often learn a

sequence of keystrokes on a computer that are required to carry out a task, such as sending out an email. The complex sequence of actions seems to "fire off" without reference to specific contexts or stimuli for specific actions. Both researchers and designers make the distinction between responses and complex response sequences.

7. **Long term memory**. This module provides the long term storage and processing of the knowledge that we require to carry out everyday activities such as studying and developing skills. It is the major source of declarative knowledge i.e. knowledge that we can declare. It also provides that information to support the tasks that need it. For example, consider when a symbol on a computer screen reminds us of something we saw once before or when we need to remember what a specific symbol means. Some tasks require only a little of our knowledge (for example, simple same different judgements) whilst other tasks depend upon much greater quantities of learned information, for example language translation.
8. **Mental models**. This module provides the capacity to create and retain the mental models that are required to conduct specific tasks, such as navigating around the University Library or around a supermarket, solving logical problems (Some As are Bs, some Bs are Cs; are some As also Cs?) or counting the windows in your home.
9. **Executive functions**. The Executive Module transfers information between the different modules, transforms information, retains a record of current progress and records the transactions / structures that are required to carry out a task or set of tasks. It also learns to create more efficient transactions / structures with feedback. The Executive Function is far from being a homunculus (a fictional person in your head that tells you what to do) but is an important component of human cognition. It is often associated with the frontal lobes of the human brain such that injuries to these areas can result in disastrous failures of executive functions.

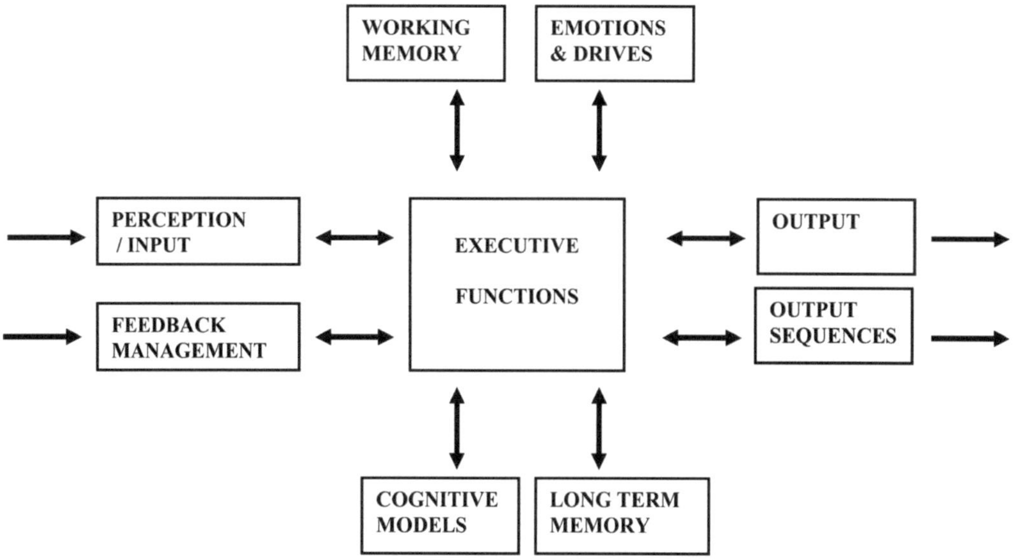

Figure 1. Simplex two

3. Learning resources for e-learning students

Learning resources are defined as information that is stored in a variety of media that supports learning, including materials for example in print, video and software formats. Considering the nine-point approach to Simplex Two, resources can be classified accordingly, relating to each of the nine components. The educationalist should consider each of the following nine fields when designing learning resources for their intended students.

1. Input resources refer to the different human senses with which information is received and understood. For example, information may be presented in different ways (e.g. audio or visual) or through multimedia (e.g. audio, visual and video). Each type of input has different types of features that may be more or less helpful for different tasks. For example, sound may be dramatic and impressive but visual materials are more persistent.
2. Feedback is considered to be essential to successful learning by most experts (e.g. Annett, 1994; Juwah et al, 2004). But it can be delivered in many different ways and through many different modalities (sight, hearing etc). Juwah et al suggest that principles of effective feedback can be identified. They tentatively suggest the following seven features of good feedback. It will facilitate self-assessment and reflection, stimulate teacher and peer dialogue, clarify the nature of good performance, (goals, criteria, standards expected), give opportunities to close the gap between actual and required performance, deliver high quality information to support positive thinking and give teachers the information that they can use to enhance teaching.
3. Working memory is now recognised as an important contributory factor to intelligent human performance and learning (for example Engle, Tuholski, Laughlin and Conway, 1999; Baddeley, 2000; Oberauer, Schulze, Wilhelm and Su¨ß, 2005). If so, the educationalist should be careful to allow the intended students to work within their working memory capacity most, if not all, the time. Learning resources should be presented in bite-sized chunks and be relatively digestible.
4. The emotions and drives of the students are important for learning success. O'Regan (2003) has concluded that emotions are central and essential to e-learning. Sankaran (2001) stressed the importance of motivation in e-learning. Clearly, learning resources must be chosen carefully to aim for a positive-emotion student experience and be suitably motivating, especially when using controversial or sensitive materials.
5. The response requirements of the developed learning resources should enable students to make appropriate responses that are neither too difficult nor arbitrary.
6. The learning resources should support the students in their attempts to develop complex and skilled response sequences.
7. The learning resources should not make unrealistic demands on the prerequisite knowledge that students must possess before they can participate in the proposed. They should not overload long-term memory.
8. The learning resources should be organised and presented to as to enable students to create suitably adequate mental models with which to structure newly acquired knowledge.
9. The students need to be supported so that they can deploy and develop their executive skills to develop overall learning strategies.

4. Technology-enhanced learning environments

Learning environments can be characterized as places arranged to enhance the learning experience. They are defined on an interdisciplinary basis based on three essential components: pedagogical functions, appropriate technologies and the social organization of education.
Widdowson (posted 21st May, 2008) asks "We can only create effective learning environments once we are clear about learning itself. What learning should young people be engaged in and what should learning be like for our 21st century learners, both today and in the future?" The author goes on to suggest some critical questions. They include (our wording) the following. What learning spaces are needed to create better opportunities for active, practical, collaborative, individual and constructive learning that engages the students? How can we design learning spaces to enable learners to develop and progress? How can measure learning environment effectiveness? Do our learning environments challenge and inspire young people? How do our learning environments support flexibility and student diversity?
We suggest that systematic and substantial answer to these questions and other related questions depends, in part, upon the development of a framework such as Simplex Two, or something better. As Widdowson (2008) concludes, the design of a learning space must be based upon an understanding of learning itself. We would also add that it should also be based on an appreciation of the diverse skills, requirements and preferences of the intended students (Adams, 2007; Adams and Granić, 2007). Clearly, learning environments must be fit for purpose (Day, 1995). One way to ensure fitness for purpose of e-learning materials is the creation and maintenance of different versions that are suitable for the different student populations (i.e. versioning: Brooks, Cooke, and Vassileva; 2003). Second, they should also inspire a sense of wonder about learning itself. To quote Albert Einstein "The most beautiful thing we can experience is the mysterious. It is the source of all true art and science. He to whom this emotion is a stranger, who can no longer pause to WONDER and stand rapt in awe, is as good as dead: his eyes are closed"
(http://www.quotationspage.com/quote/1388.html; accessed August 08).
For example, McGinnis, Bustard, Black and Charles (2008) have argued "e-learning should be enjoyed in the same way (insert: as computer games) and can be enhanced by incorporating games techniques in e-learning system design and delivery." However, Burg and Cleland (2001) have cautioned that poorly implemented computer based learning can also destroy any sense of wonder in learning. Third, learning environments must also be accessible. For example, Williams and Conlan (2007) would counteract cognitive accessibility problems by providing a means whereby users can visualize the complex space in which they are learning. In fact, accessibility problems can be found at any of the nine components of human information processing presented by Simplex Two (see above). A complementary approach is offered by Adams, Granić and Keates (2008), as shown in Table 1 below. They proposed five levels of accessibility that can be applied to an e-learning system and parallel them with the Internet layered model. They are hardware access (problems caused by lack of access to the necessary technology), connectivity access (problems with access to systems and resources), interface access (design of the interface creates accessibility difficulties), cognitive access (problems of navigation and accessing the contents of an application or website) and goal / social access (where a system allows you to access your goals). The e-learning system developer should find it a simple process to

monitor these five aspects of the accessibility of their system. These five aspects can be applied to both the specific requirements of their intended users and to the challenges set by the design of the e-learning system itself.

Comparing:	Accessibility types	Internet layered model
1	hardware access	physical
2	connectivity access	data link
3	interface access	network
4	cognitive access	transport
5	goal / social access	application

Table 1. Accessibility and the Internet layered model

5. Learning worlds

Learning worlds (or environments) are partially immersive, virtual milieu that deploy smart and adaptive teaching and learning technologies to create holistic and novel experiences based on sound pedagogical and psychological principles. The learning world or environment provides the learner with a consistent, familiar and over-arching context in which the user can access a range of different learning experiences and systems. They can also be personalised to match the requirements, strengths and weaknesses of an individual learner, creating higher levels of accessibility whilst still supporting collaborative working. For example, van Harmelen (2006) argues that learning environments can support different pedagogic methods, be collaborative or personal, easily extended or not, capable of supporting customisation or not and controlled by teachers or students or some balance of both. Learning worlds can vary significantly in a number of dimensions. First, learning worlds vary significantly in size. For example, Warburton and Pérez-García (2008) present the concept of the massive multi-user virtual environment (MUVE), whilst Blanc-Brude, Laborde and Bétrancourt (2003) present a learning micro-world. Second, learning worlds can be outdoors and mobile. For example, Chang, Shih and Chang (2006) present outdoor mobile learning, whilst most applications are located within traditional physical settings. Learning worlds can focus on different aspects of learning. Whilst, some learning worlds focus on cognitive skills (Jackson and Fagan, 2000) others focus on social factors. Skog, Hedestig and Kaptelinin (2001) report the Active Worlds system that is designed to support social interactions in 3D virtual learning spaces for distance education. The aim is to build on tacit aspects of social knowledge that are seen as critical for effective learning. A long list of these dimensions could be constructed, but the main point to be drawn is that learning worlds have the power to serve a wide variety of different learning objectives. The two caveats we would add are as follows. (a) The sheer power of the learning world concept means that it needs very careful handling. Technology for its own sake can detract from the learning experience unless learning world designs are learner centred. (b) Learning world designs should be sensitive to the accessibility requirement of the intended users.

6. The changing role of digital libraries to meet the increasing thirst for knowledge

It is clear that digital libraries contribute substantially to the provision of structured, declarative knowledge to online communities of students and scholars, who need to have substantial, accessible cognitive resources at their fingertips. Such libraries represent a major investment of both applied computing science and pedagogic expertise. They proffer potentially very valuable support for learning through the building of smart learning environments. At the moment, sad to say, digital libraries are often set behind monolithic interfaces that can offer an overwhelming richness of data. But that should not blind us as to their potential to provide smart, accessible, cognitive support for human learning in the context of the inclusive knowledge society.

There is no doubt that Digital Libraries can be an exciting and impressive way for students to glean new knowledge without straying too far from the study. They certainly offer considerable volumes of declarative knowledge to students working within the context of the modern Information Society. At the same time, some of our students find Digital Libraries to be difficult to use and the contents of Digital Libraries difficult to access. There is a considerable volume of work if we are to go beyond the simply impressive nature of the size and contents of Digital Libaries to develop the extent to which current and future digital libraries, can be made sufficiently usable, accessible and smart to support an inclusive information society and the aspiration of universal access (for example; Adams and Granić, 2007). These authors used a set of converging methods (separate measures of usability, accesibility and system smartness) to evaluate a random sample of digital libraries through their websites. They concluded that, whilst Digital Libraries are both substantial and functional repositories for knowledge, they can be improved significantly, particularly in their accessibility and smartness. They presented substantial statistical significance levels in their data. A new measure of system smartness is introduced and found to provide a useful metric for present purposes, though it is clear that further work will be needed.

7. How can learning environments be designed and evaluated for accessibility, usability and ambient smartness?

Many digital libraries are impressive in principle but often difficult to use in practice. If so, what comes after the present generation of digital libraries? One more future-proof concept is the notion of the ubiquitous knowledge environment or post-digital library. It is defined by its aims. They include the achievement of suitable levels of accessibility, usability and smartness for their structures, contents and their user interfaces. A second aim is to make the post-digital library available on a more ubiquitous and mobile basis. The first step towards such developments has been the evaluation of current digital libraries to identify their potential to support inclusive, smart ubiquitous knowledge environments (Adams and Granić, 2007). Clearly, the second step is begin to develop new designs for these ubiquitous knowledge environments, in the light of the specific design issues raised by current work. Can digital libraries become smarter and more accessible, in so doing creating ubiquitous knowledge environments? The concept of the ubiquitous knowledge environment seeks to capture the potential for convergence between current and future technologies, moving towards towards ambient intelligence and ubiquitous computing. Such knowledge environments move beyond the desktop or laptop to form part of our physical environments. Thus we should consider the creation of smart settings, with ubiquitous knowledge environments as a vital component. Access to the knowledge encapsulated would be processed through smarter everyday artifacts that deploy sensor data based responses in order to provide the users with relevant, user-model specific, situation-aware and context-of-use-aware knowledge at the point of use.

8. The design and development of more effective, technology-enhanced learning environments

Clearly, there is a long way to go in the development of better technology-enhanced learning environments. On the one hand, there is potential applicable power of new technologies that deliver learning materials and support student / system interactions in ways that are impressive, at least to the system designers and educators, if not always to all of the intended students. On the other hand, there is a growing awareness of the importance of insights into (a) the psychology of human learning coupled as well as into (b) the diversity of human learning requirements and related user modelling to capture that diversity. The danger is that we depend upon the impact of new technologies, 3D effects, virtual worlds, augmented realities, ambient intelligence in support of trivial applications etc. On the contrary, we must attain a basic level of understanding of the diversity of human learning and how to create user-sensitive methods with which to learning environments.

As discussed above, learning environments must, inter alia, be fit for purpose, usable and accessible, also responding to learner interactions in smarter ways. Drawing upon emerging technologies that are subjugated to learning objectives, the development of ubiquitous knowledge environments must also draw upon advanced design and development methodologies. Such advanced methodologies should pay sufficient attention to the evaluation of system relevance, fitness for purpoe, usability and acessibility based upon robust measurement methods.

9. How can ubiquitous learning environments be developed?

If higher standards of user satisfaction, usability, accessibility and system smartness can be achieved, then it would be possible to create convergence between technologies such as digital libraries, artificial intelligence (in the weaker sense of simulating human behaviour), ambient intelligence and ubiquitous computing. The substantive contents of such knowledge environments could be unleashed into the external, physical world rather than staying on the desktop or laptop. If so, the present methods of questionnaire based evaluation would focus not only on significant components of the smart environment like the smart digital library, but more so on an evaluation of the overall, smart environments themselves. These methods, or their successors, could be used to design and evaluate better ubiquitous knowledge environments. Access to the knowledge encapsulated would be accessed and processed through smarter everyday artefacts that deploy sensor data based responses in order to provide the users with relevant, user-model specific, situation-aware and context-of-use-aware knowledge at the point of use.

10. What new assessment methods must be developed to guide the design and development of such systems?

Clearly, Digital Libraries provide a useful and invaluable source of knowledge on a wide range of subjects, for a significant number of scholars and students. There can be few working scholars who do not make use of them. Digital Libraries are, at the moment, set behind monolithic interfaces that are typically accessed from the desktop or laptop environments in working or academic buildings. Surprisingly, however, the sample of libraries evaluated here clearly needed improvements in both accessibility and smartness. (These questionnaires are available from the authors). Clearly, if digital libraries are to form the basis for the realization of ubiquitous knowledge environments, they will become smarter and more accessible. We strongly recommend that Digital Library developers and redevelopers should evaluate their systems for user satisfaction, usability, accessibility and system smartness. One approach would be to use expert judgements but an equally important approach is to involve a sample of intended users, building useful user models in the process.

11. How can new technologies such as virtual reality applications and brain computer interfaces be applied to effective human learning?

Exciting new technologies, such as virtual reality applications and brain computer interfaces offer new potentialities for e-learning for the twenty first century. Virtual reality applications (VRAs) allow us to create virtual learning worlds in which dangerous, risky, expensive or unexplored skills can be explored and acquired. However, it is clear that the design of such virtual worlds is not easy. Whilst design heuristics can guide their design, it turns out that VRA effectiveness depends on different design points than, say, a website. This, in turn, means that developers should use VRA specific design heuristics.

In the above discussions and analyses, we have shown how a simple but innovative synthesis of key disciplines such as computing science and cognitive science, can be deployed in combination with such topics as ergonomics, e-learning, pedagogy, cognitive psychology, interactive system design, neuropsychology etc to create new learning worlds that will augment and boost human learning to meet the demands of the 21st century.

12. Conclusions and Recommendations

There are a number of important recommendations to both the practitioner and the researcher in the advancing world of e-learning environments. First, perhaps most importantly, advances in technology per se should not be confused with advances in human learning capabilities enhanced by technology. Whilst it is clear that technological innovations offer the potential of exciting new developments in e-learning in functionality, usability and accessibility, it is also now clear that new technologies can create new problems for e-learning system design. For new technologies, new design heuristics may be needed, since the critical success factors of design change, not only with different groups of intended students but also with different types of technologies. Second, this first point leads to the second point, namely the importance of user-sensitive design, where both the student and the teacher should be viewed as users of the system. The system design should not only support the requirements of each type of user, but also support true collaboration between them. The importance of prototyping, user and expert evaluations and iterative design methods should all be used to support user sensitive design. Third, powerful, effective but simple methods of evaluation of e-learning systems should be used, including functionality, fitness for purpose, usability, accessibility and system smartness. We have used a series of questionnaires that we can give you to support expert and user judgement. Clearly, there is potentially a great diversity of different types of e-learning environments, with an equally diverse range of learning objectives to be achieved. These diversities should not be seen, in themselves as problems, but rather as opportunities to make the current and growing diversity of the teachers, students, researchers and practitioners who wish to use the best and mot relevant -learning system available to them

13. References

Adams, R. (2007). Decision and Stress: Cognition and e-Accessibility in the Information Workplace. *Universal Access in the Information Society*. 5, 363-379.

Adams, R. and Granić, A. (2007). Creating Smart and Accessible Ubiquitous Knowledge Environments. *Lecture Notes in Computer Science*. 4555, 13-22. Springer Berlin / Heidelberg

Adams, R., Granić, A. and Keates, L. S. (2008). Are ambient intelligent applications more universally accessible? *In Universal Access to Novel Interaction Environments: Challenges and Opportunities* CHAIR: C. Stephanidis. In AHFE International 2008.

Annett, J. (1994). The learning of motor skills: sports science and ergonomics perspectives. *Ergonomics*, 37, 5-16.

Baddeley, A.D., Hitch, G.J. (1974). Working Memory, In G.A. Bower (Ed.), *The psychology of learning and motivation: advances in research and theory* (Vol. 8, pp. 47-89), New York: Academic Press.

Baddeley, A.D. (2000). The episodic buffer: a new component of working memory? *Trends in Cognitive Sciences*, 4, 417-423.

Blanc-Brude, T., Laborde, C. and Bétrancourt, M. (2003). Usability of speech based and multimodal interaction in a learning micro-world. IHM 2003: *Proceedings of the 15th French-speaking conference on human-computer interaction on 15eme Conference Francophone sur l'Interaction Homme-Machine*

Broadbent, D.E. (1984). The Maltese cross: A new simplistic model for memory. *The Behavioral and Brain Sciences*. 7 (1): 55-68.

Brooks, C., Cooke, J. and Vassileva, J. (2003). Versioning of Learning Objects. *Proceedings of the 3rd IEEE International Conference on Advanced Learning Technologies* 296- 297.

Burg, J. and Cleland, B. (2001). Computer-Enhanced or Computer-Enchanted? *The Magic and Mischief of Learning With Computers*. ED-MEDIA 2001 World Conference on Educational Multimedia.

Chang, C., Shih, K. & Chang, H. (2006). Some Studies on Technology Support for Outdoor Mobile Learning. In E. Pearson & P. Bohman (Eds.), *Proceedings of World Conference on Educational Multimedia, Hypermedia and Telecommunications* 2006 (pp. 1170-1177). Chesapeake, VA: AACE.

Day, C. W. (1995). Qualitative Research, Professional Development and the Role of Teacher Educators: Fitness for Purpose. *British Educational Research Journal*, 21,. 357-369.

Engle RW, Tuholski SW, Laughlin JE, Conway AR. (1999). Working memory, short-term memory, and general fluid intelligence: a latent-variable approach. *J Exp Psychol. Gen.*,128, 309-31

Ericsson, K. A., & Kintsch, W. (1995). Long-term working memory. *Psychological Review*, 102, 211-245.

Jackson, R. L. and Fagan, E. (2000) Collaboration and learning within immersive virtual reality. CVE '00: *Proceedings of the third international conference on Collaborative virtual environments*. New York, NY: ACM.

Juwah, C., Macfarlane-Dick, D., Matthew, B., Nicol, D., Ross, D. and Smith, B. (2004). Enhancing student learning through effective formative feedback. *The Higher Education Academy Generic Centre* - June 2004. (copy available from the present authors).

McGinnis, T., Bustard, D.W., Black, M. and Charles, D. (2008). Enhancing E-Learning Engagement using Design Patterns from Computer Games. *First International Conference on Advances in Computer-Human Interaction* IEEE ACHI 2008)

Milner, A.D. & Goodale, M.A. (1995) *The visual brain in action*. Oxford: Oxford University Press.

Oberauer, K., Schulze, R., Wilhelm, O. and Su¨ß, H. (2005). Working Memory and Intelligence—Their Correlation and Their Relation: Comment on Ackerman, Beier, and Boyle. *Psychological Bulletin*, 131, 61–65.

O'Regan, K. (2003). Emotion and E-Learning. *Journal of Asynchronous Learning Networks*, 7, 78-92

Sankaran, S. R. and Bui, T. (2001). Impact of Learning Strategies and Motivation on Performance: A Study in Web-Based Instruction. *Journal of Instructional Psychology*, September, 1-9.

Skog, D., Hedestig, U. & Kaptelinin, V. (2001). Supporting Social Interactions in Distance Education with a 3D Virtual Learning Space. In C. Montgomerie & J. Viteli (Eds.), *Proceedings of World Conference on Educational Multimedia, Hypermedia and Telecommunications* 2001 (pp. 1751-1752). Chesapeake, VA: AACE.

van Harmelen, M. (2006). Personal Learning Environments. *Proceedings of the Sixth International Conference on Advanced Learning Technologies* (ICALT'06)

Warburton, S. & Pérez-García, M. (2008). Motivating pupils, linking teachers through active learning with Multi-Users Virtual Environments. In *Proceedings of World Conference on Educational Multimedia, Hypermedia and Telecommunications* 2008 (pp. 3574-3578). Chesapeake, VA: AACE.

Widdowson, R. (posted 21st May, 2008). Designing effective learning environments. http://flux.futurelab.org.uk. Consulted August 08. (copy available from the present authors).

Williams, F.P. and Conlan, O. (2007). Visualizing Narrative Structures and Learning Style Information in Personalized e-Learning Systems. *Seventh IEEE International Conference on Advanced Learning Technologies* (ICALT 2007)

2

Current Challenges and Applications for Adaptive User Interfaces

Victor Alvarez-Cortes, Víctor H. Zárate, Jorge A. Ramírez Uresti and Benjamin E. Zayas

Instituto de Investigaciones Eléctricas; Tecnológico de Monterrey

México

1. Introduction

In this chapter we present the current advances in the field of adaptive user interfaces, analysing the different research efforts, the challenges involved as well as the more recent and promising directions in this field. Initially, we introduce the foundations of adaptive user interfaces, also referred in technical literature as Intelligent User Interfaces (IUIs), then we move to explore the motivation and rationale for their use, and finally we discuss the challenges they currently have to deal with. In this context, IUIs are presented as a multi-disciplinary field, with relevant research and cross-fertilized ideas derived from different areas, however special emphasis is put on the approaches taken by three core disciplines: Artificial Intelligence (AI), User Modelling (UM) and Human-Computer Interaction (HCI). After providing the foundations for IUIs, an in-depth revision for each approach is presented including the most recent findings in models, algorithms and architectures for adaptive user interfaces.

Although, adaptive user interfaces are considered a recent research field, this chapter is enriched with a state-of-the-art of IUIs applications. The material included presents the most relevant developed IUIs applied in different real domains either as a research prototype or as a complete system. A methodological analysis of these systems is presented, contrasting its advantages, limitations and domain-dependence for its success and acceptance by users. The analysis aims to uncover common principles for effective IUI design. Also, this chapter details our proposed taxonomy which is applied for the comparison of the different IUIs systems.

Finally, the chapter presents the gaps left by the approaches under analysis and concludes with a discussion of the challenges currently open, presenting a number of possible future research directions.

Las interfaces de usuario para los sistemas de computación han cambiado mucho en los últimos 20 años. Las primeras interfaces basadas en texto que utilizaban la línea de comando para acceder a los recursos del sistema operativo, han sido sustituidas por interfaces gráficas que son manipuladas a través de dispositivos de entrada como el teclado y ratón. En la actualidad, la interfaces buscan ser más intuitivas al usuario al presentar elementos gráfico de fácil asociación con elementos reales mediante el uso de metáforas (Dix et al., 2003).

Un paradigma de interacción utilizado de manera extensa en los sistemas operativos actuales es el uso de múltiples ventanas para presentar información, el uso de iconos para representar elementos del entorno como son carpetas, archivos, dispositivos, etc, junto con el uso de menús y botones, que faciliten la interacción con el sistema. A este paradigma se le conoce como WIMP (Windows, Icons, Menus, Pointers) desarrollada por Xerox PARC en los 80´s, y utilizado inicialmente por las computadoras Apple Macintosh y actualmente disponibles en otros sistemas como Microsoft Windows, OS/Motif, Risc OS y X Window System (Shneiderman & Plaisant, 2004). Sin embargo, aún con estos avances y la funcionalidad ofrecida por las interfaces de usuario de los sistemas actuales, la mayoría de ellas aún siguen siendo limitadas en cuanto al manejo de las diferencias que existentes entre los diversos usuarios de la interfaz, quedando clara que existe una limitación en el desarrollo de sistemas que puedan ser personalizados y adaptados al usuario y al entorno.
Las Interfaces Inteligentes de Usuario (IUI, por sus siglas en inglés) es un sub-campo de HCI y tiene como objetivo mejorar la interacción humano-computadora mediante el uso de nueva tecnología en dispositivos de interacción, así como a través del uso de técnicas de inteligencia artificial, que le permitan exhibir algún tipo de comportamiento inteligente o adaptivo.

2. Uso de las IUIs

Las IUIs tratan de resolver algunos de los problemas que las interfaces tradicionales, llamadas de manipulación directa (Shneiderman, 1997) no pueden afrontar.

- *Crear sistemas personalizados:* No existen dos usuarios que sean iguales y cada uno tiene diferentes hábitos, preferencias y formas de trabajar. Una interfaz inteligente puede tomar en consideración estas diferencias y proporcionar métodos personalizados de interacción. La interfaz conoce al usuario y puede usar ese conocimiento para establecer el mejor medio de comunicación con el usuario.
- *Problemas de filtrado y exceso en información:* Tratar de encontrar la información necesaria en una computadora o en Internet puede resultar una tarea complicada. Aquí una interfaz inteligente puede reducir la cantidad de información relevante en grandes base de datos. Al filtrar información irrelevante, la interfaz puede reducir la carga cognitiva del usuario. Adicionalmente una IUI puede proponer nuevas y útiles fuentes de información desconocidas al usuario.
- *Proporcionar ayuda para nuevos programas:* Los sistemas de información pueden llegar a ser muy complicados de usar al inicio. Es común que conforme el usuario empieza a entender las funcionalidades del programa, nuevas versiones o actualizaciones aparecen, incluyendo nueva funcionalidad. En esta situación un sistema inteligente de ayuda puede detectar y corregir usos incorrectos o sub-óptimos para realizar una tarea, explicar nuevos conceptos y proporcionar información para simplificar las tareas.
- *Hacerse cargo de tareas por el usuario:* Una IUI puede ver que es lo que está haciendo el usuario, entender y reconocer su intento y ocuparse de la ejecución completa de ciertas tareas, permitiéndole al usuario enfocarse en otras.
- *Otras formas de interacción:* En la actualidad los dispositivos más comunes de interacción son el teclado y el ratón. Una línea de investigación de IUI conocida como interfaces multimodales investiga nuevas formas de interacción a través de

otras modalidades de entrada y salida para interactuar con el usuario. Al proporcionarse múltiples formas de interacción, la gente con discapacidades podrá utilizar sistemas complejos de cómputo.

3. Definición y áreas relacionadas

A través de los años numerosas definiciones de inteligencia han surgido para definir sistemas y comportamientos, sin embargo no existe un consenso sobre qué se debe considerarse inteligente. No obstante, la mayoría de las definiciones mencionan la habilidad de adaptación (aprender y lidiar con nuevas situaciones), la habilidad para comunicarse y la habilidad para resolver problemas (Russell & Norvig, 2003).

Una interfaz "normal"es definida de manera simple como la comunicación entre un usuario (humano) y una máquina (Meyhew, 1999). Una extensión de esta definición para una interfaz inteligente es que utiliza algún tipo de componente inteligente para llevar a cabo la comunicación humano-computadora. Por eso también se les conoce como interfaces adaptivas, porque tienen la habilidad de adaptarse al usuario, comunicarse con él y resolverle problemas. Una definición más formal es: Las interfaces inteligentes de usuario buscan mejorar la flexibilidad, usabilidad y poder de interacción humano computadora para todos los usuarios. Al hacerlo, explotan el conocimiento de los usuarios, las tareas, herramientas y contenido, así como los dispositivos para soportar la interacción con diferentes contextos de uso (Maybury99].

Figure 1. IUIs y sus diferentes disciplinas

Debido a que la adaptación y la resolución de problemas son temas centrales de investigación en inteligencia artificial, muchas IUIs están fuertemente orientadas al uso de técnicas de IA, sin embargo no todas las IUIs tienen capacidad de aprendizaje o resolución de problemas. Muchas interfaces que se denominan inteligentes se enfocan al aspecto del canal de comunicación entre el usuario y el sistema (máquina) y generalmente aplican técnicas nuevas de interacción como procesamiento de lenguaje, seguimiento de mirada (*gaze tracking*) y reconocimiento facial. Lo cierto es que muchos campos de investigación tienen influencia en las IUIs tales como la sicología, ergonomía, factores humanos, ciencias cognitivas y otras como se muestra en la figura 1.

Una de las propiedades más importantes de las IUIs es que son diseñadas para mejorar la comunicación entre el usuario y la máquina.

No importa mucho que tipo de técnica sea utilizada para conseguir esta mejora. Una lista de varios tipos de técnicas que son usadas en las IUIs son:

- *Tecnología de entrada inteligente:* se refiere al uso de técnicas para obtener la entrada del usuario. Estas técnicas incluyen lenguaje natural (reconocimiento de habla y sistemas de diálogo), seguimiento y reconocimiento de gestos, reconocimiento de expresiones faciales y lectura de labios.
- *Modelado de usuario:* aquí se incluyen las técnicas que le permiten a un sistema mantener o inferir conocimiento acerca de un usuario basado en la entrada de información recibida.
- *Adaptividad de usuario:* comprende todas las técnicas que permiten que la interacción humano-computadora sea adaptada a diferentes usuarios y diferentes situaciones de uso.
- *Generación de explicaciones:* comprende todas las técnicas que permiten que la interacción humano-computadora sea adaptada a diferentes usuarios y diferentes situaciones de uso.
- *Personalización:* Para poder personalizar las IUIs normalmente incluyen una representación del usuario. Estos modelos de usuario registran datos acerca del comportamiento del usuario, su conocimiento y habilidades. Nuevo conocimiento del usuario se puede inferir basado en las entradas y el historial de interacción del usuario con el sistema.
- *Flexibilidad de Uso:* Para ser flexibles muchas IUIs utilizan adaptación y aprendizaje. La adaptación toma lugar en el conocimiento almacenado en el modelo del usuario al hacer nuevas inferencias al usar la entrada actual. El aprendizaje ocurre cuando cambia el conocimiento almacenado para reflejar las nuevas situaciones encontradas o nuevos datos.

4. Inteligentes y Sistema Inteligentes

Con frecuencia se comete el error de confundir lo que es una IUI con lo que es un sistema inteligente. Un sistema que muestra alguna forma de inteligencia no necesariamente es una interfaz inteligente. Existen muchos sistemas inteligentes con interfaces de usuario muy simples que no son inteligentes. Asimismo el hecho de que un sistema tenga una interfaz inteligente no nos dice nada acerca de la inteligencia que existe en el sistema. Ver figura 2.

Desafortunadamente la frontera entre un sistema y su interfaz de usuario no siempre es tan claro como en la figura y muchas veces la tecnología utilizada en una IUI también es parte del sistema, o la IUI representa en realidad la totalidad del sistema. Asimismo muchas veces se pone poco énfasis en la interfaz y su separación para ser desarrollada por un grupo especializado en interfaces y ergonomía, no siempre son una realidad. A menudo al desarrollar un sistema se le da mayor importancia a la parte interna y de algoritmos, dejando la parte de la interfaz como en componente más del sistema (Hook, 1999).

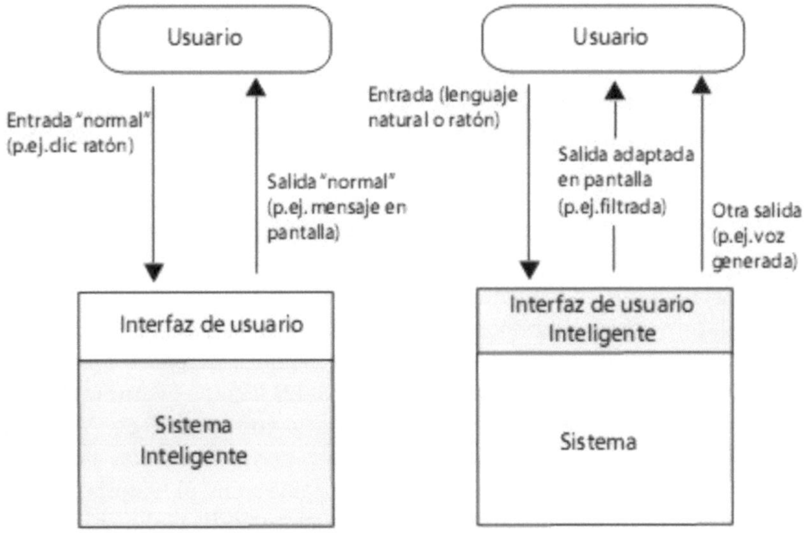

Figure 2. Sistema inteligente vs Interfaz inteligente

5. Beneficios y críticas

El campo de las IUIs en ninguna manera se encuentra maduro y aún existen problemas abiertos que deben resolverse. Quizá esta se una de las razones por la cuál las IUIs (gracias a la IA) ha recibido escepticismo de una parte de HCI. El problema central radica en que las IUIs violan principios de usabilidad aceptados dentro del desarrollo de sistemas de manipulación directa. Los trabajos de Maes en el MIT (Maes, 1994) y otro de Wernn (Wernn, 1997) advierten sobre el potencial de las interfaces inteligentes y sus capacidades, ponen de manifiesto los puntos que deben ser resueltos antes de que las IUIs sean aceptadas y usadas de manera extendida.

Para Shneiderman (Shneiderman,1997) un sistema adaptivo es impredecible y menos transparente que una interfaz tradicional. Si un sistema puede adaptar su respuesta y no da la misma salida dos veces ante la misma entrada, el sistema entonces se vuelve impredecible. Otro problema similar es el control sobre la interfaz. Las posibilidades son si el usuario toma el control y decide la siguiente acción a realizarse o si el sistema de manera autónoma con base a su conocimiento parcial toma el control y decide la siguiente acción. Esta situación ha sido abordada desde diferentes enfoques dando lugar a especializaciones dentro de las interfaces de usuario inteligentes.

Las interfaces adaptables permiten que el control lo tenga el usuario y sea él quien dirija y controle la adaptación a través de opciones para poder personalizar y adaptar la interfaz. En el otro lado encontramos las interfaces adaptivas donde el sistema tiene la inteligencia suficiente y realiza la evaluación del estado para llevar a cabo algún tipo de adaptación sin la intervención del usuario. Un esquema de interacción que ha recibido aceptación es el de iniciativa mixta o combinada, donde se comparte le interacción entre el usuario y el sistema (Armentano, 2006). Una discusión más extensa entre expertos del área de interfaces sobre las ventajas y desventajas entre las IUIs y la interfaces de manipulación directa la encontramos en el trabajo de Birnbaum (Birnbaum, 1997).

6. Aprendizaje Computacional en las IUIs

El uso de técnicas de inteligencia artificial para diseñar IUIs ha sido un enfoque que ha sido aceptado en la comunidad de interfaces y aplicado a diferentes dominios y aplicaciones.
Las técnicas reportadas en la literatura van desde los tradicionales sistemas de producción (basados en reglas) hasta técnicas más modernas como son planificación y modelos probabilísticos gráficos (Horvitz, 1998). Técnicas más recientes de IA también se han utilizado en las IUIs tales como agentes autónomos (Rich & Sidner, 1996), (Eisenstein & Rich, 2002).
Todas estas técnicas han sido utilizadas para generar diferentes grados de inteligencia o adaptabilidad y aprovechar el conocimiento que se tiene del usuario y sus tareas para proporcionar una mejor interacción y experiencia de uso del sistema.
Las técnicas y algoritmos de aprendizaje computacional (Machine Learning (ML) han tenido un rápido desarrollo ganando aceptación dentro de la comunidad de AI. El aprendizaje computacional ha sido aplicado con relativo éxito en varias dominios, principalmente en aplicaciones Web para colectar información y minar datos sobre el historial de interacción y de navegación de los usuarios (Fu, 2000). Asimismo el aprendizaje ha sido utilizado como un medio para inferir modelos de usuario (Stumpf et al., 2007) basado en datos pasados con el objeto de descubrir patrones desconocidos y adaptar el comportamiento de la interfaz.
En términos de ML, una interfaz inteligente puede ser conceptualizada como "un componente de software que mejora su capacidad para interactuar con el usuario mediante la construcción de un modelo basado en la experiencia parcial con ese usuario" (Langley, 1999). Esta definición muestra claramente que una interfaz inteligente está diseñada para interactuar con usuarios reales y humanos. Aún más, si la interfaz debe ser considerada como inteligente, entonces debe mejorar su interacción con el usuario al pasar el tiempo, considerando que una simple memorización de esas interacciones no es suficiente, sino que la mejora debe provenir como resultados de una generalización en experiencias pasadas para establecer nuevas interacciones con el usuario.
Es posible identificar dos amplias categorías de interfaces inteligentes dentro del enfoque de ML, las cuales difieren en el tipo de retroalimentación que debe proporcionar el usuario:

- *Informativas:* Este tipo de interfaz trata de seleccionar o modificar información para el usuario al presentar sólo aquellos elementos que el usuario pueda encontrar interesantes o útiles para la tarea que está realizando. Los ejemplos más comunes son los sistemas de recomendación de productos (i.e la librería en línea Amazon.com) y filtros de noticias, donde se dirige la atención de los usuarios dentro de un amplio espacio de opciones. En este tipo de sistemas la retroalimentación del usuario generalmente incluye marcar las opciones de recomendación como deseables y no deseables y evaluarlas asignando alguna puntuación. Sin embargo esta clase de interfaces distrae la atención de la tarea central, pues el usuario debe proporcionar retroalimentación. Se reporta en la literatura la existencia de métodos menos intrusivos para obtener retroalimentación al observar el proceso de acceso (Sugiyama, 2004).
- *Generativas:* Este tipo de interfaces están enfocadas principalmente a la generación de alguna estructura útil de conocimiento. Aquí se incluye programas para la preparación de documentos, hojas de cálculo, así como también sistemas para planificación y configuración. Estas áreas soportan un tipo de retroalimentación mejorada ya que el usuario puede no sólo ignorar alguna recomendación, sino

sustituirla por otra. Los tipos de retroalimentación están amarrados a los tipos de interacción que soporte la interfaz. Varios sistemas requieren que el usuario corrija acciones no deseables, lo cual es un problema de interrupción, sin embargo sistemas recientes incorporan esquemas menos instrusivos mediante la observación de las acciones del usuario. (Franklin et al., 2002).

También se reporta en la literatura que minar los registros del uso en Web es un enfoque factible para construir interfaces Web adaptivas . El historial de acceso Web constituye una fuente abundante de información que permite experimentar con conjuntos de datos reales. Los sistemas Web adaptivos le facilitan al usuario la navegación al proporcionarle accesos directos a sitios de manera personalizada. Durante el proceso de adaptación, los datos de acceso del usuario son la fuente central de información y es utilizada para construir el modelo del usuario, que refleja el patrón que el sistema infiere para los usuarios y describe varias características de los mismos. La minería de datos usando reglas de asociación se ha utilizado para minar el historial de navegación de sitios Web y también para proponer o sugerir nuevas ligas basada en un filtrado colaborativo.(Mobasher et al., 2001).

7. Modelado del usuario en la IUIs

La interfaz de usuario y el modelado del usuario (UM) pueden ser vistos como como dos lados de un mismo componente. El modelo de usuario consiste en los algoritmos que son implementados en los componentes de software mostrando el concepto de personalización desde la perspectiva del sistema. Por otro lado, la interfaz inteligente es la interfaz gráfica (GUI) y le presenta al usuario un contenido generado por el UM, mostrando la personalización desde el punto de vista del usuario como se muestra en la figura 3.

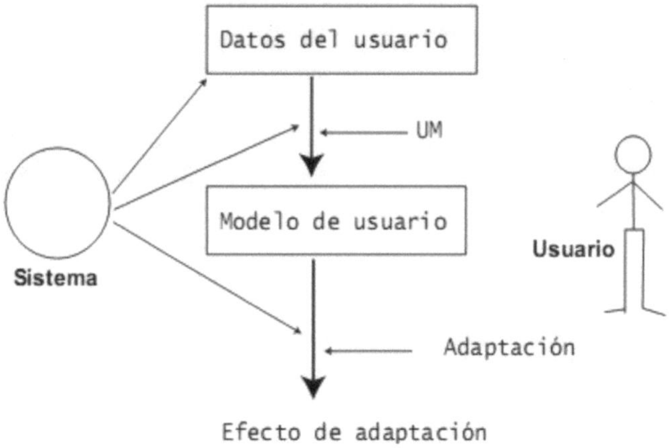

Figure 3. Dos perspectivas del modelos del usuario

Las aplicaciones de modelado de usuario pueden ser definidas como aplicaciones donde "usuarios con diferentes objetivos, intereses, niveles de experiencia, habilidades y preferencias pueden adecuar a la medida el comportamiento del programa a necesidades individuales generalmente mediante el uso de un perfil de usuario" (Kobsa, 1994)

El propósito del UM es colectar, procesar y mostrar datos adaptados al nivel de la interfaz mediante una recopilación de conocimiento de información de dos tipos.

- *Implícita:* Esta recopilación de datos involucra examinar archivos de registros como historiales de navegación o los "cookies" en un navegador (Fu, 2000). El descubrimiento de patrones en los datos permite el filtrado de contenidos y su direccionamiento y entrega basada en suposiciones hechas sobre el comportamiento del usuario. Por ejemplo, si un usuario regularmente revisa ciertos elementos (ítems) particulares, el UM identificará el patrón y puede alterar la interfaz para desplegar esos elementos y asociar el contenido en una pagina Web de acceso al usuario. Esta es una técnica automatizada de UM que no requiere de ninguna retroalimentación directa del usuario para identificar un patrón de comportamiento y modificar el contenido de acuerdo a éste.
- *Explícita:* La captura de datos explícitos involucra el análisis de datos metidos por el usuario, proporcionando información acerca de sus preferencias mediante el llenado de un perfil de usuario. Ejemplos de estos datos son la edad, sexo, ciudad, historial de compras, preferencias sobre contenidos y distribución de la información en pantalla. Esta técnica también se conoce en el área de modelado como una técnica UM informada. Esta técnica requiere la entrada de datos por parte de los usuarios y un mecanismo para reconocer patrones en las preferencias de los usuarios con el objeto de modificar la interfaz basada en esas preferencias.

Los modelos de usuario pueden ser utilizados para crear servicios personalizados mediante la adaptación a necesidades individuales usando información o técnica de filtrado colaborativo (Carenini, 2003). Los usuarios pueden tomar control sobre su interacción al elegir contenidos de manera explícita basada en perfiles de usuarios o a través de sistemas de recomendación que establezcan asociaciones entre un historial de compra individual o de navegación con el de otros usuarios similares (Kirsh-Pinheiro et al., 2005).

Una interfaz adaptiva presenta los modelos de usuario al nivel de la interfaz al desplegar contenidos personalizados (Eirinaki & Vazirgiannis, 2003). Asimismo los usuarios también tienen la oportunidad de interactuar directamente con el modelo de usuario cuando lo crean o al editar los perfiles. El modelado de usuario y la interfaz adaptiva esencialmente presentan vistas personalizadas de contenidos que pueden ahorrar tiempo para localizar información o guiar a los usuarios a contenidos disponibles y desconocidos al usuario.

En resumen, el UM es una alternativa sólida para la presentación de contenidos personalizados y es considerado una herramienta útil para el usuario que permite el uso de datos explícitos. Por otro lado existe escepticismo acerca del uso de datos implícitos para crear estereotipos imprecisos basados en complejos algoritmos de inferencia (Peyton, 2003), ya que una gran cantidad de de literatura reporta pocas pruebas con usuarios. *"Una rápida mirada de los 9 primeros años de UMUAI revela que sólo una tercera parte de los artículos incluye algún tipo de evaluación. Esto es un porcentaje muy bajo"* (Chin, 2001).

8. HCI en las IUIs

El enfoque de HCI para resolver los problemas de interacción se ha centrado en el uso de diferentes modos de interacción o modalidades para comunicar al usuario con el sistema. La idea central es realizar esta interacción de la manera más parecida a como lo hacemos los humanos. Si tomando en cuenta que los humanos percibimos el mundo a través de los sentidos (tacto, vista, oído, olfato y gusto), parece lógico la idea de unificar esta información en una computadora que sea capaz de procesarla a través de diferentes modos de acuerdo a los dispositivos disponibles (teclado, micrófono, cámara, etc.) dando lugar a una interfaces multimodal. Las interfaces multimodales combinan dos o más modos diferentes de comunicación con el objeto de mejorar el canal de interacción entre el humano y el sistema. Las interfaces multimodales actuales pueden procesar dos o más modos de entrada combinados usando tecnologías basadas en reconocimiento, con el objeto de identificar con precisión o interpretar las intenciones de comunicación del usuario (Reeves et al., 2004). Existen varios tipos de sistemas multimodales, incluyendo aquellos que procesan voz y entrada manual con lápiz o a través de pantallas sensibles al tacto y audiovisual. Las tecnologías de visión computacional y procesamiento de voz son fundamentales al desarrollo de este tipo de interfaces y son revisadas extensamente en (Oviatt et al., 2000).

Un enfoque novedoso en las interfaces multimodales es la integración de tecnología de agentes, componentes multimedia y de realidad virtual junto con técnicas de inteligencia artificial para desarrollar personajes similares a humanos que interactúan con los usuarios de una manera más natural. Mediante el uso de de visión computacional y procesamiento de voz, estos personajes animados o agentes conocidos como *ECAS Embodied Conversational Agents* representan una línea de investigación que integra varias áreas (Cassell, 2000). En estos ambientes virtuales de los ECAs, las interfaces enfrentan nuevos retos de diseño para HCI.

9. Sistemas relacionados

A continuación se presentan algunos de los sistemas reportados en la literatura de interfaces inteligentes que presentan algunas de las características de adaptación relevantes a la propuesta doctoral presentada en este documento.

9.1 Sistema SurfLen

Una de los elementos centrales de las interfaces adaptivas es su capacidad para anticipar las tareas que realizará el usuario basada en observar las acciones actuales, su comportamiento y el modelo del usuario. Una línea de investigación reportada en la literatura de IUI se basa en establecer acciones (tareas, navegación, planes, estrategias, etc.) futuras considerando el análisis del historial de las acciones pasadas del usuario (o también de un conjunto de usuarios) mediante el uso de técnicas de IA con el objeto de llevar a cabo algún tipo de razonamiento sobre dicha información e inferir la acción a seguir. El trabajo de (Fu, 2000) se ubica dentro de esta categoría, pero está enfocado a un sistema de recomendación de información basado en Web.

La hipótesis planteada por los autores es que el historial de navegación del usuario contiene información suficiente para descubrir conocimiento acerca de páginas de interés al usuario, sin la necesidad de que el usuario le asigne una calificación o tecleé información adicional, lo cual es una desventaja de los sistemas actuales. Los autores plantean que de manera activa pero silenciosa es posible mantener el seguimiento de lo que el usuario ha leído, recolectar el historial de navegación en un repositorio centralizado y aplicar técnicas de IA para descubrir conocimiento. Por ejemplo, si dos usuarios han leído varias páginas similares, podemos inferir que ambos usuarios tienen intereses similares. Este conocimiento sobre la similaridad de patrones de navegación, es usado para generar (inferir) las recomendaciones.

Para probar los planteamientos, los autores desarrollaron un prototipo de un sistema de recomendación llamado SurfLen que sugiere páginas de interés a usuarios sobre tópicos específicos. El prototipo utiliza el algoritmo de Agrawal propuesto por los autores para

generar el conjunto de reglas de asociación con el uso de una optimización apriori. La evaluación del prototipo reporta que el número de sugerencias correctas por usuario aumenta conforme el historial de navegación se vuelve más representativo de sus intereses.
La parte relevante del artículo es el uso del algoritmo de optimización A-priori de Agrawal aplicado al historial de navegación pero con el objeto de realizar recomendaciones. Asimismo el esquema propuesto con reglas de asociación ofrece ventajas sobre sistemas similares al no requerir intervención por parte del usuario. La parte débil del artículo es que las pruebas son simuladas y en un entorno controlado. En los resultados de las pruebas del prototipo se menciona que ofrece ventajas sobre otras técnicas, sin embargo no hace ninguna comparación con un sistema similar. Por otro lado, la creación de los datasets conforme se va aumentando el número de URLs y de usuarios debe resultar costoso en tiempo de procesamiento, aún con la optimización propuesta, tema que no se menciona.
El presenta artículo es relevante a a la propuesta doctoral al exponer el uso de técnicas de IA para analizar la manera en que los operadores navegan la interfaz de un sistema de supervisión y control, con el objeto de implementar el mecanismo de adaptación. Una posibilidad sería analizar el historial de navegación para operadores (experto, novato, intermedio) en situaciones (normal, emergencia) o en fases (arranque, operación, paro), para crear un patrón de navegación que me permita predecir (recomendar) el siguiente despliegue (o acción) basado en el historial de un operador (o de varios operadores similares)

9.2 Interfaces Adaptivas para Control de Procesos

El sistema reportado en (Viano et al., 2000) resulta relevante debido a que aborda el tema de las interfaces adaptivas, enfocado a interfaces de usuario para operaciones críticas tales como el control de procesos. Adicionalmente el prototipo presentado por los autores se plantea para ser utilizado en dos aplicaciones: un sistemas para el manejo de redes eléctricas y un sistema para la supervisión de una planta de generación termoeléctrica.
Los autores argumentan que debido a la complejidad cada vez mayor en los sistemas de control, las limitaciones de los operadores para manejar grandes cantidades de información en tiempo real y en situaciones de falla, junto con las exigencias para mantener la continuidad en la operación, permite considerar el enfoque de los sistemas adaptivos, los cuales pueden alterar su estructura, funcionalidad o interfaz con el objeto de acomodar las diferentes necesidades individuales o grupos de usuarios. El enfoque adaptivo que proponen permite asistir al operador en adquirir la información más relevante en cualquier contexto particular.
El planteamiento central del artículo es que el diseño de la interfaz del operador es rígido, es decir, se establece durante el tiempo de diseño, tomando en cuenta las mejores guías o prácticas recomendadas por HCI, sin embargo, una vez establecido, se mantiene durante la ejecución de la aplicación. Este mapeo entre el tipo de información que se está recibiendo de campo y la forma (y medios) utilizado para presentarlo al usuario, no es única, sino que el diseñador selecciona la que considera más efectiva y eficiente, sin embargo otros posible mapeos son descartados. Así, sin importar que tan bueno sea el diseño, será fijo con las desventajas asociadas tales como una estructura rígida, no diseñado para situaciones de emergencia, etc. La arquitectura de interfaz adaptiva propuesta considera la adaptación en la presentaci´ on de información. Los autores denominan su modelo como de "Mapeo

Flexible" basado en el estado actual del proceso, el ambiente y el conocimiento de factores humanos.
El artículo propone una arquitectura multi-agentes, con agentes para las siguientes funciones: modelo del proceso, medios, resolución de despliegue, presentación, base de datos de factores humanos y operador. Asimismo se contemplan dos principios para iniciar el mecanismo de adaptación: cuando se detecte desviación del proceso y en la desviación del operador (no reacciona de acuerdo al procedimiento esperado).
Al inicio los autores mencionan que los beneficios del enfoque propuesto se evalúan en dos prototipos, sin embargo en la sección 6 (Prototipos), se precisa que los dos prototipos están en desarrollo no se presenta ningún tipo de evaluación. La parte de aportación de este artículo a mi trabajo de investigación es la descripción de las necesidades en los sistemas de control de procesos donde un esquema adaptivo es necesario.
La parte fuerte del artículo es la arquitectura propuesta, aún cuando la explicación dada sobre los componentes y la interacción entre ellos sea escasa. Por otra parte los autores no mencionan los mecanismos de coordinación, aspecto importante y que representa un reto en los sistemas multi-agentes. En términos generales los autores no profundizan en ningún aspecto y el estado del arte que presentan es básico.

9.3 Sistema ADAPTS

El sistema ADAPTS presentado por (Brusilovsky & Cooper, 2002) aborda la utilización de diferentes modelos (tareas, usuarios y entorno) para adaptar contenido y navegación en un sistema adaptable de hiper-media. Estas características son similares a las de la propuesta doctoral, donde se plantea realizar un modelo de interfaz adaptiva de iniciativa combinada, aplicada al dominio eléctrico dentro de un sistema inteligente de ayuda con el objeto de adaptar el contenido de la información presentada, tomando en cuenta las características del usuario y el estado de la planta.
Los autores describen el sistema *ADAPTS Adaptive Diagnostics And Personalized Technical Support*, un sistema electrónico de soporte para técnicos de mantenimiento compuesto por una guía adaptiva a partir de un sistema de diagn´ ostico con acceso adaptivo a información técnica, abarcando ambos lados del proceso: qué hacer y cómo hacerlo. Es un proyecto extenso resultado de la colaboración de investigadores de la Naval Research Airs Warfare Center, Aircraft Division, Carnegie-Mellon University, University of Connecticut y la compañía Antech Systems Inc.
Un componente importante del sistema lo constituye el IETM Interactive Electronic Technical Manuals, el cual proporciona una gran cantidad de información acerca del sistema: Cómo está construido, su operación y qué hacer en caso de problemas específicos, etc. ADAPTS es un sistema adaptivo complejo que ajusta la estrategia de diagnóstico en base a quién es el técnico y qué es lo que está haciendo, adaptando dinámicamente la secuencia de configuraciones, pruebas, procedimientos de reparación/reemplazo basado en las respuestas del técnico. Asimismo integra conocimiento del dominio, tareas de mantenimiento y las características de usuario.
El modelo del usuario propuesto por los autores determina qué tarea se debe realizar, qué información técnica seleccionar para describir la tarea y cómo presentar de la manera más adecuada dicha información para un técnico particular. La problemática planteada en el artículo es que la cantidad de información potencialmente relevante en un momento dado dentro del proceso de reparación puede llegar a ser muy grande y es un reto para los técnico

encontrar la información más adecuada a su experiencia y contexto de trabajo. Para esto es necesaria llevar a cabo de manera permanente una valoración dinámica del conocimiento del técnico, su experiencia, preferencias y contexto de trabajo. En el modelo propuesto la experiencia es calculada a partir de varias evidencias sobre el nivel de experiencia del técnico que son recolectadas por el sistema al interactuar con el técnico. Asimismo ADAPTS utiliza un modelo de usuario tipo sobreposición multi-aspectos (Multi-Aspect Overlay Model) el cual resulta más expresivo, pero al mismo tiempo más complejo de generar y mantener.

Los autores presenta el sistema ADAPTS, sus modelos propuestos y cómo pueden ser utilizados para construir un sistema adaptivo, sin embargo no especifican (justifican) porque los 20 aspectos propuestos utilizados para evaluar la experiencia de los usuarios son suficientes o los adecuados. Un aspecto cuestionable es que los autores asumen en su modelo que si un usuario solicita un despliegue del IETM necesariamente lo lee, sin embargo convendría incluir algún nivel de probabilidad o tiempo para establecer esta afirmación, como lo hacen otros sistemas similares ante esta situación. Llama la atención que no se presentan datos sobre experimentos de validación, su evaluación, utilidad real, aplicación en campo, satisfacción de los usuarios, etc., a pesar de que se trata de un sistema extenso y completo..

9.4 Modelo de decisión

El enfoque propuesto en (Stephanidis et al., 1997) presenta a las interfaces inteligentes de Usuario como componentes que se caracterizan por su capacidad de adaptarse en tiempo de ejecución y tomar varias decisiones de comunicación referente al "qué", "cuando", "por qué" y "cómo" para interactuar con el usuario, todo esto mediante el empleo de una estrategia de adaptación.

El uso de modelos como una parte central para ampliar el entendimiento sobre los procesos involucrados en la adaptación de las interfaces se presenta en (Puerta, 1998), donde se hace una clara diferencia entre un modelo y una arquitectura y los objetivos que persiguen cada uno.

Los autores conceptualizan la estrategia de adaptación como un proceso de toma de decisiones, caracterizada por atributos que involucran aspectos de la interfaz de usuario que están sujetos a adaptación y denominados por los autores como "constituyentes de adaptación". Asimismo la adaptación en tiempo de ejecución implica cierto tipo de monitoreo de la interfaz con el objeto de evaluar el estado de los elementos críticos de la interacción llamados "determinantes de adaptación" y sobre los cuales se condicionan las decisiones de adaptación. Otro aspecto abordado son los Objetivos propios del proceso de adaptación. En el esquema propuesto por los autores, se establece que las adaptaciones serán realizadas mediante un conjunto de reglas, llamadas "reglas de adaptación" que en esencia y de manera simplificada lo que hacen es asignar ciertos '"constituyentes de adaptación" a "determinantes de adaptación" específicos, dado un conjunto de "Objetivos de adaptación".

Una de las motivaciones es el hecho que aunque varios enfoques han sido reportados en la literatura, actualmente no existe consenso respecto a las características, comportamiento y componentes esenciales que deben conformar las interfaces inteligentes. El problema que plantean es que los elementos críticos del proceso de adaptación (determinantes, constituyentes, objetivos y reglas) difieren sustancialmente en los sistemas actuales. Así tenemos que los sistemas existentes adaptan ciertos constituyentes predefinidos, basado en un conjunto predeterminado de determinantes, a través del uso específico de reglas, con el fin de alcanzar objetivos pre-especificados. Con lo anterior argumentan que el proceso de adaptación no es flexible y que no puede ser transferido fácilmente entre aplicaciones. Para enfrentar las limitaciones anteriores los autores proponen:

1. Utilizar un enfoque metodológico que permita la personalización del conjunto de determinantes de adaptación y constituyentes de adaptaci´ on.
2. La incorporación de los objetivos de adaptación como parte integral del proceso de adaptabilidad y.
3. la modificación de las reglas de adaptación, de acuerdo a los objetivos de adaptabilidad.

La idea central del enfoque propuesto está basada en una clara separación de los atributos, del proceso de adaptación. También se plantea que al establecer esta separación, permite que los atributos de la estrategia de adaptación puedan ser personalizados fácilmente a los requerimientos de diferentes dominios de aplicación y gruposde usuario, con lo cual podrían ser reutilizados con modificaciones menores en otras aplicaciones.

Los autores presentan una arquitectura general de una interfaz inteligente, describiendo los componentes,la interacción entre ellos y su relación con la estrategia de adaptabilidad. Asimismo se presenta de manera formal una representación de los elementos de adaptación utilizados. Concluyen el trabajo con los beneficios del enfoque propuesto, los cuales parecen ser cuestionables en varios puntos, principalmente porque no ofrecen pruebas de sus afirmaciones.

9.5 Sistemas de Iniciativa Combinada

Los sistemas de iniciativa combinada ha surgido como una alternativa a los esquemas de interacción que permite manejar la iniciativa desde una perspectiva más flexible, aunque más compleja.

El sistema presentado por Bunt (Bunt et al., 2004) describe la importancia del soporte adaptivo, un tema central dentro del campo de las interfaces adaptivas de iniciativa combinada (Horvitz, 1999), en las cuales es necesario que en ocasiones el sistema realice las adaptaciones de manera automática, asumiendo los respectivos problemas asociados tales como falta de control, transparencia y predictivilidad, y en otras, ofrecer los mecanismos para que el usuario mismo tome control y lleve a cabo la adaptación; sin embargo hay evidencias de que muchas veces el usuario no las realiza, y cuando lo hace, no es claro si lo hace de una manera efectiva (Jameson & Schwarzkopf, 2002). El artículo expone la necesidad de ofrecerle a los usuarios un esquema adaptivo que les apoye en la tarea de personalización de una interfaz.

Los autores proponen una solución de iniciativa combinada, en donde si el usuario es capaz de personalizar eficientemente por si mismo, no se requiere adaptación iniciada por el sistema. En caso contrario, el sistema puede intervenir para proporcionar asistencia. Asimismo se analiza el valor de la personalización y cómo ofrecer lo que llaman soporte adaptivo (ayudar a usuarios aprovechar ventajas de una Interfaz Adaptable). Se presenta un estudio experimental y se examinan los aspectos necesarios para que los usuarios lleven a cabo una personalización efectiva de una GUI basada en menús.

Resulta interesante el análisis que se hace sobre las características de las tareas y los comportamientos de personalización que afectan el desempeño. También se realiza un estudio con una simulación del modelo del proceso (GOMS) basado en un modelado cognitivo que genera predicciones del desempeño del usuario. Los autores analiza con datos de prueba si vale la pena realizar la personalización de la interfaz y si realmente existen beneficios.

Para probar su trabajo, se realizan 2 experimentos exploratorios utilizando el simulador GLEAN (Baumeister et al., 2000). En el primer experimento se lleva a cabo una comparación de diferentes estrategias de personalización que varían respecto al momento de su realización, es decir cuándo son realizadas y también analizan si el "overhead" de personalizar retribuye en algo. En el segundo experimento se enfocan a comparar estrategias que difieren en términos de qué funcionalidades elige agregar el usuario a la interfaz personalizada y sus implicaciones.

Como aportación del trabajo podría considerarse el uso de un modelo GOMS que le permita simular y evaluar el impacto en la personalización tomando en cuenta de manera conjunta los factores de la estrategia de personalización basada en el momento que se realiza, la frecuencia de ejecución de las tareas, su complejidad y el nivel de experiencia del usuario.

Finalmente los resultados obtenidos de los experimentos muestran la importancia de personalizar la interfaz, y consecuentemente se fortalece la justificación de "guiar" al usuario a personalizar su interfaz como una línea importante de investigación.

10. Discusión

De la revisión de la literatura de IUIs presentada en este capítulo se observa que la mayoría de los sistemas analizados son aplicados a sistemas basados en Web y de oficina o de propósito general. El sistema presentado por Viano (Viano et al., 2000) representa uno de los pocos sistemas para aplicaciones críticas, tales como las de operación y control, sin embargo a diferencia del modelo que proponemos (MIA-IC), su sistema es adaptivo y es aplicable a la visualización de contenidos únicamente, no incluyendo navegación adaptable. Asimismo el sistema MIA-IC es específico a tareas poco frecuentes y críticas, nicho que ninguno de los sistemas presentado aborda.

El sistema ADAPTs (Brusilovsky & Cooper, 2002) es similar en algunos aspectos al modelo que proponemos, ya que utiliza varios modelos para realizar la adaptación, como son un modelo de usuario, un modelo del dominio y otro de tareas similar al MIA-IC. Asimismo ADAPTs utiliza un sistema inteligente que le reporta el diagnóstico de fallas y utiliza un manual electrónico para encontrar la información que le explique al usuario cómo realizar la reparación. Esta situación parece similar a la del MIA-IC, que se conecta al sistema SAO de ayuda y realiza adaptación tanto de contenidos como de navegación.

Una diferencia importante es que ADAPTs es un sistema adaptivo, mientras que en el MIA-IC proponemos un esquema de iniciativa combinada, ofreciendo mayor flexibilidad en la interacción con el usuario. Por otra parte el énfasis del sistema ADAPTs es su complejo y novedoso modelo de usuario multi-aspectos que permite de manera dinámica establecer el nivel de experiencia del usuario en todo momento. En nuestro modelo, al tener un modelo integral se busca que la información de los diferentes modelos sea el componente que nos permita hacer más preciso el proceso de adaptación, no par la cantidad de información de los diferentes modelos, sino por la información más adecuada al operador y al estado de la planta. Otra diferencia es que ADAPTs una guia adaptiva para mantenimiento y no es para situaciones poco frecuentes o críticas.

Dado que las IUIs construyen modelos al observar el comportamiento de sus usuarios, es un reto abierto aún el generar modelos útiles mediante algoritmos que realicen un aprendizaje de manera rápida. El punto aquí no se refiere al tiempo de procesamiento en el CPU, sino al número de ejemplos de entrenamiento necesarios para generar un modelo preciso de las preferencias del usuario. La mayoría de las aplicaciones de minería de datos suponen que se tienen cantidades considerables de datos, suficientes como para inducir conocimiento preciso. En contraste, las interfaces adaptivas dependen del tiempo del usuario al utilizarlas y entonces se requiere de mecanismos de inducción que puedan proporcionar una alta precisión a partir de un conjunto pequeño de datos de entrenamiento.

Otro reto abierto es la cantidad limitada de evaluación empírica que actualmente existe para los sistemas adaptivos, por lo que más investigación es necesaria para establecer de manera medible si una interfaz adaptiva es mejor comparada a una no inteligente. Varios métodos empíricos de evaluación de usabilidad han sido utilizados y adaptados en el contexto de interfaces adaptivas, tales como entrevistas, cuestionarios, el protocolo Think Aloud (Dix at al., 2003), y otros que en esencia constituyen algunos de los métodos más usados en la validación y pruebas de los sistemas tradicionales, sin embargo su aplicabilidad a los sistemas adaptivos se considera limitado.

11. Conclusión

Aunque hemos presentado en este capítulo la investigación en el área de IUIs, sus retos y enfoque de solución con especial énfasis en el hecho que es un campo multidisciplinario, se observa que los tres enfoques que actualmente se utilizan con mayor éxito para enfrentar los retos de las IUIs aún muestran una falta de intercambio en los hallazgos y problemas enfrentados entre las disciplinas involucradas.

De la revisión de literatura se detecta que es necesaria una mayor integración e intercambio de ideas entre las diferentes disciplinas que conforman el área de interfaces inteligentes de usuario. Creemos que la investigación en el desarrollo de nuevos modelos de interfaz que integren componentes de varias disciplinas ayudará a encontrar soluciones diferentes, pues en general se observa que actualmente la investigación que se realiza tiende a favorecer el uso de los mismos conocimientos, técnicas y metodologías probadas y aceptados dentro de una misma disciplina, y la llamada fertilización cruzada aún es necesaria. -.

12. Referencias

Armentano, M.; Godoy, M. and Amandi, A. (2006) Personal assistants: Direct manipulation vs. mixed initiative interfaces. *Int.J. Hum.-Comput. Stud.*, 64(1):27-35, 2006.

Baumeister, L.K.; John, B. E. and Byrne. M. D. (2000) A com parison of tools for building GOMs models. *In CHI '00: Proceedings of the SIGCHI Conference on Human Factors in Computing Systems*, ACM Press, pages 211-214, New York, NY, USA.

Birnbaum, L.; Horvitz, E.; Kurlander, D.; Lieberman, H. ; Marks, J. and Roth, S. (1997) Compelling intelligent user interfaces. How much AI? In *IUI '97: Proceedings of the 2nd international conference on Intelligent user interfaces*, pages 173-175, New York, NY, USA.

Brusilovsky, P. and Cooper, D. W. (2002) Domain, task, and user models for an adaptive hypermedia performance support system. *In IUI '02: Proceedings of the 7th international conference on Intelligent user interfaces,* ACM Press, pages 23–30, New York, NY, USA.

Bunt, A.; Conati, C. and McGrenere, J. (2004) What role can adaptive support play in an adaptable system? *In IUI '04: Proceedings of the 9th international conference on Intelligent user interfaces,* ACM Press, pages 117–124, New York, NY, USA.

Carenini, G,; Smith, J. and Poole D. (2003) Towards more conversational and collaborative recommender systems. *In IUI '03: Proceedings of the 8th international conference on Intelligent user interfaces,* ACM Press, pages 12–18, New York, NY, USA.

Cassell, J. (2000) Embodied conversational interface agents. *Commun. ACM,* 43(4):70–78, USA.

Chin, D. (2001) Empirical evaluation of user models and user-adapted systems. *UMUAI 01', User Modeling and User-Adapted Interaction,* 11(1-2):181–194, USA.

Dix, A.; Finlay J.; Abowd G.; and Beale R. (2003) *Human-computer interaction (3rd ed.).* Prentice-Hall, Inc., Upper Saddle River, NJ, USA.

Eirinaki, M and Vazirgiannis, M. (2003) Web mining for web personalization. *ACM Trans. Inter. Tech.,* 3(1):1-27, USA.

Eisenstein, J. and Rich, C. (2002). Agents and GUIs from task models. *In IUI '02: Proceedings of the 7th international conference on Intelligent user interfaces,* ACM Press, pages 47–54, New York, NY, USA.

Franklin, D.; Budzik, J. and Hammond, K. (2002) Plan-based interfaces: keeping track of user tasks and acting to cooperate. *In Proceedings of the 7th international conference on Intelligent user interfaces,* ACM Press, pages 79–86, USA.

Fu, X.; Budzik, J. and Hammond, K. (2000) Mining navigation history for recommendation. *In IUI '00: Proceedings of the 5th international conference on Intelligent user interfaces,* ACM Press, pages 106–112, New York, NY, USA.

Hook, K. (1999) Designing and evaluating intelligent user interfaces. In *IUI '99: Proceedings of the 4th international conference on Intelligent user interfaces,* ACM Press,pages 5–6, New York, NY, USA.

Horvitz, E.; Breese, J.; Heckerman, D.; Hovel, D.; and Rommelse, K. (1998) The Lumiere project: Bayesian user modeling for inferring the goals and needs of software users. *In Proceedings of the Fourteenth Conference on Uncertainty in Artificial Intelligence,* pages 256–265, Madison, WI, USA.

Horvitz, E. (1999) Principles of mixed-initiative user interfaces. *In CHI '99: Proceedings of the SIGCHI conference on Human factors in computing systems,* ACM Press, pages 159–166, New York, NY, USA.

Jameson A. and Schwarzkopf, E. (2002) Pros and cons of controllability: An empirical study. *In AH '02: Proceedings of the Second International Conference on Adaptive Hypermedia and Adaptive Web-Based Systems,* Springer-Verlag, pages 193–202, London, UK.

Kirsch-Pinheiro, M.; Villanova-Oliver, M.; Gensel, J. and Martin H. (2005) Context-aware filtering for collaborative web systems: adapting the awareness information to the user's context. *In SAC '05: Proceedings of the 2005 ACM symposium on Applied computing,* ACM Press, pages 1668–1673, New York, NY, USA.

Kobsa, A. (1994) User modeling and user-adapted interaction. *In CHI '94: Conference companion on Human factors in computing systems,* ACM Press, pages 415-416, New York, NY, USA.

Langley, P. (1999) User modeling in adaptive interfaces. *In UM '99: Proceedings of the seventh international conference on User modeling,* Springer-Verlag New York, Inc., pages 357-370, Secaucus, NJ, USA.

Maes, P. (1994) Agents that reduce work and information overload. *Commun. ACM,* 37(7):30-40, USA.

Maybury, M. (1999) Intelligent user interfaces: an introduction. In *IUI '99: Proceedings of the 4th international conference on Intelligent user interfaces,* ACM Press, pages 3-4, New York, NY, USA.

Mayhew, D.J. (1999) *The usability engineering lifecycle: a practitioner's handbook for user interface design.* Morgan Kaufmann Publishers Inc., San Francisco, CA, USA.

Mobasher, B.; Dai, H.; Luo, T. and Nakagawa, M. (2001) Effective personalization based on association rule discovery from web usage data. *In WIDM '01: Proceedings of the 3rd international workshop on Web information and data management,* ACM Press, pages 9-15, New York, NY,USA.

Oviatt, S.; Cohen,P.; Wu, L.; Vergo, J.; Duncan, L.; Suhm, B.; Bers, J.; Holzman, T.; Winograd, T.; Landay,j.; Larson, J. and Ferro, D. (2000) Designing the user interface for multimodal speech and gesture applications: State-of-the-art systems and research directions for 2000 and beyond.

Peyton, L. (2003) Measuring and managing the effectiveness of personalization. *In ICEC '03: Proceedings of the 5th international conference on Electronic commerce,* ACM Press, pages 220-224, New York, NY, USA.

Puerta, A. R. (1998). Supporting user-centered design of adaptive user interfaces via interface models. *In Proceedings of the First Annual Workshop On Real-Time Intelligent User Interfaces For Decision Support And Information Visualization.*ACM. Press. USA.

Reeves, L.M.; Lai, J.; Larson, J. A.; Oviatt, S.; Balaji, T. S.; Buisine, S.; Collings, P.; Cohen, P.; Kraal, B.; Martin, J.; McTear, M.; Raman, T.V.; Stanney, K. M.; Su, H. and Ying Q. Guidelines for multimodal user interface design. *Commun. ACM,* 47(1):57-59. USA.

Rich, C. and Sidner, C.L. (1996). Adding a collaborative agent to graphical user interfaces. *In Proceedings of the 9th annual ACM symposium on User interface software and technology,* ACM Press, pages 21-30.

Russell S. and Norvig P. (2003) *Artificial Intelligence: A Modern Approach (2nd ed.).* Prentice-Hall, Englewood Cliffs, NJ, USA.

Shneiderman, B. and Plaisant, C. (2004) *Designing the User Interface : Strategies for Effective Human-Computer Interaction (4th ed.).* Addison-Wesley Publishing, Boston, USA.

Shneiderman, B. (1997) Direct manipulation for comprehensible, predictable and controllable user interfaces. In *IUI '97: Proceedings of the 2nd international conference on Intelligent user interfaces,* ACM Press, pages 33-39,New York, NY, USA.

Stephanidis, C.; Karagiannidis, C. and Koumpis, A. (1997) Decision making in intelligent user interfaces. *In IUI '97: Proceedings of the 2nd international conference on Intelligent user interfaces,* ACM Press, pages 195-202, New York, NY, USA.

Stumpf, S.; Rajaram, V.; Li, L.; Burnett, M.; Dietterich, T.; Sullivan, E.; Drummond, R. and Herlocker, J. (2007) Toward harnessing user feedback for machine learning. *In IUI '07: Proceedings of the 12th international conference on Intelligent user interfaces*, ACM Press, pages 82–91, New York, NY, USA.

Sugiyama, K.; Hatano, K. and Yoshikawa, M. (2004) Adaptive web search based on user profile constructed without any effort from users. *In WWW '04: Proceedings of the 13th international conference on World Wide Web*, ACM Press, pages 675–684, New York, NY, USA.

Viano, G.; Parodi, A.; Alty, J.; Khalil, C.; Angulo, I.; Biglino, D.; Crampes, M.; Vaudry, C.; Daurensan, V. and Lachaud, P. (2000) Adaptive user interface for process control based on multi-agent approach. *In AVI '00: Proceedings of the working conference on Advanced visual interfaces*, ACM Press, pages 201–204, New York, NY, USA.

Wernn, A. (1997) Local plan recognition in direct manipulation interfaces. In *Proceedings of the 2nd international conference on intelligent user interfaces*, ACM Press, pages 7–14. USA.

3

Towards a Reference Architecture for Context-Aware Services

Axel Bürkle, Wilmuth Müller and Uwe Pfirrmann
Fraunhofer Institute for Information and Data Processing
Germany

1. Introduction

This Chapter describes an infrastructure for multi-modal perceptual systems which aims at developing and realizing computer services that are delivered to humans in an implicit and unobtrusive way. The framework presented here supports the implementation of human-centric context-aware applications providing non-obtrusive assistance to participants in events such as meetings, lectures, conferences and presentations taking place in indoor "smart spaces". We emphasize on the design and implementation of an agent-based framework that supports "pluggable" service logic in the sense that the service developer can concentrate on the service logic independently of the underlying middleware. Furthermore, we give an example of the architecture's ability to support the cooperation of multiple services in a meeting scenario using an intelligent connector service and a semantic web oriented travel service.

The framework was developed as part of the project CHIL (Computers in the Human Interaction Loop). The vision of CHIL was to be able to provide context-aware human centric services which will operate in the background, provide assistance to the participants in the CHIL spaces and undertake tedious tasks in an unobtrusive way. To achieve this, significant effort had to be put in designing efficient context extraction components so that the CHIL system can acquire an accurate perspective of the current state of the CHIL space. However, the CHIL services required a much more sophisticated modelling of the actual event, rather than simple and fluctuating impressions of it. Furthermore, by nature the CHIL spaces are highly dynamic and heterogeneous; people join or leave, sensors fail or are restarted, user devices connect to the network, etc. To manage this diverse infrastructure, sophisticated techniques were necessary that can map all entities present in the CHIL system and provide information to all components which may require it.

From these facts, one can easily understand that in addition to highly sophisticated components at an individual level, another mechanism (or a combination of mechanisms) should be present which can handle this infrastructure. The CHIL Reference Architecture for Multi Modal Systems lies in the background, and provides the solid, high performance and robust backbone for the CHIL services. Each individual need is assigned to a specially designed and integrated layer which is docked to the individual component, and provides all the necessary actions to enable the component to be plugged in the CHIL framework.

2. The CHIL Project

The architecture presented in this chapter is a result of the work carried out in the FP6 research project CHIL (IP 506909) partially funded by the European Commission under the Information Society Technology (IST) program.

2.1 Project Goals

The main idea behind the CHIL project is to put Computers in the Human Interaction Loop (CHIL), rather than the other way round. Computers should proactively and implicitly attempt to take care of human needs without the necessity of explicit human specification. This implies that a service is aware of the current context of its users in order to react adequately to a user's situation and environment. Computers are repositioned in the background, discretely observe the humans and attempt to anticipate and serve their needs like electronic butlers.

To realize this goal and to overcome the lack of recognition and understanding of human activities, needs and desires as well as the absence of learning, proactive, context-aware computing services, research in the following areas was carried out within the CHIL project:

- Perceptual Technologies: Proactive, implicit services require a good description of human interaction and activities. This implies a robust description of the perceptual context as it applies to human interaction: Who is doing What, to Whom, Where and How, and Why.
- Software Infrastructure: A common and versatile software architecture serves to improve interoperability among partners and offers a market driven exchange of modules for faster integration.
- Services: Context-aware CHIL services assisting humans interacting with each other are designed, assembled and evaluated. Prototypes are continuously developed and their effectiveness explored in user studies.

2.2 CHIL Services

CHIL focuses on two situations, in which people interact with people and exchange information to realize common objectives: meetings and lecture rooms. In order to support the interaction between humans in these scenarios, the following context-aware services have been implemented:

- The **Connector** attempts to connect people at the best time and by the best media possible, whenever it is most opportune to connect them. In lieu of leaving streams of voice messages and playing phone tag, the Connector tracks and knows its masters' activities, preoccupations and their relative social relationships and mediates a proper connection at the right time between them.
- The **Memory Jog** is a personal assistant that helps its human user remember and retrieve needed facts about the world and people around him/her. By recognizing people, spaces and activities around its master, the Memory Jog can retrieve names and affiliations of other members in a group. It provides past records of previous encounters and interactions, and retrieves information relevant to the meeting.
- The **Travel Service** provides assistance with planning and rearranging itineraries. It detects if a user is going to miss a scheduled travel connection e.g. due to the delay of a meeting, and automatically searches for alternative travel possibilities. Based on user

preferences, it provides a selection of the "best" travel possibilities found. The Travel Service can either be evoked directly by the user through one of his personal devices or triggered by another CHIL service.

- The **Meeting Manager** handles all meeting related issues. For example, it keeps track of organisational meeting data, e.g. the list of planned participants and the meeting location. It can display a personalized welcome message, when a participant enters the meeting room. Furthermore, the Meeting Manager Service provides support during a meeting. One of its functionalities is to automatically start the corresponding presentation when a presenter approaches the presentation area.

Other services such as a Socially Supportive Workspace were implemented by the various CHIL partners. In addition, a series of basic services for common and elementary domain tasks are available. CHIL, however, was not intended as a project to develop specific application systems. It was intended to explore them as exemplary placeholders for the more general class of systems and services that put human-human interaction at the centre and computing services in a supporting function on the periphery, rather than the other way round.

2.3 Project Results

The CHIL consortium (15 institutes and companies in 9 countries) was one of the largest consortia tackling the above mentioned problems to-date. It has developed a research and development infrastructure by which different CHIL services can be quickly assembled, proposed and evaluated, exploiting a User Centred Design approach to ensure that the developed services answer real users' needs and demands. The CHIL project has pushed the state-of-the-art in various perceptual technologies (Stiefelhagen & Garofolo, 2007; Stiefelhagen et al., 2008). Furthermore, we have developed a highly flexible architecture employing collaborative context-aware agents, which enable the implementation and provision of the CHIL services. The effectiveness of the developed components and technologies has been demonstrated by implementing a number of CHIL services.

3. Related Work

Developing architectural frameworks supporting ubiquitous computing projects is not a recent trend. Major pervasive and ubiquitous computing projects have placed significant effort in designing such platforms that can facilitate integration, debugging, development, management and eventually deployment of the end-services.

The m4 project (multimodal meeting manager) (Wellner et al., 2005) presents a client-server architecture using JSP-generated frames in a meeting browser to produce the output of audio and video streams and services. The AMI Project (Augmented Multi-Party Interaction) (AMI, 2008), probably the project most closely related to CHIL, focuses on technologies which are integrated by a plug-in mechanism of a relatively simple, browser-based framework that allows indirect communication between the modules. Both of them concentrate on technologies and adapt existing software for integration purposes. CHIL in contrast developed an architecture that is particularly designed for the integration of and direct communication between context-aware services.

Other previous research focused on distributed middleware infrastructures (Roman et al., 2002), on architecture frameworks for developers and administrators (Grimm et al., 2000), on the design process and the development of frameworks and toolkits (Dey, 2000), on context-aware broker agents (Chen et al., 2004), on client-server architectures with a central server and multiple clients to support the management of multiple sensor input for different services (Johanson, 2002), on flexible, decentralized networks connecting dynamically changing configurations of self-identifying mobile and stationary devices (Coen et al., 1999), on architectures for coordination of I/O-devices and the exploitation of contextual information (Shafer et al., 1998), and on systems that span wearable, handheld, desktop and infrastructure computers (Garlan et al., 2002).

All these efforts justify the importance of ubiquitous computing architectures. At the same time they manifest that there is no global unified framework addressing all needs. Rather, the majority of these architectures concentrate on one or more application specific goals. A fundamental limitation of these architectures is that they assume that all context-aware components (e.g., perceptual components, situation modeling middleware) are contributed by the same technology provider, which is not always the case. CHIL as well as other emerging pervasive computing environments are composed by a variety of distributed heterogeneous components from multiple vendors. Another drawback of these architectures is that they were built upon legacy technologies and therefore do not benefit from emerging technologies (e.g., the semantic web). The CHIL architecture presented in the following sections is proposed as a reference model architecture for multi-modal perceptual systems.

4. The CHIL Reference Architecture

Due to the scale of the CHIL project with its large number of partners contributing with a diversity of technical components such as services, event and situation modelling modules, context extraction components and sensors, as well as the complexity of these components, a flexible architecture that facilitates their integration at different levels is essential. A layered architecture model was found to best meet these requirements and allow a structured method for interfacing with sensors, integrating technology components, processing sensorial input and composing services as collections of basic services.

In order to realize context-aware, proactive, and intelligent services, both context-delivering and collaborating components have to be integrated. Context is any information that can be used to characterize the situation of a person or computing entity that is considered relevant to the interaction between a user and an application (Dey, 2000). In CHIL, context is delivered both by perceptual components and learning modules. Perceptual components continuously track human activities, using all perception modalities available, and build static and dynamic models of the scene. Learning modules within the agents model the concepts and relations within the ontology. Collaboration is enabled by a set of intelligent software agents communicating on a semantic level with each other.

The result of the architecture design work is the CHIL Reference Architecture, which is an architectural framework along with a set of middleware elements facilitating the integration of services, perceptual components, sensors, actuators, and context and situation modelling scripts. The framework and the associated middleware elements facilitate integration and assembly of ubiquitous computing applications in smart spaces. Specifically, they mitigate the integration issues arising from the distributed and heterogeneous nature of pervasive, ubiquitous and context-aware computing environments.

4.1 Layer Model

The layered system architecture that facilitates the integration of these various components is presented in Fig. 1. According to the components' different functional levels such as audio and video streaming, perceptual components, sensor control, situation modelling, services and user interfaces, the architecture consists of 8 horizontal layers. They are completed by two vertical layers, the ontology and "CHIL utilities", which are accessible by all components and provide elementary functions relevant to all layers.

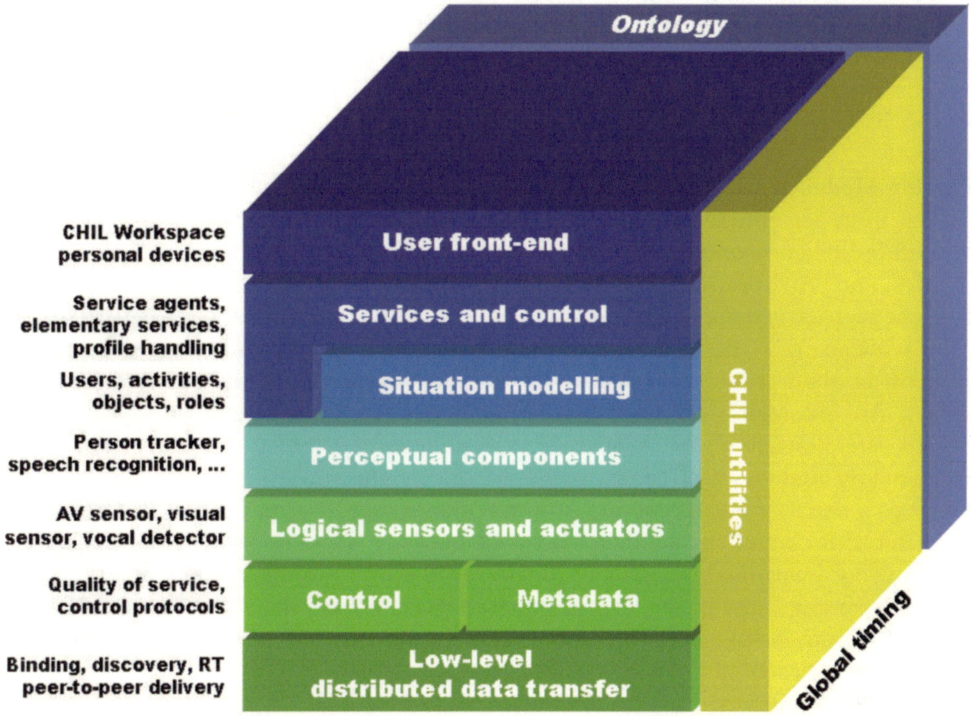

Figure 1. The CHIL architecture layer model

The lower layers deal with the management and the interpretation of continuous streams of video and audio signals in terms of event detection and situation adaptation and contain the perceptual components. The upper layers of the infrastructure enable reasoning and management of a variety of services and user interfacing devices. "User-front-end" and "Services and control" are implemented as software agents, thus the service and user interface management is based on agent communication. All layers use a common ontology as a backbone. A detailed description of the layers is given in the following section, the agent infrastructure of the CHIL system is described in detail in section 6.

4.2 Description of the Layers

User Front-End: The User Front-End contains all user related components such as the Personal Agents, Device Agents and the User Profile of a CHIL user. The Personal Agent acts as the user's personal assistant taking care of his demands. It interacts with its master through personal devices (e.g. notebook, PDA, smart phone) which are represented by corresponding Device Agents. The Device Agents are the controlling interfaces to the personal devices. The Personal Agent also provides and controls access to its master's profile and preferences, thus ensuring user data privacy. The User Profile stores personal data and service-related preferences of a user.

Services and control: The Services and Control layer contains the components which implement the different services as well as service-to-service information exchange and user-service communication. The services are implemented through software agents. The Service and Control layer comprises both the service agents and their management. The interaction with other agents within this layer and the User front-end layer follows well-defined standards and the communication mechanisms of the agent platform, while communication with the other layers follows internal mechanisms. Services are both reusable basic services as well as complex higher-level services composed of suitable basic services.

Situation Modelling: The Situation Modelling layer is the place where the situation context received from perceptual components is processed and modelled. The context information acquired by the components at this layer helps services to respond better to varying user activities and environmental changes. For example, the situating modelling answers questions such as: Is there a meeting going on in the smart room? Is there a person speaking at the whiteboard? Who is the person speaking at the whiteboard? This layer is also a collection of abstractions representing the environmental context in which users act and interact. An ontological knowledge-base maintains up-to-date state of objects (people, artefacts, situations) and their relationships. Additionally it serves as an "inference engine" that regularly deduces and generalizes facts during the process of updating the context models as a result of events coming from the underlying layer of Perceptual Components. The searched-for situations are dictated by the needs of active services, as for the detection of the level of interruptability of a particular person in a room for whom a service has to monitor incoming calls. In the CHIL Reference Architecture, the situation model takes its information from the perceptual components and produces a set of situation events that are provided to services.

Perceptual Components: Perceptual Components are software components which operate on data streams coming from various sensors such as audio, video and RFID-based position trackers, process it, interpret it, and extract information relating to people's actions. Such information may be the people's locations, IDs, hand gestures, pose recognition etc.

The CHIL Project brought together perceptual component developers from different partners; all of them were using customized tools, different operating systems, a wide variety of signal processing (and other) libraries, and in general a plenitude of equipment which was not agreed upon from the early stages of the project. However, the CHIL Project had the vision to be able to combine the developed technologies and algorithms and deliver state-of-the-art services which would exploit the whole underlying sensor and actuator infrastructure and, ideally, would be independent of the technology provider. These circumstances had to be considered when designing the Perceptual Components tier.

The design of the Perceptual Components tier does not define the parameters of the core signal processing algorithm, but pertain to the input and output data modelling aspects of it; it considers the Perceptual Component as a "black box". The design specifies and gives guidelines, how perceptual components shall operate, "advertise" themselves, subscribe to receiving a specific sensor data stream and how they shall forward their extracted context to the higher layer of the CHIL Reference Architecture. This specification incorporates all the interfaces for communicating with the sensors, the ontology and the services.

Logical Sensors and Actuators: Sensors and actuators are keys in the design and implementation of multi-modal perceptual services. They act as the "eyes and ears" of the system and provide a continuous flow of output data to the processing components which extract pertinent information by applying algorithms able to extract elementary context. This layer comprises several abstractions which wrap the sensor control and transmission components for each one of the sensors in the smart space. Several APIs for initializing the component, capturing the sensor data, for configuring the component, and for starting and stopping it are provided. Each sensor is controlled by a specified sensor controller, which provides the low-level commands to the sensor. The sensors, and therewith the logical sensor components produce a continuous flow of information which is transmitted using a particularly designed interface, the ChilFlow middleware (see below), to any consuming component in the CHIL system. Finally, each logical sensor is able to communicate with the framework's knowledge base where it can register and "advertise" itself to the rest of the framework.

Control/Metadata: Control and Metadata provide mechanisms for data annotation, synchronous and asynchronous system control, synchronizing data flows, effective storing and searching multi-media content and metadata generated by data sources.

Low-level Distributed Data Transfer: The Low-level Distributed Data Transfer layer of the CHIL Architecture is responsible for transferring high-volume and/or high-frequency data from sensors to perceptual components or between perceptual components. This layer is implemented by the ChilFlow data-transfer middleware. This middleware is heavily used by developers of perceptual components to distribute their components over several networked computers in order to exploit more computational power. In order to free developers from handling networking issues and managing the connections between components, ChilFlow offers an easy to master, yet powerful object-oriented programming interface, which provides type-safe network transparent one-to-many communication channels for data exchange between components. These communication channels are called flows. Flows provide higher abstraction level over ordinary network connections (e.g. TCP sockets) that fit the communication characteristics of components and simplify the work of the components' developers significantly.

CHIL utilities: This layer provides basic functionality that is needed by components in all layers of the framework. One particular example is global timing, an important issue in distributed, event driven systems like CHIL where time-stamped messages and streams are sent through the infrastructure.

Ontology: In order to enable the intended cognitive capabilities of the CHIL software environment, it is necessary to conceptualize entities and to formally describe relations among them. Through the ontology, CHIL software components both know the meaning of the data they are operating on and expose their functionality according to a common classification scheme.

The CHIL ontology is defined using the Web Ontology Language OWL (OWL, 2008). It comprises several modules that are physically represented by separate Web resources with distinct URLs, among them the fully integrated CHIL agent communication ontology. The idea of modularization is that software developers only need to reference those parts of the ontology that are relevant for them. Additionally, modularization increases performance, for example when deploying the agent communication subset of the ontology in order to generate software agent code.

For managing the ontological data, as well as for reasoning and detecting inconsistencies, access to an ontology is typically backed by a central knowledge base management system. The CHIL Knowledge Base Server exposes the functionality of arbitrary off-the-shelf ontology management systems by a well defined API based on OWL. As such, it provides unified access to the central ontological knowledge base for heterogeneous platforms, programming languages and communication protocols. Together with this API and the CHIL ontology, the knowledge base server constitutes the Ontology layer of the CHIL architecture.

5. Sensor Infrastructure & Context-Awareness

Sensing infrastructures are a key prerequisite for realizing context-aware applications. Within CHIL several sites have constructed in-door environments comprising multi-sensor infrastructures called "smart rooms". They include:

- Microphones and microphone arrays (Brandstein & Ward, 2001)
- Cameras (fixed, active with pan, tilt and zoom (PTZ) or panoramic (fish-eye))
- RFID-based location trackers (Ubisense, 2007)

Based on these sensor infrastructures, a variety of perceptual components have been built and evaluated such as 2D and 3D-visual perceptual components, acoustic components, audio-visual components, RFID-based location tracking, as well as output components such as multimodal speech synthesis and targeted audio.

Perceptual components derive elementary contextual information; however in general they lack information about the overall current status of the people's interactions and environmental conditions. To be able to "fuse" many of these perceptual components together in order to determine more sophisticated and meaningful states, additional middleware interfaces have been developed to facilitate the intercommunication of these components. The middleware acts as a receptor of the whole range of the elementary context cues and processes them in order to map the resulting contextual information into a complex situation. This process is called situation recognition and is a major part of every human-centric ubiquitous application. Situation recognition in our implementation follows the "network of situations" approach. This scheme allows the interconnection of distinct cases (situations), which are connected with edges, forming a directed graph. A transition from one situation to another occurs if given constraints are satisfied. As soon as this transition is feasible, the service logic is applied, and the active state is reflected by the newly reached one. Context-awareness is hence modelled by this network. Fig. 2 illustrates such a network of situations which can be used to track situations during meetings in a "smart room".

A meeting is a sequence of three main situations: "MeetingSetup", "OngoingMeeting" and "MeetingFinished". Starting with the initial "MeetingSetup" and its sub state "Arrival", the situation changes to "WelcomeParticipant" when the person identification perceptual component signals that a person is entering the room; the new person will be welcomed by displaying a message. Based on location and activity information of all attendees, the "Meeting Detector" perceptual component recognizes the start of the meeting and triggers the transition to the next main situation "OngoingMeeting". During the meeting, the body tracker perceptual component tracks the locations of the participants, detects when a person approaches or leaves the presentation area and switches the situation accordingly between the "Discussion" and "Presentation" state. The Meeting Detector again determines the end of the meeting and triggers the transition to the final "MeetingFinished" situation.

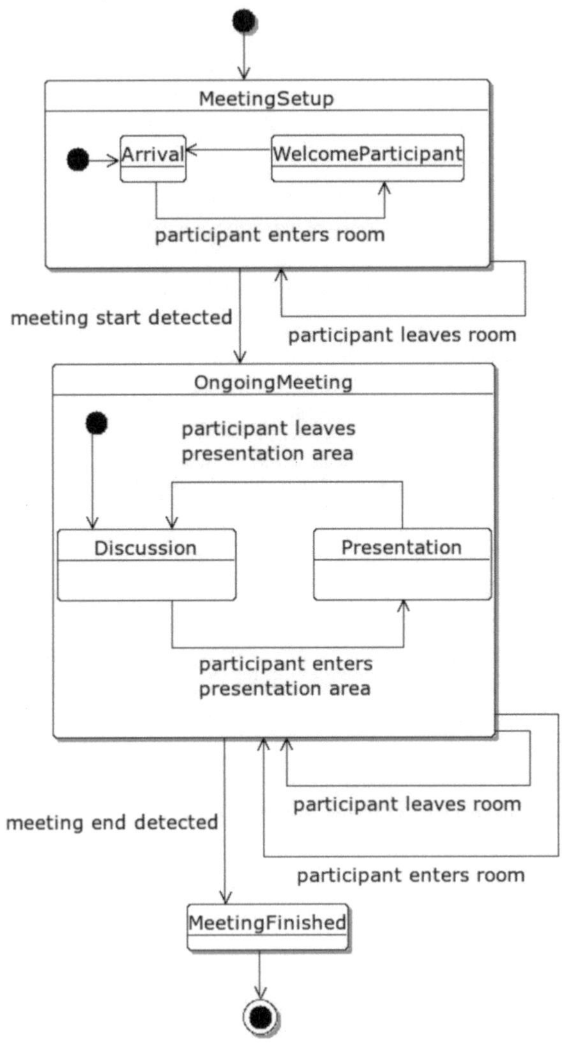

Figure 2. A "network of situations" model for tracking meetings in a smart room

6. Agent Infrastructure for Context-Aware Services

Context-aware services are usually based on complex heterogeneous distributed systems comprising sensors, actuators, perceptual components, as well as information fusion middleware. In such sophisticated systems agents are preferred (Huhns & Singh, 1999), since they are equipped with a large set of capabilities. An agent is "*...any entity that can be viewed as perceiving its environment through sensors and acting upon its environment through* *effectors"* (Russell & Norvig, 2003). Incorporating that *"An agent is a computer system, situated in some environment, that is capable of flexible autonomous action in order to meet its design objectives."* (Jennings et al., 1998) and an intelligent inter-agent communication, a multi-agent system seems to perfectly meet the challenges of such complex human-centric systems.

Autonomous agents are computational systems that inhabit some complex dynamic environment, sense and act autonomously in this environment, and by doing so, realize a set of goals or tasks for which they are designed (Maes, 1994). Hence, they meet the major requirements for the CHIL architecture: to support the integration and cooperation of autonomous, context-aware services in a heterogeneous environment. Summarized in this short term, the major goals for the infrastructure span discovery, involvement and collaboration of services as well as competition between services in order to perform a certain task the best way possible. Standardized communication mechanisms and protocols have to be considered to raise information exchange onto a semantic level and to ensure location transparency.

To this end, we have devised a multi-agent framework that meets the following target objectives:

- Facilitate the integration of diverse context-aware services developed by numerous different service providers.
- Facilitate services in leveraging basic services (e.g. sensor and actuator control) available within the smart rooms.
- Allow augmentation and evolution of the underlying infrastructure independent of the services installed in the room.
- Control user access to services.
- Support service personalization through maintaining appropriate profiles.
- Enable discovery, involvement and collaboration of services.
- Provide the human-oriented services to the end user the best way possible.

The JADE (Java Agent DEvelopment Framework) platform (JADE, 2008) was selected to be the backbone of our system as it is equipped with many features, which make it a highly flexible and secure platform. As seen in (Altmann et al., 2001), JADE performs adequately in many of the evaluation criteria which include agent mobility capabilities, administration, network traffic issues, stability, security, debugging capabilities etc. Finally, JADE is compliant to the standards for agent communication, agent management and message transfer of the IEEE Computer Society standards organization FIPA (Foundation for Intelligent Physical Agents) (FIPA, 2008).

The following sections describe the CHIL agent infrastructure and how we achieved our objectives. Moreover, they demonstrate how we realized a multi-agent system that is capable to *"solve problems that are beyond the individual capabilities or knowledge of each problem solver"* (Jennings et al., 1998).

6.1 Agent Description

The CHIL software agent infrastructure, shown in Fig. 3, is composed of three levels of agents: personal and device agents that are close to the user and offer the functionality and results of the human-centric services to the end user, basic agents providing elementary tasks like service discovery, collaboration and agent communication to the service developers, and service agents, which implement or cover the functionality of the various context-aware services.

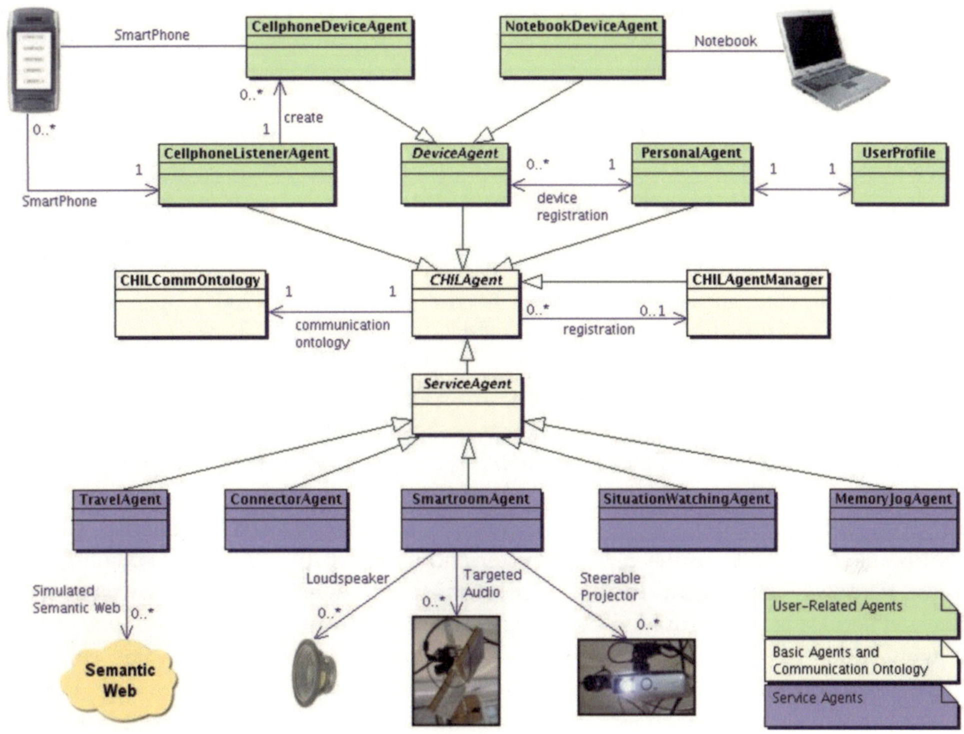

Figure 3. The CHIL software agent infrastructure

User-related Agents

Every person in the CHIL environment has a dedicated Personal Agent that acts as a personal secretary for him. Personal Agents are assigned during a login procedure and manage the complete interaction between its user and the CHIL system, supported by specialized device agents, which are bound to specific input and output devices. The Personal Agent knows what front-end devices its master has access to, how it can best receive or provide information and what input and notification types he prefers (notebook, cell phone call, SMS, targeted audio, etc.). Moreover, the Personal Agent is permanently aware of its master's context (location, environment, activity) by communicating with the Situation Watching Agent, in order to act or react in an appropriate way. Furthermore, the Personal Agent provides and controls access to its master's profile and preferences, thus ensuring user data privacy.

Similar to a user and his Personal Agent, each device has its own Device Agent that manages the complete communication between the device and a user's Personal Agent. The Notebook Device Agent handles the interaction between the graphical user front-end on the user's notebook and the user's Personal Agent, the Cell Phone Device Agent controls the communication between the Personal Agent and the user's cell phone. The Cell Phone Listener Agent supervises all incoming cell phone based requests: it watches a specific port and in case of an incoming call, it creates a Cell Phone Device Agent and passes over the socket connection to it. The newly created agent will then handle all further communication between the cell phone and the user's Personal Agent.

Basic Agents

The major basic agents in the CHIL environment are the CHIL Agent and the CHIL Agent Manager. The CHIL Agent is a subclass of the JADE Agent, which itself is the elementary agent in the JADE agent platform, and acts as the fundamental abstract class for all agents in the CHIL agent framework. It provides methods for essential agent administrative functionality (agent setup and takedown), for ontology-based messaging (create, send, receive messages, extract the message content), utility jobs like logging, and, in cooperation with the CHIL Agent Manager, for directory facilitator service (DF service) tasks such as register and deregister agents, modify agent and service descriptions and search service-providing agents based on a semantic service description. Special importance is attached to keep the agent communication conform to the FIPA (FIPA, 2008) specifications: the complete message transfer is compliant to the FIPA Interaction Protocols and the FIPA Communicative Acts and is based on a well-defined communication ontology, as recommended in the FIPA Abstract Architecture Specification.

The CHIL Agent Manager is a central instance encapsulating and adding functionality to the JADE Directory Facilitator (DF) and coordinating the selection and use of agents. Each CHIL agent registers its services with the CHIL Agent Manager, so the agent manager is, at any time, aware of all available agents, their abilities and the required resources. The CHIL Agent Manager can act both as a matchmaker and a broker. In case of an incoming service request, it knows which agents can solve the problem and which resources are needed. If the requested service can be provided by a single agent, it returns – serving as a matchmaker - the agent identifier of the capable agent to the requester, which in turn may contact the service providing agent. As a broker and in the case of a more complex problem, the CHIL Agent Manager decomposes the overall problem into sub problems, computes a problem solving strategy and invokes the subtasks on appropriate service agents. Having received all necessary partial results, it computes the overall solution and returns the final result to the initial requester.

Service Agents

Each Service Agent is associated with a specific service and provides access to the service functionality both to users and other agents. Service agents register the service functions with the CHIL Agent Manager using ontology based service descriptions, thus mapping the syntactical level of services to the semantic level of the agent community. These service descriptions can be queried both by Personal Agents in order to provide the service to human users and by other service agents, which may compose various functions from other services to supply their own one.

The basic Service Agent is an abstract ancestor class for all specific service agents; it provides the methods for the registration of service features including the necessary resources. Specialized service agents comprise the core functionality of the associated service whereas the service itself may be implemented as agent or may be covered by an agent, which then provides a suitable interface to the service. This applies to the Connector Agent, the Memory Jog Agent, the Travel Agent and the Meeting Manager Agent; the associated services have already been described in the section "CHIL Services".

Two special agents provide common abilities, which are useful for the whole agent society: the Smart Room Agent and the Situation Watching Agent. The Smart Room Agent controls the various optic and acoustic output devices in the smart room. It may communicate general messages to all attendees in the smart room by displaying them on the whiteboard or transmitting them via loudspeaker. Furthermore, it is able to notify single participants without affecting other attendees, using the steerable video projector or targeted audio, dependant on the user's preferences.

The Situation Watching Agent wraps the Situation Model of the smart room. It monitors the smart room and tracks situation specific user information such as the current location, movement and activity on different semantic levels (simple coordinates as well as hints like "attendee X approaches whiteboard"). Moreover, it can provide location information of important artefacts like notebooks, whiteboards, tables etc. Other agents may query the current situation at the Situation Watching Agent as well as subscribe to events; both information retrieving methods are supplied by well-defined access and subscription APIs to the Situation Model.

6.2 Intelligent Messaging

As proposed in the FIPA Abstract Architecture Specification (FIPA, 2008), the complete information exchange between agents is based upon a well-defined communication ontology. Thus, the semantic content of messages is preserved across agents, a concept that becomes highly important by the fact that various services are implemented by a great number of developers in different places and the necessity of these developers to understand each other correctly.

The CHIL Communication Ontology is completely defined using the Web Ontology Language OWL (OWL, 2008) and fully integrated in the overall CHIL domain ontology. It is based upon the "Simple JADE Abstract Ontology", an elementary ontology provided by JADE, which must be used for every ontology-based message exchange within the JADE agent management system. The communication ontology extends the CHIL domain ontology by tokens which are indispensable for agent communication, particularly agent actions for requesting services and response classes to hold the results of the services and return them to the requesters. The ontology classes are used in the Java environment by means of the JADE abs package, found in *jade.core.abs*. Their handling is implemented by the basic CHIL Agent, providing it to the agent community by methods for ontology-based encoding, sending, receiving and decoding ACL (Agent Communication Language) messages.

A second level of intelligent messaging is achieved by the implementation of advanced agent coordination. Coordination of agents can be performed using well-defined conversation protocols (Cost et al., 2001). As a first approach, we use the interaction protocols and communicative acts specified by FIPA (FIPA, 2008). The communication support methods of the basic CHIL Agent, supplemented by initiator and responder classes for submitting and receiving messages, ensure that the agent communication is strictly compliant to the FIPA specification. Together with the central CHIL Agent Manger as the agent coordinating instance, the FIPA compliance and the ontology-based message transfer form a highly sophisticated approach of Intelligent Messaging.

6.3 Multiple Scalable Services

In the CHIL project, several complex context-aware services have been implemented in different places and had to be integrated in one system. To minimize the integration effort and to allow the service developers to concentrate on the core service functionality, a framework for the integration of services has been highly important. Hence, one of the major goals of the CHIL agent infrastructure was to provide a mechanism that allows the distributed development of services, an easy integration and configuration and the cooperation and communication of multiple services in the CHIL system.

A simple service can easily be integrated by creating an agent which handles the framework tasks and the service control, and integrate the agent in the CHIL system. In this way the agent acts as a wrapper for the service; the agent could also embed the service logic itself.

But usually a service is more complex and requires particular functionality from other agents. For example, the Connector Service needs, in order to establish a connection the best way possible, knowledge about the user's connection preferences (phone call, SMS, notebook, audio) and the social relationship between two ore more participants (VIP, business or personal contact). For the sake of privacy, these personal information tokens must be held by the Personal Agent, although they are only used by the Connector Service. Thus, a service may require exclusive service specific functionality that is or must be realized by another agent than the service agent itself. Implementing such functionality in the agent itself implicates that all service providers which use this agent would have to synchronize the agent's code. This technique would quickly raise significant problems coordinating the implementation and configuration of software components.

6.3.1 Pluggable Behaviours

To this end, a plug-in mechanism has been designed that allows an easy integration of service specific functionality in other agents without modifying the agents' code: service specific agent behaviours are moved to pluggable handlers, which are agent independent and plugged into appropriate agents during their start-up phase. Using this mechanism, the agents themselves remain service independent, contain only the common methods and attributes all partners have agreed on, and thus become stable modules. Three types of pluggable handlers have been considered to be necessary, namely:

1. **Setup handler:** are responsible for service specific initialization and will be executed in the setup phase of an agent.
2. **Event handler**: are triggered by events from outside the agent world, e.g. the user's GUI, a perceptual component, the situation model or a web service.
3. **Responder**: are added to the agent's behaviour queue and react on incoming ontology-based ACL (Agent Communication Language) messages sent by other agents.

At start-up time each agent parses the service configuration files, determines which behaviours have to be instantiated and adds them to its behaviour queue. Since the code for this mechanism is concentrated in the basic CHIL Agent, the plug-in mechanism is available for all agents without additional implementation work for the agent developer. Moreover, the source of the configuration data could easily be switched; instead of using XML-based files, the service configuration could similarly be imported from a knowledge base.

Table 1 shows a sample implementation of a pluggable handler; the example is about a responder, which informs a user (i.e. the user's Personal Agent) about connection requests from other users.

The interface structure allows implementing the handler and the behaviour in two different classes; the handler will be recognised by the plug-in mechanism and provides the actual behaviour that will be added to the agent's behaviour queue. In this example, both are joined in one class: the responder implements the *PluggableResponder* interface and its *getAcceptedMessages* and *getBehavior* methods in order to be handled correctly by the plug-in mechanism as well as extending a generic CHIL responder behaviour and overwriting the *prepareResponse* and *prepareResultNotification* methods.

```
public class InformAboutConnectResponder
  extends CHILSimpleAchieveREResponder implements PluggableResponder {
   public InformAboutConnectResponder(Agent agent) {
      super(agent, ((PersonalAgent)agent).matchAbsOntoRequestAction
                  (new AbsAgentAction("InformAboutConnect")));
   }
   public MessageTemplate getAcceptedMessages() {
      return getPA().matchAbsOntoRequestAction(
            new AbsAgentAction("InformAboutConnect"));
   }
   public Behavior getBehavior() {
      return this;
   }
   protected ACLMessage prepareResponse(ACLMessage request)
      throws CHILFipaRefuseException {
      // create the response message
      return responseMessage;
   }
   protected ACLMessage prepareResultNotification ACLMessage request,
      ACLMessage response) throws CHILFipaFailureException {
      // create the result message
      return resultMessage;
  }
}
```

Table 1. An example of a pluggable responder for the Personal Agent accepting ontology-based messages

GetAcceptedMessages returns a JADE message template, i.e. a pattern that specifies all types of messages the responder will react to. In this case, it returns a template that accepts messages of type *request* containing the ontology-based agent action *InformAboutConnect*, the same message template that is used in the constructor. *GetBehavior* returns the actual behaviour, which realises the responder's functionality and which is added to the agent's behaviour queue. In this example it's the responder itself, but the developer may also create and return a separate behaviour object.

The *prepareResponse* and *prepareResultNotification* methods ensure FIPA compliance by implementing the agree/refuse and the failure/inform path of the FIPA Request Interaction Protocol respectively. The (optional) *prepareResponse* method receives the original request and informs the initiator, if the request is agreed to or refused. Additionally, it may start to compile the request. The (mandatory) *prepareResultNotification* completes the processing of the request and returns the results, or, in case of an error, a failure message to the initiator.

6.3.2 Scalable Services

The Pluggable Behaviours mechanism allows a service provider to plug new service specific functions in multiple agents without the need for recompilation (see Fig. 4(a)). However, to fully exploit the features of all CHIL services and to raise the functionality of the whole system beyond the sum of its components, a service must be able to define new messages, which can be understood and compiled by other services. This means that each service provider should be able to define his own service specific ontology. As a consequence, each agent participating in such a multi-service communication has to be able to handle messages from different services and to work with several service ontologies, as illustrated in Fig. 4(b). Hence, service specific ontologies have to be handled in the same way as Pluggable Behaviours: the framework must be capable to plug them in without the need for recompiling the agent's code. To this end, the Pluggable Behaviours mechanism has been extended to Scalable Services by realising a plug-in technique for service specific communication ontologies.

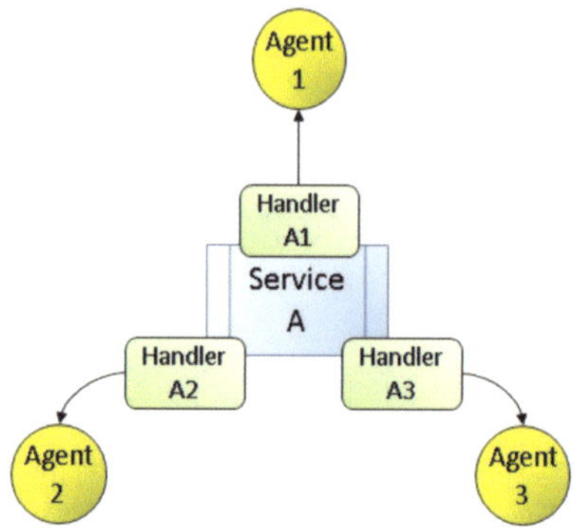

(a)

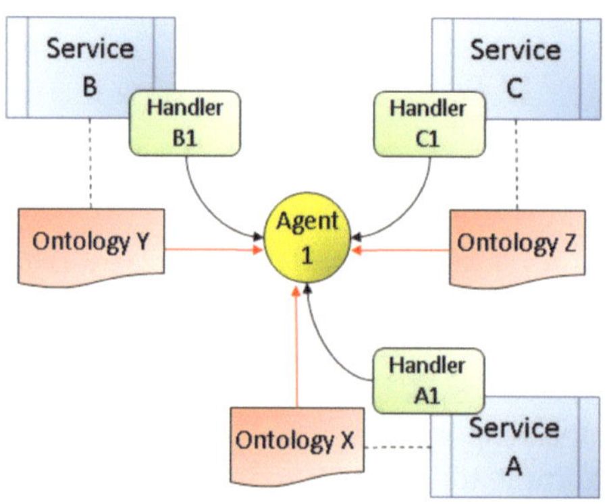

(b)

Figure 4. Pluggable Handlers and Scalable Services

A new service is specified and integrated into the CHIL system by means of a XML-based configuration file. Table 2 shows an example of a service using its own ontology and adding an event handler to the service agent and a responder to the Travel Agent. The file defines all agents participating in the service, their behaviours and the service ontology. Each pluggable handler is specified by its type (setup, event and responder) and its class name. A priority value assigned to each handler can be used to determine the order of execution, which is particularly important for setup behaviours. The service ontology is specified by a name, the namespace, the location and the class name of the ontology class. Furthermore, the configuration file provides an additional feature to system developers and administrators: it allows enabling/disabling certain functionality by simply adding/removing the appropriate configuration elements in the configuration file, without having to recompile the source code.

```
<?xml version="1.0" encoding="UTF-8"?>
<serviceconfig version="1.1"
 xmlns:xsi=http://www.w3.org/2001/XMLSchema-instance
 xsi:noNamespaceSchemaLocation="CHIL_ServiceConfig_1.1.xsd">
  <service name="YourService">
    <agent name="YourAgent">
      <handler type="event" priority="1"
       classname="yourNamespace.yourService.yourAgent.YourEventHandler"/>
    </agent>
    <agent name="TravelAgent">
      <handler type="responder" priority="1"
      classname="yourNamespace.yourService.travelAgent.YourServiceResponder"/>
    </agent>
  </service>
  <ontology
     name="YourOntology"
     namespace="http://www.owl-ontologies.com/YourServiceOntology.owl"
     locationPath="$ChilHome/lib/yourService.jar"
     className="yourNamespace.ontology.YourOntology">
  </ontology>
</serviceconfig>
```

Table 2. Sample service configuration file using multiple agents and a service-specific communication ontology

Similar to a service configuration file informing a service about all participating agents, the CHIL system is informed about all participating services: a master configuration file, also based on XML, specifies the services that are activated on system start-up by their names and the location of their configuration files. A sample can be seen in table 3.

```
<?xml version="1.0" encoding="UTF-8"?>
<services version="1.0" xmlns:xsi="http://www.w3.org/2001/XMLSchema-instance"
xsi:noNamespaceSchemaLocation="../xmlschema/CHIL_Services_1.0.xsd">
   <service name="CoreService"         configFile="CoreService.xml"/>
   <service name="MeetingService"      configFile="MeetingService.xml"/>
   <service name="ConnectorService"    configFile="ConnectorService.xml"/>
   <service name="TravelService"       configFile="TravelService.xml"/>
   <service name="MemoryJog"           configFile="MemoryJog.xml"/>
   <service name="SmartroomService"    configFile="SmartroomService.xml"/>
   <service name="SitWatchService"     configFile="SitWatchService.xml"/>
</services>
```

Table 3. Master configurations file for services

6.4 Personalisation

A CHIL computing environment aims to radically change the way we use computers. Rather than expecting a human to attend to technology, CHIL attempts to develop computer assistants that attend to human activities, interactions and intentions. Instead of reacting only to explicit user requests, such assistants proactively provide services by observing the implicit human request or need, much like a personal butler would.

Each CHIL user is described by a user profile, which contains a set of personal attributes including administrative data relevant to the CHIL system (e.g. access rights, user capabilities and characteristics) and individual personality information like professional and personal interests, contacts and the social relationships between the contacts and the user (VIP, business or personal) as well as interaction, device and notification preferences such as notebook, PDA, cell phone call, SMS, MMS, targeted audio, etc. The administrative part of the user profile is maintained by the system administrator; personal data can be added and modified by the user exclusively by means of a suitable GUI.

Access to and control of the user profile is managed by the user's Personal Agent. Thus, the Personal Agent does not only operate as a personal assistant, but also as a privacy guard to both sensitive and public user data. Since the Personal Agent is the only one having access to the user's profile, it ensures user data privacy.

The Personal Agent controls, via dedicated Device Agents, the complete interaction between its user and the CHIL system: it knows what front-end devices its master has access to, how it can best receive or send information to and from its master and what input and notification types its master prefers. Furthermore, the Personal Agent communicates (using both requests and subscriptions) with the Situation Watching Agent to be permanently updated about its master's current context (location, activity, state of the environment) and the availability of the various devices in a dynamically changing situation. Based on the static data of the user profile and the dynamic context information, the Personal Agent handles user input and connection and notification requests to its master the best way and with the most appropriate media possible.

6.5 Qualitative Advantages of the CHIL Agent Framework

The benefits of the CHIL multi-agent framework are manifold. On the one hand, the architecture undertakes a wide range of tedious tasks, easing the deployment of new services, and on the other hand it provides a transparent layer to the developer in terms of information retrieval. It offers high flexibility, scalability and reusability and it facilitates the integration of components at different levels, like

- Services,
- Perceptual Components,
- Sensors and Actuators, and
- User Interfaces.

Particularly the plug-in mechanism for agent behaviours constitutes a powerful technique for the development, test, integration, configuration and deployment of new services and components. Developers may create new agents and behaviours and use this mechanism for easy behaviour integration and agent configuration, thus facilitating and accelerating the process of development and testing. They may benefit from the reusability feature of the agent framework by including own behaviours in already existing agents in order to use the functionality of these agents. And they may profit from the flexible configuration facility,

allocate behaviours to different agents, turn behaviours and even complete services on and off, in the development and test phase as well as in the deployment and integration phase.
Another important quality factor is the use of an ontology based agent communication. Elevating the collaboration of components on a semantic level does not only augment the robustness of the system in terms of mutual understanding of internal components, but also reduces the error-proneness when integrating new components and enhances the interoperability with external systems significantly. A high level of scalability is ensured by the fact that all agents can be distributed to a theoretically unlimited number of computers.
Furthermore, the described technology for service composition enhances the scalability of the CHIL agent framework in terms of functionality. Additionally, detailed guidelines for service integrators are available, which help service developers to integrate their services into the CHIL architecture framework.

7. Prototype Implementation

The CHIL agent-based infrastructure has been utilized for implementing several non-intrusive services (cf. section 2.2) which demonstrate how this framework is appropriate for developing context-aware cooperating applications. The following paragraphs present one of the implemented example scenarios.

7.1 Example Scenario

This scenario incorporates the two CHIL services Connector Service and Travel Service and a number of elementary services such as Meeting Service and Smart Room Service. Both CHIL services are integrated into the CHIL architecture using the before described plug-in mechanism.
A meeting takes place in a CHIL smart room equipped with sensors and output devices. The presence of each meeting participant is considered to be crucial for the outcome of the meeting. Hence, the meeting will be delayed, if one of the participants is late. All meeting participants are known to the CHIL system and have CHIL-enabled personal devices, i.e. notebooks, PDAs or smart phones with a CHIL software client. Most of the participants have itineraries with flights or trains leaving shortly after the scheduled end of the meeting.
One of the participants realizes that he will be late for the meeting. He uses one of the functionalities of the Connector Service by sending an "I'm late"-notification (together with the expected arrival time) to the CHIL system from his personal device (e.g. a smart phone, see Fig. 5, left). The system then informs the other participants about the delay via the smart room devices or personal devices, dependent on the current location of the participant, user preferences and the available output media.
The Personal Agents of the other participants know the planned itineraries of their masters. Triggered by the delay message each Personal Agent determines whether the delay is likely to let its master miss his return connection. If this is the case the Personal Agent providently initiates a search for alternative connections. It provides the Travel Agent with the necessary information including user preferences, e.g. if its master prefers to fly or take a train. The Travel Agent processes the request by retrieving information from online services of railway operators, airlines and travel agencies. Eventually, it sends a list of possible connections to the Personal Agent which notifies its user. Notification is done unobtrusively taking into account the current environment situation of its master (e.g. "in meeting"), the currently

available output devices (i.e. personal devices like smart phones, PDAs, notebooks and output devices of the smart room, e.g. targeted audio or steerable video projector) and the preferred way of notification (e.g. pop-up box or voice message).

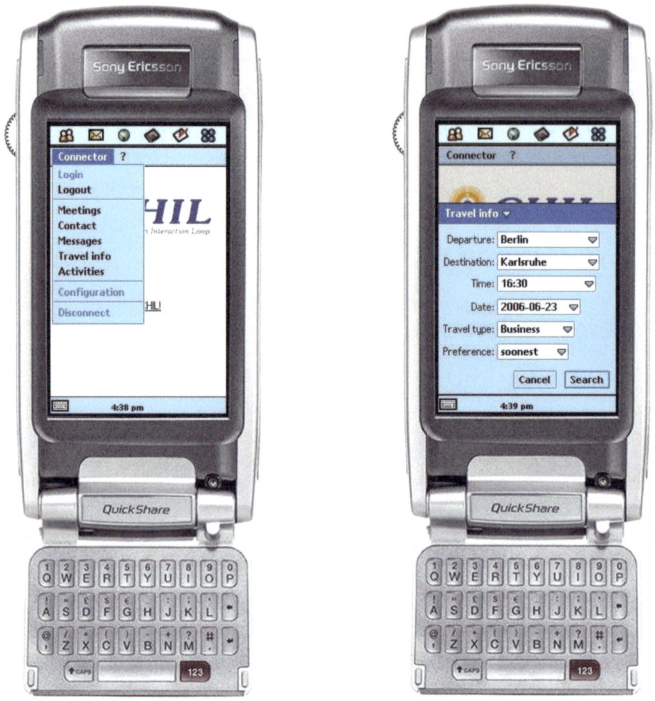

Figure 5. Smart phone version of the CHIL service access client

A possible outcome of the search could also be that the Personal Agent informs its master that he should leave the meeting as planned, since there was no suitable alternative itinerary. In case the CHIL user is not satisfied with any of the proposed itineraries or wants to look up travel connections himself, he can use his CHIL-enabled personal device to do so. Fig. 5, right, shows the query mask on a smart phone. An equivalent user front end is available for notebooks.

8. Conclusion

Developing complex sensing infrastructures, perceptual components, situation modelling components and context-aware services constitute extremely demanding research tasks. Given the tremendous effort required to setup and develop such infrastructures, we strongly believe that a framework ensuring their reusability in the scope of a range of services is of high value. This is not the case with most ubiquitous, pervasive and context-aware systems, which tend to be very tightly coupled to the underlying sensing infrastructure and middleware (Smailagic & Siewiorek, 2002; Ryan et al., 1998). It is however expedient in projects like CHIL, where a number of service developers concentrate on radically different services.

In this chapter we presented a reference architecture for context-aware services. We put the main focus on the distributed agent framework that allows developers of different services to concentrate on their service logic, while exploiting existing infrastructures for perceptual processing, information fusion, sensors and actuators control. The core concept of this framework is to decouple service logic from context-aware and sensor/actuator control middleware. Hence, service logic can be "plugged" in a specific placeholder based on well defined interfaces. The agent framework has been implemented based on the JADE environment and accordingly instantiated within real life smart rooms comprising a wide range of sensors and context-aware components. The benefits of this framework have been manifested in the development of different cooperating applications providing assistance during meetings and conferences as well as facilitating human communication.

9. References

Altmann, J.; Gruber, F.; Klug, L.; Stockner, W.; Weippl, E. (2001). Using mobile agents in real world: A survey and evaluation of agent platforms, *Proc. of the 2nd International Workshop on Infrastructure for Agents, MAS, and Scalable MAS at the 5th International Conference on Autonomous Agents,* pp. 33-39, Montreal, Canada, June 2001

AMI (2008). Augmented Multi-party Interaction (2008), Available from http://www.amiproject.org, accessed July 31, 2008

Brandstein, M.; Ward, D. (2001). *Microphone Arrays: Signal Processing Techniques and Applications,* Springer, ISBN 978-3-540-41953-2, Berlin, Germany

Chen, H.; Finin, T.; Joshi, A.; Perich, F.; Chakraborty, D.; Kagal, L. (2004). Intelligent Agents Meet the Semantic Web in Smart Spaces, *IEEE Internet Computing* 8, 6 (Nov. 2004), pp. 69-79, ISSN 1089-7801

Coen, M.; Phillips, B.; Warshawsky, N.; Weisman, L.; Peters, S.; Finin, P. (1999), Meeting the Computational Needs of Intelligent Environments: The Metaglue System, *Proceedings of MANSE'99,* pp. 201–212, Dublin, Ireland, Dec. 1999

Cost, R. S.; Labrou, Y.; and Finin, T. (2001). Coordinating agents using agent communication languages conversations. In: *Coordination of Internet agents: models, technologies, and applications,* Omicini, A.; Zambonelli, F.; Klusch, M.; Tolksdorf, R. (Eds.), pp. 183-196, Springer-Verlag, ISBN 978-3-540-41613-5, London, UK

Dey, A.K. (2000). *Providing Architectural Support for Building Context-Aware Applications,* Ph.D. dissertation, Georgia Institute of Technology, ISBN 0-493-01246-X, Atlanta, GA, USA

FIPA (2008). The Foundation for Intelligent Physical Agents, Available from http://www.fipa.org, accessed July 31, 2008

Garlan, D.; Siewiorek, D.; Smailagic, A.; Steenkiste, P. (2002). Project Aura: Towards Distraction-Free Pervasive Computing, *IEEE Pervasive Computing,* special issue on "Integrated Pervasive Computing Environments", Vol. 1, Issue 2, (April 2002), pp. 22–31, ISSN 1536-1268

Grimm, R.; Anderson, T.; Bershad, B.; Wetherall, D. (2000). A System Architecture for Pervasive Computing, *Proceedings of the 9th ACM SIGOPS European Workshop,* pp. 177–182, ISBN 1-23456-789-0, Kolding, Denmark, Sept. 2000, ACM, New York, USA

Huhns, M.N.; Singh, M.P. (1997). Agents are everywhere, *IEEE Internet Computing,* Vol. 1, Issue 1, (January 1997), pp. 87-87, ISSN 1089-7801

JADE (2008). Java Agent DEvelopment Framework, Available from http://jade.tilab.com, accessed July 31, 2008

Jennings, N.R.; Sycara, K.; Wooldridge, M. (1998). A roadmap of agent research and development. *Journal of Autonomous Agents and Multi-Agent Systems*, 1(1), (1998), pp. 7–38, ISSN 1387-2532

Johanson, B.; Fox, A.; Winograd, T. (2002). The Interactive Workspaces Project: Experiences with Ubiquitous Computing Rooms, *IEEE Pervasive Computing*, Vol. 1, Issue. 2, (Apr-Jun 2002), pp. 67–74, ISSN 1536-1268

Maes, P. (1994). Agents that reduce work and information overload. *Communications of the ACM* 37, 7 (July 1994), pp. 30-40, ISSN 0001-0782

OWL (2008). W3C Semantic Web, Web Ontology Language (OWL). Available from http://www.w3.org/2004/OWL, accessed July 31, 2008

Roman, M.; Hess, C.; Cerqueira, R.; Ranganat, A.; Campbell, R. H.; Nahrstedt, K. (2002). Gaia: A Middleware Infrastructure to Enable Active Spaces, *IEEE Pervasive Computing*, Vol. 1, No. 4, (October 2002), pp. 74–83, ISSN 1536-1268

Russell, S.J.; Norvig, P. (2003). *Artificial Intelligence: A Modern Approach*. Prentice Hall, ISBN 9780137903955

Ryan, N.; Pascoe, J.; Morse, D. (1998). Enhanced reality fieldwork: the context-aware archaeological assistant. In: *Computer Applications and Quantitative Methods in Archaeology*, V. Gaffney, M. van Leusen and S. Exxon (Eds), Oxford

Shafer, S.; Krumm, J.; Brumitt, B.; Meyers, B.; Czerwinski, M.; Robbins, D. (1998). The New EasyLiving Project at Microsoft Research, *Proc. of Joint DARPA / NIST Workshop on Smart Spaces*, pp. 127–130, July 30-31, 1998, Gaithersburg, Maryland, USA

Smailagic, A.; Siewiorek, D.P. (2002). Application Design for Wearable and Context-Aware Computers. *IEEE Pervasive Computing* 1, 4 (Oct. 2002), pp. 20-29, ISSN1536-1268

Stiefelhagen, R.; Garofolo, J. (Eds.) (2007). Multimodal Technologies for Perception of Humans, *First International Evaluation Workshop on Classification of Events, Activities and Relationships*, CLEAR 2006, Southampton, UK, April 6-7, 2006, Revised Selected Papers Series: Lecture Notes in Computer Science , Vol. 4122 Sublibrary: Image Processing, Computer Vision, Pattern Recognition, and Graphics, Springer, ISBN 978-3-540-69567-7

Stiefelhagen, R.; Bowers, R.; Fiscus, J. (Eds.) (2008). *Multimodal Technologies for Perception of Humans*, International Evaluation Workshops CLEAR 2007 and RT 2007, Baltimore, MD, USA, May 8-11, 2007, *Revised Selected Papers Series: Lecture Notes in Computer Science* , Vol. 4625, Sublibrary: Image Processing, Computer Vision, Pattern Recognition, and Graphics 2008, XIII, Springer, ISBN 978-3-540-68584-5,

Ubisense (2007). The Ubisense Precise Real-time Location System. Available from http://www.ubisense.net, accessed July 31, 2008

Wellner, P.; Flynn M. (Eds.) (2005). m4 - multimodal meeting manager. Deliverable D4.3: *Report on Final Demonstrator and Evaluation*, 25 February 2005, Available from http://www.dcs.shef.ac.uk/spandh/projects/m4/publicDelivs/D4-3.pdf, accessed July 31, 2008

4

A Robust Hand Recognition In Varying Illumination

Yoo-Joo Choi[1], Je-Sung Lee[2] and We-Duke Cho[3]
[1]*Seoul University of Venture and Information,* [2]*Korean German Institute of Technology,*
[3]*Ajou University*
South Korea

1. Introduction

As ubiquitous computing provide up-graded smart environments where humans desire to create various types of interaction for many kinds of media and information, the research in the area of Human-Computer Interaction (HCI) is being emphasized to satisfy a more convenient user interface. In particular, the gesture interaction technique has been one of the important research areas under ubiquitous computing environment since it can only utilize widespread consumer video cameras and computer vision techniques without the aid of any other devices to grasp human movements and intentions(Park, 2004; Jung, 2007). Among the gesture interaction techniques, recognition of hand poses and gestures has especially received attention due to great potential to build various and user-centric computer interfaces. The applicability of hand pose recognition is very high in applications where system users can not use existing interface devices such as a keyboard and a mouse since they are required to wear heavy protective gloves for industrial processes. Various types of gesture interfaces have been also presented in three-dimensional games based on virtual reality and these interfaces have enhanced an interest level and creativity within these environments for the users. Humans can distinguish hand poses very quickly through their complex optical systems, while it is very difficult for a computer system to rapidly and accurately understand hand poses. Therefore, many researchers have tried to simulate the human optical system, which can extract objects of interest from complex scenes and understand the context among objects. One of the major factors that disturb automatic gesture recognition is illumination change. The sudden illumination changes lead to the misunderstanding of background and foreground regions.

We propose a robust hand recognition technique that can stably extract hand contours even under sudden illumination changes. Figure 1 shows the flowchart for our proposed method. The proposed method acquires the background images for a restricted duration and calculates the mean and standard deviation for the hue and hue-gradient of each pixel within the captured background images. That is, a background model for each pixel is built. The hue and hue-gradient of the input images captured in real-time are calculated and compared to those of the background images. The foreground objects are extracted based on the difference magnitude between those of the input image and the background image. To accurately extract the tight object region of interest, we calculate the eigen value and eigen vector for the initially extracted object region and extract the object-oriented bounding box(OBB) on the optimized hand region based on the two eigen vectors. Then, the OBB region is divided into 16 sub-regions and the hand region profile is produced based on the histogram created from the number of edges for each sub-region. The profiles of nine hand poses are trained and each hand pose is recognized using a multi-class SVM algorithm.

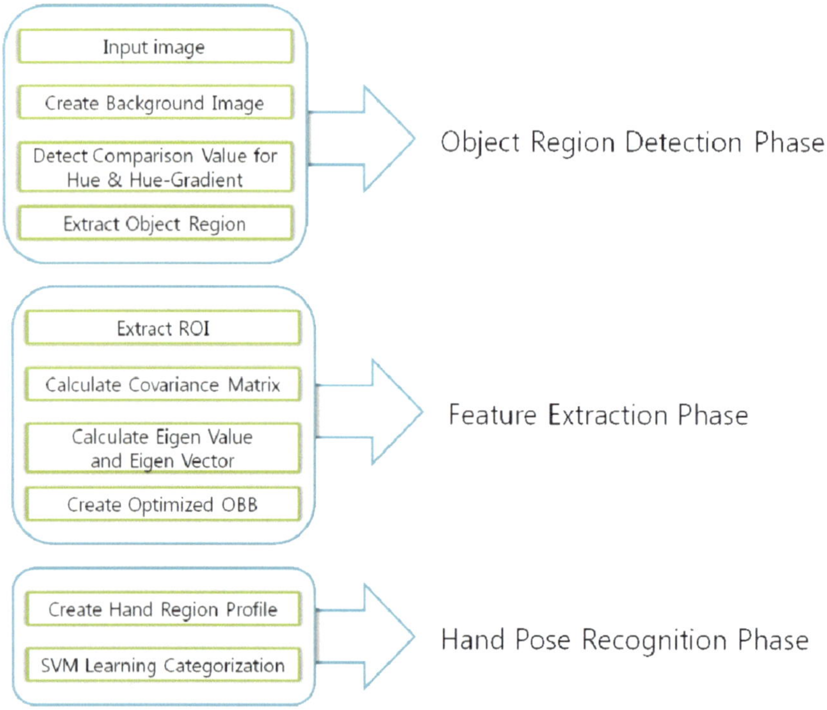

Figure 1. System flowchart

2. Previous Work

Current research of hand pose recognition can be classified into hardware sensor based methods that mostly utilize datagloves and image processing based methods that utilize two-dimensional pattern information or three-dimensional models. Since methods that use datagloves obtain three-dimensional data through sensors directly attached to the gloves in real-time, these methods make hand gesture analysis easy. However, more or less expensive equipments are required and there are problems in implementing natural interfaces since the cables are necessary to connect the equipments to the computing system. As image processing based methods, restricted approaches that uses red or green gloves to skip the complex pre-processing of the hand regions extraction have been presented (KAIST,2004). Other approaches have attempted to recognize hand movements based only on images captured from video cameras under normal lighting conditions without any specialized equipments (Park et al., 2002; Jang et al., 2004; Han, 2003; Jang et al., 2006; Tanibata et al., 2002; Licsar et al., 2005). To support general and natural interfaces, an interest in the hand pose recognition without the use of any specialized equipments or gloves have increased.

A variety of hand features have been applied for hand pose recognition. In the research proposed in (Park et al., 2002), the direction and size of the hand region was considered to determine the area of interest window and the improved CAMSHIFT algorithm was used to track the coordinates of the hand tip. The focal point of their research was in recognizing the pointing direction by extracting the coordinates of the hand tip from a single hand pose instead of various hand poses. In (Jang et al., 2004)'s research, they defined three main features for the hand pose. First, the normalized hand region on the direction and size was calculated and then from the center point of the normalized hand region, straight lines were beamed on the rotation at the regular angle. The distance on the straight line beamed from the center of the region to the outer boundary of the hand was used as the feature. The ratio of the length of the minor axis to that of major axis was also used as the hand feature. In (Han, 2003)'s research on hand pose recognition, they first estimated the entropy on the frame difference between adjacent frame images and through the distribution on the skin color, then they extracted only the hand region from the frame image. Nest, the contour of the hand was detected using a chain-code algorithm and an improved centroidal profile method was applied to recognize the hand pose on a speed of 15 frames per second. In (Jang et al., 2006)'s research, they proposed a method that divides the hand pose features into structural angles and hand outlines. They defined the relation between these hand features by using enhanced learning. Through their research, they proved the appropriateness of their proposed method by applying their method to a hand pose recognition system that uses not one but three cameras. As shown above, although many methods have been proposed for hand pose recognition, most of the research is carried out in limited situational environments with no change in lighting or the background. Thus, environment-dependent research results have been produced(Park et al., 2002; Jang et al., 2004; Han, 2003; Jang et al., 2006; Tanibata et al., 2002; Licsar et al., 2005). In contrast to the research, the application areas for hand pose recognition techniques call for environments that can handle illumination changes. Thus there is an increased demand for research on robust hand pose recognition under illumination changes. In addition, a variety of hand features that characterize the hand pose have been proposed in order to improve the success rate of the recognition, however, these features are quite complex making it difficult for real-time processing. This calls for better research in defining hand features that can efficiently and accurately represent hand poses.

3. Hand Region Extraction

3.1 Hue and Hue-Gradient Distribution of the Hand Region

The RGB color model is an additive color model that adds the three additive primaries - R(Red), G(Green), B(Blue) to create a desired color. RGB color model is sensitive to light and shadow making it difficult to extract object outlines during image processing(Kang, 2003). On the contrary, HSI color model is a user-oriented color model that is based on how humans perceive light. This model is composed of H(Hue), S(Saturation), and I(Intensity). Figure 2. Shows the HSI color model is depicted as a basic triangle and color space. Hue is expressed as an angle ranging from 0° to 360°and saturation is the radius ranging from 0 to 1. Intensity is the z axis with 0 being black and 1 being white(Kang, 2003).

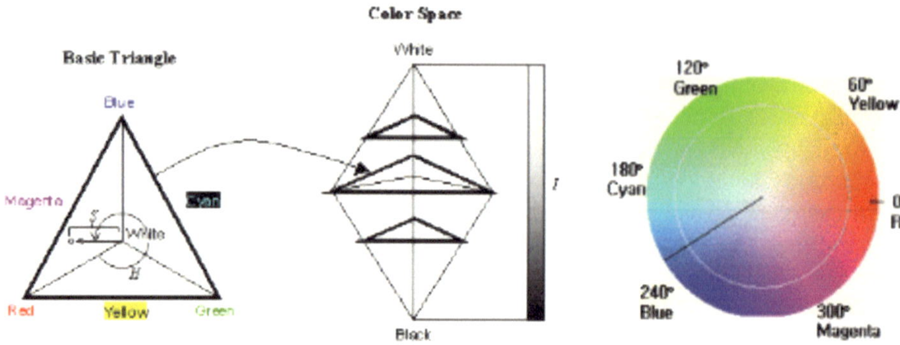

Figure 2. HSI color model

The hue component in the HSI color model represents the object's inherent color value independently from the brightness or saturation of an object. This model can be converted from the RGB model through Equation (1)(Kang, 2003). Figure 3 shows the hue and saturation difference between the hand region and the background region.

$$
\begin{aligned}
H &= \begin{cases} \theta & \text{if} \quad B \le G \\ 360-\theta & \text{if} \quad B \succ G \end{cases} \\
\theta &= \cos^{-1}\left(\frac{\frac{1}{2}[(R-G)+(R-B)]}{[(R-G)^2+(R-B)(G-B)]^{1/2}} \right) \\
S &= 1-\frac{3}{(R+G+B)}[\min(R,G,B)] \\
I &= \frac{1}{3}(R+G+B)
\end{aligned} \tag{1}
$$

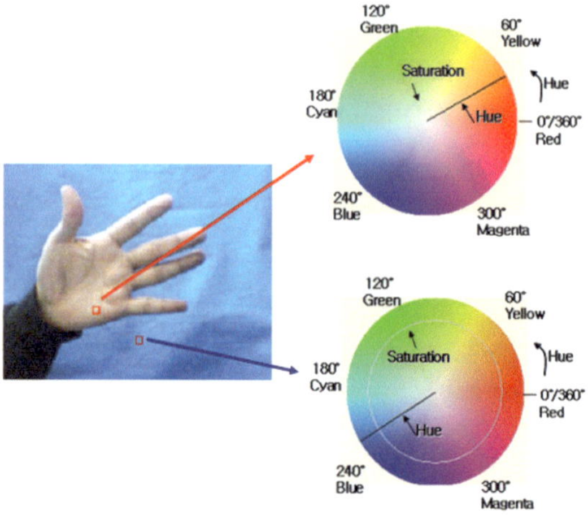

Figure 3. Hue and hue-gradient in hand region and background region

In HSI color model, components related to the color are represented by hue and saturation, and brightness is represented by intensity, which makes it easier to separate a region of interest regardless of illumination change. HSI color models are widely used in the field of interpretation of images from cameras because when there is a change in the color, all three RGB components in the RGB model are changed, whereas in the HSI model, only the hue are mainly changed. Table 1 shows the histograms for the hue image and saturation image under changes in the illumination. When there is a sudden change in the lighting condition, we can see that the histogram of the saturation is completely changed. On the other hand, although there is some change in the histogram, the distribution characteristic of the histogram of the hue is relatively preserved.

Original Image	Saturation Histogram	Hue Histogram
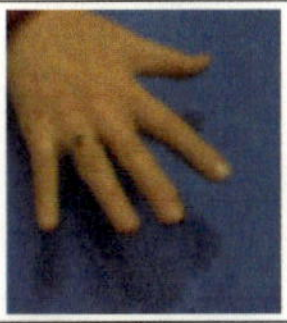	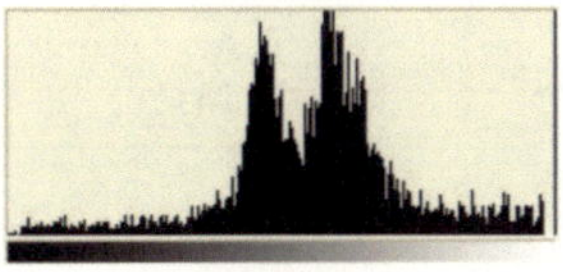	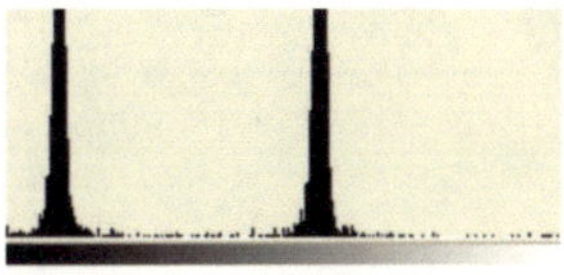
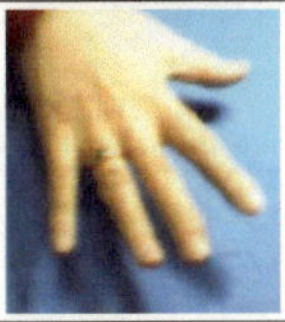	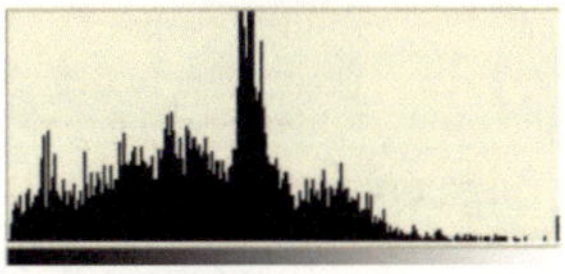	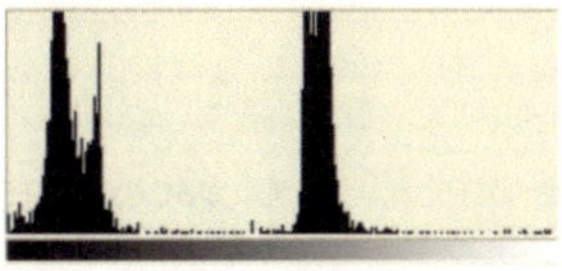

Table 1. Change of saturation and hue in response to illumination change

3.2 Background Subtraction Based On Hue and Hue-Gradient

Background subtraction is an object detection method that first obtains the average background image from frame images inputted for a set period of time, and then carries out a pixel comparison between the average background image and the incoming input image (Haritaoglu, 1998). This method is summarized as follows.

$$\begin{aligned}&\text{if } (\,|I_n(x)-B_n(x)| > T_n(x))\\&\quad x \text{ is a foreground pixel}\\&\text{else}\\&\quad x \text{ is not a foreground pixel}\end{aligned} \tag{2}$$

$B_n(x)$ is the background image pixel. In other words, if the difference between the background image pixel and the current image pixel $I_n(x)$ is bigger than the threshold $T_n(x)$, then the background pixel is regarded as the foreground pixel. In contrast to the frame subtraction methods that can only detect areas of movement in a short period of time during a scene change, background subtraction methods can detect the overall region of the moving objects. Thus object detection can be efficiently carried out if the background image well represents the current environmental condition without much change. However, if there are changes to the environment such as illumination changes and the background image does not accurately represent the actual environment anymore, the objects cannot be successfully detected using the background subtraction method. Therefore, the accuracy of the background subtraction method is highly dependent on how accurate the background model represents the current background. For accurate object detection, the background image needs to continuously learn the changing environment over time.

The hue component represents the color of the image itself and minimizes the illumination effect. The hue-gradient image maintains the background image's features and on the other hand eliminates the illumination changes and shadow effects. This section introduces a background subtraction method based on hue and hue-gradient. First, to acquire the background model image in the HSI color space, a background model that has been trained for a certain period of time is built with hue and hue-gradient of the background region. Through this model, the object is extracted by first calculating the hue and hue-gradient values when the object is inputted and then separating the foreground region from the input image by comparing the threshold defined based on the background model (Choi, 2007).

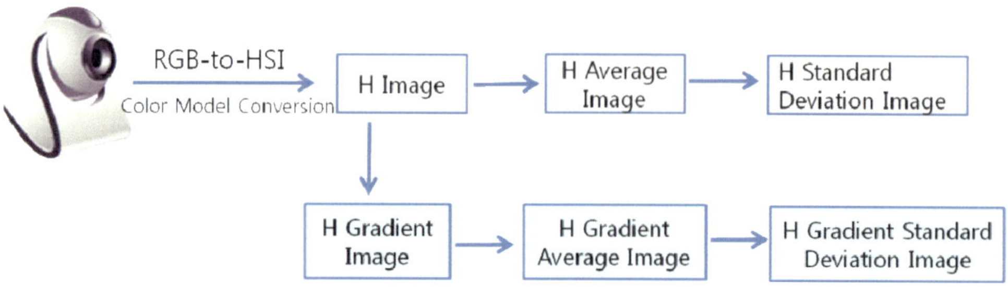

Figure 4. The procedure of background image creation

During the background learning stage, learning is carried out on both the hue component and hue-gradient value for each pixel. To measure the color change caused by general illumination changes, the background image is first acquired for a time period of T_i and then the mean and variance values for each pixel's hue is calculated.

Likewise, a sequence of background images inputted for a time period of T_i is used to calculate the hue-gradient background image. The individual pixels are used with the adjacent pixels to calculate the gradient size of the hue component value. Another averaged background image is then built with the hue-gradient component value.

The equation to calculate the hue gradient size (∇H) of each pixel in the background image is shown in Equation (3).

$$\nabla H = \sqrt{\left(H_{(x+1,y)} - H_{(x,y)}\right)^2 + \left(H_{(x,y+1)} - H_{(x,y)}\right)^2} \quad (3)$$

The equation to gradually calculate the mean and variance of the hue component for each pixel for time t is shown in Equation (4).

Mean Update :

$$\mu\left(H_i(0)\right) = H_i(0) \qquad : t = 0$$

$$\mu\left(H_i(t)\right) = (1-\alpha)\mu\left(H_i(t-1)\right) - \alpha H_i(t) \qquad : t \geq 1$$

Variance Update : (4)

$$\sigma^2\left(H_i(0)\right) = \left(H_i(1) - \mu(H_i(0))\right)^2 \qquad : t = 1$$

$$\sigma^2\left(H_i(t)\right) = (1-\alpha)\sigma^2\left(H_i(t-1)\right) + \alpha\left(H_i(t) - \mu(H_i(t))\right)^2 \qquad : t \geq 2$$

The equation to gradually calculate the hue-gradient component's mean and variance for each pixel for time t is shown in Equation (5). $\mu(\nabla H_i(0))$ is the hue-gradient mean's initial value and $\mu(\nabla H_i(t))$ is the mean at time t. $\sigma^2(\nabla H_i(0))$ is the hue-gradient variance's initial value and $\sigma^2(\nabla H_i(t))$ is the variance of hue-gradient at time t.
Mean Update :

$$\mu(\nabla H_i(0)) = \nabla H_i(0) \qquad : t = 0$$

$$\mu(\nabla H_i(t)) = (1-\alpha)\mu(\nabla H_i(t-1)) + \alpha\nabla H_i(t) \qquad : t \geq 1$$

Variance Update : (5)

$$\sigma^2(\nabla H_i(0)) = (\nabla H_i(1) - \mu(H_i(0)))^2 \qquad : t = 1$$

$$\sigma^2(\nabla H_i(t)) = (1-\alpha)\sigma^2(\nabla H_i(t-1)) + \alpha(\nabla H_i(t) - \mu(H_i(t)))^2 \qquad : t \geq 2$$

The inputted images which include the object are converted from the RGB color space to the HSI color space. If difference between the converted hue value of each pixel and that of background image is greater than the variance of background hue image, it is regarded as the object candidate region. Likewise, if difference between the hue-gradient of each pixel of the input image and that of the background image is greater than the variance of background hue-gradient image, it is regarded as the object candidate region. The region that satisfies with both conditions is extracted as the object region. The procedure of the proposed object extraction is shown in Figure 5.

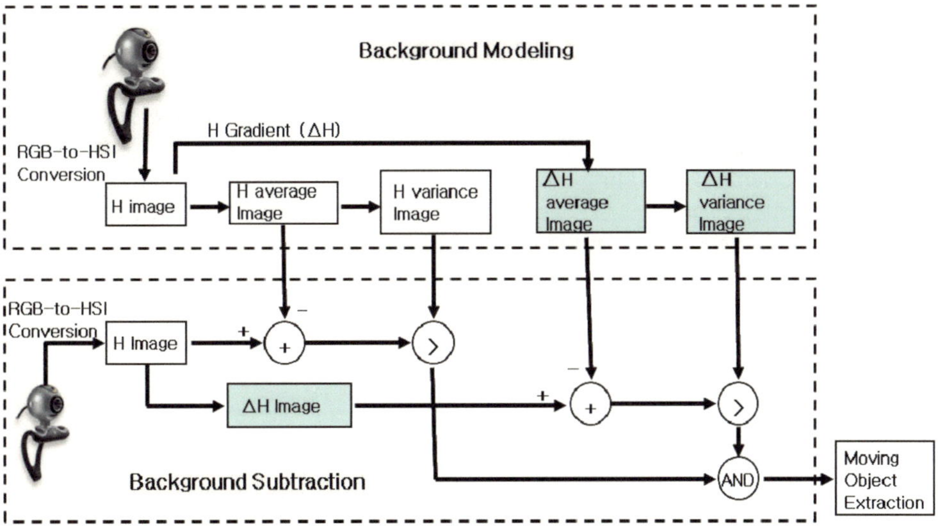

Figure 5. The Procedure of the proposed object extraction

The comparison to extract the object region is shown in Equation (6).

$$R_i(x) = \begin{cases} 1, & if\ |H_i(x) - H_{b_i}(x)| > \omega_1\sigma(H_{b_i}(x))\ and \\ & |\nabla H_i(x) - \nabla H_{h_i}(x)| > \omega_2\sigma(\nabla H_{h_i}(x)), \\ 0, & otherwise \end{cases} \qquad `(6)$$

$H_i(x)$ and $\nabla H_i(x)$ represent the hue and hue-gradient value of pixel *i* of the current input image, respectively. $H_{b_1}(x)$, $\nabla H_{b_1}(x)$, $\sigma\left(H_{b_1}(x)\right)$, and $\sigma\left(\nabla H_{b_1}(x)\right)$ represent the means of the hue and hue-gradient, variances of hue and hue-gradient of the background model, respectively. ω_1 and ω_2 each represent the weight value for the threshold region.

4. Hand Pose Recognition

4.1 Hand Pose Feature Extraction

This section presents a hand pose recognition method that recognizes the 1-9 hand sign of the sign language regardless of its direction and size. Figure 6 shows the 1-9 hand sign. 18 scalar feature values, that is, two normalized eigen values of the OBB for the detected hand region, the number of hand edge points in 16 subregions that are defined in the detected OBB, are used as features of a hand pose.

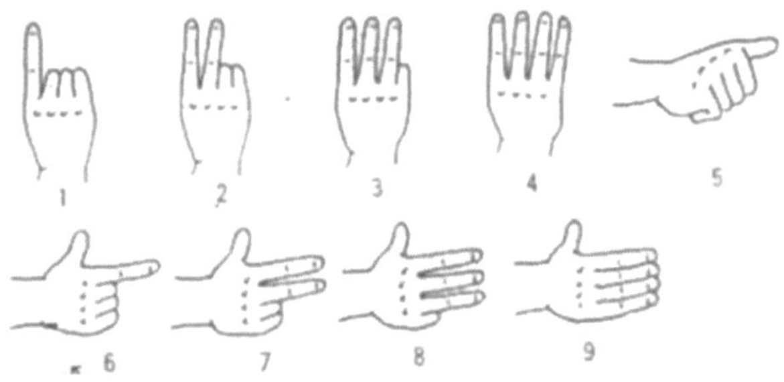

Figure 6. Numbers 1 to 9 using hand signs

4.1.1 Extraction of the eigen value and eigen vector

The detected object has different directions and sizes making image recognition difficult. To increase the success rate of the recognition of hand poses regardless of hand's direction and size, the object-oriented bounding box(OBB) is calculated by extracting the two eigen vectors for the detected hand object. The eigen vetors are preserved even though the object is rotated or scaled. Eigen value and eigen vector always form a pair (Kreyszig, 1999a). The eigen value and eigen vector are derived from the covariance matrix that expresses the specific object's fluctuating value.

Covariance matrix is the statistical criteria, which represents the changing aspect of each fluctuating value when two or more fluctuating data is given. The covariance matrix is calculated using the following equation when the samples' random data is bivariate x_i and y_i(Kreyszig, 1999b).

$$\text{If} \quad \bar{x} = \frac{1}{n}\sum_{i=0}^{n} x_i \,, \bar{y} = \frac{1}{n}\sum_{i=0}^{n} y_i$$

$$cov_{xy} = \frac{1}{n}\sum_{i=1}^{n}(x_i - \bar{x})(y_i - \bar{y}) \tag{7}$$

The covariance matrix C is

$$C = \begin{pmatrix} cov_{xx} & cov_{xy} \\ cov_{yx} & cov_{yy} \end{pmatrix} \tag{8}$$

The covariance cov_{xx} is equal to the variance of x, var_x and the cov_{yy} value is equal to the variance of y, var_y. The covariance matrix is always symmetric and has the same number of eigen vectors as the dimension of the covariance matrix. Eigen vectors are always perpendicular to each other as shown in Figure 7.

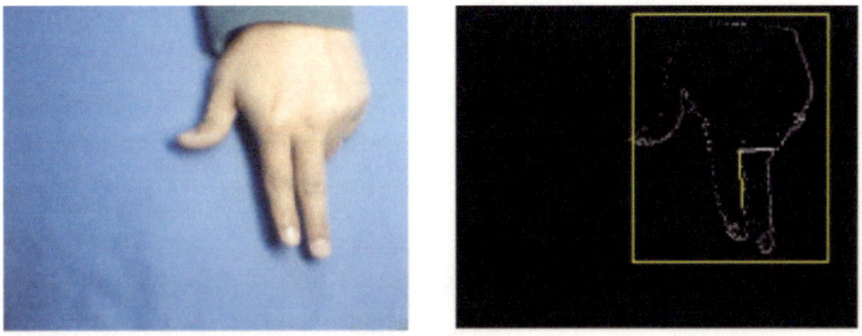

Figure 7. Example of eigen vectors for one hand pose

4.1.2 Definition of feature values

Figure 8 shows the flowchart for the OBB extraction process for a hand pose. Figure 8 (a) shows the target OBB region for the hand pose and Figure 8 (b) shows mean point A and the major/minor eigen vectors. Figure 8 (c) represents the transform to move the object coordinates to x-y coordinates. That is, the mean point is moved to the origin, and major vector and minor vector are aligned to x axis and y axis, respectively. Figure 8 (d) shows that the origin is translated to the center of the window.

To align the major and minor eigen vectors of the hand region to x axis and y axis, the matrix W is defined by eigen vectors, u_1 and u_2, as Equation (9). The contour points can be transformed to the x-y coordinates by using Equation (10).

$$W = [u_1 \dots u_n] \tag{9}$$

$$y = W^T x \tag{10}$$

After the main axes of the object are transformed, a maximally possible OBB is defined based on the variances of x and y, S_x and S_y. The reason for holding a maximally possible OBB region with the variance S_x and S_y in advance is to prevent the size of OBB from being extremely misestimated due to image noise that exist outside the hand region. The OBB is adjusted by finding the maximum contour point from the starting point on both the x and y axis' positive and negative directions within the maximally possible OBB. By defining the maximally possible OBB in advance with the variance and optimizing the OBB based on the contour point within the OBB, the error rate for false ROI extraction due to background noise can be reduced. Figure 8 (e) shows the result of the optimized OBB detection.

18 feature component values are used to recognize the hand signs representing 1 to 9 from the hand images. First, the eigen values from the two directions of the hand region is normalized using the variances of x and y within the OBB. The OBB is then subdivided into 16 regions as shown in Figure 9 and the number of overall contour pixels contained in each region is counted. Two normalized eigen values and the number of contour points for each sub-region are used as the feature information.

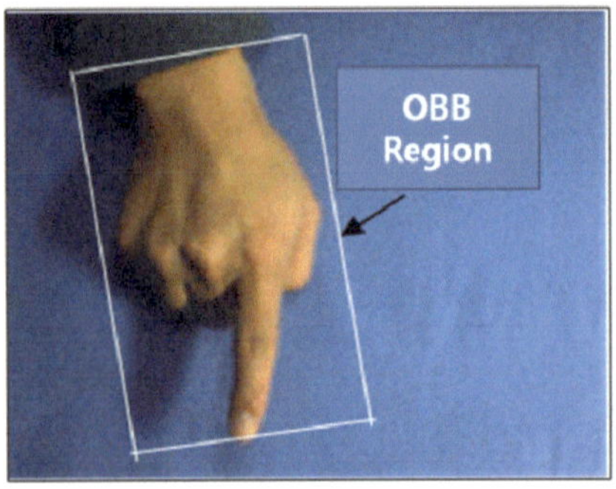

(a) Input image and OBB region of interest

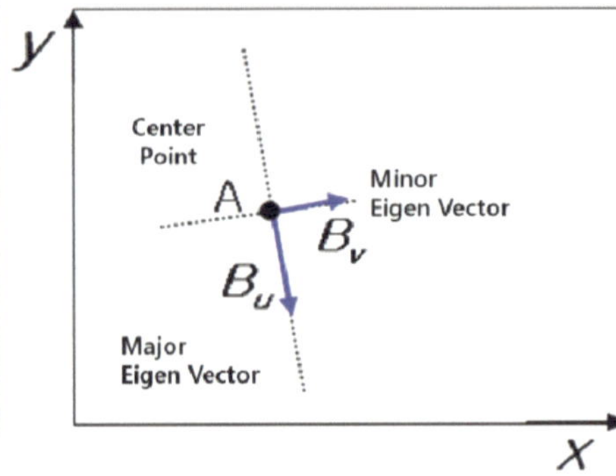

(b) Center point and eigen vectors

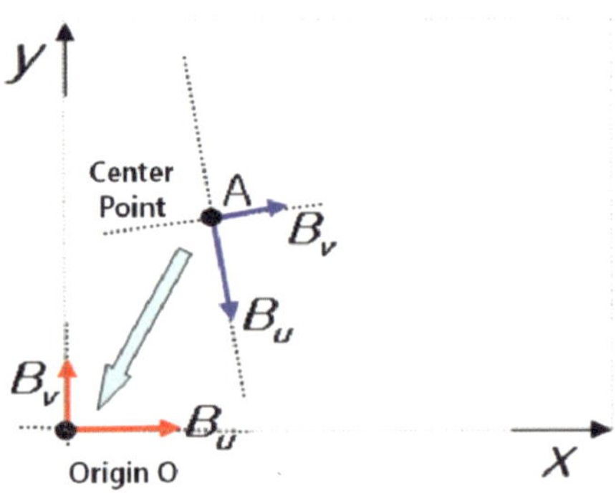

(c) Alignment of eigen vectors

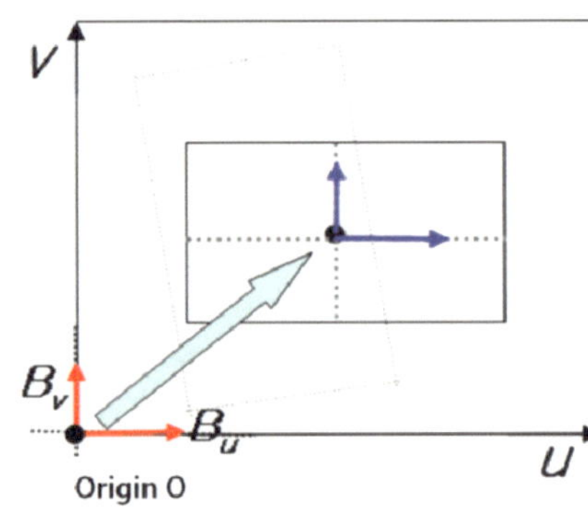

(d) Translation of origin

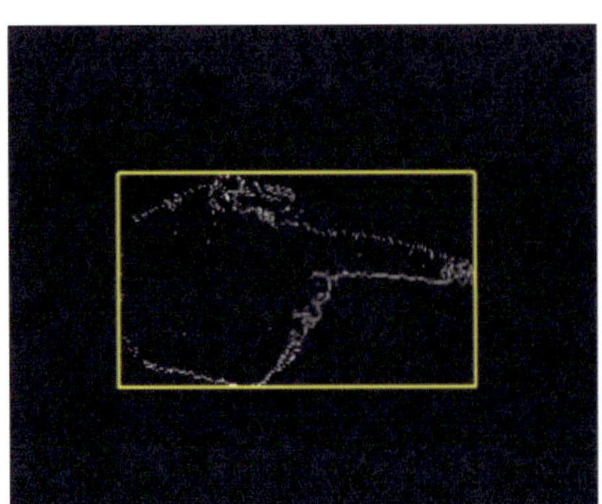

(e) optimized OBB

Figure 8. Procedure for extracting the optimized OBB

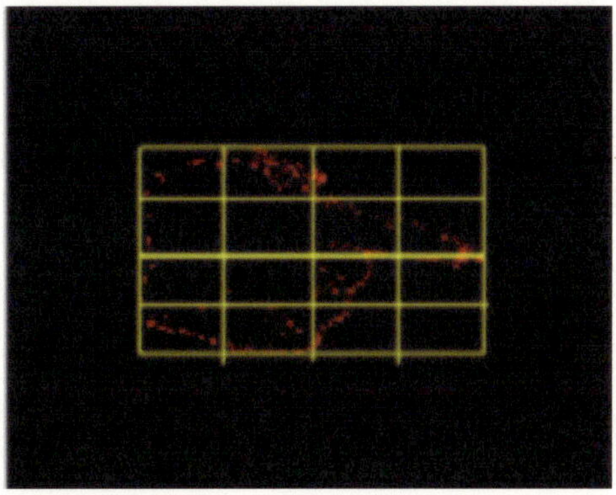

Figure 9. Sixteen sub-regions of an OBB

4.2 Recognition using SVM

SVM (Support Vector Machine) is a method that was developed by Vladimir Vapnik and his research team at AT&T Bell Research Lab. It is an object identification method that is widely used from the field of data mining to pattern recognition application areas such as face recognition(Han, 2005; Cristianini, 2000; Weida, 2002). A linear SVM is a Statistical Learning Theory(SLT) which classifies the arbitrary data based on the decision function being defined by PDF(Probability Density Function). PDF is obtained by the learning process of the training data and the categorical information.

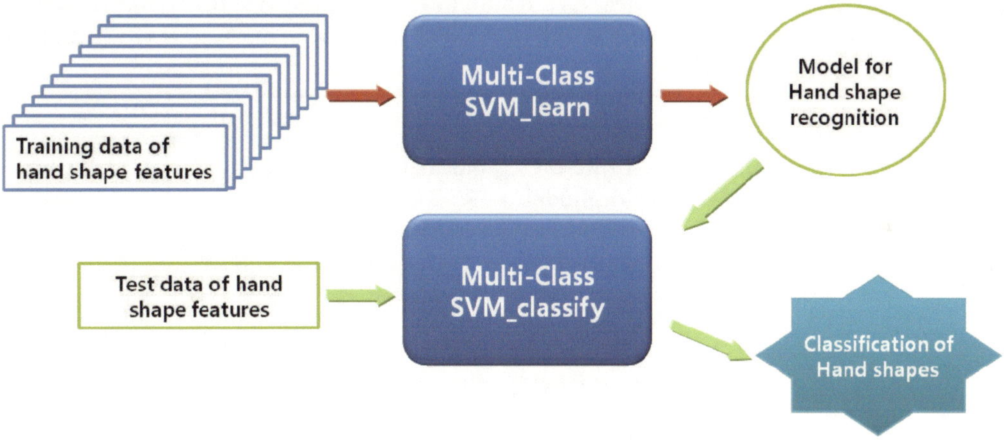

Figure 10. Procedure of hand shape recognition using SVM

SVM is an alternative learning method to polynomial, radial basis function and multi-layer perceptron. SVM can abstract patterns into higher level feature space and make globally optimal classification to be possible. Most of traditional pattern recognition methods such as neural network and statistical methods are based on empirical risk minimization(ERM) for optimal data execution, while SVM is based on the structural risk minimization(SRM), which minimizes the probability to misclassify unknown data set(Han, 2005). Originally the SVM was conceived for only dual class, but it has been expanded to multi-class classification responding to need. Expanding the SVM from a dual class to multi-class involves combining the dual class SVMs. In this section, nine hand poses are categorized using the multi-class SVM(Crammer, 2001). The

multi-class SVM technique is used on the feature values extracted from the hand poses in section 4.1 to produce the learning model. The hand pose is extracted from the real-time input images and the feature values are extracted to classify the hand pose based on the hand learning model. Figure 10 shows the process for hand pose learning and recognition using the SVM.
The training data created for the SVM learning algorithm is sorted as the class name, feature classification number, and feature value. Learning is executed in off-line by the multi-class SVM learning function. The class name is the hand sign number from the hand signs 1 to 9's classification and each class defines 18 feature values which are sorted as the feature classification number and the extracted feature value. The feature values contain the two normalize eigen values and the overall number of pixels for OBB's 16 sub-regions.

5. Experimental Results

5.1 Hand Region Detection Under Illumination Change

The testing environment set up for this experiment was implemented with Visual C++ software on a Windows XP with a Pentium-IV 3.0 GHz CPU and 1 GB of memory. Logitech Quickcam Chat camera was used to acquire input test images for the hand tracking. The images are 320 x 240 in size captured as a 24bit RGB color model.
The hue based background image was produced by converting the RGB color space into the HSI color space, and then calculating the hue and the hue-gradient's mean and variance. During the next step, the hue and hue-gradient values are extracted from the image pixels captured in real-time. The hue and hue-gradient values of the input image are compared with those of the background images. As a result, the binary image including the contour of the hand is produced. In other words, the contour of the hand is marked as white and the background is marked as black.

	(a) input image	(b)RGB color model	(c) Normalized RGB Color Model	(d) Hue	(e) Hue and H-Gradient
Bright Illumination		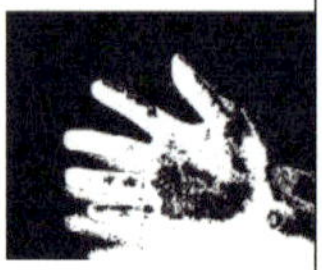			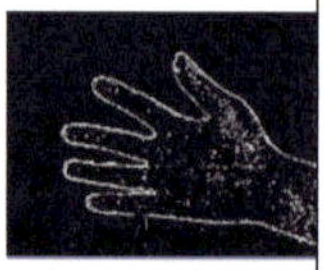
Dark Illumination	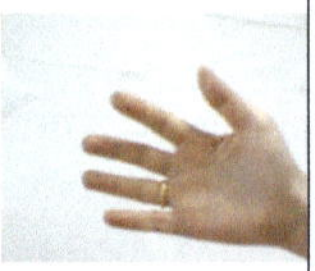		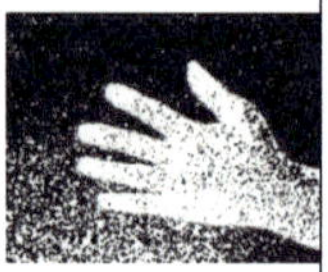		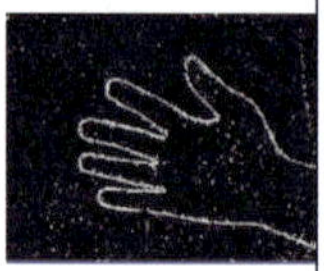

Table 2. Comparison of background subtraction methods based on different color models under sudden illumination changes

For the experiment, we compared the results of the existing methods with that of the proposed method under the exact same illumination from when the initial background was

built. Then we also compared them under drastically different illumination conditions from the initial illumination.
To create the illumination change, one condition used a 80 lm/W normal white fluorescent lighting together with a 18W 63.1 lm/W white desktop lamp directly on the hand region. The other condition eliminated the 18W 63.1 lm/W white desktop lamp and carried out the experiment to extract the hand region without rebuilding the background model for the varying illumination.

Object	Covariance Matrix		Eigen Value		Eigen Vector	
none	0 0	0 0	0	0	1 0	0 1
1	589.96 216.33	216.33 983.66	494.33	1079.3	0.91 0.4	-0.4 0.91
2	619.37 293.45	293.45 1506.82	531.11	1595.08	0.96 0.29	-0.29 0.96
3	566.75 182.57	182.57 1384.14	527.82	1423.06	0.98 0.21	-0.21 0.98
4	751.79 99.61	99.61 1468.81	738.21	1482.39	0.99 0.14	-0.14 0.99
5	931.3 5.57	5.57 585.33	585.24	931.39	0.02 1	-1 0.02
6	913.41 117.5	117.5 952.35	813.78	1051.99	0.76 0.65	-0.65 0.76
7	831.65 154.6	154.6 1278.43	783.37	1326.71	0.95 0.3	-0.3 0.95
8	832.16 28.46	28.46 1413.11	830.77	1414.51	1 0.05	-0.05 1
9	1037.26 -73.61	-73.61 1387.16	1022.4	1402.02	0.98 -0.2	0.2 0.98

Table 3. Covariance Matrix, Eigen Value and Eigen Vector's Mean on the Hand Signs 1 to 9

As shown in Table 2, when the dark and bright illumination conditions are compared, we can see that applying the proposed method better preserves the hand contour. Table 2. (b) is the binary image produced from the difference between the background image based on the RGB color model and the input image. It is the most sensitive to light change. Table 2. (c) is the result of applying normalized RGB color model as the background model. Here the contour of the hand is roughly preserved but the hand's internal noise as well as shadow noise is more prominent. Table 2. (d) is the binary image based only the HSI color model's hue value. There is an improvement from the RGB color model but it reacts to the shadows due to the illumination changes. Table 2. (e) shows that even under sudden illumination changes, the region information can be stably extracted using the proposed method.

	(a) Hand Sign 1	(b) Hand Sign 2	(c) Hand Sign 3
Eigen Vectors	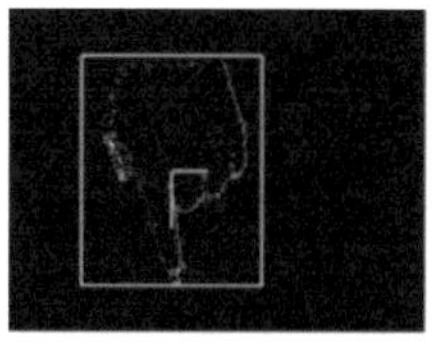	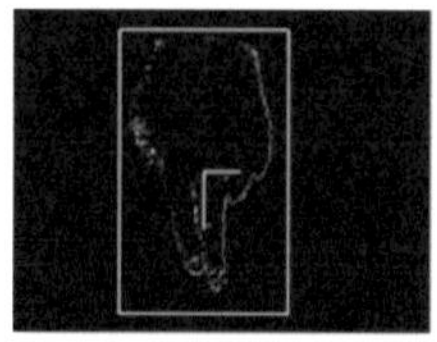	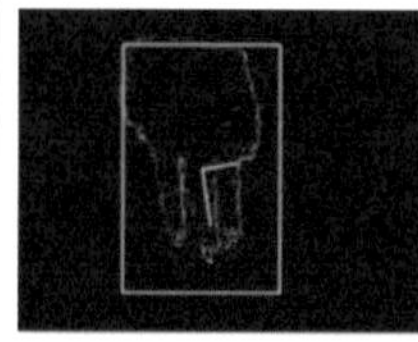
Optimized OBB	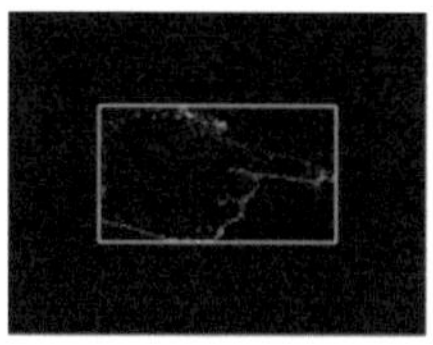	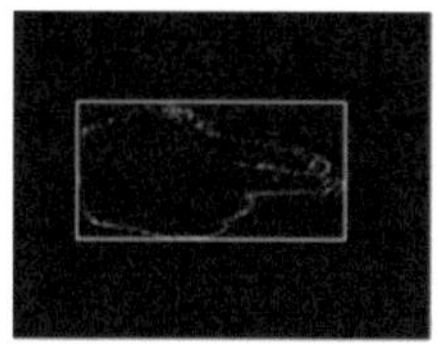	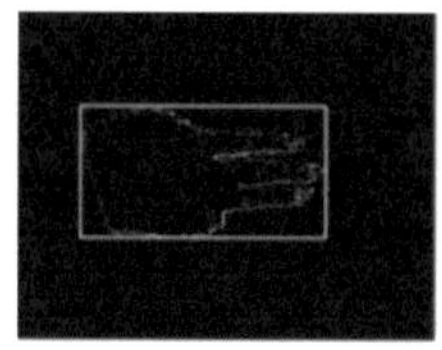
	(d) Hand Sign 4	(e) Hand Sign 5	(f) Hand Sign 6
Eigen Vectors	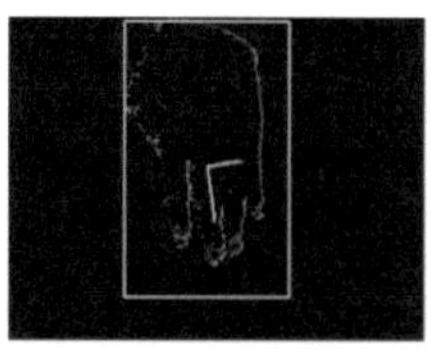	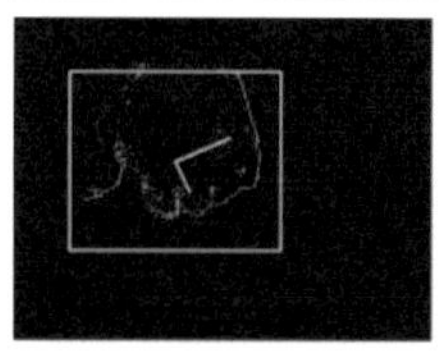	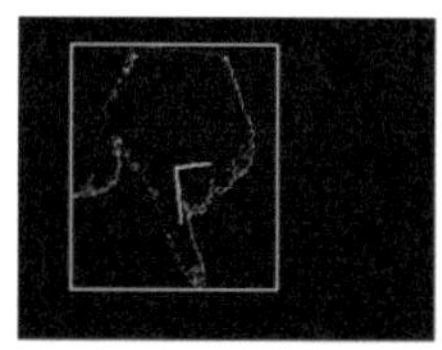
Optimized OBB	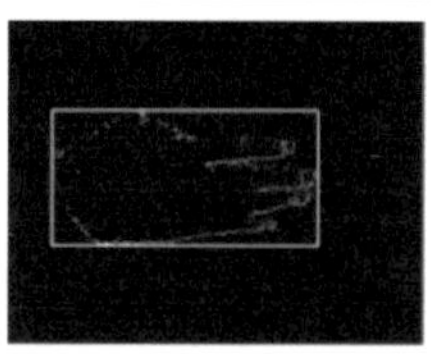	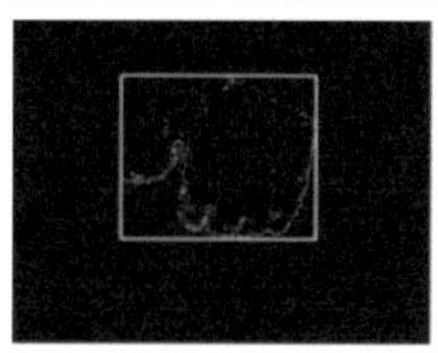	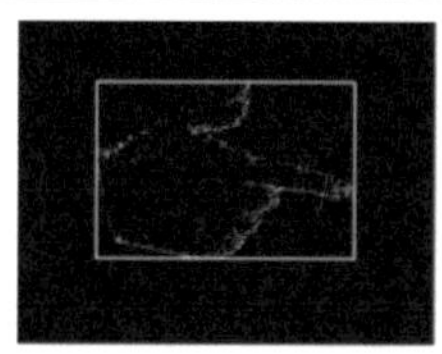
	(g) Hand Sign 7	(h) Hand Sign 8	(i) Hand Sign 9
Eigen Vectors	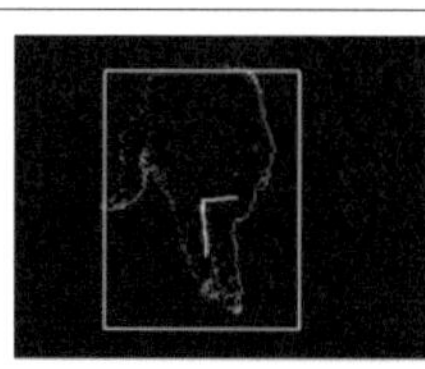	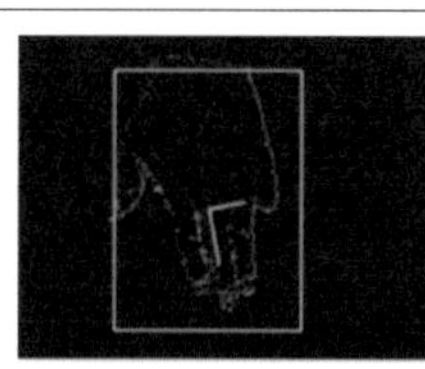	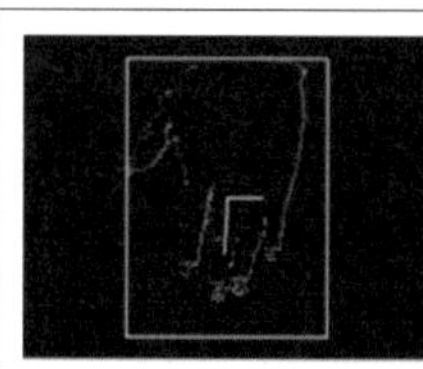
Optimized OBB	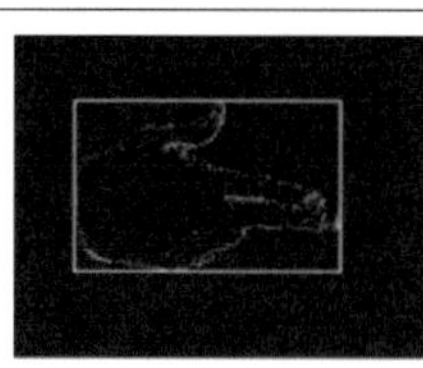	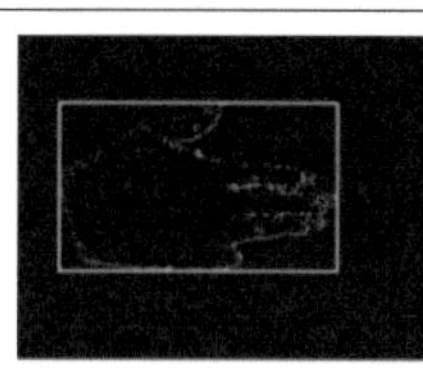	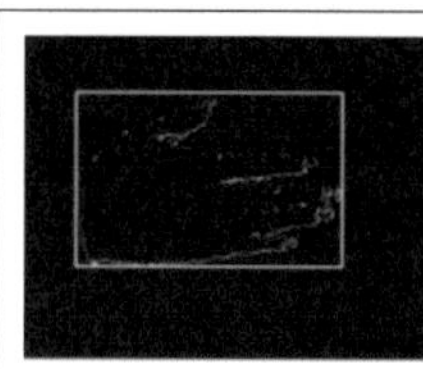

Table 4. Optimized OBB detection results on the hand signs (1-9)

Table 3. shows all the covariance matrix values as well as the eigen values and eigen vectors on the hand signs 1 to 9. Each hand sign has an eigen value proportioned to the input image object's ROI size. Figure 11 compares 90 samples for the hand signs representing from 1 to 9. When image interpretation is carried out using the correlation analysis on the major and minor eigen values, we can see that an initial classification is possible on the 1 to 9 hand signs. Table 4 shows the optimized OBB detection result for the object in the input image. The first row shows eigen vectors to be extracted from the result image of background subtraction and the second row represents the OBB optimized by transforming object coordinates using eigen vector matrix and by detecting object's outermost points.

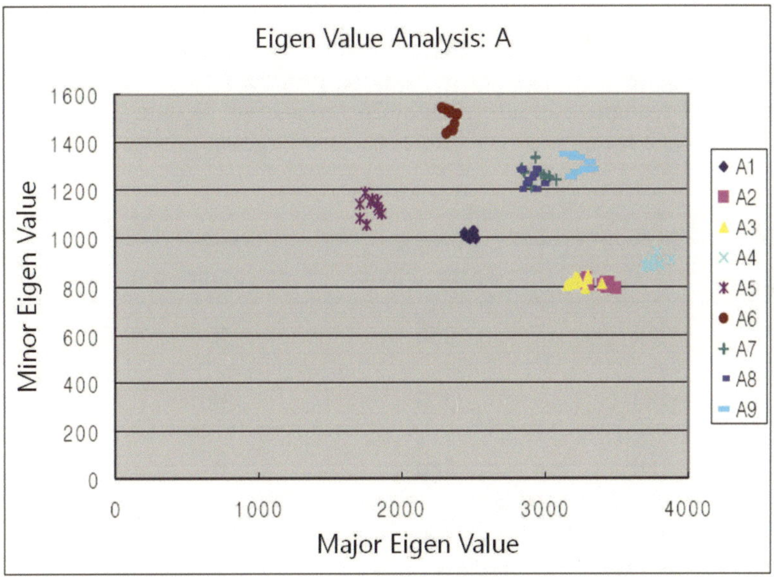

Figure 11. Two-dimensional distribution on the eigen value for hand signs 1 to 9

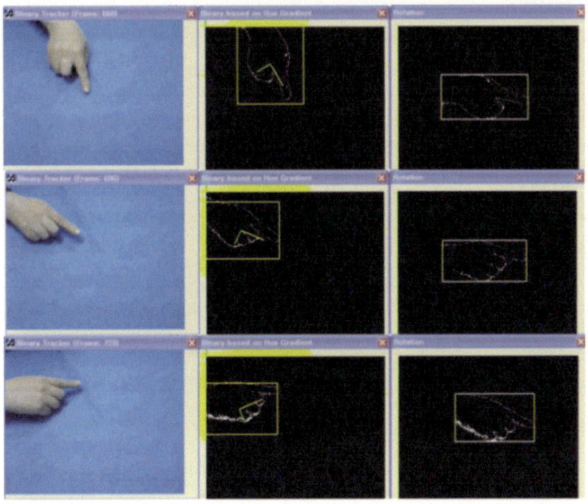

Figure 12. Optimized OBB on hand sign 1 from different directions. (Left) Input image (Middle) ROI and eigen vectors prior to optimization (Right) Optimized OBB

Figure 12. shows the OBB that has been optimized on the same hand sign 1 expressed from different angles. As we can see, even with changes in the hand direction, the normalized OBB's direction is steadily maintained and enabling stable hand recognition independent of hand direction.

5.2 Hand Recognition

The data used for this experiment consists of 1620 images - 180 images per hand sign (1 to 9). All 6 subjects individually changed hand poses on each of the hand signs resulting in 30 captured images per hand sign. 18 different hand features were learned through the SVM learning algorithm and hand recognition was performed. The result of the hand recognition is summarized in Table 5. This includes the result of failed recognition by one subject on 1,2, 4, and 7. The mean success rate of recognition on the 9 hand signs showed 92.6%.
For movies incoming at 30 frames per second, the proposed hand recognition method was able to extract and recognize hand poses at 20 frames per second. The hand recognition processing time on one frame showed 1.260 msec enabling real-time processing.

class	Number of Tests	Normal Recognition	Faulty Recognition	Recognition Rate
1	180	150	30	83.3
2	180	150	30	83.3
3	180	180	0	100
4	180	150	30	83.3
5	180	180	0	100
6	180	180	0	100
7	180	150	30	83.3
8	180	180	0	100
9	180	180	0	100
Sum	1620	1500	120	92.6

Table 5. Optimized OBB Detection Result on hand signs 1 to 9

6. Conclusions

This chapter introduced a hand pose recognition method to robustly extract objects under sudden illumination changes. The introduced method constructs the background model based on the hue and the hue-gradient, and then robustly extracts the object contours from images obtained from a fixed camera by the background subtraction. It was shown that this method stably detects the object even under various lighting conditions set by the experiment.

This research carried out a comparison experiment on the different color models for image recognition systems. The HSI color model minimizes the illumination and shadow effects and by using the hue and hue-gradient values from this color model for the background subtraction method, it showed that the proposed method sharply decreases the noise and shadow effects caused by sudden illumination changes. The optimized OBB that was produced from the extracted region is then divided into 16 sub-regions.The number of edges of the hand in that sub-region and the normalized eigen values are used for defining the hand pose feature which are then trained by the SVM learning algorithm.

This method was designed for use in gaming environments where illumination conditions can change rapidly in the limited simple environment. When the proposed method was tested in a complex environment, it was shown that if the hand region has similar color to the background region, the hand's contour was lost. In the future, this method will be expanded to include stable hand pose recognition in complex background environments.

7. References

Choi, Y.;Lee, J.;Cho W. (2007) Robust Extraction of Moving Objects based on Hue and Hue Gradient, *LNCS*, Vol. 4555, pp.784~791

Crammer, K.; Singer, Y. (2001) On the Algorithmic Implementation of Multi-class SVMs, *JMLR*

Cristianini, N. (2000) An Introduction to Support Vector Machines, *Cambridge University Press*

Han, H. (2005) Introduction to Pattern Recognition, *Hanbit Media*, pp.274~282

Han, Y. (2003) Gesture Recognition System using Motion Information, *The KIPS Transactions: PartB* , Vol. 10, No. 4, pp.473-478

Haritaoglu, I.; Davis, L.; Harwood, D. (1998) W4(Who? When? Where? What?) a real time system for detecting and tracking people. *In FGR98*

Jang, H.; Bien, Z. (2006) A Study on Vision-based Robust Hand-Posture Recognition Using Reinforcement Learning, *Journal of IEEK* : CI. Vol. 43, No.3, pp.39-49

Jang, H.; Kim, D.; Kim, J.; Jung, J.; Park, K.; Z. Zenn Bien. (2004) Decomposition approach for hand-pose recognition, *International Journals of HWRS*, Vol. 5, No.1, pp.21-25

Jung, K. (2007) "Introduction to Ubiquitous Computing: Connection to new media", *jinhan M&B*, pp. 48~63

Licsar, A.; Sziranyi, T. (2005) User-adaptive hand gesture recognition system with interactive training, *Image and Vision Computing*, Vol.23, No.12 , pp.1102-1114

Kang, D.; Ha, J. (2003) Digital Image Processing using Visual C++, SciTech Media, pp.314~322

KAIST (2004) Hand signal recognition method by subgroup based classification, Korean Patent, 10-0457928

Kreyszig, E. (1999a) Advanced Engineering Mathematics, Eight Edition, *John Wiley & Sons*, Inc., pp. 371~375

Kreyszig, E. (1999b) Advanced Engineering Mathematics, Eight Edition, *John Wiley & Sons, Inc.*, pp. 1150~1151

Park, J.; Yi, J. (2002) Efficient Fingertip Tracking and Mouse Pointer Control for Implementation of a Human Mouse, *Journal of KISS* B Vol.29, No.11, pp.851-859

Park, S. (2004) A Hierarchical Graphical Model for Recognizing Human Actions and Interactions in Video, *Disseratation of Ph.D, The University of Texas at Austin*

Tanibata, N.; Shimada, N. (2002) Extraction of Hand Features for Recognition of Sign Language Words, *The 15th International Conference on Vision Interface*, pp.391-398

Weida, Z. (2002) Linear programming support vector machines, *Pattern Recognition*, Vol.35, No.12, pp.2927-2936.

5

How Do Programmers Think?

Anthony Cox and Maryanne Fisher
Centre for Psychology and Computing, Saint Mary's University
Canada

1. Introduction

Regular expressions are an example of a regular language and are a subset of both the context free and the context sensitive languages. As the syntactic structure of many computer programming languages can be described using a context-free grammar, regular expressions can be viewed as a simplified and restricted programming language. While lacking many of the more sophisticated programming language features (e.g., types, functions), regular expressions still provide users with sequencing, alternation, and iteration constructs, and thus provide an abstract view of basic control-flow features. Concatenation can be regarded as a form of sequencing where the elements of an expression containing concatenation must occur in a specific, linear sequence. The "or" operator, represented with a vertical bar **|**, provides alternation and permits one to choose between two options, just as an "if-then-else" statement permits the choice of two alternatives. Finally, the Kleene closure, represented by a superscript asterisk * functions as an iteration operator and performs a role similar to looping constructs (e.g., "do", "while", or "for" in the C programming language). Thus, regular expressions can be viewed as simple programs with basic control-flow constructs, but with no explicit data management.

Alternatively, regular expressions are used in computer software, such as grep, vi, and Perl, as a mechanism to describe the targets of search operations. For this role, regular expressions provide a pattern description mechanism with pattern matches identifying desired search solutions. For example, the expression **[eE][nN][dD]** identifies the term "end" where the letters can independently be in upper or lower case (e.g., "eNd", "ENd", "END").

Regular languages, while being highly formalized and restrictive with regard to their expressiveness, are never-the-less a form of language. It has been documented that humans develop the ability to read before they develop the ability to write (Salvatori, 1983). Consequently, by comparing novice's skills as they learn to read (i.e., applying) and write (i.e., creating) regular expressions, one can examine the relationship of formal languages to natural languages (e.g., English) and potentially permit research on the use of natural language to be applied to computer programming. Increased understanding of regular expression use can therefore provide understanding of how we, as humans, interact with computers when using formal languages. That is, understanding the cognitive skills associated with lower level formal languages provides insight on the use of higher level imperative style languages such as Fortran, C++, or Pascal.

While there has been significant research on algorithms for automated matching and manipulation of regular expressions (Hopcraft & Ullman, 1979), there has been little research on the human element of these systems. Insight into the manipulation of regular expressions provides insight into the manipulation of formal languages, and hence on computer programming—a foundational task in human-computer interaction. In this chapter, we address this deficiency and explore the cognition underlying programming by examining performance on the manipulation of regular expressions.

The remainder of this chapter is organised as follows. A brief overview of regular expressions in the context of formal language theory is first provided. Then, we present the first of two studies that we conducted to investigate performance on expression application (i.e., matching) and creation tasks. The results of the second, revised, study are then presented, after which we describe a third study exploring the similarity between regular and Boolean expressions. Finally, the chapter concludes with an examination of some future research directions.

2. Regular Languages and Expressions

The Chomsky hierarchy of languages (Chomsky, 1959) orders languages into four classes identified by number. Each class is properly included in all lower numbered classes giving Class 0 the largest number of languages and Class 3 the smallest. In most of the literature, the language classes are identified by alternative names: recursively enumerable or phrase structured (Class 0), context sensitive (Class 1), context free (Class 2) and regular (Class 3).

Every language can be defined by a grammar or set of rules that describe valid constructions in the language. The symbols that are combined to form valid constructions are known as the alphabet, Σ, of the language. Thus, given an alphabet and a grammar it is possible to decide whether a specified sequence of symbols is a member of the language described by the grammar. Furthermore, every regular language can be described by a regular expression (Hopcraft & Ullman, 1979). Regular expressions are formed by combining the elements of Σ using three operations: concatenation, alternation and repetition (i.e., the Kleene closure). Figure 1 provides a recursive definition for well-formed regular expressions.

Given an alphabet Σ where **a** ∈ Σ, **b** ∈ Σ:

(1)	**a**	is a regular expression	
(2)	**ab**	is a regular expression	(Concatenation)
(3)	**a|b**	is a regular expression	(Alternation)
(4)	**a***	is a regular expression	(Repetition or Kleene Closure)
(5)	**(a)**	is a regular expression	(Parenthesis)

Figure 1. Well-Formed Regular Expressions

Concatenation appends two regular expressions and is the mechanism by which longer expressions are built from shorter ones. Alternation is a selection mechanism with the expression **a|b** indicating a choice in selecting either the expression **a** or the expression **b** but not both (i.e., exclusive or). Repetition describes the set of zero or more successive occurrences of an expression. Parentheses may be used to modify the order that operations are performed (i.e., precedence) or can be used to modify the scope of an operator's application. Every regular expression is equivalent to a grammar for the corresponding regular language and provides a mechanism for defining the language. Languages that are defined using only concatenation and alternation have a finite number of members while languages defined using repetition have an infinite number of members. Hence, for the alphabet, Σ = {a, b, c, d}, Figure 2 provides some examples of well-formed regular expressions and their associated regular languages.

(1)	**ab**	defines	**{ab}**
(2)	**a*b**	defines	**{b, ab, aab, aaab, ...}**
(3)	**ab***	defines	**{a, ab, abb, abbb, ...}**
(4)	**(ab)***	defines	**{λ, ab, abab, ababab, ...}**
(5)	**a | b**	defines	**{a, b}**
(6)	**ab | cd**	defines	**{abd, acd}**
(7)	**(ab) | (cd)**	defines	**{ab, cd}**
(8)	**(a | b)***	defines	**{λ, a, b, aa, ab, ba, bb, aaa, aab, aba, abb, baa, bab, bba, bbb, ...}**

Figure 2. Example Regular Expressions and Their Languages

In Figure 2, it can be seen that λ, the empty string, is a valid member of some languages. In our studies, we wished to avoid issues in coding results that contain λ. Consequently, we use a modified version of regular expressions that replaces the *, zero or more, operator with the $^+$, one or more, operator. This change, apart from excluding λ as an element of any defined language, has no other effect on the expressivity of regular expressions.

Regular languages are simple enough to be easily defined but provide sufficient flexibility for describing the results of searches. It is for this role that regular expressions are best known in the field of computer science. Another mechanism for specifying search results is Boolean algebra, as used in many information retrieval and world wide web search tools. Boolean algebra also provides an alternation (i.e., or) operator, but replaces concatenation with a conjunction (i.e., and) operator. The repetition operator does not exist in Boolean algebra, but a negation (i.e., not) operator is available. The use of Boolean algebra to specify search results has been previously studied by Green et al. (1990).

Although Boolean algebra, a logical calculus for two valued systems, and regular expressions, a restricted class of formal language, are significantly different, the common use of an alternation operator and their application for similar roles provides a link between them. The studies presented here can be seen as a first attempt at examining the relationship between the skills used in the manipulation of each system. Study 3 uses performance times to explore this similarity.

To measure performance when manipulating (e.g., creating and applying) regular expressions, we adopted the information retrieval measures of *precision,* otherwise known as accuracy, and *recall,* which is also called completeness. Precision and recall have been previously used to measure performance of Boolean search specifications (Turtle, 1994). For a search that returns a set of solutions S, where C is the complete set of possible solutions, P the precision of the search, and hence of the search specification, is defined as:

$$P = \frac{|S \cap C|}{|S|}. \quad (1)$$

In the above equation, the notation |S| is used to identify the cardinality or size of the set S (i.e., number of members in S). Precision measures the fraction of the search results that are accurate or correct. Recall measures the completeness of the search result and is the fraction of the correct results with respect to the total possible results. For the same set of solutions, R the recall of the search, is defined as:

$$R = \frac{|S \bigcap C|}{|C|}. \tag{2}$$

Specifically, our research addresses four distinct issues. First, we explore the effects of using different granularities for measuring precision and recall. It is possible that evaluating results at the character level is under-sensitive since small or single character errors may not significantly affect results. Conversely, evaluating solutions as a whole and thus at a higher level of granularity may be overly sensitive with respect to small errors. The exploration of multiple levels of granularity is intended to identify experimental results that can be attributed to overly sensitive, or conversely, insensitive measures. For example, given the string:

xxxyzzzxxxyzzxx

and the pattern **xyz**, the participant response, where the participant has underlined the matches to the pattern:

xx<u>xyz</u>zzxx<u>xyzz</u>xx

has a precision of .857 at the character level (6 of 7 characters correct) and a precision of .5 at the substring level (1 of 2 solution substrings correct). The term substring is used to indicate that match elements are substrings of the data string. To explore the relationship between these granularities, precision and recall values were calculated at both the character and substring level and then compared.

Second, we investigated the relationship between precision and recall to identify the use of specific strategies from an information retrieval perspective. We explored whether participants used a conservative strategy to improve precision at the expense of recall, or an aggressive strategy that improved recall at the expense of precision. For example, the conservative omission of a suspect, but correct solution, will have no effect upon precision, but will lower recall. We believe that regular expression use is more like natural language use than like information retrieval and will therefore demonstrate a consistent relationship between precision and recall that is not found when performing an information retrieval task.

As indicated by Salvatori (1983), writing skill can be increased by improving reading skill, but the two skills are not completely related. That is, writing and reading abilities may increase independently, which indicates their basis in different, but related, cognitive skills. Rouet (2006) classes reading comprehension as a restricted form of literacy that precedes the functional literacy needed to synthesise and express (i.e., write) ideas. Thus, it is likely that there is a relationship between pattern matching, which resembles reading in that an existing "sentence" must be understood, and pattern creation, which, like writing, requires the development of new sentences. We expect novice's matching ability to be better than their pattern creation ability in the same way that one's reading skills develop before one's writing skills.

Third, we therefore hypothesise that the incidental learning that occurs during each study will improve reading ability for regular expressions, but not writing ability, as writing skill develops more slowly than reading skill and requires more developed cognitive abilities (Salvatori, 1983). That is, participants may advance to the *interpreting* level of the Wilkinson Cognition Measure (Wilkinson, 1979) for expression matching, but not to the *generalising* level needed for accurate pattern formation.

In previous research, Ledgard et al. (1980) explored the hypothesis that making computer languages more like natural languages improves their ease of use, thus suggesting that the two types of language have some similarity that permits natural language skills to be employed when working with formal languages. However, Blackwell (2000) found that graphical notations for regular expressions exhibited improved usability over a conventional textual notation. Blackwell's finding indicates that, although there is a relationship between formal and natural language, the "content" of some formal languages (e.g., regular expressions) is better represented using other notations. On consideration of these findings, we believe that there is significant difference in the content of formal and natural language.

Fourth, it is known that in Boolean algebra the alternation operator is more difficult to use than the conjunction operator (Greene et al., 1990; Vakkari, 2000). We hypothesise that this effect will also appear in the context of regular expressions. Finding this effect would provide evidence of similar skills being applied when using the alternation operator, regardless of the context of use.

3. Study 1

Study 1 was our initial attempt at exploring the relationship between pattern application and pattern creation. The study provides some preliminary evidence that the manipulation of regular expressions is dissimilar to information retrieval.

3.1 Participants

Participants, from a diverse set of ethnic and socioeconomic backgrounds, were recruited as volunteers from various psychology classes at a major Canadian university located in a large metropolitan city. The final sample included 36 participants (age in years, $M = 20.65$, $SD = 2.23$), excluding 5 surveys we omitted due to a clearly indicated lack of task comprehension. We considered a participant as not understanding the task if he or she had less than 3 correct responses for 20 items. All participants reported that they had no previous programming experience, therefore mitigating any confounds introduced by prior experience or training in formal or programming language use.

3.2 Stimuli and Procedure

Participants were given a four-part survey. In part one, participants were given 3 minutes to study an instruction sheet that explained the formation of regular expressions. The instruction sheet was not taken from the participants and the experimenter suggested that it could be consulted for reference when completing the remainder of the survey.

In part two, participants were given 5 minutes to complete a pattern matching task. Participants were instructed to underline all occurrences of a pattern in a given string of characters. There were 10 items in the task, each having a different pattern and string. Figure 3 provides an example of a matching item.

Matching	Pattern: **bg** String: **acdbggbcgbgbedccdfabagabadefbgcccfeedbbbbbgcbabcdgcef**
Creation	A sequence of **c**'s containing one **f** and that begins and ends with a **c**. e.g., **cfc, ccfc, cfcc, cccfc, ccfcc, cfccc,** ...

Figure 3. Sample Task Items for Study One

In part three, participants were given 5 minutes to complete a pattern creation task. Participants were presented with a written description of a search solution and asked to create a regular expression that matched the solution. For the last 7 (i.e., more complex) items, examples of possible matches were provided to supplement the written description. An example of a creation task item is shown in Figure 3. The order of presentation for the matching and creation tasks was counter-balanced, such that half of the participants received the matching task first, and the rest received the creation task first.

In part four, participants answered a few demographic and follow-up questions. The demographic items addressed the age and sex of the participants while the follow-up questions examined their satisfaction with the instruction sheet and opinions on the relative difficulty of the tasks.

The generation of precision and recall values for the matching task is accomplished by counting the number of attempted, and the subset of correct solutions, and forming the appropriate ratios. For the creation task, the created strings were applied to a set of arbitrarily constructed *representative strings* and the precision and recall values calculated. The representative strings were generated by the same experimenter as the data strings of the matching task with the intent that both sets of strings contain similar character orderings and constructions.

3.3 Results

There were three hypotheses for Study 1. First, we predicted a difference in performance based on the granularity of recording pattern matches. Second, we hypothesised the existence of a relationship between precision and recall measures. Third, we predicted a relationship between pattern matching and creation abilities. Due to the number of comparisons, we adopted a conservative significance level of $\alpha = .01$ to reduce the possibility of creating a Type I error. As well, because of the unspecified direction of some hypotheses, all reported analyses are two-tailed.

To test the first hypothesis, the possibility of differences in performance due to granularity, we conducted paired-samples *t*-tests for precision and recall scores at the character and substring levels. Individual mean performance on character precision was significantly higher than substring precision, $t(35) = 12.82$, $p < .000$. Character precision yielded $M = 0.88$ ($SD = 0.08$) whereas substring precision yielded $M = 0.69$ ($SD = 0.12$). Individual mean character recall was also significantly higher than substring recall, $t(35) = 13.67$, $p <.000$; $M = 0.74$, $SD = 0.12$, and $M = 0.59$, $SD = 0.14$, respectively. We additionally conducted paired-samples correlations to examine the possibility that performance at the character level is related to performance at the substring level. For precision, character and substring performances were significantly related,

$r(35) = 0.67$, $p < .000$. There was a corresponding finding for recall, as character and substring performances were significantly related, $r(35) = 0.89$, $p < .000$.

The relationship between precision and recall was analysed by collapsing the data across task and granularity, thus generating an overall mean precision and recall value for each participant, which were significantly different; $t(35) = 8.20$, $p < .000$. Individuals' recall values were significantly lower than their precision scores; $M = 0.67$ ($SD = 0.13$) and $M = 0.79$ (SD = 0.09), respectively. In addition, there was a significant positive relationship between precision and recall; $r(35) = .75$, $p < .000$.

To examine the relationship between pattern matching and creation, we collapsed the data across granularity and performance measures to generate an overall mean matching and creation value for each participant. This comparison yielded a significant difference, $t(35) = 3.71$, $p < .001$. Creation scores were significantly lower than matching scores; $M = 0.67$ ($SD = 0.16$) and $M = 0.78$ ($SD = 0.11$), respectively. Furthermore, the scores were unrelated, $r(35) = 0.17$, $p > .01$.

3.4 Discussion

The correlations between the scores at the character and substring levels, for both precision and recall, indicate that either granularity can be used to measure performance. As expected, the values at the substring level are lower than those for the character level as a result of the fewer number of solutions and the sensitivity of the solutions to small, single character errors.

It was found that the recall scores of each participant are significantly lower than their precision scores. This effect can be partially attributed to the testing instrument, as we observed that many participants successfully identified all but one of the possible solutions for a particular item. The effect is likely the result of simple oversight and not due to an inability to identify a correct solution. One explanation could be that the participants experienced a form of repetition blindness (Kanwisher, 1987) for multiple, adjacent solutions.

As precision and recall positively correlate, there is no evidence of significant variation in individual strategy. For example, an aggressive participant could have raised all their character level matching task recall scores to 1.0 by simply underlining the entire data string. This strategy would significantly lower their precision score as a result of generating many invalid solutions. The significantly lower score for recall than for precision indicates that a conservative strategy is consistently used by participants. It is likely that participants were conscientious in their completion of the surveys and tended to err on the side of caution. Alternatively, it is also possible that since the participants were students in an educational system where performance is measured using precision, they tended to focus more on precision than on recall. The second study uses a community sample to examine this possibility. It should be noted that the high means reported for precision and recall are a result of the survey design. The initial task items were intentionally easy and designed to build confidence for the purpose of improving compliance.

The consistent application of the same strategy does not match typical information retrieval behaviour. Individuals tend to show more variation in the trade-off between precision and recall than they did in this experiment. Thus, there is evidence that when using regular expressions, participants are thinking about the expressions and not the information that is being retrieved (i.e., search targets).

Although predicted, there was no correlation between the scores for matching and creation. Examination of the completed surveys reveals that participants had considerable difficulty in creating expressions. Furthermore, consultation with experienced regular expression users indicated a belief that the creation task was much more difficult than the matching task. The number of operators used in expressions for the matching task (26) was lower than for optimal solutions in the creation task (33). The number of alphabet symbols used in matching task expressions (27) was also lower than for creation task expressions (44). The significantly lower mean on the creation task than on the matching task provides support in the belief that creation is more difficult than matching.

4. Study 2

In Study 2 we aimed to replicate the findings from Study 1, as well exploring the differences between alternation and repetition. The survey used was a revised version of that used in Study 1, with modifications to increase the similarity of presentation between the matching and creation tasks.

4.1 Participants

Participants were solicited from various community locations in the same city as Study 1, and included a manufacturing company, business office, retail outlet, athletic facilities, restaurant, and hospital. There were a total of 64 participants in the final sample (age in years, M = 25.51, SD = 8.84) excluding 1 participant who had previous programming experience and 3 who demonstrated a clear misunderstanding of the tasks (i.e., matching or creation scores less than 3). Participants' educational history, ethnicity, and socioeconomic status were diverse.

4.2 Stimuli and Procedure

In Study 2, the timing restrictions were removed and participants were given as much time as they desired for each section. As in Study 1, the tasks were counter-balanced and administered in the reverse order to half of the participants. The instruction sheet of Study 2 was improved in accordance with the anecdotal reports obtained from participants during debriefing for Study 1. The primary change was the inclusion of an example suite similar to Figure 2. Other changes included minor improvements in wording, additional instruction on the use of parentheses and deletion of the task alphabet definition. The revisions were intended to permit participants to attain the *describing* level of the Wilkinson Cognition Model (Wilkinson, 1979).

The matching task was structured similarly to Study 1, but the creation task was modified to be more like the matching task. Figure 4 provides an example of a Study 2 creation task item. The modified creation task presents participants with an underlined string, where the underlined portions represent the solutions to an applied regular expression that the participants must generate.

Creation	String:	**zzuuxyxyzyzxzzxxyyzyxyxzzyxzyyyyyzyzzzyyzywyxxwuwu**
	Solution:	

Figure 4. Study Two Creation Task Item Sample

For both matching and creation, the first 6 items were structurally identical (i.e., the same operators arranged in the same order) to an element of the example suite on the instruction sheet. Moreover, both tasks used the same 6 items but with the order varying. The remaining 4 items did not appear on the instruction sheet and can be considered as slightly more complex. The number of operators in both tasks was identical, although the creation task expressions had 3 more alphabet symbols.

As the participants were from a community-based sample, the recruiting procedure was different than for Study 1. Participants were approached by a female experimenter and asked to complete a study on pattern and language formation. The remainder of the procedure was identical.

4.3 Results

There were 4 hypotheses for Study 2, with the first and second intended to replicate the findings of the first study. Therefore, we hypothesised a difference in performance due to the granularity of recording pattern matches, and a relationship between precision and recall. Due to the improved survey, we predicted a relationship between pattern matching and creation abilities that we did not find in Study 1. Lastly, we hypothesised a difference in performance on alternation items and repetition items. As in Study 1, we employed a conservative significance level of $\alpha = .01$ and all reported analyses were two-tailed.

A paired-samples *t*-test was used to examine the possibility of differences in performance due to granularity for both precision and recall measures. Similar to Study 1, individuals' character precision ($M = 0.86$, $SD = 0.10$) was significantly higher than their substring precision ($M = 0.70$, $SD = 0.17$), $t(63) = 13.87$, $p < .000$. Likewise, mean character recall ($M = 0.81$, $SD = 0.12$) was significantly higher than substring recall ($M = .68$, $SD = 0.17$), $t(63) = 14.01$, $p < .000$. Paired-sample correlations revealed significant relationships between character and substring precision, $r(63) = 0.88$, $p < .000$, and between character and substring recall, $r(63) = 0.94$, $p < .000$.

To examine the relationship between precision and recall, we collapsed the data across task and granularity to generate an overall mean for each measure. A *t*-test resulted in significant differences, $t(63) = 5.83$, $p < .000$. As we found in Study 1, participants' recall values were significantly less than their precision values; $M = .75$ ($SD = .14$) and $M = 0.78$ ($SD = .14$), respectively. The relationship between precision and recall was again significant, $r(63) = .94$, $p < .000$.

The possibility of a relationship between pattern matching and creation was investigated by collapsing the data across granularity and performance measures to generate an overall mean for each task. Contrary to Study 1, a *t*-test did not yield significant results, $t(63) = 0.87$, $p > .01$. Also in contrast with Study 1, there was a significant relationship between matching and creation, $r(63) = 0.64$, $p < .000$. To ensure that these findings were not due to an order effect, a repeated measures Analysis of Variance (ANOVA) was conducted. This analysis yielded non-significant results for the main effect of task, $F(1,62) = 0.72$, $p > .01$, and for the interaction of the task and version; $F(1,62) = 0.16$, $p > .01$.

To assess the relationships between the tasks of pattern creation and matching and the performance measures of recall and precision, we performed four paired-samples *t*-tests. First, we paired creation precision with matching precision to examine the influence of task on precision scores, yielding $t(63) = 1.67$, $p > .01$. Second, we paired creation recall with matching recall, again to investigate the influence of task on recall scores, yielding $t(63) =$

3.03, $p < .01$. Third, we paired creation precision with creation recall to examine the influence of performance within a task, resulting in $t(63) = 1.05$, $p > .01$. Fourth, we paired matching precision with matching recall, again to assess the influence of performance within a task, yielding $t(63) = 7.33$, $p < .000$. Paired-sample correlations resulted in significant relationships for all comparisons ($p < .000$); creation precision with matching precision r = 0.63, creation recall with matching recall, $r = 0.58$, creation precision and recall, $r = 0.97$, and matching precision and recall, $r = 0.81$.

Finally, we examined the differences in performance on items containing alternation or repetition in the creation and matching tasks. For the creation task, analysis indicated significant differences between alternation and repetition items, $t(63) = 3.09$, $p < .01$. Alternation items resulted in lower values than repetition items, $M = 0.71$ ($SD = 0.33$) and M = 0.83 ($SD = 0.21$), respectively. We also compared alternation items with items containing both alternation and repetition, $t(61) = 0.06$, $p > .01$. A final comparison of repetition items with items containing both alternation and repetition revealed a significant difference, $t(61)$ = 3.35, $p < .01$. Items with both operators resulted in significantly lower values than alternation items, $M = 0.70$ ($SD = 0.28$) and $M = 0.84$ ($SD = 0.20$).

The same pattern emerged for the matching task. Analysis identified significant differences between alternation and repetition items, $t(62) = 3.75$, $p < .000$. Alternation resulted in significantly lower scores, $M = 0.72$ ($SD = 0.19$), than repetition, $M = 0.82$ ($SD = 0.18$). A comparison of alternation with items containing both repetition and alternation revealed no significant difference, $t(58) = 1.28$, $p > .01$. Finally a comparison of repetition with items containing both repetition and alternation resulted in significant differences, $t(39) = 5.29$, $p <$ .000. Repetition resulted in higher scores, $M = 0.82$ ($SD = 0.17$), than items containing both operators $M = 0.68$ ($SD = 0.19$).

4.4 Discussion

The modifications to the instruction sheet changed the participants' reported satisfaction with the instruction sheet from 44.4% (Study 1) to 70.4% (Study 2). Anecdotal reports during debriefing indicated that the addition of an example suite was the primary cause of the participants' increased satisfaction.

The replication of the correlation between character level and substring level measures provides additional evidence of the exchangeability of the two scores. Future researchers may use either scoring technique without affecting results. However, it should be noted that the high sensitivity of substring level scores, and the associated lower mean for substring level than for character level scores, may obscure small effects in performance.

Replication of the correlation between precision and recall strongly suggests the absence of any significant individual strategy differences. As a community sample was used, it is unlikely that the correlation was due to any specific occupational factor (i.e., participants being students). Participants tend to use a conservative strategy and favour accuracy over completeness. While strategy differences may exist, they are displayed with respect to the amount of conservatism a specific participant employed. No evidence exists for the use of an aggressive strategy favouring recall over precision. During debriefing, participants indicated that they focused on the actual formation of patterns and not on the strings identified by the patterns. Thus, there was no evidence to indicate a relationship between regular expression use and information retrieval skills.

There was no significant difference in the means for the matching and creation tasks, unlike in Study 1. Consequently, when the difference in task difficulty was removed, performance on matching was found to correlate with that of creation. This correlation is suggestive of a common skill set being used for both tasks. The lack of an order effect also indicates the lack of a practice effect where the first task provides practice for the second. We believe that the lack of feedback given after the first task prevented individuals from improving their skill in expression manipulation.

As found by Salvatori (1983), humans develop the ability to read before they develop the ability to write and that the abilities to read and write are related but not correlated. Thus, it is unlikely that participants' skills when manipulating regular expressions, and hence formal language, are related to our skills for reading and writing natural language. The historic relationship of computer science to mathematics provides evidence of the similarity between the two fields. Debriefing of the participants determined that they viewed regular expressions according to their formation rules and considered them as a rule-based system, much like formal mathematics. Consequently, computer programming and formal language manipulation is more akin to a rule-based system than to a new and novel language. As it is not possible to speak or hear a formal language and thereby invoke the related cognitive abilities, there is considerable difference between programming and natural languages. This difference, along with how formal language is taught and presented, likely leads to the application of different cognitive skills when programming as opposed to when using natural language.

Our findings confirm the hypothesis that alternation is more difficult than concatenation or repetition. To ensure that the alternation operator was the cause of the effect we divided items into three groups, those containing only the alternation operator, those containing only the repetition operator and those containing both. The results indicate that there was a difference between the repetition and alternation group and between the repetition and both operator group. However, there was no difference between the alternation and both operator group. This finding indicates that it is the presence of the alternation operator that is responsible for the difference and not some unidentified form of operator interaction.

5. Study 3

Study 3 further explored the differences between regular and Boolean expressions, for which it has been found that using alternation is more time consuming, and hence difficult, than using conjunction and negation. We expected to find an analogous result and hypothesised that matching regular expressions containing alternation is slower than for expressions involving concatenation and repetition.

5.1 Participants

Participants were computer science students solicited at a Canadian university. A total of 32 participants (age, in years, M = 22.56, SD = 3.68) completed the study, but 2 participants were excluded as they were unable to correctly complete more than 3 of the 20 experimental items. The participants were predominantly male (N = 2 for females) due to the current under-representation of females in informatics disciplines.

5.2 Stimuli and Procedure

Participants were asked to locate solutions to a given expression in a target string. Customised software was used to present both the expression to match and the target string containing potential solutions. Beneath the string, a sequence of 7 buttons was provided for participants to select the number of matches in the target (None, 1, 2, 3, 4, 5, More than 5). Twenty expressions were presented in random order, with participants controlling when the exposure to each item was to begin and the software measuring the time needed to identify a solution.

During analysis, only correct solutions were used since solution times for incorrect results were believed to be inaccurate. The 20 items were divided into 4 subsets of 5 items: (C) concatenation only, (CR) concatenation and repetition, (CA) concatenation and alternation, and (CAR) concatenation, alternation, and repetition.

5.3 Results

We hypothesised that, similar to the reported results for Boolean expressions, users would take longer to correctly identify matches containing alternation operators. Table 1 shows the mean times in seconds for correctly identifying solutions to the 5 items in each subset.

Group	N	Mean	SD
C	147	5.31	1.30
CR	139	7.52	1.74
CA	141	8.86	2.45
CAR	126	11.96	2.96

Table 1. Descriptive Statistics for Study Three

Paired-samples *t*-tests were used to examine the effect that alternation had on performance. The mean time for items containing alternation (CA and CAR) was significantly longer than for items not containing alternation (C and CR) $t(29) = 14.18$, $p < .000$. To ensure that the difference was not due to expression complexity, the subsets CA and CR were compared and CA was found to have a significantly longer solution times than CR, $t(29) = 6.37$, $p<.000$.

5.4 Discussion

Our results confirm the hypothesis that alternation is more difficult than repetition or concatenation. Item groups containing the "or" operator had a significantly higher mean solution time than those not containing the operator. This result was also supported by the lower scores on items containing alternation for both the matching and the creation tasks of Study 2.

We did not compare the number of items correctly solved, as we attempted to recruit participants who were skilled at manipulating regular expressions and who we expected to obtain mostly correct results. Furthermore, the expressions were not overly complex so that the majority of participants would identify correct solutions, thus causing an expected ceiling effect.

It is not surprising that participants had more difficulty manipulating expressions with alternation than those without the operator since it is documented that a similar phenomenon occurs in Boolean query systems (Greene et al., 1990). While Vakkari (2000) reports that this effect decreases with improved conceptual representation of the search task domain, it is also possible that the reported improvement is due to increased skill in the use of a Boolean system. Vakkari also describes the use of alternation as a "parallel search tactic" due to the need to simultaneously identify solutions for both elements of the construct. The data of Green et al. (1990) supports this concept of parallelism. Participants in their experiment took twice as long, 44.8 versus 24.4 seconds, on queries with disjunction alone as compared to conjunction alone. Chui and Dillon (1999) suggest that this effect is the result of a greater level in difficulty for processing disjunctive information. This explanation is supported by Johnson-Laird (1983) who postulates that human processing of logical syllogisms is limited in the number of alternative models that can be simultaneously maintained in working memory. When working memory is depleted, processing will have to be performed sequentially, increasing the time needed to solve a task. It is possible this effect is stronger in novices, as they may use working memory less efficiently while developing their cognitive skills.

We contend that the similarity of Boolean and regular expressions, with respect to increased solution times for expressions containing alternation, is due to the nature of the ideas that they are used to represent. Both can be viewed as examples of *rule-based* systems where the syntax and semantics are clearly defined by a set of rules. Unlike natural language, which can contain ambiguous, ideomatic, or metaphorical expressions, Boolean algebra and regular languages are clearly and concisely defined by a formalised set of rules. Thus, it is likely that we use similar cognitive skills for rule-based systems, and that these skills are more related to our faculties for reasoning than to those for language.

6. Future Work and Conclusions

The three experiments in this chapter consistently show that the lower recall performance on matching tasks, as a result of missed solutions for adjacent single-character substrings, is potentially due to some form of repetition blindness (Kanwisher, 1987). Performance may thus be affected by phenomena unrelated to participants' skill level. Future research will explore this hypothesis by examining the locations of missed solutions relative to similar solutions.

Pane and Myers (2000) explored the issue of pattern creation and matching in the context of Boolean algebra. They report no difference in matching performance as a result of the format of a test item. While the use of a textual and a diagrammatic expression format had no effect on matching performance, it did significantly affect creation performance. Their data suggests, on the basis of a correct versus incorrect scoring system, that creation is an easier task than matching. Participants in their study answered 72.5% of the matching tasks correctly and 89.5% of the creation tasks correctly, when averaged over both expression formats. No explanation was offered for their finding. In contrast, we obtained lower creation than matching scores in Study 1 and equivalent scores in Study 2. This apparent discrepancy in reported findings requires further investigation.

In comparison to the findings of Greene et al. (1990), our solution times for the use of alternation do not show as great a difference to those for expressions without alternation. Whereas repetition requires the location of an arbitrary number of sequential solutions, conjunction requires the location of only two solutions and is potentially faster to solve. We intend to explore this issue in future studies.

Although the research presented here has begun a highly needed exploration of the cognitive skills needed to manipulate regular expressions, there is still much to be done. We have found evidence that, contrary to expectations, the manipulation of formal language has interesting differences to the manipulation of natural language. While the domain of language application, such as the use of regular expressions for describing search targets, may influence skilled users, there was no evidence of its influence on novice users. Thus, unlike natural language, which is based on mapping terms to real-world ideas, formal languages are likely mapped to the rules that describe and define their syntax and semantics. It might be considered that computer programming has more in common with other rule-based systems such as music, game-playing, and mathematics than it has to oral and written communication.

7. References

Blackwell, A. (2001). In: *Your Wish is My Command: Giving Users the Power to Instruct Their Software,* chapter 13 - SWYN: A Visual Representation for Regular Expressions, 245-270, Morgan Kaufmann, ISBN 1558606882, San Francisco, CA, USA.

Chomsky, N. (1959). On certain formal properties of grammars. *Information and Control,* 2, 137-167, ISSN 00199958.

Chui, M. & Dillon, A. (1999). Speed and accuracy using four Boolean query systems. *Proceedings of 10th AAAI Midwest Artificial Intelligence and Cognitive Science Conference,* pp. 36–42, ISBN 1577350820, Bloomington, IN, USA.

Greene, S.; Devlin, S.; Cannata, P. & Gomez, L. (1990). No IFs, ANDs, or ORs: A study of database querying. *International Journal of Man–Machine Studies,* 32, 3, 303–326, ISSN 00207373.

Hopcroft J. & Ullman J. (1979). *Introduction to Automata Theory, Languages, and Computation.* Addison-Wesley, ISBN 020102988X, Reading, MA, USA.

Johnson-Laird, P. (1983). *Mental Models.* Harvard University Press, ISBN 0674568818, Cambridge, MA, USA.

Kanwisher, N. (1987). Repetition blindness: Type recognition without token individuation. *Cognition,* 27, 2, 117–143, ISSN 00100277.

Ledgard, H.; Whiteside, J.; Singer, A. & Seymour, W. (1980). The natural language of interactive systems. *Communications of the ACM,* 23, 10, 556-563, ISSN 00010782.

Pane, J. & Myers, B. (2000). Improving user performance on Boolean queries. *Proceedings of Conference on Human Factors in Computing Systems,* pp. 269–270, ISBN 9780201485639, The Hague, Netherlands.

Rouet, J.-F. (2006). *The Skills of Document Use: From Text Comprehension to Web-Based Learning.* Lawrence Erlbaum Associates, ISBN 0805846026 , Mahwah, NJ, USA.

Salvatori, M. (1983). Reading and writing a text: Correlations between reading and writing patterns. *College English,* 45,7, 657-666, ISSN 00100994.

Turtle, H. (1994). Natural language vs. Boolean query evaluation: A comparison of retrieval performance. *Proceedings of International Conference on Research and Development in Information Retrieval,* pp. 212–220, ISBN 354019889X, Dublin, Ireland.

Vakkari, P. (2000). Cognition and changes of search terms and tactics during task performance. *Proceedings of RIAO International Conference,* pp. 894–907, ISBN 290545007X, Paris, France.

Wilkinson, A.; Barnsley, G.; Hanna, P. & Swan, M. (1979). Assessing language development: The credition project. *Language for Learning,* 1, 2, 65, ISSN 00124576.

6

Experiential Design: Findings from Designing Engaging Interactive Environments

Peter Dalsgaard
Institute of Information and Media Studies, University of Aarhus
Denmark

1. Introduction

The objective of this chapter is to present an overview of experiential design through cases which can guide designers in understanding relations between design values, use context concerns, and interactive potentials when designing experience-oriented interactive installations and environments. Experiential design projects are complex affairs in which a number of resources and concerns are brought into play in the shaping of future design concepts For this reason, the chapter presents *an experiential design schema for interactive environments* which provides designers with a tool for capturing and comparing these concerns, as well as relating them to the scope and objectives of designing specific experience-oriented projects.

Recent years have seen an increasing interest in experience-oriented aspects of HCI, and research contributions have presented a range of approaches to integrating features of user experience in interface design. Being an emergent field of study, these approaches are however quite diverse and without a persistent formal body of knowledge. This is due to the interrelated issues that the subject can be addressed from a number of perspectives, and that it is continuously evolving as new technologies are being bought into use in ever-more use domains.

This chapter presents a practice-based approach to the field of experiential design by outlining key facets of experiential design on the basis of the author's experiences from designing seven diverse interactive installations for knowledge propagation and marketing in cooperation with public institutions and private companies. These key facets are combined in the experiential design schema for interactive environments which encompasses underlying design intentions and values, domain locations and situations, interaction styles, content types and means of engaging users.

The case installations range in scale from walk-up-and-use single-user installations to building-size responsive multi-user environments, and the use domains cover a spectrum from trade shows to open, public spaces. The common denominators for the cases discussed are a shared focus on creating engaging experiences through innovative use of interactive technologies in collaborative design processes that involve interaction designers, domain experts, and end users.

These cases are examined through the lens of a pragmatist perspective on experiential design, which is outlined and discussed on the background of recent contributions to experience-oriented interaction design. This perspective provides a theoretical foundation for exploring the interrelations between experience, interaction and engagement.

2. Background and related work within experience-oriented HCI

The increasing focus on experience-oriented aspects of HCI is the result of a combination of trends: on a societal scale, researchers and consultants have been exploring the impact of the *experience economy* (Pine & Gilmore, 1999) for a number of years, and companies as well as public institutions governments are increasing their endeavours to reap the benefits of this trend; on a technological scale, *new technologies* with the potential to expand and enrich user experiences are constantly being developed, and the experience-oriented potentials of existing technologies are being re-examined; and finally, interactive technologies are being employed in ever-more *domains* that transcend the workplace, moving into public spaces, the entertainment industry, cultural institutions, leisure activities, and not least into users' homes. With this diversity in mind, it comes as no surprise that the research community's response to addressing experience-oriented aspects of interactive technologies is highly varied. Given the intrinsic complexity of the subject, Davis (2003) contends that "experiential systems design must be radically interdisciplinary" and combine efforts and insights the fields psychology and the arts and humanities, as well as engineering and computer science. *Three approaches to experiential design* are especially relevant for the theme of this chapter, namely those that focus on products, aesthetics, or theories of experience: First, approaches such as those of Jordan (2000) and Norman (2004), take as their starting point the notion of *pleasurable products* and their design. Product-centered approaches often have their main focus on the features and qualities of the interface itself, that which can be described and studied in ostensibly objective terms. A rather different approach is to take as a starting point the notion of *aesthetics* and explore what constitutes an aesthetics of interaction, as do Petersen et al. (2004), how to engage in aesthetic criticism of interfaces, as do Bertelsen and Pold (2004) or to examine what might come from designing post- or suboptimal technologies with special regards to aesthetic qualities, as do eg. Dunne and Raby (2001). Yet another approach is to establish *theories of experience*, either by drawing on existing theories from psychology, by radically expanding or modifying these theories, or by defining new ones altogether. Proponents of this approach include Alben (2004), Forlizzi and Battarbee (2004), and Forlizzi and Ford (2000). These approaches are primarily concerned with experience as it unfolds in human-computer interaction, or in computer-mediated human-to-human interaction.

The pragmatist perspective on experiential design presented in this chapter lends partly from the first of these approaches with reference to the concern for designing engaging interactive systems, partly from the second approach with regards to an interest in exploring the aesthetic aspects of interaction. However, it is mostly aligned with the third approach through the definition and discussion of salient aspects of experience in interaction. Within the theory of experience approach, Forlizzi and Battarbee (2004) provide a more fine-grained sketch of the field of experiential design by making a distinction between *three ways of modelling experiences*: First, *product-centered models* that focus on the qualities of the interface, such as those explored in Desmet & Hekkert's 'Framework of Product Experience' (Desmet & Hekkert, 2007) which examines the interrelations between aesthetic, meaningful and emotional experiences of products. Second, *user-centered models* of human capabilities and motivations such as Hassenzahl's exploration of the user-product relation (Hassenzahl,

2003). Third, models that focus on the *interaction-centered models* in a systemic perspective, as do Forlizzi and Battarbee themselves in their understanding of experience (Forlizzi & Battarbee, 2004) as well as Petersen et al. (2004) in their call for a holistic understanding of aesthetic interaction. The pragmatist perspective on experiential design presented here is best characterized as an interaction-centered one. It is for this reason that I employ the term *experiential design,* rather than *experience design* which in some instances lends the belief that the experience itself can be designed. In contra-distinction, experiential design stresses the notion that designers may seek to imbue interactive installations and systems with certain experiential qualities, but that experience is ultimately a subjective encounter in which the experiencing user is a co-creator. This is not to say that designers cannot design with the intent of bringing about specific kinds of experience, rather it is an echo of Petersen et al's proposition that "aesthetic is not something a priori in the world, but a potential that is released in dialogue as we experience the world." Thus, a reflective combination of understandings of users, use context, and technology in the design process may result in products and systems that invite comparable experiences among a multitude of users, their subjective past experiences notwithstanding.

In addition to the abovementioned contributions, a research perspective that has heavily influenced the work presented here is that of Participatory Design (eg. Greenbaum & Kyng, 1991) which stresses the importance of integrating knowledge of users and use context in the design process. The experiences from engaging in the seven design cases has however made clear that traditional Participatory Design, which is rooted in understanding workplace challenges and concerns, is also challenged by the emergence of experiential design. In particular, methods and techniques for involving users and gaining insights into use domains conventionally employed within this tradition are in need of revision or replacement when designers move beyond the workplace. One promising recent method for gaining experiential insights is Gaver et al.'s Cultural Probes (Gaver et al., 1999) which are intended to provide designers with user-centered inspiration. The experiences drawn from designing the seven cases presented in this chapter mirror Gaver et al. who propose that user inputs are best regarded as a one of several sources of inspiration that designers draw upon, somewhat downplaying the importance of specific user inputs and instead emphasizing the role of the responsible and reflective designer whose job is to coalesce a number of experiential concerns and resources in the final design.

Moving from theoretical sources of inspiration for this paper to case-oriented ones, Bullivant has presented the most comprehensive compilation of interactive installations and environments in (Bullivant, 2006) which presents cases ranging from responsive building skins through interactive rooms to artworks. There is a clear trend in interaction design to partake in design of large-scale environments as evidenced by eg. the Urban Screens conference (www.urbanscreens.org). On a smaller scale, conferences such as Tangible & Embedded Interaction (www.tei-conf.org) are primarily oriented towards installation-size interactive systems. Manovich (2006) addresses this new domain of integrating interactive systems into environments, which he dubs *augmented space.* Interestingly, Manovich argues that some of the best examples of augmented spaces, namely Cardiff's Audio Tours and Liebeskind's Jewish Museum in Berlin, are in fact not in themselves interactive, but rather shaped by sensitivities towards digitally augmented spaces.

3. A pragmatist perspective on experiential design

Based on experiences from practical experiential design projects as well as extensive literature surveys, I propose that *pragmatism* may serve as a sound foundation for establishing a framework for addressing experiential design and highlighting key concerns across experiential design projects. First of all, pragmatism has at its core an understanding of the reciprocal, interactive process of experiencing, thinking and acting through situated inquiry and experimentation (Dewey, 1910) which can shed light on the design and use of engaging interactive environments. Second, although pragmatism emerged long before interactive systems, it has influenced a number of fields such as aesthetics and architecture, and several recent contributions to the field of interaction design have employed pragmatist concepts, which means that there are a number of sources to draw upon in developing the framework. Of particular interest here are Schön's studies of the reflective design process (Schön, 1983), McCarthy and Wright's (2004) and Petersen et al's (2004) approaches to aesthetics of interaction, and Dalsgaard's (2008) concept of inquisitive use of interactive systems.

Pragmatism originated in the United States around the end of the nineteenth century. The movement was founded by Charles Sanders Peirce, William James, and later on John Dewey. Though their works share many standpoints, they are not fully congruent, for which reason it must be emphasized that this chapter will refer to Deweyan pragmatism.

Pragmatism is so labelled due to the *primacy of practice* principle, a foundational pragmatist proposition which holds that the meaning and "truth" of concepts and ideas are to be evaluated on the basis of their consequences and implications in practice. In this light, our theories and conceptualizations can be thought of as tools or instruments for coping with the world; if they help us navigate and manipulate the world they have proved themselves in practice, although we must always be open to the possibility that they may be replaced by better-functioning theories. Pragmatism views the world as being in flux, "brimming with indeterminancy" (Shalin, 1986, p. 10), and it is through the ongoing efforts of our thinking and acting in practice that we establish order in concrete situations. In this respect, pragmatism presents a highly situated perspective on human interactions. Just as we are situated and draw upon our repertoire of habits and experiences, so are other phenomena around us situated, most notably other human agents, but also technologies and spaces which have also been shaped as tools and instruments for coping with the emergent phenomena of the world. Deweyan pragmatism has been employed to address a number of diverse domains ranging from education and art to democracy. Given the scope of this chapter, I will however focus on pragmatist understanding of aspects of special relevance for developing an experiential design schema for interactive environments, namely the closely inter-related concepts *experience, interaction* and *engagement.*

Experience

Dewey makes a clear distinction between *experience,* which is the constant stream of experience of being in the world, and *an experience,* a discrete event that stands out on the background of continuous experience. Distinct experiences often stand out because we perceive of them as being either especially *problematic,* in that they disturb our traditional understanding of practice, or *aesthetic,* arousing a sense of fulfilment. Interestingly, problematic and aesthetic experiences are often convergent, since the process of overcoming a problematic experience can result in an aesthetic experience. Both types of experiences are highly situated in practice: continuous experience because it is that which ties us to and makes us understand our history of being and acting in the world, and distinct experiences both because we give them special notice on the backdrop of our existing experience and because they are related to situations we are currently facing. The notion of distinct experience is of special concern for experiential design, in that designers within this field often seek to bring about specific and remarkable encounters through framing and shaping interaction.

A pragmatist understanding of experience has several implications for design: The continuous flow of experience prompts designers to integrate interactive systems not just into the context of physico-spatial surroundings, but also into the flow of users' experience. The notion of aesthetic experiences prompts designerly explorations into what may constitute such experiences for intended users, and which types of interactions may bring them about. Furthermore, the notion of problematic experiences prompts examinations into whether it may be preferable to present users with problematic situations (since overcoming them may ultimately lead to aesthetic experiences), and into how to design problematic situations which do not scare off users before they engage in interaction.

Interaction

In the broadest sense, interaction can defined as a person acting in a situation in order to effect certain changes while drawing upon personal and and external resources. In Deweyan pragmatism, *situation* is the assemblage of the user, other human agents, physico-spatial surroundings, available technoloies, and the established socio-cultural meanings and structures in the domain: " Situations are an intimate, interconnected functional relation involving the inquirer and the environment." (Dewey, 1938, p. 108) In this respect, resolution of a problematic situation involves changes in one or more of these aspects. This occurs over the course of time, and interaction can thus be understood as a transformations of components in the assemblage and shifts in their relations.

With specific regards to experiential design of interactive environments, a pragmatist understanding of interaction is thus highly systemic. This implies in that designers should address not just the immediate human-computer interaction at the interface, but the whole situation of interaction including the experiencing person, the physical environment (including artefacts, technologies and spaces, man-made or otherwise), socio-cultural norms and meanings, as well as other people whose intentions and actions may influence the situation over the course of time. A key interaction concern when designing engaging interactive environments is to thus to simultaneously frame a situation that invites or provokes a user to interact and to scaffold this interaction by offering access to certain resources. These resources may be inherent in the interactive system (eg. ways of controlling visual elements such as characters in a game), or they may take the form of computer-mediated access to other resources (eg. offering communication with other users). Inviting or provoking interaction is dependent on the connection between situation and the user's experience, and an effective strategy for establishing interaction is to frame a situation which stands out for the user as something which is problematic and needs to be resolved in order to achieve an experience of fulfillment.

Engagement

Based in a Deweyan understanding of experience and interaction, engagement can be understood as a focused form of interaction in which the user enters into a reciprocal

relationship which potentially effects changes in both the user and the situation. Engagement relies on a certain mode of experiencing the world, namely *inquiry*: "Inquiry is the controlled or directed transformation of an indeterminate situation into one that is so determinate in its constituents distinctions and relations as to convert the elements of the original situation into a unified whole... The resolution of a problematic situation may involve transforming the inquirer, the environment, and often both. The emphasis is on transformation." (Dewey, 1938, p. 108) Engagement can thus be defined as a a mutual process in which the user in an interactive environment encounters a problematic framing of her experience, leading to inquiry into the situation through interaction with the intended outcome of transforming the perceived practice. This change may be understood in a very literal sense, eg. that an agent transforms her physical surroundings, it may be relational – eg. that new social structures are established between people in a situation - or it may concern aspects internal to one party in the situation – eg. that an agent gains new knowledge about the situation which transforms it from problematic to comprehensible.
The notions of inquiry and transformation as key aspects of engagement prompts designers to consider the ways in which they can challenge users – eg. through evoking curiosity or establishing a competition between several users - and to examine to which extent the different parts of the situation assemblage can be altered through interaction, either literally, relationally, or internally.
This outline of a pragmatist understanding of experience, interaction and engagement serves as the basis for the experiential design schema for interactive environments presented and exemplified in the following sections.

4. A experiential design schema for interactive environments

The experiential design schema can be understood as a translation of the theoretical insights from the previous sections into an instrument that can scaffold understanding and designing engaging interactive environments. The schema contains the following salient aspects of experiential design ranging from tangible to conceptual concerns: *Scale, domain, users, situation, interaction input, interaction output, intentions, values, content* and *means of engagement*. The first aspects are very concrete, eg. it is fairly trivial to describe the scale of an interactive installation, whereas the latter aspects, particularly intention, values, content, and means of engagement, are more abstract, eg. it may be a considerable challenge to define the experiential values that an interactive environment is to evoke among users. The aspects can be understood in the following way:

- **Scale** denotes the magnitude of the installation or environment. The cases presented in this chapter range from medium-sized interactive installations to huge building-sized environments.
- **Domain** denotes the setting in which the installation or envirnment is placed. In this chapter, the case domains range from trade shows to public parks.
- **Users** denotes the number of people using or experiencing the situation, in the case examples ranging from 1 to 1000.
- **Situation** denotes the circumstances under which people will encounter the installation or environment. In the case examples, this spans serendipitous encounters when walking down a main street to consciously exploring museum exhibitions.

- **Interaction Input** denotes the ways in which users can affect or control the interaction, in the case examples ranging from facial camera tracking to tangible interaction.
- **Interaction Output** denotes the interface response, in the case examples rangning from audio of spoken words to image visualization using color-changing concrete.
- **Intentions** denotes the concrete purpose for creating an installation or environment. In the cases, this ranges from grabbing bypassing people's attention to promoting autonomous learning in museums.
- **Values** denotes the experiential qualities that an installation or environment is meant to bring about through interaction. In the cases, the experiential values range from playfulness to conveying solemn moods.
- **Content** denotes the subject matter presented in the installation or environment, in the cases ranging from simple opacity-changing windows to complex visualization of electricity production and consumption.
- **Means of Engagement** denotes the mechanisms and strategies employed to promote engagement with the installation or environment, in the cases ranging from social engagement to presented fragmented narratives that invite puzzle-solving or storytelling.

The experiential design schema for interactive environments may be used for several purposes: First, it may be used to document and compare a number of projects, as will be done in the subsequent sections of this chapter. Second, it may be employed in the design phase in order to capture and explore the relations between salient aspects of one or more design concepts. As stated, the latter aspects in the schema are more specifically related to experiential qualities, for which reason they will receive the most attention in the remainder of the chapter. When I chose also to include generic aspects of design such as size and domain, it is because aspects captured in the schema are to be construed systemically as parts of a whole. This implies that changes in one aspect will most likely cause ripples throughout other aspects in the schema. Employed actively in a design process, the schema scaffolds the crucial design competence of moving from the part to the whole and vice-versa. In capturing key aspects of a design in a compact form, the schema furthermore supports shared overview and communication, both among design team members, and between designers and other stakeholders in a design project. Viewed as a whole, the schema implies that experiential design of engaging interactive environments should entail the following design inquiries:

- Determining the over-all intentions for creating the installation or environment
- Establishing an understanding of the physico-spatial surroundings
- Establishing an understanding of potential users
- Establishing an understanding of the situation in which users encounter the installation or environment, including the habitual structures and practices
- Determining the experiential values that the installation is intended to evoke
- Exploring the potential for interactive installations to convey the intentions and values to users through the means of engagement available to them

Table 1 contains the experiential design schema for the seven cases of engaging interactive environments which will be presented and discussed in more detail in the remainder of this chapter:

	GUM FACADE	SALLING FACADE	BALDER'S PYRE	ENERGY TABLE	SILENCE & WHISPERS	AARHUS BY LIGHT	WARSAW MOMA
SCALE	Medium: Wall	Medium: Facade	Medium: Corridor	Medium: Room	Large: Tunnels	Large: Facade	Huge: Building
DOMAIN	Trade show	Dept. store	Literature center	Science centre	Cultural heritage site	Concert hall	Art museum
USERS	1-10	1-5	1-5	1-6	1-10	1-15	1-1000
DURATION	30 sec-5min	5 sec – 2 min	30 sec-5 min	5-30 min	5-30 min	1-15 min	1 min – 3 hr
SITUATION	Passing by (trade show)	Passing by (main street)	Obligatory exhibition passage point	Exhibition installation	Lingering in park	Concert hall visit or lingering in park	Museum visit or passing by
INPUT	Facial camera tracking	Movement-based camera tracking	Floor pressure sensors	Tangible interaction	Audio / Speech	Silhouette-based camera tracking	Movement-based camera tracking
OUTPUT	User-controlled spheres in 3D space	Dynamically transparent window with varying opacity	Multiple video projections (of fire engulfing users)	Responsive table display coupled with exhibited devices	Audio / Speech	Silhouettes rendered on large-scale LED facade	Thermo-chromatic concrete
INTEN-TIONS	Attention Stand out	Attention	Convey atmosphere Pause for reflection	Promote autonomous learning	Convey atmosphere and richness of place Promote story sharing	Alter perception of architecture and place Social interaction	Alter perception of architecture Seamless yet outstanding integration of IT
VALUES	Playfulness Hi-tech impression	Finesse Cutting edge technology	Solemn mood Narrative coupling	Playfulness Participation	Curiosity Respect Participation	Playfulness Participation	Subtle transformations
CONTENT	Simple: Spheres in 3D gum universe	Simple: Dynamically transparent window	Simple: Visualization of fire	Complex: Visualization of electricity production and use	Complex: Place-specific stories	Medium: Creatures Cityscape	Complex: Navigation Artwork and data visuals
MEANS OF ENGAGE-MENT	Mirroring Gameplay Social interaction	Mirroring Surprise	Immersion Narrative relations	Gameplay Learning	Curiosity Narrative unfolding	Mirroring Gameplay Social interaction	Tracing Curiosity

Table 1. The experiential design schema summarizes salient experiential design aspects for the seven interactive environments cases

5. Case presentations

The seven cases are represented in the experiential design schema in table 1. The cases have been selected on the following grounds: they all fall into the category of experiential design; they employ interactive technologies to bring about engaging experiences, often in innovative ways; the author has been involved in their design and thus has access to first hand information; and finally, they represent a broad spectrum of uses of interactive technologies for experiential purposes, for which reason they lend tehmselves well to comparisons as well as to establish a broad overview of the field. In the following sections, each environment is presented in the sequence of their scale.

The author has participated in the development of all of the cases, and with the exception of Silence and Whispers, these have been developed at in collaboration with colleagues at CAVI, the Center for Advanced Visualization and Interaction, at the University of Aarhus, Denmark. Several of the cases have been developed in collaboration with external partners from industry, as described in the individual case presentations.

Four of the cases, the Gum Facade, the Salling Facade, Balder's Funeral Pyre and Aarhus by Light, have been produced and been put into use as final products; Silence and Whispers was developed and tested at a prototype level; the Energy Table was developed as a video prototype; the Warsaw MoMA was developed as part of a comprehensive proposal for an architectural competition. Due to these incongruences, as well as the very diverse scope of the installations and environments, no directly comparable evaluations have been carried out. Rather, each environment has been evaluated on its own specific domain- and experiential-related terms.

With the scope and aim of this chapter in mind, the presentation of each case is kept at the length of one page; several of the cases have been treated in greater detail elsewhere, and this is noted in the respective sections. The descriptions focus on presenting the function of the environments as well as intentions, values and means of engagement. This is done to provide adequate grounds for discussing and comparing experiences from the cases later on.

5.1 The Gum Facade

The Gum Facade (also treated in Dalsgaard & Koefoed, 2008) is an installation developed for and in collaboration with Gumlink, a large, international chewing gum research and manufacturing company, for their booth at the world's largest annual candy and sweets trade show in Cologne, Germany.

The gum facade is placed along one of the exterior walls of the booth. It consists of four screens connected to form one large display. Above the display, a camera tracks people who approach or walk past the stand. The video feed from the camera is processed by software that identifies faces. The images of faces of passers-by are then captured and represented live, in the shape of orbs on the display. The orbs exist in a 3D space showered by small gum tablets. By moving around in front of the display, users control the orbs that interact with the showering tablets and other orbs. The purpose is to create attention and attract visitors who may otherwise not notice the stand, and the intended use-time for the console is 30 seconds to 5 minutes.

The main intentions for creating the installation was to catch the attention of bypassing convention visitors while providing a brief an introduction to Gumlink products and services.

Figure 1. The Gum Facade in use at a trade show

The use context for the installations, the sweets convention, is characterized as being simultaneously bustling and somewhat serious and restrained: A large number of visitors are present, however they are all there for business purposes (the convention is professional and not open to consumers), and as such observe certain formal behaviours, both relating to dress-codes and behaviour. The users and the use context, coupled with the Gumlink company values, thus put certain constraints on the type of installations that would fit into the domain, and the experiential values defined as conveying an image of a serious company while emphasizing Gumlink's standing as hi-tech company driven by innovation. The means of engagement employed were fairly straightforward, namely mirroring the face of bypassers in the spheres, providing a simple gameplay, and inviting social interaction among passers-by. The Gum Facade was moderately successful in that it functioned quite well technically and served well as an ornamentation of the Gumlink stand; however, few visitors engaged in interaction, likely due to concerns about losing face in a professional business environment.

5.2 The Salling Facade - Dynamically Transparent Windows

The Dynamically Transparent Windows is a facade installation developed for and in collaboration with Salling, a major Danish department store. The Dynamically Transparent Windows are installed in a 5 meter section of the main street facade of Salling and respond to movements of people passing by. Using a camera, passers-by are tracked, and the data is processed by a system that controls custom-built interactive windows on the facade. The windows are fitted with electro-chromatic foil that can change from opaque to transparent when an electric current runs through it. By using thin strips of the foil, narrow bands on the facade change in order to reveal what is on display in the store when people walk by in a five-by-two-meter zone outside window. The facade uses various interaction modes in order to lure the by-passers near and make them explore the display, primarily through hiding the displayed items until people walk by.

Arguably the simplest of the installations presented in this chapter, the main intention of the facade is to attract the attention of potential shoppers. The main values guiding this process is to convey a sense of finesse and cutting-edge technology to by-passers. The main means of engagement is the element of surprise to se a window that has the until now unseen opacity-changing property, and in a straightforward sense the mirroring of by-passers: the facade is opaque, but when you enter in front of it, the it 'opens up' of you by making the strips in front of you transparent. The installation was in place at Salling for five weeks, during which we made a number of observations. The intentional use of the installation was quite limited, one likely reason being that the strategy of obscuring the items until display was overwhelmed by almost every other display on the main street, which in contrast screamed out for attention. As such, the Dynamically Transparent Windows were largely unsuccessful when employed in the main street setting.

Figure 2. The Salling Facade - images from a prototype and from the actual installation

5.3 Balder's Funeral Pyre

Balder's Funeral Pyre (also treated in Dalsgaard & Halskov, 2006) is an interactive environment designed for and in collaboration with 7th Heaven, an organization whose objective is stimulate reading among children. The environment was custom designed for a centre for Scandinavian children's literature as part of a series of interactive installations in which visitors experience settings and moods of the stories from Norse mythology. The Balder's Funeral Pyre installation is a 7 meter long and 1.5 meter wide corridor, in which one of the sides is a 6 meter long and 2 meter high rear projection of fire. The fire is digitally produced using a particle system with hundreds of bit map images of fire, which together with 14 on/off pressure sensors in the floor enable interaction with the fire. When no one is in the corridor, the flames glow low above the floor, but when someone enters the corridor, a lager fire erupts where the person is standing. As the person proceeds down the corridor, more explosions erupt near them, and eventually the person is immersed in flames.

The main intention of the environment is to Convey the story and mood of Balder's funeral at sea. Balder is a god figure from Norse mythology, in which his death marks a dramatic narrative event: Balder is killed, and this spells the beginning of the end of the mythological world, culminating in the apocalyptic Ragnarok that lays waste to the heavens and the earth. At his funeral, Balder's body is placed upon a ship that is ignited and set off to sea.

The experiential values were developed to underscore this story in collaboration with 7th Heaven: Convey an atmosphere that instils a solemn mood to emphasize the importance of the story and provide provide room for reflection upon what it means in the broader context of Norse mythology. The most direct means of engagement is the concrete experience of being slowly immersed in flames when entering and moving through the corridor. A more subtle means of engagement was in part shaped by 7th Heaven, who operate with a general strategy of conveying moods and atmospheres and hinting at story elements rather than retelling stories word by word; this is intended to encourage children to read the stories themselves. Thus, the environment creates a link to users' pre-existing knowledge and experiences, partly by employing the imagery and evoking the mood of the specific story, partly through placing the installation as a passing point at the middle of the childrens' movement through the literature center, mirroring how the story is in the middle of the over-arching narrative of Norse mythology. The environment was moderately successful: users responded very well to the final concept in testing, however the final production was marred by a limited budget for which reason it was perceived as somewhat unfinished.

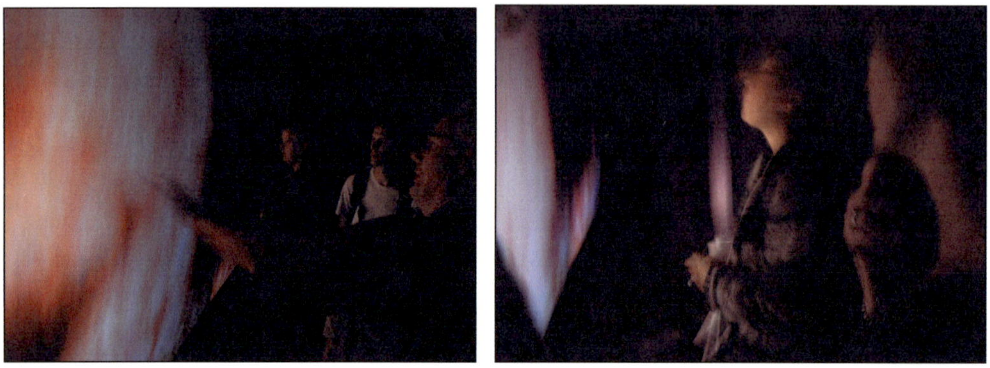

Figure 3. Users explore Balder's Funeral Pyre

5.4 The Energy Table

The Energy Table (also treated in Dalsgaard & Halskov, 2006) is a video prototype developed for The Danish Electricity Museum, a science and cultural heritage museum. The museum hosts varying special exhibitions and a number of permanent exhibit varying from a fully functional water plant to large Tesla coils, small experimental setups, electrical machinery etc. The museum visitors are include school classes and private visitors who attend lectures, follow guided tours, and explore the museum's exhibits on their own.

The Energy Table is a full-room environment. At the centre is a table, above which are mounted a camera and a projector. On the table are six miniatures of power generators, e.g. a windmill and a water power plant. Additionally, there are five to ten miniatures of devices that correspond to full-size devices placed around the table. When visitors stand next to a miniature power generator, they activate it, indicated by a glowing aura projected from above. They can now use physical icons, Electricons, to create flows of energy on the table by physically placing and moving the Electricons on the table. They can lead energy to the miniature devices on the table, thus activating the full-size devices in the room. The devices require different amounts of energy, and visitors can collaborate by combining flows of energy. The various Electricons function as switches, resistance, batteries etc., allowing for the execution of a wide variety of scenarios. The table can also be set up for the visitors to meet certain objectives, thus acting as a board for playing power games.

The intentions behind The Energy Table was to provide visitors with information about natural and technological phenomena that are invisible to the naked eye, primarily energy production and consumption, and to engage visitors in a manner which invites them to explore exhibits on their own. For these reasons, the guiding values were to instil a sense of playfulness and participation, and to evoke a sense of coherence between the installation and existing museum artefacts and surroundings. The primary means of engagement are on an installation-specific level to establish a gameplay structure for producing and consuming energy and to foster curiosity for learning about these phenomena, and on a social level to foster visitor-to-visitor interaction. Since The Energy Table was not put into final production, it is not known whether or not the product will be successful.

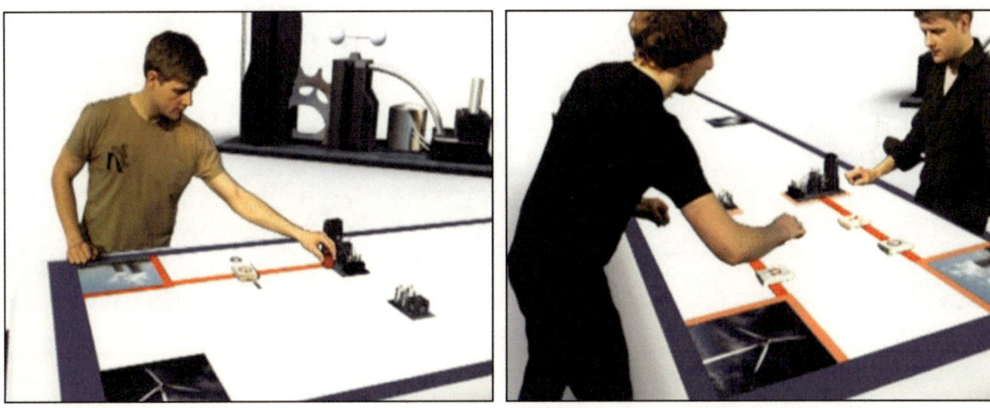

Figure 4. Images from The Energy Table video prototype

5.5 Silence and Whispers

Silence and Whispers (also treated in Dalsgaard, 2008) is a conceptual mixed reality installation created in 2006 as a cross-disciplinary collaboration between four interaction design researchers, including the author. Silence and Whispers was developed and located on Suomenlinna, a series of islands in the Helsinki harbour entrance. Suomenlinna served as a naval fortress and 1748 until the end of World War I, and simultaneuosly the islands housed detention camps. Today, there is a close-knit community of inhabitant on the islands that also serve one of the most popular public recreative area in Finland. Furthermore, Suomenlinna hosts an open prison facility. The primary intention underlying the design of Silence and Whispers is to collect and convey stories that reflect this multi-layered cultural history. Near King's Gate on the southern island of Gustavssvärd, faint whispers emanate from a shadowy cave. When visitors step inside the cave, they hear audio fragments of ominous stories and folklore from Suomenlinna. These stories, collected from resident islanders and visitors with strong relations to Suomenlinna, tell of events and myths not presented in official historic documentation. In addition to the audio fragments, stories and rumours are written in chalk on the cave walls. Some written fragments retell the same stories as the audio snippets.

The values underlying the design were to bring about a brooding atmospehere, to evoke a sense of respect for the history of the place, and to bring about a sense of co-participation. A primary means of engagement is to play on curiosity through the fragmented unfolding of narratives - the further visitors move into the darkness of the cave, the more disturbing the stories, and in order to view the gloomiest stories, visitors can light matches to reveal them in short glimpses. Another means of engagement is the option for visitors to contribute themselves: Pieces of chalk are left in the cave, and visitors can write down their own stories. In this way, the installation evolves and expands over time as old stories are erased or washed away and new ones are added to the cave walls. It was planned but not implemented to include an audio input option for visitors to tell their own stories, which would then also be fragmented and spread throughout the caves. As an experiential prototype, Silence and Whispers was relatively successful, in that users responded very well to the atmosphere and means of engagement inherent in the environment; we are currently exploring the possibility of realizing the final concept in a different setting.

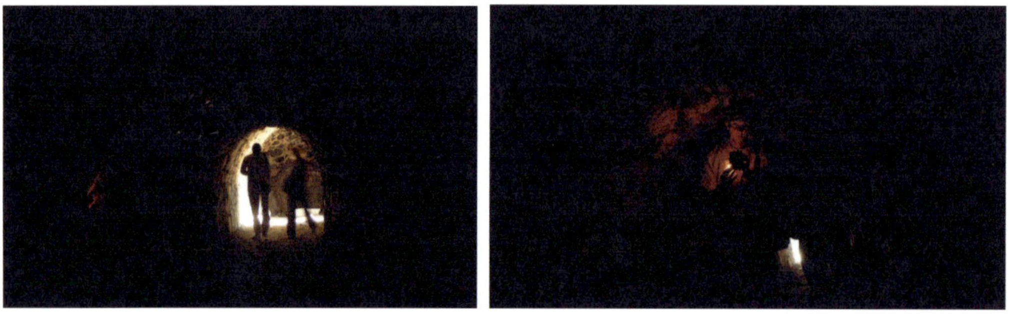

Figure 5. Visitors explore Silence and Whispers

5.6 Aarhus by Light

Aarhus by Light was an interactive facade developed by CAVI for Concert Hall Aarhus, Denmark, in use in February and March 2008. The interactive facade consists of 180 m2 LED displays which are highly transparent and can be arranged in 2x2 meter sections. The displays form an organic shape that becomes part of the distinct architecture of the concert hall. Luminous creatures live in the facade on the backdrop of an ever-transforming skyline that mirrors Aarhus. On the path towards the concert hall, a number of sensors capture the movements of passers-by and transform them to silhouettes on the facade. In this way, users can contact and play with the luminous creatures, eg. they may push them around or wave to them, and the creatures may respond by kicking or waving back. The tracking and animation software has been programmed from the ground up for the occasion by CAVI in C++. MaxMSP/Jitter was used extensively during prototyping of interaction and tracking. The character animation (done by animation company Wall of Pixels) as well as the Skyline was made in Flash.

The intention behind Aarhus by Light was to alter the perception of Concert Hall Aarhus (which has traditionally appealed to either children or middle-aged and old people, demographic groups which the concert hall seeks to expand) and the park surrounding it (primarily used as a transit zone in the city rather than a place for resting and relaxing), as well as to experiment with the newly developed LED displays. The intended values were to promote playfulness and participation, which was primarily addressed through the possibility of interacting with the luminous creatures in the facade. In continuation of this, the means of engagement were the gameplay potentials and the social interaction in the interaction zones. Furthermore, the mirroring of users as large silhouettes on the facade served as a prominent and straightforward means of engagement. Aarhus by Light was very successful in several respects: almost all visitors interacted with it, and a large majority enjoyed it, it generated a lot of attention and press of benefit for the involved stakeholders, and finally it served as a fruitful research experiment both with regards to technical and user-oriented concerns.

Figure 6. Aarhus by Light in use at Concert Hall Aarhus

5.7 The Warsaw Museum of Modern Art

This concept (also treated in Dalsgaard et al., 2008), which contains three interactive elements, was developed by CAVI as part of a complete proposal for an architectural competition for a new modern art museum (MoMA) in Warsaw, Poland developed by BIG (Bjarke Ingels Group), a Danish architectural firm.

The interactive components of the museum all make use of thermo-chromatic concrete (TCC), a material which has the property of enabling a concrete façade to become a display in its own right. Simply put, this is a type of concrete that slowly changes color as it is heated, and through controlling heating elements the building itself can act as a display. Three concepts were developed for the use of TCC in the Warsaw MoMA: 1) Visualization of exhibited artwork on ceilings and floors, 2) traces on ceilings and floors of visitors' movements throughout the museum, and 3) schematic vsualizations on walls of visitor data and statistics. The concepts are illustrated in figure 7:

The intentions for the conceps were to examine the properties of TCC to create a seamless yet innovative and outstanding integration of interactive systems to visualize exhibition contents and to guide visitors through the traces which would indicate the most popular exhibitions as well as 'hidden treasures'. The main values guiding this process was to present subtle transformations of the building though the use of TCC to alter the perception of architecture, and ultimately to convey the feeling of a living and mutable museum building responding to what goes on inside of it in terms of exhibitions and visitor actions. Due to the size and number of potential users, the means of engagement were primarily non-participative in the form of immersion and intrigue, although visitors would also see their movements as traces in the building (as per concept 2).

Figure 7. TCC used in three way in the Warsaw Museum of Modern Art

The BIG/CAVI proposal entered the final round of selections for the MoMA competition, but ultimately another proposal was selected; the TCC concept is however being refined in collaboration between CAVI and BIG. For this reason the environment may be considered a moderate success, however on the basis of the information available at the present time, it is not possible to determine how well the final product would be received.

6. Findings from designing engaging interactive environments

Some design disciplines are well-established, for which reason it is possible to observe and extract successful patterns for design. Examples of this include Alexander's pattern language of architecture (Alexander, 1977), or the Alexander-inspired patterns for interface accumulated by Tidwell (2005). Since this field of experiential design of interactive environments is emergent, such endeavours are in all probability premature within this field. In some instances, this is because the phenomena you wish to study as a researcher are not yet present, for which reason you have to engage in design projects to create them; eg. Aarhus by Light sprang from a research agenda of studying how social interaction and the perception of public places might be affected or transformed by media facades, a phenomenon which did not become observable until the environment was designed and put into use in practice. In other instances, it is because access to interesting aspects of cutting-edge environments and installations are not accessible to researchers due to designers' disinterest in divulging their trade secrets. The seven design cases are markedly diverse and as such they do not lend themselves to direct comparative evaluation. Rather, they offer a background for analyzing and discussing general experiences from engaging in in-situ design experiments carried out to explore the field of experiential design. In doing so, I shall focus on issues of success and failure, interrelations between values and intentions, place-specific concerns, and means of engagement. These discussions are summarized in a series of general experiential design considerations in the conclusion.

6.1 Success and failure of experiential interactive environments

Evaluating the success and failure of the installations is no mean feat: first, they are intended for different domains and situations; second, they are not all final products and as such not directly comparable; third, it is not always straightforward to define success and failure of experiential environments. With regards to final products, Aarhus by Light was without a doubt the most successful. It was a hit with users, it achieved the objectives and intentions posed in advance and delivered on the intended experiential values, and finally it served as a rich source for research insights. However, it may be more interesting to look at the Salling Facade, the least successful of the cases. The installation was thoroughly tested technically, and the prototype was user-tested in other settings, including a stand at a technology convention, before being deployed in the main street setting. Nevertheless, in situ observations coupled with analysis of recorded video revealed that it did not meet the intention of grabbing the attention of by-passers, and very few people would stop to interact with it. This finding led our attention to the general behaviour of by-passers on the main street, and studies of their behaviour revealed that very few people would actually stop to study what was presented in regular window displays. Even though not very many people interacted with the installation, it did likely generate a bit more interest than a non-interactive window display. In this manner, the project can be seen as quite successful in terms of generating research insights, although unsuccessful in practice. The relative failure of the Salling Facade however also led us to compare it to the success of Aarhus by Light: the main street offers people a great number of inputs, many of which appear quite similar the Salling Facade at first glance, whereas Aarhus by Light was immediately recognizable to people, both because of the scale and because it stood out on the backdrop of people's past experiences. As a means for stimulating immediate interest, this indicates that installations and environments should stand out, but in a recognizable way. This points to the highly situated nature of experiential design: determining the failure and success of installations and environments is done in practice, and there can be a number of influential factors which may not be known in advance.

6.2 Working with intentions and values

A distinctive feature of the process of developing the seven cases was the work that went into integrating intentions and values into the design process. Intentions and values were in most cases identified in the early stages of a project, often in collaboration with other stakeholders and based on studies of the use domain and situation. This was done to establish guiding tenets for design decisions. The process of designing Balder's Funeral Pyre sheds light on how this can take place in practice. Based on the nature of the myth of Balder and discussions with stakeholders from 7th Heaven, we sought to convey emotional qualities and a sense of slowness, which guided the design toward a subtle interaction with very simple content, the fire. During the design process, a more complex visualization, with dissolving imagery from Norse mythology, was discussed as an alternative that would stimulate children to play with the fire. A number of user tests of prototypes were carried with children in order to evaluate use patterns and the impact and impression of the installation. These tests made it clear that the more complex visualization would encourage playful interaction from visitors, whereas the simple version would result in a relatively passive and reflective usage. The established values of instilling a solemn mood and making room for reflection consequently made it clear that we should opt for the simple version of the installation. In the case that several stakeholders are involved in a project, it can be particularly valuable to take the effort to define the intentions and values, first because this establishes a common ground in between the stakeholders, and second because it empowers designers with foundation for making design moves and decisions without constantly seeking the consent of other stakeholders.

This being said, it is often a challenge to determine values that are specific enough to form a foundation for making informed design decisions. One strategy that worked well in several projects was to include anti-values in design discussions, ie. statements that reflect the opposite of the intended values for the installations. Altough we have not worked with anti-values in a systematic way, retrospective analyses indicate shared anti-values were formulated and referred to throughout many of the design processes. One example of an anti-value can be found in the case of Balder's Funeral Pyre, in which we deliberately steered clear of the anti-value "Spirited playfulness" since it would likely conflict with the solemn and reflective values that we aimed for.

6.3 Place-specific concerns

Based on the insights from evaluating failures and successes of the environments and using values as design guidelines, it is evident that an understanding of the *place* in which an environment or installation is located is essential. Drawing on geographer Yi-Fu Tuan (1997), Harrison and Dourish (1996) define place as follows: "... a place is a space which is invested with understandings of behavioral appropriateness, cultural expectations, and so forth."

In a pragmatist understanding, place may be construed as the assembly of shared socio-cultural meanings attributed to a space and the situations which habitually play out in it. The notion of places in combination with technology is thus of particular interest to interaction designers, for these are the materials which may be formed through design. Places and technologies embedded in them play a twofold role in that at the same time as they are framing and shaping our experience, they also provide means to transforming it since they scaffold our knowing and doing. Spaces and technologies also carry with them past histories and potential future trajectories since they are crystallizations of prior practice and contain latent possibilities for future events.

This makes it clear that the designer's understanding of place is of great importance for the outcome of experiential design of interactive environments. It can be argued that the relative failure of the Salling Facade, and to a certain extent of the Gum Facade, are due to a lack of understanding of the place-specific practices into which they were placed. In contrast, much effort went into examining the place into which Aarhus by Light was located with respect to architecture as well as to the understandings and practices associated with the concert hall and the park surrounding it. This expands both the role and responsibility of the interaction designer beyond the immediate interface to encompass the whole situation, "the assemblage of the user, other human agents, physico-spatial surroundings, available technoloies, and the established socio-cultural meanings and structures in the domain" as presented in section 3.

6.4 Means of engagement

The consequences of this expansion of the designer's role entail increased demands, but they also offer new possibilities and open up the design space. One area of experiential design in which this is the case is with regards to means of engagement. In some of the cases, the means of engagement pertain to aspects of interaction design which may be regarded as traditional, eg. establishing a suitably challenging gameplay through the design of interface and content in the case of the Energy Table. In other cases, however, the means of engagement are about framing situations which include further aspects of the situation, eg. in the case of Aarhus by Light, an important means of engagement is social interaction, in the sense that exploring the environment is often inspired by and done in collaboration with others.

The means of engagement presented in this chapter only scratch the surface of what is possible within experiential design of interactive environments. Designers may look for further examples both within interaction design, eg. Dalsgaard (2008) who presents a number of strategies for promoting inquisitive use of installations, and the Digital Experience blog (www.digitalexperience.dk) which is a repository for hundreds of inspiring experiential design projects, or within other disciplines such as architecture, film-making and education, eg. Arnone (2004) who presents numerous strategies for fostering curiosity in learning situations.

Proper means of engagement are also closely related to the scale and content of the environment or installation. A general trend in the cases described here is that there is an inverse relation between the scale and number of users and the complexity of the content: The larger the environment and the higher the number of users, the lower the potential complexity of the installation. This may change as the field evolves and interaction designers explore and develop new modes of interaction and content dissemination. The complexity of the content is of course also related to the situation and the potential time of interaction, eg. it would make little sense to convey complex information in the Salling Facade case, since many by-passers are only briefly exposed to the installation.

7. Conclusions and future work

The interest in exploring and developing experience-oriented aspects of HCI is growing, and numerous approaches and perspectives on the field are emerging.

This chapter has aimed at providing an practice-based overview of one part of the field, namely the design of engaging interactive environments, based on insights from participation in and evaluations of concrete design projects. This participation in concrete projects has allowed for insights into not only the function of the designed environments, but also into their becoming.

The central component of the chapter is the experiential design schema for interactive environments, which comprises the following key concerns: scale, domain, users, duration, situation, input, output, intentions, values, content, and means of engagement. The schema can be used analytically to gain an overview of the field, and to focus on interrelations between key concerns. It can also be used in the design process, both as a source of inspiration using the cases presented, to capture and relate aspects of the concrete design process, or to compare multiple avenues for design.

The components of the design schema are based on a pragmatist perspective on experiential design. This perspective stresses the situated and reciprocal processes of experiencing, thinking and acting, and presents a framework for understanding the relations between experience and interaction through engaged inquiry.

The experiential design schema has served as the common ground for presenting and discussing seven cases spanning a wide range of interactive environments design. Although these cases represent but a minor fraction of the field, the findings from them offer informed insights into some of the main issues facing interaction designers venturing into this field. As is evident from the discussions of the cases, a well-substantiated theoretical approach combined with practice-based experiences is no guarantee for creating successful designs, and there are still many open questions beckoning examination by thoughtful design researchers. On the basis of the cases, there are however a number of key considerations to take into account when designing engaging interactive environments:

- ***Designing with the entire interaction situation in mind***: Interaction unfolds in a situation that encompasses the experiencing agent, other agents, the physical environment, socio-cultural structures, and technologies; all of these interrelated aspects affect the experience of interaction and can be leveraged to present occasions for specific experiences to occur.
- ***Establishing connections between past, present and future experience***: Distinct experiences occur on the backdrop of existing histories of experience, and establishing connections between disctinct and continuous experience is a key concern.
- ***Tapping into the meaning of place***: Installations and environments are often brought into places that carry with them well-established consensual meanings and practices which the designer should bring into the design process, whether the objective is to establish a fit into the place or to stand out.
- ***Integrating values into design***: Integrating discussions and definitions of intentions and values can guide experiential design from early phases throughout the process - consider which ways of doing so are suitable.
- ***Utilizing means of engagement beyond the interface***: A number of strategies may be used to encourage inquiry among users; consider both those situated at the interface and those beyond, and whether they may be combined.
- ***Employing curiosity and occasions for social interaction and reciprocal change as motivational dynamics***: Of particular success for inviting inquiry and interaction seem to be the arousal of curiosity, the potential for social interaction, and the experience of reciprocal change in which both the experiencer and the situation are transformed. All of these may be brought about through a wide array of strategies.

8. Acknowledgements

The projects have been carried out over a period of four years and involved a multitude of collaborators. The author would like to thank these collaborators, both at the university and beyond, none mentioned, none forgotten.

Special thanks to my PhD advisor, Professor Kim Halskov, with whom I have worked closely in developing and reserarching interactive environments at CAVI and published several papers about experiential design in the past.

The Salling Facade, the Gum Facade, the Energy Table and Balder's Funeral Pyre are part of the "Experience-oriented Applications of Digital technology in Knowledge Dissemination and Marketing" project, which is funded by The Danish Ministry of Science, Technology and Innovation (The IT-corridor). Nordes, the Nordic Design Research network, provided the occasion to develop Silence and Whispers. Aarhus by Light and the Warsaw MoMA research has been funded by the Danish Council for Strategic Research, grant number 2128-07-0011 (Digital Urban Living) and grant number 07-014564 (Media Façades).

8. References

Alben, L. (2004). Quality of Experience: Defining the Criteria for Effective Interaction Design. *Interactions* Vol. 3 No .3 May+June 1996, ACM Publishers, 2004.

Alexander C. (1977). *A Pattern Language*. New York: Oxford University Press.

Arnone, M. P. (2004). *Using Instructional Design Strategies To Foster Curiosity*. ERIC Digest 2004-3.

Bertelsen, O.W. and Pold, S. (2004). Criticism as an approach to interface aesthetics. *Proceedings NordiCHI 2004*, pp. 23–32.

Bullivant, L. (1996). *Responsive Environments. Architecture, Art and Design*. V&A Publications, London.

Dalsgaard, P & Halskov, K. (2006): Real Life Experiences with Experience Design. *Proceedings of NordiCHI 2006.*

Dalsgaard, P. (2008): Designing for Inquisitive Use. *Proceedings of Designing Interactive Systems (DIS) 2008*, Cape Town, South Africa.

Dalsgaard, P. & Koefoed, K. (2008). Performing Perception: Staging Aesthetics of Interaction. Accepted for publication in *Transactions on Computer-Human Interaction (TOCHI:) Special Issue on Aesthetics of Interaction.*

Dalsgaard, P., Halskov, K. & Nielsen, R. (2008): Maps for Design Reflection. Accepted for publication in *Artifact.*

Davis, M. (2003), Theoretical Foundations for Experiential Systems Design. *Proceedings of ETP'03*, Berkeley, California.

Desmet, P.M.A., & Hekkert, P. (2007). Framework of product experience. *International Journal of Design*, Vol. 1 No. 1, pp. 13-23.

Dewey, J. (1910). *How We Think*. Dover Publications, Mineola, NY.

Dewey, J. (1938). *Logic: The Theory of Inquiry*. Holt, Rinehart and Winston, New York.

Dunne, A. & Raby, F. (2001). *Design Noir: The Secret Life of Electronic Objects*. Berkhauser, Berlin, Germany.

Forlizzi, J. & Battarbee, K. (2004). Understanding Experience in Interactive Systems. *Proceedings DIS 2004*, pp. 261-268.

Forlizzi, J. & Ford, S. (2000). The Building Blocks of Experience: An Early Framework for Interaction Designers. *Proceedings of DIS 2000*, pp. 419-423.

Gaver, B., Dunne, T. & Pacenti, E. (1999). Cultural Probes. *Interactions: New Visions of Human-Computer Interaction*, Vol. 6 No. 1, pp. 21-29.

Greenbaum, J. and Kyng, M. (eds.) (1991). *Design at Work: Cooperative Design of Computer Systems*. Lawrence Erlbaum Associates, Hillsdale, NJ.

Harrison, S. & Dourish, P. (1996). Re-Place-ing Space: The Roles of Place and Space in Collaborative Systems. *Proceedings of CSCW 1996*, Cambridge, MA, USE.

Hassenzahl, M. (2003). The Thing and I: Understanding the Relationship Between User and Product. In Blythe, M.A., Overbeeke, K., Monk, A.F. and Wright, P.C. (Eds.) (2003). *Funology: From Usability to Enjoyment*. Kluwer Academic Publishers, Dordrecht, pp. 31-42.

Jordan, P.W. (2000). *Designing Pleasurable Products: An Introduction to the New Human Factors.* Taylor and Francis, London, England.

Manovich, L. (2006). The poetics of augmented space. *Visual Communication*, Vol. 5, No. 2, pp. 219-240.

McCarthy, J. Wright, P. (2004). *Technology as Experience*. MIT Press.

Norman, D. (2004). *Emotional design: why we love (or hate) everyday things*. Basic Books, New York, NY.

Petersen, M.G., Iversen, O.S., Krogh, P. and Ludvigsen, M. (2004). Aesthetic interaction. *Proceedings DIS 2004*, pp. 269-276.

Pine, B.J. II & Gilmore, J.H. (1999*). The Experience Economy*. Harvard Business School Press, 1997.

Schön D. (1983). *The Reflective Practitioner*. MIT Press, Cambridge, MA.
Shalin, D. (1986). Pragmatism and Social Interactionism. *American Sociological Review*, Vol. 51, No. 1 (Feb., 1986), pp. 9-29
Tidwell, J. (2005) *Designing Interfaces: Patterns for Effective Interaction Design*. Sebastopol, CA: O'Reilly.
Tuan, Y. (1977). *Space and place: the perspective of experience*. University of Minnesota Press, Minneapolis.

7

Evaluation of Human Cognitive Characteristics in Interaction with Computer

Nebojša Đorđević and Dejan Rančić
University of Niš, Faculty of Electronic Engineering
Serbia

1. Introduction

Research results from the past several years indicate significant influence of human-computer interaction (HCI) on computer system development, which, combined with technological development, enabled their application in almost every branch of human activity (Jacob et al., 2007). HCI can be defined as "a field of study related to design, evaluation and implementation of interactive computer systems used by humans, which also includes research of the main phenomena that surround it" (Dix et al., 1998).

Multidisciplinary nature of human-computer interaction requires contribution from different science disciplines, especially from computer science, cognitive psychology, social and organizational psychology, ergonomics and human factors, computer-aided design and engineering, artificial intelligence, linguistics, philosophy, sociology and anthropology.

Main goal of HCI is to improve interaction between the user and the computer in order to make computers more user friendly and designed systems more usable. Understanding physical, intellectual and personal differences between potential users defines the level of understanding and fulfilling user needs. Regarding different human perceptual, cognitive and motor abilities can lead to universally usable interface development. In HCI, knowledge of the capabilities and hitations of the human operator is used for the design of systems, software, tasks, tools, environments, and organizations. The purpose is generally to improve productivity while providing a safe, comfortable and satisfying experience for the operator (Helander et al., 1997).

In this Chapter, we have presented some new research results on HCI methodologies. An extension of cognitive model for HCI - XUAN/t, based on decomposition of user dialogue into elementary actions (GOMS) is described. Using this model, descriptions of elementary (sensor, cognitive and motor) actions performed by user and system are introduced sequentially, as they will happen.

In order to evaluate user performance in interaction with interface, based on the described model and psychometric concepts, we have developed software CASE tool for testing sensomotor abilities of user in human-computer interaction. Software CASE tool arranges tests into test groups for psychosensomotor and memory capabilities. Test construction is based on recognition of activities in user-computer interaction, prominent user characteristics and the measurement method of individual production results. Taking into account different aspects of user profiles confronts us with the challenges of physical, cognitive, perceptual, personal and cultural differences between users. Test concept allows program-led testing of the target group and precisely quantifies user performance. Every experimental result is just a piece of a mosaic in the human performance in interaction with information systems based on computers. User test results are persistently stored in a database and available for further statistical analysis. Case study is carried out using XUAN/t interaction model and supporting CASE tool with group of 234 users and the numerical results verifying the proposed model are presented in the Chapter.

The main research goal was suitability verification of different HCI techniques for special user groups. In this study we have obtained an efficient tool for making user profiles. The software tool enables graphical interpretation of the results, calculation of different statistical parameters, visual analyses of the tested groups averaged results and easy creation of the user profiles.

The Chapter is organized as follows. After short introduction, second section gives an overview of research results in the area of HCI related to our work. Our extension of the existing XUAN interaction model - XUAN/t model is described in third section while forth section explains details of testing methodology according to proposed model. The description of the software CASE tool we have developed in order to support the proposed model as well as description of several characteristic tests are given in fifth section. Obtained results of the case study we have carried out are given in sixth section, while the last, seventh section concludes the Chapter.

2. Related work

The most important element in HCI is user interface (UI). User articulates his requests to the system via dialogue with the interface. Interface is the point at which human-computer interaction occurs. Physical interaction with end user is provided using hardware (input and output devices) and software interaction interface elements. User interface, as an interaction medium of the system, represents "software component of the application which transforms user actions into one or more requests to the functional application component, and which provides the user with feedback about the results of its actions" (Myers & Rosson, 1992).

Key concepts of graphic interfaces are based on the WIMP metaphor, which includes key elements of the interface: Window, Icon, Menu and Pointer.

The importance of user interface and human-computer interactions was noticed in the late 1970ties. In 1982 this caused a development of an independent research group, which, in 1992, had formed HCI as a special discipline (Dix et al., 1998).

The subject of HCI research is human being and everything related to human being: work, environment and technology. Classification of HCI methodologies was made based on the method by which end user is incorporated into system development (Brown, 1997):

- *User centered development* - provides system development FOR the user based on feedback information from the user during the entire process of system development.
- *System development WITH users* – development of user participation which promotes system development in user environment (manufacturing facilities, offices, etc.) rather than within software companies.
- *System development based on taking the user into account* - this approach uses cognitive modeling of end users in order to understand user behavior in a certain situation and why one system is better than the other.

Cognitive modeling provides a description of user in interaction with the computer system; it provides a model of user's knowledge, understanding, intentions and mental processing. Description level differ from technique to technique and ranges from high-level goals and results regarding thinking about a problem all the way to the level of motor activities of the user such as pressing a key on a keyboard or a mouse click. Research of these techniques is done by psychologists, as well as computer science specialists.

Alternative cognitive abilities model, based on cortical functions, is also known as "simultaneous and successive syntheses model" (Das et al., 1975). In both information processing ways, simultaneous as well as successive way, the memorizing processes are integration core enabling functioning of the whole integration (including perception and cognitive processes).

Classification of cognitive models is based on whether the focus is on the user and its task, or on transformation of the task into interaction language (Dix et al., 1998):

- Hierarchical presentation of user's tasks and goals (GOMS);
- Linguistic and grammar levels;
- Models of physical level.

GOMS (*Goals, Operators, Methods and Selection*) (Kieras & Arbor, 1988) model consists of the following elements:

- ***Goals*** - are results of user's task and they describe what the user is trying to accomplish.
- ***Operators*** - are basic actions which the user must take while working with a computer system. Operators can act on a system (pressing a key) or on the mental state of the user (reading a message). Detail level of the operators is flexible and it varies based on the task, on the user and on the designer.
- ***Methods*** - are step sequences which need to be performed in order to reach a given goal. A step in the method consists of operators.
- ***Selection rules*** - provide prediction on which method will be used in reaching a given goal in case there are different methods to reach the goal.

Models of the physical level relate to human motor skills and describe user's goals that are realizable in a short time period. An example is KLM model (*Keystroke-Level Model*) (Card et al., 1980) used for determining user's performance with a given interface. In this mode, the task of accomplishing a goal is given in two stages:

- *Task acquisition*, during which user makes a mental picture of how to reach a given goal, and
- *Task execution* using the system.

Task acquisition closely connects KLM with GOMS level that gives an overview of the tasks for a given goal. KLM decomposes the phase of task performance into five different physical operators (pressing a key on a keyboard, pressing a mouse button, moving a cursor to a desired position, moving a hand from keyboard to mouse and reverse, and drawing lines using a mouse), one mental operator (mental preparation of user for physical action) and one system response operator (user can ignore this operator unless he is required to wait for system response). Each operator is given a time period for its action. By summing these time periods we get estimated time for completion of those tasks for a given goal. Precision of the KLM model depends on the experience of the designer, because he is required to make a realistic decision about the abilities of end user. Obviously, the development of high quality user interface is impossible without cognitive modeling and techniques.

Interaction models are descriptions of user inputs, application actions and obtained outputs. The models are based on formalisms, which ensure their implementation within interface development tools.

One of the oldest and most general interaction models is PIE model (Dix et al., 1998), which describes user inputs (from keyboard or mouse) and output to user (on a screen or a printer).

User Action Notification (UAN) model (Harrison & Duke, 1995) was developed by system designers in order to understand the complexity of interactions with regard to the system, rather than the user. UAN model efficiently describes (and identifies) four elements of interaction in a way understandable to all participants in software development. Also, it does not differentiate between text and graphic interfaces, thus supporting each interaction technique. A drawback of this model is its approach to interactions by regarding the system only, without taking into account the other participant, the human being. This problem was overcome in the XUAN (*eXtended User Action Notification*) model (Gray et al., 1994), which equally treats both the system and the user. XUAN model treats the user and the system in terms of their visible, in case of the user articulated, internal actions. The advantage of XUAN model is that it includes human mental action. Its drawback is excluding the state of the interface, which can lead to its inconsistency.

3. Extension of XUAN Interaction Model

In order to evaluate user performance as realistically as possible, we have extend the mentioned interaction models (UAN, XUAN). Our extended model - called XUAN/t (*eXtended User Action Notification per Time*) treats equally the complexity of interactions, both from the system and from the user. The proposed model is given in table form (Fig. 1), that is divided into two parts. The first part of the table contains two rows in which descriptions of the user`s mental or sensory as well as articulated or motor activities are given. The second part of the table contains three rows in which interface descriptions (visible actions and interface conditions) and internal system actions (core) are given. Separation arrow dividing these two parts represents a point at which human-computer interaction occurs, and it also represents a time scale. Activities are also presented graphically on the time scale. Graphic presentation also provides visual interpretation of position, order and duration of each activity.

With the aim to efficiently estimate the number of actions and time duration of the entire task, a complex dialogue is decomposed into elementary actions using GOMS model. Descriptions of elementary actions by the user and by the system are entered sequentially in order of occurrence. The time needed for completion of each activity is given. Estimated time is determined by summing the times required for individual activities. In this way, the proposed model provides interpretation of action descriptions with empirical variables, which can be evaluated.

In XUAN/t model, time component is based on the duration of individual elementary actions; it is limited by given events as reference points. The user initiates these events, but they occur in the system. The system can register them precisely in order to determine the beginning and the end of each activity. The model is intuitive and it can be easily supported with available software tools.

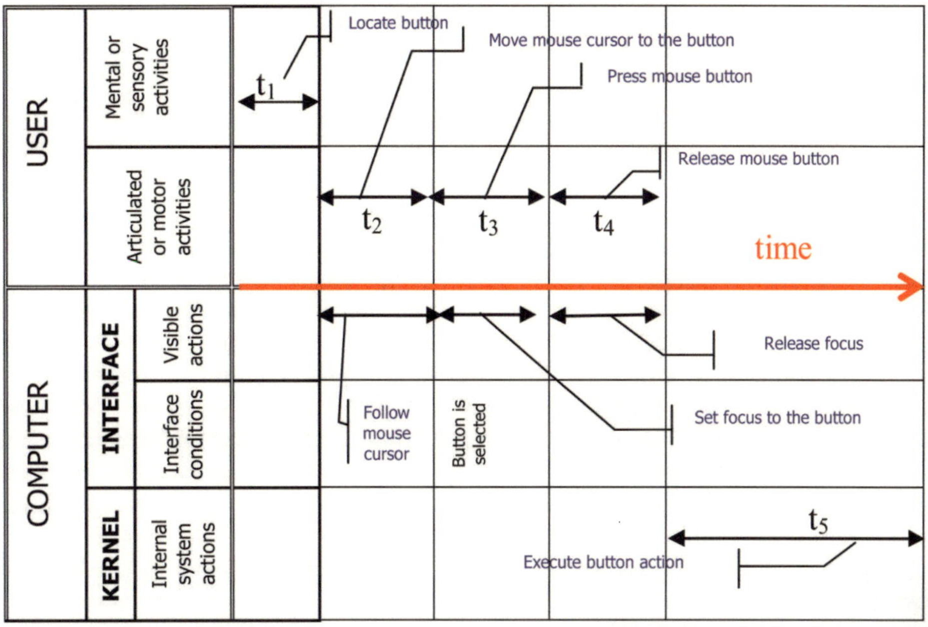

Figure 1. XUAN/t model of a click-on-a-program-field of the user interface

4. Testing Cognitive Characteristics Using XUAN/t Model

Understanding physical, intellectual and personal differences between potential users defines the level of understanding and fulfilling user needs. Regarding different human perceptual, cognitive and motoric abilities can lead to universally usable interface development. Taking into account different aspects of user profiles confronts us with the challenges of physical, cognitive, perceptual, personal and cultural differences between users.

A lot of tasks from everyday work are tightly bound to perception, so designers should be aware of the boundaries of human perception (Ware, 2001). The eyesight is especially important because the speed of human reaction depends on various visual stimuli, such as the time to accommodate to a very bright or very dim light, ability to recognize the appropriate part of a context, determine the speed or route of the moving point, etc. Visual sense reacts differently to different colors depending on spectral boundaries and color sensibility. The other senses, like these of hearing and touch, are also important.

The working environment can neither be ignored. Well-designed working environment increases user satisfaction, increases the speed of achieving the goal and reduces the number of errors. There is plenty of working environment aspects that should be taken into account such as: luminance level, albedo reduction, balance of light and glint, noise and vibrations, temperature, air flow and humidity, and the equipment temperature. Even the most elegant screen design loses its preference in noisy, dark and conglomerate environment. Such environment does not only reduce the working speed and increases errors, but also discourages even the most motivated users.

The classical methods of experimental psychology are under the constant development in order to cope with complicated cognitive tasks, specific to human interaction, on one side, and to computers on the other.

The reliable and valid results of the interface performance rating can be achieved by observing the user efficiency through the repetitive assignment of similar tasks in similar environment conditions.

The most important prerequisite to design an efficient interactive system is understanding of the user's cognitive and perceptual abilities (Wickens & Hollands, 2004; Ashcraft, 2001; Goldstein, 2002). Modern computer systems are based on human ability to fast interpret affection of sense organs and respond with a sequence of complex actions. In the short time intervals, (measured in milliseconds), users perceive changes on their screens and react adequately. The Ergonomics Abstracts journal (Ergonomics Abstracts journal, 2007) has published the classification of human cognitive process: short and working memory; long and semantic memory; problem resolution and reflection; decision and risk estimation; linguistic communication and understanding; search, pictures, and sensor memory and learning, skill development, knowledge acquisition and concept creation. That reference also specifies a set of factors which qualify users' perceptual and motoric performance: awaking and vigilance; weariness and the lack of sleep; sensor load (mentally); awareness of the results and loopback information; monotony and boredom; sense limits; healthy food and diet; fear, nervousness, mood, emotion; drugs, smoking and alcohol and physical rhythms.

According to the mentioned recommendations, we perform evaluation of user's cognitive characteristics by using specific tests designed for evaluation of certain characteristics and obtaining the user profile. Test construction is based on recognition of activities in user-computer interaction, prominent user characteristics and the method of measurement of individual production results. There are several steps during user-computer interaction, which we grouped into sensory, cognitive and motor activities.

Within sensory activities, we isolated the processes in which human being is gaining knowledge about phenomena and events around him such as:

- Impact of physical and chemical processes from the environment on human senses;
- Initiation of certain physiological processes in nerve cells of the sensory organs;
- Transmission of nerve excitation by neurons to the primary sensor zone in cortex,
- Initiation of a psychological response, which enables the human to become aware of the stimuli, which acted on the sensory organ.

In order to articulate his demands, user utilizes certain interaction elements of user interface (hardware and software), which enable his physical interaction with the computer. In physical interaction with hardware device, user makes a voluntary activity, which is coordinated with visual senses (from the primary sensory zone) and kinesthetic senses (from the motor cortex). Kinesthetic senses provide muscle coordination and development of skills for performing different complex movements while working.

Based on the described model and psychometric concepts, we developed software CASE tool for evaluation of human cognitive characteristics in interaction with the computer (Djordjević & Rančić, 2007).

5. Developed Software CASE Tool

In order to support new XUAN/t model, we have developed MS Access based software CASE tool that provides input of user identification data as well as user characteristics (Fig. 2). Using that tool, it is possible to determine the test list, and define general and particular test conditions.

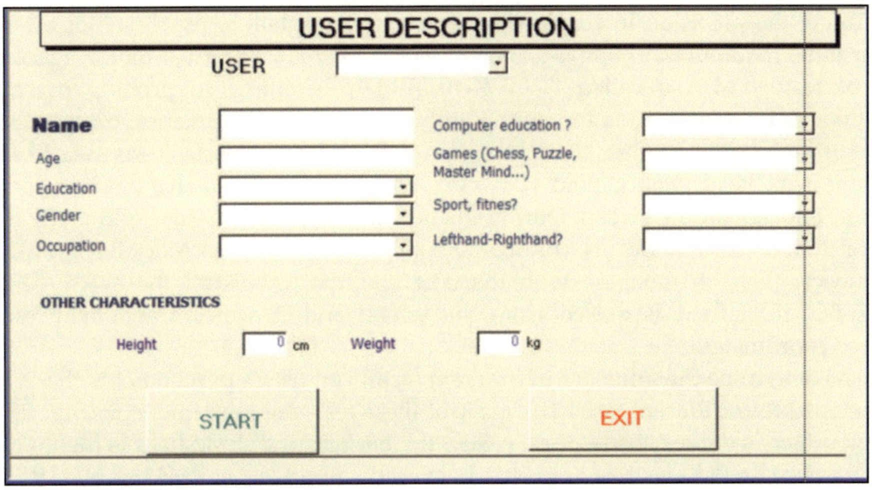

Figure 2. User description input form

In order to test all users under the same conditions it is necessary to define general conditions (screen resolution, mouse speed, etc.) and determine particular conditions of the micro surrounding (noise, light, temperature, etc.). During testing, tests are given in predetermined order with time limits. Testing depends on the choice of tests given on the list. Test groups related to perceiving, information processing and motor activities include tests of memory, sensory and psychomotor abilities.

5.1. Sensory Ability Tests

Cognitive processes, which represent response to specific stimulation, are represented using visual-information processing model (Atkinson & Shiffrin, 1968). According to that model, available information comes to special user´s sensory register and remains in it about one second. Physical characteristics of the stimulation are determined at this level. After that, information is erased from the register (has been forgotten) or transferred into the user´s short-time memory. At this level, some information has been lost, while the rest (along with information from user´s long-time memory) has influence on user response. The goal of sensory ability tests (perception) is to determine reaction times of users to visual (TP1) and audio (TP2) stimuli. User's abilities in domains of seeing, hearing and kinesthetic senses are tested. The test lasts 20 seconds, during which time user is stimulated with series of stochastic visual and auditory stimuli. User's task is to react as quickly as possible by pressing a certain key (LIGHT-OFF, RINGER-OFF), confirming registration of the tested stimuli. The CASE tool registers time lapse between giving the stimuli and user's response, as an evaluation parameter.

5.2. Psychomotor Tests

In order to articulate his demands, user utilizes certain interaction elements of user interface (hardware and software), enabling his physical interaction with the computer. In physical interaction with hardware device, user makes a voluntary activity, which is coordinated with visual senses (from the primary sensory zone) and kinesthetic senses (from the motor cortex). Kinesthetic senses provide muscle coordination and development of skills for performing different complex movements while working. The goal of psychomotor tests is

to determine the precision in coordination, object manipulation, psychomotor orientation, reaction time, manipulation aptness and the ability of making visual-motor guesses. First group of tests (PM), so called "CLICK-A-FIELD", is aimed to probing psychomotor orientation, visual-motor guessing ability and coordinated manipulation of user-computer interaction tools, coordination of individual senses and body parts. Tests last 20 seconds, and user's task is to click a field (1×1 cm), which cyclically, using random coordinate generator, appears on the screen. During the test, the software on-line continually registers times related to certain events (PRESS-MOUSE-BUTTON, RELEASE-MOUSE-BUTTON) and connects them in database with the user and the test. After the event, RELEASE-MOUSE-BUTTON field is erased from the screen and it appears at a new randomly generated coordinates.
In order to determine the influence of different factors on user's psychomotor characteristics we developed four different tests. The goals of these tests are the same, however: PM1 field on the interface is darker shade of gray than the background; PM2 field is highlighted red on the interface; in PM3 test the field is 1×3 cm on the interface; in PM4 test after RELEASE-MOUSE-BUTTON event a beep sound is given in order to provide audio stimuli.

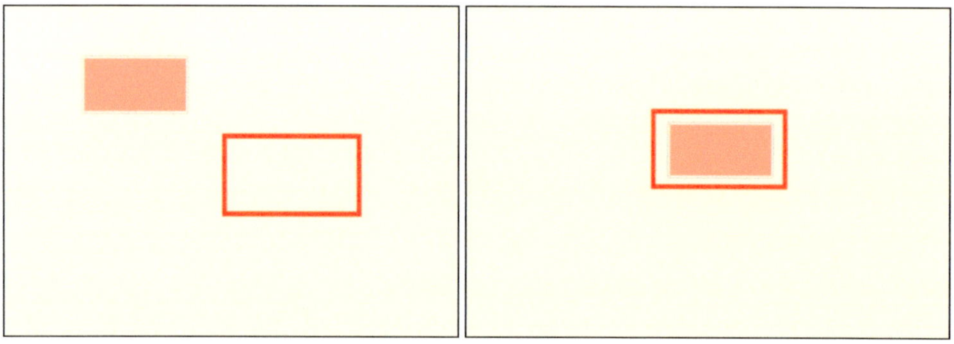

Figure 3. Test PM5 - "DRAG-ME" test

In order to determine precision and ability of fast, easy, correct and coordinated manipulation of visual objects with interaction technique of dragging objects on the screen, we have developed PM5 test (called "DRAG-ME") (Fig. 3). Test lasts 20 seconds, and user's task is to click on a red rectangular object on the screen and drag it into a rectangular window with red borders. After each attempt the object on the screen appears at a different randomly generated coordinates. The software on-line registers successful attempts.

5.3. Memory Tests

Memory is information-process structure composed from three components: sensory, short-time and long-time memory (Sperling, 1963). All memory components are necessary for successful information memorizing. Memory subsystem for sensory information deals with sensory representation of visual or audio event, which stimulates user sense during very short period. User´s short-time memory represents activity center in information processing system with limited capacity. In this zone, information comes from both sensory as well as user´s long-time memory subsystem (Sperling, 1963). Information in long-time memory is persistent with potentially unlimited capacity. Crucial characteristic of long-time memory is that information, which is memorized, may differ from the original information because of the user´s experience as well as other information influence.

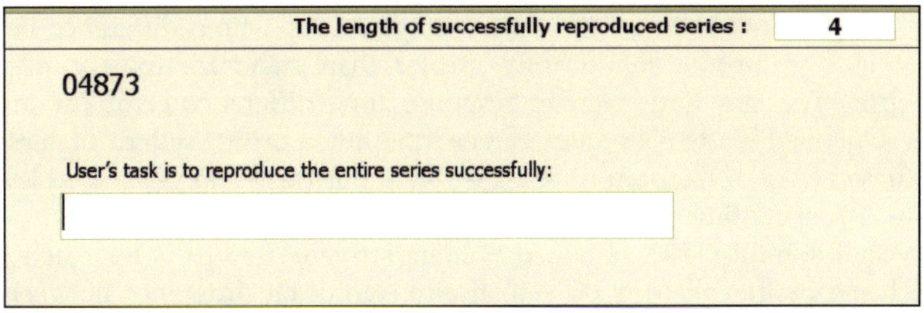

Figure 4. Test TM1: Memory test

The main goal of memory tests (TM1) is to investigate memory span through the ability of immediate reproduction of a series of elements after only one viewing of the series. This test is not time limited, it lasts until the first unsuccessful reproduction is made (Fig. 4). User can see, in a certain time interval, series of randomly generated numerical signs of given length. Presentation time of the series is proportional to the length of series. User's task is to reproduce the entire series successfully. This step is repeated with each series one sign longer.

We have also developed two more tests with the same scenario as TM1 tests, with a certain difference: in TM2 tests, generated series are composed using letter signs only, while in TM3 tests, the series are composed using alphanumeric signs. The software CASE tool registers the longest length of successfully reproduced series as a memory span parameter.

6. Case Study

In order to acquire HCI ability information from different user groups, we have performed special tests on group of 234 users. The group includes n1=116 male and n2=118 female users. We have performed statistical analysis on obtained results in average reaction time on visual as well as audio stimuli in order to discover statistically significant difference between different user groups. For statistically significant difference estimation we used Student's t-test (Spiegel, 1992), which is based on average reaction time difference between two independent user groups (with limitation that n1+n2 should be greater than 60).

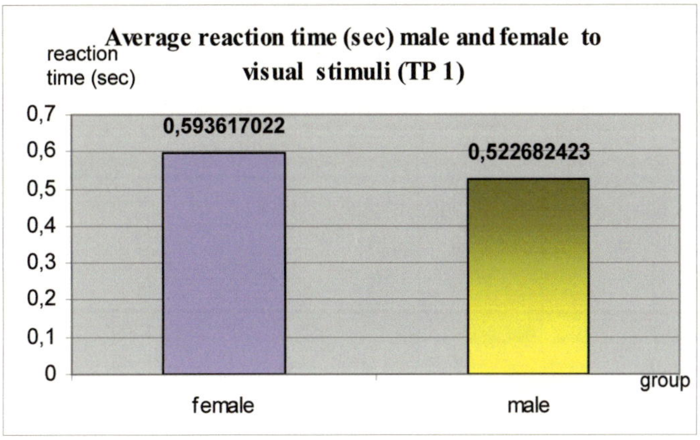

Figure 5. Average reaction time for male and female group in sensory ability tests (visual stimuli)

Hypothesis acceptance condition was that average reaction time difference between two independent user groups is significantly greater than standard average response time difference error. The standard average response time difference error for our test was 0.089419 sec. Obtained Student's t-value can be interpreted using Student's tables for limit t-values for chosen level of freedom n1+n2-2 (=232 in our case) and significant level ($p=0.01$, which means 99% of confidence).

In case of visual stimuli (TP1), obtained Student's t-value $t=0.79$ is less then limit value $t=2.58$, which means that there is no statistically significant difference between male and female users (Fig. 5). The difference is consequence of random variance, the samples belongs to the same basic set.

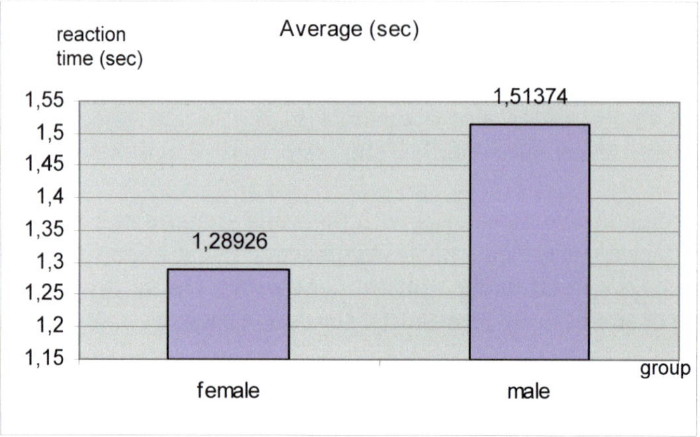

Figure 6. Average reaction time for male and female group in psychomotor ability tests (psychomotor orientation)

But, in the case of psychomotor orientation tests (PM), average response time was 1.51374 sec for male and 1.28926 sec for female users. Obtained t-value $t=2.06$ is greater than limit value $t=1.96$, which means (with 95% confidence, $p<0.05$) that there is statistically significant difference between male and female users (Fig. 6).

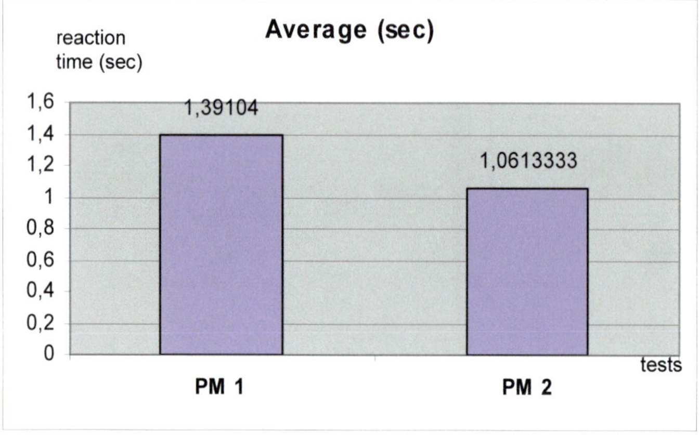

Figure 7. Average time in psychomotor tests with small and significant contrast difference in button color

Nevertheless, in case of psychomotor orientation tests with small (PM1) as well as significant (PM2) contrast difference in button color, average response time for entire testing population (both male and female users) was 1.39104 for PM1 tests and 1.06133 sec for PM2 tests. Since obtained t-value t=3.9567 is greater than limit value t=2.58, which means (with 99% confidence) it follows that there is statistically significant difference in response time between cases with small and significant contrast difference in button color (Fig. 7).

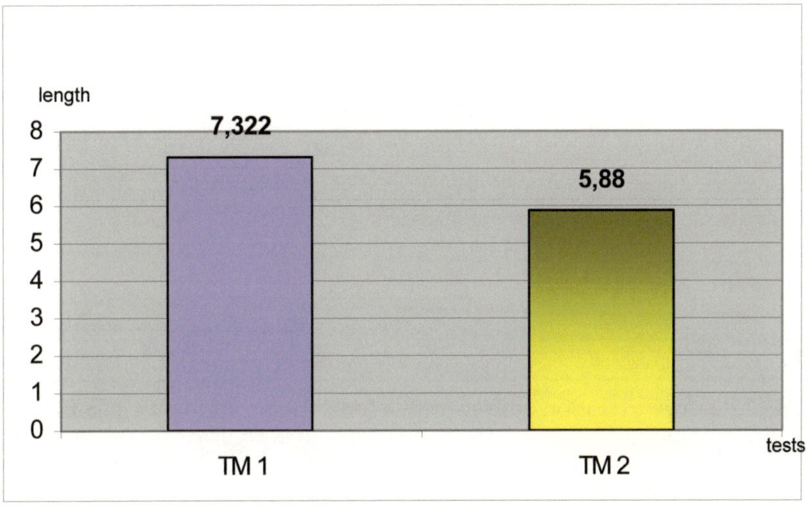

Figure 8. Average length of randomly generated signs sequence in memory tests

For the memory tests we used randomly generated numbers with average length of 7.322 numerical signs (for TM1 test) and randomly generated signs with average length of 5.88 letter signs (for TM2 test) (Fig. 8). Obtained t-value t=4.79 is greater than limit value t=2.58, which means (with 99% confidence) that there is statistically significant difference in average length of repeated sequence for numbers and letter signs.

7. Conclusion

Understanding physical, intellectual and personal differences between potential users defines the level of understanding and fulfilling user needs. Regarding different human perceptual, cognitive and motor abilities can lead to universally usable interface development. Taking into account different aspects of user profiles confronts us with the challenges of physical, cognitive, perceptual, personal and cultural differences between users. In order to evaluate user performance in interaction with interface, we extend the concepts of existing XUAN interaction model. Extended model is named XUAN/t and extension is related to the equal treatment of interaction complexity both from the system and user. Based on the described model and psychometric concepts we have developed software CASE tool for testing cognitive as well as psychomotor abilities of user in human-computer interaction. Test concept allows program-led testing of the target group and precisely quantifies user performance.

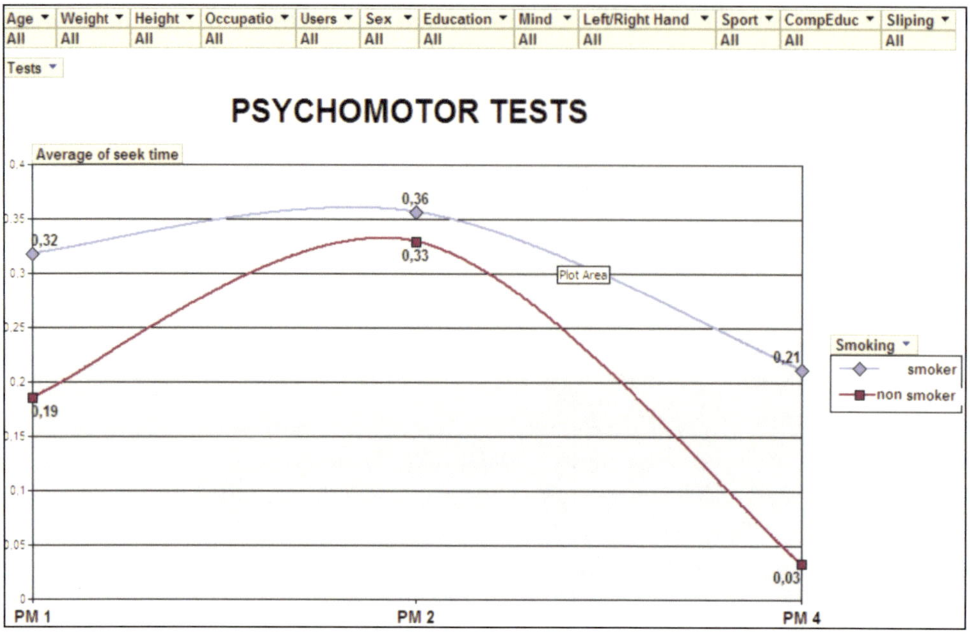

Figure 9. Graphical interpretation of user profile for smokers and nonsmokers

The developed software is efficient tool for making user profiles (smokers and nonsmokers, for example - Fig. 9). The software CASE tool enables graphical interpretation of the results, plenty of statistical calculations (Fig. 10), visual analyses of the tested groups averaged results and easy creation of user profiles.

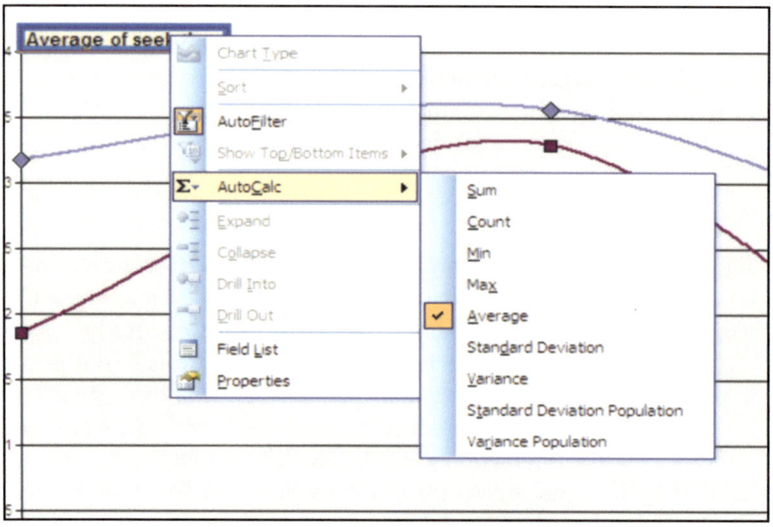

Figure 10. Set of the software CASE tool statistical calculations

In order to verify the extended interaction model (XUAN/t) as well as the developed software CASE tool, we have carried out case study for acquiring HCI ability information from different user groups. For this purpose, we have performed special tests on group of

234 users (116 male and 118 female users). Using our software tool, we have performed statistical analysis on obtained results in average reaction time on visual as well as audio stimuli in order to discover statistically significant difference between different user groups. Differentiation of tested users is utilized to determine compatibility of individual interaction models with given target groups. Qualitative analysis of obtained results provides recommendations for individual interface parts design suitable for the target group.
A future work should be based on extension of a set of user characteristics which qualify perceptual and motoric performance, as well as a set of tests using different interaction techniques. In that way we will obtain better software tool for reliable user groups profiling, enabling software designers to develop much suitable user interface for the chosen target group.

8. References

Ashcraft, M. H. (2001), *Cognition,* Third Edition, Prentice-Hall, Englewood Cliffs, NJ.

Atkinson R. C. & Shiffrin, R. M. (1968), Human Memory: a proposed system and its control processes, In: K. W. Spence and J. T. Spence (eds.): *The Psychology of Learning and Motivation,* vol. 2, New York, Academic Press, pp. 89-195.

Brown, J. (1997), HCI and Requirements Engineering - Exploring Human-Computer Interaction and Software Engineering Methodologies for the Creation of Interactive Software, *SIGCHI Bulletin,* vol. 29(1).

Card, S. K.; Moran, T. P. & Newell, A. (1980), The Keystroke-Level Model for user performance with interactive systems, *Communications of the ACM,* vol. 23, pp. 396-410.

Das, J. P.; Kirbi, J. & Jarman, R. F. (1975), Simultaneous and successive syntheses: An alternative model for cognitive abilities, *Psychological Bulletin,* 82, 1, pp. 87-103.

Dix, A.; Finlay, J., Abowd, G. & Beale, R. (1998), *Human-Computer Interaction,* 2nd ed. Prentice Hall Europe.

Djordjević, N. & Rančić, D., (2007), Software Tool for Evaluation of Human Cognitive Characteristics in Interaction with Computer, *Proceedings of the 8th International Conference on Telecommunications in Modern Satellite, Cable and Broadcasting Services – TELSIKS 2007,* pp. 446-449, ISBN: 978-1-4244-1467-3, Niš, Serbia, September, 2007.

Ergonomics Abstracts–the journal (2007): www.eee.bham.ac.uk/eiac/eiac7.htm

Goldstein, E. B. (2002), *Sensation and Perception:* 6th Edition, Wadsworth Publishing, Pacific Grove, CA.

Gray, P.; England, D. & McGowan, S., (1994) XUAN: Enhancing UAN to Capture Temporal Relationships among Actions, *Proceedings of the HCI'94 Conference on People and Computers IX,* pp. 301-312.

Harrison, M. D. & Duke, D. J. (1995), A review of formalisms for describing interactive behavior, *In the Software Engineering and Human-Computer Interaction – Notes in Computer Science,* vol. (896), Springer-Verlag, pp. 49-75.

Helander, M. G.; Landauer, T. K. & Prabhu, P. V., editors. (1997), *Handbook* of *Hurnan-Computer Interaction,*. Elsevier Science, Amsterdam.

Jacob, R. J. K.; Girouard, A., Hirshfield, L. M., Horn, M. S., Shaer, O., Solovey & E., Zigelbaum, J. (2007), Reality-based interaction: unifying the new generation of interaction styles, *Proceedings of ACM CHI 2007 Conference on Human Factors in Computing Systems,* vol. 2, pp. 2465-2470.

Kieras, D. E & Arbor, A. (1988), Towards a Practical GOMS Model Methodology for User Interface Design, In M. Helander: *Handbook of Human-Computer Interaction*, Elsevier Science Publishers B. V. (North Holland), pp. 135-202.

Myers, B. A. & M. B. Rosson (1992), *Survey on user interface programming*, In P. Bauersfeld, J.Bennett and G. Lynch, editors, *CHI'92 Conference Proceedings on Human Factors in Computing Systems*, pp. 195-202, ACM Press, New York.

Sperling, G. A. (1963): A model for visual memory tasks, *Human Factors*, 5, pp. 19-31.

Spiegel, M. R. (1992), *Theory and Problems of Probability and Statistics*, New York: McGraw-Hill.

Ware, C. (2004), *Information Visualization: Perception for Design*, 2nd edition, Morgan Kaufmann Publishers, San Francisco, CA.

Wickens, D. & Hollands, G. (2004), *Engineering Psychology and Human Performance*, Prentice-Hall, Englewood Cliffs, NJ.

8

Audio Interfaces for Improved Accessibility

Carlos Duarte and Luís Carriço
LaSIGE and Faculty of Sciences, University of Lisbon
Portugal

1. Introduction

According to the World Health Organization the number of people with visual impairments worldwide in 2002 was in excess of 161 million, of whom about 37 million were blind (Resnikoff et al., 2004). Although the visually impaired population is not uniformly distributed over the world, estimates for the developed countries, including the United States of America and European Union countries, go up to more than 20 million visually impaired people. Even if considering only the numbers for the developed countries, there are large numbers of population being prevented to fully access, depending on the severity of their visual impairment, today's software applications, which are mostly based on visual interaction.
The limitations to the visually impaired population caused by this reliance on visual interaction are felt both on the input and output ends of the interaction spectrum. Considering the use of visual output modalities, the limitations can range from total content inaccessibility felt by blind users, to minor limitations that are still detrimental to the user experience. These include small font sizes that make it hard to read, colour selections disregarding the problem of the colour blind population, and other presentation related issues. Input modalities are also extremely reliant on visual interaction. Although even the blind population is capable of using the traditional keyboard, pointing devices, like the mouse, are unusable by people with serious visual limitations, which hinder their perception of the pointer representation on screen.
In order to improve accessibility, alternative modalities must be considered. Audio interaction is the most promising alternative to visual interaction for visually impaired users, as the recommendations toward using screen readers and voice recognition software show (W3C, 2008; Sutton, 2002). It can be used alone for users with severe visual impairments who won't benefit from any kind of visual representation, or it can be used as a complementary or redundant modality for visual interaction, assuming greater or lesser relevance in accordance to the visual impairment level of the user population.
This chapter reflects on how audio interaction can improve interface accessibility, and shows its usefulness by describing the development of an audio based interface for Digital Talking Book (DTB) listening. DTBs are primarily targeted at blind and vision impaired users, but their development under the Universal Accessibility (Stephanidis & Savidis, 2001) umbrella can extend their usage to settings where sighted users operate in constrained environments that restrict visual interaction.
The chapter begins with a short summary of the issues pertaining to DTB presentation. This is relevant since a DTB player will be the application used to illustrate how audio interaction

can increase interface accessibility. This is followed in section 3 by a study comparing the use of auditory icons, earcons and speech in an audio only interface for a DTB player. The different techniques are evaluated according to the identification errors made, and subjective measures of understandability, intrusiveness, and likability. Section 4 presents the recommendations resulting from this study.

These recommendations are then accounted for during the development of a DTB player for two platforms: a desktop and a PDA. Section 5 will present the development of the DTB player for both platforms. The DTB player uses audio feedback to support non visual interaction. Books are recorded in audio streams which are played back to the user. The audio streams are synchronized with the books textual content allowing for visual presentation if required and supporting a set of additional features, which include improved navigation mechanisms and annotations support. Navigation possibilities are offered through the table of contents, and user defined bookmarks. The DTB player interface also supports annotation reading and creation. Audio annotations can be created using the devices' audio recording features. In visual operation, multimedia annotations consisting of images and videos can also be created and visualized.

For visually impaired users, and for visually constraining environments, it is necessary to rely on audio based awareness raising mechanisms. These are integrated into the interface to alert to the presence of navigation elements and existing annotations. The two versions presented in section 5 are visual based, but are introduced to lay the ground for the audio only version presented in section 6, which makes use of the recommendations from section 4 for presentation, and introduces pointer less based interaction, allowing blind users to control the application with a reduced number of keys.

Finally, section 7 presents the conclusions.

2. Digital Talking Book Presentation

Digital recordings of book narrations synchronized with their textual counterpart allow for the development of DTBs, supporting advanced navigation and searching capabilities, with the potential to improve the book reading experience for visually impaired users. By introducing the possibility to present, using different output media, the different elements comprising a book (text, tables, and images) we reach the notion of Rich Digital Book (Carriço et al., 2006). These books, in addition to presenting visually or audibly the book's textual content, also present the other elements, and offer support for creating and reading annotations.

Current DTB players do not explore all the possibilities that the DTB format offers. The more advanced players are executed on PC platforms, and require visual interaction for all but the most basic operations, behaving like screen readers, and defeating the purpose to serve blind users (Duarte & Carriço, 2005).

The DTB format, possessing similarities with HTML, has, nevertheless, some advantages from an application building perspective. The most important one is the complete separation of document structure from presentation. Presentation is completely handled by the player, and absent from the digital book document. Navigation wise, the user should be able to move freely inside the book, and access its content at a fine level of detail. The table of contents should also be navigable. One major difference between a DTB player and a HTML browser is the support offered for annotating content. Mechanisms to prevent the reader becoming lost inside the book, and to raise awareness to the presence of annotations and other elements, like images, are also needed.

To solve these problems in an audio only environment (speech recognition plus auditory display) we have tested several approaches. Concerning the auditory display, playback of pre-recorded books may be complemented by three other solutions: pre-recorded speech cues, auditory icons (Gaver, 1986) and earcons (Blattner et al., 1989). These solutions are used to convey context information and navigational cues, and their comparison is presented in the following section.

3. A Study of Audio Presentation Techniques in Rich Digital Talking Books

DTBs are capable of presenting their contents either on screen or through speech, recorded or synthesized. Besides the main content presentation, other book elements also have to be presented when working in an audio only environment. This means that the table of contents and the annotations must have an audio representation also. If an annotation is a voice annotation this is straightforward. If it is a text annotation, its content can be reproduced using a speech synthesizer.

However, in an audio only environment, not only content has to be transmitted, but the entire narration context has to be available in an audible format, thus enabling the listener to form an accurate image of the surrounding elements. For this to be possible the listener must be aware of annotations and images present in the book, as well as be able to know what is her/his position in the book whenever desired.

To understand how to better transmit this information to the listener, we evaluated three techniques for improving the listener awareness to the different DTB elements: speech, auditory icons and earcons.

Using speech for transmitting context information is perhaps the easiest of the three approaches, involving just the selection and recording or synthesis of the words to employ. While for certain applications this may not be a trivial task, in the DTB context, where the elements are well identified, it is an uncomplicated one. Speech can also be expected to be the technique where the message meaning is most easily understandable by the listener.

However, the use of speech can have disadvantages also. Since the book's content is being narrated, there will be two audio tracks presenting information in the same manner. If the presented messages are long they can disrupt the reading experience, become too intrusive, or even make it harder to listen to the main content if both tracks are played back simultaneously (Petrie et al., 1998). Furthermore, for voice messages to be understood, the listener must know the language in which the messages are spoken.

Auditory icons have been defined by Gaver (Gaver, 1997) as "*Everyday sounds mapped to computer events by analogy with everyday sound-producing events*". Due to this nature, auditory icons share with voice commands the ease of understanding, if enough care is put into the auditory icons selection, ensuring appropriate and intuitive mappings between the sounds and what they represent in the interface. However, there may be cases where it may be difficult, and even impossible, to find a sound to map to abstract interface events or components (Brewster, 2002). In the DTB domain, certain concepts are abstract enough to make it harder to find an everyday sound to map to, e.g. the beginning of a chapter.

Earcons are "*abstract, synthetic tones that can be used in structured combinations to create auditory messages*" (Brewster, 1994). They can be used in the situations where there are no intuitive sound to represent an interface's event. This gives them the advantage of being able to represent any event or interaction with the interface. They are based on an abstract mapping between a music-like sound and the interface events, which means that, at least initially, they have to be explicitly learned.

There are four types of earcons (Blattner et al., 1989): one-element, compound, hierarchical and transformational, allowing them to be used in every situation, and even giving them the flexibility to be concatenated, in a process similar to building sentences out of words (Brewster, 1994). Guidelines on how to build earcons are also available (Brewster et al., 1995), identifying timbre, rhythm, pitch and register as sound characteristics that can be used to effectively differentiate one earcon from the others.

3.1 Experimental Setting

In order to understand what solutions are more appropriate for the different DTB elements, and how they can be used, an experiment was set up, evaluating the use of the three different techniques, in a purely audio version of the DTB interface. To better focus on this goal we conducted a Wizard of Oz evaluation, with just the features required for an audio environment.

Four elements, essential for contextual awareness, were the subject of evaluation: beginning of a new chapter, current chapter number, presence of an annotation and presence of an image. A pre-recorded narration of the book "O Senhor Ventura" by a professional narrator was used in the experiment. Four excerpts of the narration, each making use of different audio feedback techniques, were prepared:

1. The first excerpt, six minutes and 39 seconds long, consisted of four chapters. Chapter beginnings, the presence of annotations, and the presence of images were signaled with earcons. The current chapter number was transmitted by speech recordings. When listening to the chapter number, the book's narration was paused.
2. The second excerpt, seven minutes and 38 seconds long, consisted of three chapters. Chapter beginnings were announced by a speech recording of the chapter number. Speech was also used to signal the presence of images and annotations. User requests for chapter numbers were answered with earcons, with no interruption of the book's narration.
3. The third excerpt, six minutes and 36 seconds long, consisted of three chapters. Chapter beginnings were announced with an earcon. Auditory icons signaled the presence of images and annotations. Speech recordings were used to transmit the chapter number, without pausing the book's narration.
4. The fourth and last excerpt, six minutes and three seconds long, consisted of three chapters. All feedback was given using earcons. The chapter number announcements paused the book's narration.

The speech used consisted of pre-recordings of the words "*annotation*", "*image*", and of the chapter numbers. Each chapter number was recorded on its own, meaning that there were no composition of recordings of individual numerals.

Auditory icons were used to signal the presence of images and annotations. For the image signal, the sound a photographic camera shutter closing was employed. The sound's duration was 600 milliseconds. For annotations, the sound of a typewriter was used. This sound's duration was 3 seconds and 50 milliseconds. This last sound was larger than the first because it was expected to be more difficult to recognize.

Earcons were designed to signal chapter beginnings, presence of images and annotations, and chapter numbers. Figure 1 presents the earcons used in the evaluation procedure. To promote ease of identification, each earcon is designed according to the earcon design guidelines (Brewster et al., 1995). Different timbres are employed: chapter beginnings - marimba; images - synth bass; annotations - trombone; numerals 1 to 4 - acoustic piano; numerals 5 to 9 - organ; and numeral 0 - tubular bells. The earcons for chapter numbers were divided into three groups corresponding to numerals 1 to 4, numerals 5 to 9 and the numeral zero. The numerals 1 to 4 are played with the same timbre, each numeral consisting of one more note than the previous, played in an ascendant scale. The numerals 5 to 9 are played with another timbre, following the same principles, but with each note played in a descendant scale. The numeral zero is played with yet another timbre. Numbers above 9 were composed with sequential presentation of the individual numerals (e.g. the number 15 is presented by playing the numeral 1 followed by the numeral 5). The interval used between numerals when composing numbers was 400 milliseconds.

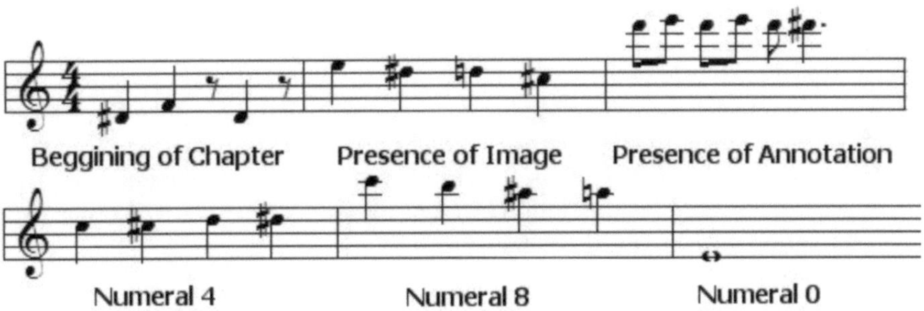

Figure 1. Earcons: Beginning of chapter, presence of image and annotation, and three examples of numeral used for chapter numbers

3.2 Experimental Procedure

Seven participants aged between 21 and 26, one female and six males, undertook the experiment. The experiment was a within-participants factorial design with two independent variables. The first independent variable was the type of auditory feedback technique used. The second variable defined how the current chapter number was presented: with or without interruption of the main narration. Dependent variables were the number of correct identifications of book elements, and subjective measures of understandability, intrusiveness and satisfaction. The main hypothesis was that varying the type of auditory feedback used would lead to different levels of understandability, intrusiveness and satisfaction.

The experiment began with the presentation phase, where the participants were introduced to the different auditory feedback techniques. In this phase the participants were asked to recognize the sounds used as auditory icons, and to associate them with one of the features of the DTB player. This was followed by the presentation of the different earcons, repeated as many times as wished. When the participants felt comfortable with the earcons, these were played back twice in a different order, to test the recall rate. The construction of numbers from the numeral earcons was then explained to the participants. The participants were then asked to identify twelve numbers represented by earcons. This phase ended with the replay of earcons used for beginning of chapter, images and annotations.

The testing phase consisted in the presentation of the four book excerpts. During the excerpts presentation, participants were allowed to use three commands: pause and play, for controlling playback (no forward or backward movement was allowed) and another command to inquire the current reading position. The participants were asked to perform two tasks during excerpt presentation: one task consisted in keeping count of the number of annotations (or images - this varied from excerpt to excerpt) in that excerpt; the second task consisted in identifying, for all occurrences of images (or annotations), the current chapter number, writing it down and delivering it to the test coordinator, immediately after recognizing the audio cue. After each excerpt, the participants answered a questionnaire, rating the techniques used in the excerpt in terms of their understandability, intrusiveness, and satisfaction. Rating scales ranged from zero to nine, with zero meaning it was hard to understand the sound's meaning, the sound was very intrusive, and unpleasant. Nine corresponded to a sound with an easily identifiable meaning, not intrusive, and pleasant to listen to.

3.3 Results

The preparation phase allowed for the individual evaluation of the auditory icons and earcons, while their use as part of an application was evaluated during the next phase.
The auditory icons were correctly identified by all the participants. The sound of the camera shutter closing was associated with the image element by all participants. The typewriter sound was associated with the annotation element by six participants. The other participant associated the sound with the image element.
The three earcons for chapter beginning, images and annotations, presented twice to each participant, were correctly identified by just three participants. One participant was not able to correctly interpret the chapter beginning and annotations earcons in the first round, exchanging their meanings. Two participants exchanged the meanings of the annotations and images earcons in both rounds of presentation. The other participant exchanged the meanings of the beginning of chapter and images earcons in both rounds. No clear misinterpretation pattern was identified. It is possible that all these misinterpretations are due to the participants not having heard the earcons enough times to correctly recall them.
The twelve number earcons for the number identification task represented the numbers 62, 8, 17, 2, 46, 93, 2, 30, 11, 54, 66, 9. Four were single digit numbers, six were composed by earcons of different timbres, and two by earcons of the same timbre. Three participants correctly identified all numbers (the same participants that had correctly identified all the earcons previously). Two participants incorrectly identified two numbers, and the other two participants incorrectly identified five numbers. The fourteen errors, out of the 84 numbers played, can be divided in the following categories: wrong count of notes in a numeral (e.g. identifying a three when a two as played) - 8; wrong association of timbre to numeral (e.g. identifying a two when a six was played) - 3; wrong interpretation of the pause between two notes (e.g. identifying a two when an eleven was played) - 3.The total percentage of correctly identified numbers was 83.3%.

3.3.1 Testing Phase Results

The four excerpts of the book played back to the seven participants contained a total of 385 fixed audio cues divided in the following way: 210 in the form of earcons, 84 in the form of auditory icons and 91 in the form of spoken messages. We will use this number of fixed audio cues as the corpus for comparison between the different techniques. To arrive at the total number of audio cues, the number of times the chapter number was requested would have to be added.

When considering the identification of audio cues, we expected that both speech and auditory icons would be identified correctly every time. This was indeed the case, with all participants identifying correctly all the elements when presented with these two techniques. When the elements were presented by earcons, the recognition rate lowered to 89.05%., corresponding to a total of 23 misinterpreted earcons over the 7 experiments. The percentages of incorrect interpretations by book element were as follows: 15.71% for the beginning of chapter earcon, 14.29% for the presence of images earcon, and 2.86% for the presence of annotations earcon. This might lead to believe that the beginning of chapter earcon and the presence of images earcons can be misinterpreted one for the other. We can further detail the analysis by looking at how the participants were interpreting the earcons. All the incorrectly identified presence of images earcons were mistaken for presence of annotations, and 72.73% of the beginning of chapter earcons were mistaken for presence of annotations (18.18% were mistaken for numerals and 9.09% for presence of images earcons). These results reveal that the beginning of chapter and the presence of images earcons are not being mistaken one for the other, but are being interpreted as presence of annotations earcons. This is somewhat surprising, since the presence of annotations earcon was correctly identified 97.14% of the times it was played.

The next results report the subjective measures obtained from the questionnaires. The first measure, understandability, can be expected to have a similar outcome to the identification results presented above. Thus, we expected higher values of understandability for speech and auditory icons than for earcons. Figure 2 presents the average understandability for the four elements, by type of audio cue used.

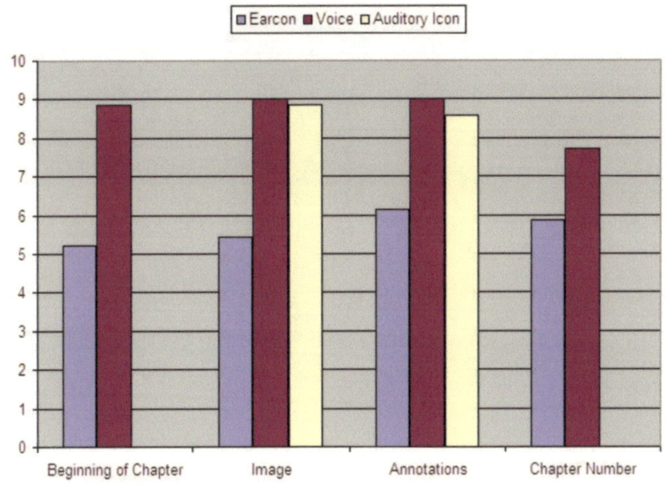

Figure 2. Understandability of the different auditory cues used

To determine if the differences shown are statistically significant two t-tests (one for the beginning of chapter and chapter numbers auditory cues) and two ANOVA tests (one for the presence of images and other for the presence of annotations) were carried out. The t-test comparing the beginning of chapter results found a significant increase ($t(19) = 3.55$, $p <$

0.01) in understandability when speech was used instead of earcons. The t-test comparing the results for chapter numbers between earcons and speech also revealed a significant increase in understandability ($t(26) = 3.03$, $p < 0.01$). The ANOVA for the presence of image cues between earcons, speech and auditory icons was also found to be significant ($F(2, 18) = 40.98$, $p < 0.001$). Post hoc Tukey HSD tests found earcons to have significant lower understandability than speech ($HSD = 11.31$, $p < 0.01$) and auditory icons ($HSD = 10.85$, $p < 0.01$), and no difference between speech and auditory icons. The ANOVA for the presence of annotations understandability when using earcons, speech and auditory icons was also significant ($F(2, 18) = 10.47$, $p < 0.001$). Once again, post hoc Tukey HSD test showed that earcons had significant lower understandability than speech ($HSD = 6.00$, $p < 0.01$) and auditory icons ($HSD = 5.10$, $p < 0.01$). No significant difference was found between speech and auditory icons.

Figure 3 presents the average results for the intrusion rating of the three auditory cues employed (higher values mean less intrusive sounds). Once again, two t-tests and two ANOVA tests were performed to determine if the differences are statistically significant. The t-tests for the beginning of chapter and chapter number comparisons did not identify any significant results. The ANOVA for the intrusiveness when presenting images comparing earcons, speech and auditory icons found a significant difference ($F(2, 18) = 4.01$, $p < 0.05$). Post hoc Tukey HSD tests however did not find significant results between any pair of results. t-tests with the Bonferroni adjustment found that earcons were significantly more intrusive than auditory icons for signaling the presence of an image ($t(12) = 3.62$, $p < 0.05$). The ANOVA test for the presentation of annotations with earcons, speech and auditory icons found a statistically significant difference. The post hoc Tukey HSD tests identified once again that earcons were more intrusive than auditory icons ($HSD = 4.56$, $p < 0.05$).

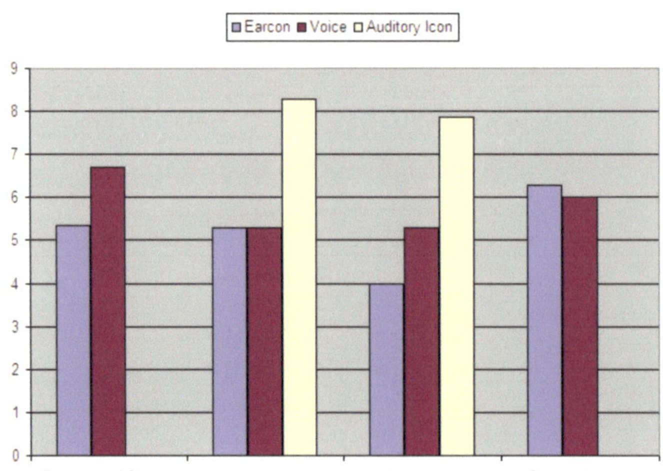

Figure 3. Intrusion of the different auditory cues used. Higher values correspond to less intrusive sounds

Figure 4 presents the average results for the satisfaction rating. The same t-tests and ANOVA tests were applied. The t-test for the beginning of chapter feedback revealed that participants found speech more pleasurable than the earcons ($t(19) = 3.28$, $p < 0.01$). Chapter numbers presented with speech were also found to be significantly more pleasurable than with earcons ($t(26) = 2.71$, $p < 0.05$). The ANOVA test for the presentation of image presence with earcons, speech and auditory icons found a significant difference ($F(2, 18) = 36.06$, $p < 0.001$). Post hoc Tukey HSD confirms that participants found earcons to be significantly less pleasurable than speech (HSD = 8.65, $p < 0.01$) and auditory icons (HSD = 11.54, $p < 0.01$). The corresponding ANOVA test for annotation presence signaling with earcons, speech and auditory icons also found a significant difference ($F(2, 18) = 13.67$, $p < 0.001$). Post hoc Tukey HSD tests once again confirmed that earcons were found to be significantly less pleasurable than speech (HSD = 5.43, $p < 0.01$) and auditory icons (HSD = 7.06, $p < 0.01$).

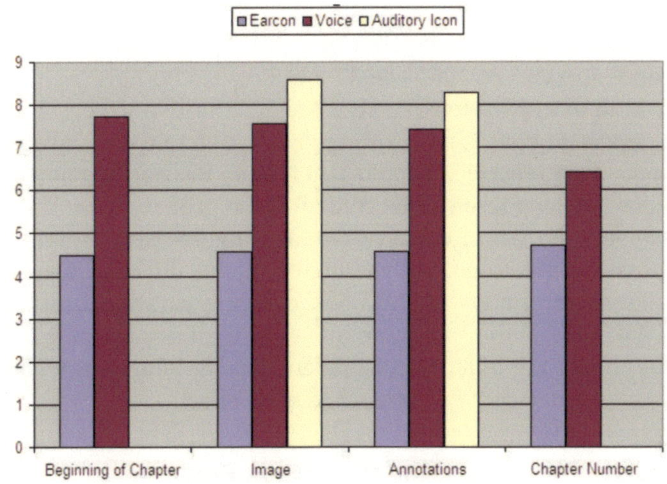

Figure 4. Satisfaction with the different auditory cues used

The effect of interrupting the narration of the main content when presenting the current chapter number on the subjective ratings was also studied. However no significant results were found for understandability, intrusion and satisfaction ratings, which points to the important factor for these ratings being the type of audio feedback technique employed.

4. Audio Design Recommendations

The results presented in the previous section indicate that auditory icons and spoken messages should be preferred to earcons in the design of audio DTB players' interfaces. Earcons proved to be more prone to identification errors, and accordingly, test participants found them less suited to transmit the correct meaning. In addition, the results also show that participants found earcons the least pleasurable of all the evaluated techniques. When considering the intrusion results, earcons and speech achieve comparable results, but both techniques were considered significantly more intrusive than auditory icons.

Observations made during the experiments support these results. It was common amongst test participants to need more time to identify the meaning of a sound when presented with earcons. This is supported by the number of times most participants requested a pause in excerpts which made use of earcons to signal the presence of images or annotations, compared to other excerpts. Another evidence was the request for chapter numbers when they were presented using earcons in comparison with other techniques. Although some participants did the request just for confirmation (the correct number was already written down) it nevertheless shows that participants felt less secure with the earcons.

When comparing test performance on the first and last excerpts, which were the ones which relied most in earcons, all measures evolved positively with the exception of the understandability of the earcon for signaling the presence of an image (average of the answers dropped slightly from 5.43 to 5.29) and the intrusiveness for chapter beginnings, presence of images and annotations. The greatest evolutions were felt in the understandability and likability of the presence of annotations and chapter numbers earcons. This may imply that with more time to familiarize with the earcons used, the measures could continue to evolve positively. However, one cannot be sure until further tests confirm this hypothesis.

For applications sharing the characteristics of a DTB player, we recommend the use of auditory icons and speech. As the events needing audio feedback might not occur frequently in this kind of applications, earcons are at a disadvantage, since it will be harder to memorize and associate their sound with an event, due to the mentioned low frequency of events. The events comprehension should also require the least amount of cognitive effort by the listener, since listening to the book content is the primary task. This is another factor that impacts negatively the use of earcons. We also suggest that auditory icons should be used whenever possible, due to normally being of shorter duration than speech messages. This means smaller interruptions of the book content narration. Another advantage of auditory icons is the fact that they are more universal than any language that may be used, thus requiring less effort for interface development. For the situations where it is difficult to find an auditory icon, then speech can be used to good effect.

5. Visually Enabled Versions of the Rich Book Player

Although ultimately targeting blind users, other visually impaired users can still benefit from the visual component present in the Rich Book Player. Additionally, under Universal Accessibility concerns, the visual component may or may not be used, depending on the context, but the application operation should not be impacted by its presence or absence. As such, the next sections will present two versions of the Rich Book Player, with both visual and audio components. First, a brief overview of a desktop version will be introduced. After, a mobile version will be more thoroughly explained, since that version is the basis for the audio only version.

5.1 The Desktop Rich Book Player

By combining the possibilities offered by multimodal interaction and interface adaptability we have developed the Rich Book Player, an adaptive multimodal Digital Talking Book player (Duarte & Carriço, 2006) for desktop PCs. This player can present book content visually and audibly, in an independent or synchronized fashion. The audio presentation can be based on previously recorded narrations or on synthesized speech. The player also supports user annotations, and the presentation of accompanying media, like other sounds and images. In addition to keyboard and mouse inputs, speech recognition is also supported. Due to the adaptive nature of the player, the use of each modality can be enabled or disabled during the reading experience.

Figure 5 shows the visual interface of the Rich Book Player. All the main presentation components are visible in the figure: the book's main content, the table of contents, the figures' panel and the annotations' panel. Their arrangement (size and position) can be changed by the reader, or as a result of the player's adaptation. The other visual component, not present in figure 5, is the search panel. Highlights are used in the main content to indicate the presence of annotated text and of text referencing images. The table of contents, figures and the annotations panels can be shown or hidden. This decision can be taken by the user and by the system, with the system behavior adapting to the user behavior through its adaptation mechanisms. Whenever there is a figure or an annotation to present and the corresponding panel is hidden, the system may choose to present it immediately or may choose to warn the user to its presence. The warnings are done in both visual and audio modalities.

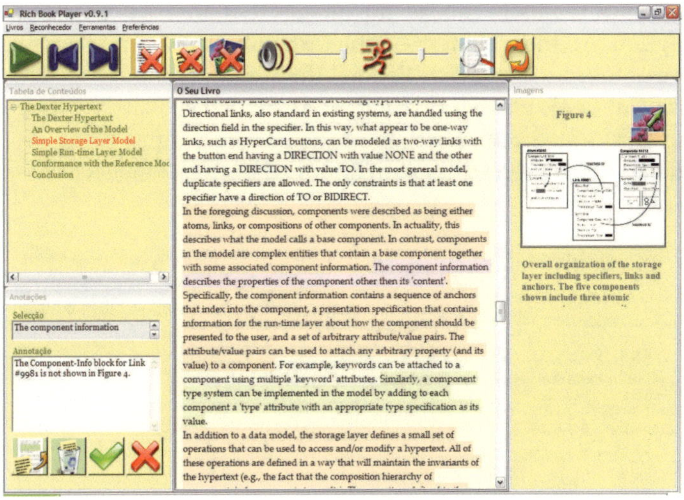

Figure 5. The Rich Book Player's interface. The center window presents the book's main content. On the top left is the table of contents. On the bottom left is the annotations panel. On the right is the figures panel. The content being presented in the player is the article "The Dexter Hypermedia Reference Model", by Halasz and Schwartz

All the visual interaction components have a corresponding audio interaction element, with one exception. Since the speech recognizer currently used in the player does not support free speech recognition, annotations have to be entered by means of a keyboard. All the other commands can be given using either the visual elements or speech commands.

5.2 The Mobile Rich Book Player

The mobile version of the Rich Book Player was developed with three main goals in mind: 1) Allow for an anytime, anywhere entertaining and pleasant reading experience; 2) Retain as much as possible of the features available in the desktop version; 3) Support a similar look and feel and foster coherence between both applications.

To achieve these goals, architectural and interaction changes had to be made with regard to the desktop version. The two major limitations of the mobile platform are the limited screen size and processing power.

5.2.1 Main Components Display

Figure 5 displays the main components of the Rich Book Player: main content, table of contents, annotations and images windows. On the desktop version it is possible to display all the components simultaneously and users can find the arrangement that best suits them.

Due to the much smaller screen size of the mobile device it is impossible to follow the same approach.
Figure 6 presents the main content view of the mobile version of the Rich Book Player. The four main areas of interaction can be seen in the figure. On the top, three tabs allow for the selection of the current view. The left tab opens the content view (figure 6, left). The tab header is used to display the current chapter number, which, in this way, is quickly available to the user. The middle tab displays the annotations view. This is the view used to read previously entered annotations and write new ones. The right tab is the images view (figure 6, right). In this tab users can see the images that are part of the book, together with their title and caption. All these contents, book text, annotations and images are displayed in the biggest of the interaction areas. Bellow this area is a toolbar which displays the commands to control book playback, navigation, and other features. The final interaction area is the menu bar located at the bottom of the screen. Besides being used to present the menu, the menu bar is also used to display command buttons whenever necessary.

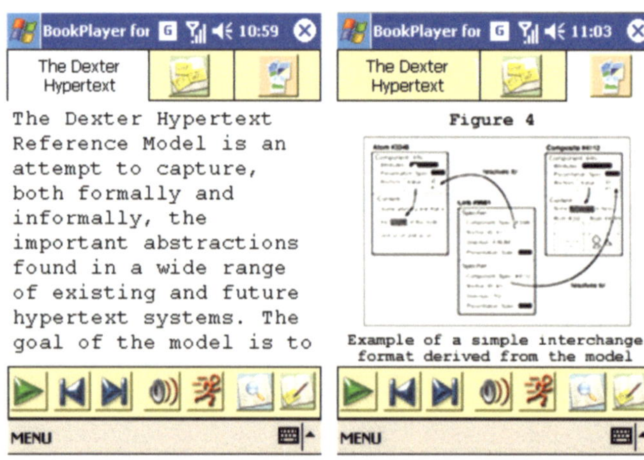

Figure 6. The mobile Rich Book Player. Main content view on the left and images view on the right

Of the four main components of the desktop version, three of them were already mentioned and although they cannot be displayed simultaneously as in the desktop version, they all can be displayed on their own view. The component not yet mentioned is the table of contents. This component has been downgraded to a menu entry and retained just one of its functions. In the desktop version, the table of contents was used to display the current chapter being read, by highlighting its entry, and as a navigation mechanism, allowing users to jump to a particular chapter by selecting its entry. In the mobile version, only the navigation function was retained. The current chapter feedback is now provided as the header of the main content tab.

5.2.2 Annotation Creation and Display

Creating annotations is a two stage process. The user must first select the text to be annotated and only after that enter the annotation. The text selection process is done by selecting the text in the main content view with the stylus and then pressing the create

annotation button (the rightmost button in the toolbar). This takes the user to the annotations view in create annotation mode (figure 7, left).
In the annotations view, the user is still able to see the selected text while entering the annotation. When the text box is selected, the virtual keyboard is displayed, and the *confirm* and *cancel* buttons are reallocated to the menu bar (figure 7, right).

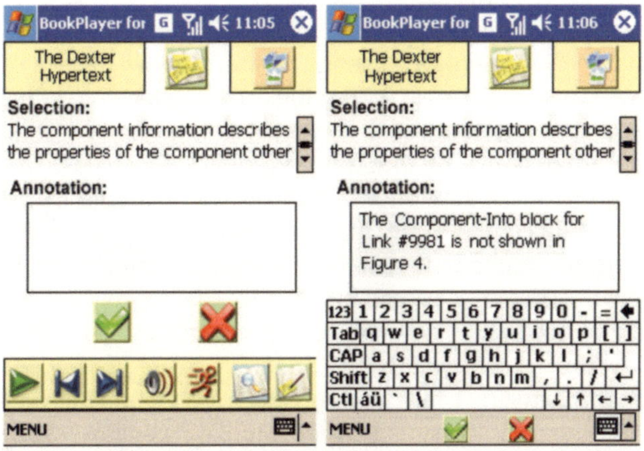

Figure 7. Annotations view during an annotation creation process. On the right, buttons are reallocated to the menu bar when using the virtual keyboard

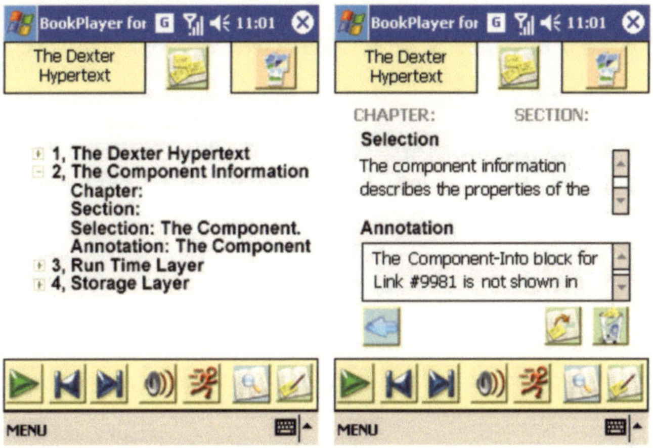

Figure 8. Annotations view in annotation creation mode. Annotations menu on the left, and details of an annotation on the right

Figure 8 presents the annotations view in annotation display mode. When the user changes to the annotations tab, the annotations menu (figure 8, left) displays all the existing annotations in a tree view. By selecting one of the annotations the user is taken to the annotations detail view (figure 8, right). In this view the user can read the current annotation, edit the annotation (which means going to annotation creation mode), delete the annotation, and navigate to the text that has been annotated. The navigation buttons in the toolbar, which in the content view navigate to the next and previous pages, in this view navigate to the next and previous annotations.

5.2.3 Speech Recordings and Synchronization

The main feature distinguishing a Digital Book Player from an e-book player is the possibility to present the book's content using speech, either recorded or synthesized. The desktop version of the Rich Book Player supports both modes of speech presentation. The mobile version currently supports the presentation of recorded speech, using the *Windows Media Player for Pocket PC* for playback.

Speech presentation opens up interaction possibilities that are not available with a visual only interface. With speech, users can change tabs and view images or read annotations while listening to the narration, thus avoiding the forced pause in reading if speech had not been available. Speech also allows users to access the book content without having to look at the device, allowing usage scenarios that, up until now, were available only with portable music devices, but without the limitations of those. For example, performing a search in such a device is extremely cumbersome. In comparison, with the mobile Rich Book Player, search is extremely simple due to the presence of a digital version of the book's text.

With the benefits of incorporating speech into the interface new challenges are uncovered. With speech comes the need for synchronization mechanisms. The application needs these to be able to know when and what images and annotations to present. We were able to port the synchronization mechanism of the desktop version to the mobile version without losing synchronization granularity, meaning the mobile version also supports word synchronization. The synchronization mechanism only had to be adapted to the page concept, introduced in the mobile version, which was absent from the desktop version. The synchronization mechanism allows the application to turn to the next page when the narration reaches the end of the current one. It is also used to visually highlight the word currently being spoken, in order to make the narration easier to follow when the user chooses to both read and listen to the book.

5.2.4 Awareness Raising Mechanisms

Images and annotations require a notification system to alert the user to their presence. Users just listening to the narration need to be alerted through sound signals, while users reading the text need to be alerted through visual signals. Both mechanisms coexist also in the mobile version of the Rich Book Player. Following the recommendations presented in section 4, auditory icons are played when the narration reaches a page with annotations or associated images. Visually, when the user reaches such a page, the annotations or images tabs flash to indicate the presence of an annotation or image.

5.2.5 Pagination

One of the main presentation and interaction differences between the desktop and mobile versions of the Rich Book Player is the introduction of the page concept in the mobile version. The main motivation behind this decision was the desire to avoid the use of scroll bars to read the book. With moderate to large books even small scroll bar movements might give origin to large displacements of the text being displayed, which would quickly turn into a usability problem. Loading a text control with the books full content could also raise performance issues.

To support changing font and font sizes while reading the book, the pagination is executed in real-time. Whenever a book is loaded, or the font settings are altered, a new pagination is started. This implies storing the current reading point (when speech playback is active) or current page (when speech playback is inactive), repaginate, and present the page of the current reading point. Several choices are possible for the pagination starting point. Starting the pagination algorithm from the book's first page would mean the user would have to wait a variable period for the display to refresh. This period would vary depending on the current reading point. Reading points near the end of book would mean substantially longer waiting periods, due to the lack of processing power of most mobile devices. Starting the pagination from the current reading point, would mean pages with different contents would result from runs of the algorithm with different starting points, even with the same font settings. This might confuse users used to pages holding the same contents on print books. Both approaches raise usability issues. To overcome these issues we employed the notion of forced page break. A forced page break is a location in the text that is guaranteed to be at the start of a page. Employing this notion, the pagination algorithm always produces the same results for the same font settings. The pagination starts from the first forced page break prior to the current reading point and runs to the first forced page break after the current reading point. Since we can control the frequency of forced page breaks, we can guarantee an upper limit on the time that is necessary to paginate until the current reading point, thus assuring the user will not have to wait unacceptably long periods and the pages stay coherent with every run. After this stretch of the book is paginated, the algorithm can run in the background, paginating the rest of the book. Possible choices of forced page breaks, which will be adequate in most situations, are all the entries in the table of contents. This has the added benefit of page breaks being associated with structural book elements, which is something a reader would expect, or, at least, not find confusing.

5.2.6 Adapting the Layout to the Device

Nowadays, mobile devices exist with a multitude of screen resolutions, and even with the possibility of altering the screen orientation. The Rich Book Player visual layout is able to adapt itself to changes in orientation and to different screen resolutions. Figure 9 presents the layout of the Rich Book Player in landscape mode.

Besides changing the layout of the different interface components, a changing in screen orientation also requires a new run of the pagination algorithm, as described in the previous section.

5.2.7 Performance and Storage

The book's presentation involves parallel processing of three threads: the main interaction thread with audio playback, the synchronization thread and the pagination thread. This might impose some performance constraints on the reproduction platform. We have tested the Rich Book Player on two devices: an HP iPAQ h5500 with a 400 MHz XScale processor, 40 MB ROM and 128 MB RAM running Microsoft's Pocket PC 2003, and a QTEK 9100, with a 200 MHz TI OMAP 850 processor, 128 MB ROM and 64 MB RAM running Microsoft's Windows Mobile 5. We have successfully been able to use the application on both devices to read a book of circa 25000 words (a 279 Kb text file), corresponding to a narration with 2 hours and 15 minutes, recorded in a 158 Mb mp3 file.

Due to the size of the audio files, books will have to be made available in storage cards, since it cannot be expected that internal storage of the mobile devices be able to hold such large amounts of data. The Digital Talking Books can be shared between the two platforms, as well as annotations that have been made in one platform can also be read in the other.

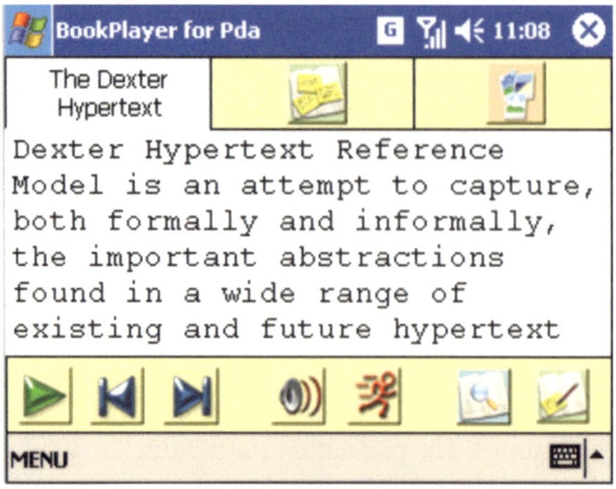

Figure 9. The Rich Book Player layout in landscape mode

6. The Audio Only Version of the Rich Book Player

The audio only version of the Rich Book Player is based on the mobile version described in the previous section. With regard to output capabilities, the mobile version, which incorporates the recommendations from section 4, as described before, is close to fully usable by blind users. This is due to the fact that book contents are recorded in mp3 files, which are played back during book presentation. Additionally, the awareness mechanisms presented are also audio based, like the annotations and image awareness mechanisms which make use of auditory icons. The main issue that is not solved in the player's interface is the presentation of all non-audio annotations. These include text annotations, created using the device's keyboard, and photo or video annotations, captured through the device's camera. Text annotations can be delivered to blind users through speech synthesis when available. Photo or video annotations are currently undeliverable, unless the annotation's author creates an audio file with the annotation description, which could be played back, instead of the default annotation presentation. These limitations do not impact the operation of the Rich Book Player for single use, since a blind user would not write annotations (or use the camera for annotating) when presented with the possibility to speak annotations and have them recorded and latter played back. These limitations are only felt in collaborative scenarios, where the annotations could be shared between readers of the same book. In these scenarios, visually created annotations would be impossible to render using only audio enabled devices.

Concerning the mobile version as described previously, to allow for a completely non-visual interaction, the greatest changes have to impact the input interaction mechanisms. Currently, input is completely visually oriented: button selections, text input, tab selection, menu entries, and text selection. All these tasks rely on stylus operation, which requires the user to be able to look at the screen to know the position of each element to operate. For non-visual operation, an alternative input mean is required. Due to the processing power limitations of current mobile devices, this alternative should not rely on automated speech recognition. It should rely instead on available input capabilities, which can be reliably

employed by blind users. On current mobile devices, the alternative can only be the physical input buttons, which afford recognition by blind users.
It can be safely assumed that all mobile devices (PDAs, mobile phones, with the exception of the iPhone which is not visually impaired friendly) possess a minimal set of physical buttons: a joystick or four directional buttons, with the accompanying selection button, and two more selection buttons. Figure 10 presents this set of buttons in a typical PDA arrangement. Buttons 1, 2 and 7 are selection buttons. Buttons 3, 4, 5 and 6 are directional buttons. Different devices might have a larger number of buttons, but to try to make the application the more device independent as possible, only these seven buttons will be considered from this point forward.

Figure 10. Typical PDA keyboard, with at least 7 different buttons

To enable a fully non-visual operation of the application, all the input commands have to be mapped to these seven buttons. Since there are more than seven commands in the Rich Book Player interface, it will be necessary to map the interface to different states, where each button will have a different meaning. To fully map all the operations, different state diagrams were defined.
Figure 11 presents the first state diagram, representing the key mappings under normal playback. As can be seen in the figure, during playback the directional keys are used to navigate the content. Up and down keys (keys 3 and 4) are used to advance or go back one chapter. Left and right keys (keys 5 and 6) are used to advance or go back one page. The user can pause the playback by pressing key 7. The same key will resume playback when paused. To access the main menu, the user can press the right selection key (key 2). This takes the user to another set of key binding states. During playback, whenever the user wishes to create an annotation, he or she should press the left selection key (key 1). The same key is used to listen to an annotation, whenever the playback reaches a point when there is one available to listen. Annotation creation and annotation listening are also states with different key bindings.
Figure 12 presents the key bindings and state changes when the user is consulting the main menu. As seen before, the main menu is accessed by pressing the right selection key during playback. The same key closes the main menu and takes the user back to the playback mode. In the main menu, the up and down directional keys cycle through all the menu options, with the currently available option being spoken by the interface immediately after the cycling. In this way, the user is aware of what option if available at every instant. This is fundamental when the user is not yet familiar with the menu contents. Later, when the user gets to know the menu contents, he or she does not have to wait for the spoken feedback,

being able to press the selection keys immediately, thus taking advantage of the acquired expertise. If the user selects (using keys 1 or 7) the options "Faster" or "Slower", the application returns to the playback mode, with the playback speed adjusted as per the user's request. If the option selected is "Load" the user will be taken to the book loading mode, and after completing the book selection, the operation resumes in playback mode. The user has two other options available in the main menu. Selecting "TOC" takes the user to the Table of Contents menu. In there, the up and down directional keys cycle through the table of contents entries. In a similar fashion to what happens with the main menu entries, the table of content entries are also spoken by the interface, thus allowing the user to become aware to what chapter or section is currently selected. After selecting one of the entries of the table of contents, the operation is returned to the playback mode, starting from the beginning of the selected table of contents entry. The other option available in the main menu is "Annotations". Selecting this option takes the user to the Annotations menu. This operates in a similar manner to the other menus. Up and down directional keys cycle through the options, and keys 1 or 7 select the annotation which the user desires to listen. After each cycling key press, the annotation identifier is spoken to the user.

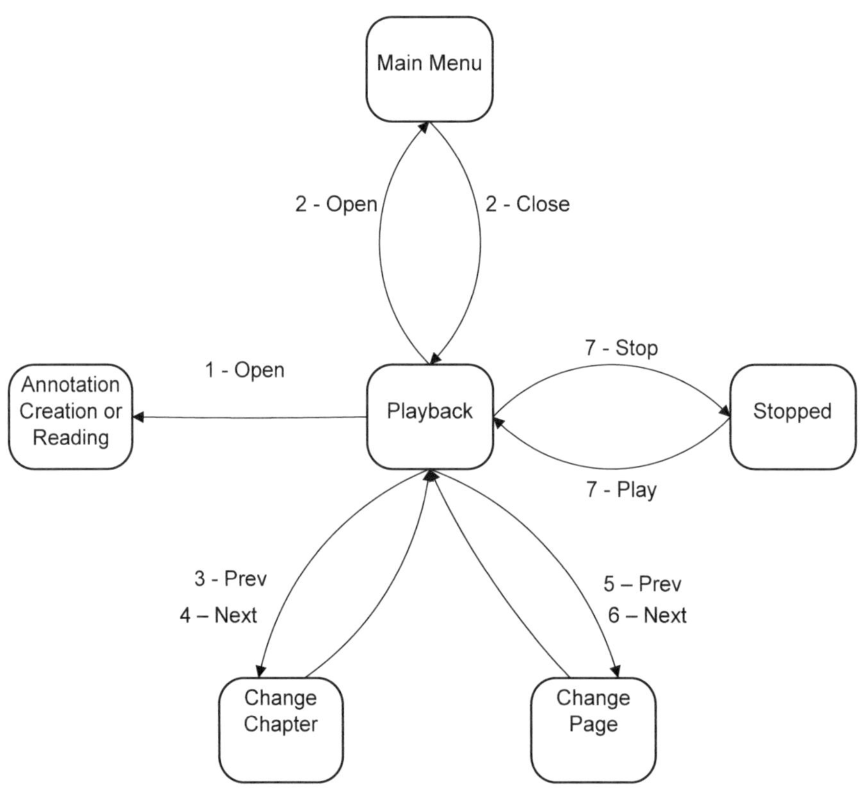

Figure 11. Key mappings and state changes for normal playback conditions

Finally, figure 13 presents the key mappings and state changes for annotation creation and reading operations. In annotation reading mode, left and right directional arrows cycle through available annotations, while the up directional arrow repeats the current annotation. If the user presses the left selection key (key 1), she will be asked if she wishes to delete the current annotation. This operation can be acknowledge by pressing key 2, or cancelled by pressing key 1. Notice the acknowledgment key is a different key from the one that starts the operation in order to avoid situations where the user presses the same key twice by mistake. If the delete is confirmed the application resumes the book playback. If it is not, the application returns to the Annotations menu. In addition to being able to delete an annotation, the user can also modify it. To achieve this, the key 7 must be pressed. This will take the user to the same operation mode that is called when the user creates an annotation from the playback mode. The user is then asked to utter the required annotation content. When finished the user presses the left selection key. The application then requests confirmation. If the user is satisfied with the recorded annotation she confirms by pressing the right selection key which saves the annotations and returns to playback mode. If not, the operation can be cancelled by pressing the left selection key. The application then asks the user if she wishes to repeat the recording. If the answer is affirmative, the process begins again. If the answer is negative then the operation is cancelled without any annotation being recorded, and playback ensues.

Comparing the audio only version with the other versions of the Rich Book Player, the main lacking feature is image support. However, since the target population for this version are blind users, there is no need to visually display the images. Instead, if there is a recorded description of the image content, it can be processed in exactly the same fashion as an annotation. If there is no recorded description of the image, it can be disregarded, since there is no way to present it to a blind user.

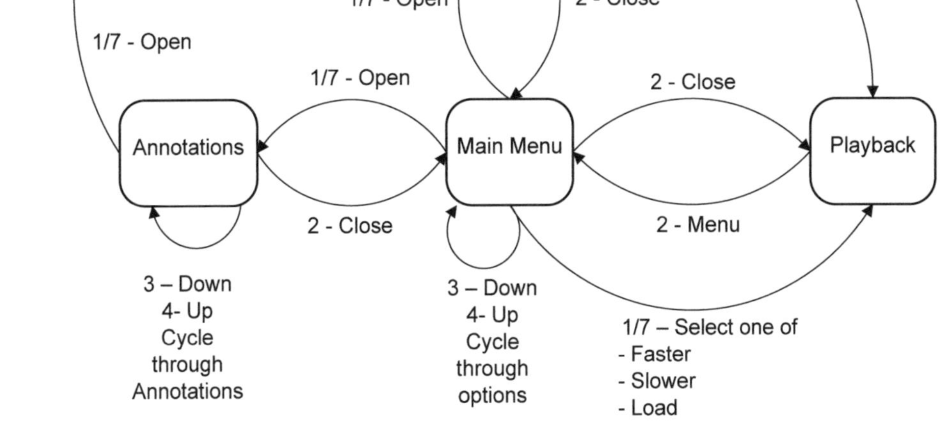

Figure 12. Key mappings and state changes for menu operation

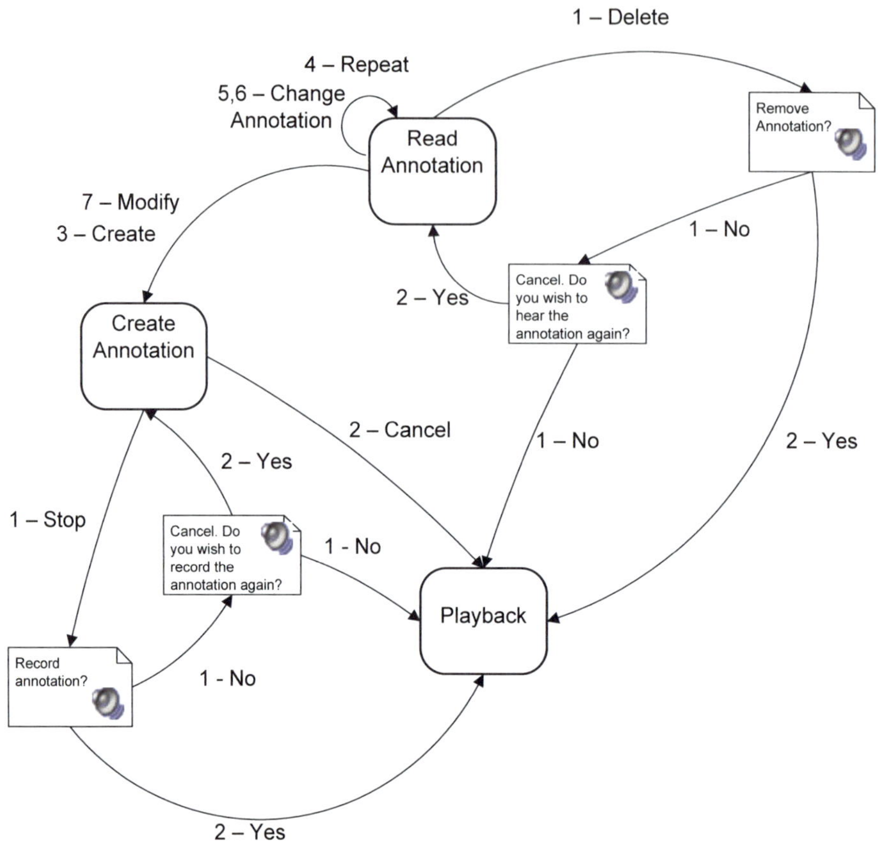

Figure 13. Key mappings and state changes for annotation reading and creation operations

7. Conclusion

This chapter focused on how endowing interfaces with audio interaction capabilities can improve their accessibility. To exemplify this outcome the development of several versions of a Digital Talking Book player was presented. This allowed us to show it is possible to maintain the same set of features while stripping the interface of visual components, and still keep it usable for the visually impaired population.

The interface development concerns focused on both ends of the interaction spectrum: the input and the output. Both these are traditionally very reliant on visual information. To overcome this dependence, visual output was replaced by audio output. On the input side, touch interaction, which is completely based on specific locations on the screen, thus requiring visual inspection, was replaced by mapping all the input options to a minimal set of physical buttons available on the majority of interaction devices, which are able to afford their locations to blind users. This, together with audio feedback, proved capable to convey to blind users the complete interaction features provided by a Digital Talking Book player.

In this chapter we begun by presenting a study of different audio techniques for transmitting awareness information, which compared speech recordings, auditory icons and earcons. The study results suggest the use of auditory icons combined with speech whenever necessary, in detriment to the use of earcons, for applications with the characteristics of a Digital Talking Book player.

These results were then applied to the development of the Rich Book Player, being essential to increase the usability and accessibility of the mobile version. This same version was used as the foundation of the audio only version of the Rich Book Player. The fundamental difference between the two versions was given by the introduction of the possibility to operate all the commands from the mobile device physical input buttons. In this fashion, all of the application's functionalities are made available through the device's input buttons, complemented with audio feedback, waiving the necessity of using the stylus, and making the application fully accessible to visually impaired users.

This means that a final version, with the full audio interaction capabilities combined with the visual features of the mobile version, can be said to follow the guidelines of Universally Accessible applications. This version makes itself accessible and usable to users with and without visual impairments. Furthermore, non visually impaired users can still use the application in all kinds of settings, even the ones where visual attention needs to be focused elsewhere, by taking advantage of the multiple input and output modalities available.

8. References

Blattner, M.; Sumikawa, D. & Greenberg, R. (1989). Earcons and Icons: Their Structure and Common Design Principles. *Human-Computer Interaction*, Vol. 4, No. 1, pp. 11-44, ISSN 0737-0024

Brewster, S. (1994). *Providing a Strucutred Method for Integrating Non-Speech Audio into Human-Computer Interfaces*. PhD Thesis. Department of Computer Science, University of Glasgow

Brewster, S.; Wright, P. & Edwards, A. (1995). Experimentally derived guidelines for the creation of earcons. *Proceedings of the British Computer Society Human-Computer Interaction Group Annual Conference*, pp. 155-159, Huddersfield, UK, August 1995, Cambridge University Press

Brewster, S. (2002). Overcoming the lack of screen space on mobile computers. *Personal and Ubiquitous Computing*, Vol. 6, No. 3, May 2002, pp. 188-205, ISSN 1617-4909

Carriço, L.; Duarte, C.; Lopes, R.; Rodrigues, M. & Guimarães, N. (2005). Building Rich User Interfaces for Digital Talking Books, In: *Computer-Aided Design of User Interfaces IV*, Jacob, R.; Limbourg, Q. & Vanderdonckt, J., (Ed.), 335-348, Springer-Verlag, ISBN: 1-4020-3145-9 (Print) 1-4020-3304-4 (e-book), Berlin Heidelberg

Duarte, C. & Carriço, L. (2005). Users and Usage Driven Adaptation of Digital Talking Books, *Proceedings of the 11th International Conference on Human-Computer Interaction*, Las Vegas, Nevada, USA, July 2005, Lawrence Erlbaum Associates, Inc.

Duarte, C. & Carriço, L. (2006). A Conceptual Framework for Developing Adaptive Multimodal Applications, *Proceedings of the 11th ACM International Conference on Intelligent User Interfaces*, pp. 132-139, Sydney, Australia, January 2006, ACM Press, New York

Gaver, W. (1986). Auditory Icons: Using Sound in Computer Interfaces. *Human-Computer Interaction*, Vol. 2, No. 2, pp. 167-177, ISSN 0737-0024

Gaver, W. (1997). Auditory Interfaces, In: *Handbook of Human-Computer Interaction, 2nd edition*, Helander, M., Landauer, T. & Prabhu, P., (Ed.), pp. 1003-1041, Elsevier, ISBN 0444818766, Amsterdam

Petrie, H.; Johnson, V.; Furner, S. & Strothotte, T. (1998). Design Lifecycles and Wearable Computers for Users with Disabilities. *Proceedings of the First International Workshop of Human Computer Interaction with Mobile Devices*, Glasgow, Scotland, May 1998, Department of Computing Science, University of Glasgow, Glasgow

Resnikoff, S.; Pascolini, D.; Etya'ale, D.; Kocur, I.; Pararajasegaram, R.; Pokharel, G. & Mariotti, S. (2004). Global data on visual impairment in the year 2002. *Bulletin of the World Health Organization*, Vol. 82, No. 11, November 2004, pp. 844-852, ISSN 0042-9686

Stephanidis, C. & Savidis, A. (2001). Universal Access in the Information Society: Methods, Tools, and Interaction Technologies. *Universal Access in the Information Society*, Vol. 1, No. 1, June 2001, pp. 40-55, ISSN 1615-5289

Sutton, J. (2002). *A Guide to Making Documents Accessible to People Who Are Blind or Visually Impaired*, American Council of the Blind, Washington, DC

W3C (2008). Web Accessibility Inititative. Available at http://www.w3.org/WAI/

9

Intelligent Interfaces for Technology-Enhanced Learning

Andrina Granić
Faculty of Science, University of Split
Croatia

1. Introduction

Current research in the field of Human-Computer Interaction (HCI), through its user-centred, user sensitive and learner-centred design approaches, places the requirements of the individual as the focus of all theoretical and practical advances, stressing the importance to design technologies for human needs. The role of transparent interfaces and adjustable interactions, suited to different particular needs, thus becomes even more important for users' success. Users with a wide variety of background, abilities, motivations and goals are using computers for quite diverse purposes. In such contexts of knowledge society for all, the role of system interfaces that are more closely tailored to the way people naturally work, live and acquire knowledge is unquestionably important. Intelligent User Interfaces (IUIs) have been advocated as means for making systems individualized or personalized, thus enhancing the systems flexibility and attractiveness. The ability to adapt is one frequently cited indication of intelligence. This implies the adaptation of the interface behaviour to user's individual characteristics, therefore generally relying upon the use of user models.

The chapter elaborates on intelligent interfaces for Technology-Enhanced Learning (TEL) systems, stressing the need to move from the traditional one-size-fits-all paradigm to adaptive and personalized one that takes into account various users' personal characteristics. In order to enrich the process of knowledge acquisition and enhance the system ability to improve the learning experience, TEL systems need to adapt continuously to their users. This can be achieved by initiating and updating a relevant user model. Although acknowledging that differences among individuals have an effect on learning, as of now, user modelling has not yet happened as expected in addressing the variety of the learning environment in terms of personalization and individual user profiles.

First, the chapter introduces TEL system with interaction style adaptation developed in order to support intelligent tutoring. The main objective of a research is both, to improve the learning experience and increase the system's intelligent behaviour. The system offers interaction adaptivity through the provision of suitable interaction styles rather then functionality. Different interface types along with adequate interaction styles are automatically switched basing on knowledge about the individual user and her/his interaction session, which is acquired dynamically during run-time. The user model developed to support interface adaptation strongly relies on user individual differences. In order to consider innovations in user sensitive research, the engaged user model should be enhanced with personal characteristics that affect learning and its outcomes. Second, an experimental study aiming to examine the affect of users' individual differences in technology-enhanced environment specifically of the ones which need to be accommodated through the system's intelligent behaviour is presented and evaluated. Personal user features assumed to affect learning process and learning outcomes are clearly identified and the methods how to measure them are determined. The study indicated that motivation to learn along with to expectations of learning in TEL environment significantly affects on users' learning achievement. Consequently, an appropriate user model should be engaged in order to accommodate users' characteristics which have an impact on learning process, thus ensuring system accurate usage. The chapter presents how an employment of user sensitive research provides strong foundations for designing usable and effective TEL systems within responsive environments that motivate, engage and inspire learners of this emerging knowledge society for all.

2. Background to the Research

HCI research acknowledges that understanding users' needs are at the core of successful designs for information society technology (IST) products and services. In the emerging knowledge society for all, system user interfaces that are more closely tailored to the way people naturally work, live and acquire knowledge are unquestionably important. The role of an intuitive interface and a flexible interaction suited to different needs, preferences and interests becomes even more important for the users' success, as users with a wide variety of background, skills, interests, expertise, goals and learning styles are using computers for quite diverse purposes (Benyon *et al.*, 2001). This leads to *user-centred design approaches*, a philosophy which places the users at the centre of design (Norman & Draper, 1986) and a process that focuses on cognitive factors (such as perception, memory, learning, problem-solving, etc.) as they come into play during users' interactions with applications (Adams, 2007; Zaharias, 2005). *User sensitive design* can be advocated as one of the natural and most appropriate methodologies developed out of user-centred design (Gregor *et al.*, 2002). The central concept of user sensitive design is an equal focus on user requirements and the diversity of such requirements in the population of intended users.

Additionally, in order to take into account the unique needs of users as learners, a shift from user-centred to *learner-sensitive design* is needed (Soloway *et al.*, 1994). This approach entails understanding and considering who is the user, what are her/his needs, what we want her/him to learn, how is (s)he going to learn it and how are we going to support her/him in achieving the learning objectives. As a result, a variety of learners' types must be considered due to characteristics revealing user individual differences like personal learning styles and strategies, diverse experience in the learning domain as well as previously acquired knowledge and abilities.

Intelligent User Interfaces (IUIs) are being suggested as means for making systems individualized or personalized, thus enhancing the systems flexibility and attractiveness (Benyon & Murray, 2000; Hook, 2000). IUIs should facilitate a more natural interaction between users and computers, not attempting to imitate human-human communication, but instead aiding the human-computer interaction process in diverse areas. The intelligence in an interface can for example make the system adapt to the needs of different users, take initiative and make suggestions to the user, learn new concepts and techniques or provide explanation of its actions, *cf.* (Benyon & Murray, 2000a; Lieberman, 1997). A focus on human interaction and on a measure of adaptivity to differing user requirements and needs is emphasized. "One frequently cited indication of intelligence is the ability to adapt", as highlighted in (McTear, 2000, p. 324), implying the ability to adapt output to the level of understanding and interests of individual users. A suitable framework for taking into account users' heterogeneity has provided (Schneider-Hufschmidt *et al.*, 1993):

- *adaptable systems*, by allowing the user to control the systems' customization and
- *adaptive systems*, by tailoring systems' appearance and behaviour to each user's individual characteristics.

Adaptive interface generally relies upon the use of *user models* (UMs). User modelling has been concerned with developing systems that provide such an adaptivity by collecting information and assumptions about particular users, such as their goals, skills, preferences, and knowledge, and then using this information to control the system's output (Kobsa, 1995; McTear, 2000; Brusilovsky *et al.*, 2007). The information in the user model is "a representation of the knowledge and preferences which the system believes that a user possesses" (Benyon and Murray, 1993, p. 205). Therefore, while some of the information in the user model may be relatively static and long-term, other information may be updated dynamically as the user interacts with the system. This information is used in various ways to provide adaptivity, i.e., to enable the system to adjust its functionality and/or the communication according to the needs of individual users, needs that may also change over time (Dieterich *et al.*, 1993).

System intelligent/adaptive behaviour strongly relies on *user individual differences*, the claim which is already confirmed and empirically proved by HCI research (Egan, 1988; Ford & Chen 2000; Dillon & Watson, 1996; Jennings *et al.*, 1991; Magoulas & Chen, 2004; Brusilovsky *et al.*, 2007). Such assumption is in line with related studies completed by the authors; see for example (Granić *et al.*, 2007). When considering adaptation of systems to individual use, user personality and cognitive factors have to be taken into account because of their higher resistance to change. Moreover, it is useful to exploit a certain amount of "stable" knowledge about the user, conveyed through long-term characteristics, containing information about user's level of expertise with computers in general, her/his expertise with the system in particular, as well as familiarity with the system's underlying task domain. Certain information related to user's preferences or current goals conveyed through short-term user characteristics should also be considered. Table 1 provides taxonomy of key user characteristics for system adjustment presented in (Granić & Nakić, 2007). Those features are generally categorized as:

- personal user characteristics, quite stable over time and independent from the system, where we can differentiate
  - general personal characteristics, including characteristics that reflect internal psychological state and
  - previously acquired knowledge as well as user abilities, along with
- system-dependent user characteristics, the most changeable category of characteristics as related to particular system.

Nevertheless, as range and complexity of interactive system increases, understanding how the system can dynamically capture relevant user needs and features as well as subsequently adapt its interaction, has become vital for designing intuitive and effective interfaces in diverse areas as intelligent hypermedia, recommender systems, intelligent filtering, explanation systems, intelligent help and technology-enhanced learning.

		A	B	C	D	E	F
personal characteristics	Gender	•	•			•	•
	Age		•			•	
	Personality & Emotions	•	•	•		•	•
previously acquired knowledge and abilities	Experience	•	•	•	•	•	•
	Cognitive Abilities	•			•	•	•
	Psycho-motor Skills			•		•	•
	Technical Aptitudes		•		•		
	Domain Knowledge	•	•	•	•	•	•
system dependent characteristics	Goals & Requirements			•		•	•
	Motivation			•		•	•
	Expectations			•			•

Table 1. User characteristics revealing individual differences; A (Benyon & Murray, 1993), B (Egan, 1988), C (Browne *et al.*, 1990), D (Norico & Stanley, 1989), E (Dillon & Watson, 1988), F (Rothrock *et al.*, 2002)

2.1 Technology-Enhanced Learning

Technology-Enhance Learning (TEL) uses Information and Communication Technology (ICT) to secure advancements in learning. By taking advancements as the objective, it goes beyond the attempt to reproduce classical ways of teaching via technologies. TEL combines but places equal emphasis on all three dimensions: technologies, learning and enhancement or improvements in learning (Manson, 2007). Learning should be delivered seamlessly, providing knowledge without interruption to people's normal work, thus implying holistic and systemic views of learners and their environments (Spector & Anderson, 2000). In this context, greater emphasis should be placed on informal and distributed learning. Tools and technologies to support distributed learners are likely to become more sophisticated and more prevalent, further removing the traditional boundaries between learning and working. In such a context the focus on learners appears well established in principle, but the practice of taking learners for what they are and as they are has yet to catch up (Sampson *et al.*, 2004). The second noticeable trend is on the individualization of learning, specifically the tailoring of pedagogy, curriculum and learning support to meet the needs and aspirations of individual learners, irrespective of ability, culture or social status. These is accompanied by the shift to assessing learning outcomes and doing this according to the learner's progress and needs; see for example (ERCIM News, 2007)

Apparently the appropriate use of the technologies should result in improvements in learning – making it more effective and more efficient. It has been claimed that although "technology is often touted as the great salvation of education, an easy way to customize learning to individual needs, it rarely lives up to this broad expectation" (Healey, 1999, p. 398). It seems that too much of this research is being driven by technical possibilities, while paying inadequate attention to the area of application and improvement of the quality of knowledge acquisition. The result was an over-ambitious and pre-mature attempt to eliminate the teacher's role in the educational environment (Kinshuk *et al.*, 2001). Besides, while acknowledging the important relation between individual differences and education has a long history, *cf.* (Cronbach & Snow, 1977), user modelling has not yet really succeeded in addressing the variety and richness of the educational environment. Namely simply acknowledging against systematically empirically verifying that differences among individuals in the terms of personal user profiles or characteristics have an effect on learning are two diverse things (Shute & Towle, 2003).

Although a lot of work still has to be done, there are attempts in TEL architectures which attribute individualization and end-user acceptability, emphasizing the need to consider diverse users' individual characteristics, e.g. (Ayersman & von Minden, 1995; Shute & Towle, 2003; Ahmad *et al.*, 2004; Brusilovsky & Millan, 2007). The process of knowledge acquisition should be enriched and system ability to improve the learning experience and increase the system intelligent behaviour enhanced. It has been argued that the solution is to be found in TEL systems that are accessible and usable to the intended populations of users, provide a high quality learner and teacher/tutor experience at the same time supporting rather than replacing the teacher, reflect best practice in learning psychology, can adapt to the needs and individual characteristics of diverse users thus employing a valid user (learner) model, *cf.* (Adams, 2007).

2.2 User Modelling for Technology-Enhanced Learning

Currently technology-enhanced learning systems are moving from the traditional one-size-fits-all paradigm to adaptive and personalized systems that take into account various users' individual differences. In order to be effective and usable, at the same time supporting individualization of learning, TEL systems need to adapt continuously to their users as they gain more domain knowledge while learning. However, adaptive TEL systems are still facing difficulties also including the following: (i) insufficiently utilized potential of flexibility and interaction styles in implementing a successful interface, (ii) only a limited number of user (i.e., learner and/or teacher) characteristics for adaptation are tracked, (iv) ineffective integration mechanism of the learner model with the interaction engine, (iii) there exists neither a widely accepted inventory of relevant adaptation types the system should be able to undertake, nor a definite study on the impact of these adaptations on user learning and performance. Additionally, so far user modelling research has not yet succeeded in dealing with the diversity of the learning and teaching settings. Namely, learning takes place in different social contexts involving diverse learners with different personal preferences, prior knowledge, skills and competences as well as learning goals. Moreover, at the onset of the learning process, when a user first accesses TEL system, the initiation of the user model requires explicit user actions that may require time and effort the user is not willing to invest.

Consequently, as the alternative to customary user interfaces, adaptive TEL systems are supposed to build a model of characteristics, preferences and/or goals of each individual user and use it throughout the interaction, in order to personalize it. This can be achieved by initiating and updating a relevant user model (Kobsa, 1995; Rich, 1999). In general, the quality of the personalized service provided by a system to its user depends largely on the characteristics of the UMs, e.g., how accurate it is, what amount of information it stores, and whether this information is up to date. Hence, as a general rule, the more information is stored in the UM, namely the more knowledge the system has obtained about the user, the better the quality of the service will be. In this context, quality refers to the capability of the system to better assess the learner knowledge in the studied domain, as well as his/her background and capabilities, so to tailor the learning process accordingly. In practice, obtaining sufficient user modelling data is difficult. This is especially important at the initial stages of the interaction with the user, when little information about the user is available. At these stages, all existing user modelling techniques face the bootstrapping problem, although recent research in ubiquitous user modelling suggests the idea of "user models mediation" (Berkovsky *et al.*, 2008).

While acknowledging that differences among individuals have an effect on learning, as of now user modelling in TEL field has not yet happened as expected in addressing the variety of the learning environment in terms of personalization and individual user profiles, especially at the initial stages of TEL system use. Learners are diverse and have different requirements such as their individual learning style, personality and cognitive factors, individual background knowledge and abilities. Many studies have been conducted on this subject; see for example (Egan, 1988; Benyon & Murray, 1993; Browne *et al.*, 1990; Chen *et al.*, 2000; Juvina & van Oostendorp, 2006) for reviews in the HCI field in general, in addition to work of (Ayersman & von Minden, 1995; Ford & Chen, 2000; Liegle & Janicki, 2006) in the TEL area in particular. However, obtained results are not quite consistent since the effect of individual characteristics on user performance with particular system greatly depends on the system alone (Browne *et al.*, 1990). Even though some of user individual differences can be assimilated by users' education or by interface redesign, a number of these differences will certainly need to be accommodated through adaptive interface behaviour what implies engaging a user model into a technology-enhanced learning system.

In the following two approaches to user modelling for TEL systems are presented and evaluated. Both studies are aiming to examine the affect of users' individual differences in technology-enhanced environment specifically of the ones which need to be accommodated through the system's intelligent behaviour.

3. Individual Differences and Interaction Style Adaptation

Following previous discussion, the role of proper interface design turns out to be central in both improving the learning experience and increasing the system's intelligent behaviour. Technology-enhanced learning systems are still inadequate with respect to the interaction mechanisms they provide. The adaptation effect, like in adaptive hypermedia and web systems, is usually limited to adaptive navigation, selection and/or on-screen presentation adaptivity (Brusilovsky & Maybury, 2002; Brusilovsky *et al.*, 2007). This is the motivation that led us to focus our research on intelligent (i.e., adaptive) interaction which would support intelligent tutoring. Our prototype system, developed in order to validate the approach, is an arbitrary domain knowledge generator with adaptive interface denoted Adaptive Knowledge Base Builder (AKBB) (Granić, 2006). It builds on the continuing research in the area of intelligent learning and teaching systems which has been performed in the last time and resulted with a number of operative systems, all based on the TEx-Sys model (Stankov, 2005).

3.1 AKBB, an Adaptive Knowledge Base Builder

AKBB enforces a simple adaptive mechanism, which selects the most appropriate interface out of a number of them according to run-time tracing of user behaviour. Fig. 1 illustrates AKBB's mixed mode interface style. The system offers interaction adaptivity through the provision of suitable interaction styles rather than functionality, cf. (Dieterich *et al.*, 1993), or the "educational aspects" of the interface. Different interface types along with adequate interaction styles are automatically switched basing on knowledge about the individual user and her/his interaction session, which is acquired dynamically during run-time. In this way it is an example of a self-adaptation (*ibid.*), where the system itself observes the communication, decides whether to adapt or not and generates and executes the adaptation as well. Parameters that control style swapping strongly rely on user individual differences. Specific values for user characteristics may be explicitly specified either by the user, captured directly from user actions or derived by the AKBB inference engine. Conforming to the initial discussion of self-adaptation, it is important to determine those parameters that are inferred and quantified from the interaction. These include the subsequent ones:

- user level of experience in computer usage in general and in usage of the AKBB system itself; these characteristics are taken into account because of their influence on successful task accomplishment, what is based on general results of user analysis and
- cognitive and individual characteristic of the user, i.e., spatial ability, which has relevance to users' use of AKBB different interface styles.

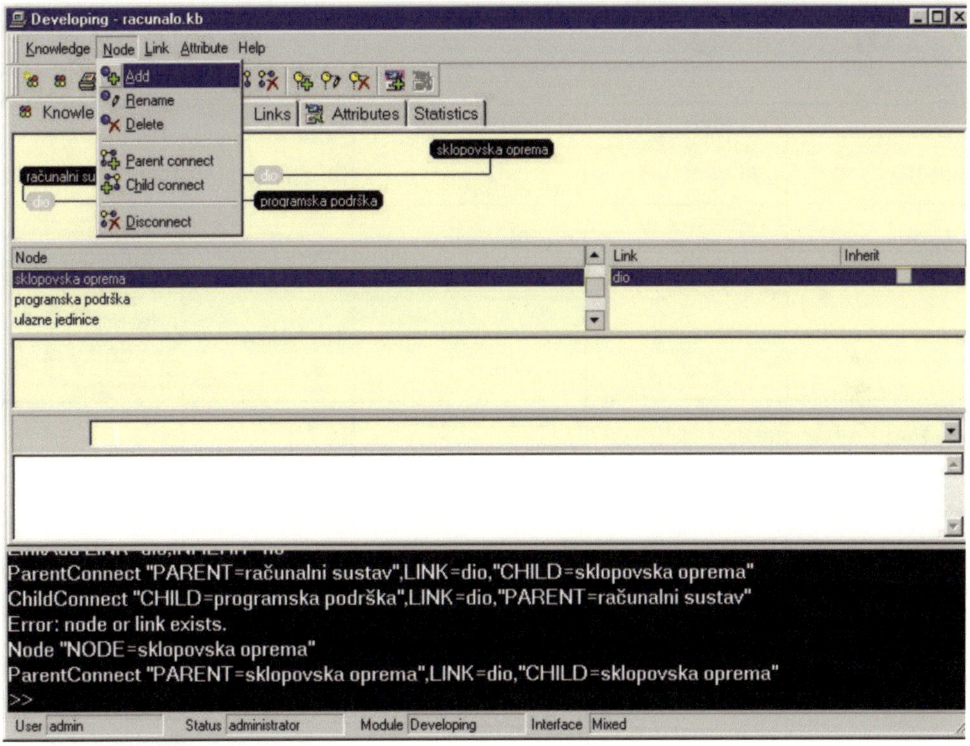

Figure 1. Screenshot of AKBB user interface

As postulated by an "architecture" or reference model for adaptive user interfaces (Benyon, 1993; Benyon & Murray, 2000a), AKBB uses three models for its operation:

- *user model*, based on monitoring the user in run-time,
- *system model*, storing system characteristics that are adaptive and

- *interaction model*, defining the actual interface adaptation through parameter values obtained from the interaction, along with all the relevant inferences and adaptations.

System Model. The system model specifies those AKBB characteristics that illustrate adaptivity. In order to describe system changing characteristics, each one of the levels - task, logical and physical - has to be specified in terms of the respective aspects, as illustrated in Table 2.

Level	Measuring Concept	Parameter Name	Value
Task Level	generation of arbitrary domain knowledge base	task	{1..N}
Logical Level	execution of a logical function	subtask	{1..N}
	wrong syntax; wrong semantics	error	{1..N}
Physical Level	adequate interaction style	interface	{command, mixed, graphical}

Table 2. AKBB System Model

	Parameter Name	Measuring Concept	Value	Initial Value
Cognitive Level	spatial ability	inferred from interaction	{high, low}	high
Experience Profile	experience in command languages	inferred from interaction	{high, low}	inferred at the beginning of interaction
	incidence of system usage	inferred from interaction	{high, low, none}	inferred at the beginning of interaction
Personal Profile	task	from interaction dialog	{1..N}	null
	subtask	from interaction dialog	{1..N}	null
	total subtasks	from interaction dialog	{1..N}	inferred at the beginning of interaction
	error	from interaction dialog	{1..N}	null
	total errors	from interaction dialog	{1..N}	inferred at the beginning of interaction
	interface	from interaction dialog	{command, mixed, graphical}	command

Table 3. AKBB User Model

User Model. The construction of a user model usually requires stating many assumptions about users' skills, knowledge, needs and preferences, as well as about their behaviour and interaction with the system. The user model developed to support AKBB interface adaptation is based on knowledge about the individual user and her/his interaction session that is dynamically acquired during run-time. It allows the current knowledge of the user to be combined with two additional models - the system model and the interaction one. Among the variety of user individual characteristics (cf. for example Table 1), we have considered the following:

- spatial ability, user cognitive characteristic offering a measure of her/his ability to conceptualize the spatial relationships between desktop objects,
- experience in command languages, characteristic concerning user experience in computer system usage in general and
- incidence of system usage, characteristic which regards user familiarity with the system itself.

Note that not all individual differences introduced in Table 1 have been considered in this research. The characteristics which were taken into account in the the offered classification are denoted as previously acquired knowledge and abilities.

Consequently, parameters from both cognitive and experience profile levels as well as parameters from the personal profile are continuously updated on-the-fly in order to record all the relevant aspects of the interaction (see Table 3).

Interaction Model. The interaction model describes the actual AKBB interface adaptation, by including user interaction history along with a set of inference and adaptivity rules. The dialog record logs all the necessary data related to the interaction. This encompasses user model updating, data on successfully completed subtasks and errors committed thereupon as well. In order to accomplish concrete adaptations, a set of inference and adaptivity rules is employed as follows:

1. values of the parameters maintained in the user model (spatial ability, experience in command language, incidence of system usage) are constantly updated as the result of an employment of *a set of five inference rules*, corresponding to user's individuality and her/his changing knowledge and behaviour during the interaction;
2. *a set of twelve adaptivity rules* provides actualization of interface adaptation in accordance to the updated parameter values in the user model.

As an illustration, one AKBB inference rule and three adaptivity rules are offered below.

{Inference rule no. 2}
if total subtasks = 0
  then incidence = none
  else
    if interface = command
      then incidence = high
    if interface = mixed
      then incidence = low
    if interface = graphical
      then incidence = low

{Adaptivity rule no. 1}
if spatial ability = high
  AND experience = high
  AND incidence = high
then interface = successor(interface)

{Adaptivity rule no. 5}
if spatial ability = high
  AND experience = low
  AND incidence = low
then interface = interface

{Adaptivity rule no. 9}
if spatial ability = low
  AND experience = high
  AND incidence = no
then interface = predecessor(interface)

Three different interface types with suitable interaction styles implemented are: (i) a command interface, enabling interaction through a command line only, (ii) a graphical interface and (iii) a mixed interface, combining the former two.

3.2 Discussion

One of the key problems in the development of adaptive systems is the inadequacy of available evaluation methods and techniques. There is still a lack of evaluation studies (Weibelzahl, 2005) capable of distinguishing the adaptive features of the system from general usability. Furthermore, it has long been acknowledged that systems based on user modelling and adaptivity are associated with a number of usability problems, which sometimes out-weight the benefits of adaptation (Jameson, 2005). Although AKBB evaluation is outside the scope of this chapter, obtained results and conclusions are in line with the above mentioned claims. The applied scenario-based usability evaluation, as a combination of behaviour and opinion based measurements, enabled us to quantify usability in terms of users' performance and satisfaction, see for example (Granić, 2008). According to the achieved results, the main directions for AKBB interface redesign are offered and directions of future work identified:

- the information needed for AKBB user model is collected indirectly by inferring users' proficiencies and attitudes through their interaction with the interface; such approach to user information gathering can be augmented by explicitly asking the users about their preferences or acquiring their goals from questionnaires;
- the presentation of domain knowledge failed to convey in a transparent way the semantics of the linked domain knowledge objects, thus impeding users in obtaining a clear and unambiguous view of a particular subject matter; in order to hide as much as possible the internal structure of the domain knowledge base, the knowledge presentation should be redesigned;
- some work should be conducted in order to provide the users more control both by disabling automatic adaptation and by incorporating manual selection for swapping the operation mode;

- adaptation of communication enables AKBB users to perform the same tasks whether adaptation takes place or not, while conversely potential adaptation of functionality will provide users with the opportunity to employ new or more complex system function;
- further research will be needed to determine whether an AKBB adaptive interface is measurably better than a non-adaptive one and under what circumstances the benefit is more valuable than the apparent loss of control due to unexpected adaptations of the interface.

Nevertheless, the acquired experience indicates that useful evaluation with a significant identification of interface limitations can be performed quite easily and quickly. Conversely, it raised a series of questions which, in order to be clarified, require further comprehensive research, the more so if the employment of universal design within TEL context is considered (Granić & Ćukušić, 2007).

4. Individual Differences and Learning Outcomes

The experimental study (Granić & Nakić, 2007; Granić & Adams, 2008) aimed to question existence and level of interaction among users' individual differences and learning outcomes accomplished while using a TEL system. Personal user features assumed to affect learning process were clearly identified and the methods how to measure them were determined. We have classified characteristics to be measured according to the categorization presented in Table 1 - user personal characteristics, previously acquired knowledge and abilities along with system dependent characteristics. Note that not all individual differences from the presented classification have been examined in this study.

4.1 Research Methodology

Subjects and Research Instruments. Twenty-four undergraduate students (6 males and 18 females) of the second year of a university program were recruited. Since we intended to use an application related to the domain of programming, we have randomly selected students among volunteers who yet did not take an Introduction to Programming course. The participants of the study have been told that their achievement in the exam would have only experimental use and would not affect their future exam grades.

Assessed users' characteristics, which might have the impact on learning process and consequently learning outcomes, were grouped as following:

- intelligence and personality characteristics, including emotional stability, extraversion, mental stability and honesty level,
- previously acquired knowledge and abilities, comprising experience in using computers and Internet as well as background knowledge to material supposed to be learned during the experimental session and
- system dependent characteristics, including motivation to learn programming and expectations from learning in TEL environment.

Intelligence and personality factors were measured by *standard psychological tests*, D-48 and EPQ (Petz *et al.*, 2005). Intelligence test (D-48) measured general mental abilities, while personality test (EPQ) measured dimension of emotional stability/instability, extraversion/introversion, mental stability/psychoticism and honesty/dissimulation level.

A questionnaire was designed in order to obtain data about students' gender, prior experience in using computer and Internet, motivation to learn, expectations from TEL systems in general and also expectations and satisfaction with used e-learning application in particular. Students' grades from previously passed exam on Introduction to Computer Science course were regarded as indicators of their background knowledge required to learn programming.

Interaction with a TEL system comprised learning programming basics as well as testing acquired knowledge with quiz embedded in the learning module of the application. System used to test students' knowledge is an intelligent learning and teaching system based on the TEx-Sys model (Stankov, 2005). We consider it as well-accepted instrument for this research since its effectiveness has been evaluated in several case studies and it has been shown that system can support at least 20 users at a time. Participants of the experiment were already familiar with the system functionality since they have already used it for other university courses. However, the students never accessed learning modules or quiz related to a course Programming I, the one selected to facilitate in this study.

Procedure and Results. Experiment was conducted through few steps illustrated in Fig. 2. Firstly, a psychologist and a HCI expert interviewed the experimental group of students to get an insight into some general characteristics of the group in order to design a questionnaire. The students have been introduced with nature and purpose of the experiment as well. Few days after the introductory interview the participants were invited to take intelligence test and personality test.

EXPERIMENTAL PROCEDURE

Step 1: Introductory Interview

Step 2: Intelligence and Personality Test

Step 3: e-Learning Session on Particular Domain Knowledge

Step 4: e-Testing of Domain Knowledge

Step 5: Multiple Choice Questionnaire

Figure 2. Five-step experimental procedure

Two experimental sessions in an on-line classroom were conducted for groups of twelve students at a time. Students were not allowed to take notes or use any external learning material, paper or on-line, besides the lessons related to the selected subject matter. They were free to learn for 30 minutes, and then began to test acquired knowledge on a quiz belonging to the TEL system. Time for testing was limited to 15 minutes and all participants completed the quiz at given time. After the quiz, students were asked to fill in the multiple choice questionnaire.

Although the main objective of the research was to investigate the influence of user individual differences on their learning outcomes, it was interesting to see if there were any connections among individual differences of the users themselves. Some interesting correlations were found between intelligence and personality factors obtained by tests with other user characteristics gained by questionnaire. Those results are given in Table 4. Significant correlations were found between mental stability and motivation ($r = -0.50$, $p <$

0.05) and also between emotional stability and expectations from using the system ($r = -0.45$, $p < 0.05$). This means that mentally stable students are more motivated to learn programming then mentally unstable or "more neurotic" students. Analogous, emotionally stable students have greater expectations from learning than emotionally unstable or "more psychotic" students.

Highly significant correlation was found between students' prior experience in using computers and Internet and their background knowledge required to learn programming ($r = 0.62$, $p < 0.01$) as expected. It seems that students' intelligence and dimension of extraversion/introversion are not associated with any other individual characteristics.

	Intelligence	Emotional Stability	Extraversion	Mental Stability	Experience
Experience	0.22	-0.28	0.19	-0.18	
Motivation	-0.17	-0.08	0.07	-0.50*	0.16
Expectations	-0.11	-0.45*	0.36	-0.26	0.01
Background Knowledge	0.39	-0.28	0.06	-0.11	0.62**

Table 4. Pearson correlations between user individual characteristics
* Significant correlations at level of $p < 0.05$
** Significant correlations at level of $p < 0.01$

Correlations between students' individual differences and their learning outcomes accomplished with a system are shown in Table 5. Apparently there are no associations between intelligence and personality factors with learning outcomes. Considering other user characteristics, it seems that only motivation to learn programming in addition to expectations of learning has statistically significant impact on knowledge acquired through interaction with the system ($p < 0.05$).

Analysis by age and by prior experience in using concrete system was not conducted because individual differences among participants were minor in those variables. Moreover analysis by gender would be inadequate as well because of the small samples.

	Intelligence	Emotional Stability	Extraversion	Mental Stability	Experience	Motivation and Expectation	Background Knowledge
Acquired Knowledge	0.05	-0.29	-0.00	-0.15	0.29	0.42*	0.26

Table 5. Pearson correlations between user individual characteristics and knowledge acquired on TEL system
* Significant correlations at level of $p < 0.05$

Additionally, subject group was split by the mean of their scores on the intelligence test. Correlation coefficients with learning outcomes were calculated for both high ($N = 14$) and low ($N = 10$) intelligence group separately. Apparently, students from low intelligence group made much more effort in knowledge acquisition with the system and achieved better results in quiz assessment then expected ($r = 0.74^*$, $p < 0.05$) comparing to the ones from high intelligence group ($r = -0.41$, $p < 0.05$). Because of very small sample, this result should not be used for generalization purpose, but for further research in order to clarify this and as similar issues. It seems that some of these results could have great internal validity if they confirm themselves on a larger sample.

4.2 Discussion

There are numerous studies reporting minor influences of personality factors on predictions of user performance (reviewed in (Dillon & Watson, 1996)) or no influence at all (Egan, 1988), so the perceived lack of associations between intelligence and personality with learning outcomes in our analysis was not quite unexpected.

Nevertheless, thorough interpretation and observation of the obtained results revealed some shortcomings of applied methodology. First of all, the sample we analyzed was too small and too homogenous to give us strong grounds for generalization of the results. All participants of the experiment were students of the same age, with comparable background knowledge and experiences, intellectual capabilities and motivation for graduating. Similar experiment with larger sample of more diverse users would certainly provide more reliable results.

Besides the necessity to enlarge number and diversity of participants, we have found certain procedural issues in need of refinement in the further research as well:

- instead of intelligence and personality testing, a cognitive test should be completed with the aim to identify some important components of human cognition,
- knowledge acquired in the TEL environment should be measured more accurately, the best as a gain between pre-test and post-test scores,
- pre-test score could be exploited as a measure of background knowledge,
- time required to complete the post-test could be used as an additional measure of learning outcome for each participant,
- questionnaires for measuring independent variables (age, gender, experience, motivation and expectations) for more perceptively measurement should be designed more thoroughly, implying amplification of the quantity of questions regarding particular issue as well as giving special attention to the sequencing of questions and
- reliability analysis of prepared questionnaire should be conducted prior to its involvement into the study.

Accordingly, we consider this study as an experiment that gave us important directions to establish an enhanced user sensitive methodology in our future research.

5. Conclusion

Within emerging knowledge society for all, intelligent user interfaces should aid the human-computer interaction process in diverse areas. Namely, users with a variety of characteristics are using computers for quite diverse purposes. In such context the role of intuitive and transparent interaction tailored to unique personal requirements is crucial and the role of intelligent (i.e. adaptive) interfaces becomes unquestionable. Our research has been focused on the employment of intelligence in interfaces for technology-enhanced learning (TEL) systems in order to personalize them for individual use. Such an interface adjusted to individual differences of each particular user should provide her/him more pleasant learning experience, resulting in higher knowledge achievement.

The chapter initially elaborates on the intelligent interface of Adaptive Knowledge Base Builder (AKBB), a type of TEL system. AKBB is an arbitrary domain knowledge generator which provides intelligent interaction in the sense of adaptation to user personal differences and behaviour. It offers the users three different interface types (command, mixed and graphical) with suitable interaction styles. The user model developed to support AKBB interface adaptation is based on knowledge about the individual user and her/his interaction session that is dynamically acquired during run-time. The AKBB system design is briefly presented and evaluation results summarized. Although related experience and achieved results were encouraging, the "sophistication" of the adaptation mechanism is required. The user model should be redesigned, further acknowledging and considering user personal differences that have an effect on learning and which certainly need to be accommodated through an adaptive interface.

Consequently, the empirical study aiming to examine the affect of users' individual differences on their learning outcomes achieved within TEL environment is conducted. Personal user features assumed to affect learning process were identified and the methods how to measure them determined. We have analyzed interrelations among quantified personal characteristics and found highly significant correlation between students' prior experience in using computers and internet with their background knowledge, but similar connection of experience and learning outcomes was not found. This experiment indicated that motivation to learn in addition to expectations of learning in TEL environment significantly affects on users' learning achievement. Aware of the great sensitivity of results to the sample (which had certain limitations), instead of generalization of presented results we have used them to determine the guidelines for developing further research design.

Considering similar studies and our own experience, it can be concluded that most of users' characteristics which have an impact on learning process and learning outcomes should be accommodated through an adaptive interface, with an employment of satisfactory user model. Additional research is clearly needed to be conducted in order to provide stronger foundations for a redesign and improvement of an adaptation mechanism for TEL systems.

6. Acknowledgments

This chapter describes the results of research being carried out within the project 177-0361994-1998 Usability and Adaptivity of Interfaces for Intelligent Authoring Shells funded by Ministry of Science, Education and Sports of the Republic of Croatia.

7. References

Adams, R. (2007). User Modeling for Intelligent Interfaces in e-Learning. *Lecture Notes in Computer Science*, LNCS 4556 (2007), pp. 473-480, Springer-Verlag, Berlin Heidelberg

Ahmad, A-R., Basir, O. & Hassanein, K. (2004). Adaptive User Interfaces for Intelligent e-Learning: Issues and Trends, *Proceedings of the Fourth International Conference on Electronic Business*, ICEB2004, pp. 925-934, Beijing, China, December 5-9, 2004.

Ayersman, D.J. & von Minden, A. (1995). Individual Differences, Computers, and Instruction, *Computers in Human Behaviour*, Vol. 11, No. 3-4, pp. 371-390.

Benyon, D. & Murray, D. (2000). *Interacting with Computers. Special issue on intelligent interface technology*, Vol. 12

Benyon, D. & Murray, D. (2000a). Editorial. Special issue on intelligent interface technology: editor's introduction, *Interacting with Computers*, Vol. 12, pp. 315–322.

Benyon, D. & Murray, D. (1993). Developing Adaptive Systems to Fit Individual Aptitudes, *Proceedings of the 1st international conference on Intelligent user interfaces*, pp. 115-121, January 4-7, 1993, Orlando, Florida, USA

Benyon, D., Crerar A. & Wilkinson, S. (2001). Individual Differences and Inclusive Design, In: *User Interfaces for All – Concepts, Methods and Tools*. Stephanidis, C. (Ed.), pp. 21-46, Mahwah, NJ: Lawrence Erlbaum Associates, Inc.

Berkovsky, S., Kuflik, T. & Ricci, F. (2008). Mediation of user models for enhanced personalization in recommender systems, accepted to *User Modeling and User-Adapted Interaction* (UMUAI). DOI 10.1007/s11257-007-9042-9 [available on line] http://www.springerlink.com/content/jt48g17025r8v567/

Browne, D., Norman, M. & Rithes, D. (1990). Why Build Adaptive Systems? In: *Adaptive User Interfaces*, Browne, D., Totterdell, P. & Norman, M. (Eds.), pp. 15-59, Academic Press. Inc., London.

Brusilovsky, P. & Milan, E. (2007). User Models for Adaptive Hypermedia and Adaptive Educational Systems, In: *The Adaptive Web. Methods and Strategies of Web Personalization*, Brusilovsky, P., Kobsa, A. & Nejdl, W. (Eds.), pp. 3-53, LNCS 4321 (2007), Springer-Verlag, Berlin Heidelberg

Brusilovsky, P., Kobsa, A. & Nejdl, W. (Eds.) (2007). *The Adaptive Web. Methods and Strategies of Web Personalization*, LNCS 4321 (2007), Springer-Verlag, Berlin Heidelberg

Brusilovsky, P & Maybury, M. (2002). From Adaptive Hypermedia to the Adaptive Web, *Communications of the ACM*, Vol. 45, No. 5, pp. 31-33.

Chen, C., Czerwinski, M. & Macredie, R. (2000). Individual Differences in Virtual Environments - Introduction and overview, *Journal of the American Society for Information Science*, Vol. 51, No. 6, pp. 499-507.

Cronbach, L.J. & Snow, R.E. (1977). *Aptitudes and instructional methods: A handbook for research on interactions*, New York: Irvington

Dillon, A. & Watson, C. (1996). User Analysis in HCI - The Historical Lessons from Individual Differences Research. *International Journal on Human-Computer Studies*, Vol. 45, pp. 619-637.

Dieterich, H., Malinowski, U., Kühme, T. & Schneider-Hufschmidt, M. (1993). State of the Art in Adaptive User Interfaces, In: *Adaptive User Interfaces: Principles and Practice*, Schneider-Hufschmidt, M., Kühme, T. & Malinowski, U. (Eds.), pp. 11-48, Elsevier Science B.V. Publishers (North-Holland).

Egan, D. (1988). Individual Differences in Human-Computer Interaction, In: *Handbook of Human-Computer Interaction*, Helander, M. (Ed.), pp. 543-568, Elsevier Science B.V. Publishers, North-Holland

ERCIM News (2007). Special: Technology-Enhanced Learning, Number 71, October 2007, [available on line] http://ercim-news.ercim.org/images/stories/EN71/EN71-web.pdf

Ford, N. & Chen, S.Y. (2000). Individual Differences, Hypermedia Navigation and Learning: An Empirical Study, *Journal of Educational Multimedia and Hypermedia*, Vol. 9, No. 4 , pp. 281-311.

Granić, A. (2008). Experience with Usability Evaluation of e-Learning Systems. *Universal Access in the Information Society*, Springer [available on line] DOI 10.1007/s10209-008-0118-z.

Granić A. (2002). Foundation of Adaptive Interfaces for Computerized Educational Systems. Ph.D. Diss. University of Zagreb, Faculty of Electrical Engineering and Computing, Zagreb, Croatia (in Croatian)

Granić, A. & Adams, R. (2008). User Sensitive Research in e-Learning: Exploring the Role of User Individual Characteristics. *Universal Access in the Information Society,* Springer (accepted for publication)

Granić, A. & Nakić, J. (2007). Designing intelligent interfaces for e-learning systems: the role of user individual characteristics, *Lecture Notes in Computer Science,* LNCS 4556. pp. 627-636, Springer-Verlag, Berlin Heidelberg

Granić, A. & Ćukušić, M. (2007). Universal Design within the Context of e-Learning, *Lecture Notes in Computer Science,* LNCS 4556 (2007), pp. 617–626, Springer-Verlag, Berlin Heidelberg

Granić, A., Stankov, S. and Nakić, J. (2007). Designing Intelligent Tutors to Adapt Individual Interaction. *Lecture Notes in Computer Science,* LNCS 4397 (2007), pp. 137-153, Springer-Verlag, Berlin Heidelberg

Gregor, P., Newell, A.F. & Zajicek, M. (2002). Designing for dynamic diversity - interfaces for older people, *The Fifth International ACM Conference on Assistive Technologies,* ASSETS 2002, pp. 151-156, 8-10 July, Edinburgh, Scotland.

Healey, D. (1999). Theory and Research: Autonomy in Language Learning, In: *CALL Environments: Research, Practice and Critical Issues,* Egbert, J. & Hanson-Smith, E. (Eds.), pp. 391-402, Alexandria, VA: Teachers of English to Speakers of Other Languages, Inc.

Hook, K.. (2000). Steps to Take Before Intelligent User Interfaces Become Real, *Interacting with Computers,* Vol. 12, pp. 409-426, Elsevier Science B.V.

Jameson, A. (2005). User Modeling Meets Usability Goals, In: *User Modeling: Proceedings of the Tenth International Conference,* Ardissono, L. & Mitrović, A. (Eds.), Berlin: Springer

Jennings, F., Benyon, D. & Murray, D. (1991). Adapting systems to differences between individuals, *Acta Psychologica,* Vol. 78, pp. 243-256.

Juvina, I. & van Oostendorp, H. (2006). Individual Differences and Behavioral Metrics Involved in Modeling web Navigation, *Universal Access in the Information Society,* Vol. 4, No. 3, pp. 258-269.

Kinshuk, Patel, A. & Russell, D. (2001). Intelligent and adaptive systems, In: *Handbook on Information Technologies for Education and Training,* Collis, B., Adelsberger, H. & Pawlowski, J. (Eds.), pp. 79-92, Springer

Kobsa, A. (1995). Supporting User Interfaces for All through User Modeling, *Proceedings of the 6th International Conference on Human-Computer Interaction,* HCI International 1995, pp. 155-157, Yokohama, Japan,. [available on line] http://www.ics.uci.edu/~kobsa/papers/1995-HCI95-kobsa.pdf

Lieberman, H. (1997). Introduction to intelligent interfaces. [available on line] http://web.media.mit.edu/~lieber/Teaching/Int-Int/Int-Int-Intro.html

Liegle, J.O. & Janicki, T.N. (2006). The Effect of Learning Styles on the Navigation Needs of Web-based Learners, *Computers in Human Behavior,* Vol. 22, pp. 885-898.

Magoulas, G. & Chen, S. (2004). Proceedings of the AH 2004 Workshop, Workshop on Individual differences in Adaptive Hypermedia, The 3rd International Conference on Adaptive Hypermedia and Adaptive Web-based Systems, August 23 - 26, 2004, Eindhoven, Netherlands

Manson, P. (2007). Technology-Enhanced Learning: Supporting Learning in the 21st Century, Keynote ERCIM NEWS Special: Technology-Enhanced Learning, No. 71, p. 3.

McTear, M.F. (2000). Intelligent interface technology: from theory to reality? *Interacting with Computers* , Vol. 12, pp. 323–336.

Norcio, A. & Stanley, J. (1989). Adaptive Human-Computer Interfaces: A Literature Survey and Perspective, *IEEE Transactions on System, Man and Cybernetics*, Vol. 19, No. 2, pp. 399-408.

Norman, D. & Draper, S.W. (1986). *User Centred System Design*. Erlbaum, Hillsdale NJ

Petz, B., et al.. (2005). Psychological Dictionary (Psihologijski rječnik). Naklada Slap, Jastrebarsko (in Croatian)

Rich, E. (1999). Users are individuals: individualizing user models, *International Journal on Human-Computer Studies*, Vol. 51, pp. 323-338.

Rothrock, L., Koubek, R., Fuchsm, F., Haas, M. & Salvendy, G. (2002). Review and Reappraisal of Adaptive Interfaces: Toward Biologically Inspired Paradigms, *Theoretical Issues in Ergonomics Science*, Vol. 3, No. 1, pp. 47-84, Taylor and Francis Ltd.

Sampson, D. G., Spector, J. M., Devedzic, V. & Kinshuk (2004). Remarks on the Variety and Significance of Advanced Learning Technologies, *Educational Technology & Society*, Vol. 7, No. 2, pp. 14-18.

Schneider-Hufschmidt, M., Kühme, T. & Malinowski, U. (Eds.) (1993). *Adaptive User Interfaces: Principles and Practice*. North-Holland, Elsevier Science Publishers B.V.

Shute, V. & Towle, B. (2003). Adaptive e-learning, *Educational Psychologist*, Vol. 38, No. 2, pp. 105-114.

Soloway, E., Guzdial, M. & Hay, K.E. (1994). Learner-Centred Design: The Challenge for HCI in the 21st Century, *Interactions* Vol. 1, pp. 36–48.

Spector, J. M. & Anderson, T. M. (Eds.) (2000). *Integrated and holistic perspectives on learning, instruction and technology: Understanding complexity*, Dordrecht: Kluwer Academic.

Stankov, S. (2005). Principal Investigating Project TP-02/0177-01 Web-oriented Intelligent Hypermedial Authoring Shell. Ministry of Science and Technology of the Republic of Croatia (2003-2005)

Weibelzahl, S. (2005). Problems and pitfalls in the evaluation of adaptive systems, In: *Adaptable and Adaptive Hypermedia Systems*, Chen, S. & Magoulas, G. (Eds.), pp. 285-299, Hershey, PA: IRM Press

Zaharias, P. (2005). E-learning design quality: A holistic conceptual framework, In: *Encyclopaedia of Distance Learning*, Howard, C., Boettcher, J., Justice, L., Schenk, K., Rogers, P.L. & Berg, G.A. (Eds.), Vol. II. New York, NY: Idea Publishing.

10

Design of Text Comprehension Activities with RETUDISAuth

Grammatiki Tsaganou and Maria Grigoriadou
University of Athens, Dept. of Informatics & Telecommunications
Greece

1. Introduction

The cognitive psychological approach in text comprehension suggests that the internal variables of the reader hold a primary role in text comprehension, such as his personal goals, interests and pre-existing knowledge. However, cognitive science does not ignore the influence of the text form, in which factors such as text cohesion and logical coherence of facts presented have been proved to be significant elements that facilitate its comprehension (DeCorte et al., 1982). Recent discussions, directions and research results on text comprehension concern the structural analysis of science texts and cognitive aspects of text elements, such as causal relationships between text elements. Different studies on text comprehension have focused their interest on the sentence structure presented by the text (Brown & Day, 1983; Kintsch, 1998). Sentence structure of a text could be organized on the basis of hierarchy in order to allow the importance of sentences in the text to be revealed (Van Dijk, & Kintsch, 1983). In approaching text comprehension, researchers examine issues that focus on assisting comprehension through text summarization (Brown & Day, 1983) by improving text coherence (McNamara, 1996; Kintsch, 1998; Graesser & Tipping, 1999) or assisting the design of the text form and text activities (Baudet & Denhière, 1992).

Text comprehension theory of Baudet & Denhière, supports that readers build mental representations of information contained in the text during the comprehension process. Primary role should be attributed to the understanding of cognitive categories such as entity, state, event and action as well as temporal and causal relationships connecting these structures (Leon & Penalba, 2002). This consideration deals with text comprehension as the attribution of meanings to causal and temporal connections between occurrences in the text. Furthermore, the organization and structure of cognitive representation should involve three system types: relational system, transformational system and teleological system and should be examined on micro and macro-levels (Baudet & Denhière, 1992). The design of the structure of text activities is important in order to enhance learning in an educational system.

In order to make the information in such activities available to target users (students, teachers, researchers, authors, educators) new efforts have emerged to bring together novel methodologies and technologies. Authoring such activities demands an authoring system which involves knowledge acquisition, design process and managing a large amount of complex information. Authoring tools offer the appropriate structure and guide authors to

import and elaborate educational material (text, questions, dialogues etc.). Researchers have been investigated Intelligent Tutoring Systems (ITS) with authoring tools almost since the beginning of ITS research and authoring systems have been built (Koedinger & Anderson, 1995; Schultz et al., 2003). An authoring tool is a generalized framework along with a user interface that allows non programmers to formalize their knowledge (Koedinger & Anderson, 1995; Ritter & Blessing, 1998; Wong & Chan, 1997). Part of authoring an ITS is the systematic decomposition of the subject matter into a set of related text elements. Each authoring system provides tools or cues which assist the author in this process of breaking down and elaborating the content to the necessary level of detail according to an instructional model. There are intelligent adaptive hypermedia systems like CALAT (Muray, 2003) and GETMAS (Wong & Chan, 1997) that their functions overlap those from both the above categories. There are also expert systems, like Dempndtr8 (Blessing, 2003), IRIS-tutor (Arruarte et al., 2003) which include rule-based cognitive models of problem solving expertise and observe learner behaviour in order to build a learner model.
In this chapter we outline the process of structuring technical text educational material with questions and dialogue activities for text comprehension in the educational environment of ReTuDiS (Reflective Tutorial Dialogue System), using its' authoring tool, ReTuDiSAuth. The technical text presented as an example concerns "Local Network Operation". Authors are guided to organize and structure text and activities involving the relational, transformational and teleological system and make descriptions on micro and macro-levels. The system supports text comprehension using questions and dialogue activities, adapted to different learner profiles. In this work we also report on evaluation results of the use of ReTuDiSAuth as an authoring tool.

2. Text Comprehension Theory

In order to examine the representation constructed by learners during the comprehension process of a text, primary role should be attributed to the understanding of the cognitive categories entity, state, event and action (Baudet & Denhière, 1992). The term entity refers to the atoms, units or persons participating in the representation structure. The term state describes a situation in which no change occurs in the course of time. The term event refers to an effect, which causes changes but is not provoked by human intervention. The event can be coincidental or provoked by human intervention, e.g. by a machine. An action causes changes but is originating by a man but is originating by a human intervention. Text comprehension is considered as the attribution of meaning to causal connections between occurrences in the text. Learners compose a representation of the text, which contains the cognitive categories: entity, state, event and action. For the interpretation of learners' cognitive processes their discourse is analysed, in order to trace the recognition (or not) of the cognitive categories.
Furthermore, text analysis in relation to the cognitive categories does not suffice (Baudet & Denhière, 1992). The organization and structure of cognitive representation should involve three system types: relational system, transformational system and teleological system.

- The relational system represents a state in which there are entities of the possible world and no change occurs in the course of time, whereas part to whole relations define a hierarchy in the structure of the system.
- The transformational system represents complex events of the world or events' sequences which provoke transformation of static states. When a transformational

system is causal then it is described as a causal path between events. When it is temporal the changes are temporal. Part to whole relations between events and macro-events define a hierarchy in the system.

- The teleological system is organized in a tree of goals and sub-goals and within a time period its' initial state, defined by the present entities, their relations and the values of their properties, changes turning into a final state performing in that way the predefined goal.

The organization and structure of cognitive representation should also be examined on micro and macro-levels. Mental representations capture elements of the surface text, of the referential meaning of the text, and of the interpretation of the referential meaning, thus constructing a micro-world of characters, objects, spatial settings, actions, events, feelings etc. The person who reads a text gradually constructs the microstructure of the text representation, i.e. the states, event and compound actions of the world described in the text as well as the time and causal relationships that interlock those structures.

On a micro-level scale, in order a person, to be able to explain the operation of a technical system, has to construct a representation of the "natural flow of things", where every new event should be causally explained by the conditions of events which have already occurred. The creation of a text that allows a precise description of a technical system and facilitates readers in constructing its microstructure representation must involve: (a) the description of the units that constitute the system based on the causal relationship which unites them and (b) the description of event sequence taking place in these units in respect of the cause affecting them as well as of the changes they bring to the state of the system.

On macro-level, the development of the macrostructure by readers is achieved through the reconstruction of the microstructure and the establishment of a hierarchical structure with goals and sub-goals. The creation of a text which facilitates readers in constructing its macrostructure representation for a system must involve the teleological hierarchical structure of goals and sub-goals of the various operations as well as their implications.

3. Authoring Tools

ITS authoring is both a design process and a process of knowledge articulation. While authoring tools are becoming more common and proving to be increasingly effective they are difficult and expensive to build. Authoring tools use methods to achieve the following goals (Ainsworth et al., 2003) a) decrease the effort of authoring (time and cost), b) allow others to take part in the design process c) help the author articulate or organize his domain knowledge d) support good design principles concerning the pedagogy and the interface and e) allow quick evaluation cycles.

Authoring tools achieve the above goals using various of methods. Authoring systems use methods to simplify and automate authoring and knowledge acquisition. Part of authoring an ITS is the systematic decomposition of the subject matter into a set of related elements, for example a hierarchy. Each authoring system provides tools or cues which assist the author in this process of breaking down and elaborating the content to the necessary level of detail according to an instructional model.

Authoring tools allow non-programmers to build tutors by incorporating a particular model or framework to scaffold the task (Muray, 2003). Learner modelling process requires making certain choices, and it is in these choices that the learning process is located (Kay, 2001). We do not learn much from looking at a model, we learn from models by building them and using them (Jonassen, 2004; Morgan, 1999). Learning from building models involves finding out what elements fit together in order to represent the world of the model. The design of dialogue activities for adaptive learning supported by appropriate authoring tools attracts the interest of many researchers and educators in inventing new methodologies for effective teaching and learning. The authoring process activates authors to decompose the subject matter into a set of related elements to discover what elements fit together in order to represent a concept, for example a hierarchy. The authoring process, as a process of choosing, organizing, structuring and linking educational material becomes a process of learning.

Authoring tools for text comprehension have to discover and offer mechanisms which help authors design activities for the diagnosis of learners' difficulties in comprehending texts. They offer the appropriate structure and guidance in order the author to be able to import and elaborate educational material (text, questions, dialogues etc.). There has been a growing concern about scientific text comprehension (Brown & Day, 1983). Efficient teaching and learning requires that educators should be familiar with the difficulties which learners are likely to face.

3.1 ReTuDiS System

ReTuDiS is a diagnosis and open learner modelling tutorial dialogue system for text comprehension. The system infers learners' cognitive profile in order to construct and revise the learner model with the learners' participation (Tsaganou et al., 2004). ReTuDiS consists of two parts: the Diagnosis part and the Dialogue part.

The diagnosis part of ReTuDiS approaches learner's text comprehension supporting the theory of Baudet & Denhière that learner's representation of the text contains the cognitive categories: event, state and action (Baudet & Denhière, 1992). The system engages learners in an activity which includes reading comprehension of text and answering question-pairs by selecting between given alternative answers. Learners' answers are used for diagnosing learners' text comprehension. Learners have to study all the text to comprehend it and select answers from the given alternative answers, in order to express their position on certain issues and support it by a justification. The diagnosis part infers learners' cognitive profile and his learner model.

The underlying theory beyond the dialogue part of ReTuDiS is the Theory of Inquiry Teaching (Collins, 1987). ReTuDiS approaches dialogue activities based on theories of dialogue management, strategies, tactics and plans which promote reflection in learning. The dialogue part is based on the learners' cognitive profile, inferred by the diagnosis part, the learners' answers to question-pairs and the selected dialogue strategy offered by the system. The dialogue part of ReTuDiS engages the learner in personalized reflective dialogues in order to revise the learner model with the participation of the learner (Tsaganou et al., 2004). The dialogue generator activates the appropriate for the learner sequence of dialogue-parts, and using the dialogue plan, dynamically constructs the individualized learning dialogue.

3.2 ReTuDiSAuth

ReTuDiSAuth, the authoring tool of system ReTuDiS, offers an environment that lays out the appropriate parameters an author needs to define. The authoring tool supports users registered as teachers or administrators. Teachers have the authority to create new activities or edit existing ones. Administrators of the system have the authority to manage the base of the users of the ReTuDiS and the educational material. The environment offers the tools and the shell (Figure 1). The tools, which add interactivity to the system and support authors to import educational material, are the following:

Text fields. These fields are designed to help authors enhance their own educational material into the system for example, titles of activities, texts, questions.

Pop-up menus. The menus are designed to help authors select from predefined by the teacher or by the system values or defaults such as: categories of activities, characterizations of answers, teaching strategies.

The knowledge base. This data base includes the educational material of text, questions, and dialogues.

Association buttons. They are buttons designed to help authors establish causal relationships between text elements such as text-unities and make associations such as between educational material and learners' profiles, teaching strategies and learners' profiles, learners' profiles and dialogue plans.

Guidance tips. They are information tips designed to support the author by giving back the appropriate feedback to his actions that is confirmation or not of the completion of each step.

Administrative tools. These tools are for managing the lists of users, the roles of the users (teachers or students), the categories of activities, the activities, reports on carried out activities (log files for each student).

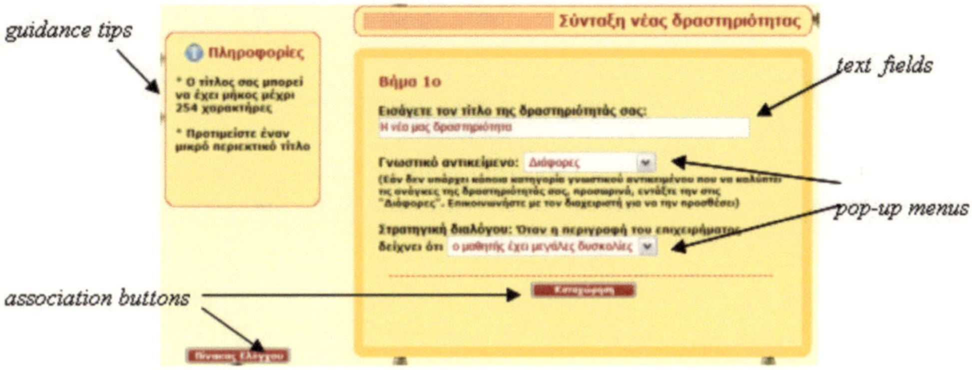

Figure 1. The ReTuDiSAuth: Tools for structuring and elaborating a dialogue activity

The shell delivers the educational material according to the instructions generated by the author using the tools in combination with its predetermined defaults. A semantic network is created by the author using the association buttons. The nodes of the network represent the elements of the material and the branches represent possible paths followed by the learner while participating in instructional activities. While delivering the educational material to a learner in a specified manner the shell constructs his learner model. The values of the learner model change over the activity course as the learner participates in dialogues.

4. Text Structuring with RETUDISAuth

School and university text-books usually include texts not structured according to any theory of text comprehension. Authors of such texts usually ignore micro and macro structure. Research held with participation of 60 students studying Didactics of Informatics in the Department of Informatics and Telecommunications, University of Athens during the academic year 2006-2007, asked students to select texts and write questions for text comprehension (Tsaganou & Grigoriadou, 2008). The research results indicated that selected texts embody mainly descriptions of micro structure, whereas descriptions of macro structure were very poor or fragmentary. On the other hand, questions reported by the students included descriptions of macro structure.

Structuring a text is a demanding process. The text should be organized and structured in order to include descriptions on micro and macro-level representation of the knowledge domain. Since this is difficult, authors can lie heavy on the construction of the appropriate questions about the text. ReTuDiSAuth involves the author in the following processes concerning text, questions and dialogue structure (Tsaganou et al., 2004; Grigoriadou & Tsaganou, 2007).

Text structure

The author selects the text from a text-book and identifies the cognitive categories. He separates the text in sections, each of which represents a cognitive category and gives a phrase as a title for every section. Titles help in organizing the structure of the questions and dialogues activities. The author specifies the cognitive categories involved and the number of them. For example, in case of technical text are used four cognitive categories: entity, state, event and action. In case of historical text have been used three cognitive categories: state, event and action (Tsaganou et al, 2004; Grigoriadou et al., 2005; Grigoriadou & Kanidis, 2003).

Questions with alternative answers

For every section the author submits simple questions or question-pairs to the system and the related alternative answers. The first question in a question-pair is related to the section and the learner's alternative answer concerning this question is declared to the system as position. The second question is related to the learner's justification concerning a position and is declared to the system as justification. Position and justification represent the causal relationships in the text. Each question or question–pair refers to a description on micro-level of the relational system: (a) description of units that constitute the system, (b) description of part to whole relations connecting system units and (c) description of static states of the units. Or to a description of the transformational system: (a) description of events and events' sequence taking place in these units, (b) description of causal and temporal relationships between events and the changes bringing on the static states. The teleological system includes description of the system on macro-level throughout a "tree" of predefined goals and sub-goals for every transformation of the system from one state to another.

Local Network Operation

A computer network is often classified as being either a local area network (LAN), a metropolitan area network (MAN) or a wide area network (WAN). Another means of classifying networks is based on the topology of the network, which refers to the pattern in which the machines are connected. Three popular topologies are: (1) bus, in which the machines are connected to a common communication line called a bus, (2) ring, in which the machines are connected in circular fashion and (3) star, in which one machine serves as a central focal point to which all the others are connected.

A bus topology is designed with each node connected directly to a high-data speed bus. Nodes communicate across the network by passing packets of data through the bus (they read and write data -in the form of packets). Packets placed on the bus, transfer messages to nodes. A message includes the receiver's address, which specifies the network address of the target node. A node watches the bus continuously and reads the target address of each packet. After that, the node compares the address with its own, and if they are the same, then reads the message of the packet, otherwise ignores it. When a node is ready to broadcast a message, waits until the bus is free and then begins passing it to the bus. If a node uses the bus it watches it and can be aware of any other node using the bus at the same time. In that case both nodes stop using the bus waiting until one of them accidentally attempts to us it. When a limited number of packets are simultaneously transmitted throughout the bus, them this competence strategy is successful. The bus topology network can work even in case of disconnection of a node (Brookshear, 2005) .....

Question 1 (Identification of local network units).

1) In a local network which of the following is a node.

- A server
- A packet
- A bus

Question 2 (Identification of events and events' sequence).

2a) In a bus topology network, what happens in case there is an interruption (a cut off) of the bus. Select one of the following answers.

- the network crashes (non scientific)
- the network continuous to work properly (towards scientific)
- the network is divided into two independent networks each one working properly (scientific)

2b) Justify your answer by selecting one of the following answers.

- because all nodes are connected with the bus and they cannot communicate if there is a cut off (non scientific)
- because all nodes have spare connections between each other that can operate without the bus (towards scientific)
- because a bus network needs only a central bus to connect the nodes to (scientific)

Figure 2. Text fragment and questions with alternative answers given by a student

In Figure 2, Question 1 is related to description of units that constitute the local network system (relational system). Question 2 is related to description of events taking place in the system, relationships between events and the changes bringing from one state to another (transformational system).

Dialogue structure

Defining argument completeness. For every question-pair the combination of the learner's position and the corresponding justification constitutes the learner's argument. Arguments are classified as complete, when both position and justification are scientific. Otherwise the argument is non-complete. The author defines the different degrees of argument completeness. Possible values of argument completeness are: complete, almost complete, intermediate, nearly incomplete and incomplete.

Forming dialogues. The author creates a library consisting of specific dialogue-parts for all combinations of possible answers and associates them with the corresponding answers. Each specific dialogue-part is designed to remedy a particular learning difficulty. The specific dialogue-parts are dependent on the specific text. The specific dialogue-parts of different types are associated with predefined and embedded in the system dialogue tactics

Forming dialogue tactics. Dialogue tactics, inspired by the general teaching strategies (Collins, 1987; Graesser, 2001), are hints or Socratic-style dialogues. Tactics correspond to different levels of dialogue concerning the specific subject matter and involve learners in activities which promote reflection. The author defines the dialogue tactics which have the following forms: (a) picks positive or negative examples, (b) picks counterexamples, (c) generates hypothesis, (d) makes learner to form hypothesis, (e) makes learner to test hypothesis, (f) entraps the learner, (g) traces consequences to a contradiction or faulty knowledge of a learner and (h) promotes questioning authority.

Selecting dialogue strategy. The choice of the dialogue strategy is decided in the beginning. Example of a strategy embedded in the system is the following (Grigoriadou et al., 2005): "The system sorts learners' argument classifications in a list according to decreasing degree of argument completeness. The tutorial dialogue begins with a discussion about the unity for which the learner seems to face less learning difficulties. The system generates the sequence of dialogue-parts for this unity. Then the system prepares the next dialogue-part, based on the results of the previous dialogue-part".

Selecting dialogue tactics. Predefined dialogue tactics are accessed throughout a pop-up menu. The author selects a predefined dialogue tactic and formulates the dialogue-part.

Planning dialogue. For the selected teaching strategy and depending on the learner profile the system constructs the initial dialogue plan for the learner. The system uses: (a) the general dialogue-parts, which include typical dialogue-parts, concerning participation of the learner in dialogue, encouragement, motivation, agreement or not with the system, guidance etc. and (b) the specific dialogue-parts that were previously entered by the author according to the appropriate dialogue goals and tactics. During entering the author has made the appropriate associations between contradicting answers (contradictions between learner's position and his justification concerning causal relationships in the text) and dialogue-parts for all possible combination of answers. So as, the system becomes able to initiate the dialogue and generate dynamically the appropriate dialogue in response to the learners' feedback during the dialogue process.

Defining learners' profiles. Learners can be described as belonging to one of a set of author-defined learner profiles taking into account the number of learner's arguments with high degree of argument completeness.

5. Evaluation

Formative evaluation, concerning the use of ReTuDiSAuth for text structuring, was conducted with the participation of 26 postgraduate students and 6 experts in informatics domain at the University of Athens. Evaluation aimed at further revisions, modifications and improvements of ReTuDiSAuth as well as of ReTuDiS system (Muray, 2003). The participants were given explanations about the aims of the authoring tool.

Students were asked to participate in the evaluation process and perform representative tasks: (a) to prepare source material text and questions with alternative answers of their choice and (b) to use the system for the construction of dialogue activities. Each student proposed a two pages text, three question- pairs with alternative answers involving causal relationships and specific dialogues-parts.

Experts used the material proposed by the students in order to identify and comment issues concerning specific problems or deficiencies users face in formulating learning goals, questions and tutoring dialogues and the educational benefits of the process.

Both students and experts were given a questionnaire and commented about usability, learnability and efficiency:

- the depth to which the system can infer a learner's knowledge, respond accordingly and teach
- if the system can support dialogue activities on different knowledge domains
- how easy non-programmers can learn to use the system
- how quickly a trained user can construct questions and dialogue activities
- the amount of resources needed to construct questions and dialogue activities

Moreover, experts were asked to comment about:

- how much the underlying instructional model of the system constrains the author
- the sources of teaching and domain expertise
- the level of expertise /background of the target authors.

In general, most of the experts faced minor difficulties in using the interface. Experts spent more time to overcome difficulties in structuring the text and matching text paragraphs with cognitive categories. Experts commended about the quantity and the quality of questions made by the students. They identified as beneficial the method used for training students, which may be potential teachers, for the improvement of their authoring skills for text-based dialogue activities.

6. Conclusions

Research results of the effectiveness of ReTuDiSAuth environment as an authoring tool for structuring educational text material were presented. Students experimented in the environment and designed text, questions and dialogue activities that promote learners' reflection. Evaluation got hold of representative users: graduate students and experts.

We explored the role of the learner in authoring environment. Analysis of the current study indicated that authoring makes students improve their authoring skills and become familiar with text structuring and question constructing. Educational benefit of this process was the way the environment easily allowed students to add educational material by taking advantage of the system's interactive features. Experts found the system appropriate for the education of postgraduate students as teacher and authors, by offering them considerable power to construct appropriate domain material, create effective learning environments and test their own teaching strategies.

Currently, we are exploring improvement of the system concerning direct specification of causal connections between text elements during text structuring. Moreover, as ReTuDiS does offer significant advantages for classroom use and generate important learning outcomes, we plan further research into the evaluation of the system in complex classroom conditions and compare results in different knowledge domains.

7. References

Ainsworth, S., Major, N., Grimshaw, S., Hays, M., Underwood, J, Williams, B. et al. R. (2003). REDEEM: Simple Intelligent Tutoring Systems from Usable Tools. In: *Authoring Tools for Advanced Technology Learning Environments,* Murray, T., Blessing, S., Ainsworth, S. (Eds.), 205-232, Kluwer Academic Publishers, ISBN:1402017723, The Netherlands.

Arruarte, A., Ferrero, B., Fernandez-Castro, I., Urretavizcya, M., Alvarez, A., & Greer, J. (2003). The IRIS Authoring Tool. In: *Authoring Tools for Advanced Technology Learning Environments,* Murray, T., Blessing, S., Ainsworth, S. (Eds.), 233-267, Kluwer Academic Publishers, ISBN:1402017723, The Netherlands .

Blessing, S., (2003). A Programming by Demonstration Authoring Tool for Model-Tracing tutors. In: *Authoring Tools for Advanced Technology Learning Environments,* Murray, T., Blessing, S., Ainsworth, S. (Eds.), 93-119, Kluwer Academic Publishers, ISBN:1402017723, The Netherlands.

Baudet, S., & Denhière, G. (1992). *Lecture Comprehension de Texte et Science Cognitive,* Presses Universitaires de France, Paris.

Brookshear J G. (2005). *Computer Science: An Overview,* Pearson International Edition, 9th Edition.

Brown, A.L., & Day, J.D. (1983). Macrorules for summarizing texts: The development of expertise. *Journal of Verbal Learning and Verbal Behavior,* 22 1–14.

Collins, Al. (1987). A Sample Dialogue Based on a Theory of Inquiry Teaching. In: *Instructional Theories in Action,* Reigeluth, Ch. (Ed.), 181-199, Lawrence Erlbaum Associates Inc., Hillsdale.

DeCorte, E. Verschaffel, L. & DeWin, L. (1982). Influence of rewording verbal problems on children's problem representations and solutions. *Journal of Educational Psychology,* 77, 460-470.

Graesser, A. (2001). Teaching Tactics and Dialog in Auto-Tutor, *International Journal of Artificial Intelligence in Education,* 12 257-279.

Graesser, A. & Tipping, P. (1999). Understanding Texts. In: *A Companion to Cognitive Science,* Bechtel, W. & Graham, G. (Eds.), Blackwell, Malden MA.

Grigoriadou, M., & Kanidis, V. (2003). Cognitive Aspects in Teaching the Computer Cache Memory with Learning Activities based on a Coherent Technical Text and a Simulation Program. *Proceedings of the 6th Hellenic European Conference on Computer Mathematics & its Applications (HERCMA03) - Minisymposium: Informatics in Cognitive Sciences*, 429-235, LEA Publishers, Athens, Greece .

Grigoriadou, M., Tsaganou, G., & Cavoura, Th. (2005). Historical Text Comprehension Reflective Tutorial Dialogue System, *Educational Technology & Society Journal*, Special issue, 8(40), 31-40.

Grigoriadou, M., Tsaganou, G., (2007). Authoring Tools for Structuring Text Based Activities, *Proceedings of the 4th International Conference on Universal Access in Human-Computer Interaction (UAHCI 2007)*, Volume 7, 319-328, LNCS_4556, ISBN: 978-3-540-73282-2, Beijing, P.R. China.

Jonassen, D., (2004). Model Building for Conceptual Change: Using Computers as Cognitive Tools. *Proceedings of the 4rd Panellenic Conference with International Participation: Information and Communication Technologies in Education (ETPE2004)*, Grigoriadou, M., Raptis, A., Vosniadou, S. & Kynigos, X. (Eds.), 4-17, Athens, Greece.

Leon, J., Penalba, G. (2002). Understanding Causality and Temporal Sequence in Scientific Discourse. In: *The Psychology of Science Text Comprehension*, Otero, J., Leon, J., Graesser, A. (Eds.), Lawrence Earlbaum Associates, Publishers, London.

Kay, J. (2001). Learner control. *User Modeling and User-Adapted Interaction*, 11, 11-127.

Kintsch, W. (1998). *Compréhension: a paradigm for cognition*, Cambridge University Press, UK.

Koedinger, K. & Anderson, J. (1995). Intelligent Tutoring Goes to the Big City. *International Journal of Artificial Inteligence in Education*, 8, 30-43.

McNamara, D.S., Kintsch, E., Songer, N.B., & Kintsch, W. (1996). Are good texts always better? Text coherence, background knowledge, and levels of understanding in learning from text. *Cognition and Instruction*, 14, 1-43

Morgan, M.S. (1999). Learning from Models. In: *Models as mediators: Perspectives on natural and social science*, M.S. Morgan & M. Morrison (Eds.), 347-388, Cambridge: Cambridge University Press.

Muray, T. (2003). An Overview of Intelligent Tutoring System Authoring Tools: Updated analysis of the state of the art. In: *Authoring Tools for Advanced Technology Learning Environments*, Murray, T., Blessing, S., Ainsworth, S. (Eds.), 491-544, Kluwer Academic Publishers, ISBN:1402017723, The Netherlands,.

Ritter, S., & Blessing, S. (1998). Authoring tools for Component-Based Learning Environments. *Journal of the Learning Science*, 7(1), 107-132.

Schultz, K., Bratt, E. O., Clark, B., Peters, S., Ponbarry, H. & Treeratpituk, P. (2003). A Scalable, Reusable, Conversational Tutor: SCoT. *Proceedings of the 11th International Conference on Artificial Intelligence in Education Workshop: Tutorial Dialogue Systems*, 367-377, Sydney, Australia.

Tsaganou, G., Grigoriadou, M., Cavoura, Th., Koutra, D., (2003). Evaluating an Intelligent Diagnosis System of Historical Text Comprehension. *Expert Systems with Applications*, 25(4), 493-502, ISSN: 0957-4174.

Tsaganou, G., Grigoriadou, M. & Cavoura, Th. (2004). W-ReTuDiS: a Reflective Tutorial Dialogue System. *Proceedings of the 4rd Panellenic Conference with International Participation: Information and Communication Technologies in Education,* Grigoriadou, M., Raptis, A., Vosniadou, S. & Kynigos, X. (Eds.), 738-746, Athens, Greece.

Tsaganou, G., Grigoriadou, M., (2008). «Text and Dialogue Structure Analysis Matching a Theory of Text Comprehension». *Proceeding of 4th Hellenic Conference "Didactics of informatics"*, Komis B. (eds.), 333-342, Patra, Greece, ISBN 978-960-6759-07-9.

Van Dijk, T.A., & Kintsch, W. (1983). *Strategies of discourse comprehension.* Academic Press, ISBN-10: 0127120505, New York.

Wong, W. K. & Chan, T. W. (1997). A Multimedia Authoring System for Crafting Topic Hierarchy, Learning Strategies and Intelligent Models. *International Journal of Artificial Intelligence in Education*, 8(1), 71-96, ISSN 1560-4292.

11

Computer-based Cognitive and Socio-emotional Training in Psychopathology

Ouriel Grynszpan
Centre Émotion, Centre National de la Recherche Scientifique(UMR 7593),
Univeristy Pierre & Marie Curie
France

1. Introduction

Recent years have witnessed a growing interest of psychopathology for therapeutic uses of Information and Communication Technologies (ICT). Researchers and clinicians are carrying out interdisciplinary projects and empirical investigations of computer-based treatments dedicated to the rehabilitation of psychiatric patients. Some projects gave rise to practical implementations in clinical settings, a quite publicized example being the use of virtual reality for treating various forms of phobias and anxiety disorders. Companies specialized in developing software intended for psychotherapy are starting to emerge. Academic networks are being formed to exchange ideas and results, with international conferences organized regularly for the purpose of bringing together researchers from various disciplines including computer sciences, psychology and psychiatry. Examples of the multiple aspects of this new and dynamic field of research will be provided throughout the present chapter.

Literature mentions several potential advantages of computers for clinical interventions in psychopathology. Patients seem to adhere to treatments based on computer usage: computers are thought to be stimulating and entertaining (Field et al., 1997; Medalia, 2001). In the same time, they are non-judgmental in case of failure (Bellucci et al., 2002) and their virtual environment is free from danger (Moore et al., 2005). The user has total control over the computer and can repeat any action as many times as she or he wishes (Field et al., 1997; Panyan, 1984). Moreover, the computer offers rich multisensorial stimuli (Bosseler & Massaro, 2003; Medalia, 2001; Panyan, 1984) with precise and immediate feedback (Bellucci et al., 2002; Bosseler & Massaro, 2003; Burda et al., 1994). Computers are considered adequate for implementing treatment procedures as they provide structured and standardized tasks (Bellucci et al., 2002), while enabling the tasks to be personalized (Medalia et al., 2001). Automatic online recording of the patient's performances is also seen as an advantage (Field et al., 1997; Panyan, 1984). Moreover, literature emphasizes the economical advantages of computers. There usage appears to be cost effective in terms of reducing therapist time (Burda et al., 1994). However, authors also suspect problems could arise from computer-based treatments, such as difficulties to generalize learning acquired on the computer to everyday life (Bernard-Opitz et al., 2001).

This chapter intends to illustrate the interdisciplinary approaches of computer-based treatments for psychiatric rehabilitation. It starts with a brief overview of issues regarding treatment in psychopathology and distinguishes three paradigms guiding computer-based approaches: compensation, desensitization and training. The present chapter is especially devoted to computer-based treatments that adhere to the training paradigm. It then reviews the literature on computer-based cognitive and socio-emotional training in psychopathology. The literature survey is illustrated by two specific categories of psychopathological disorders: schizophrenia and autism. Computer-assisted cognitive remediation is described for schizophrenia where it has been evaluated by a number of studies. Socio-emotional training examples are presented for autism, where an emerging body of literature addresses computerized training of social interactions and emotional processing. Following the literature review, the chapter describes a longitudinal pilot study that investigated both cognitive and socio-emotional computer-based training in the case of autism. The interconnections between cognitive remediation and socio-emotional training are discussed in the light of this exploratory investigation and relevant literature. Finally, the chapter concludes with future research directions.

2. Treatment issues in psychopathology

2.1 From symptoms to social dysfunction

Computer-based treatments target a wide range of deficiencies, from neurocognitive functioning to social and emotional regulation. As described by Craig (2006), psychopathological disorders imply difficulties permeating the whole life of the individual. Symptoms may be regarded as the basic impairments, as they form the core features of the disorder. Functional disabilities occur in the process of performing everyday tasks for which individuals experience difficulties as a consequence of their symptoms. For instance, shopping or cooking can be a challenging activity for people with memory losses or poor concentration. Commuting by public transportation can be very stressful for a person having agoraphobia. Symptoms and disabilities most often result in a serious handicap, exposing the concerned individual to social stigma and impeding social and professional integration. Professional outcomes seem to be especially compromised and the trend appears to be worsening. For example, Craig (2006) indicates that the employment rates for people with severe psychiatric illnesses in the UK are lower now than they use to be fifty years ago. There may be various explanations for this state of fact. Current jobs are more demanding in terms of cognitive performances, while opportunities for low skilled manufacturing jobs are decreasing. The wide use of computers in modern economy may be a drawback for some impaired individuals as it requires high level cognitive skills and rapid adaptation. Another important reason may derive from the medication side-effects, for instance sedation. Obviously, the various aspects of psychiatric disorders that were just described are closely intertwined: symptoms and cognitive impairments are determinant factors influencing functional disabilities and social incapacities, reversely social exclusion can have devastating effects on mood and self-esteem, eventually leading to depression or anxiety that worsen the symptomatic profile. Potential targets for computer-based approaches are thus threefold. Firstly, they may address the basic impairments including symptoms and cognitive deficiencies. Secondly, they can be used for helping the individual in everyday tasks, thus decreasing disabilities. Thirdly, they can assist in overcoming social

and professional obstacles. Research projects usually aim mainly at one of these three targets, while acknowledging the possible influence on the other two.
Computer-based interventions in psychopathology depend on the critical issue of adapting the features of computer technology to the specificities of psychopathological disorders. The fact that psychopathological disorders are permeating every aspect of the individual's life without being easily associated with a specific functional capacity makes it all the more complex to define suitable technology. This contrasts with many physical disabilities, as for example lower limbs palsy that hinders locomotion but leaves rather unaltered the skills necessary for deskwork. In the latter case, the functional incapacity appears to be more clearly defined and can therefore be more readily addressed by technology with various types of high-tech wheelchairs for instance. As for psychopathological disorders, researchers experience difficulties in circumventing the functional implications and the treatment needs to cover altogether symptoms and cognitive alterations, functional disabilities and social withdrawal. Another limiting factor that complicates the work of defining suitable technology is the lack of knowledge about the etiology of various psychopathological disorders. Reviews on autism (Happé & Frith, 1996) and on schizophrenia (Walker et al., 2004) reveal that the causes of these disorders have still not been fully uncovered by research. The contemporary perspective in many psychiatric disorders assumes that a single syndrome may encompass different subgroups with various possible etiologies. Hence, specialists tend to consider psychiatric disorders as spectrums rather than as uniform entities. Multiple explanatory theories for the same syndrome coexist and frequently compete. Their predictions about the impact of various therapeutic approaches can be contradictory, thus complicating the task of researchers trying to design appropriate computer-based interventions. Adapting computer technology for treatment of psychiatric disorders is an adventurous endeavor requiring thorough interdisciplinary understanding of both psychopathology and computer sciences.

2.2 Paradigms of computer uses

Current computer-based treatments in psychopathology seem to follow mainly three paradigms: compensation of disabilities, desensitization to anxiety or addictive craving and training of cognitive, social and emotional functioning. The compensation approach seeks to alleviate the disabilities provoked by the symptoms and cognitive deficiencies through the use of assistive technological devices. In a review of the matter, LoPresti and colleagues (2004) underline the analogy with prostheses in physical or sensorial handicaps. Compensation proceeds by providing a device designed to assist the individual in performing cognitive tasks for which she or he encounters difficulties. Examples may be found in neurology. For instance, Wilson and colleagues (2001) developed a paging system that was tested with 143 patients having neurological disorders. The paging system would compensate for memory losses by sending reminders at the right date and time about tasks that had to be carried out. Results of a randomized control trial showed a substantial increase in task completion due to the pager system. The desensitization paradigm is used extensively for phobias, anxiety disorders and addiction. Desensitization relies on the classic biological principle of habituation, according to which the neural response to a stimulus is attenuated by repeated exposure to this stimulus (Castellucci et al., 1978). In psychotherapy, desensitization to an anxiety provoking stimulus or an addictive craving is achieved by gradual exposure of patients to the critical stimulus. Virtual reality appears especially appropriate for this therapeutic paradigm as it enables exposure to fake stimuli that are realistic enough for habituation to occur. Virtual reality's role in clinical practice is rapidly expanding. For instance, virtual reality therapies are used for treating victims of terrorist attacks having post stress disorders (Difede et al., 2002; Josman et al., 2006). Some companies have specialized in virtual reality development for psychopathology, as for instance „Virtually Better©" (www.virtuallybetter.com) that design virtual environments intended for exposure to addictive craving. Lastly, the cognitive and socio-emotional training paradigm refers to teaching methods based on the active participation of the patient and repeated practice of specific tasks. The rest of the present chapter is devoted to describing in more details the computer-based approaches that adhere to this paradigm. The following sections start by presenting training programs focusing on basic cognitive functions, also known as cognitive remediation. Programs intended for social and emotional enhancement are described latter on.

3. Computer Assisted Cognitive Remediation (CACR)

3.1 Rationale

Cognitive remediation refers to teaching methods aiming at helping patients acquire or regain basic cognitive abilities. These techniques were initially devised for patients with neurological disabilities such as cerebral palsy or stroke. For the last two decades, they have been progressively introduced in psychiatric settings as well. These teaching methods target fundamental cognitive skills such as attention, memory and executive functions. The term "executive functions" traditionally refers to a set of cognitive functions that encompasses planning, working memory, impulse control, inhibition, shifting set as well as the initiation and monitoring of action (Hill, 2004). During cognitive remediation therapy, patients are required to complete sets of cognitive tasks. Attention remediation typically involves exercising vigilance and the ability to select among multiple stimuli. Tasks targeting memory can for example train the ability to remember lists of items over a short period of time. Remediation of executive functions often employs problem-solving tasks such as the Towers of Hanoi (Bracy, 1981). Cognitive remediation approaches often include individual coaching by a therapist. The role of the therapist can vary from merely encouraging the patient (Bellucci et al., 2002) to guiding the patient through efficient use of relevant cognitive strategies (Medalia et al., 2001). As often in psychopathology, there are various models for applying cognitive remediation. Models vary depending on the theoretical background that supports their psychological validity. The reader may consult (Wykes & van der Gaag, 2001) for a review on the different theories employed in cognitive remediation. Computer-based approaches are especially convenient for training models relying on repeated practice of standardized tasks. These approaches are based on the premise that intense and regular training on tasks involving deficient cognitive functions can help in improving these functions although they are altered. Two theoretical arguments support this view. Firstly, literature states that computer exercises hold opportunities for learning novel strategies that enable bypassing impaired abilities (Kurtz et al., 2007). Secondly, repeated practice in a multimedia environment is believed to hasten cortical reorganization (Butti et al., 1998).

Neurobiological research supports the idea that exercise and stimulation in a rich environment accelerates neural plasticity. Kandel (1998) illustrates neural plasticity with the example of separate maps of the surface of the body contained in the postcentral gyrus of the primary somatic sensory cortex. These cortical maps are dynamic and not static. Their expansion or retraction depends on the particular use of the associated area of the body. Experiments on animals have shown the influence of external stimulation on synaptic plasticity. For instance, Knott and colleagues (2002) investigated the effect of whiskers' stimulation in adult mice and found that after 24 hours of continuous stimulation, the synaptic density in the cortical zone associated with the whiskers had increased by 36%. Similarly to synaptic plasticity, exercise and environmental stimulation appear to favor the increase of neurogenesis, associated with improved memory function (Van Praag et al., 2002). Neurogenesis refers to the generation of new functional neurons in adult animals, which has been especially observed in the hippocampus of the mouse (Van Praag et al., 2002). This corpus of research agrees with the framework for psychiatry introduced by Kandel (1998) according to whom learning mechanisms involving epigenetic regulation of neural processes are the basic principles underlying psychotherapy.

Computer-Assisted Cognitive Remediation (CACR) is supported by neurobiological observations of the positive effect of repeated practice on neural plasticity. However, as emphasized by Wykes and van der Gaag (2001), continued practice on a particular cognitive task may not impact performances on other tasks, even if they rely on the same type of cognitive operations. This CACR model of cognitive remediation could therefore bear the potential drawback that acquired skills would not generalized to untrained tasks.

3.2 The example of schizophrenia

This section focuses on schizophrenia to illustrate computer-assisted cognitive remediation in psychopathology. The prevalence of schizophrenia is estimated at around 1% of the total population (Walker et al., 2004). Schizophrenia is a disorder characterized by at least two of the following symptoms that must be present for at least one month: delusion, hallucination, disorganized speech, grossly disorganized or catatonic behavior and negative symptoms such as affective flattening, alogia, avolition (APA, 1994). Moreover, the diagnosis includes a decline in social and occupational functioning since the onset of illness. Schizophrenia is subdivided into five types: paranoid, disorganized, catatonic, undifferentiated and residual. The paranoid type is characterized by preoccupation with delusions or hallucinations. The disorganized type includes disorganized speech, disorganized behavior and flat or inappropriate affect. In the catatonic type, the following symptoms predominate: motor immobility or excessive motor activity, negativism or mutism, peculiar movements and bizarre posturing, echolalia or echopraxia. The undifferentiated type refers to patients who cannot be classified in any other types. Finally, the residual type is used when positive symptoms (delusion, disorganized speech, disorganized or catatonic behavior) are not prominent anymore, although some attenuated symptoms are still present.

Beside symptoms listed in the diagnosis, schizophrenia is associated with a broad cognitive impairment involving every domain of functioning. Heinrichs and Zakzanis (1998) report that between 61% and 78% of people with schizophrenia exhibit a cognitive deficit. Individuals show a high heterogeneity of cognitive performances with some having mild or no deficit and others being profoundly impaired. A recent consensus (Nuechterlein et al., 2004) has been established for classifying cognitive deficiencies into the following categories: Speed of Processing, Attention/Vigilance, Working Memory, Verbal Learning and Memory, Visual Learning and Memory, Reasoning and Problem Solving, Verbal Comprehension and Social Cognition. Although these cognitive domains may be impaired in individuals with schizophrenia, they are considered liable to improve given an appropriate treatment. The only exception is Verbal Comprehension, which is considered resistant to change.

3.3 Clinical evaluations

As mentioned earlier, a major possible drawback of CACR is suspected to be the lack of generalization of acquired skills on untrained tasks. Hence, the studies presented here have been selected on the basis that they employ assessment tasks that are different from tasks used during training.

Several randomized controlled trials have been conducted to evaluate the effectiveness of CACR in schizophrenia (Bell et al., 2001; Bellucci et al., 2002; Burda et al., 1994; Field et al., 1997; Greig et al., 2007; Hogarty et al., 2004; Kurtz et al., 2007; Medalia et al., 2000; Medalia et al., 2001; Sartory et al., 2005; Vauth et al., 2005). Most have reported improvements of cognitive performances, with some exceptions as for example Field and colleagues (1997) and Medalia and colleagues (2000). Studies report improvements in various cognitive domains such as: speed of processing (Bellucci et al., 2002; Burda et al., 1994; Hogarty et al., 2004; Kurtz et al., 2007; Sartory et al., 2005), attention (Vauth et al., 2005), working memory (Bell et al., 2001; Burda et al., 1994; Hogarty et al., 2004; Kurtz et al., 2007), verbal memory (Bellucci et al., 2002; Burda et al., 1994; Hogarty et al., 2004; Kurtz et al., 2007; Sartory et al., 2005; Vauth et al., 2005), visual memory (Kurtz et al., 2006), reasoning and problem solving (Bell et al., 2001; Hogarty et al., 2004; Kurtz et al., 2007; Medalia et al., 2001) and social cognition (Bell et al., 2001; Hogarty et al., 2004).

Bellucci and colleagues (2002) investigated the effect of CACR on symptoms. Their experiment included 34 adults with schizophrenia randomly assigned to either a CACR group or a wait list control group. The CACR group received biweekly half-hour computer sessions for 8 weeks. They employed "Capitain's Log" software (Sandford & Browne, 1988), which is specialized for cognitive remediation. Results indicated that the CACR group had improved on measures of verbal learning and memory, concentration and executive functions. Moreover, patients receiving CACR demonstrated greater reduction of negative symptoms compared to the control group. The study of Bellucci and colleagues (2002) thus suggests that CACR could have an influence beyond cognitive impairments and impact symptoms as well.

Researchers have also investigated if CACR could combine with other therapies so as to increase positive outcomes. Given that cognitive impairments are limiting factors for occupational functioning and professional integration, the combination of CACR with vocational rehabilitation raises interest. Bell and colleagues (2001) combined Work Therapy (WT), which is based on adapted employments including coaching and counseling, with Neurocognitive Enhancement Therapy (NET), which includes computer-assisted cognitive remediation, social information processing groups and work feedback groups. NET relies on PSSCogRehab software (Bracy, 1981) that was initially design for the rehabilitation of neurological patients. In a randomized controlled trial, 65 patients were assigned either to NET combined with WT or to WT only. The treatment lasted 26 weeks, on the basis of 2 or 3 computer sessions par week. The authors found that the combination of NET with WT showed greater improvements on measures of executive functions and working memory. These results were replicated in a latter study that also investigated NET combined with a vocational therapy (Greig et al., 2007). Following a similar path, Vauth and colleagues (2005) tested the combination of a computer-assisted cognitive training with vocational rehabilitation. They compared this combination with vocational rehabilitation alone in a randomized controlled trial including 138 participants with schizophrenia. The group receiving the combined therapies showed greater improvement on attention and verbal memory. Moreover, this group had a higher rate of successful job placement in a follow-up assessment 12 month after the end of the treatment. The three just mentioned studies suggest that CACR can help to improve vocational outcomes, which seems extremely relevant given the functional disabilities and occupational decline associated with schizophrenia.

The influence of CACR on social cognition is yet less obvious. As described above, trials assessing CACR report positive outcomes concerning cognitive impairments, symptoms and occupational disabilities. Few studies evaluated the possible impact on social abilities. Bell and colleagues (2001) report a progression of affect recognition, but this result was not replicated in a latter study (Greig et al., 2007). Hogarty and colleagues (2004) assessed social competencies in a two years randomized controlled trial including 121 patients. The treatment intervention they were experimenting is called cognitive enhancement therapy and includes CACR combined with social cognitive group exercises. Their results showed improvements on measures of social cognition and social adjustment after two years of treatment. Such improvements were not observable at the end of the first year. Computer-based training programs especially dedicated to social cognition have recently been developed (Silver et al., 2004; Wölwer et al., 2005). They essentially focus on emotion recognition and management. Wölwer and colleagues (2005) evaluated a computerized training program called "Tackling Affect Recognition" (TAR) in a randomized controlled trial involving 77 patients with schizophrenia. They compared this program with a traditional form of CACR. According to their results, remediation of emotional recognition was achievable with the TAR program but not with classical CACR. Silver and colleagues (2004) conducted a pilot study of a brief training intervention using software developed for teaching children with autism about emotions. Participants with schizophrenia improved on measures of emotion recognition. The next section describes computer-based social and emotional training in more details, based on the example of autism.

4. Computer-based socio-emotional training

4.1 The example of autism

Autism is defined as a pervasive developmental disorder (APA, 1994). The diagnosis is determined on the basis of the following triad of criteria: qualitative impairment in social interaction; qualitative impairment in communication; restricted, repetitive and stereotyped patterns of behavior, interests and activities. First signs leading to diagnosis appear before the age of 3 years. Both verbal and non-verbal communications are altered. The disorder strongly affects social interactions. Individuals' cognitive profiles vary considerably along the autism spectrum, despite the general common impairments defined in the diagnosis. Autism is frequently but not necessarily paired with intellectual retardation (Happé & Frith, 1996). Autism associated with normal or high IQ (Intelligence Quotient) is referred to as high functioning autism. People with high functioning autism may have a well-developed vocabulary but nevertheless have profound difficulties to understand social norms and sustain reciprocal social interactions (Volkmar, 1987).

Nadel and colleagues (2000) conducted an experiment showing that despite profound social disorders, people with autism could develop social expectations from others. Moreover, people with high functioning autism are reported to hold average performances in recognizing basic emotional facial expressions (Baron-Cohen et al., 1997), although their cerebral activity might differ from people without autism on such tasks (Critchley et al., 2000). The social dysfunctions arise when emotions are associated with a dynamic context. People with autism often fail to use perceived social and emotional information to self-regulate their own behaviour with an ongoing social situation (Loveland, 2005). Contextualizing problems pervade the entire social disorder in autism.

4.2 Empirical investigations

Computer science projects are being carried out and experimented to provide educational software for people with autism in the fields of emotional and social interactions. Bernard-Opitz and colleagues (2001) studied 10 sessions of training based on software used for social behavior education. Children had to find a solution to different scenarios involving characters in problematic social conflicts, for example two children arguing over who can use a slide first. They compared a group of 8 children with autism and a group of 8 children without autism. While the performances of both groups improved, the progression of the group without autism was steadier. Generalization of the acquired social skills to real life appeared to be possible when real situations were similar to those that had been trained on the computer. Leonard and colleagues (2002) designed a virtual reality system aimed at teaching social skills to people with high functioning autism. They evaluated the system with 6 adolescents. The virtual reality environment simulated a coffee house. Participants had to perform several social tasks inspired from real life situations, such as finding a place to sit without disturbing other clients. Results showed progression in dealing with the social situation that had been simulated. Generalization of learning was effective in real situations similar to the virtual environment but failed when the context differed. These experiments highlight the difficulties of transferring skills acquired during training to other contexts.

Collaborative use of educational software has also been explored. Rajendran and Mitchell (2000) conducted two case studies where the experimenter and the participant played together using a software game designed to foster adequate social responses. The game consisted of cartoons featuring two characters. The speech and thought bubbles of each character had to be filled in by the players. The experimenter played one character and the participant played the other one. Results showed no evidence of social skills improvement, but participants' performances increased on measures of executive functions. The authors suggested that, although the game they used targeted social skills, it could additionally involve various executive functions for planning dialogues and flexibility for alternating between thought and speech bubbles.

Several software projects focus on the use of Animated Conversational Agents (ACA) for teaching social skills to people with autism. ACA are considered relevant for practicing social and emotional skills because they communicate through modalities such as speech, facial expressions and gesture that are inspired from human communication. Moreover, while resembling human characters, researchers believe ACA can enable to control the interactions at a suitable level for people with autism. Bosseler and Massaro (2003) developed a language-learning tool based on a virtual 3-D talking head. The virtual head could realistically simulate the articulary movements of the mouth and tongue during speech. Eight children with autism were trained during 6 month with this tool. Pre-tests, post-tests and follow-up tests revealed that children acquired new vocabulary and that learning was maintained 30 days after the end of the training. Tartaro and Cassell (2006) designed an ACA used for training children with autism in collaborative storytelling. The ACA looked like a child and could communicate through speech, gesture and gaze. Moreover it was authorable, which means the child could specify and plan its interactions and control it during storytelling sessions with another person.

In an attempt to investigate the competencies of people with high functioning autism in understanding the emotions displayed by an ACA, Moore and colleagues (2005) conducted an experiment where participants were required to associate the facial expressions of virtual characters (happy, sad, angry, and frightened) with emotions or emotionally connoted social situations. The results showed some evidence that people with high functioning autism could assign the appropriate emotional facial expressions to the ACA, coherently with the social context. Golan and Baron-Cohen (2006) designed and evaluated a multimedia application to train recognition of complex emotions (such as embarrassment, insincerity, etc.) in both visual and auditory channels for people with high-functioning autism. Their application presented series of emotions in silent films of faces, faceless voice recordings and videos of emotionally connoted situations. Nineteen participants with high-functioning autism were trained with the software during 10-15 weeks. Participants improved in emotion recognition of faces and voices separately, but there was no evidence of progression concerning the holistic tasks involving videos that required integrating information from facial, vocal and contextual sources. The next section presents a study that addressed the latter point by exploring the ability to use facial expressions in the context of a dialogue.

5. Study on parallel training of cognitive and socio-emotional skills in autism

5.1 Training objectives

The goal of the study presented here was to explore a computer-based approach combining cognitive remediation and socio-emotional training for high-functioning autism. In the socio-emotional field, the training tackled contextualization difficulties attributed to autism with a specific focus on pragmatics. The main communication deficiency in autism relates to pragmatics (Paul, 1987). Authors report that people with high functioning autism have a tendency to interpret speech literally rather than in reference to a context (Attwood, 1998). They experience difficulties in interpreting pragmatic speech that conveys irony and metaphors (Happé, 1993). Jolliffe and Baron-Cohen (1999) carried out an experiment where participants had to understand a short text containing a semantically ambiguous word that required the context to be correctly interpreted. Participants had to choose between three possible interpretations of the ambiguity: the contextually correct interpretation, a literal and out of context interpretation and an erroneous non-literal interpretation. Results showed that participants with autism chose the literal interpretation more often than healthy controls. They tended to omit context although it was necessary for interpreting the text.

The main neurocognitive deficit targeted by the computer-based training described in this section was the executive dysfunction attributed to autism (Russell, 1996). The executive dysfunction theory in autism derives from analogies with patients sustaining brain injuries in the frontal lobes regions. As explained earlier, executive functions refer to cognitive constructs considered responsible for controlling behaviour, planning activities, inhibiting inappropriate responses and taking initiatives (Hill, 2004). People with autism are considered having difficulties with tasks involving inhibition of an appropriate response and flexibility of attention (Hughes & Russell, 1993). The training software designed for the present study consisted of a visuospatial planning game.

5.2 Experimental protocol

The study presented here was part of a broader experimental protocol that used a pre-post test design to assess a three months training using software games. The entire experimentation comprised 13 sessions. The first and the last sessions were dedicated to assessment. The training program was composed of the 11 in-between sessions. The training comprised three phases: a preparatory phase to introduce the software tasks (sessions 1 to 3), a mass training phase (sessions 4 to 8) and a final phase testing particular interface modalities described below (sessions 9 to 11). The focus here is on the final phase and especially on the last two sessions (sessions 10 and 11) for which participants were assumed to have acquired experience on the usage of the tested interface modalities.
As recruiting school students with high functioning autism is a complex procedure, the study was restrained to a small number of participants. Two groups took part in the experiment: a clinical group including 10 teenagers diagnosed with high functioning autism according to the DSM IV criteria (APA, 1994), and a typical group of 10 children without autism. The typical group served as a reference base for the clinical group. The groups were matched on developmental age and academic level. Participants attended the training individually and were assisted by an experimenter. They managed the software games using the mouse, on personal computers running Windows®. Participants were volunteers and their parents' written informed consent was requested and obtained. For more details about the experimental protocol, see (Grynszpan et al., 2007a).

5.3 Software games

An experimental software platform was developed to explore training with computer games. A software game (called "What to choose?") was designed for training pragmatics. It presented series of social scenarios displayed as written dialogues between two characters. Dialogues contained semantically ambiguous phrases that could be disambiguated only by taking into account the context. Pragmatic ambiguities relied on irony or metaphors. The game's interface prompted the user to select one of three assertions about each dialogue. Those three assertions followed a similar pattern to the one used in the experiment of Jolliffe and Baron-Cohen (1999): one assertion was a contextually correct interpretation of the pragmatic ambiguity, one was an out of context literal interpretation of the ambiguity and one was an erroneous non-literal interpretation.
To examine the impact of emotional facial expressions as pragmatic cues, the game included an interface modality which bounded each utterance of the dialogue to a 3-D image of the character's facial expression. When the user clicked on an utterance in the dialogue, the associated facial expression was displayed. For example, in Fig. 1, the 4th utterance in the dialogue is a metaphor and should not be interpreted literally. This utterance is associated with a facial expression of happiness so as to emphasize the contrast between what the character says literally and what she feels. The characters could display five emotional facial expressions (joy, sadness, fear, surprise, anger) as well as a neutral facial expression. These facial expressions were based on Ekman's descriptions (2003) and designed with Poser 5® from Curious Lab. The dialogue was displayed textually on the screen and uttered by a synthetic voice (IBM ViaVoice®).

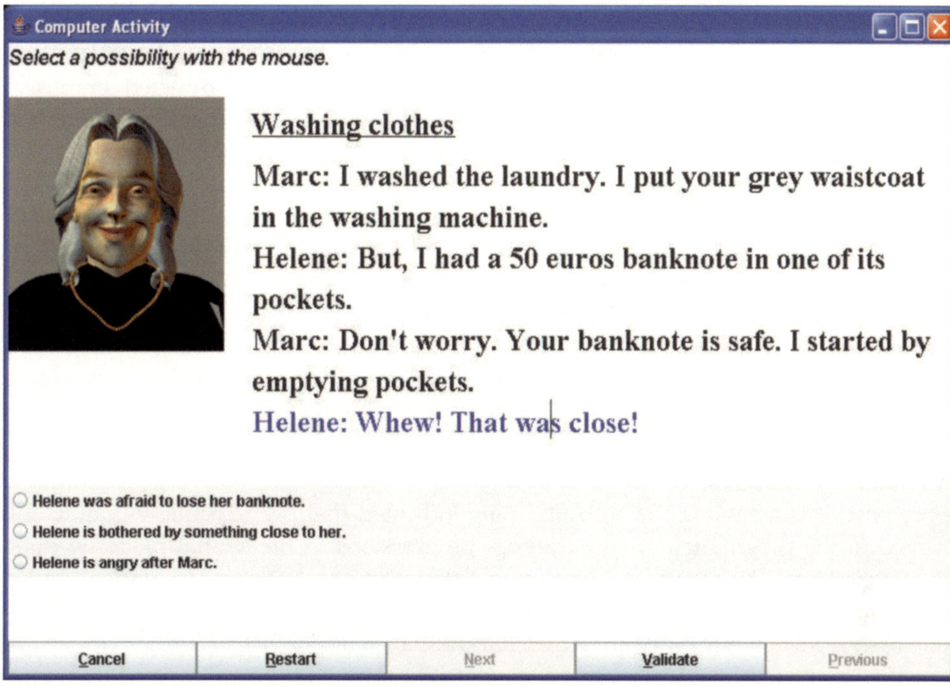

Figure 1. An example of the "What to choose" game with the facial expressions modality. The facial expression of "happiness" was displayed when the user clicked on the 4th utterance. This example is an English translation of the French dialogue that was actually used

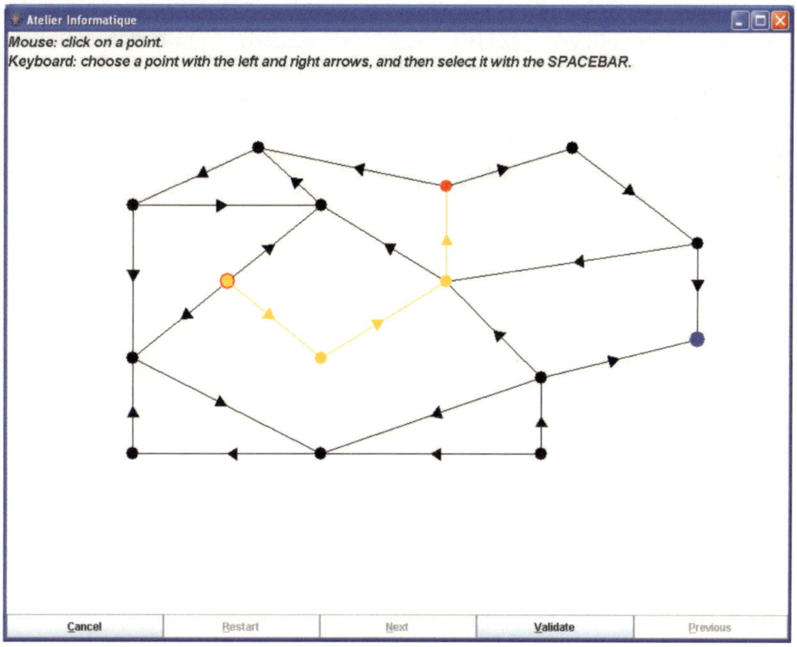

Figure 2. An example of the "Labyrinth" game. Participants would trace a route by clicking on successive nodes of the graph. The route that participants traced appeared in yellow

The game used for training visuospatial planning was called "Labyrinth" (Fig. 2). It displayed graphs where participants had to find a path between two nodes. Graphs were either directed or non-directed, although the main focus was on directed graphs. The directions of the edges were represented by arrows. The rule induced by directed edges was reinforced by the interface: an edge could not be crossed in the direction opposite to its arrow. Participants would click on successive nodes of the graph to trace a route. The route they traced appeared in a lighter colour than the rest of the graph. The interface enabled participants to come back to the previous node of the route, by clicking on the "Cancel" button. The route would not be modified on the interface if the participant tried to click on a node that was not connected to the route's current node by an edge with the appropriate direction. Indeed, these clicks were considered illegal in the context of the game's rules. The user's clicks were recorded in log files with a flag indicating whether they were legal or illegal.

5.4 Results and discussion

The pre-post tests assessing the entire training indicated that participants with autism had improved in the pragmatic domain whereas progressions in the spatial planning domain were less obvious. The overall evaluation of the training is discussed in another paper. It reveals that participants with autism experienced difficulties that could be linked to the executive dysfunction attributed to autism (Grynszpan et al., 2007a).

The results presented here focus on the peculiarities shown by participants with autism in handling of the above presented software. The typical group had significantly higher success rates than the clinical group on the "What to choose?" game. The details of the statistical analysis and the subsequent discussion may be found in (Grynszpan et al., 2008). The disambiguation cues provided by the facial expressions did not seem to help overcome the contextualizing deficiency of participants with autism. Qualitative observations and quantitative analysis suggest that participants with autism did not use facial expressions appropriately. Using facial expressions along with the text of the dialogue required users to shift their attention from one source of information to another, thus involving attention set-shifting skills considered linked to the executive dysfunction in autism (Hughes & Russell, 1993).

The executive dysfunction appears to impact performances in the visuospatial planning game as well. The results on the "Labyrinth" game show that the clinical group made significantly more illegal moves and backtracked significantly more than the typical group (Grynszpan et al., 2007b). This suggests that the clinical group relied to a greater extent on a trial and error strategy, which is the least demanding strategy in terms of planning and inhibiting inappropriate responses. Hence, the influence of the executive dysfunction attributed to autism was apparent in the two training games.

6. Conclusion

The present chapter reviewed two types of computer-based training approaches in psychopathology: cognitive remediation and socio-emotional training. The example of schizophrenia was employed for illustrating cognitive remediation and socio-emotional training was described in experiments involving autism. Following the literature review, this chapter described a longitudinal pilot study that investigated both cognitive

remediation and socio-emotional computer-based training in the case of autism. The analysis of data from this study suggests that the executive dysfunction attributed to autism could account for results in both types of training. Developers need to take into account the particular cognitive dysfunction attributed to a psychopathological disorder when designing training software intended for this disorder. These outcomes emphasize the need for further research on the specific software design principles in psychopathology that differ from design premises based on typical users.
The influence of computer-assisted cognitive remediation on social cognition has recently received increased attention. Several research projects presented in this chapter are closing the gap between cognitive remediation and socio-emotion training. Future research should explore these treatments for other psychopathological disorders, such as depression or anxiety.

7. Acknowledgments

I would like to thank the staff and pupils of the Parisian special classroom for teenagers with autism in the "Collège Stanislas". I am also grateful to the staff and pupils of the children's centre of Orsay.

8. References

APA (American Psychiatric Association) (1994) *Diagnostic and Statistical Manual of Mental Disorders – Fourth Edition (DSM-IV)*, American Psychiatric Association, Washington D.C.

Attwood, T. (1998) *Asperger syndrome, A guide for Parents and Professionals*, Jessica Kingsley, London

Baron-Cohen, S., Jolliffe, T., Mortimore, C., Robertson, M. (1997). Another advanced test of theory of mind: evidence from very high functioning adults with autism or asperger syndrome, *Journal of Child Psychology and Psychiatry*, 38, 7, 813-822

Bell, M., Bryson, G., Greig, T., Corcoran, C., Wexler, B.E. (2001) Neurocognitive enhancement therapy with work therapy: effects on neuropsychological test performance, *Archives of General Psychiatry*, 58, 8, 763-768

Bellucci, D.M., Glaberman, K., Haslam, N. (2002) Computer-assisted cognitive rehabilitation reduces negative symptoms in the severely mentally ill, *Schizophrenia Research*, 59, 225-232

Bernard-Opitz, V., Sriram, N., Nakhoda-Sapuan, S. (2001) Enhancing Social Problem Solving in Children with Autism and Normal Children Through Computer-Assisted Instruction, *Journal of Autism and Developmental Disorders*, 31, 4, 377-384

Bosseler, A., Massaro, D.W. (2003) Development and evaluation of a computer-animated tutor for vocabulary and language learning in children with autism, *Journal of Autism Developmental Disorders*, 33, 6, 653-672

Bracy, O. (1981) *PSSCogRehab Software*, Psychological Software Services Inc., Indianapolis, IN, USA, available at: http://www.neuroscience.cnter.com/pss/psscogrehab.html

Burda, P.C., Starkey, T.W., Dominguez, F., Vera, V. (1994) Computer-Assisted Cognitive Rehabilitation of Chronic Psychiatric Inpatients, *Computers in Human Behavior*, 10, 3, 359-368

Butti, G., Buzzelli, S., Fiori, M., Giaquinto, S. (1998) Observations on Mentally Impaired Elderly Patients Treated with THINKable, a Computerized Cognitive Remediation, *Archives of Gerontology and Geriatrics*, 26, 5, 49-56

Castellucci, V.F., Carew, T.J., Kandel, E.R. (1978) Cellular analysis of long-term habituation of the gill-withdrawal reflex of Aplysia californica, *Science*, 202, 4374, 1306-1308

Craig, T. (2006) What is Psychiatric Rehabilitation? In: *Part1. Enabling Recovery: The Principles and Practice of Rehabilitation Psychiatry*, Glenn Roberts, Sarah Davenport, Frank Holloway & Theresa Tattan (Ed.), 3-17, Gaskell (Royal College of Psychiatrists), Cromwell Press Limited, ISBN: 1-904671-30-6, Trowbridge, UK.

Critchley, H.D., Daly, E.M., Bullmore, E.T., Williams, S.C.R., Van Amelsvoort, T.V., Robertson, D.M., Rowe, A., Phillips, M., McAlonan, G., Howlin, P., Murphy, D.G.M. (2000), The functional neuroanatomy of social behaviour - Changes in cerebral blood flow when people with autistic disorder process facial expressions, *Brain*, 123, 11, 2203-2212

Difede, J., Hoffman, H., Jaysinghe, N. (2002) Innovative Use of Virtual Reality Technology in the Treatment of PTSD in the Aftermath of September 11, *Psychiatric Services*, 53, 1083-1085

Ekman, P. (2003) *Emotions Revealed*, Weidenfeld & Nicolson, London

Field, C.D., Galletly, C., Anderson, D., Walker, P. (1997) Computer-aided cognitive rehabilitation: possible application to the attentional deficit of schizophrenia, a report of negative results, *Perceptual and motor skills*, 85, 3 Pt 1, 995-1002

Golan, O., Baron-Cohen, S. (2006) Systemizing empathy: Teaching adults with Asperger syndrome or high-functioning autism to recognize complex emotions using interactive multimedia, *Development and Psychopathology*, 18, 591-617

Greig, T.C., Zito, W., Wexler, B.E., Fiszdon, J., Bell, M.D. (2007) Improved cognitive function in schizophrenia after one year of cognitive training and vocational services, *Schizophrenia Research*, 96, 156-161

Grynszpan, O., Martin, J.C., Nadel, J. (2007a) Exploring the influence of task assignment and output modalities on computerized training for autism, *Interaction Studies*, 8, 2, 241-266

Grynszpan, O., Martin, J.C., Nadel, J. (2007b) What influences Human Computer Interaction in Autism? *Proceedings of the 6th IEEE International Conference on Development and Learning*, July 11-13th, London, UK

Grynszpan, O., Martin, J.C., Nadel, J. (2008) Multimedia interfaces for users with high functioning autism: an empirical investigation, *International Journal of Human-Computer Studies*, 66, 628-639

Happé, F. (1993) Communicative competence and theory of mind in autism: A test of relevance theory, *Cognition*, 48, 101-119

Happé, F., Frith, U. (1996) The neuropsychology of autism, *Brain*, 119, 1377-1400

Heinrichs, R.W., Zakzanis, K.K. (1998) Neurocognitive Deficit in Schizophrenia: A Quantitative Review of the Evidence, *Neuropsychology*, 2, 3, 426-445

Hill, E.L. (2004) Evaluating the theory of executive dysfunction in autism, *Developmental Review*, 24, 189-223

Hogarty, G.E., Flesher, S., Ulrich, R., Carter, M., Greenwald, D., Pogue-Geile, M., Kechavan, M., Cooley, S., DiBarry, A.L., Garrett, A., Parepally, H., Zoretich, R. (2004) Cognitive enhancement therapy for schizophrenia: effects of a 2-year randomized trial on cognition and behavior, *Archives of General Psychiatry*, 61, 9, 866-876

Hughes, C., Russell, J. (1993) Autistic children's difficulty with mental disengagement from an object: Its implications for theories of autism, *Developmental Psychology*, 29, 498-510

Jolliffe, T., Baron-Cohen, S. (1999) A test of central coherence theory: linguistic processing in high-functioning adults with autism or Asperger syndrome: is local coherence impaired? *Cognition*, 71, 2, 149-185

Josman, N., Somer, E., Reisberg, A., Weiss, P.L., Garcia-Palacios, A., Hoffman, H. (2006) BusWorld: Designing a Virtual Environment for Past-Traumatic Stress Disorder in Israel: A Protocol, *CyberPsychology & Behavior*, 9, 2, 241-244

Kandel, E.R. (1998) A New Intellectual Framework for Psychiatry, *American Journal of Psychiatry*, 155, 4, 457-469

Knott, GW., Quairiaux, C., Genoud, C., Welker, E. (2002) Formation of dentritic spines with GABAergic synapses induced by whisker stimulation in adult mice, *Neuron*, 34, 265-273

Kurtz, M.M., Seltzer, J.C., Shagan, D.S., Thime, W.R., Wexler, B.E. (2007) Computer-assisted cognitive remediation in schizophrenia: What is the active ingredient?, *Schizophrenia Research*, 89, 1-3, 251-260

Leonard, A., Mitchell P., Parsons S. (2002), Finding a place to sit: a preliminary investigation into the effectiveness of virtual environments for social skills training for people with autistic spectrum disorders. *Proceedings of the 4th International Conference on Disability, Virtual Reality and Associated Technology*, pp. 249-258, ISBN 0704911434, Veszprém, Hongrie.

LoPresti, E.F., Mihailidis, A., Kirsch, N. (2004) Assistive technology for cognitive rehabilitation: State of the art, *Neuropsychological Rehabilitation*, 14, 1/2, 5-39

Loveland, K.A. (2005) Social-emotional impairment and self-regulation in autism spectrum disorders, In: *Emotional Development: Recent research advances*, J. Nadel & D. Muir (Ed.), 365-382, Oxford University Press, Oxford

Medalia, A., Revheim, N., Casey, M. (2000) Remediation of memory disorders in schizophrenia, *Psychological Medicine*, 30, 1451-1459

Medalia, A., Revheim, N., Casey, M. (2001) The Remediation of Problem-Solving Skills in Schizophrenia, *Schizophrenia Bulletin*, 27, 2, 259-267

Moore, D., Cheng, Y., McGrath, P., Powell, N.J. (2005) Collaborative Virtual Environment Technology for People with Autism, *Focus on Autism and Other Developmental Disorders*, 20, 4, 231-243

Nadel, J., Croue, S., Mattlinger, M.J., Canet, P., Hudelot, C., Lecuyer, C., Martini, M. (2000). Do children with autism have expectancies about the social behaviour of unfamiliar people? *Autism*, 4, 2, 133-145

Nuechterlein, K.H., Barch, D.M., Gold, J.M., Goldberg, T.E., Green, M.F., Heaton, R.K. (2004) Identification of separable cognitive factors in schizophrenia, *Schizophrenia Research*, 72, 29-39

Panyan, M.V. (1984) Computer Technology for Autistic Students, *Journal of Autism and Developmental Disorders*, 14, 4, 375-382

Paul, R. (1987) Communication. In: *Handbook of Autism and Pervasive Developmental Disorders*, D.J. Cohen, A.M. Donnellan & R. Paul (Ed.), 61-84, John Wiley & Sons, New York

Rajendran, G., Mitchell, P. (2000) Computer mediated interaction in Asperger's syndrome : the Bubble Dialogue program, *Computer & Education*, 35, 189-207

Russell, J. (1996) *Agency Its Role in Mental Development*, Taylor&Francis, Erlbaum, UK

Sandford, J.A., Browne, R.J. (1988) Capitain's *Log Cognitive System*, Brain Train, Richmond, VA, USA, available at: http://www.braintrain.com/educators/captains_log/captainslog_educator.htm

Sartory, G., Zorn, C., Groetzinger, G., Windgassen, K. (2005) Computerized cognitive remediation improves verbal learning and processing speed in schizophrenia, *Schizophrenia Research*, 75, 2-3, 219-223

Silver, H., Goodman, C., Knoll, G., Isakov, V. (2004) Brief emotion training improves recognition of facial emotions in chronic schizophrenia. A pilot study, *Psychiatry Research*, 128, 2, 147-154. Erratum in: *Psychiatry Research* 2004 Nov 30, 129, 1, 113

Tartaro, A., Cassell, J. (2006) Authorable Virtual Peers for Autism Spectrum Disorders, *Proceedings of the Workshop on Language-Enabled Educational Technology at the 17th European Conference on Artificial Intelligence (ECAI06)*, Riva del Garda, Italy

Van Praag, H., Schinder, A.F., Christie, B.R., Toni, N., Palmer, T.D., Gage, F.H. (2002) Functional neurogenesis in the adult hippocampus, *Nature*, 415, 1030-1034

Vauth, R., Corrigan, P.W., Clauss, M., Dietl, M., Dreher-Rudolph, M., Stieglitz, R.D., Vater, R. (2005) Cognitive Strategies Versus Self-Management Skills as Adjunct to Vocational Rehabilitation, *Schizophrenia Bulletin*, 31, 1, 55-66

Volkmar, F.R. (1987). Social Development. In: *Handbook of Autism and Pervasive Developmental Disorders*, D.J. Cohen, A.M. Donnellan & R. Paul (Ed.), 61-84, John Wiley & Sons, New York.

Walker, E., Kestler, L., Bollini, A., Hochman, K.M. (2004) Schizophrenia: Etiology and Course, *Annual Review of Psychology*, 55, 401-430

Wilson, B.A., Emslie, H.C., Quirk, K., Evans, J.J. (2001) Reducing everyday memory and planning problems by means of a paging system: a randomised control study, *Journal of Neurology, Neurosurgery and Psychiatry*, 70, 477-482

Wölwer, W., Frommann, N., Halfmann, S., Piaszek, A., Streit, M., Gaebel, W. (2005) Remediation of impairments in facial affect recognition in schizophrenia: efficacy and specificity of a new training program, *Schizophrenia Research*, 80, 2-3, 295-303

Wykes, T., van der Gaag, M. (2001) Is it time to develop a new cognitive therapy for psychosis - Cognitive Remediation Therapy (CRT)?, *Clinical Psychology Review*, 21, 81, 1227-1256

12

Facial Expression Recognition as an Implicit Customers' Feedback

Zolidah Kasiran, Saadiah Yahya (Dr) and Zaidah Ibrahim
Faculty of Information Technology & Quantitative Science, Universiti Teknologi MARA Malaysia

1 Introduction

In social interaction, face is playing an important role. Social psychology researches had agreed that among the three mediums in communication, facial expression is the one that is always active. Mehrabian [1] indicated that the verbal part of a message contributes only for 7 percent to the effect of the message as a whole; the vocal part contributes for 38 percent, while facial expression of the speaker contributes for 55 percent to the effect of the spoken message.

Psychologists Paul Ekman and Friesen in 1978 had come with a method to classifying muscle movement to measure the facial expression. This method, which later became the mostly used in classifying facial movement in behavioral science, is called Facial Action Coding System (FACS). Most of the research work on Facial Expression Recognition refers to the Facial Action Coding System. Paul Ekman [2], believed that basic emotion is universal, though he challenge those who can claim otherwise. The universality of emotion expression proposed by (Ekman,1999) was supported by various researchers. The study of emotion universality [3] using American and Indian to recognize emotion expression of 45 selected pictures had convinced that there is existence of universality in emotion expression. People from different backgrounds display similar expression in respond to similar stimuli [4], but it is reasonable to expect local variations. Thus Ekman suggested that extreme positions regarding the universality of emotion are incomplete. Seven Basic emotions established are; happy, sadness, anger, surprise, fear, disgust, and contempt.

2 Related Work

The research, facial expression analysis received significant attention with the wide range of commercial application and more feasible technologies available. All the existing methods for automated facial expression recognition are mainly based on three steps: face acquisition, facial extraction and facial expression identification from the observed facial image or image sequence.

The works of facial expression analysis has evolved from recognizing expression in static image to video and in simple background to complex background with different pose and illumination changes. Facial feature extraction is another challenging step and most of the works in extracting facial feature employed either motion-based method or deformation of face. Motion-based[[5, 6] method focuses directly on the occurring changes in the face due to the facial expression while deformation-based[[7-9] have to rely on neutral face images or face model in order to extract facial features that are relevant to facial action. The processing of the facial feature could be done either locally or holistically where the face is process by focusing on facial feature areas that are prone to changes or the whole face to the latter.

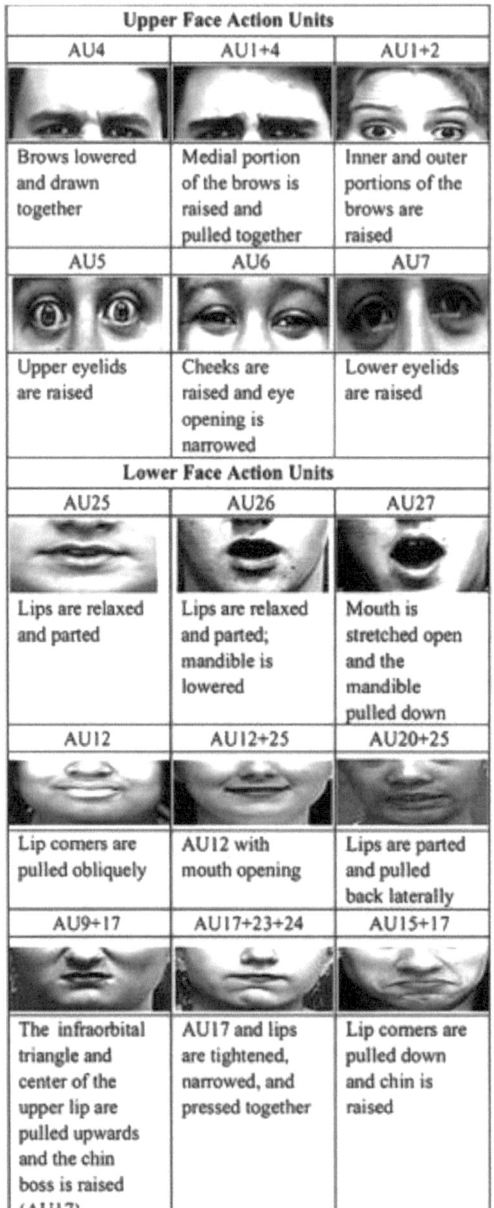

Figure 1. Sample Aus coded in FACS (Ekman and Friesen 78)

Research in machine learning techniques for spontaneous facial expression recognition that involves muscles movement have been widely conducted [10, 11]. In order to capture the facial expressions, Facial Action Coding System (FACS) has been developed[12, 13]. FACS identifies all visually distinguishable facial activity that relates to individual facial muscles in expressing different expressions, such as, happy, sad, angry, surprise, fear and disgust on the basis of 44 action units (AU). Each AU has a numeric code that relates to the different expression. Figure 1 show some examples of the AUs coded in FACS and the muscle groups involved in each action.

2.1 Tracking

The first step in automatic facial expression recognition is to track the face in the video sequences. Tracking of object motions like the head or the face in a video sequence is important for good facial expression classification. Object motion can be the result of either camera motion with static object or object motion with static camera. Discussions on various tracking techniques can be found in [14-17]. This tracking can be achieved by detecting:

- Skin color using Gaussian models, histogram analysis and color probability distribution
- Geometric features like corners of the eyes, mouth, iris, brow or cheek
- 2D template model
- Deformable contours (also known as snakes) of objects like eyes and mouth

Figure 2(a) - 1(c) illustrate some samples on the face tracking techniques. Once the facial expression features have been extracted, they can be transferred to the facial expression recognition for facial expression classification.

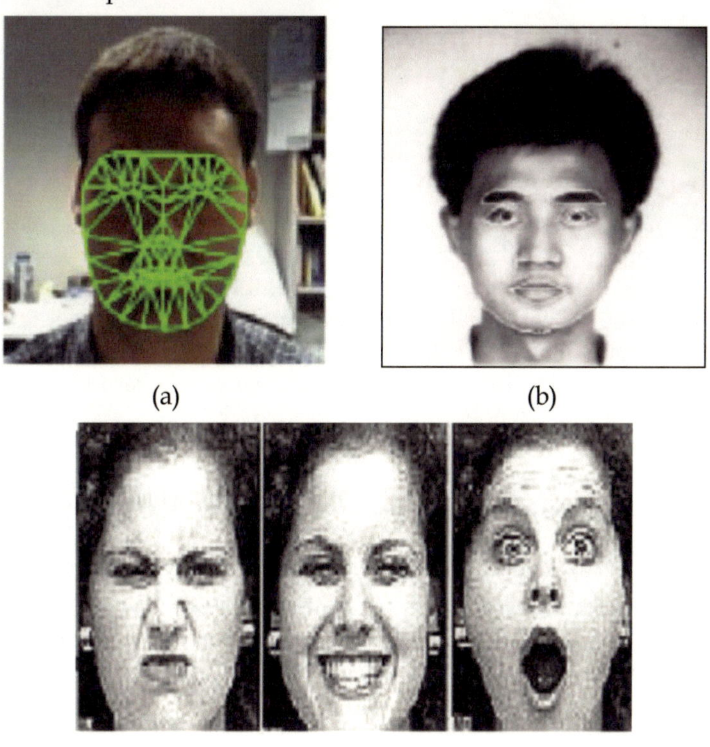

(a) (b)

(c)

Figure 2. (a) Face tracking using 2D model, (b) Face tracking using active contour, c) Face tracking using contours of objects like corners of eyes and mouth (Wang and Singh 03)

2.2 Facial expression recognition techniques

There exist various techniques for facial expression recognition. Among the popular ones are artificial neural network (ANN)[18-20] and support vector machines (SVM)[21, 22]. ANNs were inspired from brain modeling studies that consists of layered network of artificial neurons (AN) [14]. An AN receives a vector of input signals, either from the environment or from other ANs. Each input signal is multiplied with a weight that is randomly selected to strengthen or deplete the input signal. Then, the output signal is produced by applying an activation function. Learning process is conducted by adjusting the values of the weight. An ANN may consist of multi-layers of AN but usually it consist of an input layer, hidden layers and output layer. Each AN in each layer is connected to other AN in the other layers. A typical architecture of the ANN is shown in Figure 3.

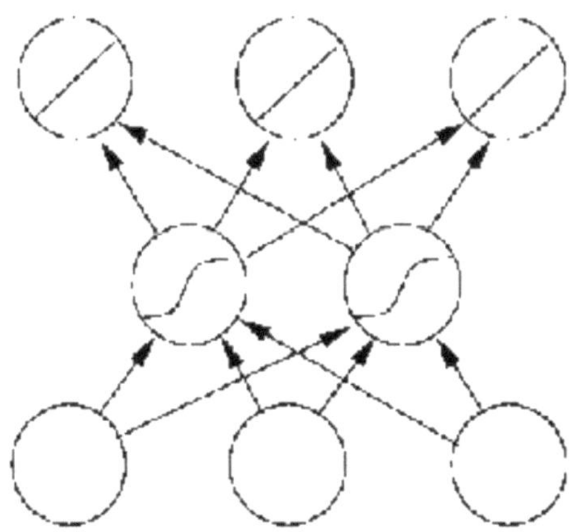

Figure 3. Typical architecture of an ANN

In facial expression recognition, the input nodes for the input layer may be represented as a vector of the color probability distribution of an image if the skin color is being used as the input features. If geometric features are being used, then the vectors may be the distance between the coordinates of the facial features like the top and bottom of the mouth or the eyes. Training process will be conducted to train the ANN by applying either a supervised or unsupervised learning algorithm. In supervised learning, a set of input and the target output is shown to the ANN while in unsupervised ANN, the ANN will cluster the input data into various patterns. Back propagation is one of the widely used supervised learning algorithms. Self-organizing map (SOM) is an example of an unsupervised ANN. Then, testing phase can be performed to measure the classification rate. Feedforward neural network (FFNN) and backpropagation neural network (BPNN) are two of the widely used supervised learning algorithms and enhancements have been made to the FFNN and BPNN to improve the classification performance. Constructive FFNN has been applied in [18] where a two-dimensional discrete cosine transform (DCT) for the entire face image has been used as the feature vector. The vertical distance, size and angle for the eyebrows, eyes and mouth have been used as the feature vector in [20] with enhanced FFNN classifier. Similar feature vectors have also being applied for the SVM in [21]. Self-organizing map (SOM) is an example of an unsupervised ANN. Then, testing phase can be performed to measure the classification rate. A 2D-template model is being used for the SVM in [22].

The SVM formulation uses the Structural Risk Minimization (SRM) principle while the ANN formulation uses the Empirical Risk Minimization (ERM). SRM minimizes an upper bound on the expected risk, while ERM minimizes the error on the training data[23].
The works of facial expression had been implement in many area such as security, biometric, robotic and Human Computer Interaction and [24] had suggest the ideal system that all of stages of facial expression analysis are to be performed automatically from face detection to facial expression information extraction and facial expression classification. The characteristics of automatic facial expression classifier are also mentioned as in Table 1 and Table 2.

	Characteristic
1	Automatic facial image acquisition
2	Subjects of any age, ethnicity and outlook
3	Deals with variation in lightning
4	Deals with partially occluded faces
5	No special markers/ make-up required
6	Deals with rigid head motions
7	Automatic Face detection
8	Automatic facial expression data extraction
9	Deal with inaccurate facial expression data
10	Automatic facial expression classification
11	Distinguishes all possible expression
12	Deals with unilateral facial changes
13	Obeys anatomical rules

Table 1. General Characteristic of automatic facial expression classifier

	CHARACTERISTIC
1.	Distinguishes all 44 facial actions
2.	Quantifies facial action codes
3	# interpretation categories unlimited
4.	Features adaptive learning facility
5.	Assigns quantified interpretation labels
6.	Assign multiple interpretation labels
7.	Features real time processing

Table 2. Characteristic of automatic facial expression classifier in Behavioral Science and HCI

Researcher [25] is an active researcher in facial expression area and she evaluates few face recognition and facial expression recognition techniques under various resolutions. The author found that the combination of technique gave a better result and the lowest resolution that the technique can still perform is 36x48.

3. Facial Expression And Satisfaction Level

Recent advances in image analysis and pattern recognition open up the possibility of automatic detection and classification of emotional and conversational facial signals. Possible area that could use the advance technology of Facial expression recognition system is the customer satisfaction measurement. The expression of customer being served at the counter is captured to evaluate the satisfaction of the customer. This multimedia approach of customer satisfaction measurement is an alternative of the conventional way of collecting customers' response.

Quality measurement and improvement have been an important agenda in many organizations to stay competitive. A good quality measurement needs a good instrument and most of the literature on quality service measurement is based on customer's perception, which is translated into numbers using likert scale. Perception is very subjective and complicated to be translated into numbers. Thus it is important to have a new way of collecting information that is more precise and scientific to make performance measurement more meaningful.

The objective of this work is to measure the satisfaction level of the new students during the registration process. Five parties were involves during the registration of new students at INTEC, UITM; Admission & Record, Bursary, Accommodation and Sponsor. The students were informed that their picture would be taken during the registration process for academic research purposes. The video was captured during the last transactions of the registration process, which is at the sponsors counter. To ease the registration process, the setup of the registration counters was arranged such that all involved parties for the registration were placed at the ad hoc registration venue.

4. Challenges Of Collecting User Satisfaction Based On Facial Expression

Facial expression recognition system may be able to classify intangible values like customer satisfaction. The system involve seven steps namely; identifying the best technique in facial expression, acquiring a library of images for system training, installing the appropriate camera and hardware/software at the identified location for the data collection, capturing the images in the real environment (as the customer is being served at the counter), storing the captured images in the database, processing the images, and store the processed result in the database. Figure 4 illustrates the process of image processing.

In facial expression analysis, mouth and eyes features are playing an important role and both features should be visible in order to extract the correct expression. [26, 27]works focus on upper and frontal view of facial features which are eye brows and eyes, while [28] works focus on recognizing facial expression in profile image sequence. Multistate face component models have been developed by [29] to handle different head pose. Different states head pose have to use different face component model to ensure the robustness of the systems. For example, a lip model of the front face does not work for a profile face.

Based on the different appearances of different components, different geometric models are used to model the component's location, shape, and appearance. Each component employs a multistate model corresponding to different component states. For example, a three state lip model is defined to describe the lip states whether it is opened, closed, and tightly closed. A two state eye model is used to model opened and closed eye. There is one state for brow and cheek. Present and absent are use to model the states of the transient facial features. Seven head states (left, leftfront, front, rightfront, right, down, and up) are shown in Figure5.

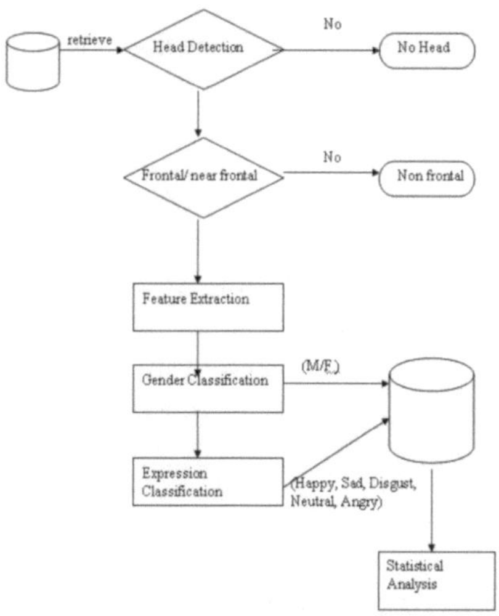

Figure 4. Sequence Image processing

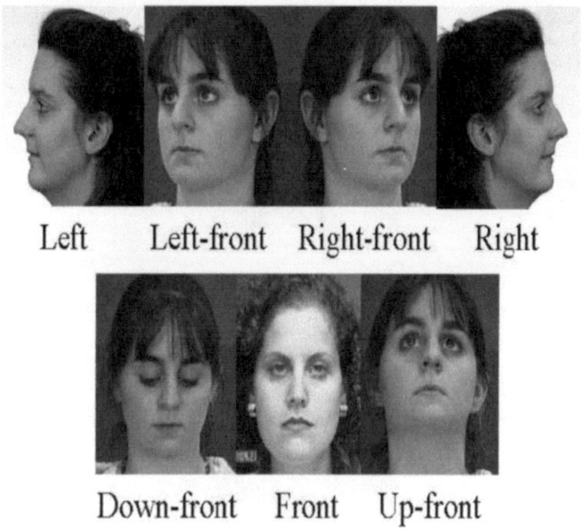

Figure 5. Multistate Face Model

Most of data collections for the available databases are set up in the laboratory where the facial expressions were not spontaneous. Though few researchers have been conducting the research on the spontaneous behavior., their work ([30],[31]) collect the data by recording the subject while there were interviewed on a selected topic in controlled environment but the subjects were free to move their heads and out-of plan head was presents during the discourse.

Affective computing which apply the automatic facial recognition techniques is getting more attention ([32],[33],[9],[34]). The main idea of affective computing is that the computer could better adjust its behavior to user's current emotion. In this user-centered research, the data were collected by mounting the camera on the computer monitor and user's facial expression was captured during user interaction with the systems. The software will intelligently change its behavior according to the expression of the users. If the user's facial expression show a sad expression, the software will interpret that user do not understand how to use the systems. The data is gathered and store in the database to be use later on how much the user happy with the systems. Affective computing have little challenges in collecting the data because user is always facing the monitor while using the systems and thus frontal or near frontal view is not so hard to obtain.

Facial expression application for spontaneous behavior such as at the counter service of student registration may have problem in data collection due to physical counter set up. On the normal counter service, staff on duty was seated behind a table while the customers (student) who was being served was either sitting down or standing up. When the customer is seated in front of the staff, the staff may obstruct the customer. Hence the frontal view is not possible. While when the customer is standing up forces the customer (student) to look down at the table and makes the image capturing very difficult. During the service, both student and staff were moving their head and obstructing the camera from capturing the student's face as shown in figure 6 (a).

The images in the database set up from laboratory making sure that the face is not occluded by the subject's hair as in figure 6 (b). Though the down-front face state have been mentioned by [29], in real environment , subjects tend look down that make it hard to track the mouth and eyes (figure 6 (c)-(e)).

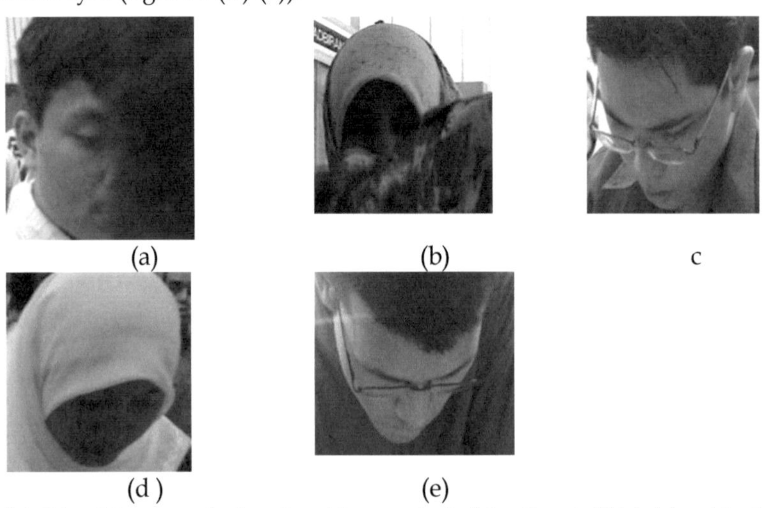

Figure 6. (a)-(b) subject was facing front but occluded by the staff (c)-(e) subject were facing down

5. Conclusion

The facial expression recognition has attracted intense attention from various group of computer vision research team and many techniques had been developed and many areas of application could benefit from it. The performance of an ANN may depend on the number of the training data or the parameters of the ANN like the learning rate or the threshold value. Similar experiments for the SVM can also be conducted. Thus, various experiments in tuning the values of the ANN and SVM parameters need to be made in order to maximize the classification performance. Comparative study between ANN and SVM for image classification could also be performed since the same training and testing data could be applied. Future research could be made to compare the classification performance between ANN and SVM and there is always room for further enhancements for both techniques in improving the performance.

The effort of facial expression capturing in the real environment has been elaborated. The challenges and difficulties encountered when performing the experimentation were also highlighted. This work should be able to substantiate the holistic customer satisfaction study from the facial expression perspective rather than from the conventional customer satisfaction survey. The finding may benefit all enterprises that are concerned with their customer satisfaction in order to ascertain good management of supply chain and hence sustain strategic advantages and competitiveness.

6. References

Mehrabian, A., *Nonverbal Communication.* 1972, Chicago: Aldine Atherton Inc. [1]

Ekman, P., Basic Emotion, in *Handbook of Cognition and Emotion.* Su, T.D.a. M.Power(Eds.), Editor. 1999, John Wiley & Sons, Ltd: Sussex, UK. [2]

Ahalya Hejmadi, R.J.D., Paul Rozin, Exploring Hindu India Emotion Expression: Evidence for Accurate Recognition by Americans and Indians. *Psychological Science,* 2000. 11[3].

Abigail A Marsh, H.A.E., Nalini Ambay, NonVerbal "Accents": Cultural Differences in Facial Expressions of Emotion. *Psychological Science,* 2003. 14[4].

Masahiro Nishiyama, H.K., Takatsugu Hirayama, Takashi Matsuyama. Facial Expression representation based on timing structures in faces. in *IEE Int' workshop on Analysis Modeling of faces and Gestures.* 2005. [5]

Lee, K.K.C., Human expression and Intention via motion analysis:Learning, recognition and ystem implementation, in Graduate School. 2004, The Chinese University of Hong Kong. [6]

Pantic M, R.L.J.M. An expert system for multiple emotional classification of facial expressions. in *IEEE International Conference on Tools with Artificial Intelligence,.* 1999. [7]

Fadi Dornaika, F.D. Simultaneous facial action tracking and expression recognition using particle filter. in *Internation Conference on Computer Vision.* 2005. [8]

Zhihong Zeng, J.T., Ming Liu, Tong Zhang, Nicholas Rizzoto, Zhenqiu Zhang. Bimodal HCI-related Affect Recognition. in I*nternational Conference Multimodal Interfaces.* 2004. State College, PA, USA. [9]

Zeng, Z., Spontaneous emotional facaial expression detection. *Journal of Multimedia,* 2006. 1(5). [10]

M. S. Bartlett, J.R.M., G. Littlewort, B. Braathen, Frank M. G., Claudia Lainscsek, Ian Fasel, Javier Movellan, Automatic Recognition of facial actions in spontaneous expressions. *Journal of Multimedia,* 2006. [11]

Ekman P, F., Facial Action Coding System: A Technique for the measurement of facial Movement. 1998: *Consulting Psychologist Press.* [12]

Rossenberg, E.P.a., What the Face Reveals: Basic and Applied Studies of Spontaneous Expression using the Facial Action Coding System. 1998: Oxford University Press. [13]

S, W.J.J.a.S., Video Analysis of Human Dynamics- A survey. *Real-Time Imaging* 9, 2003. [14]

Beat Fasel, a.L.J., Automatic Facial Expression Analysis : A survey. *Pattern Recognition*, 2003. 36. [15]

Maja Pantic, I.P.a.R. Facial Action Recognition in Face Profile Image Sequence. in *IEEE International Conference on Multimedia and Expo*. 2002. [16]

Chuang E S, D.H.a.B.C. Facial Expression Space Learning. in 10th *Pacific Conference on Cumputer Graphics and Application*. 2002. [17]

K, M.L.a.K. Facial Expression Recognition using Constructive Feedforward Neural Network. in *IEEE Transaction on Systems Man nad Cybernatics*. 2004. [18]

Dang P, s.H., Ham F and Lewis F L. Facial expression Recognition Using Two Stage Neural Network. in *Mediterranean Conference on Control and Automation*. 2007. [19]

C, T.S.C.a.C.K., Automatic Facial Expression Recognition System using Neural Networks. *IEEE Transactions on Pattern Analysis and Machine Intelligence*, 2007. [20]

Littlewort G, b.M.S., Fasel I, Susskind J and Movellan J, Dynamics of Facial Expression Extracted Automatically From Video. *Image and Vision Computing*, 2006. 24. [21]

Sebe N, L., M S, Sun Y, Cohen I, gevers T and Huang T S, Authentic Facial Expression Analysis. *Image Facial Analysis*, 2007. 25. [22]

C, B., A tutorial on Support Vector machines For Pattern Recognition. *Data mining Knowledge Discovery*, 1998. 2. [23]

Pantic Maja, a.L.J.M.R. Self-adaptive Expert System for Facial Expression Analysis. in *International Conference on System, Man and Cybernetic*. 2000b. [24]

Tian, Y. Evaluation of Face Resolution for Expression Analysis. in *IEEE Wokshop on face Processing in Video* (FPIV'04). 2004. Washington DC. [25]

Ashish Kapoor, Y.Q., Rosalind W Picard. Fully automatic upper facial action recognition. in *IEEE Int' workshop on Analysis and Modeling of Faces and Gestures*. 2003. [26]

Takeo Kanade, Y.T., T. Kanade, J. F. Cohn and Jeffrey F. Cohn. Comprehensive Database for Facial Expression Analysis. in *Fourth IEEE International Conference on Automatic Face and Gesture Recognition*. 2000. [27]

Pantic M, I.P., Rothkrantz L.J.M. Facial action recognition in Face profile image sequence. in *IEEE Int Conf on Multimedia and Expo*. 2002. Laussane. [28]

Yingli Tian, T.K., Jeffrey F Cohn, Multistate based facial feature tracking and detection. 1999. [29]

M. S. Bartlett, J.R.M., G. Littlewort, B. Braathen, Frank M. G., Claudia Lainscsek,Ian Fasel, Javier Movellan. Fully automatic facial action recognition in spontaneous behavior. in *7th Int. Conference on Automatic Face & Gesture Recognition*. 2006. [30]

Jeffrey F Cohn, P.E., Measuring Facial Action by Manual Coding, Facial EMG, and Automatic Facial Image Analysis, in *Handbook of nonverbal behavior research methods in the effective sciences*, R.R.K.S. J.A Harrigan, Editor. 2004, Oxford: NY. [31]

Amr Goneid, R.E.K. Facial Feature Analysis of Spontaneous Facial Expression. in *10th International Artificial Intelligent Conferences*. 2002. [32]

Lesley Axelrod, K.H. E-motional advantage: Performance and satisfaction gains with affective computing. in *HCI 2005*. 2005. [33]

Abdolhossein Sarrafzadeh, H.G.H., Chao Fan, Scott P Overmyer. Facial Expression Analysis for Estimating Learner's Emotional State in Intelligent Tutoring Systems. in *IEEE Conference on Advanced Learning Technologies*(ICALT'03). 2003. [34]

13

Natural Interaction Framework for Navigation Systems on Mobile Devices

Ceren Kayalar and Selim Balcisoy
Sabanci University
Turkey

1. Introduction

Mobile Augmented Reality (AR) applications based on navigation frameworks try to promote interaction beyond the desktop by employing wearable sensors, which collect user's position, orientation or diverse types of activities. Most navigation frameworks track location and heading of the user in the global coordinate frame using Global Positioning System (GPS) data. On the other hand, in the wearable computing area researchers studied angular data of human body segments in the local coordinate frame using inertial orientation trackers.

In this work, we introduce a combination of global and local coordinate frame approaches and provide a context-aware interaction framework for mobile devices by seamlessly changing Graphical User Interfaces (GUIs) for pedestrians navigating and working in urban environments. The system is designed and tested both on a Personal Digital Assistant (PDA) based navigation system prototype and ultra mobile PC based archaeological fieldwork assistant prototype. In both cases, the computing device is mounted with a GPS receiver and inertial orientation tracker. We introduce a method to estimate orientation of a mobile user's hand. The recognition algorithm is based on state transitions triggered by time-line analysis of pitch angle and angular velocity of the orientation tracker. The prototype system can differentiate between three postures successfully. We associated each posture with different contexts which are of interest for pedestrian navigation systems: investigation, navigation and idle.

We introduce the idea that once orientation trackers became part of mobile computers, they can be used to create natural interaction techniques with mobile computers. Currently, we are integrating our interaction ideas to a Mobile AR system, which is designed to assist fieldwork in archaeological excavation sites.

2. Related Work

As the technology evolves rapidly; faster, smaller and multifunctional mobile computing devices integrate into our daily lives. Most common mobile devices, i.e. mobile phones and PDAs, are not only serving to make phone calls, send/receive text messages, check e-mails, write documents or watch video; beyond, they are capable of rendering complex 3D graphical environments and connecting with diverse positioning or orientation devices through faster communication interfaces. Naturally, computer graphics researchers begin to

exploit mobile computing devices as core device for Virtual Reality (VR) and Augmented Reality (AR) applications.
However, these applications should take advantage of the system's mobility by offering novel interaction techniques and user interfaces, which reduce the users' effort while providing relevant data. The decision about which information is relevant under which conditions and how to react to it is taken by the application designer, so the mobile AR application is informative about the real environment without distracting the user. Extracting such results requires observing the environmental conditions, collecting data, analyzing it and obtaining statistical results about possible user activities and context.

2.1 Context-Aware Mobile AR Systems

AR is an active research area in Computer Graphics. It is the discipline of augmenting real-time video images with computer generated 3D graphics in real-time. As defined by Azuma, an AR application should satisfy the following properties: combines real and virtual, interactive in real-time, registered in 3D (Azuma, 1997).
The users of mobile systems are pedestrians or traveling in vehicle, hence interacting with the environment while using a mobile phone or PDA. Most of such systems are deaf and blind to anything occurring in the environment other than change in position. But mobile AR applications, which combine the real world with computer generated graphics, are

- increasing the richness of human-computer interaction,
- preventing perception distraction,
- offering more useful computational services than regular mobile applications by increasing the perceived information level,
- minimizing explicit interaction effort of users.

These applications take full advantage of context-awareness and provide us the sense of being acquainted by the application interactively and intelligently, where context is defined as any environmental information that is relevant to the interaction between the user and the application, and that can be sensed by the application (Salber, 2000). Some example research systems are *ArcheoGuide*, real-time virtual reconstruction of a cultural heritage site's remains (Vlahakis et al., 2002); *Backseat Gaming*, a mobile AR game about finding virtual clues of a kidnapping case by interacting with the roadside objects (Brunnberg & Juhlin, 2003); and *MARS*, a mobile AR tour-guide system (Höllerer et al., 1999).

2.2 Mobile Navigation Applications

Two crucial services that are usually provided by most mobile guides are navigation support and information delivery. Navigation support allows users to obtain directions to navigate in an environment and to locate themselves and points of interest in the surrounding area. Information delivery provides users information about the point of interests located in the visiting area (Burigat & Chittaro, 2005).
Cyberguide project defines several prototypes of a mobile context-aware tour guide, which are aware of the user's current location and as well as a history of past locations (Abowd et al., 1997). This project is partitioned into components with different functionalities: map, information, communication and positioning. Prototypes are built on Apple MessagePad and pen based PC platforms acquiring position data from GPS (outdoor) and IR (indoor). Cyberguide was one of the first complete prototypes clarifying the thoughts on how context-

aware computing provides value to the emerging technology promising to release the user from the desktop paradigm of interaction.

Another example, *LAMP3D* is a system for location-aware presentation of VRML (Virtual Reality Modeling Language) content on mobile devices. This system is used to provide tourists with a 3D visualization of the environment they are exploring, synchronized with the physical world through the use of GPS data; tourists can easily obtain information on the objects they see in the real world by directly selecting them in the VRML world (using a pointing device such as the PDA stylus or their fingers) (Burigat & Chittaro, 2005).

2.3 Activity Recognition

As emphasized by Salber, another important context attribute is activity (Salber, 2000). Beyond determining a person's current location, by recognizing what she/he is doing using diverse types of sensors or wearable computers, novel interaction mechanisms can be created.

Detection and recognition of upper body postures and gestures are also studied by several research groups. The proposed methods aim generically to aid daily life, reduce human effort to use computing systems and integrate computers into the environment seamlessly.

Amft et al. introduced a recognition system for detecting arm gestures related to human meal intake (Amft et al., 2005). The idea of this project is based on dietary monitoring used by health professionals. They mounted two orientation sensors on the wrist and upper arm to detect gestures, i.e. moving the arm towards the mouth and back.

Recognizing arm postures is used to introduce a new technique for entering text into a mobile phone. Orientation of the tilt sensor mounted mobile phone is used to resolve the ambiguity faced by standard text entry technique. Tilting the phone in one of four directions chooses which character on a particular key to enter (Wigdor & Balakrishnan, 2003). They also reported that 20 to 50 Hz sampling rates are required for robust tilt implementations.

2.4 Interaction Paradigms

Before the advent of wireless, mobile and handheld technologies, prevailing paradigm in interaction design was to develop applications for the desktop, where the user is interacting with keyboard, mouse and looking to a monitor. The term, which unifies concepts of GUIs representing the user's desk accessories and the whole desktop environment, is the *desktop metaphor*. Mostly such an interface is based on WIMP (windows, icons, mouse and pointers) using a regular monitor. However, recent trends in interaction paradigms try to promote beyond the desktop.

2.4.1 Ubiquitous computing

The interaction paradigm for ubiquitous computing is based on technology disappearing in the background, which means we would be no longer aware of the computers in the environment while they are integrated seamlessly into the physical world, interacting with each other and extending human capabilities. Mark Weiser, the founder of ubiquitous computing, built a prototype system called "tabs, pads and boards", which consist of hundreds of computers equivalent in size of post-it notes, sheets of paper and blackboards (Weiser, 1995). These computing devices are to be used in office environments without noticing that they are computers and offering more functions than desktop metaphor.

2.4.2 Wearable computing

Researchers try to embed technologies in everyday environment. Wearable computing focuses on systems which people can wear or mount on the clothes. Such a system allows the user interact with and take advantage of digital information while moving in the physical world.

A complete wearable framework, which consists of a backpack containing a laptop with a wireless interface, a positioning system, an orientation tracker, a see-through Head Mounted Display (HMD) and a camera doesn't introduce a natural interaction mechanism, because it prevents the user move freely. Rather than this heavy setup, a mixed reality platform consisting of a PDA with localization and orienting capabilities and a lightweight see-through HMD operates with same capabilities and allows a free movement, natural interaction to the user (Peternier et al., 2006).

Due to the small screen space of PDAs, screen based interaction mechanisms controlled with UI widgets are confusing and ineffective. Thus, small screen space forces the interaction mechanisms to be more natural. If the interaction is provided with widgets on the PDA screen, these widgets must be large enough to be distinguished from the content on display and to be practical for relevant interaction. This fact limits the displayed content size, and it is better to build natural interaction mechanisms and avoid virtual interface widgets.

Höllerer et al. introduced a gaze-directed selection mechanism for outdoor UI interaction in their mobile augmented reality system. The display unit of this system is a see-through head-mounted display, which augments the real world with virtual labels and flags. Gaze-directed selection is accomplished by the user orienting her/his head so the desired object's projection is closer than any other to the center of the head-mounted display (Höllerer et al., 1999).

2.5 Visualizing Data on Small Screen

Most of the previous work on location-aware mobile guides uses 2D maps of the area where the user is located; pinpointing her position and usually providing visual information on the nearest points of interest and on the paths she has to follow to reach specific destinations. Maps are powerful tools for navigation because of the richness of information they can supply and the rate at which people can absorb this information.

Rakkolainen and Vainio have proposed a system that combines a 2D map of an area with a 3D representation of what users currently see in the physical world; study the effects of 3D graphics on navigation and way finding in an urban environment (Rakkolainen & Vainio, 2001). They concluded that 3D models help users to recognize landmarks and find routes in cities more easily than traditional 2D maps. The prototype was implemented on a laptop computer, not on a PDA. Moreover this project was focused only on navigation support and no information delivery service was provided about point of interests.

Realistic visualization of large and complex 3D models, such as those used in mobile guides, is a very important task for other application areas as well: scientific simulation, training, CAD, and so on. However, mobile devices do not include the specialized hardware typical of high-quality graphics boards, thus it is not always possible to obtain a good quality level for the visualization. A possible approach to this problem is to carry out rendering on a powerful remote server (or a cluster of workstations) connected through a wireless network and display the results on the mobile device as a video sequence (Lamberti et al., 2003). This solution has two advantages: the data to be visualized is processed by specialized hardware, thus bypassing the problem of the low computational power of mobile devices, and the source data is not transmitted to the client device, thus allowing for data independence. On the other side, due to the limited bandwidth of current wireless networks, this remote computation solution needs complex algorithms for the preparation of the data to be transmitted.

2.6 View Management for AR Applications

Designing a 2D or 3D graphical user interface (UI) for augmented reality applications is a challenge in different manners;

- according to the changing viewing direction, the UI components must be relocated to maintain visibility,
- virtual objects can disappear in front of the real world scene because of lighting and rendering parameters,
- any annotations or virtual objects can overlap each other in a crowded scene.

Such problems have been discussed by researchers under the term view management. Bell et al. defined view management for interactive 3D user interfaces as of maintaining visual constraints on the projections of objects on the view plane, such as locating related objects near each other, or preventing objects from occluding each other (Bell et al., 2001). Azuma and Furmanski handled this discussion from 2D point of view and according to their research; view management is about the spatial layout of 2D virtual annotations in the view plane of augmented and mixed reality applications (Azuma & Furmanski, 2003).

Other than the layout of annotations, text readability is affected from the interference of the background texture in the dynamically changing AR environment. Leykin and Tuceryan introduced a pattern recognition approach to automatically determine if a text placed on a particular background would be readable or not (Leykin & Tuceryan, 2004).

3. Mobile Augmented Reality System

3.1 Hardware components

The proposed mobile AR system provides a context-aware interaction framework for pedestrian, wandering in urban environments. As reported in relevant research based on navigation, it is important to acquire what the user's geographic position is and where she is looking at. In addition to these context-attributes, this research provides a natural interaction mechanism to the navigation system by inferring application dependent arm posture. These services are implemented and tested with two hardware configurations:

PDA prototype (Figure 1):

- HP iPAQ Pocket PC h2200 series operating on Pocket PC 2003 with Intel XScale 400MHz processor, 64MB RAM, and 320x240 pixels 64K color TFT display.
- Fortuna GPS receiver is connected to PDA via Bluetooth and sends global positioning data in National Marine Electronics Association (NMEA) 0183 format with a frequency of 1 Hz.
- InertiaCube2 is an inertial orientation tracking system and provides angular data in 3 degrees-of-freedom with a frequency of 180 Hz. It is connected to PDA via Sync port and uses an RS-232 interface.

Ultra-mobile PC prototype (Figure 2):

- Sony VAIO UX 280p operating on Windows XP with an internal camera capable of capture videos in 640x480 resolution.
- GPS receiver used in this prototype is the same as the one in PDA prototype.
- XSens' MTx is an inertial measurement unit and provides 3 degrees-of-freedom angular data with a frequency of 100 Hz. It is connected via USB.

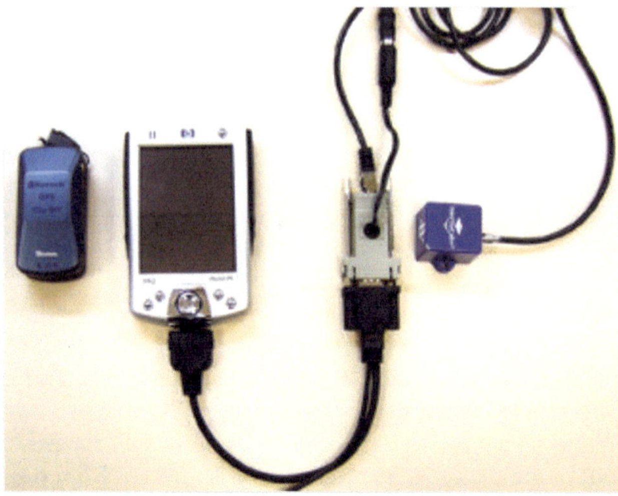

Figure 1. PDA based hardware prototype

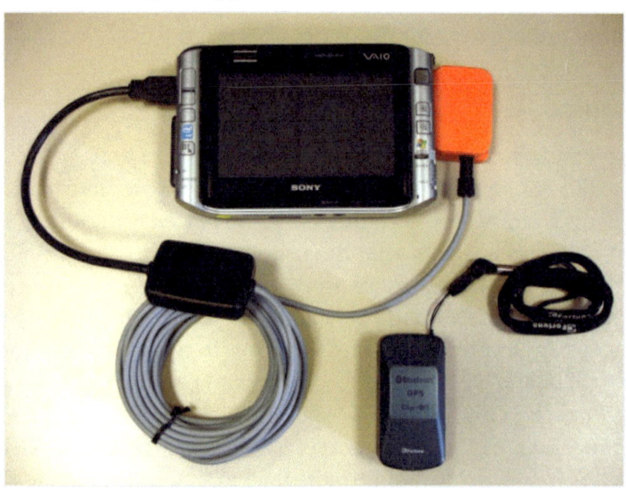

Figure 2. Ultra-mobile PC based hardware prototype

3.2 Software components

Software in the mobile and ubiquitous computing area is expected to be modular, simply modifiable to accommodate for new user needs, expectations, and a constantly changing environment. To implement the navigation application a diverse set of APIs are integrated to the development environment. Table 1 lists the libraries, which we used in our system.

System hardware	User Interface, Windowing / Rendering	Video and Image Processing	Sensor Communication	Data Handling
PDA prototype	• Vincent Mobile 3D Rendering Library (OpenGL | ES) • GLUT | ES Windowing Library	-	• InertiaCube2 Software Development Kit for Pocket PC 2003 • Bluetooth Communication Interface	-
Ultra Mobile PC prototype	• OpenGL Library • Freetype Font Library	OpenCV Library	• MTx Software Development Kit • Bluetooth Communication Interface	• PostgreSQL 8.3.1 (PostGIS included) • Libpqxx 2.6.9

Table 1. Software components of two hardware prototypes

4. Posture Recognition

As mentioned in the related work section, all of the orientation tracker work is based on either to assist precise tracking and positioning of the user in space or gesture recognition using several sensors. In this work, the goal is to create a stable differentiation mechanism between several arm postures and map them to several application dependent contexts.

The developed recognition algorithm is based on state transitions triggered by time-line analysis of orientation and angular velocity of the sensor. The angle between user's forearm and upper arm is obtained from the orientation sensor as pitch angle, α, and analyzed to recognize different postures. We have gathered sample data from mobile users with various walking speeds, while moving their hands between three postures:

- *vertical*, where pitch angle is around 0°,
- *horizontal*, where pitch angle is around 90°,
- *idle*, where the hand may move freely (Figure 3).

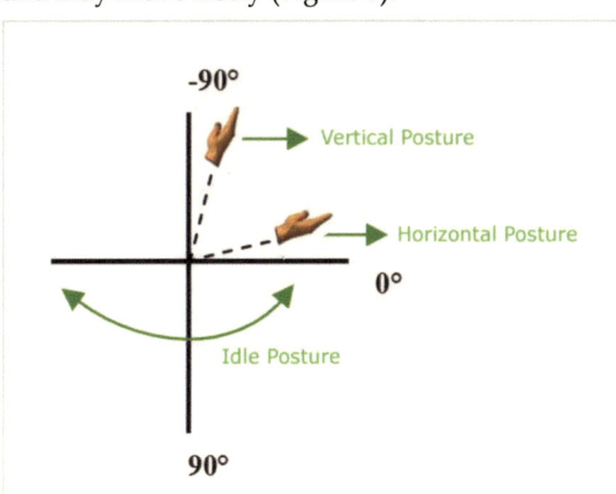

Figure 3. Drawing of target three hand postures from side view

Figure 4 shows pitch angle measurements of the user's arm movement in three different conditions: standing, walking, and running. Transitions between diverse arm postures can be inferred from the top left plot of Figure 4: For 0s ≤ t < 5s, the posture is on idle state. After this interval the user moves her hand up and stabilizes on horizontal posture until t ≈ 10s. For 10s < t < 20s, the user moves her hand down, stabilizes on idle state and moves her hand up. For 20s ≤ t < 27s, vertical posture is observed, and so on.
The measurements indicate that with the increase of velocity the noise on the measured signal increases significantly. The noise can be observed on the top right plot of Figure 4, where the transition from idle posture to horizontal posture is not clearly recognizable at t ≈ 40. Our current algorithm performs acceptably with users walking with low speed but the accuracy decreases significantly with increased speed due to the high frequency noise introduced into data by walking and running motion.

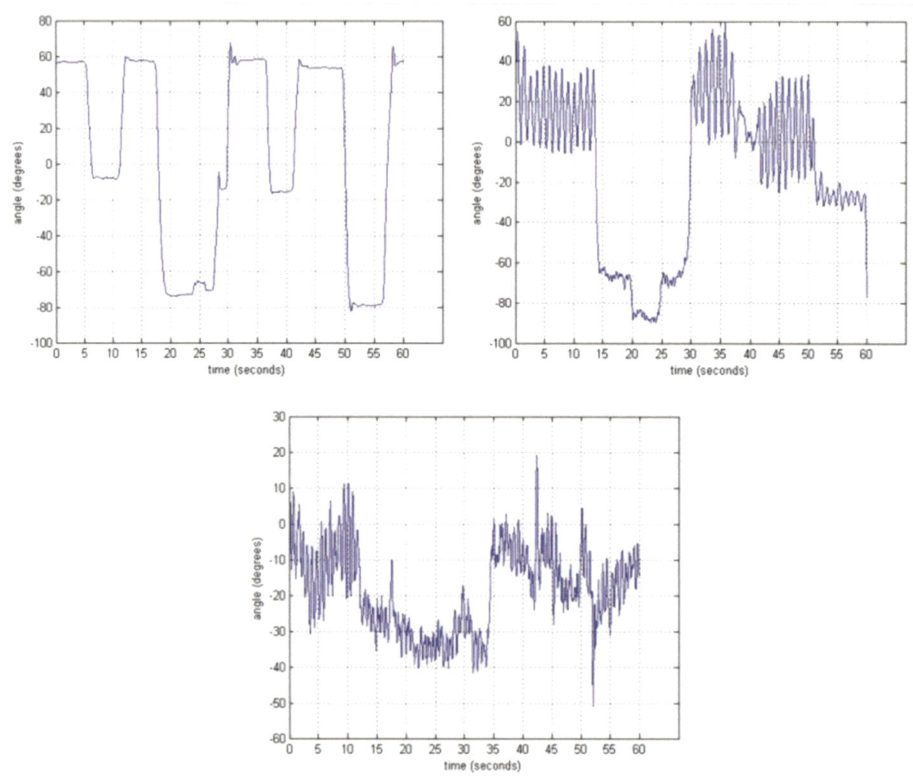

Figure 4. Pitch angle measurements while user is stationary (top left), walking (top right), and running (bottom). Data is collected with MTx

We implemented a sliding window to detect changes of the hand on pitch angle, α. A window, which contains five angle values obtained in time interval [t-1, t-5], is created at each time step and upcoming angle is estimated by multiplying them with increasing weights.

$$0.1 * \alpha_i + 0.1 * \alpha_{i+1} + 0.1 * \alpha_{i+2} + 0.2 * \alpha_{i+3} + 0.5 * \alpha_{i+4} = \alpha_{estimated} \quad (1)$$

The $\alpha_{estimated}$ angle is compared with the measured angle α_{i+5} to identify if the hand is moving up or down.

$$\alpha_{i+5} > \alpha_{estimated} \Rightarrow downside\ change \tag{2}$$

$$\alpha_{i+5} < \alpha_{estimated} \Rightarrow upside\ change \tag{3}$$

$$\alpha_{i+5} \cong \alpha_{estimated} \Rightarrow no\ change \begin{cases} \alpha_{i+5} \rightarrow -90°, & vertical \\ \alpha_{i+5} \rightarrow 0°, & horizontal \end{cases} \tag{4}$$

However using the pitch angle in one single direction is not sufficient enough to have robust posture recognition. We have also evaluated the case, where the user performs short tilts (rotations around the longitudinal axis) causing an inference on the state transition. For such cases, a filter is implemented on the system which increased the state transition accuracy.

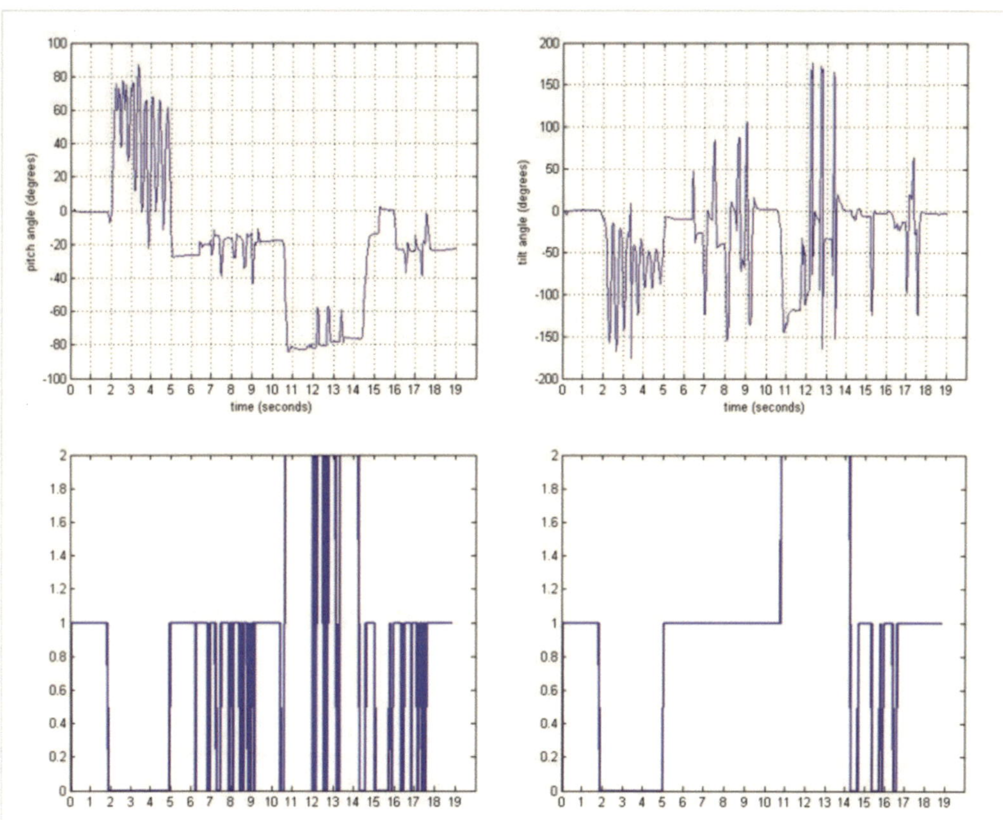

Figure 5. Sample pitch angle measurement (top left). Tilt measurement of the same posture (top right) causing erroneous estimation - 0: idle state, 1: navigation state, 2: investigation state (bottom left) and increased estimation accuracy with tilt filter (bottom, right). Data is collected with InertiaCube2

Figure 5 shows plots of sample pitch and tilt angle measurements of the same motion and corresponding state estimations. For 7s< t <9s, tilt angle is increasing and decreasing instantly (top right plot, Figure 5) which affects the pitch angle. In spite of the fact that the user holds her hand stable around -20° during angular data measurement, the top left plot of Figure 5 shows that the pitch angle is changing up to 20°. Same erroneous measurement can be observed for 11s < t < 15s. These unexpected changes cause inaccurate state estimation (bottom left plot, Figure 5). Therefore, estimation accuracy is increased (bottom right plot, Figure 5) by introducing the system with a tilt angle filter, which locks the state to the previous one if major changes occur on tilt angles.

The system becomes unstable and produces erroneous results when users perform other occasional movement patterns. Therefore we have introduced an additional data, angular velocity, to the recognition system. The change of angular velocity together with the angle allows us more stable recognition results.

Finally we developed a finite state machine to map all possible postures into one of the three states: investigation, navigation and idle (Figure 6). The investigation state is when a user holds a mobile terminal in vertical position to use it in an augmented reality context. In this condition the user needs to investigate point of interests and receives environmental information according to her gaze direction in the local coordinate frame. The navigation state is when a user holds a mobile terminal in horizontal position to use it to render maps or Geographic Information System (GIS) information. Thus, the user receives environmental information in the global coordinate frame. There is a third idle state, where the user is not in either posture and moves her hand freely. In this state, rendering is minimized to allow power save property.

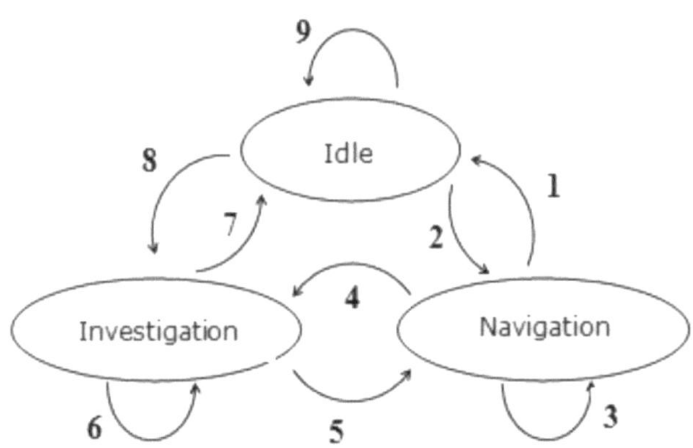

Figure 6. State transitions

The conditions satisfying the state transitions in Figure 6 are defined in Figure 7. In this algorithm, firstly, the estimated pitch angle value is compared with the angular value perceived from the orientation sensor at that time step. If they are approximately equal, user's arm posture is estimated to be stable and either in investigation or navigation state (3rd and 6th columns of the table in Figure 7). Other enumerated transitions include conditions which define possible changes between states, i.e. while arm posture is on idle state and the user moves her hand upwards, then it is possible to switch state to navigation or upside change on arm posture continues and state is switched to investigation. The state estimation algorithm is empowered by introducing angular velocity and tilt angle filter to the system.

Unexpected arm movements of the user can affect the accuracy of the system. While the user holds the PDA in horizontal or vertical position (navigation or investigation state) and suddenly performs fast upward or downward movements with her hand, i.e. waving to somebody, the system is stabilized in the former state with a tolerably accuracy rate.

We performed a user study to examine the accuracy of our system. In this test, all possible state transitions emphasized in Figure 6 are performed. The overall accuracy rate is calculated as approximately %87. Performing sudden up-down movements in navigation state and investigation state produced some erroneous results.

1	2	3	4	5	6	7	8	9
$\alpha > 0°$ $\omega < -0.75$ $\Delta\alpha < 0$	$\alpha > 0°$ $\omega > 0.75$ $\Delta\alpha > 0$	$\alpha \approx 0°$ $\omega \approx 0$ $\Delta\alpha \approx 0$	$\alpha < 0°$ $\omega < -0.75$ $\Delta\alpha < 0$	$\alpha < 0°$ $\omega > 0.75$ $\Delta\alpha > 0$	$\alpha \approx 90°$ $\omega \approx 0$ $\Delta\alpha \approx 0$	$\alpha > 0°$ $\omega > 0.75$ $\Delta\alpha > 0$	$\alpha < 0°$ $\omega < -0.75$ $\Delta\alpha < 0$	$\alpha > 0°$ $\lvert\omega\rvert > 0.75$ $\Delta\alpha \neq 0$

$\omega = angular\ velocity\ (rad/s)$

$\Delta\alpha = \alpha_{true} - \alpha_{estimated}$

Figure 7. Conditions defined to change system states

5. Case Studies

5.1 Navigation system for campus environment

After connecting necessary hardware and building software components, the prototype system is studied with a context-aware pedestrian navigation application. Location, orientation, and activity of the user are the affecting context attributes. As a standard navigation system working outdoors, this application locates the user using GPS data and gives information about the point of interests around. Moreover, it offers different interfaces by changing them seamlessly according to the user's arm posture. This feature is achieved by mounting the orientation tracker to the Pocket PC's rear and integrating the posture recognition algorithm discussed in the previous section. Currently, power is supplied to the orientation tracker only with a power adapter. A battery pack connection must be built carefully. Therefore, the interface transition mechanism could only be tested indoors with previously collected GPS data.

The navigation application is tested in our university campus, but it is possible to add different environment data and run the navigation system without doing massive changes in code. This modularity increases the scalability of the prototype.

The screen captures of three application dependent interfaces can be observed in Figure 8. The *idle state* is where the user is moving her hand freely, possibly not looking at the screen. Thus rendering is minimized to save battery power. The *navigation state* is where the user holds her hand in approximately horizontal posture (Figure 3) and the campus buildings are represented in 3D coordinate system. During this state, the user can get information about her position in the area, heading and speed. Campus buildings are labeled with their names and represented with rectangular shapes changing size according to the distance to the user, i.e. if the distance decreases the height of the building increases by a predefined scale. The user can change the view by rotating the camera using hardware buttons. The size of the buildings' names change according to the position of the camera to maintain visibility. The *investigation state* is where the user lifts the PDA in her gaze direction. In this state, the campus buildings are placed in user's local coordinate system and change their position as the user changes her heading and position. We intended to switch to an augmented reality view but the rendering capabilities of the PDA didn't guarantee the video processing requirements. Thus we improved our ideas in the following case study using an ultra mobile PC.

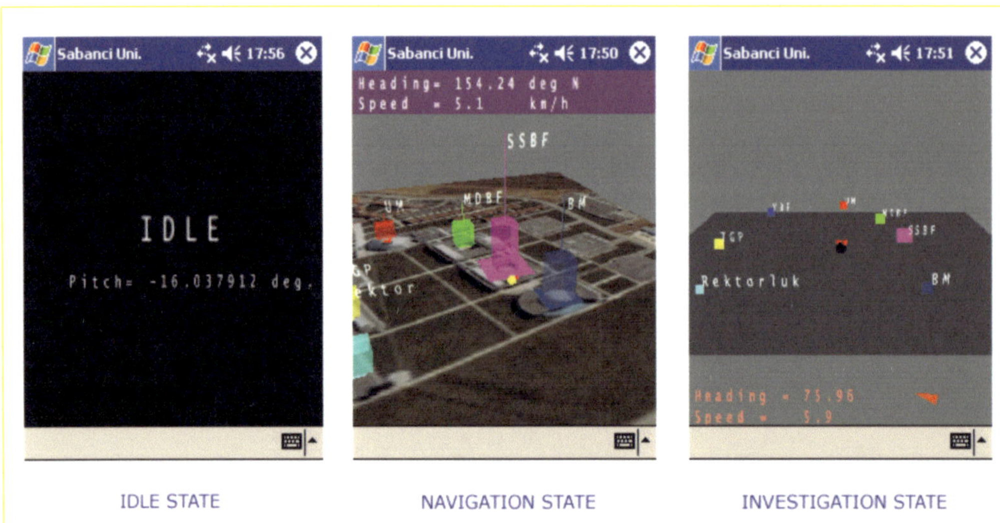

Figure 8. Screenshots from PDA screen displaying three application dependent contexts

5.2 Mobile AR system for archaeological excavations

Currently, we are working on this case study and integrating our interaction ideas to an archaeological fieldwork assistant tool.

Archaeological site excavation is a destructive and irreversible process. Archaeologists try to follow the phases of the excavation using traditional methods, i.e. querying access databases, examining excel sheets, analyzing Computer-aided design (CAD) files etc. According to archaeologists, there is a certain need to visualize and analyze the previously collected data and completed work. Over the past years, researchers have developed virtual reality and augmented reality applications for cultural heritage sites. The current applications are mainly focused on AR context, where 3D virtual objects are integrated into the real environment in real-time. They can be classified into two main categories: mobile tour guides (Vlahakis et al., 2002; Vlahakis et al., 2004) and reconstructive tools of remains (Benko et al., 2004; Green et al., 2001). Although there are examples of excavation analyzers in indoor augmented reality and 3D virtual reality contexts, there is no such application which offers real-time on site digital assistance using outdoor augmented reality. We are testing our tool in Yenikapi Marmaray rescue excavation site in Istanbul. This site is an exciting discovery for the history of Istanbul because archaeologists revealed the ancient port of Constantinople, which was the capital of the Roman Empire for centuries.

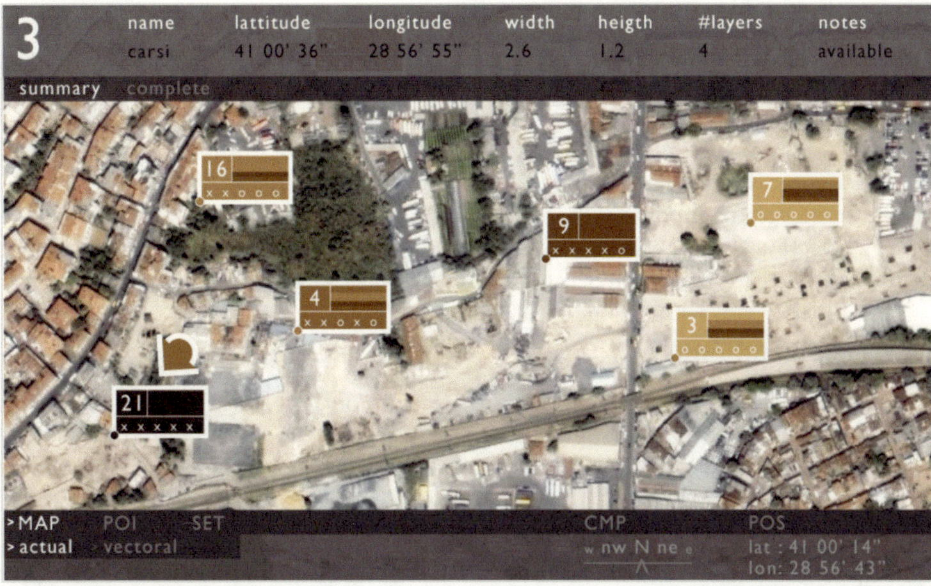

Figure 9. Navigation interface (aerial view) displays the information sheet of a POI

Figure 10. 3D modeling interface

We mapped the states in Figure 6, except the idle state, into two different viewing options of the site: navigation interface (aerial view) and rough 3D modeling interface. The navigation interface is where the archaeologist holds ultra mobile PC in approximately horizontal posture as shown in Figure 3. The point-of-interests (POI) are archaeological artefacts, i.e. in our case, remains of port walls, which are pinned to their actual locations on the aerial view (Figure 9). The color coding of each POI represents how much work is completed for that POI, i.e. as the color gets darker the completeness of the work decreases. The archaeologist can observe her location and orientation on the excavation area. Each POI has its own data sheet, which is editable in this interface. If the archaeologist wants to investigate a POI in detail, she walks to that POI using the navigation interface and as she stands in front of the POI, she lifts the ultra mobile PC to her gaze direction. Using the state transition mechanism introduced in the posture recognition section, the 3D modeling interface is enabled. The real-time video capture of the POI is mapped to the interface and a 2D plan of that POI is given as a reference for modeling on the screen. The archaeologist can start the modeling process by selecting the real corners of the wall according to the corresponding reference points in an augmented reality interface (Figure 10).

6. Conclusion and Future Work

In this research, we introduced a posture recognition system to integrate a natural interaction mechanism to mobile devices. The system consists of an inertial measurement unit attached to a mobile device (PDA or ultra mobile PC) to distinguish between two different postures of the hand and an idle state. This data can be used to differentiate between three states, which enable to switch between different interfaces seamlessly. We tested our approach on two different hardware prototypes.

In the global coordinate frame, we used GPS sensor data to locate the user, acquire her gaze direction, embed GIS data and provide information about point of interests. In the local coordinate frame, we used orientation sensor data to allow the user interact with the mobile device while performing natural arm postures and perceive information on different user interfaces. By combining these interaction techniques of global and local coordinate frame, we provide a context-aware interaction framework for pedestrian navigation systems on mobile devices by seamlessly changing graphical user interfaces.

We want to improve our approach by introducing different interaction techniques in mobile augmented reality context by employing wearable sensors. Since augmented reality is the discipline of augmenting the real world with computer generated graphics, and the user is interacting with the real environment, the interaction methods used in these applications must feel more realistic and natural.

7. References

Abowd, G. D.; Atkeson, C. G.; Hong J.; Long S.; Kooper R. & Pinkerton M. (1997). Cyberguide: A mobile context-aware tour guide. *ACM Wireless Networks*, Vol. 3, No. 5 (October 1997), pp. 421-433, ISSN: 1022-0038

Amft, O.; Junker, H. & Troster, G. (2005). Detection of eating and drinking arm gestures using inertial body-worn sensors, *Proceedings of 9th IEEE International Symposium of Wearable Computers*, pp. 160-163, ISBN: 0-7695-2419-2, Osaka, Japan, October 2005, IEEE Computer Society, Los Alamitos, CA, USA

Azuma, R. (1997). A Survey of Augmented Reality. *Presence: Teleoperators and Virtual Environments*, Vol. 6, No. 4, August 1997, pp. 355—385, ISSN: 1054-7460

Azuma, R. & Furmanski, C. (2003). Evaluating Label Placement for Augmented Reality View Management. *Proceedings of ISMAR 2003*, pp. 66–75, ISBN: 0-7695-2006-5, Tokyo, Japan, October 2003, IEEE Computer Society, Washington, DC, USA

Bell, B.; Feiner, S. & Höllerer, T. (2001). View Management for Virtual and Augmented Reality. *Proceedings of UIST'01*, pp. 101–110, ISBN: 1-58113-438-X, Orlando, Florida, USA, November 2001, ACM Press, New York, NY, USA

Benko, H.; Ishak, E. & Feiner, S. (2004). Collaborative Mixed Reality Visualization of an Archaeological Excavation. *Proceedings of the 3rd IEEE and ACM International Symposium on Mixed and Augmented Reality*, pp. 132-140, ISBN: 0-7695-2191-6, Arlington, VA, USA, November 2004, IEEE Computer Society, Washington, DC, USA

Brunnberg, L. & Juhlin, O. (2003). Motion and Spatiality in a Gaming Situation - Enhancing Mobile Computer Games with the Highway Experience. *Proceedings of Interact 2003*, pp. 407-414, ISBN: 1-58603-363-8, Zurich, Switzerland, September 2003, IOS Press

Burigat S. & Chittaro L. (2005). Location-aware visualization of VRML models in GPS-based mobile guides. *Proceedings of the 10th international conference on 3D Web technology*, pp. 57–64, ISBN: 1-59593-012-4, Bangor, United Kingdom, March 2005, ACM Press, New York, NY, USA

Green, D.; Cosmas, J.; Itagaki, T.; Waelkens, M.; Degeest, R. & Grabczewski E. (2001). A Real Time 3D Stratigraphic Visual Simulation System for Archaeological Analysis and Hypothesis Testing. *Proceedings of the Conference on Virtual Reality, Archeology, and Cultural Heritage*, pp. 271–278, ISBN: 1-58113-447-9, Glyfada, Greece, November 2001, ACM Press, New York, NY, USA

Höllerer, T.; Feiner, S.; Terauchi, T.; Rashid, G. & Hallaway, D. (1999). Exploring MARS: developing indoor and outdoor user interfaces to a mobile augmented reality system. *Computers and Graphics*, Vol. 23, No. 6, December 1999, pp. 779-785, ISSN: 0097-8493.

Lamberti, F.; Zunino, C.; Sanna, A.; Fiume, A. & Maniezzo, M. (2003). An Accelerated Remote Graphics Architecture for PDAs. *Proceedings of Web3D 2003*, pp. 55-61, ISBN: 1-58113-644-7, Saint Malo, France, March 2003, ACM Press, New York, NY, USA

Leykin, A. & Tuceryan, M. (2004). Automatic Determination of Text Readability over Textured Backgrounds for Augmented Reality Systems. *Proceedings of ISMAR 2004*, pp. 224-230, ISBN: 0-7695-2191-6, Arlington, VA, USA, November 2004, IEEE Computer Society, Washington, DC, USA

Peternier, A.; Vexo, F. & Thalmann, D. (2006). Wearable Mixed Reality System in Less Than 1 Pound. *Proceedings of Eurographics Symposium on Virtual Environments*, pp. 35-44, Lisbon, Portugal, May 2006, Eurographics Association

Rakkolainen, T. & Vainio, T. (2001). A 3D city info for mobile users. *Computers and Graphics*, Vol. 25, No. 4, August 2001, pp. 619-625, ISSN: 0097-8493

Salber, D. (2000). Context-awareness and multimodality. *Proceedings of the First Workshop on Multimodal Interfaces*, Grenoble, France, May 2000

Vlahakis, V.; Ioannidis, N.; Karigiannis, J.; Tsotros, M.; Gounaris, M.; Stricker, D.; Gleue, T.; Daehne, P. & Almeida, L. (2002). Archeoguide: An Augmented Reality Guide for Archaeological Sites. *IEEE Computer Graphics and Applications*, Vol. 22, No. 5, September 2002, pp. 52-60, ISSN: 0272-1716

Vlahakis, V.; Demiris, A. & Ioannidis, N. (2004). A Novel Approach to Context-Sensitive Guided e-Tours in Cultural Sites: "Light" Augmented Reality on PDAs. *Proceedings of VAST '04,* pp. 57–66, ISBN: 3-905673-18-5, Oudenaarde, Belgium, December 2004, Eurographics Association

Weiser, M. (1995). The computer for the 21st century, In: *Human-computer interaction: toward the year 2000,* Baecker, R.M.; Grudin, J.; Buxton W.A.S. & Greenberg, S., pp. 933-940, Morgan Kaufmann Publishers Inc., ISBN: 1-55860-246-1, San Francisco, CA, USA

Wigdor, D. & Balakrishnan, R. (2003). TiltText: Using Tilt for Text Input to Mobile Phones. *Proceedings of UIST 2003,* pp. 81-90, ISBN: 1-58113-636-6, Vancouver, Canada, November 2003, ACM Press, New York, NY, USA

14

Review of Human-Computer Interaction Issues in Image Retrieval

Mohammed Lamine Kherfi
Department of Mathematics and Computer Science, Université du Québec à Trois-Rivières
Canada

Abstract:

Image retrieval is an active area of research, which is growing very rapidly. Indeed, stimulated by the rapid growth in storage capacity and processing speed, the number of images in electronic collections and the World Wide Web has considerably increased over the last few years. However, with this abundance of information, people are continuously looking for tools that help them find the image(s) they are looking for within a reasonable amount of time. These tools are image retrieval engines.

When using an image retrieval engine, the user is continuously interacting with the machine. First, he[1] uses the system's interface to formulate a query that expresses his needs. Second, he provides feedback about the retrieved results at each search iteration. This allows the engine to provide more accurate results by using relevance feedback (RF) techniques. Third, he may be asked to assign a goodness score or weight to each image retrieved, which helps evaluating the system's performance.

In this chapter, we will review the main interactions between human and the machine in the context of image retrieval. We will address several issues, including:

Query formulation:

- How the user expresses his needs and what he is looking for
- The different ways the query can be formulated: keywords-based, sentence-based, query by example image, query by sketch, query by feature values, composite queries, etc.
- Query by region of interest (ROI) vs. global query.
- Queries with positive example only vs. queries with both positive and negative examples.
- Page zero problem: finding a good image to initiate a retrieval session.

Relevance feedback: we will try to answer questions like:

- Why do systems use relevance feedback?
- How can the user express his needs during the relevance feedback process
- How this information is exploited by the system to perform operations like feature selection or the identification of the sought image.

---

[1] Note that the masculine gender has been used strictly to facilitate reading, and is to be understood to include the feminine.

- The different families of RF techniques.
- Relevance feedback with retrieval memory, i.e., taking into account the value of old iteration queries when constructing the new one.
- Whether it is useful for the system to create user profiles, and the challenges it has to face.
- The number of RF iterations required to obtain satisfactory results.

Viewing retrieval results:

- Existing viewing techniques: 2D linear presentation, 3D-based presentation, etc.
- Different ways the resulting images may be ordered and presented to the user: similarity-ordered, time-ordered, event-ordered, etc.

Evaluation of the retrieval performance by the user:

- How the user can express his satisfaction/dissatisfaction about the retrieved images
- What about the ground truth in image retrieval evaluation?
- System response time and its influence on user satisfaction.
- The ease of use of the system's interface.

Other issues:

- User's needs: He may be looking for a specific image, for images that meet a given need (e.g. illustrate a concept) or simply browsing the collection looking for potentially "good" images.
- Etc.

1. Introduction

In the last two decades, the number of images in electronic collections has increased considerably. This is due to several factors, including:

- The substantial drop in prices of image acquisition devices. These devices include digital cameras, video cameras, cellular phones, surveillance cameras, scanners that can digitize analog images, etc. This drop in price has resulted in many people now owning these devices, which allows them to create personal collections. In addition, these images end up on Web pages and are thus available to the general public. Professional collections are no less substantial. For example, many museums have several hundred thousands of images representing their collections. Another example is the images used in medicine for different purposes, including learning, diagnosis and decision-making.
- The increase of storage capacity and lower prices for storage devices (hard disks, CDs, DVDs, external hard disks, etc.). Within only a few years, the size of a normal hard disk, for example, has gone from a few megabytes to several hundreds of gigabytes. Today, an ordinary user can have the space needed in his computer to store several millions of images.

In addition to this, and due to the development of new technologies, which allow to share images across the Internet and all types of networks, people can now access tons of images that were not accessible before.

This availability of information, however, created a new need that did not exist before: to find desired images within a reasonable time. This stimulated the emergence of a new area of research, which is currently rapidly developing, namely image retrieval. The main objective of this area of research is to develop tools that can help the user find the desired images within a reasonable time. These tools are generally called image retrieval engines, or image retrieval systems.

Different scenarios are possible for image retrieval. The most common scenario is the following:

1. The engine allows the user to create his query. It may be a text box in which the user enters keywords describing what he is searching. It may also involve a set of images from which the user can choose several as examples. Other ways of creating the query are also possible, as we will see later in the chapter.
2. The user creates his query.
3. The engine searches by comparing the query against the images in the collection.
4. The engine displays the resulting images for the user.
5. If the user is satisfied or simply wants to end the retrieval session, he stops. If not, he gives feedback about these results.
6. The engine uses this information and tries to find the most relevant results, and then moves to Step 4.

Human beings are at the centre of any image retrieval method since it is primarily their needs that the retrieval engine must cater to. In this way, the person who uses the services of a retrieval engine is in continuous interaction with it, and, at different stages: creating the query, examining the results, evaluating the engine, etc. The objective of this chapter is to provide an overview of the different steps during which the user interacts with the machine in the context of image retrieval. We should point out that this chapter is in no way a survey of existing image retrieval engines and retrieval techniques. The user interested by this type of survey can find a lot of good articles in the literature. For example, [1][2][3][4] and [5].

The chapter has been organized as follows: Section 2 discusses the different types of interactions between human and the engine, whereas Section 3 explores the different tools at the user's disposal for creating his query and the manner in which this query can be created. In Section 4, we will discuss similarity measures and their link with human judgement, and in Section 5, will focus on relevance feedback. In Section 6, we will delve into more detail about the different methods of viewing the results, and Section 7 covers engine performance evaluation. We will end the chapter with a short conclusion.

2. Interaction Modes Between the User and the Engine

User needs and the manner in which users search for images vary from person to person, and even for a given user at different times:

- Some users have a specific idea of what they are looking for, whereas others simply want to navigate through the database (DB) in search of an image that will catch their interest.
- Some users are looking for a single image whereas others are looking for several.
- Some are looking for a specific image (an image they have already seen), whereas others are looking for any image that could meet a given requirement (e.g. to illustrate a newspaper article).

Depending on the type of user and the user's needs, his way of interacting with the engine may vary. Two different methods of interaction can be identified, namely query-based search and browsing through a catalogue. For example, if the user is interested by a specific image, the search function may work best for him. If, however, the user does not have a clear idea about what he is looking for, but simply wants to explore the DB to find potentially good images, browsing through a catalogue may be very useful. By drilling down in the catalogue, he can better pinpoint his needs and more accurately identify what he is looking for.

The first style of interaction, namely query-based search, can be summarized as follows. The user uses the engine interface to create his query. This query may be textual or visual as we will see in Section 3. A good interface must be easy to use, and must allow the user to express his needs (e.g. example images must be available). After the user has created his query, the engine searches through the DB to retrieve the corresponding images. This involves extracting features, calculating similarity measures between the query and images in the DB, possibly using an index, as well as sorting images based on similarity. Once the results are obtained, they are displayed to the user on the engine interface. A good engine must enable the user to give more details on what he is searching for, which helps the engine refine the results via what is called Relevance Feedback. All these aspects will be explained in detail in subsequent sections.

For the second method, browsing, the system starts by creating a catalogue by grouping similar images within a given class. This similarity can be calculated in terms of visual elements, semantic concepts, or both. It is best if the catalogue is hierarchical, which means that each theme at an upper level is subdivided into subthemes. Once the catalogue has been created, the user can browse the DB by starting with a theme, and then search by either drilling down through the sub-themes or moving across horizontally to other related themes. At any time he may decide to change theme or to simply end the browsing session.

3. Query Formulation:

As we mentioned above, machine-user interactions can be done through a query or by browsing through a catalogue. In the first case, the user must start by formulating a query, whereas the second method does not require a query. In this section, we will focus on the first scenario.

The first communication between the user and the image retrieval engine takes place when creating the query. Indeed, the engine needs to understand which image(s) the user needs in order to meet this requirement. Creating the query is a delicate problem and more difficult than it seems. Two questions arise at this point: 1) For the user, the challenge is to describe images that the user needs by using the few tools at his disposal; and 2) For the system, the challenge is to understand what the user wants based on the query he formulated. However, note that considerable advances have been made over the past few years, which facilitates interactions between the user and engine during the query formulation. In the rest of the section, we will look at the main existing techniques.

The user expresses his needs using text:

The first image retrieval engines used the same query formulation technique as the previous text retrieval engines. This technique involves allowing the user to provide a textual description of what he is looking for. The textual description can be either a group of keywords or a sentence.

Keyword queries:

The user expresses his needs by providing a keyword, such as in the following query: I am looking for an image that contains "an apple". Most engines enable the user to provide several keywords. An example of this type of query could be: I am looking for images that contain "oranges and apples". When the query is made up of several keywords, they may be combined using different logical connectors, such as AND, OR and NOT. This method of formulating queries is directly derived from text search techniques.

Query by sentence:
For this type of query, the user provides a sentence that describes what he is looking for. An example of this type of query could be: I am looking for "an image in which people are eating in a park". The challenge with this type of query is to analyze the sentence in order to extract the most important words to the user. Another challenge involves understanding the exact meaning of the sentence, since a sentence is not a simple group of words without any order or links. For example, the word "Impala" can have different meaning depending on the sentence in which it is found. If the user creates the query "Find me a herd of impala", the engine must understand that he is talking about the animal. However, if he says: "Find me a Chevrolet Impala on the road", the engine must interpret it as the car, and not the animal.

Discussion:
Creating the query using a textual description presents a certain number of advantages:

- This is a natural way of allowing the user to express himself as he does in everyday life.
- It allows to re-use an entire arsenal of text-search techniques, which were developed over the years.
- It was noted by several researchers that text more easily captures semantic concepts associated with images. Imagine, for example, a user who is searching for images describing the concept "Joy". As we will see a little later, the current content-based search techniques have great difficulty in extracting this concept from images automatically. If text is used, however, it becomes entirely possible to answer the query provided that certain images are annotated with this word.

This being said, a text-based search is not without its problems:

- First of all, this technique becomes unusable when the collection does not contain any text along with the images. This is unfortunately the case for most personal image collections. People often do not take the time to add text to their personal photos. Many of them just empty out their acquisition devices (cameras, etc.) by recopying the images onto their hard disk. This is also the case for many professional collections.
- Secondly, even if the images are annotated with text, this annotation can be very subjective. The same image can be annotated with different words by different annotators. According to [6], the annotation tells us more about the annotator than about the image itself.
- The text depends on the language. In order to be able to search in a DB in which the images were annotated by using a given language, there must be tools that translate queries into other languages to the annotation language.
- If images are surrounded by text, such as on a Web page, this text may be used in their indexing. This technique is used by certain retrieval engines on the Web. The problem however arises from the fact that it is not easy to determine which words are relevant to the image, and which words are not.

- Text does not go beyond a certain degree of refinement. For example, we went to Google Image [53] and searched using the word "Goose". We found the images in Fig. 1. on the first page of results.

Figure 1. Search results using the word "Goose"

All these images do indeed contain geese. What happens now if you are interested in images containing geese, but that must also visually resemble of the image in Fig. 2? This image contains a single goose, in a very specific position, with very specific wings and colours, water of a given colour and texture, etc. It is impossible to describe all these details using text, which demonstrates the limitation of the capacity of text to go beyond a certain level of refinement. We will look at how searches using an example image can get round this obstacle.

Figure 2. [54] Illustration of the limitation of text to describe the content of an image

- A picture is worth a thousand words: It can contain many objects with a given layout, very specific colour shades and shapes that cannot be described with text. Take the image in Fig. 3, for example. It contains houses that are shaped in a specific way, cars of specific makes, models and colours, trees, lawn, poles, etc. All these objects are set up in a particular way. How could we describe the entire content of this image in words?

Figure 3. [55] A picture is worth a thousand words

The user expresses his needs using images:

The limitations of text-based retrieval that we have mentioned earlier have led certain researchers to wonder whether it would be better to let the images speak for themselves. In other words, the idea was to allow the user to formulate his queries using images, and then the system would quite simply find the images that resemble them. Of course, responding to these queries that only contain images means that different techniques must be used than with textual queries. This new method was called content-based image retrieval or CBIR. As part of content-based searches, the query can be formulated in different ways, which we will summarize below. However, note that a certain number of steps are common to most methods:

1. A certain number of visual descriptors must be extracted from all the DB images. This extraction must be done a priori, i.e., before even allow the user to perform searches.
2. In general, the same visual descriptors must be extracted from the query.
3. The comparison between the query and a DB image comes down to comparing between their visual descriptors.

Query in which the user provides the value of each feature

Some engines, such as [7], have chosen this technique, which involves asking the user to provide the numerical value of each feature. If, for example, each image is described by colour moments and Fourier descriptors of its shapes, it is then up to the user to provide the numerical value for these features. It is clear that creating this type of query is, for various reasons, very difficult, if not impossible, for the user, even if he is a specialist in image processing. First of all, the ordinary user ignores the meaning of features, such as colour moments or Fourier descriptors. Secondly, it is extremely difficult, even for a specialist, to translate one's needs (the image that he is searching for) into a set of numerical values.

Query based on example image(s)

This is definitely the most successful content-based technique. The principle of this technique is simple: the user selects an example image, and then the engine finds images that resemble it. Several variations have been proposed:

Query with one example image versus query with several example images:

In its simplest form, retrieval by example image can be summarized as follows:

1. The engine starts by proposing to the user a number of images from the DB.
2. The user selects one of these images to say "Find me images that look like this".
3. The engine browses through the DB looking for the images that resemble the query, and then returns the results to the user.

The images that the engine proposes at the beginning may be chosen randomly or intelligently (e.g. an image from each family). In general, wisely choosing these images can make the search easier, more productive and quicker.

Many engines allow the user to create a query with several example images. In this case, the example images can be combined by using logical connectors, such as AND, OR, NOT, etc. At the time of the search, the images that make up the query may be combined in different ways and at different levels. They can be combined at feature level by calculating, for example, an average of all these images, and then by comparing this average with the images in the DB. The combination can also be made using set operations. If the user is looking for images that resemble Image A AND Image B, then the engine can start by searching all images that resemble A, and then all images that resemble B, and the result will be the intersection of the two sets.

Later we will see that certain engines make use of the fact that the user chooses several example images to perform feature selection. However, note that certain models need many example images to be able to select features. This can be restrictive and requires much work on the part of the user, which is not always guaranteed.

Query by global image versus query by region of interest:

Certain retrieval engines do not allow the user to select part of an image as the query. If an image is selected, it is taken as a whole. However, it was noted in different situations that the user may be interested in part of an image, instead of the entire image. An example of this is the user who is looking for a given object regardless of the background on which it appears. In this case, allowing the user to select part of the image as a query can considerably improve search results.

Searching by regions of interest can be summarized as follows:

- During feature extraction phase, each image is first segmented into regions; then each region is represented by a set of descriptors.
- The user creates his query by selecting one or more example regions. Certain engines require the regions to be chosen within a single image whereas others allow to select regions from different images. In addition, certain engines enable the user to choose regions as negative examples.
- Once the query has been created, the engine searches through the collection images for those that can be described by the combination of example regions.

- When it involves comparing a single region with another, different similarity measures can be applied, including probabilistic measures and distances. The problem becomes more complex, however, when comparing two groups of regions: the first coming from the query, while the second comes from the DB image. To perform this comparison, different techniques were adopted, including fuzzy logic [8] and set operations.

Lastly, note that nothing prevents the retrieval engine from letting the user to combine global images and regions of interest in the same query. A possible example would be "I am looking for images that resemble Image I but without Object O."

Queries with positive example versus queries with negative example:

Over the past decade, researchers have realized the importance of negative examples and the additional possibilities these offered for creating queries. The negative example can let the user express what he does not want, which helps solve several problems during image retrieval, including noise and miss. Noise is the set of images that the user does not want, but that are returned by the engine. Miss designates all images that should have been returned, but were not. There can be different reasons for these two problems: a user who did not express his needs well, an engine that was not successful in understanding these needs, etc. The negative example can be used as a way of reducing noise and miss. By selecting a few images as negative examples, the user tells the engine that these must be skipped (as well as any image resembling them) in the results of the next iteration, which reduce the amount of noise. As well, the images skipped will be replaced by more relevant images, which reduces miss.

Some of the other advantages of negative examples include:

- It allows to target certain parts of the search space that the positive example alone cannot do. It also finds classes of results that have complex forms in the search space.
- It can sometimes solve the Page zero problem, which we will discuss at the end of this section
- It helps better select features.

Many engines enable the user to combine positive examples with the negative examples when formulating the query. Some engines allow users to introduce the negative example since the first iteration whereas others allow users to use it only for the second iteration, i.e., to refine the results. Technically, the negative example was modelled in different ways, including optimization models [9], probabilistic models [10] and set models [11].

Note that the negative example alone does not really allow to create a query due to its multi-modality. Indeed: if you know what someone does not want, this does not give you enough indication to know what he wants. For example, if a user does not want images of cars, this can mean that he is looking for trees, buildings, the sea, grass, works of art or anything else.

Queries by sketch and queries by predefined icons

Two other mechanisms for creating the query have been adopted by certain engines. The first involves allowing the user to make a sketch that roughly represents what he is looking for, such as in [12]. The user can use the mouse or a electronic pen to make the sketch. As well, the engine can allow the user to colour the objects being drawn.

The second mechanism involves letting the user "make" his own query image. The engine starts by proposing a list of icons, each representing a well-defined object, such as the sky, sea, sun, a car, etc. The user can select icons that interest him and put them in the right place on a "canvas", which represents his query image. The engine of [12] allows this type of query.

These two ways of creating the query can be useful in certain situations:

- They sometimes help in the case of a *target search*, i.e., a user who searches for a specific image that he has already seen. However, in the case of a *group search* or when the user does not have a specific description of the image content that he is looking for (e.g. he wants to find any image that can illustrate a given concept), these types of queries may be unsuitable.
- They allow to create certain simple queries (e.g. an object on a background). However, they do not allow to describe complex images, such as images with a multitude of objects.
- They can help solve the Page zero problem. When the user cannot find the right image to start the search from those proposed by the engine, the sketch or icons can help serve as a starting point. He starts by making a sketch or placing several icons, and then the engine searches for a few corresponding images, and lastly the user uses some of these images to create his query.

However, these types of queries are fraught with a number of problems:

- They depend largely on the ability of the user to express his needs by using the sketch, which is not easy given the difficulty that some users have with sketching, especially with a mouse or a electronic pen.
- Many users do not have the time or patience needed to place icons or draw a sketch for each search iteration.
- Another difficulty crops up when searching and comparing since the engine must compare two things that are not of the same type: a sketch and an image. One possible solution consists of comparing the shape of the drawn objects or selected icons with the shapes extracted from the DB image. Another possible solution would be using shape and object recognition. Automatic annotation could also be used.

Given their limitations, these two types of queries cannot be used alone in an engine. They must be combined with other methods, such as query by example images.

Discussion:

Content-based retrieval includes a certain number of advantages, including:

- The fact that it can be used even if the DB does not contain any text. Indeed, in this case, the text-based search becomes unusable, and the only way would be to base the search on the content of the images.
- It works well with very complex images and with those containing many objects that cannot be described with text.
- It allows a level of refinement that text cannot. For example, looking for images that visually resemble the image in Fig. 2 is quite possible using a search with example images.
- The content of images is more objective than text.

Content-based search also have a certain number of challenges:

- Extraction of visual features.
- Semantic gap.
- The page zero problem.

Each of these challenges is discussed below:

Extraction of visual features:

The fact of designing and extracting visual features which accurately represents the content of images is perhaps the pillar of content-based search. A multitude of features are proposed in the literature. They can be grouped in different families. The first family describes the colour and includes histograms, moments, etc. The second family describes the texture and includes the co-occurrence matrix, Gabor filter, autocovariance, etc. The third family describes the shape: this includes invariant moments, Fourier descriptors, edge points, etc. The fourth family involves mixed features that describe more than one aspect, such as the correlogram, which describes both colour and texture. Other features were also proposed to describe the structure, points of interest, etc. Extraction of features is a problem that is not completely resolved and much work remains to be done, especially regarding features that can capture the semantic content of images.

Semantic gap:

Although it works well for users interested in the visual content of images, content-based search have much difficulty in capturing semantics. For example, imagine a user who is searching for images that can be associated with the concept "Lunch". A search on the Web using Google Image [53] provides the results in Fig. 4. Although these images describe this concept, there is little or no visual resemblance between them. How, then, can the content-based search meet this query? This lack of connection between the visual content of an image and the semantic concepts that may be associated with it is known as the Semantic Gap.

Different solutions were proposed to alleviate this problem. Some simply combine the content of images with text, since text better captures semantics. Others use relevance feedback in order to better understand what the user wants. However, note that the problem of semantic gap is far from resolved. It is the greatest challenge that the new generation of content-based retrieval engines face.

Figure 4. Results of the search using the word "Lunch"

Page zero problem:

It sometimes happens that none of the images proposed by the engine resemble what the user is looking for, and therefore cannot be used to create the query. This is known as the page zero problem. Several solutions can be applied to solve or alleviate this problem. Certain engines allow the user to select another set of images from the DB, which can serve as examples. Other engines allow the user to provide his own example image, i.e., an image that is not in the DB. However, this should not be the only option possible seeing that the user does not always have the images to describe what he wants. Queries containing several example images can also provide some solutions to the page zero problem, insomuch as each of these images contains part of what the user wants. Queries by region can also be useful. For example, imagine that, from the images being proposed by the engine, only one contains the object that the user wants, but that this same image contains other objects that the user does not want. In this case, forcing the user to choose the integrality of the image is restrictive whereas allowing him to select only the object that interests him provides more flexibility. The negative example can also contribute to solve the problem of page zero. As we explained earlier, the negative example reduces miss; and, when miss is reduced, the odds will be greater that the user finds new images that resemble what he is looking for. These images can therefore be used to create the query, which allows to overcome the page zero problem. Another possible solution for this problem is to start with a textual query and then refine it using example images, assuming of course that the engine supports textual queries. Lastly, note that the queries made using sketches and icons sometimes help solve this problem, as we explained earlier.

Combining different types of queries

Each way of creating the query is better suited for a given type of search, and meets a specific need. Text-based search allows to find images based on their semantics. Content-based search allows finding them based on their visual content, and is indispensable in the case of non-annotated DBs. As well, specific method of creating queries, such as sketches and icons, allow to solve certain problems, including the page zero problem. We think that combining all these types of queries in the same engine could only be an advantage. More tools would be available to the user, which would help him better express his needs. A possible scenario would be to conduct a two-step search. During the first step, the text is used to limit the search space to the set of images that relate to the same theme as the query. During the second step, the visual aspect is used to refine the results and sort them according to their visual resemblance with the query.

4. Similarity and Human Judgement

In the case of text-based search, matching techniques are generally used to compare terms contained in the query and those accompanying the images. If, however, the search is based on content, similarity techniques are more appropriate since rigid matching does not work in most situations. Indeed, requiring that an image be an exact match to the query to be returned to the user is a very restrictive choice and may return no result. Even images that are very similar to the query are almost never an exact copy of it. This is due to a certain number of variations and imperfections: difference in scale, angle, position, and object orientation, etc. Unlike matching, similarity does not require equality among images. It simply involves calculating a level of resemblance between the query and each image in the DB, and then sorting these images in decreasing order based on this degree of resemblance.

In image retrieval, a good similarity measure must be as close as possible to human judgement. This is justified by the fact that, in the end, it is the need of a person that should be met, and it is him who will judge whether the results are relevant or irrelevant. Because of this, similarity is a complex cognitive process that involves different disciplines, including psychology, mathematics and computers.

Old models consider similarity as a distance in the feature space, which assumes that it meets the following conditions: non-negativity, identity of indiscernables, symmetry and triangular inequality [13]. However, experimental studies have shown that these conditions are not always met.

The *Thurstone* and *Shepard* models, where the base idea comes from [13], represent a second family of similarity models. These models can be seen as a generalization of distances. See [14] for a good review of these methods. In these models, the similarity between two stimuli (images in our case) is a function of the distance, which is Minkowski's distance, given by $d(x,y)=\left[\sum_{k=1}^{n}|x_k-y_k|^{\gamma}\right]^{\frac{1}{\gamma}}$.

Later, other models were developed. These models drop the distance model, which allows them to eliminate the conditions mentioned earlier. We can talk about the work of Amos Tversky [15], which proposed the famous *feature contrast model*. Instead of considering stimuli as points in the metric space, Tversky characterizes them as a set of features. Let us assume that a and b are two stimuli, and that A and B are their respective sets of features. The work of Tversky stipulates that similarity can be obtained by calculating a linear combination of functions of common features ($A \cap B$) and discriminatory features ($A - B$) and ($B - A$). Mathematically, the similarity can be formulated as follows: $S(a,b) = f(A \cap B) - \alpha f(A - B) - \beta f(B - A)$, where f is a positive function and α and β are two constants.

Some work, including [16], noted that all stimuli do not influence the perception of similarity according to the same mechanism. For some of them, a distance may be appropriate and correspond to test results. Others, however, require more complex models.

Before ending this section, we would like to say a few words on the similarity between colours, because colour is a feature that is largely used when searching for images. Colour can be characterized in different ways including histograms and colour moments. As well, it can be represented in different spaces: RGB, HSV, XYZ or even L*a*b*. It was noted that certain spaces correspond better to human judgement than others. For a space to be considered close to human judgement, the following conditions must be established: two colours that are distinct to humans must be found far from one another within this space, and two colours that are similar to humans must be close to one another within this space. For example, the L*a*b* space was often used since it approached human judgement. Lastly, for similarity measures used with histograms, different measures were used, including Euclidian distance [9], the Earth Mover Distance (EMD) [17] and histogram intersection [18].

5. The User and Relevance Feedback (RF):

Problem: Why do we need RF?

The user who interacts with an image retrieval engine expresses his needs through query formulation. However, due to imperfections at different levels, it is not unusual for the user to not be able to express his needs correctly or the engine to not succeed in understanding these needs. Different problems may lie at the origin of this lack of understanding between the user and engine. First of all, there is the semantic gap. Often the user is interested by the semantics of images (e.g. I am looking for images that illustrate joy), whereas the engine relies on their visual content. The opposite may also occur: a user interested by the visual content of images versus an engine that only takes into account the semantic concepts extracted from the text, for example. Secondly, there is the weakness of the visual features to correctly represent the images. In spite of the progress made these past few years in feature extraction, a lot of work remains to be done before we can rely on features to adequately represent the content of images and even less so their semantics. Thirdly, there is the disparity between the similarity measures used by the engine and human judgement of the similarity between the images. The page zero problem is the fourth problem. It occurs when no image proposed by the engine resembles what the user is looking for, and cannot therefore be used as an example image. Fifth, there is the subjectivity of the text in the representation of images. The user of the engine and the person who annotated the images do not necessarily have the same point of interest, which means they will not use the same terms to describe the same image. Consequently, at the time of carrying out the search, the user will have a lot of problems finding this image. Other difficulties also crop up when we use text: synonyms, dependence on language and culture, etc.

Relevance feedback as a solution:
Relevance Feedback (RF) was introduced as a technique to overcome or alleviate the aforementioned problems. RF was first used in search techniques in the mid-sixties. Its objective is to improve retrieval precision during the iterations, based on the information the user provides about the relevance of the retrieved results. The first work on RF includes [19], [20] and [21]. Motivaed by the improvement it achieved in text retrieval, image retrieval researchers very quickly understood the role that RF could play in image retrieval, and have integrated it into their engines.

How does the user express his needs during the RF process?
The concept of RF is to ask the user to provide feedback regarding the results returned by the engine at each iteration. Using this mecanism, the user explicitly or implicitly provides more information on the images he likes and those he does not like as well as on the features that interest him and those that do not.
In concrete terms, RF can be carried out in different ways:

- The engine can ask the user to choose from the images returned at each iteration the ones that he finds relevant (positive examples) and the ones he finds not relevant (negative examples). It can also ask the user to assign a weight to each image. For a positive example image, a high weight means that it resembles very much what the user is looking for, whereas a low weight means that it resembles the user's idea a little. For a negative example image, a low weight means that similar images would not be appreciated, whereas a high weight means that the user definitely does not want similar images returned.
- The engine can ask the user to explicitly assign a weight to each feature used. However, this can be restrictive given that the normal user ignores the significance of features. In addition, even for a specialist, it is difficult to say whether a given feature is important or not to find what he is looking for. To resolve this problem, many engines guess the importance of features without explicitly asking the user. This information can be deduced from the example images that the user provides, as we will see in this section.

- Some engines ask the user to choose between the use of textual features, visual features or a combination of both.

What can RF do?
After the user has provided his feedback about the results of an iteration, this information is used to improve the results in different ways [10][5]. It helps to understand what the user is looking for, i.e., to identify the image(s) in his head. It also helps determine the importance he gives to each feature, which will then be used to define the similarity measures that best reflect his judgement.

The different RF techniques:
Early CBIR systems that adopted RF were built on the vector model in information retrieval theory. They used the query-point movement technique, and/or the axis re-weighting technique [22]. In the query-point movement technique, the ideal query point is moved toward the positive example and away from the negative example. Examples of systems that have adopted this technique include [23] and [24]. Rocchio's formula [25] has been frequently used to perform query-point movement. In the axis re-weighting technique, the main goal is to assign more importance to features according to which example images are close to each other, and less importance to other features. This can be justified by the fact that, if the variance of the query images is high along a given axis, any value on this axis is apparently acceptable to the user, and therefore this axis should be given a low weight, and vice versa [22]. An example of axis re-weighting models can be found in [23], where each feature is weighted with the inverse of its standard deviation.
More recently, some researchers have considered RF to be a classification problem in which example images provided by the user are employed to train a classifier, which is then used to classify the database into images that are relevant to the query and those that are not. Bayesian models have been used in systems like [26] and [27], which support image classes that assign a high membership probability to positive example images and penalize classes that assign a high membership probability to negative example images. SVMs have also been used in RF [28] [5]. Examples include [29] and [30]. Some systems first train an SVM classifier using positive and negative examples, and then use it to divide the database into relevant images and irrelevant ones. Considering RF as a classification problem may entail some difficulties, however. First, in a typical classification problem, each item (image) belongs to one or more clearly defined classes, whereas, in image retrieval, human subjectivity makes it difficult to assign a given image to a given class [31]. Second, classification does not always provide a ranking of the retrieved images in terms of their resemblance to the query, which may be necessary for some applications.
Other researchers consider RF to be a learning problem in which examples fed back by the user are used to train a model, which is then used for retrieval. Techniques used include self-organizing maps (SOMs), Bayesian frameworks and decision trees. In [32] for example, SOMs are used to measure similarity between images. In [33], a Bayesian framework is used to predict what target image users want, given the action they undertook. In turn, [34] proposes an RF model that, for each retrieval iteration, learns a decision tree to uncover a common thread uniting all images marked as relevant. This tree is then used as a model for inferring which of the unseen images the user would most likely want. The initial drawback of learning methods is the lack of data. Indeed, users usually provide a small number of feedback images in the retrieval process, while these algorithms need a large number of

examples for training. For example, after extensive experimentation with the system described in [9], we found that people rarely give more than a few images as feedback, while the model, in order to be trained correctly, needs a number of images at least equal to the dimension of the largest feature. It would be inconceivable to ask the user to select several dozen images in each retrieval step, because this can make the retrieval process very slow and cumbersome.

Some researchers considered RF to be a distance optimization problem whose solutions are the parameters that make it possible to find the ideal query, weight the features, and transform the feature space into a new one that corresponds better to the user. Examples of such models include [9], [22] and [35]. In these models, RF is formulated as a minimization problem whose solutions are the optimal query and a weight matrix, which is used to define a generalized ellipsoid distance as a measure of similarity between images. The basic idea of those models is to enhance features for which example images are close to each other. When the query embeds some negative examples, they enhance features that distinguish clearly between positive and negative examples, and neglect those that do not. Like learning techniques, optimization techniques suffer from the problem of lack of data, and different attempts have been made to address it, like in [36], where the authors introduce the regularization method and the null-space method.

Type of user and user influence on RF strategy:

For relevance feedback, two different strategies can be used [28]. The first strategy is the most common. It involves providing the user, at each iteration, with the most relevant images that the engine was able to identify. The second strategy involves returning the more informative images and trying to obtain as much information as possible from the user. This helps to better pinpoint the range or set of images that the user is searching for. In [37] and [38] for example, at each iteration, two images are presented to the user, who must choose the one that most matches what he is looking for.

The difference between the two strategies is that the first one assumes that the user is impatient and therefore must be provided with the best results as quickly as possible or else he could end the retrieval session. The second technique assumes that the user will cooperate [39]. It attempts to ask him as many questions as possible to learn more about what he is looking for. Note that both techniques can be combined in the same system [40]. For example, at each iteration, the system can provide the user with the most relevant images and ask him some optional questions (if he wants to answer them) to better understand what he wants.

Relevance feedback with or without memory:

When processing a given iteration query, some RF models take into account older queries (previous iterations), whereas others only look at the query of the current iteration. The first family could be called "models with memory" and the second "models without memory". Models with memory assume that the user is consistent in his choices, i.e., that, during a given session, he continues to search for the same images and does not change his intention. Models without memory do not make this hypothesis. Therefore, when the user is consistent, the precision of models with memory increases throughout the iterations. Some studies, including [41], have noted, however, that the user often changes his intention while searching. In this case, a model without memory may be the most appropriate. Technically, models with memory consider the new search target as a combination (linear or otherwise) of the very last query and the queries from previous iterations.

Creating user profiles:
The concept of memory discussed in the previous subsection can be expanded even further. The engine can, for example, try to create a profile for each user. It must first identify each user in a unique manner. This can be done by asking him to identify himself each time he uses the engine by entering his user name and password for example. Other techniques, such as IP address or cookies, also can be used to identify the user or his machine. The second step is to memorize the preferences of each user when he performs search. The third step consists of using these preferences in the future to improve search precision. Let's take an example. User X created Query Q at a given moment. According to the his feedback, the engine understands that he was satisfied with the results obtained. In the future, if this same user submits the same query, it would be intelligent on the part of the engine to return the same results. However, if the user is not satisfied, the same results should not be returned. User preferences go beyond the set of resulting images. The user may have a preference for a given feature versus others, a type of query (e.g. text-based) versus others (e.g. content-based), etc. All this information can be stored by the engine for future use. Once individual profiles have been created, the engine can make a classification in order to discover the different user classes and preferences of the members of each class. This classification can be cross-referenced with their other attributes: age, sex, language, culture, etc.
Lastly, we should note that the creation of profile poses a certain number of challenges. The largest challenge is the potential cooperation of the users: to create profiles, users must be willing to identify themselves or provide certain personal information. This sometimes goes against protecting the user's privacy.

Helping the user create his query and provide feedback:
Sometime it is best to guide the user throughout the search process: from query formulation to relevance feedback to obtaining results. From the user's point of view, this assistance can make search easier and more attractive. The engine, in turn, can better understand the user's needs to better serve him.
This help can be provided in different ways:

- Help the user choose the query mode that best suits him from those offered by the engine: textual query, example image query, etc.
- Provide the user with some tips for creating his query, as is done by the engines of [42] and [43].
- When the engine asks the user to enter the importance he gives to each feature, explain to him at least the meaning of each of these features.
- Step by step and by asking a certain number of questions, the engine can have the user express his need in a more specific manner. For example, for the first step, the engine may propose a set of image families (animals, cars, landscapes, etc.) and ask the user to choose the family that corresponds to his search. Once the user has made his choice, the engine proposes the list of subfamilies, and so forth, until the desired results have been obtained.
- Guide the user, as in [37] and [38], where, at each step, the engine asks the user to choose the image that best meets what he is looking for between two images proposed.

- An "Advanced Search" function, found in certain Web retrieval engines, can be very useful. It enables the user to give more details about what he is looking for: file format (jpg, gif, bmp, etc.), file size, image dimensions, greyscale or colour, a photo versus a sketch versus a synthesized image, etc.
- Hints that appear automatically when the mouse moves over certain elements in the interface.
- Add a "What is it?" button beside certain elements in the interface so that the user can, if he so wishes, better understand their meanings.

While helping the user is definitely appreciated, we must however determine how far this help can go before it produces a negative effect. In extreme cases, we could require the user to take training so that he can benefit from all engine functionalities. However, we must remember that many users do not have the desire, patience or time to take this training. It therefore becomes an obstacle that purely and simply pushes them to abandon such an engine.

6. Results Visualisation:

1D Visualisation versus several D Visualisation:

Once the search has been performed, the engine must display the results to the user. The most used and traditional method is to present the results linearly with images ordered based on their resemblance to the query, starting with the closest match. We can call this way of presenting results the one-dimensional method. However, we should note that most engines use the fact that the screen is two-dimensional (2-D) and present the results on several lines where the first line has the most relevant images from left to right, as though reading a book.

Other methods of viewing search results have been proposed:

1. The system can use two features—which may be multidimensional—to represent images. All images in the DB are displayed in a 2-D plan, with the query image in the centre. Both axes of the plane each represent a feature. The position of a DB image on each axis is proportional to its dissimilarity to the query with regard to the feature concerned. In [44], for example, both axes represent the RGB and HSV histograms respectively. The X-axis of each DB Image I is obtained from the intersection of the RGB histograms of I and the query, with a positive sign if the entropy of the RGB histogram of I is lower than the entropy of the RGB histogram of the query. The Y-axis is calculated in the same way, but by using the HSV histograms.
2. Since most retrieval engines use more than two features to represent images, the method described in 1) cannot be used in a 2-D plan. It can, however, be generalized as follows: start by representing the images in the multidimensional feature space, and then project them in a 2-D space (plan). It is this plan that the user will see displayed, with his query in the middle. In order to minimize loss of information due to projection, techniques such as Principal Component Analysis (PCA) can be applied. This method was used in [45]. It not only allows to display images based on their similarity to the query, but also based on resemblance between them.
3. Some engines, such as [46], visualize images in a 3D virtual reality space. The three axes can each represent a feature as in 1) or a combination of features after projection, as in 2). In [46], for example, the axes represent colour, texture and structure

respectively. The engine can enable the user to view the results based on each axis taken individually, or even view them from any angle (combination of axes).

4. In certain engines, such as [47], the query image is displayed in the middle, and then surrounded by similar images. The size and position (distance) of each image from the query is proportional to its similarity to the query. In addition, [47] proposes two ways of displaying these images: either in concentric rings or in a spiral.
5. Some engines, such as [48], use Self-organized maps (SOM) for viewing collections of images.

Note that some of these methods can also be used when formulating the query. They can also be seen as a hybrid solution between the query and navigation.

All these viewing methods can be improved by combining them with the following techniques:

- Image size: during display, the size of each image can be in proportion to its similarity to the query.
- Zoom function: enable the user to zoom in to see more detail of a part of the collection or to zoom out to have a more global view.
- Reduce overlapping: When projecting, many similar images can be found in the same small zone, which means that some of them hide others. This effect is known as overlapping. This problem becomes even more serious when the collection contains many images. Most of the time, it is not possible to eliminate overlapping completely. However, it can be reduced by using optimization or heuristic algorithms, which attempt to find the position of each image that is as close as possible to its original position and that minimizes overlapping with its neighbours. Displaying images in small sizes with the Zoom option also alleviates this problem. However, the images should not be too small, since users will not appreciate this. The article, [49], analyzes and proposes a few solutions to these problems.

Size of image displayed to the user:

Whether during query creation, relevance feedback or results display, images must be displayed to the user. The issue that this section looks at is the choice of dimensions for the images displayed: Should the actual dimensions be kept, or modified, and why? The most natural choice would be to have each image keep its actual dimensions. However, this may have certain disadvantages:

- The actual dimensions of an image may be very large. The interface may not be able to display them. As well, displaying a large image may require greater calculation capacity and therefore take lots of memory.
- The different images can have different sizes. It is neither convenient nor attractive to present images of different sizes on the same interface.

Instead, the dimensions of each image should be adapted to the interface. We could replace each image with a thumbnail, for example, while giving the user the option of viewing the original image if he so wishes. The size of the thumbnail should be proportional to the original dimensions in order not to distort the image. In general, a thumbnail is smaller than the original image. However, thumbnails should not be too small. If they are, the user will have to view the original image each time to be able to see the details and decide whether the image interests him. This could be cumbersome and slow down the search process [41].

Presentation order of results:

Another issue that should be raised is: In which order should results appear? There are several possible solutions. The most common is to present them in decreasing order of similarity to the query. Other solutions are also possible:

- In chronological order according to creation date.
- By event: images taken during a given event are presented together. This could be family events or otherwise. An example of an event could be "Our camping trip in 1998" or even "Wedding of X family member". This way of presenting assumes that we know the event related to each image. It works well with certain collections of personal or family images.
- Hierarchically: different classes of images are displayed to the user, who can then choose the class that he wants to visit. This way of presenting the results is similar to browsing through a catalogue.
- A combination of all these choices.

Number of images to return to the user and interrogation technique:

Another issue that must be addressed is identifying the number of images to return to the user and how to find these images. Two main query techniques were used by most retrieval engines: The k nearest neighbours and the neighbours whose distance from the query (or dissimilarity) is below a certain threshold ε. If we use the first technique, a certain number of problems must be addressed. The first is choosing the number k. This choice however is not necessary for small DBs. The engine can simply sort all the images in the DB according to their resemblance to the query, and then return the first ones to the user, while giving him the option of viewing more results. For large DBs, using an index becomes essential. If this index is available, the search will be limited to the classes closest to the query, which leads us to searching in a smaller DB as in the previous case. The second problem is that the images returned may not resemble the query, especially when the number of relevant images in the DB is low.

When the second technique is used, the value of ε must first be determined. In order for the results to have meaning, a threshold under which all the images actually resemble the query must be chosen. Sometimes we have to define a variable threshold that changes depending on the query. The problem with the threshold technique is that it depends considerably on Recall. If it is too low, it might not return any results, and if it is high, it could return too many results. In the latter case, the results can be truncated by limiting them to the k nearest neighbours to the query, which brings us back to the first technique. The engine can also sort the results, display the first ones to the user and give him the option of viewing others.

Regardless of the query technique adopted, using an index is only useful when the DB is very large. An appropriate indexing technique limits the search to the most relevant classes, which helps increase precision of results and reduce search time.

Viewing on small devices and adapting:

These past few years, the use of portable devices (PDA, cell phones, Palm Pilot, etc.) has increased substantially. These tools are used for various purposes, including browsing the Internet, accessing multimedia collections and searching on the Web. Creating retrieval engines for these devices or adapting existing engines to them will help meet a growing need. Recently, some researchers have taken an interest in this issue. For example, [50], [51] and [52].

When a retrieval engine is developed for these devices, client-server applications can be used, in which the server runs on the computer to allow access to and searching in the DB, while the client runs on the portable device. Portable devices are different from a conventional computer. They are subject to additional limitations. The first constraint is the size of their screens, which are smaller than a regular computer screen. Therefore, the client interface and the size of images displayed must be adapted based on to this limitation. For example, the client program can display a single image at a time, but while giving the user the option of scrolling through the page to see more images. The second constraint is the reduced data transfer speed. The server must therefore limit as much as possible the number of images and data sent to the client. The third constraint is their rather limited calculation capacity. The server must perform a maximum number of operations, leaving the client only with the simplest things to do, like displaying results.

7. Users as a Retrieval Engine Evaluator

A retrieval engine is created to meet the needs of the user. The user must therefore be satisfied with the services offered by the engine. According to Section 2, there are two types of services: query-based search and catalogue browsing. In this section, we will look at issues related to evaluating each of these services.

Evaluating the search function:
The most common evaluation scenario is the following. We start with several retrieval sessions by changing the query each time. Once results have been obtained, they are evaluated by being assigned scores as to their relevance versus the query. These scores can be assigned by humans or obtained from preclassification of the DB. The scores of the different sessions are then combined, for example, using a weighted average, which allows to obtain different performance indicators, including Precision and Recall.
Therefore, it can be deduced that evaluating the search function of an engine requires three components, namely, an image DB, ground truth and evaluation measurements, as detailed below.

Image collection or DB:
In order to ensure an objective evaluation, the image collection used must meet a certain number of criteria. First it must be large enough to allow evaluation of the scalability of the engine. Next it must correspond to the objectives for which the engine was designed. If the engine was developed for personal photos, for example, it must be evaluated on a collection of personal photos, and if it was developed for art images, it must be evaluated on a collection of art images. While remaining within the engine's domain, the collection must be as diverse as possible in order to evaluate the ability of the engine to find images from different categories. Lastly, note that several collections have been used to evaluate search engines. The most commonly used is that from Corel [37].

Ground truth:
Ground truth allows to judge whether the images returned by the engine are relevant or not. Two types of ground truth are generally used: human judgement and preclassified DBs.
Human judgement is a good indicator, because, in the end, it is humans that will be using the engine. If they see the results as being relevant, then we can say that the engine is

precise. In order to ensure that the evaluation by people is objective, we must follow a certain number of recommendations:

- The number of users: A significant number of users must participate in the evaluation process in order to limit the effect of subjectivity from certain people.
- The users must be representative of the population who will be using the engine: the level of expertise in the field, level of instruction, age, sex, preferences, etc. For example, if the engine is for the general public, the evaluators should not all be experts in image processing.
- Sometimes training is required so that a person can use the engine. This training must be as concise and easy as possible; if not, users might not use the engine.

When the ground truth comes from a prior classification of the DB, a high score is automatically assigned to any image belonging to the same class as the query, whereas a low score, zero or even a negative score, is assigned to images from other classes. However, similar classes must be monitored: an image from a class resembling the query should not be considered as poor, even if it is not as good as an image coming from the same class as the query.

Particular attention must be given to preclassification. The fact of relying on preclassification to evaluate the engine implicitly assumes that it is perfect: imprecise preclassification would completely distort our evaluation. Preclassification can be obtained in different ways. It can be carried out by humans, which brings us back to the first type of ground truth, or it could be done by the machine with little or no human intervention.

Evaluation measurements:

Two of the most commonly used measurements are Precision (*Pr*) and Recall (*Re*). Precision measures the proportion of good images versus the total number of images returned to the user. Recall measures the proportion of good images returned to the user among all good images in the DB. Noise, which is the opposite of Precision, was also used. It represents the proportion of irrelevant images from all images returned to the user. Certain variations of Precision and Recall take into account image rank: the most relevant images must appear in the first positions. Once calculated, Precision and Recall can be represented by curves. Some authors draw the curve $Pr = f(Re)$. A good system should provide high Precision regardless of the Recall value. However, if Recall is low, as in the case of certain image collections, this measurement becomes unsuitable. Other authors replace it with $Pr = f(\mathrm{Sc})$, where Scope *Sc* is the number of images returned to the user.

Evaluation of the browsing function:

In order to provide browsing services to users, the engine must start by indexing the DB. This operation involves dividing the DB into classes, and then dividing each class into subclasses. The first thing to evaluate here is the class quality. A good class must be coherent and complete. Coherence means that the images assigned to this class resemble each other. An example of an incoherent class would be a class that contains images of apples, cars and horses. Completeness means that we find, in a given class, all the images that should be assigned to it. We can draw a parallel between Coherence and Precision on the one hand, and Completeness and Recall on the other.

As in the case for search, to evaluate the cataloguing, a DB is needed on which the algorithm will be applied and a ground truth can be used to judge relevance. The collection must be carefully selected. As for the ground truth, it can be provided by humans.

The catalogue can be evaluated based on the total number of images it contains, the diversity of subjects it covers, whether it is hierarchical or not, the inter-class and inter-level relationships, the option of moving from theme to theme, ease of use, etc. Some of these measurements, such as the total number of images covered by the catalogue, are objective. They can be calculated without requiring any judgement from the user.

Other evaluation criteria
A certain number of other criteria could also be used when evaluating:

Number of images indexed:
It is more difficult, but more useful, to index several hundreds of thousands of images than to index only a few dozens. An engine can be evaluated based on the number of images it indexes.

User-friendliness:
One of the attributes that makes a retrieval engine successful is how easy it is to use. The interface must be user-friendly on all levels: formulating the query, displaying results, relevance feedback, etc.

Response time:
Response time can also influence user satisfaction. A system, even if it provides relatively precise results, that takes too long will not be appreciated by users. The response time for a query can be influenced by:

- Prior extraction of features: extracting the features of images first means large time savings, since the engine will not have to do it at the time of the search. The only thing left for it to do is compare the query with the DB images. All known engines extract features ahead of time.
- The number of features used and their sizes: increasing the number of features or increasing the size of a few features generally increases the comparison time, and, in turn, the response time.
- Similarity measures used: certain similarity measures are quick to calculate whereas others take longer, which directly affects searching time.
- The fact of using an index: the index restricts the search space to classes that most resemble the query, which considerably reduces the searching time.

Refinement and number of iterations:
It is always a good idea for the engine to provide the user with the option of refining the results via relevance feedback. However, the number of iterations required to obtain good results should be minimal.

8. Conclusion

When a user uses an image retrieval engine, he is in constant interaction with the engine, be it to create the query, provide feedback, view the results or evaluate engine performance. In this chapter, we have looked at most of these aspects. The retrieval engine must meet human needs. Therefore, it must be as close as possible to them. In particular, it must use the features that capture the semantic content of images, use similarity measures that resemble human judgment, have a user-friendly interface, etc. A lot of work has been done to that effect over the past few years; however, we believe much remains to be done.

9. References

R. Datta, D. Joshi, J. Li and J. Z. Wang. Image Retrieval: Ideas, Influences, and Trends of the New Age. *ACM Computing Surveys*, Vol. 40, No. 2, 2008 [1]

A. W. M. Smeulders, M. Worring, S. Santini, A. Gupta and Ramesh Jain. Content-Based Image Retrieval at the End of the Early Years. *IEEE Transactions on Pattern Analysis and Machine Intelligence*, Vol. 22, No. 12, pp. 1349-1380, 2000. [2]

M. L. Kherfi, D. Ziou and A. Bernardi. Image Retrieval from the World Wide Web: Issues, Techniques, and Systems. *ACM Computing Surveys*. Volume 36, No 1, pp. 35 - 67, March 2004. [3]

R. C. Veltkamp and M. Tanase. Content-Based Image Retrieval Systems: A Survey. *Technical Report* UU-CS-2000-34, Department of Computing Science, Utrecht University, October 28, 2002. [4]

Y. Liu, D. Zhang, G. Lu and W.-Y. Ma. A Survey of Content-Based Image Retrieval with High-Level Semantics. *Pattern Recognition*, Vol 40, N 1, pp. 262 - 282, 2007[5]

R. Jain. World-Wide Maze. *IEEE MultiMedia*, Vol 2, N 2, 1995. [6]

G. Wei, D. LI, and I. K. Sethi. Web-WISE: Compressed Image Retrieval over the Web. In *IAPR International Workshop on Multimedia Information Analysis and Retrieval*, 33–46. 1998. [7]

Jia Li James Z. Wang Gio Wiederhold. IRM: Integrated Region Matching for Image Retrieval. *ACM Multimedia* 2000. 147-156. [8]

M. L. Kherfi, D. Ziou and A. Bernardi. Combining Positive and Negative Examples in Relevance Feedback for Content-based Image Retrieval. *Journal of Visual Communication and Image Representation*, Vol 14, pp. 428–457, 2003. [9]

M. L. Kherfi and D. Ziou. Relevance Feedback for CBIR: A New Approach Based on Probabilistic Feature Weighting With Positive and Negative Examples *IEEE Transactions on Image Processing*, Vol. 15, No. 4, April 2006. [10]

T. P. Minka, R. W. Picard. Interactive learning using a Society of Models. In *IEEE Conference on Computer Vision and Pattern Recognition*, San Francisco, pp. 447–452, 1996. [11]

M. S. Lew. Next generation Web Searches for Visual Content. *IEEE Computer*. Vol 33, No 11, pp. 46–53, 2000. [12]

L. L. Thurstone. A Law of Comparative Judgement. *Psychological Review*, 34:273-286, 1927. [13]

D. M. Ennis and N. L. Johnson. Thurstone-Shepard Similarity Models as Special Cases of Moment Generating Functions. *Journal of of Mathematical Psychology*, 37:104-110, 1993. [14]

A. Tversky. Features of Similarity. *Psychological Review*, 84(4):327-352, 1977. [15]

F G. Ashby and N. A. Perrin. Toward a Unified Theory of Similarity and Recognition. *Psychological Review*, 95(1):124-150, 1998. [16]

Y. Rubner, C. Tomasi and L. J. Guibas. A Metric for Distribution with Applications to Image Databases. In *IEEE ICCV*, 1998. [17]

M.J. Swain, and B.H. Ballard. Color Indexing. *International Journal of Computer Vision*. Vol 7, No 1, 11 - 32, 1991. [18]

J. J. Rocchio Jr. Relevance Feedback in Information Retrieval. In *The Smart System – Experiments in Automatic Document Processing*. Englewood Cliffs, NJ: Prentice-Hall, pp. 313–323, 1971. [19]

E. Ide. New Experiments in Relevance Feedback. In *The Smart System-Experiments in Automatic Document Processing*. Englewood Cliffs, NJ: Prentice-Hall, pp. 337–354, 1971. [20]

G. Salton. Relevance Feedback and the Optimization of Retrieval Effectiveness. In *The Smart System – Experiments in Automatic Document Processing*. Englewood Cliffs, NJ: Prentice-Hall, pp. 324–336, 1971. [21]

Y. Ishikawa, R. Subramanya and C. Faloutsos. Mindreader: Querying Databases Through Multiple Examples. In *24th International Conference on Very Large Databases*, New York, pp. 433–438, 1998. [22]

Y. Rui, T. S. Huang and S. Mehrotra. Content-Based Image Retrieval with Relevance Feedback in MARS. In *IEEE International Conference on Image Processing*, Santa Barbara, CA, pp. 815–818, 1997. [23]

H. Müller, W. Müller, D. M. Squire, S. Marchand-Maillet and T. Pun. Strategies for Positive and Negative Relevance Feedback in *Image Retrieval. Computer Vision Group*, Computer Center, University of Geneva, Geneva, Switzerland, Technical Report, 2000. [24]

J. J. Rocchio Jr. Relevance Feedback in Information Retrieval. In *The Smart System – Experiments in Automatic Document Processing*. Englewood Cliffs, NJ: Prentice-Hall, pp. 313–323, 1971. [25]

N. Vasconcelos and A. Lippman. Learning from User Feedback in *Image Retrieval Systems*. Neur. Inf. Process. Syst., 1999. [26]

C. Meilhac and C. Nastar. Relevance Feedback and Category Search in Image Databases. In *IEEE International Conference on Multimedia Computing and Systems*, Florence, Italy, pp. 512–517, 1999. [27]

M. Crucianu, M. Ferecatu and N. Boujemaa. Relevance Feedback for Image Retrieval: a Short Survey. In *State of the Art in Audiovisual Content-Based Retrieval, Information Universal Access and Interaction, Including Datamodels and Languages*, Report of the DELOS2 European Network of Excellence, 2004. [28]

D. Tao and X. Tang. Random Sampling Based SVM for Relevance Feedback Image Retrieval. In *International Conference on Computer Vision and Pattern Recognition*, Washington, DC, 2004. [29]

S. Tong and E. Chang. Support Vector Machine Active Learning for Image Retrieval. In *ACM Multimedia Conference*, Ottawa, ON, Canada, 2001. [30]

Z. Su, H.-J. Zhang, S. Li, and S. Ma. Relevance Feedback in Content-Based Image Retrieval: Bayesian Framework, Feature Sub-spaces, and Progressive Learning. *IEEE Transactions on Image Processing*, Vol. 12, No. 8, pp. 924–937, Aug. 2003. [31]

J. Laaksonen, M. Koskela and E. Oja. PicSOM: Self-Organizing Maps for Content-based Image Retrieval. In *International Joint Conference on Neural Networks*, Washington, DC, 1999. [32]

I. J. Cox, T. P. Minka, T. V. Papathomas and P. N. Yianilos. The Bayesian Image Retrieval System, PicHunter: Theory, Implementation, and Psychophysical Experiments. *IEEE Transactions on Image Processing*, Vol. 9, No. 1, pp. 20–37, Jan. 2000. [33]

S. D. MacArthur, C. E. Brodley and C.-R. Shyu. Relevance Feedback Decision Trees in Content-based Image Retrieval. In *IEEE Workshop on Content-based Access of Image and Video Libraries*, Hilton Head, SC, 2000. [34]

Y. Rui and T. S. Huang. Optimizing Learning in Image Retrieval. In *IEEE International Conference on Computer Vision and Pattern Recognition*, Hilton Head, SC, 2000. [35]

D. Tao and X. Tang. Nonparametric Discriminant Analysis in Relevance Feedback for Content-based Image Retrieval. In *International Conference on Pattern Recognition*, Cambridge, U.K., 2004. [36]

www.corel.com[37]

I. J. Cox, M. L. Miller, S. M. Omohundro and P. N. Yianilos. An Optimized Interaction Strategy for Bayesian Relevance Feedback. In *IEEE Conference on Computer Vision and Pattern Recognition*, pp. 553-558, 1998. [38]

X. S. Zhou and T. S. Huang. Relevance Feedback in Image Retrieval: A Comprehensive Review. In *IEEE CVPR Workshop on Content-based Access of Image and Video Libraries* (CBAIVL), 2001[39]

K. Tieu and P. Viola. Boosting Image Retrieval. In *IEEE Conference on Computer Vision and Pattern Recognition*, South Carolina, 2000. [40]

A.A. Goodrum, M.M. Bejune and A.C. Siochi. A State Transition Analysis of Image Search Patterns on the Web. *In International Conference on Image and Video Retrieval*, pages 269–278. Lecture Notes in Computer Science, Vol. 2728, Springer, 2003. [41]

A. Jaimes, K. Omura, T. Nagamine and K. Hirata. Memory Cues for Meeting Video Retrieval. In *CARPE Workshop*, ACM Multimedia, 2004. [42]

T. Nagamine, A. Jaimes, K. Omura and K Hirata. A Visuospatial Memory Cue System for Meeting Video Retrieval. In *ACM Multimedia* (Demonstration), 2004. [43]

Le Thi Lan. Interface de visualisation avec retour de pertinence pour la recherche d'images. In *des 1ères Rencontres Jeunes Chercheurs en Recherche d'Information*, 2004. [44]

B. Moghaddam, Q. Tian and T. Huang. Spatial Visualization for Content-Based Image Retrieval. *Technical Report* 2001-53. MITSUBISHI ELECTRIC RESEARCH LABORATORIES, February 2002. [45]

M. Nakazato and T. S. Huang. 3D MARS : Immersive Virtual Reality for Content-based Image Retrieval. *IEEE International Conference on Multimedia and Expo*, 2001. [46]

R. S. Torres, C. G. Silva, C. B. Medeiros and H. V. Rocha. Visual Structures for Image Browsing. *ACM CIKM'03*, New Orleans, Louisiana, USA, November 2003. [47]

D. Deng J. Zhang and M. Purvis. Visualisation and Comparison of Image Collections based on Self-organised Maps. *Australasian Workshop on Data Mining and Web Intelligence*, Dunedin. Conferences in Research and Practice in Information Technology, Vol. 32, 2004. [48]

G.P. Nguyen and M. Worring. Interactive Access to Large Image Collections Using Similarity-based Visualization. *Journal of Visual Languages and Computing*, 2006. [49]

S. Boutemedjet and D. Ziou. A Graphical Model for Context-Aware Visual Content Recommendation. *IEEE Transactions on Multimedia*, Vol. 10, No. 1, Jan. 2008. [50]

E. Bertini, A. Cali, T. Catarci, S. Gabrielli and S. Kimani. Interaction-based Adaptation for Small Screen Devices. *Lecture Notes in Computer Science* 3538, 277-281, 2005. [51]

L. Q. Chen, X. Xie, X. Fan, W. Y. Ma, H. J. Zhang and H. Q. Zhou. A Visual Attention Model for Adapting Images on Small Displays. *Multimedia Systems* Vol. 9, No. 4, 353-364, 2003. [52]

http://images.google.com/ [53]

http://www.wallpaperbase.com [54]

http://research.microsoft.com/research/downloads/Details/b94de342-60dc-45d0-830b-9f6eff91b301/Details.aspx [55]

15

Smart SoftPhone Device for Networked Audio-Visual QoS/QoE Discovery & Measurement

Jinsul Kim
Digital Media Laboratory, Information and Communications University
Republic of Korea

1. Introduction

Today Multimedia over IP (MoIP) service is provided through the various access networks to Internet, allowing users to get service anytime and anywhere. To control many resources for QoS/QoE guaranteed services over converged networks, developing smart devices and applications applying pervasive network and computing are one of the hot research issues today. The ISO 8402 vocabulary defines quality as the totality of features and characteristics of a product or services that bear on its ability to satisfy stated and implied needs. Quality of Service (QoS) is the collective effect of service performance which determines the degree of satisfaction of the user of the service (from ITU-T E.8001). And then, Quality of Experience (QoE) is a term to allow for subjective as well as objective measures of QoS, performance and all aspects of the interaction (experience) with the service or product (from SLA management handbook). Both QoS and QoE are described very well with networked multimedia application services such as MoIP, IPTV, and mobile IPTV from most recently research (Kim et al., 2008). Due to the shared nature of current network structures, guaranteeing the QoS/QoE of Internet applications from an end-to-end is sometimes difficult and then it has been requested to develop smart devices which have multi-modal functionality for ubiquitous network and computing environment. There are two different aspects, i.e. 'network' and 'multimedia' that are both closely coupled in many critical issues such as QoS, QoE, etc., for MoIP services. An important problem is to provide realtime QoS/QoE-guaranteed multimedia services over packet-based networks. The problem is still unsolved because there are many parameters affecting quality between network and multimedia. In order to solve the problem, a study on QoS/QoE parameters discovery and measurement is necessary.

IP networks are on a steep slope of innovation that will make them the long-term carrier of all types of traffic, including multimedia services in the Next Generation Network (NGN) environment today. However, such networks are not designed for QoS/QoE guaranteed realtime multimedia communication because their variable characteristics (e.g. due to bandwidth, packet loss, delay, etc.) lead to a deterioration in voice/video quality. A major challenge in such networks is how to measure voice/video quality accurately and efficiently considering network resources that provide QoS/QoE-guaranteed services.

In this chapter, we design smart SoftPhone device for guaranteeing human perceived_QoS/QoE which can discover and measure various network parameters during realtime service through IP network. The smart SoftPhone for discovering and measuring of QoS/QoE-factors in realtime consists of four main blocks that is in order to control and measure various parameters independently based on SIP/UDP/RTP protocol during the end-to-end multimedia (voice and video) service. Also, we provide message report procedures and management schemes to guarantee QoS/QoE based on using smart SoftPhone device. In order to report quality parameters optimally during establishing call sessions for MoIP service, we design critical management module blocks for quality reporting. To sum up, for the performance evaluation of the smart SoftPhone with scientific exactitude of quality factors, we examine the proposed technique based on the realtime phone-call service through heterogeneous network. The experimental results confirm that the developed smart SoftPhone is very useful to quality-measuring for the quality guaranteed realtime MoIP service and then it could also be applied to improve quality as a packet compensation device. Finally, we propose QoS/QoE delivery and assessment methodology by model design and performance analysis in considering heterogeneous network and terminals.

The organization of this chapter is as follows. Section 2 describes previous approaches on the identification and characterization of MoIP services by using related works. In section 3, we design modules of smart SoftPhone for quality resource discovery and measurement. The message procedures are presented for call establishing and releasing. In section 4, we describe user, terminal, and network-aware QoS/QoE supported methods with personal mobile broadcasting services. In section 5, RTCP-XR based block types are introduced to monitoring and managing media quality for MoIP services. Section 6 and section 7 present measurement methods with performance evaluations for voice and video quality. Finally, section 8 concludes the chapter.

2. Previous Works

There have been many related research and development efforts in the field of QoS management and measurement for the past decade. Also, today multimedia quality management aspects of QoE have become an important issue with the development of realtime applications such as IP-phones, TV-conferencing and video streaming over IP networks. Specifically, when voice/video data is mixed with various application data, there are worries that there will be a critical degradation in voice/video quality. For the measurement of network parameters, many useful management schemes have been proposed in this research area (Imai et al., 2006). Managing and Controlling of QoS/QoE-factors in realtime is required importantly for stable MoIP service. An important factor for MoIP-quality control technique involves the rate control, which is based largely on network impairments such as jitter, delay, packet loss rate, etc due to the network congestions (Eejaie et al., 1999) (Beritelli et al., 2002). In order to support application services based on the NGN, an end-to-end QoS monitoring tool is developed with qualified performance analysis (Kim et al., 2006).

The different parts of multimedia have different perceptual importance and each part of multimedia does not contribute equally to the overall media quality. Voice/video packets that are perceptually more important are marked, i.e. acquire priority in our approach. If there is any congestion, the packets are less likely to be dropped than the packets that are of less perceptual importance. The QoS schemes which are based on the priority marking are open loop ones and do not make use of changes in the network (Cole & Rosenbluth, 2001).

Currently, most interactive multimedia applications use the realtime transport protocol (RTP) for data transmission with realtime constraints. RTP runs on top of existing transport protocols, typically UDP, and provides realtime applications with end-to-end delivery services such as payload type identification and delivery monitoring. RTP provides transport of data with a notion of time to enable the receiver to reconstruct the timing information of the sender. Besides, RTP messages contain a message sequence number to allow applications to detect packet loss, packet duplication, or packet reordering. RTP is extended by the RTP control protocol (RTCP) that exchanges member information in an on-going session. RTCP monitors the data delivery and provides the users with some statistical functionality. The receivers can use RTCP as a feedback mechanism to notify the sender about the quality of an on-going session. The original RTCP provides overall feedback on the quality of end-to-end networks (Schulzrinne et al., 2005). However, the standard RTCP packet type is defined for quality control in realtime without bidirectional quality reporting and managing procedures in detail through IP networks. The RTP Control Protocol-Extended Reports (RTCP-XR) are management protocol which defines a set of metrics that contains information for assessing the media quality by the IETF (Friedman et al., 2003). The RTCP-XR reports the packet loss rate, the packet discard rate and the distribution of lost/discarded packets. The loss/discard distribution describes calls in terms of bursts (periods during which the loss/discard rate is high enough to cause noticeable quality degradation) and gaps (periods during which lost or discarded packets occur infrequently and hence quality is generally acceptable). To guarantee quality, the RTCP-XR can report the quality directly in terms of the estimated ***R***-factor or the mean opinion score (MOS). The ***R***-factor is a conversational-quality metric in the range of 0 to 100. And the both MOS-LQ and MOS-CQ are in the range of 1 to 5. The RTCP-XR can be implemented as software is integrated into IP phones and gateways inexpensively. Then the messages containing key call-quality-related metrics are exchanged periodically through SoftPhones. However, the RTCP-XR is adequate to monitor the QoS-factor on end-to-end MoIP networks because it doesn't have media quality monitoring functionality. To solve this problem, we propose upgrading some components in the RTCP-XR scheme. Because current IP networks are not designed to support the QoS, quality measurement becomes more important and urgent for more reliable higher quality multi-media services over IP networks. We explore impact of individual packet loss, delay, and jitter on the perceptual media quality on the smart SoftPhone as one of MoIP systems. The evaluation of MoIP service quality is carried out by firstly encoding the input media pre-modified with given network parameter values, and then decoded to generate degraded output signals.
In this paper, we implement smart SoftPhone device for guaranteeing QoS/QoE which can discover and measure various network parameters such as jitter, delay, and packet loss rate, etc., and then propose an end-to-end quality management scheme with the realtime message report procedures to manage the QoS/QoE-factors. The newly presented QoS-factor transmission mechanism for QoE related QoS-factors managing over IP networks is assessed with the performance analysis in the realtime transmission of QoS parameters through various IP networks.

3. Smart SoftPhone Module Design for Discovering and Measuring

In this section, we clarify and design each functionality blocks which are carried on smart SoftPhone for discovering and measuring call-quality over IP network in realtime. There are ten different technical functionality, i.e. 'SIP Stack Module', 'Codec Module', 'RTP Module', 'RTCP-XR Module', 'Transport Module', 'Measurement Module', 'UA Communication Module', 'User Communication Module', 'User Interface Module' and 'Control Module' (Kim et al., 2007).

3.1 Modeling of Smart SoftPhone Functionality

In order to discover and measure quality status, we design 11 critical modules for User Agents (UA) as illustrated in Fig. 1. It comprises in four main blocks and each module is defined as follows:

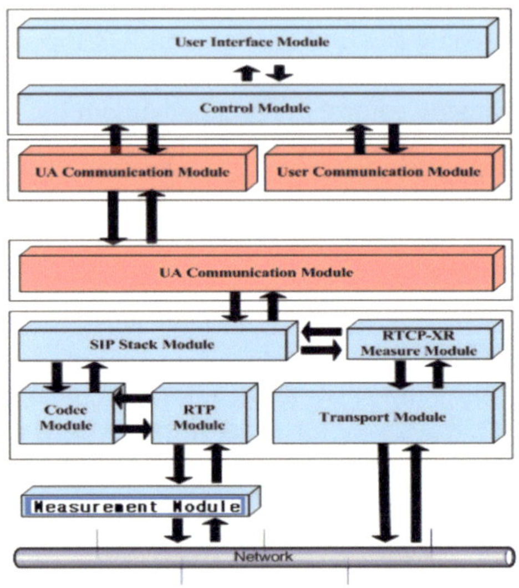

Figure 1. Main blocks and modules of smart SoftPhone functionality

* SIP Stack Module -
- Analysis of every sending/receiving messages and creation response messages
- Sending to transport module after adding suitable parameter and header for sending message
- Analysis of parameter and header in receiving message from transport module
- Management and application of SoftPhone information, channel information, codec information, etc.
- Notify codec module of sender's codec information from SDP of receiving message and negotiate with receiver's codec
- Save up session and codec information

* Codec Module –
- Providing the encoding and decoding function about two different voice/video codecs
- Processing of codec (encoding/decoding) and rate value based on SDP information of sender/receiver from SIP stack module

* RTP Module –
- Sending created data from codec module to receiver SoftPhone through RTP protocol

* RTCP-XR Measure Module –
    - Formation of quality parameters for monitoring and sending/receiving information of quality parameters to SIP stack/transport modules
* Transport Module -
    - Address messages from SIP stack module to network
    - Address receiving message from network to SIP stack module
* Measurement Module –
    - Measure voice/video quality by using packet and rate which is received from RTP module and network
* UA Communication Module -
    - For requesting call connection, interchange of information to SIP stack module and establish SIP session connection
    - Address information to control module in order to show information of SIP message to user
* User Communication Module -
    - Sending and receiving of input information through UDP protocol
* User Interface Module -
    - User give any command by using GUI and sending information to control module
* Control Module -
    - Management of UA communication, user communication, and user information modules
    - Management of various optional information module

3.2 Blocks and Modules for Call Session Control & Quality Management

In this work, we propose realtime message report procedures and management scheme between MoIP-Quality Management (QM) server and smart SoftPhones. The proposed method for the realtime message reporting and management consists of four main processing blocks, as illustrated in Fig. 2. These four different processing modules implement call session module, UDP communication module, quality report message management module and quality measurement/computation/processing modules. All of the call session messages are addressed to quality report message management module by UDP communication. After call-setup is completed, QoS-factors is measuring followed by computation of each quality parameters base on the message processing. Followed by each session establish and release, quality report messages are also recorded in database management module immediately.

An endpoint of SIP based Softswitch (SSW) is known as smart SoftPhone (UA). That is, SIP client loosely denotes SIP end points where UAs run, such as SoftPhones. SSW is intermediated network elements between the end points and engages in the routing of SIP messages from a UA to other UA based on a logical SIP address. SSW also performs functions of authentication, authorization, and signaling compression. A logical SIP URI address consists of a domain and identifies a UA ID number. The UAs belonging to a particular domain register their locations with the SIP registrar of that domain by means of a REGISTER message. Fig. 3 shows SIP based SSW connection between UA#1-SoftPhone and UA#2-SoftPhone.

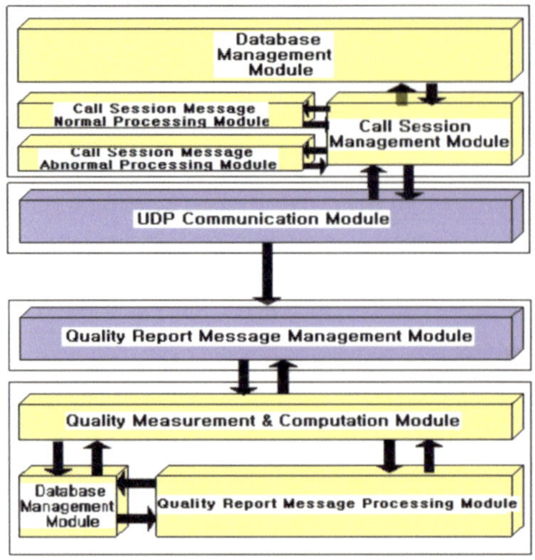

Figure 2. Main blocks and modules for call session control & quality management

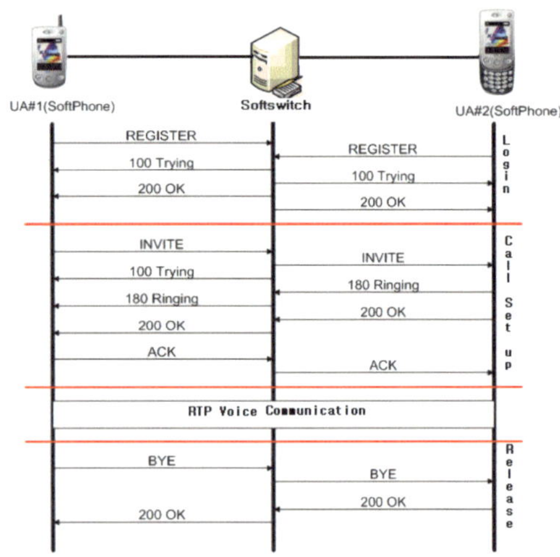

Figure 3. Procedures of call establish/release between Softswitch and smart SoftPhone

4. User, Terminal, and Network-Aware QoS/QoE Guaranteed MoIP Services

For the techniques of new challenging over application source levels we focus on the relationship of user terminals and media streaming sources to support user perceived quality of experience (QoE) based on high quality of service between heterogeneous terminals and heterogeneous networks. These techniques depend on the characteristics of media processing and terminal capabilities such as LCD panel size, resolution, etc., on the heterogeneous network environment.

4.1 IP-based Personal Mobile Broadcasting Services

IP-based communications over a wide area have become more and more popular because of the emerging wireless IP networks and services. However, multimedia transmission and streaming may suffer from an unreliable Internet connection and heterogeneous bandwidth to the different receivers. The multimedia streaming service, which is aware of the network resource, is still a critical topic for the user perceived QoS/QoE guaranteed service. For example, if users wish to call and watch callee on the media phone, they will require resource to support QoS/QoE. The bandwidth allocation in the distribution network will be very different for these two users in order to ensure that both users get the same QoE. The bit rate required for the delivery of content at a fixed quality varies. Therefore, the priority of any individual media stream must correspondingly be allowed to vary both over time and from one stream to another.

Also, the personal mobile broadcasting service as one of MoIP services considers that the QoE-guaranteed media contents are transferred seamlessly between heterogeneous devices based on each user profile. The user currently has various handheld devices. It is always possible to buy an additional new device and use more than one at the same time. In this case, in order to maintain a high QoE-guaranteed media service for specific devices that a user owns, all of the terminal capability information is associated with each user subscription profile on the home subscription server (HSS) system. The HSS function is defined as one of the subdivided functions of IP multimedia subsystem (IMS) service network that is contained in the initial filter criteria.

There is a need to be able to coordinate the access to the supporting terminal capability and user profile information so that they can receive their interesting context service from the originating device to the target client device. This service involves seamlessly transferring QoE-guaranteed video and displaying it between different devices based on user profiles. In order to display the proper scene, HSS, application server (AS), and SSW systems are composed to provide video streams seamlessly for the heterogeneous devices environment. These systems consider both the terminal capability and the user profile for personal mbile broadcasting service as shown in Fig. 4. The HSS system controls and matches all of the profile information in terms of service providers, users and devices. Call session control function (CSCF) can either play the role of a proxy (P)-, interrogating (I)-, or serving (S)-CSCF for seamless session controls.

The personal mobile broadcasting service is more suited for transferring realtime sessions. It is basically to support capturing the session control information from the originating terminal device and transferring them to the target terminal device. This is done by a session control function that allows a user to have heterogeneous mobile devices. For the scenarios to provide a personal mobile broadcasting service, the provider would first find an available network resource for streaming (e.g., bandwidth, multicast address). Then, it would give this information to a content providing end-user that is controlled by the HSS. This example is shown in Fig. 4 as explicated at a football stadium. Second, the content providing end-user sends an extracting video stream by first considering the LCD panel sizes of heterogeneous devices. It also considers an actual broadcasting video stream with multicast or multiple unicasts by using the information in the AS. Third, the receiving client in the mobile environment may be able to select a specific content. This will be based on user profile and terminal capability with logical source information provided by content search results. In this process, service control functions may participate in session routing information gathered by the SSW. This message contains actual content address and session information for receiving it. Fourth, receiving client devices in the mobile environment can request a content delivery function to join the session. Receiving client devices obtain the content from the content delivery function which is designed and located in the AS. The providing functions in the HSS, SSW and AS control all of the service providers, end-users and terminal capability, together.

The contents provider provides a video stream on many heterogeneous devices such as a cellular phone, PDA, computer, HDTV (IPTV), etc. These devices have various LCD panel sizes and different resolutions from small to big considering heterogeneous networks (e.g., WLAN, Wibro, CDMA). The viewer can feel very uncomfortable if the multimedia contents just transfers from a widescreen sized LCD panel to a small sized LCD panel without considering the resolution and aspect ratios. The user cannot recognize what the scene describes on the device in the mobile service environment. Quality degradation due to down sampling, up-sampling, en(de)coding, etc in the delivery channel can happen for personal mobile broadcasting service.

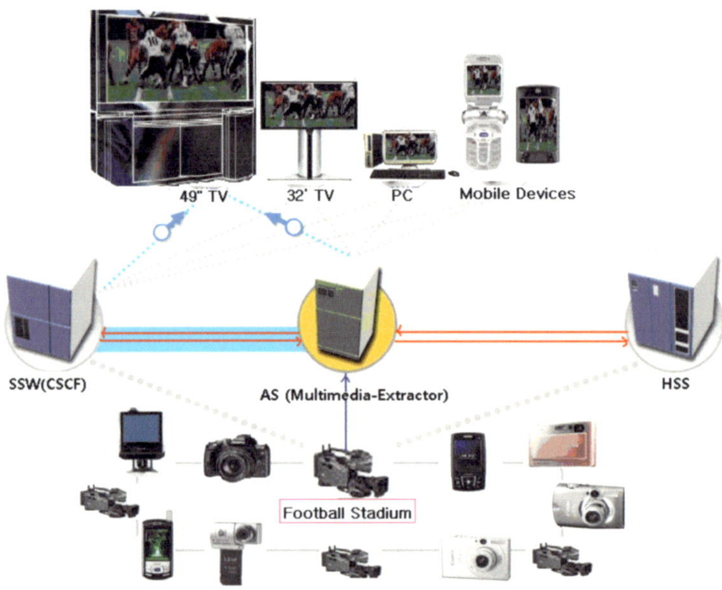

Figure 4. Configuration of personal mobile broadcasting service with considering terminals capability and user profiles

The term resolution is often used as a pixel count and as the spatial dimension in a digital imaging which is captured and displayed on device. The resolution is defined by three cases: Low Resolution (LR), High Resolution (HR), and Super Resolution (SR). Consider the following case: a low resolution image captured by a mobile phone has a resolution of 128 * 128 and we would like to display it on a higher resolution screen of 1024 * 768. Then, SR processing techniques are needed so that the blurring effect can be reduced to improve user perceived QoE. In this case, some more complicated processing techniques are required to convert the LR image to a higher one. The aspect ratio of an image is defined as its width divided by height. If an image is displayed on a device with an aspect ratio different from that of an image, the modification is required, and it is still an interesting issue for frame rate conversion (Telkap, 1995). The resolutions of commonly used displays and several commonly used aspect ratios for various applications are shown in Table 1 (Lee et al., 2007).

	Resolution	Aspect ratio
SDTV	640 * 480	4:3
HDTV	1920*1080	16:9
Computer-VGA	640*480	4:3
Cellular phone	128*128	1:1
PDA	320*200/480*320	5:4

Table 1. Frame resolution and aspect ratio comparison of heterogeneous devices

5. Quality Management for QoS/QoE Guaranteed MoIP Services

The RTP protocol is used for transmitting realtime data information and the RTCP, for sending the control information. The main function of the RTCP is to provide a detailed representation of the voice packets exchanged during an RTP session. Its structure includes the sender report (SR) and the receiver report (RR) transmitted periodically to all participants in the session. It aims at providing a feedback on the quality of the transmission (e.g., delay, jitter, packet loss, etc.), where transmitters send "sender reports" and receivers send "receiver reports" using the RTCP-XR. While the SR includes transmission and reception information for active senders in the session, the RR would also contain the reception information for non-active senders. The MoIP-QM server receives the QoS-factor followed by messages procedure and reports QoS information for the monitoring QoS-factor every 2 seconds.

5.1 RTCP-XR based Quality Monitoring and Management for MoIP Services

For the management of bidirectionial quality resources, we have developed a RTCP-based packet structure to provide an end-to-end transmission controlling method that can report delay, jitter, and packet losses in a timely manner. Our packet structure is similar to the RTCP extended report, which is primarily defined to provide more detailed statistics, particularly for multicast applications. In our case, the RTCP-XR scheme is specifically designed to report delay, jitter, and packet losses for every frame of voice signal. Also, the loss and the discard rates are designed to be calculated for each session at the end-receiver in order to measure realtime values. The original RTCP-XR packet type defined that can be used for speech quality monitoring. However, it is not familiar with realtime speech quality reporting for conversational speech through IP networks. Thus, we modified the RTCP-XR packet scheme in order for reporting and monitoring of bidirectional quality because MoIP communication services such as Internet phone, cellular phone, etc must be recognized as dialogical speech.

For the delay as one of the significant QoS-factor, BT-1 is formatted with both sub-block 1 and sub-block 2. SSRC_1 and SRRC_2 are for the sender and the receiver numbers which are defined randomly. The DLRR in sub-block-1 reports one way delay between the sender and the receiver. The DLRR in sub-block-2 reports the round trip delay which is measured using one way delay information from DLLR in sub-block-1. Fig. 5 shows the message format-II of BT-1 for delay monitoring. In Fig. 6, the information of the jitter and the packets is controlled in BT-2. At first, in order to manage the jitter, we categorize it into three levels of min_jitter, max_jitter, and mean-jitter. Those are reported as the cumulative effects of jitter values obtained through the jitter buffer in our cases. Second, to get the realtime communication, speech quality monitoring field of packet count information of the RTP/RTCP is included in the report block. The Tx/Rx RTP Packets format in BT-2 is designed for monitoring sender/receiver RTP. The Rx RTCP Packets are the RTCP-XR packets which are received at the MoIP-QM server, and the Tx RTCP Packets are the RTCP XR packets which are sent from the SoftPhone to the MoIP-QM server. The final result value of the cumulative packet loss is also included in the BT-2 scheme. The format of the BT-3 scheme is similar to the standard RTCP-XR. However, the loss and the discard rates are computed as soon as the call session is established by using the cumulative packets which is controlled on BT-2. The accuracy of the realtime counter for each packet is really critical point. Specially, for time synchronization, we set our current execution time of SoftPhone by using the NTP (National Time Protocol). That is, time of the host system is designed to be synchronized to the national standard time. Finally, by applying the QoS-factor obtained from speech quality measurement in UA, the MOS and MOS-CQ are defined separately Other factors in BT-3 are added to the standard format scheme as shown in Fig. 7.

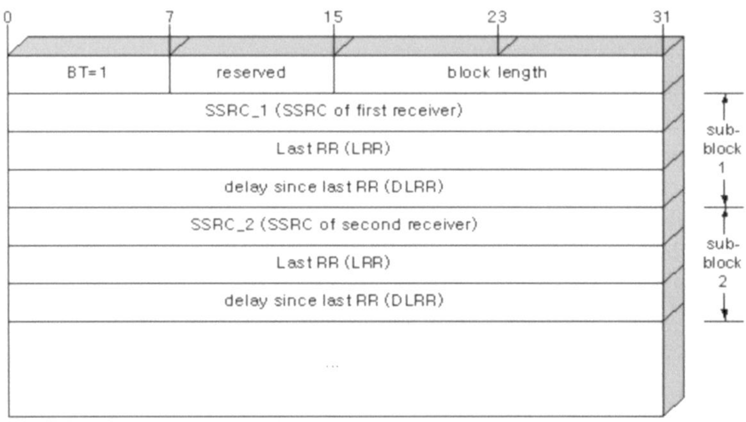

Figure 5. BT=1 delay monitoring for transmission control

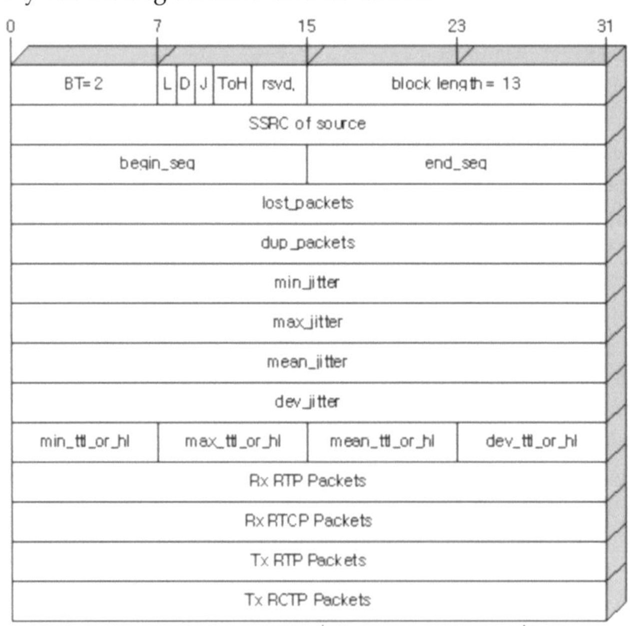

Figure 6. BT=2 jitter, packets for transmission control

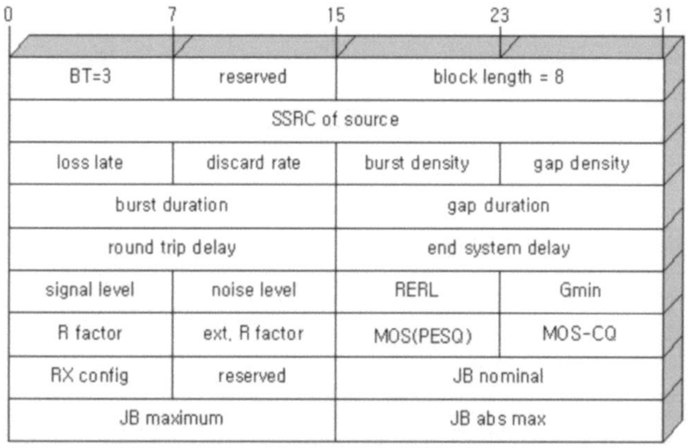

Figure 7. BT=3 loss & discard late, MOS (PESQ), & MOS-CQ for transmission control

6. Voice Quality for QoS/QoE Guaranteed MoIP Services

We propose method of the realtime message report procedures and management schemes for the quality guaranteed MoIP services above. The QoS/QoE-factors control mechanism is experimented with applying Packet Loss Concealment (PLC) algorithm under different packet loss simulating conditions using G.711 and G.729A codecs. When packet losses occur over IP networks, the PLC algorithms employed in speech codecs reconstruct lost speech frames based on the previously received speech information. The PLC algorithm in G.711 Appendix I repeatedly inserts pitch period which is detected from the previous speech in history butter which is called the pitch period replication method. The PLC algorithm employed in G.729A estimates an excitation signal and synthesis filter parameters from last frame which is good condition. To prove the efficiency of the proposed message procedures and management schemes for QoS/QoE-factor control, we evaluate packet loss rate with G.711 and G.729A codecs and then the management scheme is proved as following improvement of results in this chapter.

6.1 Voice Quality Measurement for MoIP Services

Because present IP networks are not designed to support the QoS, the quality measurement becomes more important and urgent for more reliable higher quality multimedia services over IP networks. We explore the impact of the individual packet loss, the delay, and the jitter on the perceptual speech quality in MoIP systems. The MoIP service quality evaluation is carried out by firstly encoding the input speech pre-modified with given network parameter values and then decoded to generate degraded output speech signals. In order to obtain an end-to-end (E2E) MOS between the caller-UA and the callee-UA, we apply the PESQ and the E-Model method. In detail, to obtain the ***R*** factors for E2E measurement over the IP network we need to get ***Id, Ie, Is*** and ***Ij***. Here, ***Ij*** is newly defined as in equation (1) to represent the E2E jitter parameter.

$$R\text{-}factor = R0 - Is - Id - Ij - Ie + A \qquad (1)$$

The ITU-T Recommendation provides most of the values and methods to get parameter values except ***Ie*** for codecs, ***Id*** and ***Ij***. First, we obtain ***Ie*** value after the PESQ algorithm applied. Second, we apply the PESQ values to ***Ie*** value of R-factor. We measure the E2E ***Id*** and ***Ij*** from our current network environment. By combining ***Ie, Id*** and ***Ij,*** the final ***R***-factor could be computed for the E2E QoS performance results. Finally, obtained ***R***-factor is reconverted to MOS by using equation (2), which is redefined by the ITU-T SG12.

$$\begin{cases} R \leq 6.5: \ MOS = 1 \\ 6.5 \leq R \leq 100: \ MOS = 1 - \frac{7}{1000}R + \frac{7}{6250}R^2 - \frac{7}{1000000}R^3 \\ R \geq 100: \ MOS = 4.5 \end{cases} \tag{2}$$

6.2 Experimental Environment and Performance Evaluation

To model various packet loss environments, we design burst and random packet losses with 0%, 3%, 5%, and 10% loss rates, and it is considered that a packet contains 1 speech frame, 2 speech frames, or 3 speech frames.

Loss type \ PLC		No PLC			Applied PLC		
		PESQ	R	MOS	PESQ	R	MOS
Random	0%	4.2	93	4.4	4.2	93	4.4
	3%	3.5	71	3.6	3.8	78	3.9
	5%	3.0	59	3.0	3.4	68	3.5
	10%	2.5	48	2.5	3.0	58	3.0
Burst	0%	4.2	93	4.4	4.2	93	4.4
	3%	3.2	64	3.3	3.2	65	3.4
	5%	3.0	57	3.0	3.3	64	3.3
	10%	2.7	50	2.6	2.8	53	2.7

Table 2. Result for realtime environment with G.711

Loss type \ PLC		No PLC			Applied PLC		
		PESQ	R	MOS	PESQ	R	MOS
Random	0%	3.5	72	3.7	3.5	72	3.7
	3%	3.2	63	3.4	3.3	68	3.5
	5%	3.1	62	3.2	3.2	65	3.4
	10%	2.9	57	2.9	3.0	58	3.0
Burst	0%	3.5	72	3.7	3.5	72	3.7
	3%	3.2	64	3.3	3.3	67	3.5
	5%	3.1	61	3.2	3.2	64	3.2
	10%	2.9	56	2.9	3.0	57	2.9

Table 3. Result for realtime environment with G.729A

For the performance evaluation of PLC algorithm based on proposed management scheme, we use the systemic evaluation method called PESQ, defined by ITU-T Recommendation P.862 for objective assessment of quality. After comparing an original signal with a degraded one, the output of PESQ provides a score from -0.5 to 4.5 as a MOS-like score. The reference speech for the real-time environment simulation is the decoded speech without any packet loss, respectively. In the real-time environment, after getting the measured value from PESQ evaluation method, the value is applied to the E-Model evaluation method and then, finally, the MOS is acquired.

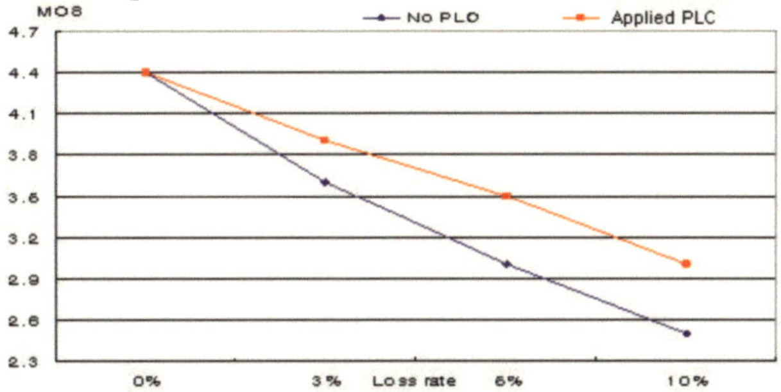

Figure 8. MOS result for random losses with G.711

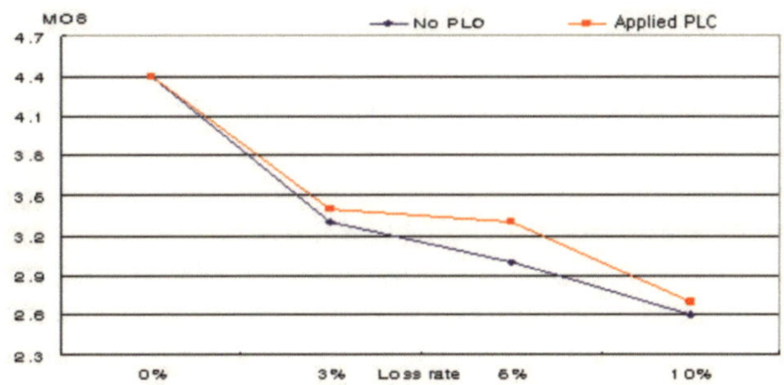

Figure 9. MOS result for burst losses with G.711

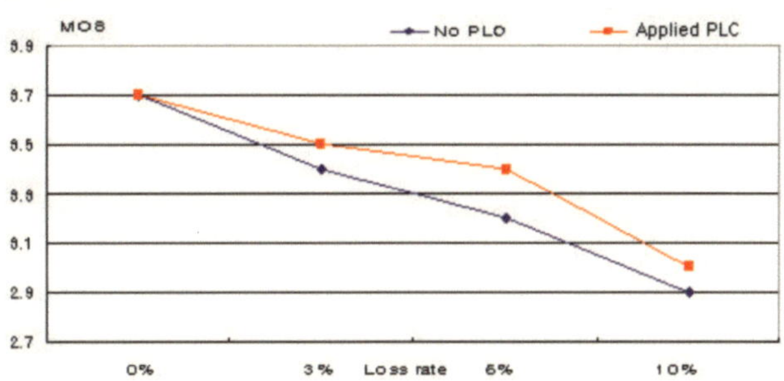

Figure 10. MOS result for random losses with G.729A

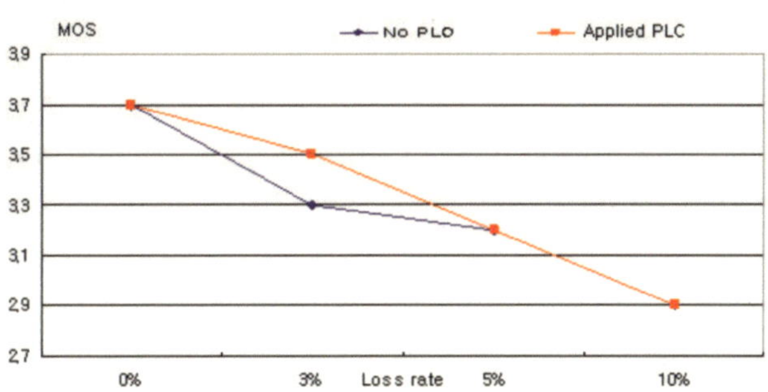

Figure 11. MOS result for burst losses with G.729A

We use 200 Korean dialogue speech utterances from 2 male and 2 female speakers as test data. The duration of each utterance is about 10 seconds. The simulation result shows that the QoS-factor transmission control mechanisms with applying PLC algorithms achieve the distinguished result for the realtime speech quality monitoring than other MoIP systems which use the standard scheme without applying PLC algorithm during conversation through IP-based network environment. In the following result tables, 'fpp' refers to frame per packet. The performance of the PLC algorithm in G.711 and G.729A is compared to that of the no-PLC algorithm employed in G.711 and G.729A. In Table 2, the results of PLC performance evaluation for G.711 in realtime environment are summarized by the measurement methods of PESQ, the R-factor, and the MOS. The applied PLC achieves the PESQ gains between 0.1 and 0.3 for packet loss. The corresponding gains for the R-factors and the MOS scores are also achieved by these PESQ gains. High gains are achieved at random losses with high loss rates as shown in Table 2 (in Fig. 8 and 9). In Table 3, the results of PLC performance evaluation for G.729A in real-time environment are also summarized by the measurement methods of PESQ, the R-factor, and the MOS. The PLC algorithm achieves the PESQ gain of 0.1 for all types of loss. The corresponding gains for the R-factors and the MOS scores are achieved by these PESQ gains. Finally, even though the MOS is not highly improved for burst losses, the MOS gain of 0.1 is generally achieved as shown in Table 3 (in Fig. 10 and 11).

6.3 Implementation of SoftPhone and MoIP-QM Server

The main part of the smart SoftPhone is implemented in MFC and C# in .Net environment for delivering and measuring of QoS/QoE-factors with various parameters transmission control in realtime. As illustrated in Fig. 12 (a), the realtime MoIP packets delivering and measuring function on the smart SoftPhone is designed as various GUI function to manage an end-to-end media quality over IP network. Smart SoftPhone has functionality for media (voice/video) communication with other devices through SIP stack. The SIP stack implement to connect between network and any user's GUI of smart SoftPhone. We use vocal 1.5.0 server in order for role of SSW, which is registration, establish, and release from smart SoftPhone. The user can call session establish and release by using GUI on smart SoftPhone which display the SIP message for sending and receiving to user. By the SIP message, the user checks current situation in realtime between caller and callee. Also, it measures voice quality by using objective measurement method which is called PESQ as standard from ITU-T and has reporting function network parameters which follows by RTCP-XR formation especially to monitoring QoS/QoE-factors. While the sessions establish and release by phone, three different RTCP-based packet structures BTs are modeled by realtime information such as caller ID, callee ID, delay, jitter, packet loss, packet discard, etc., for each frame of speech signal. For speech signal measurement, our smart SoftPhone designs to control of encoding/decoding voice packets in G.711 and G.729A as shown in Fig. 12 (a). One important objective point with the implementation is to explore the measured values of PESQ, ***R-factor*** and MOS with time synchronization of each session at the end-sender and end-receiver by using NTP.

MoIP-QM server is implemented in Delphi and C# in .Net environment followed by the structure of BT=1, BT=2, and BT=3 for monitoring of QoS/QoE-factor transmission control in realtime. While the sessions establish and release by SoftPhone, three different RTCP-based packet structures BTs are modeled by realtime information.

Two main parts of MoIP-QM server, the request and response are designed based on message procedures while call session is opened, and then jitter, delay, etc., per packet are reported and described visually on MoIP-QM server as shown in Fig. 12 (b).

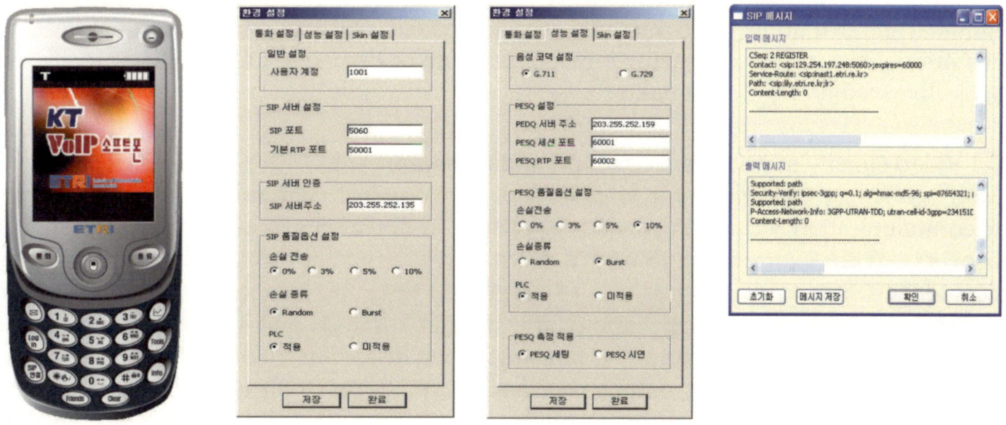

(a) Smart SoftPhone (UA) with control interfaces

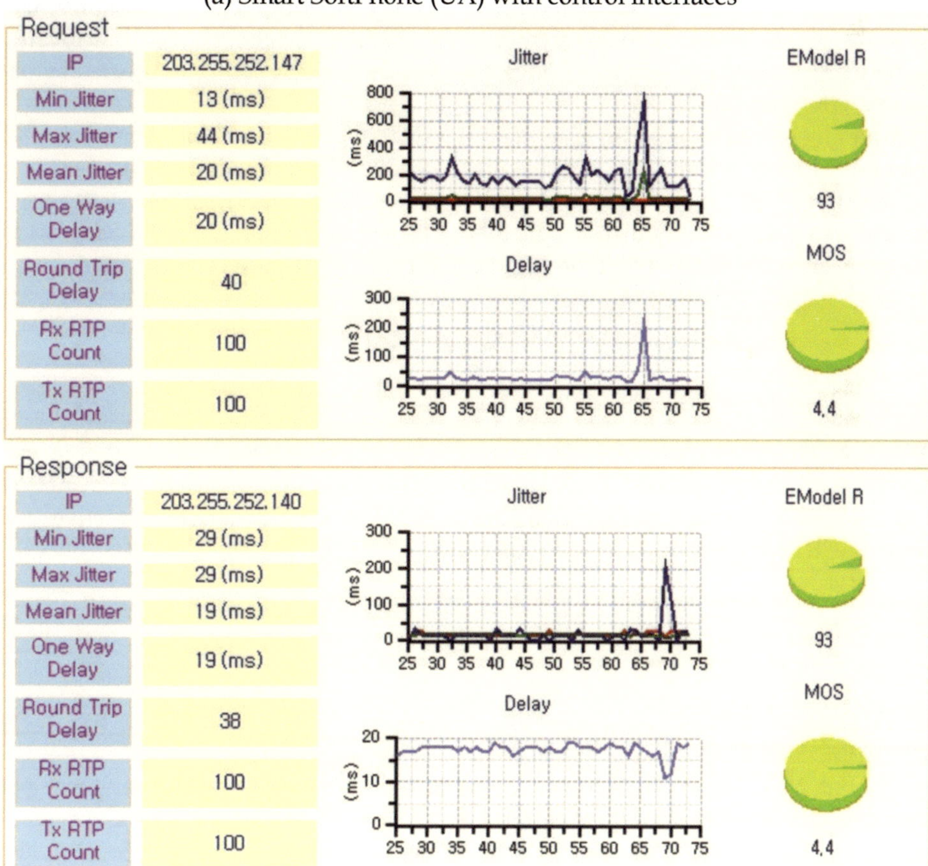

(b) MoIP-QM server with QoS/QoE-factors measurement

Figure 12. Implementation of SoftPhone and MoIP-QM server

7. Video Quality Measurement for QoS/QoE Guaranteed MoIP Services

Video quality for MoIP services can be affected by variety of factors such as video coders, transmission type, bandwidth limitation etc. We need to measure video quality in a fundamental requirement in modern communications systems for technical, legal and commercial reasons. Video quality measurement can be carried out using either objective or subjective methods of video quality.

7.1 Video Quality Indicators Extraction and Measurement

MoIP service can be defined as a kind of convergence service composed of broadcasting and telecommunication sectors. In this sense, various multimedia can be provided through IP networks with interactivity. Since MoIP services are very sensitive to the network degradation such as packet loss, out of order, and jitter, the quality of service cannot be guaranteed. With considering various effects both network and video levels for MoIP service, several distortions including blurring, block distortion, color error, jerkiness, edge busyness, etc. aspects of user perceived QoE, occur during transmitting and encoding/decoding processes times. At the measuring points, block distortion, blurring effects, and color error mainly happen on the video source. From the transport area, we can assess at the points where there are areas before/after the IP network and before/after the access network. Color error, jerkiness, edge busyness, etc., in the source is affected by packet loss, delay, jitter, etc.

Degradation measures, which can give the numerical information of video quality, play an important role. Most researchers have used many forms of quantitative quality metrics such as the mean squared error (MSE) and peak-to-noise ratio (PSNR) as Full Reference (FR) based objective video quality measure method. The most common objective criterion is the mean square error (MSE). The MSE of original and processed image refer to (3).

$$MSE = \frac{1}{M.N}\sum_{x=1}^{M}\sum_{y=1}^{N}| f(x,y) - \tilde{f}(x,y)|^2 \tag{3}$$

where $f(x,y)$ is the original image, $\tilde{f}(x,y)$ is the processed image, $\boldsymbol{M}$ and $\boldsymbol{N}$ are the height and width of the images. Peak Signal-to-Noise Ratio (PSNR) is another widely used way to measure all image quality evaluation. PSNR is a MSE derived objective quality measure. PSNR is defined in (4) where peak signal strength is assumed as 255.

$$PSNR = 10\log_{10}\frac{255^2}{MSE} \tag{4}$$

However, since pixel values of original and degraded videos are used in the full-reference model in MSE and PSNR, computational burden is very large.

Also, although MSE and PSNR metrics are simple and widely used metric results are poorly correlated with subjective rating since they do not model the human visual system. The example for comparing MSE and PSNR values is shown in Fig. 13. People feel uncomfortable in spite of the same PSNR among the image.

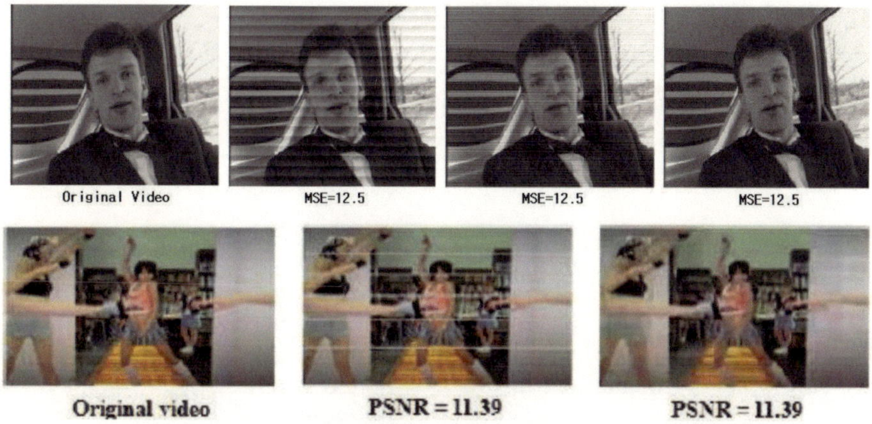

Figure 13. Correlation between MSE/PSNR results and subjective rating

It is necessary to develop new objective metrics in order to reflect network based QoS-status aware end-user perceived QoE indicators for accurate prediction and measurement in considering correlation with subjective measurement.

Error	Model	Method	Cause
Blurring	RR	Comparing edge standard deviation between OS and PS	Encoding/ Decoding
Block distortion	RR	Estimation using edge of vertical/horizontal direction and weight of around pixels	Encoding/ Decoding/ Network Transport
Color error	RR	Comparing hue and saturation between OS and PS	Encoding/ Decoding/ Network Transport
Edge busyness	RR	Comparing edge average values between OS and PS	Network Transport
Jerkiness	NR	Freezing frame extraction using edge difference between frames	Network Transport

Table 4. Video quality indicators

The current issue in the area is to measure in realtime with face value which service providers really want the greatest accuracy. Thus, our focus is prediction and measurement quality of the distorted video contents frames with considering user perceived QoE, basically, and then the several additional proposed methods are useful for applying to estimation of networked-QoS aware video-QoE indicators base on reduced-reference (RR) for blurring, block distortion, color error, and edge busyness/no-reference (NR) for jerkiness video measurement method. In Table 4, we briefly present the cause of errors and key of measuring method.

In the RR model, extracted features of the original and degraded videos are used instead of all pixel values. Perceptual video quality is computed by using these features. Finally, no-reference models use only the degraded video sequence without using the original video sequence. Although the NR model is very fast, accuracy for measuring degradation cannot be guaranteed. The perceptual objective video quality models are shown in Fig. 14.

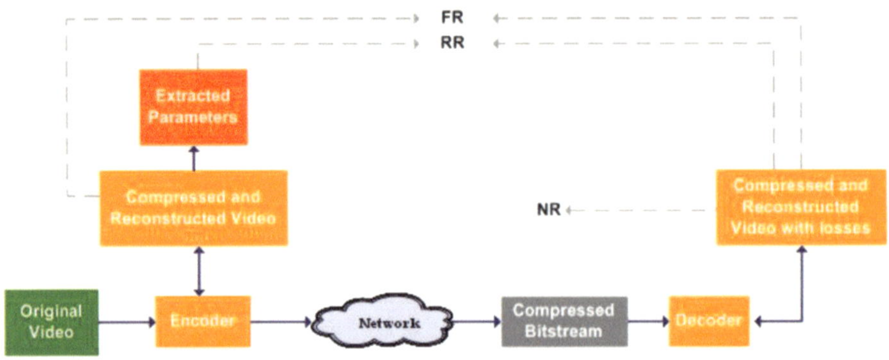

Figure 14. Perceptual video quality measurement model

7.2 Hybrid Objective Metrics for Video Quality Measurement

Differences in quality of video are due to loss compression/decompression as well as transmission errors, which lead to artifacts in the received viewing contents. The amount of artifacts and visibility of these distortions strongly depend on the video contents. There are two types of quality to measure and to verify digital video quality which is delivered to the end user to identify content quality degradation: objective and subjective quality. Both of these are to develop Video Quality Metrics (VQM) which is intended to provide calculated values that are strongly correlated with a viewers' assessment. In this research, we mention above five indicators which include blurring, block distortion, edge busyness, color error, and jerkiness according to the whole transmission process which can produce artifacts to digital video QoE. We design hybrid VQM model which is defined in (5).

$$VQM = a \times E_{edge} + b \times E_{block} + c \times E_{blur} + d \times E_{color} - E_{jerky} + C \quad (5)$$

We use the multiple linear regression analysis. If we suppose as $y = a + bx$, it can be described by the results of QoE indicators and subjective MOS as in $(x_1, y_1), (x_2, y_2), \cdots, (x_n, y_n)$, and then to get linear coefficient a, b, the procedure is as follows,

$$\Pi = \sum_{i=1}^{n} [y_i - f(x_i)]^2 = \sum_{i=1}^{n} [y_i - (a + bx_i)]^2 \quad (6)$$

By differentiation of a, b, as follows, and then define by x, y

$$\frac{\partial \Pi}{\partial a} = 2\sum_{i=1}^{n}[y_i - (a + bx_i)] = 0$$
$$\frac{\partial \Pi}{\partial b} = 2\sum_{i=1}^{n} x_i[y_i - (a + bx_i)] = 0 \quad (7)$$

$$\sum_{i=1}^{n} y_i = a\sum_{i=1}^{n} 1 + b\sum_{i=1}^{n} x_i$$
$$\sum_{i=1}^{n} x_i y_i = a\sum_{i=1}^{n} x_i + b\sum_{i=1}^{n} x_i^2 \quad (8)$$

Finally, linear coefficient a, and b are as follows, and then from the equation, coefficients a, b, c, d, C for the hybrid VQM is a = -17.809, b = -3.352, c = 5.340, d = 32.191, C = 4.424 from the equation (5).

$$a = \frac{(\sum_{i=1}^{n} y_i)(\sum_{i=1}^{n} x_i^2) - (\sum_{i=1}^{n} x_i)(\sum_{i=1}^{n} x_i y_i)}{n\sum_{i=1}^{n} x_i^2 - (\sum_{i=1}^{n} x_i)^2}, \quad b = \frac{n\sum_{i=1}^{n} x_i y_i - (\sum_{i=1}^{n} x_i)(\sum_{i=1}^{n} y_i)}{n\sum_{i=1}^{n} x_i^2 - (\sum_{i=1}^{n} x_i)^2} \quad (9)$$

Finally, we design the hybrid VQM model as follows,

$$VQM = -17.809E_{edge} - 3.352E_{block} + 5.340E_{blur} + 32.191E_{color} - E_{jerky} + 4.424 \quad (10)$$

7.3 Heterogeneous Networks and Terminals-Aware for MoIP Services

The content providing end-user sends an extracting video stream by first considering the LCD panel sizes of heterogeneous devices. The personal mobile broadcasting contents provider provides a video stream on many heterogeneous handheld devices such as a cellular phone, PDA, computer, etc. These devices have various LCD panel sizes and different resolutions from small to big considering heterogeneous networks (e.g., WLAN, WIMAX, (W)CDMA). The viewer can feel very uncomfortable if the multimedia contents just transfer from a widescreen sized LCD panel to a small sized LCD panel without considering the resolution and aspect ratios. The user cannot recognize what the scene describes on the device in the personal mobile broadcasting service environment. Quality degradation due to down sampling, up-sampling, en(de)coding, etc in the delivery channel can happen for the personal mobile broadcasting service.

Table 5 shows the results packet loss rates with considering LCD panel size of heterogeneous terminals in their bandwidth limitation when the personal mobile broadcasting services deliver video content to their various target terminals through heterogeneous networks which has different LCD size. We consider VGA (resolution: 649*480, 150kbps (video), 192kbps (audio)), CIF(resolution: 356*288, 75kbps (video), 192kbps (audio)), QVGA(resolution: 320*240, 63kbps (video), 192kbps (audio)), QCIF(resolution: 178*144, 41kbps (video), 192kbps (audio)), Cellular Phone Size (resolution: 128*128, 34kbps (video), 192kbps (audio)) with same commercial content for heterogeneous handheld devices.

Handover (HO) Time		No HO	30.0s	60.5s	90.5s
Analysis Section		0.0s ~ 10.0s	25.5s ~ 35.5s	55.5s ~ 65.5s	85.5s ~ 95.5s
Source	HO delay	LAN(100M)	WLAN(11M)	WiMAX(5M)	WCDMA(384Kb)
VGA (Computer, SDTV)	0.0ms	0/1731	42/803	90/1325	271/1457
	0.3ms	0/1045	103/1077	58/1513	276/792
	0.7ms	0/953	89/960	108/1012	1002/1680
CIF (PDA-I)	0.0ms	0/635	72/791	7/703	87/579
	0.3ms	0/642	27/518	102/770	194/794
	0.7ms	0/913	148/1062	49/520	94/559
QVGA (PDA-II)	0.0ms	0/667	30/601	7/945	78/569
	0.3ms	0/518	42/720	48/457	82/711
	0.7ms	0/509	35/431	57/847	159/699
QCIF (Cellular Phone-I)	0.0ms	0/538	19/398	1/431	11/500
	0.3ms	0/430	22/390	34/394	31/336
	0.7ms	0/391	54/442	36/446	43/454
Cellular Phone	0.0ms	0/343	19/338	0/327	4/386
	0.3ms	0/478	20/355	30/322	39/353
	0.7ms	0/385	35/386	30/308	33/316

Table 5. HO in heterogeneous networks/terminals for the personal mobile broadcasting service

The display of a specific target scene considering the context-aware viewer's visual sight is one of the important facts in providing QoE-guaranteed viewer centric mobile broadcasting service (Kim et al, 2008). When the original contents used for a big LCD panel are transferred to a small LCD panel, the video sequence captured for normal viewing on a standard IPTV may have an adverse effect. The viewer trying to view the image on the smaller display may have uncomfortable experiences. In order to provide the QoE guaranteed service to satisfy the visual perception of the viewer, the specific context based extracting methodology should be applied to the contents on devices with considering LCD panel size of the targeted device, together.

8. Conclusion

The demand on the guaranteed QoS/QoE of the flexible audio-visual content through the heterogeneous networks and the display heterogeneous terminals will increase as much as the MoIP service has been developed rapidly in residential and business communication markets.

- In this chapter, several related active research issues of Mobile IPTV service are highlighted and some new research directions have been pointed out.
- Provide critical message procedures applying RTCP-XR based packet structures BTs to manage call session with quality factors such as jitter, delay, loss, etc.
- Design management module for call session and for quality reporting using SoftPhone.
- Present QoS/QoE-factors transmission control mechanism
- Assess voice quality with a performance analysis of the PLC algorithms
- Derive video quality guaranteed technologies that enable end-to-end personal mobile broadcasting service in a heterogeneous environment.
- Ability to correlate the impact of networking resource, terminal capability, and user profile at each of the media stream applications.

Finally, our proposed methods of transmission procedure and management scheme using SoftPhone are very useful to manage QoS/QoE audio-visual quality through IP network. Also, hybrid objective metric is very useful for user perceived QoE-aware video quality measurement.

9. References

Beritelli, F.; Ruggeri, G. & Schembra, G. (2002). TCP-Friendly Transmission of Voice over IP, *Proceedings of IEEE International Conference on Communications,* pp. 1204-1208, 0-7803-7400-2, April 2002, New York, USA

Cole, R. G. & Rosenbluth, J. H. (2001). Voice over IP Performance Monitoring, *ACM SIGCOMM Computer Communications Review,* Vol. 31, No.2, April 2001, pp. 9-24, 0146-4833

Eejaie, R.; Handley, M. & Estrin, D. (1999). RAP: An End-to-end Rate-based Congestion Control Mechanism for Realtime Streams in the Internet, *Proceedings of IEEE INFOCOM,* pp. 21-25, 0-7803-5417-6, March 1999, New York, USA

Friedman, T.; Caceres, R. & Clark, A. (2003). RTP Control Protocol Extended Reports, *IETF RFC* 3611, Nov. 2003

Imai, S.; Yamada, A.; Ueno, H.; Nakamichi, K. & Chugo, A. (2006). Voice Quality Management for IP Networks based on Automatic Change Detection of Monitoring Data, *Proceedings of APNOMS, LNCS* (Lecture Notes in Computer Science) Springer-Verlag, Berlin Heidelberg, Vol. 4238, pp. 27-29, September 2006, 0302-9743

ITU-T Recommendation G.711 Appendix I. (1999). A High Quality Low-Complexity Algorithm for Packet Loss Concealment with G.711, *ITU-T,* Sept. 1999

ITU-T Recommendation G.729 Annex A. (1996). Coding of Speech at 8 kbit/s using Conjugate-Structure Algebraic-Code-Excited-Linear-Prediction (CS-ACELP), *ITU-T,* Nov. 1996

Kim, C. C.; Shin, S. C.; Ha, S. Y.; Han S. Y. & Kim, Y. J. (2006). End-to-End QoS Monitoring Tool Development and Performance Analysis for NGN, *Proceedings of APNOMS,* LNCS (Lecture Notes in Computer Science), Springer-Verlag, Berlin Heidelberg, Vol. 4238, pp. 332-341, September 2006, 0302-9743

Kim, J. S.; Hahn, M. S. & Lee, H. W. (2007). Smart SoftPhone Device for the Network Quality Parameters Discovery and Measurement, *HCI International 2007,* LNCS (Lecture Notes in Computer Science), Springer-Verlag, Berlin Heidelberg, Vol. 4555, pp. 898-907, January 2007, 0302-9743

Kim, J. S.; Um, T. W.; Won, R.; Lee, B.S. & Hahn, M. S. (2008). Heterogeneous Networks and Terminal-Aware QoS/QoE-Guaranteed Mobile IPTV services, *IEEE Comm. Maga.,* Vol.46, No.5, May 2008, pp.110-117, 0163-6804

Lee, M. S.; Shen, M. Y.; Kuo, C. C. & Yoneyama, A. (2007). Techniques for Flexible Image/Video Resolution Conversion with Heterogeneous Terminals, *IEEE Comm. Maga.,* Vol. 45, No. 1, Jan. 2007, pp. 61-67, 0163-6804

Park, C. S.; Wang, T. S. & Ko, S. J. (2007). Error Concealment using Inter-Layer Correlation for Scalable Video Coding, *ETRI Journal,* Vol. 29, No. 3, June 2007, pp. 390-392, 1225-6463

Recommendation J.149. (2004). Method for Specifying Accuracy and Cross-Calibration of Video Quality Metrics (VQM), *ITU-T,* March, 2004

Schulzrinne, H.; Casner, S.; Frederick, R. & Jacobson, V. (2005). RTP: A Transport Protocol for Real-Time Application, *IETF RFC 3550,* July 2005

Schwarz, H.; Marpe, D. & Wiegand, T. (2005). Comparison of MCTF and Closed-Loop Hierarchical B Pictures, *ITU-T & ISO/IEC JTC1, JVT-P059,* July 2005

Telkap, A. M. (1995). *Digital Video Processing,* Prentice Hall, Englewwod Cliffs, NJ, 1995

16

Sonification System of Maps for Blind

Gintautas Daunys and Vidas Lauruska
Siauliai University
Lithuania

1. Introduction

Creating, manipulating, accessing, and sharing information such as pictures, maps, charts and other visualisations as well as mathematical data and tables are fundamental skills needed for life. Visualisation is commonly used within almost every scientific field. Visually impaired people have very restricted access to information presented in these visual ways and it is currently very hard for them to create, manipulate and communicate such information.

For visually impaired people other information presentation ways must be found, which would replace visual information. The solution is to transform visual information to stimulus which could be perceived by other human sensor systems, which are functioning normally. A touch sense is used for a long time due to Braille reading system. Nowadays dynamic Braille displays are used for situations where more discreet communication is required. However, Braille displays are expensive and can not be widely used.

A sense of hearing is the other choice. It seems that exploitation of hearing doesn't require expensive hardware because a sound system is present in all new computers. One solution is to use a screen-reader and a voice synthesiser to access information on a computer. The screen reader extracts textual information from the computer's video memory and sends it to the speech synthesiser to speak it. Such technology generally only allows access in a linear manner (for example from the top left corner of the screen) and non-textual information such as pictures and diagrams are not easily displayed in this manner. It is difficult to present information where the spatial relationships between the data are important.

The term "sonification" comes from the Latin word "sonus" which means sound. Sonification is the method of information transfered by non-speech audio signals. By means of such signals a visually impaired user could explore computer screen if the sound output is related to area over which computer cursor currently is present.

The aim of this study is to create a model of system for map sonification. The system must use a cheap hardware, for example, usual sound system and tablet. The main component of the system is computer software, which enables sonification of an imaginable display. The term "map" must be understood in a wide sense –vector graphic picture divided to the relatively large area constant colour regions.

Shortly about the structure of the paper. The related works are analysed in the second section. The third section is devoted to the method. Firstly, non-speech sound characteristics most suitable for sonification are analysed. After that XML based maps presentation format is discussed. Finally, a model of sonification is presented and its functionality is described. The details of implementation are discussed in the fourth section. Finally, the fifth section is devoted to the discussion about sonification and the achieved results.

2. Related works

One of the first approaches of sonification signals used in human computer interaction is called earcons (Blattner et al., 1989). Sounds used for earcons should be constructed in such a way that they are easy to remember, understand and recognise. It can be a digitised sound, a sound created by a synthesiser, a single note, a motive, or even a single pitch. Rhythm can be used within earcons to characterise the sound and makes it more memorable (Deutsch, 1980). The guidelines were provided for the creation of earcons (Brewster et al., 1995; Lemmens, 2005). Example of their use is conveying of error messages, to provide information and feedback to the user about computer entities. Presentation of earcons can be accelerated by playing two earcons together (Brewster et al., 1994, McGookin & Brewster, 2004).

A method for line graph sonification invented in the mid 1980s was called SoundGraphs (Mansur et al., 1985). Movement along the x-axis in time causes notes of different pitches to be played, where the frequency of each note is determined by the value of the graph at that time. It was established by experiments with fourteen subjects that after a small amount of training, test subjects were able to identify the overall qualities of the data, such as linearity, monotonicity, and symmetry. The flexibility, speed, cost-effectiveness, and greater measure of independence provided for the blind or sight-impaired using SoundGraphs was demonstrated.

In the late 1980s a system called Soundtrack was developed (Edwards, 1989). It is a word processor for visually impaired people. The interface consists of auditory objects. An auditory object is defined by its spatial location, a name, an action, and a tone. One constraint applied was that objects cannot overlap. Their layout is, therefore, based on grid arrangements. Two forms of sound are used in the interface: musical tones and synthetic speech. Tones are used to communicate imprecise information quickly and speech is used to give more precise information more slowly. Speech is used to communicate die contents of documents being processed. An object's tone is sounded when the mouse is moved to point to it and the name of the object pointed to is spoken if the user presses the mouse button. The tones used in Soundtrack are simple square waves of differing pitch. The pitch varies with position, increasing from left to right and bottom to top. The edges of the screen are marked with another distinctive tone. Auditory objects are structured into two levels. At the upper level, the user interacts with an auditory screen comprising eight auditory windows. As the user moves the mouse across the window boundaries, their tones are sounded and their names can be ascertained, as previously described. To progress the interacting at the second level, the user activates a window, by double clicking the mouse button within that window. The same protocol applies within an activated window, so that each (sub)object has a tone and a name that are produced. Soundtrack demonstrated that a WIMP-style auditory interface could be designed for visually impaired users. Further improvements and experiments investigations are described in paper (Pitt and Edwards, 1995).

A diagram reader program for the visually impaired (Kennel, 1996) (called AudioGraph) enabled blind and visually impaired users to read diagrams with the aid of touch panel and an auditory output display. The experiments under the AudioGraph experimental platform described in this paper aimed to investigate whether structured musical stimuli can be used to communicate similar graphical information.

Invention of haptic devices leaded to design of multi-modal interfaces to access graphical information. An example of haptic system is Pantograph (Dufresne et al., 1995). The idea of multimodal access was realised in the research project PC-ACCESS (Martial and Garon, 1996). A similar technique was also used in the GUIB system in which graphics were communicated using sound and text using synthesised voice or Braille (Mynatt and Weber, 1994). There are known also later attempts to combine haptic and auditory (Jansson & Larsson, 2002).

Other approach is coding scheme based on a pixel-frequency association (Capelle et al,1998). The sensory substitution model can now be summarized as follows. According to model of vision, the acquired image matrix is first convolved by an edge detector filter and, second, converted into a multiresolution image. Then, coupling between the model of vision and the inverse model of audition is achieved by assigning a specific sinusoidal tone to each pixel of this multiresolution image; the amplitude of each sine wave is modulated by the grey level of the corresponding pixel. Finally, according to the inverse model of audition, the left and right complex sounds consist of weighted summations of these sinusoidal tones.

The experimental research (Rigas & Alty, 2005) indicated that the rising pitch metaphor can be successfully employed to communicate spatial information in user interfaces or multimedia systems. It was found that users interpreted better short sequences of notes (e.g., 6, 10 or 12). Longer sequences or groups of notes introduced an error in users' interpretation. Typically, 50–60% of the whole data was within +-3: Users successfully navigated an auditory cursor and recognised simple geometrical shapes. These results would enable the continuation of this work by introducing more shapes and enlarging the resolution of the 40 x 40 grid which was used as a basis for these experiments. The same research team (Rigas & Alty, 2005) carried out experiments of use of structured musical stimuli.

Tactile (embossed) maps were designed for this purpose. Until recently, the use of tactile maps has been very limited, as most of the maps have been produced by hand, for example using string and glue. Recent developments facilitated the production of cost effective maps. For example: printers, new types of papers and new types of ink.

An experiment found out that the tactile display did not improve performance when audio was present. The mouse appears to have some design deficiencies that means it is not useful on its own. However, as discussed above, when combined with other modalities it can be effective. Traditional methods of accessing diagrams use raised paper, allowing a teacher and student to work together by providing a visual representation of the diagram to the teacher and a tactile version to the student.

Providing accessible tactile diagrams through this method is not a trivial task. Is was noted that a direct translation of a visual diagram to a tactile diagram is in most cases not sufficient to provide accessible tactile diagrams. The data generated are static, and can be slow and expensive and error prone to alter and recreate. Further to this, for situations where the teacher and student are not collocated, this shared access to the workspace is not available through this method. For these reasons, there have been work examining computer-based technologies as an alternative to the raised paper.

In the TeDUB project (Technical Drawings Understanding for the Blind) (Horstmann et al, 2004) the system was developed, which aim is providing blind computer users with an accessible representation of technical diagrams. The TeDUB system consists of two separate parts: one for the semi-automatic analysis of images containing diagrams from a number of formally defined domains and one for the representation of previously analysed material to blind people. The joystick was used for navigation through drawings.

In the recent work (Zhao et al, 2008) sonification was used to convey data (plots) information to visually impaired user.

3. Method

3.1 Sounds

Humans can perceive a wide range of frequencies. The maximum range we can hear is from 20Hz to 20kHz. This decreases with age so that at 70 a listener might only hear a maximum of 10kHz.

Perception of sounds is characterised by three basic features: pitch, timbre, and loudness. They are subjective attributes that cannot be expressed in physical units or measured by physical means.

Pitch is the perceived frequency of a sound. In the case of a pure tone, its primary objective correlate is the physical attribute frequency, but the tone's intensity, duration, and temporal envelope also have a well established influence on its pitch (Houtsma, 1995). If a tone is complex and contains many sinusoids with different frequencies, which is usually the case with natural sounds, we also may hear a single pitch.

Our auditory memory seems to be particularly good at storing and retrieving pitch relationships, given that most people can easily recognize tones or melodies and sing them more or less correctly. This ability to recognize and reproduce frequency ratios is often referred to as perfect relative pitch. Some people possess the ability to identify the pitch of sounds on an absolute. This relatively rare ability is referred to as perfect absolute pitch.

Loudness may be defined as that attribute of auditory sensation that corresponds most closely to the physical measure of sound intensity, although, this definition is not accurate in all circumstances. Loudness is often regarded as a global attribute of a sound, so that we usually talk about the overall loudness of a sound rather than describe separately the loudness in individual frequency regions. Sounds of between 1kHz and 5kHz sound louder at the same intensity level than those outside that frequency range. Humans can perceive a very wide range of intensities.

The traditional definition for timbre used in ANSI standard is by exclusion. It is the quality of a sound by which a listener can tell that two sounds of the same loudness and pitch are dissimilar. This definition does not tell us what timbre is. The sense of timbre comes from the properties of the vibration pattern. Timbre is the attribute of auditory sensation in terms of which a listener can judge two sounds with the same loudness and pitch to be dissimilar. It is what makes a violin sound different to a piano even if both are playing the same pitch at the same loudness. Even though its structure is not well understood it is one of the most important attributes of sound that an interface designer can use.

The analysis indicates that non-trained people better rely on relative changes of sound than on absolute values.

3.2 Format of maps

Nowadays vector graphics format is widely used to store digitized maps. Often rich interactive maps are published in web using SVG file format (W3C, 2003). SVG is an XML markup language for describing two-dimensional vector graphics. It is an open standard created by the World Wide Web Consortium. The available fill and stroke options, symbols and markers enable higher quality map graphics.

As a XML based language, SVG supports foreign namespaces. It is possible to define new elements or add new attributes. Elements and attributes in a foreign namespace have a prefix and a colon before the element or attribute name. Elements and attributes in foreign namespaces that the SVG viewer does not know, are ignored. However, they can be read and written by script. Foreign namespaces are used to introduce new elements (e.g. GUI elements, scalebars) and for the attachment of non-graphical attributes to SVG graphic elements (W3C, 2003).

Most suitable software for browsing interactive SVG maps some years ago was plugin Adobe SVG Viewer, available for all major platforms and browsers (Linux, MacOSX, Solaris, Windows) which earlier could be downloaded free from the Adobe SVG homepage. Exist and commercial products as MapViewSVG from ESRI (ESRI , 2008).

```
<path id="Finland"
fill="rgb(128,255,128)" M140 76C139.82
70.67 133.284 62.11 127 63.46C119.30 65.11
117.69 71.50 109.00 66.48C98.81 60.59
100.58 49.34 93.58 41.11C86.38 32.65 83.01
40.97 83 48L77 46L96 75C105.89 76.76
118.67 89.71 120.09 100C121.01 106.62
117.20 113.69 116 120L123 127 .... C143.73
65.90 144.32 72.16 140 76 z"/>
```

Figure 1. Map with contour of Finland and example of contour description

Mapping represents a perfect application of SVG because maps are, by nature, vector layered representations of the earth. The SVG grammar allows the same layering concepts that are so crucial to Geographic Information Systems (GIS). Since maps are graphics that depict our environment, there is a great need for maps to be informative and interactive. SVG provides this interaction with very high quality output capability, directly on the web. Because of the complexity of geographic data (projection, coordinate systems, complex objects, etc.), the current SVG specification (W3C, 2003) does not contain all the

particularities of a GIS particularities. However, the current specification is sufficient to help the mapping community produce open source interactive maps in SVG format. Figure 1 is a example of represent map of Finland using SVG format.
The hierarchical structure of file for storing map is shown in Figure 2 (Daunys & Lauruska, 2006). There are shown only main elements. All map has text field with information about the map. This is information for presentation to user by speech synthesis. Other elements of the first level represent regions of maps. Actually, region is graphical tag of SVG, which describes contour of region. This tag has attributes related to sound, text and similar. Sound attribute allows to indicate sound file, which is played when cursor is over region. Text attribute is devoted to information about selected region.

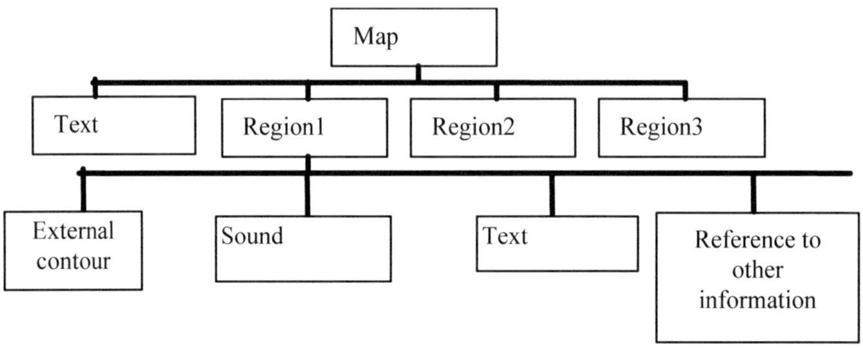

Figure 2. The hierarchical structure for maps information storage in XML format file

3.3 System model

First we consider the system hardware. Computer mouse is optional graphic-input device. The device use relative motion, so when the user hits the edge he or she needs merely to pick up the mouse and drop it back. It is convenient during usual work with computer applications, but maps exploration system is one of exceptions. In our application we need devices which give absolute coordinates. There are two choices: tablet and touchscreen. For graphical input on desktop or laptop computer we selected digitiser (tablet) as cheaper and more accurate device. PC computer have sound system and installed Microsoft Windows XP (Service Pack2) operation system.
Created sonification software without executable file has resources (collections of WAV and XML format files) and configuration file.
Software must implement these actions:

- loading default system configuration;
- selection of XML file;
- parsing of XML file;
- handling of mouse move events or menu options.

Moving of pen on tablet invokes mouse movement event in computer OS. Mouse events must initiate the generation of non speech sound. Mouse coordinates are defined and by them it is determined, over which region the mouse is present. If the mouse is on the same region as previously, now changes are done to played wav file. If the mouse goes to the new region, correspondingly, the old sound file is stopped and new file is started to play. Additionally, the distance of cursor point to the region boundary is measured to give alert signal if cursor is approaching the boundary of region.

The algorithm for determination of distance is next. The initial direction angle and the step for angle increase are selected. By default angle is equal to 0 degrees and step is equal to 5 degrees. We go from cursor point by the given angle while we reach boundary. Boundary is reached when pixel colour changes. Then we calculate Euclidean distance from cursor point to point on the boundary. The obtained value is stored in the array. Next direction is selected by adding angle step to current direction angle. And again point on boundary and distances is found (Figure 3 (a)). From the array of distances, which is plotted in Figure 3 (b), minimal distance is defined.

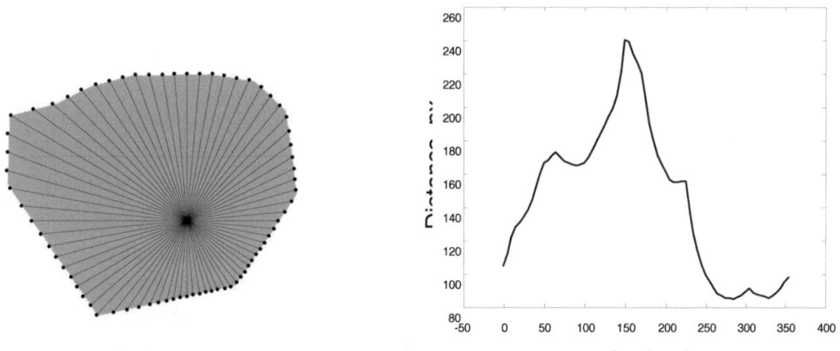

a) b)

Figure 3. Determination of minimal distance from cursor point to boundary of region: a) points on boundary detection in all directions, b) plot of distances between cursor point and boundary points

If minimal distance is lower than threshold then alerting signal is issued. The volume of sound is increased when distance decreases.

4. Implementation

In this section we will discuss implementation issues of the sonification system. For coding we selected C# language. We used the free Microsoft Visual C# 2008 Express Edition. The Windows application is based on ***System.Windows.Forms*** assembly.

The developed software must be very stable because it will be impossible for a disabled to solve a software crash and respond to unpredicted dialog boxes. Best guarantee for stability should be found in widely used technologies. In recent years the .NET Framework by Microsoft has brought the ability to write much more robust and secure code on the Windows platform. Furthermore, .NET Framework is not operating system specific; there exist some projects where .NET Framework is implemented in other OS. For example, one of the projects is Mono leaded by Novel.

One of the advantages of .NET Framework is its automatic memory cleaning, so called garbage collection. It is carried out when managed code is used. One of the simplest ways for managed code programming is the use of C# language.

.NET Framework promises good options for interoperability. It is easy to combine code written in different .NET languages because all code is first translated into CIL (Common Intermediate Language). CTS (Common Type System) also exists and ensures compatibility

of parameter types in functions calls. It is simpler to invoke methods on COM objects. There are also some choices for cross-machine communication between managed modules.
The parsing of SVG document was implemented using XLINQ library functions, other called as LINQ to XML library. The abbrevation LINQ stands for *NET Language-Integrated Query*. LINQ defines a set of general purpose standard query operators that allow traversal, filter, and projection operations to be expressed in any .NET-based programming language. The standard query operators allow queries to be applied to any **IEnumerable<T>**-based information source. XLINQ provides both DOM and XQuery/XPath like functionality in a consistent programming experience across the different LINQ-enabled data access technologies.
We used object-oriented programming technology. XLINQ allows parse data from XML file directly to classes of graphical objects.
Graphical rendering was implemented with Windows GDI+ functions. PictureBox control allows draw stable pictures. Included bitmap in it allows organise navigation plane.
For speech synthesis we used Speech library from NET. Framework version 3.0. It allows not only synthesize English speech but also some effects as emphasis of words or speech rate changes by 5 levels.
Only one software component was used outside .NET Framework. It was DirectSound library from Microsoft DirectX version 9c. Attractive features of DirectSound are advanced sound playing control: some files in the same time with independent parameters control.

5. Discussion

The differences of visual and auditory systems are pointed by Brewster (Brewster, 2002). Our visual system gives us detailed information about a small area of focus whereas our auditory system provides general information from all around, alerting us to things outside. Visual system has a good spatial resolution, while auditory system has preference in time resolution. So it is impossible to convey the same information by these two information channels.
In the sonification report (Kramer & Walker, 1999) it is stated that progress in sonification will require specific research directed at developing predictive design principles. There is also indicated about the need of research by interdisciplinary teams with funding that is intended to advance the field of sonification directly, rather than relying on progress through a related but peripheral agenda.
Analysis shows that there many different sonification efforts including solutions for visually impaired but they are more as project results and are not widely available.
The described sonification system can be easily implemented and easily integrated to bigger projects. The improvements mostly can concern selection of sounds.

6. Conclusions

XML format files were successfully used for preparing information for sonification. The developed model of sonification was successfully implemented using free software development tools: Microsoft Visual C# 2008 Express Edition and Microsoft DirectSound library.

7. References

Alty, J.L., Rigas, D. (2005). Exploring the use of structured musical stimuli to communicate simple diagrams: the role of context. *International Journal of Human-Computer Studies*, 62, 21–40, 1071-5819

Blattner, M.M., Sumikawa, D.A., & Greenberg, P.M. (1989). Earcons and icons: their structure and common design principles. *Human Computer Interaction*, 4(1), 11-44, 0737-0024

Brewster, S.A. (2002). Non-speech auditory output. In: *Human-Computer Interaction Handbook*, Jacko, J.A. and Sears, A. (Eds), Chap. 12, 220-239. Lawrence Erlbaum Associates, 0805844686, NJ

Brewster, S.A., Wright, P.C., Edwards, A.D.N. (1994). Parallel earcons: reducing the length of audio messages. *International Journal of Human–Computer Studies*, 43(2), 153–175, 1071-5819

Brewster, S.A., Wright, P.C., Edwards, A.D.N. (1995). Experimentally derived guidelines for the creation of earcons. In: Allen, G., Wilkinson, J., Wright, P. (Eds.), *Adjunct Proceedings of HCI'95: people and Computers*, Huddersfield, British Computer Society, pp. 155–159.

Capelle, C.; Trullemans, C.; Amo, P.& Veraart, C. (1998). A Real-Time Experimental Prototype for Enhancement of Vision Rehabilitation Using Auditory Substitution, *IEEE Transactions on Biomedical. Eng*ineering, vol. BME-45, pp. 1279-1293, 0018-9294

Daunys, G., Lauruska V. (2006). Maps Sonification System Using Digitiser for Visually Impaired Children. Lecture Notes in Computer Science, 4061, 12-15, 0302-9743

Deutsch, D. (1980). The processing of structured and unstructured tonal sequences. *Perception and Psychophysics*, 28(5), 381-389, 0031-5117.

Edwards, A. D. N. (1989). Soundtrack: An auditory interface for blind users. *Human Computer Interaction*, 4(1), 45-66, 0736-6906

ESRI homepage. http://www.esri.com

Horstmann, M.; Hagen, C., King, A., Dijkstra, S., Crombie, D., Evans, D.G., Ioannidis, G., Blenkhorn, P., Herzog, O. & Schlieder, Ch. (2004). TeDUB: Automatic Interpretation and Presentation of Technical Diagrams for Blind People. *Proceedings of the Conference and Workshop on Assistive Technologies for Vision and Hearing Impairment* CVHI 2004, *CVHI'2004*, pp. 112-118, Granada, Spain. CD-ROM publication

Houtsma, A.J.M. (1995). Pitch Perception. In: *Hearing*, Moore B.C.J.(Eds), 267-295, 0-12-505626-5, Academic Press

Jansson, G. & Larsson, K. (2002). Identification of Haptic Virtual Objects with Different Degrees of Complexity. *Proceedings of Eurohaptics 2002*, pp. 57-60, Edinburgh, July 2002, University of Edinburg

Kramer, G., & Walker, B. (Eds.). (1999). Sonification report: Status of the field and research agenda. Available online http://www.icad.org/websiteV2.0/References/nsf.html

Kennel, A.R. (1996). Audiograf:a diagram-reader for the blind. *Proceedings of ASSETS'96*, pp. 51–56, 0-89791-776-6, Vancouver, April 1996, ACM, New York

Lemmens, P. (2005). Using the major and minor mode to create affectively-charged earcons. In: *Proceedings of International Conference on Auditory Display*, Limerick, Ireland, July 2005 Available online http://www.idc.ul.ie /icad2005/downloads/f98.pdf

Liard, C.; Beghdadi, A. (2001). An Audiodisplay Tool For Visually Impaired People: The Sound Screen System, *International Symposium on Signal Processing and its Applications (ISSPA)*, volume 1, pp. 108–121, Kuala Lumpur, Malaysia.

Mansur, D. L., Blattner, M., & Joy, K. (1985). Sound-graphs: A numerical data analysis method for the blind. *Journal of Medical Systems*, 9, 163-174, 0148-5598

Martial, O., Dufresne, A. (1993). Audicon: easy access to graphical user interfaces for blind persons, designing for and with people, *Proceedings ofFifth International Conference on Human–Computer Interaction*, pp. 808–813, 0-444-89540-X, Orlando, Florida, USA, August 1993, Elsevier

Martial, O., Garon, S., 1996. How the visually impaired learn to work with windows. In:Burger, D. (Ed.), *Proceedings of the New Technologies in the Education of the Handicapped*, pp. 249–255, Paris, Colloque INSERM, John Libbey Eurotext Ltd.

McGookin, D. K., & Brewster, S. A. (2004). Understanding concurrent earcons: Applying auditory scene analysis principles to concurrent earcon recognition. *ACM Transactions on Applied Perception, 1*(2), 120-155, 1544-3558

Mynatt, E.D., Weber, G., 1994. Nonvisual presentation of graphical user interfaces: contrasting two approaches. In: *Proceedings of the CHI'94 Conference on Human Factors in Computer Systems*, pp. 166–172, 0-89791-650-6, ACM, New York

Pitt, I.J., Edwards, A.D.N., 1995. Pointing in an auditory interface for blind users. In: *Proceedings of the IEEE International Conference on Systems, Man and Cybernetics: Intelligent systems for the 21st Century*, pp. 280–285, 0-7803-2559-1, Vancouver, October 1995, IEEE

Rigas, D., Alty, J. (2005). The rising pitch metaphor:an empirical study. *Int. J. Human-Computer Studies*, 62, 1–20, 1071-5819

Rossing, T. D. and Houtsma, A.J.M. (1986). Effects of signal envelope on the pitch of short sinusoidal tones. *Journal of the Acoustical Society of America*, 79, 1926-1933, 0001-4966.

W3C (2003). Scalable Vector Graphics (SVG) 1.1 specification. Available online http://www.w3.org

Zhao, H., Plaisant, C., Shneiderman, B., Lazar, J. (2008). Data Sonification for Users with Visual Impairment: A Case Study with Georeferenced Data. *ACM Transactions on Computer-Human Interaction*, 15, 1, 4:1-4:28, 1073-0616

17

Advancing the Multidisciplinary Nature of HCI in an Undergraduate Course

Cynthia Y. Lester
Tuskegee University
USA

1. Introduction

The aim of this chapter is to describe the development of an undergraduate Human Computer Interaction (HCI) course that is taught from a multidisciplinary perspective to a multidisciplinary audience using themes from the various disciplines that are encompassed within HCI. Consequently, the goals of this chapter are to:

- Describe HCI
- Introduce HCI as a multidisciplinary field
- Expound on the various disciplines encompassed within HCI
- Describe the development of an undergraduate course from a multidisciplinary prospective
- Suggest ideas for future work

2. What is HCI?

2.1 Overview

Technology is a mainstay in today's society. Whether at home, school, or in the workplace, people use technological systems. Consequently, the average user is now less likely to understand the systems of today as compared to the users of 30 years ago. Therefore, the designers and developers of these systems must ensure that the systems are designed with the three "use" words in mind so that the product is successful. Hence, the system must be useful, usable, and used (Dix, et al., 2004). The last of the "use" terms has not been a major factor until recently, thereby making the discipline of human-computer interaction increasingly more important.

Human-computer interaction has been described in various ways. Some definitions suggest that it is concerned with how people use computers so that they can meet users' needs, while other researchers define HCI as a field that is concerned with researching and designing computer-based systems for people (Benyon, et al., 1998; Sharp, et al., 2007). Still other researchers define HCI as a discipline that involves the design, implementation and evaluation of interactive computing systems for human use and with the study of major phenomena surrounding them (Preece, et al., 1994). However, no matter what definition is chosen to define HCI, the concept that all these definitions have in common is the idea of the technological system interacting with users in a seamless manner to meet users' needs.

2.2 The human user

The human user may be an individual or a group of users who employ the computer to accomplish a task. The human user may be a novice, intermediate, or expert who uses the technological system. Further, the human user may be a child using the system to complete a homework assignment or an adult performing a task at work. Additionally, the human user may be a person who has a physical or cognitive limitation which impacts his/her use with the computer-based system. No matter who the human user is, the goal when interacting with a computer system is to have a seamless interaction which accomplishes the task.

2.3 The computer system

According to the *Random House Unabridged Dictionary*, a computer is defined as an electronic device designed to accept data, perform prescribed mathematical and logical operations at high speed, and display the results of these operations (2006). However, as computers become more complex, users expect more than just a display of the results of their operations. The term computer system is used to represent technology and technological systems. Consequently, technology or technological systems encompass many different aspects of computing. Users now require their systems to be able to provide answers to questions, to store various forms of information such as music, pictures, and videos, to create a virtual experience that physically may be unattainable, and to understand verbal, visual, audio, and tactile feedback, all with the click of a button. As the human user becomes to depend on these technological systems more, the interaction between the user and the system becomes more complex.

2.4 The interaction

Interaction is the communication between the user and the computer system. For computer systems to continue their wide spread popularity and to be used effectively, the computer system must be well designed. According to Sharp, Rogers, and Preece, a central concern of interaction design is to develop an interactive system that is usable (2007). More specifically, the computer system must be easy to use, easy to learn, thereby creating a user experience that is pleasing to the user. Consequently, when exploring the definition of interaction, four major components are present which include:

- The end user
- The person who has to perform a particular task
- The context in which the interaction takes place
- The technological systems that is being used

Each of these components has its own qualities and should be considered in the interaction between the computer system and the user. In his bestselling book, *The Design of Everyday Things*, Donald Norman writes about these components and how each must interact with the other, suggesting that the common design principles of visibility and affordance help to improve interaction (2002). The principle of visibility emphasizes the idea that the features of the system in which the user interacts should be clearly visible and accessible to human sense organs, which improves the interaction between the action and the actual operation (Norman, 2002). The principle of affordance as suggested by Jef Raskin, should accommodate visibility such that the method of interacting with the system should be apparent, just by looking at it (2000).

Therefore, in order to create an effective user experience, a designer of an interactive computer system must understand the user for which the system is being created, the technological system that is being developed and the interaction that will take place between the user and the computer system. An ideal designer of these systems would have expertise in a wide variety of topics which include but are not limited to psychology, sociology, ergonomics, computer science and engineering, business, art and graphic design, and technical writing. However, it is impractical to assert that any one designer should have expertise in all these areas. Furthermore, when the concepts of HCI are introduced to students who eventually become designers of these systems, the course is typically taught in a computer science department, by a computer science professor, to computer science majors.

3. HCI as a Multidisciplinary Field

3.1 The discipline of HCI

HCI is a field that brings many disciplines together and is regarded as a highly multi-disciplinary field. There are several main disciplines that are encompassed within HCI. Figure 1 provides a graphical representation of the many academic fields that are often included in HCI. This section will briefly introduce the disciplines and suggest why each is an important area of HCI and is therefore, relevant for inclusion in an undergraduate HCI course.

Figure 1. The Disciplines of HCI

3.2 Art and Graphic Design

In order to design products that are useful, usable, and used, the disciplines of art and graphic design are essential. While psychologists bring to the field of HCI the understanding of how humans act and react to technology, and computer scientists and engineers design and develop the computer systems, and the area of human factors enhances knowledge about the physical environment in which the system will be used and the social sciences help obtain accurate descriptions about the user, without the areas of art and graphic design, most systems would not be used. Artists and graphic designers put a "face" on the system and thereby with a good design and use of color, artists and graphic designers help to make the interaction between the user and the system enjoyable and seamless. Graphic designers often use typography, visual arts and rules for page layouts to assist with the design of an interface for a system. Meanwhile, the discipline of art brings to HCI a creative process by which interaction takes place between the user and the computer system. Artists help to bridge the gap between designing the system for the user and making the system usable by the user.

3.3 Business

The business field is wide. Various areas of business include business administration, accounting, economics, finance, management, and sales and marketing. At the core of each of these areas lies a knowledge base that HCI uses to its benefit. Whether it includes how to sale and market a computer system that capitalizes on user sensory interaction with a system, or if it includes e-commerce management, all the areas of business contribute to the HCI discipline. While all cannot be covered in an undergraduate course in HCI, it is important for students to understand the role that business plays within the discipline.

3.4 Engineering

ABET, Inc., the recognized accrediting agency for college and university programs in applied science, computing, engineering, and technology, has defined engineering as "[T]he creative application of scientific principles to design or develop structures, machines, apparatus, or manufacturing processes, or works utilizing them singly or in combination; or to construct or operate the same with full cognizance of their design; or to forecast their behavior under specific operating conditions; all as respects an intended function, economics of operation and safety to life and property." Engineering plays a very specific role in HCI ensuring that systems are designed and developed according to specifications.

3.5 Ergonomics and Human Factors

The term ergonomics originally coined in Europe or its United States counterpart, human factors, is traditionally the study of the physical characteristics of interaction (Dix, et al., 2004). More specially the discipline is concerned with how the controls are designed, the physical qualities of the screen, and the physical environment in which the interaction between the user and the system takes place. The goal of human factors is to optimize human well-being and overall system performance.

The discipline of human factors is important to the field of HCI as it focuses on the user's capabilities and limitations. For example, the arrangement of controls and how information is displayed, the physical environment of the user such as whether the user will be sitting or standing, using the system in a lighted room of artificial or natural light, and how color will be used, are some of the many human factors studied which contribute to the field of HCI. Consequently, students must understand how human factors impact system performance.

3.6 Technical Writing

Technical writing is concerned with the presentation of information that helps a reader solve a specific problem. Technical writing has been called a form of technical communication that is frequently used to demystify technical terms and language. Technical communicators write and design many kinds of professional documents which include but are not limited to manuals, lab reports, web pages and proposals. Often students have been exposed to writing and creating documents during their undergraduate career, but many have not written documents that explain technical concepts. Technical writing contributes to the field of HCI as it provides a form of communication that helps to enhance the interaction between the user and the computer system.

3.7 Computer Science

Computer science is a discipline that is concerned with the study and the science of theories and methods that underlie technological systems. Computer science can also be thought of as the study of computer hardware, and the study, design and implementation of computer software. HCI for many years has been thought to be a sub-discipline of computer science. However, as computer systems become more complex, requiring a heightened level of interaction between the user and the computer system, HCI encompasses the field of computer science as it does many other disciplines.

Computer system design includes a variety of activities that range from hardware design to interface design. Consequently, careful interface design plays an essential role in the overall design of interaction between the user and the computer system. The themes from computer science's software design are therefore, very prominent in the user interface design of HCI.

3.8 Social Sciences

Although, HCI has often been linked with the "hard sciences" of computer science and engineering, it is the "soft sciences" of sociology and anthropology that bring to the forefront of the discipline the impact and influence that technology has on its users. A major concern of the social sciences is to understand the interaction between the computer system and the user both during and after the event. Therefore, the reasons for including the social sciences in HCI are to obtain a more accurate description of the interaction between users, their tasks, the technological systems that they use and the environment in which they use the systems (Preece et al., 1994).

3.9 Information Systems

Information systems sometimes called management information systems, is considered to play a major role in HCI. Information systems, is an applied discipline that studies the processes of the creation, operation, and social contexts and consequences of systems that manipulate information. It also includes the analysis, development, and management of systems.

The area of information systems has two distinguishing features that place information systems within the context of HCI: (1) business application and (2) management orientations (Zhang, 2004). Consequently, information systems works well as one of the many disciplines of HCI because it is concerned with the study in which humans interact with information, technologies, and tasks in business, organizational, and cultural environments. Simply put the discipline of information systems helps HCI to go beyond the theoretical concepts of computer science to a more applied approach while taking into account issues related to social and organizational constructs.

3.10 Math and Statistics

Evaluation is concerned with gathering information about the usability of a system in order to improve system performance (Benyon et at., 1993). Without evaluation, user requirements may not be met or system performance may be low, all leading to an unpleasant user experience. However, in order to evaluate a system, data concerning the user's interaction with the system and the user's attitudes towards the system must be collected and analyzed. Consequently math, primarily statistics, plays an important role in the evaluation of a system and the user.

Statistical testing helps to present the results of evaluation in a useful and meaningful manner. Consequently, if researchers are observing the behavior between the user and the computer repeatedly, comparing one group of users to another group of users, studying one group of users comprised of individuals differing from one another, or simply presenting background information on a group of users, statistics is needed.

3.11 Cognitive Psychology

In order to design a product for the user, it is important to know the user's capabilities and limitations. The discipline of cognitive psychology provides knowledge of the user's perceptual, cognitive and problem-solving skills. Cognitive psychology is needed in order to understand the manner in which humans act and react. More importantly, cognitive psychology is used to understand how users will interact with technological systems and devices.

Of particular interest to HCI is the human information processing system which is akin to the computer information processing system. The human information processing system, according to various researchers consists of three subsystems which include: the perceptual system, which handles sensory information; the motor system, which controls actions; and, the cognitive system which provides the processing needed to connect the sensory information with the motor system (Card, et al., 1983). The computer information system includes: input devices which accepts information by apparatuses such as a keyboard or mouse; output devices which include peripheral devices; and, the central processing unit which combines the arithmetic and logic unit with the control unit to transform user input to output. Figure 2 shows the correlation between the human information processing system and the computer information processing system.

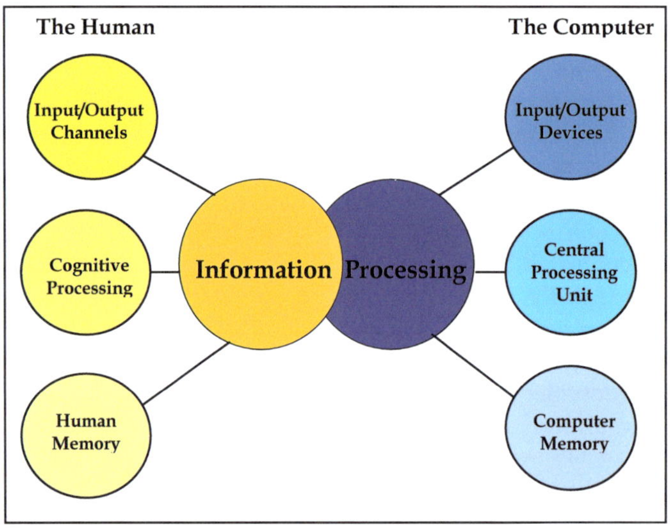

Figure 2. Information Processing

4. The HCI Curriculum

In 1988, the ACM Special Interest Group in Computer-Human Interaction organized and created a Curriculum Development Group (CDG) whose specific task was to produce a set of recommendations for education in HCI. The CDG acknowledged the multidisciplinary nature of the field, but also stated that the HCI undergraduate curriculum should be embedded within an existing disciplinary curriculum, namely computing programs (ACM 1991). Computing programs were chosen because the CDG felt that the computing disciplines "are a natural place to start" since the programs cover a broad spectrum in computing (ACM, 1991). Consequently, a review of many undergraduate programs found that HCI was typically taught in computer science departments with a heavy focus on user interface design. Yet the CDG acknowledged that "ideally" an HCI specialist would be generally comfortable in handling technological issues, the needs of individuals, and handling the concerns of their organizations and workgroups (ACM, 1991). Therefore, to prepare students with the skills needed to handle the human component of the HCI discipline, similar courses were found in Psychology Departments with a heavy emphasis on human factors, cognitive science and problem-solving principles.

With this premise in mind, the idea of the newly developed course in HCI was to draw a cross section of students from the various disciplines on campus to provide them with the basic knowledge of HCI principles taught from a multidisciplinary perspective. It was the intent of the newly developed course to bridge the gap between the courses and to offer a multidisciplinary learning experience to an undergraduate multidisciplinary audience.

The next section describes the development of an undergraduate human computer interaction course that was developed and taught from a multidisciplinary perspective to a multidisciplinary audience using themes from the various disciplines that are encompassed within HCI.

5. A New Approach

Prior to spring semester 2005, a HCI course had not been offered. Students received some instruction in HCI principles in several of the upper-level division computer programming courses that they took or in the senior level software engineering course required for all computer science majors. However, the only students enrolled in these courses were computer science students. Consequently, the new course had to be structured so that students who were majoring in other disciplines could take the course and not feel intimidated by the computer programming requirements sometimes associated with the computer science major and upper level division computer science courses. Furthermore, since the new course was designed to cater to a multidisciplinary audience, the focus of the course could not merely be on user interface design but also would include discussion on the human user, the interaction between the user and the computer system, and on the evaluation of computer systems. The new approach to the course focuses on developing a course that encompasses the themes central to HCI.

To further incorporate the concepts of a multidisciplinary learning experience, a different teaching approach was incorporated. The next section introduces various teaching methods and explains why the facilitator teaching style using peer teaching was ultimately chosen and employed as the teaching style for the HCI course.

5.1 Teaching style

Education literature states there are four styles of teaching (Grasha, 1994). To ascertain the most appropriate teaching strategy for the development of a new HCI course, the four teaching styles, formal authority, demonstrator/personal model, facilitator, and delegator were assessed. A brief description of each is presented in the next sections.

5.1.1 Formal authority

The formal authority teaching style is an instructor-centered approach where the instructor is responsible for providing and controlling the flow of the content and the student is expected to receive the content. The advantage of this method is that the instructor provides the instruction, knowledge and skills, and therefore the material is thoroughly conveyed. The disadvantages of this method are that a heavy display of knowledge can be intimidating to less experienced students and students do not build relationships with their peers because team work and collaboration are not fostered.

5.1.2 Demonstrator

The demonstrator/personal model approach is also an instructor-centered approach where the instructor demonstrates the skills that students are expected to learn. This approach encourages student participation and instructors adapt their presentation to include various learning styles. The advantage of the demonstrator/personal model method includes an emphasis on direct observation. However, the disadvantages to this approach conclude that some instructors may be too rigid and therefore discourage a personalized approach by students and if they cannot complete the task as effectively as the teacher, some students may become discouraged and frustrated.

5.1.3 Facilitator

The facilitator method is a student-centered approach. The instructor acts as a facilitator and the responsibility is placed on the student to achieve results for various tasks. This type of teaching style fosters independent learning as well as collaborative learning. The instructor typically designs group activities which necessitate active learning, student-to-student collaboration and problem-solving. The learning situations and activities require student processing and application of course content in creative and original ways. This type of teaching approach provides options or alternatives for students and encourages higher-level thinking skills. The limitation to this approach is that it is time-consuming to prepare materials and the instructor and materials must be flexible.

5.1.4 Delegator

The delegator teaching style is a student-centered approach where the instructor delegates and places the control and the responsibility for learning on the students and/or groups of students. The delegator method often gives students a choice in designing and implementing their own complex learning projects while the instructor acts in a consultative role. The advantages to this approach include high levels of collaboration and active learning. However, the limitations to this approach conclude that much of the control and responsibility for learning is placed on individuals or groups of students, which may not be the best environment for some students.

The facilitator teaching style was chosen because it is a student-centered approach which shifts the focus of activity from the teacher to the learners. This method includes active learning, collaborative learning and inductive teaching and learning (Felder, 1996). The facilitator teaching style has been stated to work best for students who are comfortable with independent learning and who can actively participate and collaborate with other students (Grasha, 1994). In particular, this approach was chosen because in education literature, the method has been shown to increase students' motivation to learn, to lead to a greater retention of knowledge, and to positively impact attitudes toward the subject material being taught (Bonwell, 1991; Johnson & Johnson, 1994; Meyer & Jones 1993). Additionally, the method places a strong emphasis on collaborative learning.

5.2 Collaborative learning

Students learn best when they are actively involved and engaged in the learning process. In educational environments, study groups are often formed to gain better insight on course topics through collaborative efforts. Collaborative learning is defined as the grouping and/or pairing of students for the purpose of achieving an academic goal (Gokhale, 1995). Davis reported that regardless of the subject matter, students working in small groups tend to learn more of what is taught and retain it longer, than when the same content is presented in other more traditional instructional formats (1993).

Supporters of collaborative learning suggest that the active exchange of ideas within small groups not only increases interest among group participants, but also helps to improve critical thinking skills. The shared learning environment allows students to engage in discussion, take responsibility for their own learning, hence becoming critical thinkers (Gokhale, 1995) Students are responsible for their own learning as well as the learning of others. Research has shown that collaborative learning encourages the use of high-level cognitive strategies, critical thinking, and positive attitudes toward learning (Wang & Lin, 2006). Further, Johnson and Johnson suggest that collaborative learning has a positive influence on student academic performance (1994).

5.3 Peer teaching

Collaborative learning takes on a variety of forms, one of which is peer teaching. Peer teaching is one of the oldest forms of collaborative learning in American education with its roots in the one-room schoolhouse educational setting. Peer teaching is defined as students learning from and with each other in ways which are mutually beneficial and involve sharing knowledge, ideas and experience between participants (Rubin & Herbert, 1998). Plimmer and Amor reported in their evaluation of student responses in an HCI course that fostered peer teaching, that there was a substantial sharing of knowledge and that students found this exchange useful (2006). The study further found that the sharing of existing knowledge with peers enriched the learning experience and contributed to an appreciation of the multiple disciplines encompassed within HCI. Similarly, in a study conducted by Rubin and Herbert found that the benefits to the peer teacher included a sense of empowerment, an increased sense of mastery and self-efficacy (1998). It has been further suggested that the peer being taught learned more, than from traditional, teacher-centered approaches.

6. Course Development

6.1 Course description

The description of the course, *CSCI 499G – Human Computer Interface,* is to provide students with an introduction to human computer interaction and to also expose them to current research topics within the field.

The prerequisites for the course are at least junior standing (a completion of at least sixty credit hours) with a minimum of two computer science courses, one of which had to be a programming course. The prerequisites were chosen to ensure that students had some programming experience and that they had completed many of the general university requirements some of which included courses in the social sciences and humanities where some of these concepts would be used in the HCI course.

6.2 Learning outcomes

Learning outcomes are extremely important when developing a course. The learning outcomes describe the specific knowledge and skills that students are expected to acquire. The learning outcomes for *CSCI 499G* included the following, and at the end of the course a student should be able to:

- Clearly state what the multidisciplinary nature of human computer interaction is and its origin.
- Identify the different areas of study within and current research topics related to the HCI discipline.
- Identify the basic psychological and physiological attributes of computer users.
- Describe and identify the components and devices of computer systems.
- Describe the fundamentals of the HCI design process.

To meet the objectives of the course outcomes, the content of the course included:

- Introduction to HCI
- The Human Component of HCI
- The Computer Component
- Interaction Basics
- The Design Process
- Evaluative Techniques
- Current Topics in HCI

Table 1 is an outline of the topics covered during the sixteen week semester (Lester, 2007).

WEEK	TOPIC
1	Introduction
2	Historical Perspective of HCI
3	Chapter 1 - The Human
4	Chapter 1 - The Human
5	Chapter 2 - The Computer
6	Chapter 2 – The Computer
7	Chapter 3 – The Interaction
8	Chapter 3 – The Interaction *Midterm Examination*
9	**SPRING BREAK** **NO CLASS**
10	Chapter 5 – Interaction design basics
11	Chapter 7 – Design rules
12	Chapter 9 – Evaluation techniques
13	Chapter 9 – Evaluation techniques
14	Chapter 10 – Universal design
15	Chapter 10 – Universal design
16	Putting it all together
17	*Final Examination*

Table 1. Weekly course schedule

Students were assessed through homework, three class projects, and a paper in special topics. Additionally, two exams were administered.

The next section presents how homework and class projects were designed and used to introduce to students the multidisciplinary nature of HCI.

7. Student Assessment

7.1 Homework

The homework assigned was not the typical homework of answering questions taken from class readings or from the questions at the end of each chapter of the required course textbook. Instead, homework was taken from human engineering exercises (Bailey, 1996). These exercises required students to solicit random volunteers, ask the volunteers to perform specific tasks, and then to submit a report. The report was to be type-written and no more than two pages in length. The report contained the following sections:

- Purpose of the study
- Method used
- Results
- Discussion of results
- Concluding thoughts

Often, computer science and engineering students receive no formal instruction on how to conduct a study using human participants or how to write and submit a scientific report. By choosing this homework method, the concepts within the social sciences, technical writing, and human factors disciplines were reinforced.

7.2 Class projects

There were three class projects assigned during the course of the sixteen week semester. The projects were designed such that each incorporated some aspect from the many disciplines encompassed within HCI. Each project was named after a popular American television show to encourage active student involvement and to create an environment where real-world applications could be used. Students used collaborative learning and peer teaching to complete the projects.

7.2.1 Project I

Project I was named *Extreme Makeover*. The television show features a home that is in desperate need of repair and renovation. The class project required students to redesign the interface of a display device. The students were asked to create a physical prototype of the device. Specific instructions for the creation of the prototype included that the device could not be any larger than one 8½ X 11" sheet of paper and no smaller than the size of regular-sized PDA. The device could not weigh more than one (1) pound. Additionally, the device should use text entry or a positioning, pointing, or drawing device.

Additionally, in creating a physical device, students were also required to produce a technical document. The document included the following: a statement of the problem and introduction to the device; an outline of the specifications for the device; an explanation of how the device was to be used; a statement about the skills that the user of the device must possess, if any (is training necessary?); a statement concerning the sensory channels needed to operate the device; as well as the advantages and limitations of the design.

The project encouraged students to be creative and focused on the principles found in the disciplines of art and graphic design, cognitive psychology, ergonomics and human factors, and technical writing. Students were assessed on the written report as well as the creativity and presumed usability of physical prototype.

7.2.2 Project II

Project II was named *Design on a Dime*. The television show features homeowners who would like to redesign one room of their home, using limited financial resources. The class project required students to design and develop a user interface for a clothing store that needed to track inventory. Students were only asked to create the interfaces which allowed employees to input a product number and determine if the merchandise existed and how much of the merchandise was in stock; hence, the concept of design using limited resources was utilized. Additionally, students were asked to create a persona that described the core user group, a scenario that described an example of how the ordering tool would be used and a network diagram that illustrated the main screens or states of the ordering tool.

Also, as in Project I, students were asked to submit a technical report. The report included a statement of the problem and an introduction to the ordering tool, the description of the ordering tool, the persona, the scenario, the network diagram, an illustration or figure of the first screen for the ordering tool and also the advantages and limitations of the design.

For Project II, the main focus was on the concepts found in the information systems, computer science, engineering and the business disciplines. Computer programming was required for this project. However, the focus was not to design and develop a program, but to concentrate on the interface that the employees would use and the business concepts required for this type of development. Technical writing was also a focus in this project. Students were assessed on the screen design and layout, and also on usability including learnability, flexibility, and robustness. Students were also assessed on the written report.

7.2.3 Project III

Project III was called *America's Next Top Model*. The television show focuses on the search for the next super runway model. The objective of Project III was to use the experimental evaluation technique discussed in class to conduct an evaluation. More specifically, the class project required students to solicit random participants (no fewer than six and no more than ten) who evaluated two interfaces of various web search engines. Students were asked to develop two testable hypotheses, to use descriptive statistics to make inferences about the population and to also display results from statistical tests. While it was explained to the students that the population size limited the type of statistical tests that could be used, the idea was expose students to experimental evaluation.

A written report was required from the students which included: a statement of the problem; an introduction to the search engines, including the important features of each and an illustration of each; a description of the evaluative technique used, including the stated hypotheses; the results; a discussion of the results and concluding thoughts; and an appendix containing the hard copies of the end user survey. An end user survey created by the author was provided to the students.

The project focused on the concepts of data collection, evaluation, analysis of data, and presentation of results. The principles found in the disciplines of the social sciences, cognitive psychology, math, primarily statistics, were the focus of this project. Students were assessed on the written report.

7.3 Special topics in HCI

Students were asked to select any current topic in the HCI field to research, which was not presently covered in class. Students were required to write a research paper on the topic and to present the paper in class. The paper was to be type-written and between eight and ten pages in length. The parts of the paper included: an introduction to the topic; a review of the literature on the topic; an analysis of the topic; and a summary and concluding thoughts. Additionally, students were required to follow either the *IEEE Computer Society Style Guide* or *The Publication Manual of the American Psychological Association*.

The focus of this project was the multidisciplinary nature of HCI. Students were assessed on degree of content, scholarly synthesis of literature, organization, grammar, and style.

8. Discussion

The course has been offered twice, once during the spring 2005 semester and again during the spring 2007 semester. Students were asked to complete a short survey after the completion of the course. The review of the survey revealed the following:

- Students left the course with an appreciation for the various disciplines that are encompassed within the HCI discipline
- Students understood the need for user interface design and that it was important to include the user throughout the design lifecycle
- Interface design is much harder than just choosing colors and buttons
- The creation of an evaluation tool is difficult and that users do not always answer the questions in the manner requested
- Users do not always use the interface in the manner in which they are requested

When asked about the course itself, the students expressed the following:

- Although nervous at first about the course set-up, students stated that they enjoyed the material and the computing majors expressed a desire for more courses that promoted a student-centered teaching approach
- They enjoyed using collaborative learning to complete the projects
- They liked the idea of presenting their projects and the paper on the selected special topic which provided them with an opportunity to practice public speaking
- They enjoyed taking classes with "other" majors which provided a different perspective as it related to problem-solving

9. Limitations and Future Work

9.1 Limitations and challenges

Developing a course that is multidisciplinary in nature proved to be quite challenging. This section describes some of the challenges that the author encountered.

One of the challenges that the author encountered was the use of the facilitator style teaching pedagogy during class meetings. Many of the computer science and engineering students expressed their discomfort with this approach because they had no prior experience with a student-centered approach to learning. Consequently, getting the students to understand that formal authority was only one style of teaching and that other methods exist was quite difficult. However, the psychology students who were familiar with this teaching style were quite comfortable from the onset.

Another challenge was getting non-computer science majors to register for the course. Many students still see computer science as programming, only. Therefore, encouraging a cross section of students to enroll in the course proved to be quite difficult. The majority of students who enrolled in the course both semesters were computer science, engineering, and psychology majors.

An additional challenge was selecting course projects for students of varying ability. Although the students liked the idea that projects were based on popular television shows, ones to which they could relate, students still expressed certain levels of discomfort. While the students from the technical disciplines were very sure of their computing ability, they were less confident with their technical writing skills, and with the disciplines that related to human factors. Similarly, the students with a major in psychology were quite comfortable with human factors topics and less confident with the technical subject matter. This finding is consistent with prior research which suggests that although multidisciplinary approaches in HCI courses introduce the work practice of various disciplines, the designing of these types of learning experiences is difficult (Adamczyk & Twidale, 2007).

9.2 Suggestions for future work

Now that the course has been taught twice with the next offering proposed for the spring 2009 semester, the author has decided to make the following changes:

- Infuse both the formal authority and facilitator teaching styles into class meetings so that despite the discipline, students are comfortable with the teaching style
- Promote the course as an interdisciplinary offering so that students from other disciplines (i.e., sociology, business, etc.) will be encouraged to enroll in the course
- Continue the development of additional course projects that focus on the multidisciplinary nature of the field
- Develop a quantitative survey so that student survey responses can be measured and analyzed
- Continue to emphasize the multidisciplinary theme throughout the course
- Invite guest lecturers from industry and other academicians who focus on HCI research

10. Implications

A well-known HCI mantra is "users perform tasks using computers (Sharpe et al., 2007)." The implication from this statement is that designers and developers of these systems must understand the user, the technological system and the tasks that the users expect to perform. More specifically, in order to create an effective user experience, a designer of an interactive computer system must understand the user for which the system is being created, the technological system that is being developed and the interaction that will take place between the user and the computer system.

An ideal designer of these systems would have expertise that ranges in a wide variety of topics which include but are not limited to psychology, sociology, ergonomics, computer science and engineering, business, art and graphic design, and technical writing. However, it is not possible for one person to be proficient in all areas. Therefore, if we as educators are to provide our students with the tools needed for leadership roles within the development process of HCI, we need to consider the development of a truly interdisciplinary course. The course should encompass the themes central to the HCI discipline and integrate the paradigms from various discipline-oriented perspectives.

It is the intent of the author to expand the dialogue that is already taking place between educators from various disciplines. It is the expectation that the infusion of the multidisciplinary themes of HCI into an undergraduate course leads to the creation of effective user experiences where the designers of interactive computer systems understand the user for which the system is being created, the technological system that is being developed and the interaction that will take place between the user and the computer system.

11. Conclusion

In summary, the aim of this chapter was to: describe HCI; introduce HCI as a multidisciplinary field; expound on the various disciplines encompassed within HCI; describe the development of an undergraduate course from a multidisciplinary prospective; and, to suggest ideas for future work. HCI has been described in a multitude of ways; however, the main theme of HCI emphasizes the idea of the technological system interacting with users in a seamless manner to meet users' needs. Therefore to meet the needs of the user, HCI interleaves the "soft skills" with technical proficiency. As a result the field of HCI is constantly changing and becoming more complex as user expectations of technical systems becomes greater. Consequently, human-computer interaction will continue to make advances and so will its multidisciplinary nature.

12. Acknowledgments

This work was supported in part by a grant from the National Science Foundation, Research Infrastructure in Materials Science and Engineering.
The author wishes to thank Dr. S. Jeelani; Dr. H. Narang; and, Ms. L. Bufford of Tuskegee University, for their resources and support. The author also wishes to thank Dr. V. Lester of Tuskegee University for her editorial comments. Additionally, the author wishes to thank Mrs. A. King of the University of Alabama at Birmingham for her assistance with the figures and Mr. M. Hobson of the University of Illinois for his contributions to the manuscript.

13. About the Author

Cynthia Lester is an Assistant Professor of Computer Science at Tuskegee University, Tuskegee, Alabama. She joined the Tuskegee University faculty in her current rank in 2005. Dr. Lester earned the B.S. degree in Computer Science from Prairie View A&M University, Prairie View, Texas and both the M.S. and Ph.D. degrees from The University of Alabama, Tuscaloosa, Alabama. Her area of specialization is Human Computer Interaction with a special interest in gender differences in computer-related usage. Other areas of research include computer science education, software engineering, secure software development, and human factors engineering. Dr. Lester is a member of several social and professional organizations and has presented her published research at national and international conferences.

14. References

Adamczyk, P. & Twidale, M.B. (2007). Supporting Multidisciplinary Collaboration: Requirements for Novel HCI Education. *CHI 2007 Proceedings, Learning & Education. pp.* 1073 - 1076, 978-1-59593-593-9, San Jose, CA, April 2007, Association of Computing Machinery, New York City.

Bailey, R.W. (1996). *Human Performance Engineering. 3rd Edition.* Prentice Hall, 0-13-149634-4, Upper Saddle River, NJ

Benyon, D; Davies, G; Keller, L.; Preece, J & Rogers, Y. (1998). *A Guide to Usability*, Addison Wesley, 0-201-6278-X, Reading, MA

Bonwell, C.C. & Eison, J.A. (1991). Active learning: Creating excitement in the classroom. *ASHE-ERIC Higher Education Report No. 1.* Washington, DC: George Washington University.

Card, S.K.; Moran, T.P & Newell, A. (1983). *The Psychology of Human-Computer Interaction, Lawrence* Earlbaum Associates, 0-898-592437, Mahwah, NJ

Davis, B.G. (1983). *Tools for Teaching.* San Francisco: Jossey-Bass Publishers. 978-1-55542-568-5, Hoboken, NJ

Dix, A.; Finlay, J; Abowd, G.B & Beale, R. (2004). *Human-Computer Interaction.* Prentice Hall, 0130-461091, Boston, MA

Felder, R.M., & Brent, R. (1996). Navigating the Bumpy Road to Student-Centered Instruction. *College Teaching.* Vol. 44 (43-47)

Gokhale, A. (1995). Collaborative learning enhances critical thinking. *Journal of Technology Education* 7, no. 1. 1995.

Grasha, A.F. (1994). A matter of style: The teacher as expert, formal authority, personal model, facilitator, and delegator. *College Teaching*. Vol. 42, (42-149)

Johnson, R. T & Johnson, D.W. (1994). An Overview of collaborative learning. *Creativity and Collaborative Learning;* Baltimore: Brookes Press. [Electronic Version]. http://www.cooperation.org/pages/overviewpaper.html (Assessed on August 31, 2006).

Lester, C. (2007). *CSCI 499-G Human Computer Interface Course Syllabus.* Department of Computer Science, Tuskegee, University. http://www.tuskegee.blackboard.com

Meyers, C., & Jones, T.B. (1993). *Promoting active learning: Strategies for the college classroom.* Jossey Bass, 1-55542-524-0, San Francisco, CA

Norman, D. (2002). *The Design of Everyday Things.* MIT Press, 978-0-262-64037-4, Cambridge, MA

Plimmer, B. & Amor, R. (2006). Peer teaching extends HCI learning. *Proceedings of the 11th Annual SIGCSE Conference on Innovation and Technology in Computer Science Education.* 1-59593-055-8, Bologna, Italy, June 26-28, Association for Computing Machinery, New York City

Preece, J.; Rogers, Y.; Sharp, H.; Benyon, D.; Holland, S. & Carey, T. (1994). *Human-Computer Interaction.* Addison Wesley, 0-201-62769-8, Reading, MA

Raskin, J. (2000). *The Humane Interface.* Addison Wesley, 0-2-1-37937-6, Boston, MA

Rubin, L. & Herbert, C. (1998). Model for active learning: Collaborative peer teaching. *College Teaching* Washington, Vol. 46, No. (26-31)

Sharpe, H.; Rogers, Y. & Preece, J. (2007). *Interaction design: beyond human-computer interaction 2nd ed.* John Wiley & Sons Ltd, 978-0-470-01866-8, England

Wang, S. & Lin, S. (2006). The effects of group composition of self-efficacy and collective efficacy on computer-supported collaborative learning. *Computer and Human Behavior.* Volume 23, Issue 5 (2256-2268) 0747-5632

Zhang, P; Nah, F. & Preece, J. (2004). HCI Studies in MIS. *Behaviour & Information Technology,* Vol. 23, No. 3, 147-151.

ACM/IEEE-CS Joint Curriculum Task Force. (1991). *Computing Curricula 1991,* ACM Baltimore, MD. (Order No. 201880).

ABET, Inc. (1998-2008). Accessed June 2008. http://www.abet.org/

Computer. Def. 1. (2005). *Random House Unabridged Dictionary.* 0-375-40383-3, New York, NY

18

Simple Guidelines for Testing VR Applications

Livatino Salvatore[1] and Koeffel Christina[2]
[1]*Electronic, Communication and El. Engineering, University of Hertfordshire*
[2]*Center for Usability Research and Engineering*
[1]*United Kingdom,* [2]*Austria*

1. Abstract

In recent years the number of virtual reality (VR) applications and devices employed in companies as well as in research facilities has increased remarkably. The applications developed call for human-computer interaction, which in turn calls for system and usability evaluations. These evaluations are usually conducted by means of measurement of human behaviour including aspects of perception, action, and task-performance. Traditionally, evaluations are held in specially designed usability laboratories but the new tendency requires researchers and even students that are non-experts in the field of usability, to evaluate applications. Hence, these studies take place at the premises of laboratories at universities or research institutes. This raises the question of whether non-experts are able to conduct evaluations in a professional manner. Furthermore, the evaluation issue calls for multi- and inter- disciplinary collaboration, where technical expertise is combined with humanistic knowledge and methodology. Several experts in the field of VR, as well as in the field of usability studies, call for producing helpful guidelines in order to be able to evaluate VR applications. This chapter gives an overview of the problem and introduces a guideline for evaluations of VR applications which aims to assist researchers in evaluating VR devices and installations,and in particular usability novices. This chapter also aims to facilitate multidisciplinary activities through the use of an evaluation guideline which would be simple and focused on VR. The applicability and usefulness of the proposed guideline are based on the authors' experience in supervising and coordinating several university student projects related to the development of VR visualization technologies and applications. Furthermore, the guideline has been tested through several case studies where students were asked to evaluate their final year projects. The results showed how the proposed guideline could successfully be employed by non-experts to carry out pilot and formal evaluations. Therefore, this chapter is expected to represent a valuable reference for students and non-usability experts who design VR systems or applications and wish to run a user study to assess usefulness and general usability characteristics of their products.

2. Introduction

In recent years VR applications started to be used more commonly. If a few years ago only big institutions had the budget to acquire devices such as a CAVE or a head mounted display, today the spread of interactive applications and their commercial use has opened a

wide market accessible to a larger range of activities and budgets. This has also raised interest in the ways of using VR devices. Research institutions are exploring new possibilities and new interaction tools, to support and enhance the ideal use of VR facilities.
There is a large range of possible applications in VR, not only for product development and laboratory simulation, such as computer-aided design, data visualization, training, but also for entertainment purposes, such as computer games, art and tourism. The full potential of those techniques has not entirely been explored by now, e.g. only few games suitable for VR devices are available so far.
The VR evolution also raises the question of usability to assess the relevance and user friendliness of the proposed applications. Especially since each VR device has a diverse operational area, there is a large range of possible uses depending on the given circumstances. In order to assess the overall usability of the system and to figure out which kind of device and system setting should better be used on what application, usability evaluations of systems are conducted.
In the last 20 years, since the introduction of usability to a wider audience (also comprising non experts), amongst others by Jakob Nielsen (Nielsen, 1993), the development of usable applications whose usability is evaluated through user-tests has increased in importance. Companies offering consultancy in this area have been established, e.g. USECON[1], which most of the time dispose of professional usability laboratories. Nevertheless, only few research establishments, especially from an interdisciplinary background, have access to such facilities.
The number of people developing VR devices increases steadily. Amongst them there are computer-scientists and engineers, including also a remarkable number of students, who are often required to conduct user studies by themselves. Most of those technically educated people are not specialists in conducting evaluations.
Unfortunately, at the current state little work can be found in form of helping instructions or guidelines for the specific area of VR. Although evaluations and usability in general are a common and well known area and there are several books available on this topic, it has to be considered that VR is a modern and not standardized subject. Furthermore, students usually do not have a large amount of time for developing their applications or doing their research. Big companies or universities specializing in this field have more resources at hand. Students typically have up to one year of time to develop and test a project. Therefore most of the guidelines introduced have to be simplified in order to be able to be applied in a reasonable amount of time. Nevertheless, they have to be as accurate as possible.
The purpose of this chapter is to describe a simple guideline for running usability studies with a focus on VR applications. The guideline consists of a number of directives exposed with a certain level of detail, while still being a compact set (as required for a handbook), and of easy understanding.
This chapter is expected to represent a precious reference for students and non usability experts that undertake the design of a new VR application and wish to run a pilot or formal user study to assess effectiveness and general usability characteristics of their product.
Section 3 provides an overview of related work which supports the argumentation for a simplified and focused guideline. Section 4 introduces the guideline concept in terms of a multidisciplinary facilitator. Section 5 presents the objective and approach of the chapter.

[1] USECON, The Usability Consultants, http://www.usecon.com/

Section 6 presents the suggested basic set of evaluation guidelines to be considered when performing a user study. A case study where the proposed guideline has been adopted is described in section 7.

3. Related Work

Renowned specialists in the field of VR, who are conducting usability studies and perform research in this field, call for a general guideline for evaluations in VR.

Joseph Gabbard states in (Gabbard, 1997) the urge for a handbook or more professional help for conducting usability studies in the field of VR. In his thesis, Gabbard proposes a taxonomy for conducting user studies connected to VR. Gabbard offers a very precise and detailed list of inputs for conducting usability studies. He introduces an approach which starts at the beginning of the product life-cycle and comprises assets for the tasks the participants should conduct as well as for the specific applications that are employed for the usability study. Although written in 1997, most of the inputs are still valid, nevertheless, there is no section about the state-of-the-art included in his thesis - a point that he tried to cover in his following work.

In particular, Gabbard et al. published a paper in 1999, describing a new methodology treating the usability process of products employed in the field of VR (Gabbard et al., 1999). They divide the interaction development into behavioural and constructional development. Because of this user-centered and developer-centered approach, they describe a four-step usability process including user task analysis, expert guideline-based evaluation, formative user-centered evaluation and summative comparative evaluations. Gabbard et al. further mention the lack of professional guidelines in VR. Although they describe a well-structured process, the guidelines still consist of expert-based approaches that are hard to be executed by non-experts in the field of usability.

Bach and Scaping, (Bach & Scaping, 2004) are also very involved in this area and point out the lack of a guideline that not only treats one VR device, but is a general handbook for all VR facilities available. Further they mention that usability tests in the field of VR could get very complicated, since the technology used is very complex. In general, they give a good overview of the main obstacles one might encounter while conducting usability studies in this area. Bach and Scaping specify the most significant differences between common user studies and user studies accomplished in the field of VR. They also point out that most of the VR devices are multi-user compatible, whereas regular 2D devices are not. Since the ergonomic knowledge in the field of VR is very rare, they suggest combining some already existing methods of evaluations with new ideas.

In his paper about usability of VR systems, Timothy Marsh criticizes the absence of a general guideline for 3D applications (Marsh, 1999). He proposes further research to investigate the precise definition of VR, to detect the differences in the evaluation methods from normal 2D usability studies, to investigate existing research approaches and to develop studies for a future research plan.

Sutcliffe and Gault (Sutcliffe & Gault, 2004) introduce a new possibility of heuristic evaluations for VR applications. Their method is based on the heuristics introduced by Nielsen (Nielsen, 1993). They assembled a set of 12 heuristics and conducted 2 test studies using them. The results show, that not all heuristics are suitable for all kinds of applications and devices. Sutcliffe et al. consider the heuristics developed to be a new and important extension to expert-based human-computer interaction (HCI) evaluation methods and they deem it to be superior to Nielsen's original approach concerning VR applications.

In 2006 Karaseitanidis et al., (Karaseitanidis et al., 2006), used the VIEW-IT tool (view inspection tool) developed by Tromp and Nichols (Tromp & Nichols, 2003) for a new kind of evaluation method, following the "VIEW of the Future" project. They decided not only to rely on traditional questionnaires, but to use psycho-physiological and neurophysiologic measures like the estimation of mental workload, stress, strain, level of cognitive performance, alertness and arousal. For assessing these factors, which are not able to be measured with "common" usability methods, they made use of electroencephalography (EEG), event-related potentials (ERP), electrocardiography (ECG), blood pressure and more. Furthermore they made a socio-economic assessment to identify future domains for VR facilities.

As can be seen from the above presented works, the methods and approaches introduced almost exclusively focus on expert-based evaluation methods and are therefore not suited for novices in the area of usability.

4. A Multi-Disciplinary Subject

Measurement of human behaviour is a main subject of the humanistic community (e.g. psycho-physiologists, psychologists), whose studies have recently also targeted VR related topics (e.g. presence, immersion). The humanistic community typically lacks technical knowledge which sometime leads to proposing inapplicable studies or studies of difficult comprehension by many among the technical people.

VR technology is, on the other hand, mostly developed by the technical community (e.g. computer scientists, engineers). However, in this community there are many not familiar with conducting human-based evaluations and therefore struggling with designing a systematic usability study, hence, desiring simple guidelines or, in other words, an evaluation "handbook".

While multi- and inter- disciplinary research activities are being promoted and carried out both at research and educational level, a synergic interaction between the technical and humanistic communities is still out of reach for many researchers who have typically been educated monodisciplinary.

Interaction between different communities has often led to contrasts, misunderstandings and slow development. The authors of this chapter and their department colleagues have experience with problematic situations due to multidisciplinary cooperation in recently established interdisciplinary educations, such as Medialogy[2], and in projects at European level, e.g. Benogo[3], Puppet[4].

The aim for this guideline is also to support multidisciplinary activities by functioning as facilitator of multidisciplinary interaction when performing evaluation studies in VR. In

2 Medialogy is a new interdisciplinary study at Aalborg University, Denmark. http://www.media.aau.dk.

3 Benogo (Being There Without Going), EU-FP6 RTD (IST-FET) project. Coordinator: Aalborg University, Denmark, 2002-2005. http://www.benogo.dk

4 Puppet (The Educational Puppet Theatre Of Virtual Worlds), EU-ESPRIT-LTR project under i3 – (Experimental School Environment). Coordinator: Aalborg University, 1998-2001. http://www.cvmt.dk/projects/puppet.

particular, by reducing interaction among different disciplines when this may not be needed. For example, when non-usability experts aim at performing pilot/formal performance evaluations or when evaluations are planned after product development and not earlier in the process (such as for industrial products).

Although user studies in VR should generally involve multidisciplinary collaborations because of their complexity, the authors of this chapter believe that it is beneficial to provide VR technical developers with a handbook containing a precise guideline on how to perform usability tests. A concept also supported by the experts mentioned in the previous section.

5. Aim and Approach

The aim of this chapter is a simple evaluation guideline specifically targeting usability studies in VR. The guideline is designed for "non-experts" to provide them with a simple but scientifically valid reference on how to run and design usability evaluations. We propose the guideline to be achieved from the analysis of representative and well assessed scientific work in the field, e.g. articles from major international journals and conferences.

We have researched and analyzed the state of the art in evaluations connected to VR in some of our
previous work, (Koeffel, 2007; Koeffel, 2008). In particular, more than 30 representative literature works concerned with evaluation of VR displays have been analyzed, and 15 of them have been chosen for a deeper study (Bayyari & Tudoreanu, 2006; Christou et al., 2006; Cliburn & Krantz, 2008; Demiralp et al., 2006; Elmqvist & Tudoreanu, 2006; Fink et al., 2004; McMahan et al, 2006; Ni et al., 2006; Patel et al., 2006; Qi et al., 2006; Sutcliffe et al., 2006; Takatalo et al., 2008; Vinayagamoorthy et al., 2006; Wang et al., 2006; Wilcox et al., 2006). The analyzed papers represent a determined cross-section of the mostly treated areas in VR and are related to the analysis of different visual display technologies in VR applications.

Since the field of VR represents a wide area which is surely hard to cover with a general guideline, we decided to leave out acoustic and haptic devices. Furthermore, not all visual displays are considered, e.g. head mounted displays, since it was our goal to show case studies through experimentation with available facilities (though, including a large panoramic wall and a 6-sided CAVE).

Generally, one major issue in visual display technology in VR, covered in some of the considered papers, is the display size. Among other topics of interest: exploration and remote driving, information rich VRs, influence of the real world and occlusions in VR, and use of different VR facilities.

The Fishtank VR facility is evaluated against the CAVE in two different types of user studies conducted by Demiralp et al., (Demiralp et al., 2006). Ni et al. investigate the connection between display size and task performance in information-rich VR, (Ni et al., 2006). Bayyari and Tudoreanu investigate the impact of immersive VR displays on user performance and comprehension (Bayyari & Tudoreanu, 2006). Cliburn and Krantz conduct a user study in order to assess the impact of stereoscopic visualization and multiple displays on user performance (Cliburn & Krantz, 2008).

The users' performance in real and virtual environments is investigated by Fink et al. (Fink et al., 2004). A similar study is conducted by Sutcliffe et al., who compare interaction in real world and virtual environments (Sutcliffe et al., 2006). In (Wang et al., 2006), Wang et al. evaluate the effects of real world distraction on user performance in VR. The effectiveness of occlusion reduction techniques is investigated by Elmqvist and Tudoreanu in (Elmqvist &

Tudoreanu, 2006). Using the results of an empirical study, Qi et al. develop guidelines to ease the choice of display environment for specific volume visualization problems (Qi et al., 2006).

The performance and usability of different 3D interaction devices is investigated by Patel et al. (Patel et al., 2006). The importance of posture and facial expressions of virtual characters in virtual environments is explored by Vinayagamoorthy et al. (Vinayagamoorthy et al., 2006). Wilcox et al. evaluate whether or not people perceive a violation of their interpersonal space when using VR (Wilcox et al., 2006). Takatalo et al. present a framework for measuring human experience in virtual environments in (Takatalo et al., 2008). McMahan et al. introduce a study that separates 3D interaction techniques and the level of immersion since it is very difficult to compare different VR systems, (McMahan et al, 2006). The development and evaluation of a large-scale multimodal VR simulation suitable for the visualization of cultural heritage sites and architectural planning is described by Christou et al. (Christou et al., 2006).

The most significant information about the user studies conducted in the analyzed papers had been collected, classified, and used as a base for our analysis.

The data collected comprehends:

- The goal of the user study.
- The number of participants.
- Data connected to the participants such as their vision or attitudes.
- The setup in use.
- The number of tasks to complete, their nature and the completion time.
- The statistical and graphical types of evaluation.

All the collected data has then been evaluated statistically.

The idea of a "handbook" together with its content have then been developed, (Koeffel, 2008), presented to the research community (Livatino & Koeffel, 2007), and further improved based on the acquired experience.

The proposed guideline merges existing traditional approaches in evaluation and the state of the art in evaluating VR applications. For the traditional part especially Nielsen (Nielsen, 1993), Rubin (Rubin, 1994) and Faulkner (Faulkner, 2000) appeared to be relevant.

The guideline addresses two areas:

1. General suggestions on how to design usability studies.
2. VR specific aspects of usability studies.

The general recommendations of the first part can be understood as the basics of user testing, which can also be found in the literature, such as (Faulkner, 2000; Nielsen, 1993; Nielsen & Mack, 1994; Rubin, 1994; Sarodnick & Brau, 2006). The proposed guideline comprises a summary of the suggestions offered in the above mentioned sources and because of the generality of this part, the provided information can also be adapted and applied to different areas of VR.

The second part includes VR specific aspects such as the number of participants employed in user studies in the field of VR, the kind of questionnaires used or statistical measures employed to obtain results, etc.

The Guideline has been tested through user studies, (one of them is briefly described in section 7). The results and experience obtained from those studies combined with the authors' experience in conducting user tests, have allowed for improving and completing the guideline to the stage presented here.

The proposed guideline contains the basis of a recommendation on the most important steps for designing, planning and conducting a usability study in the field of VR. It is accompanied by a case study to facilitate implementation and conceptual understanding.

6. Evaluation Guidelines

This section describes the proposed set of directives for the evaluation of VR applications. The following paragraphs are divided into sub-sections addressing specific aspects. The content of the description is based on selected literature in the field of VR that we have investigated. The test designer is left with some freedom of choice depending on: the guideline specific aspects, application context, available time, and pre-determined objectives. To support the designer's decision in making a choice, the guideline often directly refers to the results of our investigation in specific aspects in terms of percentage of literature works.

6.1 Research Question

Before starting to build a setup for an evaluation, the research question for the usability study needs to be formulated. A general research question defining the purpose of the entire project should already exist; nevertheless a specific research question should be formulated for the special purpose of the evaluation. This defines the main subject of the study.
It is very important to create a strong and valid research question that summarizes the goal of the evaluation in only one sentence/paragraph.
It is essential that the purpose of the entire project as well as the evaluation is clear to everybody on the project/evaluation team. Additionally, the research question should help to formulate the hypothesis we want the project to be tested against.

6.2 Ethics

Since user tests are conducted with humans, it is essential to assure that there will be no harm to the participants and that their personal rights are maintained, (Burdea & Coiffet, 2003). Users' mental and physical health must not be at risk and they need to be informed about potential hazards. Furthermore, users have to be able to stop whenever they feel uncomfortable and desire the test to end.
Certain universities dispose of an ethical department that administrates all studies and evaluations conducted involving humans. In this case, the researchers have to apply to this committee and do have to obey certain rules. If the university where the evaluation is supposed to take place does not dispose of such a department, ethical considerations have to be taken into account as well. Especially when there is no board reviewing the studies, one has to make sure that all ethical concerns are respected. Furthermore also legal considerations of the country where the study is planned,should be reviewed.
Virtual reality applications offer many possible risks to the participants of a user study, e.g. in cases when new devices are invented and tested or when existing devices have not entirely been tested for health risks. Additional hazards can appear through the use of HMD's, backpacks or laser diodes. Different mechanical devices in use, such as haptic tools can endanger the participants' health when applied incorrectly. Side-effects such as the occurrence of cybersickness need attention when using VR applications. They might even require a participant to stop the test.

6.3 Evaluation Method

At the very beginning of each user study it is important to choose and define the appropriate evaluation methods applicable to the setup to be tested. According to Jakob Nielsen these are: performance measures, thinking aloud, questionnaires, interviews, logging actual use and user feedback. These evaluation methods can also be applied in a combined version.

Depending on the time when the evaluation takes place and the kind of data collected, one can distinguish between formative and summative user studies. Formative usability evaluations usually take place several times during the development cycle of a product to collect data of prototypes. Typically summative evaluations are applied at the end of a project, for example, to compare different products. Formative user studies are rare in VR. According to our statistical evaluation, all of the 19 user studies investigated were conducted as summative studies.

When comparing two or more different VR devices/applications (summative evaluation), one can decide whether to use a within or between subjects design. Between subjects studies are more common in VR. A statistical analysis conducted in (Koeffel, 2008) has shown that a total of 61% of user studies in VR were designed as between subjects studies.

6.4 Setup

In our recommendations the setup is distinguished into the testing environment and the technological setup.

- **Testing environment**

  Evaluations conducted by students and academic researchers usually take place in the facilities of universities. In some cases universities dispose of their own usability labs for conducting evaluations, but in most of the cases the evaluations occur in computer labs or classrooms. Since classrooms are not always comfortable (and hard to find relaxing), while it is required that the participants feel at ease, it is very important to create a comfortable environment. It has to be avoided the presence of people that are not involved in the project, the presence of those running around hectically and preparing the evaluation, and other distractions such as loud noises.

  It is generally important not to give the participants unnecessary information about the project or to bias the results by telling the users some weaknesses or previous results. If the user study requires a test monitor logging data while the participants perform the testing, it is fundamental that he/she respects the participants' privacy by not sitting too close to them. Furthermore, any kind of stress and emotional pressure has to be kept away from the participants in order not to influence the results.

- **Technological setup**

  Student and research evaluations often base on an already finished project (summative evaluations), referring to the hardware and/or the software. Therefore the technological setup might already be given. Considering the different VR setups, it is very important to assure that all needed devices are at the test monitors' disposal on the day(s) of the usability study. Furthermore it is very important to test if the application, the software, and the data logging, are well functioning. Since VR devices and applications are still considered to be "new technology" they are sometimes unstable and tend not to work all the time. Hence, it is crucial to organize and reserve technical facilities and rooms, and to inspect the functionalities of the project to be tested.

6.5 Participants

Several fundamental elements of evaluations are related to participants. Before recruiting volunteers, it is very important to investigate the target population of the user study. Therefore users with the desired attributes such as age, gender, education, experience with VR, computer experience, gaming experience, visual abilities, etc. can be selected. Generally, it is advisable to test user groups with a great internal variance. Especially in the field of VR, it is utterly important to recruit users from different age groups, gender and experience.

The results of our research indicate that around 71 percent of the participants were male and only 29 percent were female, which means that men are participating in user studies in the field of VR twice as often as women. This could be acceptable in case of men being the main users of a VR product. In general, a careful selection of participants according to expected system users is important.

Concerning the number of participants, it mainly depends on the kind of user study conducted (i.e. formative or summative evaluation, between or within subjects design, etc.). Generally, usability experts (Faulkner, 2000; Nielsen, 1993; Nielsen & Mack, 1994; Rubin, 1994) hold that 2 to 4 participants suffice for conducting a representative pilot study, and 5 to 20 participants suffice for conducting a formal user study. Nevertheless, more recent approaches on evaluations in the field of VR have suggested testing a higher number of participants in order to obtain meaningful results.

A number of approximately 23 participants is suggested for within subject designs and 32 for between subject designs. In case of pilot studies, a minimum number of 6 participants is proposed. These figures are based on our literature analysis.

Participants are typically volunteers and/or they do not receive any financial compensation. Nevertheless, it is highly recommended to hand the participants a small token of appreciation after finishing the user study.

6.6 Forms

Forms are different documents that are handed to the participants during the course of a user study. Concerning the forms given to the participants, this guideline conforms to the traditional approaches introduced in (Nielsen, 1993; Rubin, 1994) and the results of the statistical analysis of relevant literature in (Koeffel, 2008). Therefore we recommend the use of the following forms:

- **Information sheet:** The information sheet (also called test script) provides an overview of the entire testing process. This form should be handed to the participants at the very beginning before the actual testing, and it should contain information about: the title of the project, names and contact information, introduction to the project, duration of the study, tasks to be completed, and the possibility to withdraw from the study at any time. In 5 out of the 18 studies investigated, the participants have reported to have received written or displayed information before the testing process.
- **Consent form:** The consent form states that the researchers are allowed to use and publish the data collected during the user study. This may also include eventually taken pictures or videos. It is a reassurance for the participants that their data will not be used for any other purpose than the one explained in the consent form and/or in the information sheet. For the researcher this form is a legal reassurance that he/she is allowed to use and publish the obtained data.

- **Questionnaires:** Generally questionnaires should contain the information required by the research question which is not possible to be collected automatically through data logging and performance measures. Therefore, mostly subjective qualitative data is collected using questionnaires. Special issues should be treated in questionnaires in order to emphasize the conclusion and the results of the data collection. Questionnaires can provide answers about personal feelings or preferences. We distinguish among: screening, pre-test, device, post-test, background, presence, simulator sickness, and the EVE-experience questionnaire.
- **Task scenarios:** It might be necessary to provide participants with a task scenario (describing each step in detail) for each task he/she should complete. This allows every participant to gain the same amount of information. Furthermore it clarifies the knowledge necessary to complete a given task.
- **Data collection forms:** Experience has shown that it is not always sufficient to auto-log data using software. Sometimes it is necessary that the test monitor writes down notes or information during a task session. This can be additional information such as time or estimates expressed by participants.
- **Thank you form:** In addition to the possible personal gratification that participants may receive by taking part in a user study, a thank you letter should also be handed to them. This is important in order to formally thank the participants and tell them where to find further information about the progress of the project, e.g. published papers.

The forms should be adapted to the needs of the user study. Generally we suggest the employment of semantic differentials as answering options.

6.7 Schedule

It is essential to estimate the overall completion time per participant and to prepare a schedule showing the sequence of participants and their assigned tasks. In particular, the schedule should include: timing of the single tasks, overall completion time, the sequence of the tasks per participant, possible breaks, time needed for introduction and debriefing, room locations, etc.

The studies analyzed indicate an overall completion time per participant that ranges from 23 to 240 minutes with an average completion time of 45 minutes. This time includes the time from when a participant arrived at the testing facility until the time he/she left.

In the field of VR it is very important to keep the single task sessions as well as the overall completion time as short as possible. A maximum of 30 minutes per task is recommended by Bowman et al. (Bowman et al., 2002). Too long sessions might cause exhaustion of the participants and side effects such as cyber-sickness, which could negatively affect the results. It is important to counterbalance the sequence of the single tasks in order to avoid learning effects and biasing of the results.

6.8 Test Monitor and Spectators

The role of each person present during the user study has to be predefined. Especially the test monitor should be well instructed and capable to serve his/her purpose.

The test monitor is present during all parts of the usability study and interacts with the participants. If possible somebody who has ground knowledge in usability (especially evaluations) should be employed as test monitor. In case that there is no expert in usability available, the person in the role of test monitor should acquire basic knowledge in this area.

The test monitor should be able to comfortably interact with the participants, which requires an open and friendly personality (i.e. a "people-person"). It is also important that the test monitor does not get too close to the participants physically as well as mentally, to give them some privacy.
In case other people than the test monitor and the participant, are present during a test session, e.g. technical staff, VR project development team, spectators, etc., they should be introduced to participants at the beginning and the roles of the spectators need to be defined clearly. Generally, the number of spectators during a testing session should be kept small since they tend to make the users nervous. If not part of the research question, spectators should avoid talking during task sessions. This is especially crucial for VR applications, since distractions such as loud noises might disturb the sense of presence.
Since VR systems are still considered new technology and unstable, it might happen that the participant gets frustrated because something is not working properly or it is very difficult to accomplish. In such a case, the test monitor should not judge the participant or the system by expressing that e.g. "this error always occurs" or otherwise by negatively influencing the user. The test monitor should encourage the participant to go on as long as possible.

6.9 Test Plan

When forming the idea of conducting an evaluation, a test plan should be created. This document contains in principle every kind of knowledge necessary for the user study. The test plan describes the main content of the usability study. It serves as the basic document for communication to other people that might be involved in the user study (e.g. second test monitor).
Using the test plan every involved person knows the main principles and ideas behind the evaluation. Therefore open questions and misunderstandings can be clarified. Furthermore, the test plan describes the resources needed and gives an overview of the milestones already accomplished. A properly formulated test plan for user studies in the field of VR should contain the following items:

- **Purpose**: The purpose describes the research question and the main problems treated as well as the current state of the art of the project.
- **Problem statement/test objectives**: The problem statement treats the main issues and questions connected to the evaluation, e.g. the questions derived from the hypothesis.
- **User profile**: The user profile describes the target group and the participants to be acquired for the study.
- **Test design**: The test design includes decisions about the entire session of the usability study, such as the evaluation method, e.g. if doing a between or within subjects evaluation. Furthermore the test design specifically describes each single step during the user study, starting from the arrival of the participants until the time they leave.
- **Task list**: The task list describes every task and subtask that the participants will be asked to accomplish and on which VR device tasks are accomplished.
- **Test environment/equipment**: This section elaborates the test environment and equipment used in the test, e.g. VR devices and rooms needed.
- **Test monitor role**: The description of the test monitor role includes information about the test monitor and possible spectators.
- **Evaluation measures**: The evaluation measures should be described on a list enumerating all data collected during the user study (data logging, questionnaires, etc.).

- **Report contents and presentation**: This section gives a short preview on the data contained in the final test report and the presentation of the results obtained during the user study.

6.10 Pilot Study

It is generally recommended to perform a pilot study before testing a project in a formal user study. The pilot study should be conducted in the same way as the formal study and each participant should be treated as if he/she were in the formal study (including the forms to be used).

The pilot study is useful for removing errors from the project/setup, debug the test design, debug the experimental design, detect biased questions in the questionnaires, refine the questionnaires and detect the overall time necessary per participant. Furthermore, rooms and technical facilities should be tested of their functionality.

A minimum number of 6 participants is suggested, (see sub-section 6.5 for more details). In general, the more participants are tested, the more indicative the results are.

The pilot study is essential in case of problems that may not be predicted and only occur during the study.

6.11 Formal Study

In an ideal case, a pilot study has been conducted before the formal study and the results of the pilot study have been taken into account when planning and conducting the formal study. If required, additional tests could be conducted at the very beginning of the study in order to categorize the participants. Furthermore, a practice session should be administrated for all testing activities which need a test-user to become acquainted with system commands and behaviour. In our literature an average of 4.1 tasks are accomplished per participant in practice sessions.

In order to avoid negative side effects (such as motion sickness) and fatigue, long enough breaks should be held between the single task sessions.

Concerning the variables chosen for the evaluation, the most frequently used independent variables (factors) are related to: display type and size, chosen virtual environment, stereoscopic visualization, etc. The most popular dependent variables are subjective measures (obtained from questionnaires). The most used are completion time and response accuracy.

The number of possible tasks which users are asked to complete during an evaluation may vary largely. An average of 28.7 trials accomplished by one participant during a user study was detected in the analyzed works. The most frequently employed categories of tasks in our literature research may represent a typical example. These are:

1. Navigation (Bayyari & Tudoreanu, 2006; Cliburn & Krantz, 2008 ; Fink et al., 2007; Ni et al., 2006; Patel et al., 2006; Takatalo et al, 2008, Vinayagamoorthy et al., 2006; Wang et al., 2006).
2. Manipulation (Christou et al., 2006; McMahan et al., 2006; Patel et al., 2006; Sutcliffe et al., 2006).
3. Counting (Bayyari & Tudoreanu, 2006; Elmqvist et al., 2006; Qi et al., 2006; Vinayagamoorthy et al., 2006; Wang et al., 2006).

Among other tasks completed less frequently by the participants: estimation, prediction, search and observation.

6.12 Results and Presentation

Another important part of conducting usability studies is the processing and evaluation of the collected data. The processing of the results can be very complex and time consuming since most of the time a lot of data is collected. Therefore it is recommended to employ statistical tools. The most frequently used are: mean, median, frequency distribution, Bonferroni, standard deviation, t-test, and ANOVA (Analysis of Variance).

For the graphical display of the gained data, frequency distributions (in form of histograms) are very popular (83% of the cases in our investigation). Their main purpose is to display error rates and time. As inferential statistics the analysis of variance (ANOVA) is used the most to detect the statistical significance of test results. The ANOVA is a common method of separating the effects of multiple investigation factors (independent variables) on evaluation measures (dependent variables). The ANOVA examines which factors have a significant influence on a dependent variable by comparing the variance within a factor to the variance between factors, (Wanger et al. 1992).

A one-way ANOVA is to be used to estimate the effect of one factor (independent variable) on one of the evaluation measure. A two-way ANOVA is to be used to estimate the effect of two factors (independent variables) on one evaluation measures. According to the literature it is hard to analyze more than two factors using an ANOVA.

In case the effect of a factor is to be estimated on more than one evaluation measure, a multivariate ANOVA (MANOVA) should be applied. A MANOVA is an extension of the ANOVA that reports for multiple dependent variables.

The results of ANOVA's should be displayed in tables, while bar graphs are most used to display descriptive statistics.

7. Case Study

This section briefly presents a case study where the proposed guideline has been applied to. Although it is not imperative to conduct a case study to asses our guideline, we believe this could illustrate its usefulness and application possibilities, and it would facilitate implementation and understanding of the underlying concept.

We have run several case studies over the last few years in order to assess and improve the proposed guideline. The presented case study is related to an innovative use of VR technologies in Telerobotics. The study focuses on a mobile robot teleguide application, (Livatino et al. 2007), which included:

- Qualitative evaluation on user preferences for different VR technologies (Desktop, CAVE, Panorama).
- Quantitative evaluation to support the comparative study, to analyze the advantage of using stereoscopic over monoscopic viewing, and to examine the influence of the user's cognitive profile on his/her performance.

The case study took place at the facilities of Aalborg University in Aalborg (VR Media Lab) and Copenhagen (Medialogy Lab).

The proposed study aimed at improving and extending previous evaluations conducted with different VR facilities, (Livatino & Privitera, 2006). We ran the tests on the three VR facilities represented in figure 1. They are: 3D desktop in mono and stereo; large panoramic wall in mono and stereo; a 6-sided CAVE in stereo only.

7.1 Problem Statement

The problem statement of our case study (part of the test plan, see sub-section 6.9) had three hypotheses. They are:

- Users performing tasks employing stereo visualization perform better than users performing the same tasks employing mono visualization.
- The same task is not performed with the same efficiency and accuracy on different VR facilities.
- The level of visual attention influences the performance of participants in Teleoperation tasks.

Figure 1. The VR devices tested in the case study are located at the VR Media Lab and Medialogy Lab at the Aalborg University in Aalborg and Copenhagen, Denmark. They are: a 160°panoramic wall with 8x3 m. screen (top-left), a 3D desktop equipped with shutter glasses (bottom-left), and a 2.5 m^3 6-sided CAVE (top and bottom right). The right figures show the CAVE structure (bottom) and a representative view from inside the CAVE (top)

7.2 Participants

Ten users took part in the evaluation study. The case study required around 2 hours per participant to be completed. All participants had basic to medium experience with VR devices. Experience in playing computer games was also taken into account as experience in VR. Figure 2 shows a user during the evaluation.

7.3 Evaluation Method

As different types of VR devices were compared against each other, the case study was designed as summative evaluation. Because of the limited number of participants and the difficulty of finding equally skilled participants, a within subjects design was preferred over a between subjects design. Therefore each participant fulfilled the same amount of tasks on all available VR devices.

Figure 2. A user during the evaluation on the 3D desktop

7.4 Procedure

The test procedure is part of the test design, (see sub-section 6.9). In our particular case it started with an introduction, then a visual attention test was performed to classify the participants' level of selective visual attention. The users were then asked to teleguide a robot within an interactive test, during which quantitative data were recorded. The last step comprehended the completion of pre-designed questionnaires to acquire qualitative data referring to the users' experience with different VR technologies.

We decided to turn special attention on the counterbalancing of the tasks as well as the sequence during the entire user study to avoid fatigue and learning effects. This required the participants to perform the tests according to a precise schedule.

Practice sessions were administrated before testing. A debriefing phase ended the test session.

7.5 Forms and Questionnaires

As suggested in the guideline, we used a consent form, an information sheet, and different questionnaires for background information and the relation between the different VR devices employed in the test.

During the pilot study the participants were asked to fill in four different questionnaires, one after each task and one at the end of the user study (see Figure 3). The questionnaires contained questions related to users' background, their experience and gaming abilities (e.g. hours per week), specific questions on five proposed judgment categories (adequacy the application, realism, immersion, 3D impression and viewing comfort), and users' overall impression after the user study.

7.6 Evaluation Measures

The following evaluation measures (part of the test plan, see sub-section 6.9), were collected and calculated for the quantitative and qualitative evaluation.

For the quantitative evaluation:

- The numbers of collisions during single driving tasks, (Collision Avoidance test).
- Time to complete each driving task, (Time Completion test).
- Errors made while estimating the relative distance (Access Width Estimation test).
- Number and percentage of tasks completed correctly (Collision Avoidance and Access Width Estimation tests).

For the qualitative evaluation:

- Adequacy of the task to the application, (Adequacy to application).
- The realism of the visual feedback, (Realism).
- Sense of presence, (Immersion).
- Depth impression, (3D impression).
- The user's viewing confort, (Viewing comfort).

The numbers received from the "device questionnaires" were combined with the background and post-test questionnaire.

During the evaluation of the data, the questions were grouped into five categories corresponding to the five qualitative judgement categories, in order to be able to compare the results in each area. The 7 scale semantic differentials were used for the answer of the questionnaires.

Figure 3. The prepared testing setup including the forms handed to the participants (top) and participants filling in questionnaires (bottom)

7.7 Result Analysis and Discussion

The collected evaluation measures were analyzed through inferential and descriptive statistics and the results were graphically represented by diagrams. In the following some comments on the obtained results are reported while all gathered data can be found in (Koeffel, 2007).

The results on the Panorama and the 3D desktop showed an increased number of collisions with mono visualization compared to stereo visualization.

As for the average completion time needed for the driving task, the participants performed best on the 3D desktop (using either mono or stereo visualization), then on the panorama and CAVE. The participants performed worst on the CAVE. These resulte are shown in figure 4.

Most of the errors in estimating the distance were made using the CAVE. Nevertheless, the CAVE was the facility that users declared to prefer over the others.

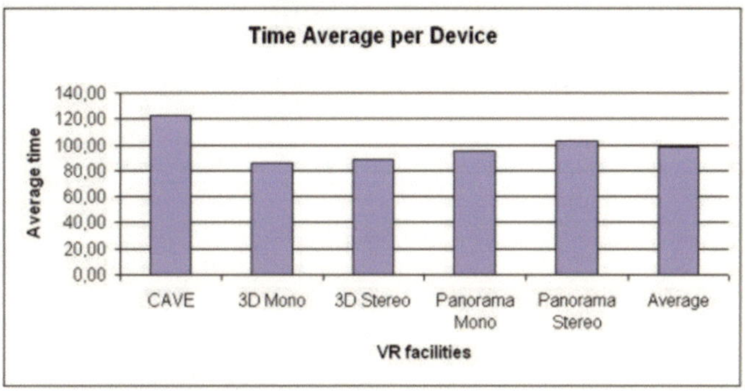

Figure 4. The average completion time per device. As can be seen the users performed slightly faster on the desktop system (mono and stereo), denoted as 3D Mono and 3D Stereo

For what concerns the qualitative evaluation, the CAVE was voted to be most immersive (as expected) while the 3D desktop using mono visualization seemed to be less immersive. The 3D impression and Realism categories emphasized the CAVE as the most appreciated device, while the Viewing comfort was judged without significant differences among all facilities. Figure 5 shows bar diagrams for each judgment category.

When reviewing the overall ranking provided by the post-test and background questionnaire, the CAVE appears again to be the best and most liked device (Figure 6). This goes along with the considerations of Demiralp et al. (Demiralp et al., 2006), telling that "looking-out" tasks (i.e. where the user views the world from inside-out as in our case), require users to use their peripheral vision more than "looking-in" tasks (e.g. small object manipulation). Large and fully surrounding displays also present environment characteristics closer to their real dimension, and in addition the possibility for body interaction allows for a more natural behaviour.

Most of the results of the inferential statistics (ANOVA) did not show significant differences. Though, some clear tendency could be noted. Few significant improvements were found, e.g. the correlation of the number of collisions when using the panorama in stereo instead of mono.

Concerning the analysis related to the influence of the users' selective visual attention, the separation between the single user-classes was based on the median time employed to perform the TAP test. The results showed a trend: users with high-level visual attention performed significantly better in the Collision Avoidance and the Access Width estimation test in the panorama using stereo viewing than with mono visualization (see Figure 7).

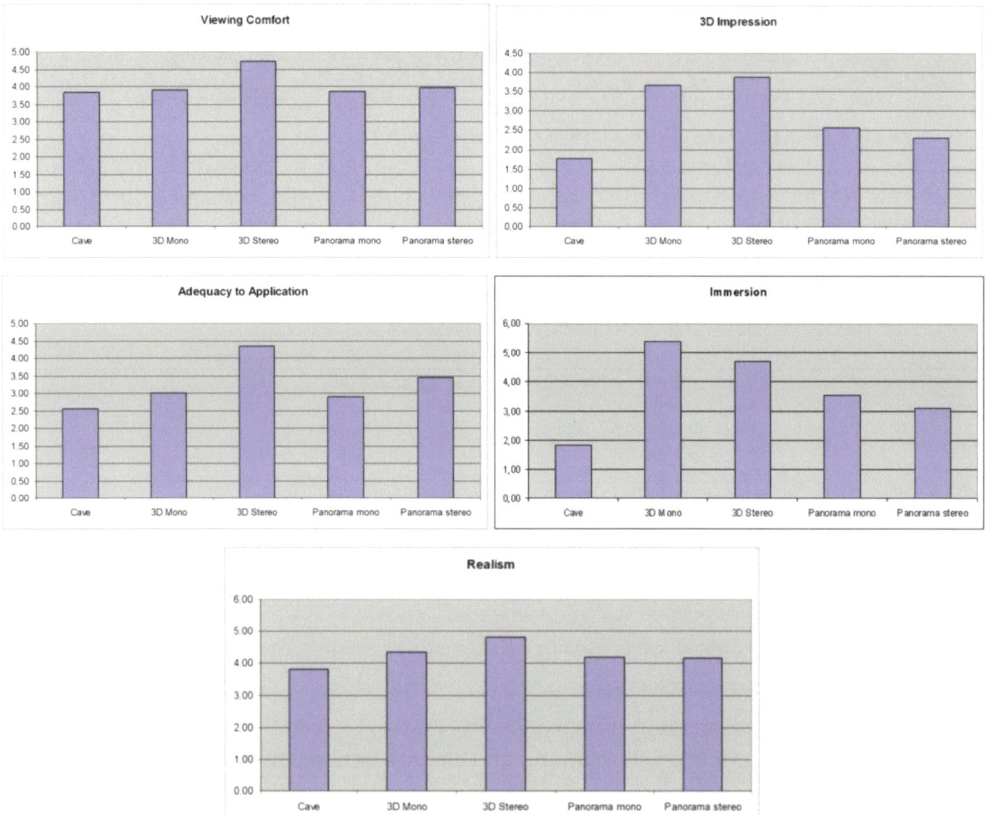

Figure 5. The qualitative results for the categories: Viewing comfort, 3D impression, Adequacy to the application, Immersion and Realism. The 7 scale semantic differentials, ranging from -3 to 3, were converted to a 1 to 7 range for computational purposes

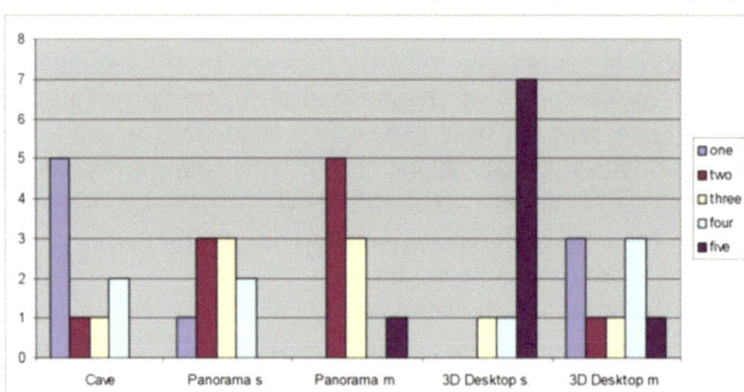

Figure 6. The overall results of the qualitative evaluation indicating that the CAVE was the most appreciated device

Further data processing led to relevant findings. For example, there is a statistically significant difference in the number of collisions between participants that are frequently playing computer games and participants that do not play computer games at all, Figure 8 shows this result.

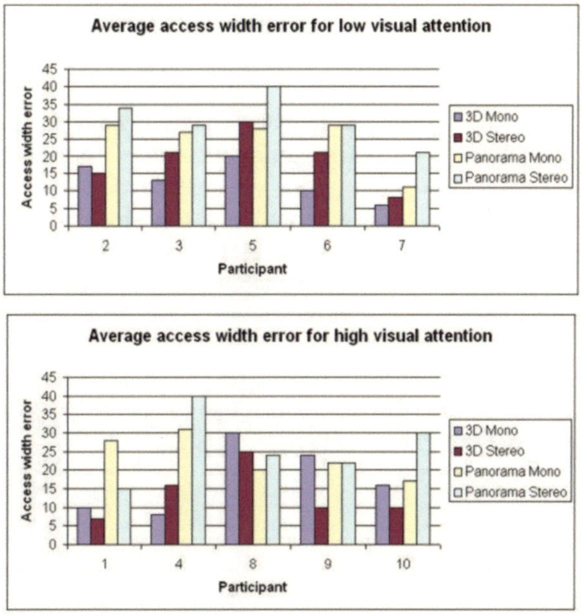

Figure 7. The users' performance of the Access Width estimation on different devices. The top diagram indicates the results for users with a low level of visual attention; the bottom one depicts the results of users with a high level of visual attention

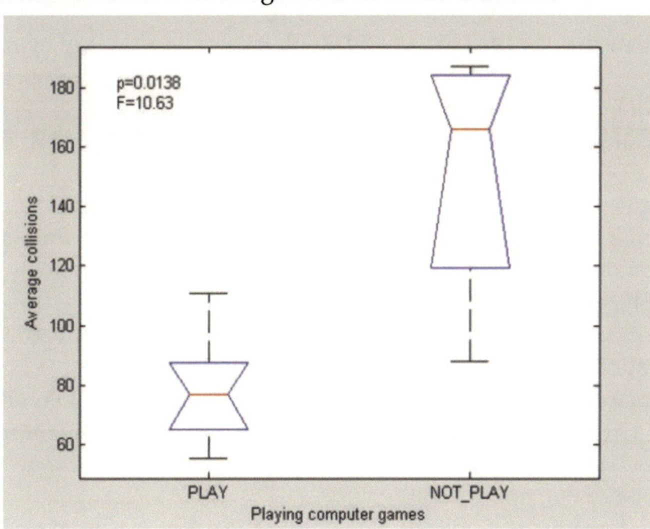

Figure 8. The difference in the users'performance (Collision Avoidance) when playing computer games frequently and when not playing computer games at all, ($p=0.0138$, $F=10.63$)

8. Conclusion

The present chapter introduced a guideline for usability evaluation of VR applications. The need for an effort in this direction was underlined in the related literature works. The proposed work targets researchers and students who are not experts in the field of evaluation and usability in general. The guideline is therefore designed to represent a simple set of directives (a handbook) which would assist users drawing up plans and conducting pilot and formal studies.

The chapter briefly introduces multidisciplinary issues related to the evaluation of VR applications and it claims how such guideline may represent a facilitator for multidisciplinary collaborations.

The introduction to the guideline is accompanied by a case study to provide the reader with a practical example of its applicability and to ease its comprehension.

The guideline was judged by users as reasonable and appropriate to the problem. We believe that students and researchers with limited expertise in usability evaluations, as well as those constrained in time, might profit from its content.

Human-Computer Interaction is a subject area in great expansion. There will be therefore an increasing need for user studies and usability evaluations. We believe that a guideline concept as the one proposed will certainly become popular.

9. References

Bach, C. & Scapin, D. L. (2004). Obstacles and perspectives for evaluating mixed reality systems usability.

Bayyari, A. & Tudoreanu, M.E. (2006). The impact of immersive virtual reality displays on the understanding of data visualization. In *VRST '06: Proceedings of the ACM symposium on Virtual reality software and technology*, Limassol, Cyprus, Nov. 2006, pp 368–371.

Bowman, D.A., Gabbard, J.L. & Hix, D. (2002). A survey of usability evaluation in virtual environments: classification and comparison of methods. In *Presence: Teleoperation in . Virtual Environments*, 11(4):404-424

Burdea, G.C., & Coiffet, P. (2003). *Virtual Reality Technology*, John Wiley & Sons, Inc., second edition, ISBN 978-0471360896

Christou, C., Angus, C., Loscos, C., Dettori, A. & Roussou, M. (2006), A versatile large-scale multimodal vr system for cultural heritage visualization. *In Proc. of VRST'06: ACM symposium on Virtual Reality Software and Technology*, Limassol, Cyprus, Nov. 2006, pp.133-140.

Cliburn, D. & Krantz, J. (2008). Towards an effective low-cost virtual reality display system for education. *Journal of Computing. Small Coll.*, 23(3):147–153

Demiralp, C., Jackson, C.D., Karelitz, D.B., Zhang, S. & Laidlaw, D.H. (2006). CAVE and fishtank virtual-reality displays: A qualitative and quantitative comparison. *In proc. of IEEE Transactions on Visualization and Computer Graphics*, vol. 12, no. 3, (May/June, 2006). pp. 323-330,

Elmqvist, N. & Tudoreanu, M. E. (2006). Evaluating the effectiveness of occlusion reduction techniques for 3D virtual environments. In *proc. of VRST'06: ACM Symposium on Virtual Reality Software and Technology*. Limassol, Cyprus, Nov. 2006.

Faulkner, X. (2000). Usability engineering. Palgrave Macmillan, ISBN 978-0333773215

Fink, P.W., Foo, P.S. & Warren W.H.(2007). Obstacle avoidance during walking in real and virtual environments. *ACM Transaction of Applied Perception.*, 4(1):2

Gabbard, J.L. (1997). A taxonomy of usability characteristics in virtual environments, *Master's Thesis*, Virginia Polytechnic Institute and State University, Blacksburg, Virginia

Gabbard, J. L., Hix, D., & Swan, J. E. (1999). User-centered design and evaluation of virtual environments. *In proc. of IEEE Computer. Graphics. Applications.* 19, 6 (Nov. 1999), 51-59.

Karaseitanidis, I., Amditis, A., Patel, H., Sharples, S., Bekiaris, E., Bullinger, A., & Tromp, J. (2006). Evaluation of virtual reality products and applications from individual, organizational and societal perspectives- the "VIEW" case study. *Int. Journal of Human Perception in Computer Studies* 64, 3 (Mar. 2006), 251-266.

Kasik, D.J., Troy, J.J., Amorosi, S.R., Murray, M.O. & Swamy, S.N. (2002). Evaluating graphics displays for complex 3D models. *IEEE Computer Graphics and Applications*,vol.22, no.3, (May/Jun 2002) pp.56-64

Koeffel, C. (2007). Evaluation methods for virtual reality applications, *Tech.Rep.* Medialogy, Aalborg University, Denmark, 2007.

Koeffel, C. (2008). Handbook for evaluation studies in vr for non-experts, *Tech.Rep.* Medialogy, Aalborg University, Denmark, 2008.

Livatino, S. & Koeffel, C. (2007), Handbook for evaluation studies in virtual reality. *In proc. of VECIMS '07: IEEE Int. Conference in Virtual Environments, Human-Computer Interface and Measurement Systems,*, Ostuni, Italy, 2007

Livatino, S., Gambin, T., Mosiej L, & Koeffel, C. (2007). Exploring critial aspects in vr-based mobile robot teleguide. *In proc. of RA'2007: Robotics and Applications conference,* Wurzburg, Germany, 2008

Livatino, S. & Privitera, F. (2006). Stereo visualization and virtual reality displays. *In proc. of Vis2006: IEEE Visualization 2006 conference,* Baltimore, USA, November, 2006.

Malkondu, E. (2007). The study of the camera parameters in remote robot teledriving. *Master's thesis,* Aalborg University, Denmark, 2007.

Marsh, T. 1999. Evaluation of virtual reality systems for usability. In *CHI '99 Extended Abstracts on Human Factors in Computing Systems* (Pittsburgh, Pennsylvania, May 15 - 20, 1999). CHI '99. ACM, New York, NY, 61-62.

McMahan, R.P., Gorton, D., Gresock, J., McConnell, W. & Bowman, D.A. (2006). Separating the effects of level of immersion and 3d interaction techniques. *In proc. of VRST '06: ACM symposium on Virtual Reality Software and Technology,* Limassol, Cyprus, Nov. 2006 pp. 108–111

Ni, T., Bowman, D. A., & Chen, J. (2006). Increased display size and resolution improve task performance in information-rich virtual environments. *In Proc. of Graphics Interface 2006,* Quebec, Canada, June 07 - 09, 2006. (ACM Int. Conference Proceeding Series, vol. 137. Canadian Information Processing Society, Toronto, Ont., Canada, 139-146).

Nielsen, J. (1993). *Usability engineering,* Morgan Kaufmann, ISBN 978-0125184069

Nielsen, J., & Mack R.L. (1994). *Usability Inspection Methods,* John Wiley & Sons, New York, USA, May 1994, ISBN 978-0471018773

Patel, H., Stefani, O., Sharples, S., Hoffmann, H., Karaseitanidis, I. & Amditis, A.(2006). Human centred design of 3-d interaction devices to control virtual environments. *Int. Journal of. Human Perception in Computer Studis.*, 64(3):207–220

Qi, W., Russell, I., Taylor, M., Healey, C.G. & Martens, J.B. (2006). A comparison of immersive hmd, fish tank vr and fish tank with haptics displays for volume visualization. *In proc. APGV '06: 3rd Symposium on Applied Perception in Graphics and Visualization*, New York, NY, USA, pages 51–58

Rubin, J. (1994). *Handbook of Usability Testing: How to Plan, Design, and Conduct Effective Tests.* John Wiley & Sons, ISBN 978-0471594031

Sarodnick, F., & Brau, H. (2006). *Methoden der Usability Evaluation, Wissenschaftliche Grundlagen und praktische Anwendung*, Hans Huber Verlag, ISBN 978-3456842004

Sutcliffe, A. & Gault, B. (2004). Heuristic evaluation of virtual reality applications, *Interacting with Computers*, Volume 16, Issue 4, (August 2004) Pages 831-849

Sutcliffe, A., Gault, B., Fernando, T. & Tan, K. (2006). Investigating interaction in cave virtual environments. *ACM Transaction Compute.-HumanInteraction*, 13(2):235–267

Takatalo, J., Nyman, G. & Laaksonen, L.(2008). Components of human experience in virtual environments. *Computer Human Behaviour*., 24(1):1–15

Tromp, J.G. & Nichols, S.C. (2003). VIEW-IT: a vr/cad inspection tool for use in industry. *In proc. of the HCI International 2003 Conference*, Crete, 22-27 June.

Vinayagamoorthy, V., Brogni, A., Steed, A. & Slater, M.(2006). The role of posture in the communication of affect in an immersive virtual environment. *In proc. VRCIA '06:ACM international conference on Virtual reality continuum and its applications*, New York, NY, USA, 2006, pp 229–236

Wanger, L.R., Ferweda J.A., Greenberg, D.P. (1992). Perceiving spatial reletionships in computer generated images. *In Proc. of IEEE Computer Graphics and Animation.*

Wang, Y., Otitoju, K., Liu, T., Kim, S., & Bowman, D. A. (2006). Evaluating the effects of real world distraction on user performance in virtual environments. *In Proc. of VRST'06: ACM Symposium on Virtual Reality Software and Technology.* Limassol, Cyprus, Nov. 2006.

Wilcox, L.M., Allison, R.S., Elfassy, S. & Grelik, C. (2006). Personal space in virtual reality. *ACM Transaction of. Applied Perception*, 3(4):412-428.

19

Mobile Device Interaction in Ubiquitous Computing

Thorsten Mahler and Michael Weber
University of Ulm, Institute of Media Informatics
Germany

1. From Computing Machines to Personal Computers

The 20th century has seen the rise of the computer. In the early days of the 40s a computer was a big machine filling a whole room working with bulbs. New technologies decreased its size to a machine as big as a closet, sometime later to a size fitting onto a desk. Along with the miniaturization the new technology made the computer as we know it today affordable for the everyday user. This made the personal computer to an omnipresent and universal tool for a vast number of users with very different expertise.

The human computer interface has evolved tremendously since its first days. Early computers had to be reconfigured through cables on patch fields and operated by switches. With the introduction of text displays and keyboards computers became a direct interactive tool being operated primarily through command line interfaces. The invention of graphic user interfaces and the mouse as a pointing device led to graphical window systems, the desktop metaphor and direct manipulation.

Notably, the inventions enabling these graphical user interfaces persistent until today where made years before their first useful application. The first mouse, presented in 1968 by Douglas Englebart did not get much attention because there was no need for a pointing device as there was no graphical user interface. The graphical user interface was invented in 1981 by Xerox Parc and introduced to the broad public three years later with the Apple Macintosh. Currently we are in a similar situation concerning interaction styles and metaphors in ubiquitous computing. Several exemplified solutions are being reported, but the breakthrough of the most likely to be used metaphors and interaction techniques is not revealed yet. (see for example Norman, 1998)

Besides the development of new technologies, we can observe a dramatic shift in the typical user of a computer from operators and programmers to non-expert users, which are most often not specifically trained to use computers. This leads towards user centred development and design approaches to better cover and understand the needs of the various user groups and to incorporate this knowledge into the design process and the products.

1.1 The Paradox of Technology

From the invention of first computing machines to today's personal computers we can state the turning away from technology centred design to user centred design. This tendency holds for the development of hardware but is especially true for the evolution of the user interface. But this development is not linear (see Fig. 1). Rather, the invention of new technology and its application makes new devices hard to use, the complexity level is high. After a while, when the technology is mastered and the needed interaction paradigms are identified, the complexity level drops. Along with it, users are getting accustomed to the technology, the usage get easier and easier. Some time later, the mature interface for the new device is found and people use the technology naturally, the complexity level gets low, the device usable. When this point is reached, new features will be added to the device making it more complex again, resulting in a rising complexity level. The paradox of technology starts again (Norman, 1988).

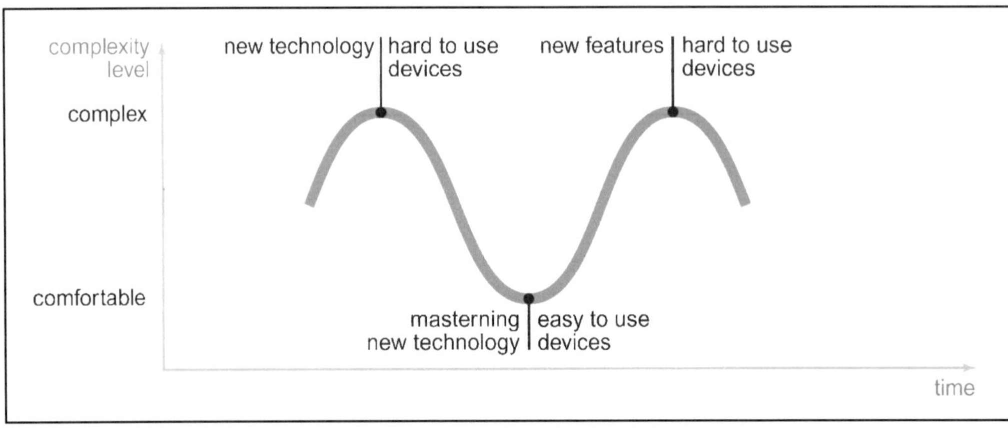

Figure 1. The Paradox of Technology (figure developed after Norman, 1988)

1.2 The vision of Transparency and Ubiquity: Ubiquitous Computing

The development of ever smaller, faster and more equipped devices makes way for mobile computing resulting in a change of the ways computer are used. Mobile computers free the user from his desktop, due to the portability of devices and also due to wireless communication technologies. However, the increasing number of devices carried posse new problems but allow for new ways of interaction. A user nowadays does not work with only one computer but with an ever increasing number of devices as more and more devices get computerized. These devices invade our homes and environments with effects not yet known and not yet understood. But concepts are evolving to deal with the new challenges and ways are researched to make the new possibilities usable and comfortable for everyday use (Messeter, 2004).

In his visionary article "The computer in the 21st century" Mark Weiser (Weiser, 1991) formulates the next step in computerization. He coined the term ubiquitous computing. In his vision the miniaturization of the computer is leading to a world with computers everywhere enhancing artefacts intertwining the real and the virtual world. He states the renouncing of the personal computer as a single universal tool. Instead his vision propagates the use of multiple connected and invisible computers together. The furthermost implication of his vision and the goal of the new paradigm are the human centred direct interaction and problem solving in the real world as he states *"ubiquitous computing, [...], resides in the human world and pose no barrier to personal interactions"* (Weiser, 1991).

In consequence the human user is able to concentrate on his task on hand eliminating the struggle with today's interfaces as they are unnoticeably being pushed to the background. The final goal is a world enhanced by computers being seamlessly integrated into our real life and our surroundings. There shall not be a technical barrier as there is today for lots of non expert users. Instead the computer should be integrated seamlessly, the user not being aware of its presence.

1.3 Virtuality Continuum

The convergence of virtual and real worlds exceeds the bounds of traditional understanding of computing and slowly blurs the formerly clearly separable areas. This is one major characteristic of interaction in ubiquitous computing where we witness the integration and merging of the physical world represented by real life objects and the virtual world represented by computer-generated visualizations or digital data in general.
Milgram and Kishino (Milgram & Kishino, 1994) conceived the range of possible mixtures as the Virtuality Continuum (Fig. 2). At the one end (on the left of the figure) there are real environments consisting only of real objects, at the other extreme there are purely virtual environments. Depending on the extent of virtuality, Milgram and Kishino distinguish between Augmented Reality (AR) and Augmented Virtuality (AV). They call this span Mixed Reality (MR).

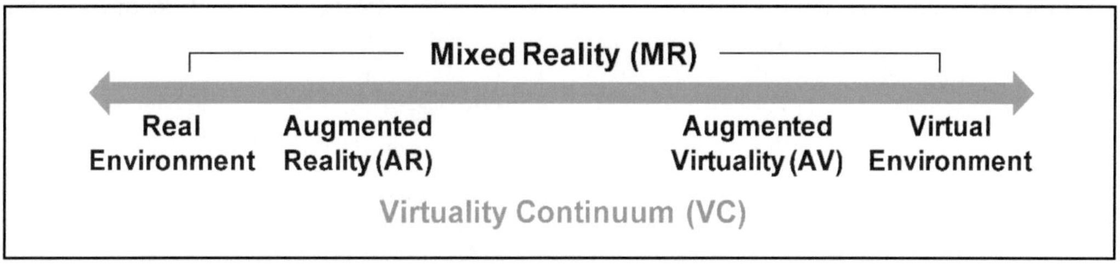

Figure 2. The Virtuality Continuum (Milgram & Kishino, 1994)

According to Azuma a Virtual Environment, more commonly known as Virtual Reality (VR) is a completely synthetic immersive world in which the user has no notion of the real world around him. In contrast to that, Augmented Reality (AR) rather uses superimposition to enhance the real world wit virtual objects. Thus, the user stays in the real world and virtual objects are composed into the real scene (Azuma, 1997).
The goal of Milgram and Kishino is to describe a taxonomy to distinguish and categorize projects in the field of Mixed Reality and set them in relation with respect to their degrees of reality or virtuality. Thus they define virtuality as a fully closed computer generated world in which the user can totally immerse. Such a virtual reality does not necessarily convey the laws of physics of time, it only has to be consistent and reasonable enough to be able to immerse. Such virtual worlds are produced by projection screens surrounding the user potentially wearing shutter-glasses to get a 3-D impression (Weber & Hermann, 2008).
Milgram and Kishino propose three aspects to further clarify the merging of real and virtual worlds. On first extend they distinguish which Extend of World Knowledge is known. This unites the degree of knowledge of the whereabouts of objects in a special mixed reality environment with their understanding. Only a complete understanding of every object and every object's specific location makes a fully immersive and superimposed mixed reality possible. Without the exact positioning and registration in the scenery the relation of objects

cannot be visualized seamlessly. Without the understanding of objects their specific behaviour cannot be simulated. Furthermore an enhanced visual representation is not possible without specific knowledge of objects (cf. also to section 1.5).
The second dimension Milgram and Kishino define is the reproduction fidelity which denotes the quality with which the whole mixed reality scene is presented. It is clear, that high resolution representations with high colour quality and depth differ from simple wire frame representations. So this dimension tackles the quality of the rendering of virtual objects as well as the reproduction of real objects.
Finally they define the dimension Extend of Presence Metaphor (EPM). The EPM denotes on which extend the user feels present in the Mixed Reality. This dimension has a strong relation with the used hardware of the mixed reality application. Is it egocentric or exocentric, is the system real time capable and does it allow for seamless immersion.
Mixed Reality makes use of real world objects to some extent. The immersion gets harder and harder to be achieved the more interaction with the real environment shall be supported. Therefore the virtual objects have to behave more and more like real objects if a consistent feel of the whole Mixed Reality is desired.
Notably, Milgram and Kishino focus on visual displays, which are by far the most important output technology being used for Mixed Reality. Nevertheless, there are other thinkable virtual augmentations to reality such as auditory or haptic augmentation. Whereas Cohen focuses on enhancing user interfaces by speech (Cohen, 1992), Rath and Rocchesso for example use pure sound to enhance interaction. Their rolling ball example renders a bar to a virtual balance, feedback on the configuration is given by sound, which a rolling ball would make, when rolling according to the angle in which the bar is held (Rath & Rocchesso, 2005). Another possibility lies in the haptic feedback of virtual objects (Shimoga, 1992). However, this needs a considerable lot of additional hardware like gloves which results in a more invasive application.

1.4 Tangible Interaction

With the vision of ubiquitous computing and its final goal to bring the virtual world into the real world it is only consequent to affect the virtual representations and objects through interaction with real life artefacts. As described by Holmquist et al. (Holmquist et al., 2004) there is a lot of research done in this domain focussing on different aspects according to the primary goal they pursue: graspable interface, tangible interface, physical interface, embodied interface, to name just a few. Yet the principal goal remains the same, the enrichment of virtual interaction by physicality.
One of the first to describe this link are Ishii and Ullmer in their paper "Tangible Bits" (Ishii & Ullmer, 1997). Based on their observation that, by now, we are living almost constantly wired between the physical environment and cyberspace, they introduce the coupling of everyday objects with virtual information, the coupling of "Bits and Atoms" as they call it, to overcome this division and "rejoin the richness of physical world HCI like in pre-computer era". Their visionary tangible bits allow for natural interaction rendering real life objects into tools, their interaction having effect on virtual objects. Such interaction is not only limited to objects as such but can also take place with a whole room, a wall or a space in general. Additionally Ishii and Ullmer tackle a very important fact: they distinguish between in focus action and background awareness. Following our natural way of perceiving our surrounding, ubiquitous computing and spatial interaction allow for

peripheral perception and ambient artefacts. Consequently they develop the vision of ubiquitous computing into multi-sensory interaction and experience of digital information situated in natural space.

To clear the understanding of tangible interfaces Hornecker and Buur present a framework for tangible interaction concepts (Hornecker & Buur, 2006). They describe four criteria on which basis they rate tangible interfaces as being shown in Fig. 3.

Tangible Interaction

Tangible Manipulation	Spatial Interaction	Embodied Facilitation	Expressive Representation
Haptic Direct Manipulation	Inhabited Space	Embodied Constraints	Representational Significance
	Configurable Materials		
Lightweight Interaction	Non-fragmented Visibility	Multiple Access Points	Externalization
	Full Body Interac-tion		
Isomorph Effects	Performative Action	Tailored Representations	Perceived Coupling

Figure 3. Tangible Interaction Framework (Hornecker & Buur, 2006)

The first dimension, Tangible Manipulation, reflects the bodily interaction with a physical object. As each object for tangible interaction is simultaneously interaction device, interface and object the key aspects here are the quality of the mapping between action and effect along with the direct manipulation and how explorative the interface is. This tackles above all whether the effects of the object interaction are easily reversible and thus easy learning of object functionality is feasible.

The second dimension tackles the space in which the interaction takes place. The pure action of manipulating an object requires movement in space and particularly movement of the body itself. The sole body can even be seen as a special interface. Thus this category measures how the performative action itself has influence on the effect. Furthermore it tackles the meaning of space itself, if the position or the configuration of an object is meaningful and moreover if these properties can be configured.

Embodied Facilitation questions the constraints introduced by the object. To unburden the user interfaces should build on users' experience and the physical shape of the object should inspire the user with the desired action and effect. Detached from the Embodied Facilitation, the dimension Expressive Representation is proposed to measure the mapping itself. How clear is the coupling of the digital and real representation and are they of the same strength and importance. Does the object represent the virtual data and is it perceived as that. Hornecker and Buur describe this as being able to use objects as "props to act with", giving discussion a focus. Another interesting point made here is the transition of digital benefits. This dimension also measures to which extend props can record their configuration themselves and thus for example being able to undo changes, a functionality we are very used to in digital life. (Hornecker & Buur, 2006)

Besides the elaboration of the framework, Hornecker and Buur mention another very interesting point: The possibility of digitally enhancing real objects allows for bringing together hard, complicated task with simple objects. The most direct mappings may therefore not always be the best way as this reduces the opportunities of rich interaction and manipulation of virtual information.

2. Enhancing Everyday Objects

The merge of the virtual and real world leads to problems concerning the handling of augmented objects and their digital representative.
different people. She particularly examined the connection people make between memories and physical objects. Especially the connection between personal souvenirs and holiday memories are characterized and based on the results a tangible user interface for personal objects created (van den Hoven & Eggen, 2005). Their work with personal souvenirs shows another interesting point. Physical objects can already be connected with a mental model. That means that personal objects have personal meaning for a single user or very few users. They also define the term generic objects as a physical object that is not bound to an existing mental model for multiple users (van den Hoven & Eggen, 2004).
If we expand these findings on everyday objects, ready mades, we can find up to three different links for a physically enhanced object:

1. Physical linkage introduced by physical constraints and learned knowledge about the used object.
2. Personal linkage between a known object and a personal occurrence.
3. Digital linkage between the object and the digital representative.

The potential of personal objects and the affiliated existing mental model is recognized as one of the most interesting couplings for tangible interfaces by other researchers as well (see Ullmer & Ishii, 2001).
The desired seamless augmentation introduces the problem, that users are not always aware of the artefact's functions. As described above the unawareness can be due to different reasons: The physical linkage of the object may contradict the digital representation. For instance the learned knowledge about an object may be completely rational in a certain context but not understandable per se. For instance, in the MediaCup project augmented cups can detect whether they hold freshly brewed coffee and if there are other cups in the vicinity; if so, automatically a meeting context is assumed and the room is booked for the group (Beigl et al., 2001).
The personal or social linkage of an object may contradict a digital representative or may not be obvious for certain people.
The digital linkage is per se not existent in the real world and thus may remain undiscovered at all. Or, what is even more undesirable, interaction with a certain digitally enhanced object can trigger completely unexpected and unforeseen digital actions.
Clearly, these breaks in the mental model of our mixed surroundings are of no great impact at the time of set up. But as technology constantly pushes the bounds further and further these problems are important research challenges, not only for special solutions, but especially for complex and mixed environments.
Closely coupled with the raised problem of digital awareness is the question of how an object gets linked to a digital representation in general. To clarify this question we propose to divide the problem into three parts, the starting problem, the configuration problem and the interaction problem.

Clearly, the use of beforehand unknown personal objects introduces the problem of how to link an object with a certain digital representation or action. This is especially true for objects that do not have an enhancement. So this is the question of how to supply an object with functionality in the first place.
Related to the starting problem is the question of how a linkage between object and digital representation can be changed or adjusted. We call this the configuration problem. In contrast to the starting problem, changes and adjustments have to be done while running the system because the very nature of mixed reality is the seamless integration and therefore the use of objects as an integral part. In conclusion this prohibits a shutdown and restart of a complete system. This is especially true for coming mixed reality environments will be inherently multi user systems.
This poses a third question: the question of how to interact with a real physical object on a purely digital basis. The interface itself is widely recognized to be an integral part of an enhanced object (see for example Ishii & Ullmer, 1997) but how interfaces could look like in mixed reality environment needs further investigation. This is especially true for ready-made objects that do not need a display of its digital representative in everyday use. This duality of transparency and reflectivity is discussed from different points of view by many researchers. Chalmers (Chalmers, 2004) elaborates the coexistence of "seamful" technology and seamless interaction tracing back to philosophical hermeneutics (e.g. Heidegger, 1927) and semiotics. Bolter and Gromala (Bolter & Gromala, 2004) point to the duality of transparency and reflectivity from an aesthetic point of view and Bødker points out the importance of re-appearing interfaces for experience and reflexivity (Bødker, 2006). In conclusion, in a physical world constantly interweaved with virtual reality and filled with digitally enriched objects, it remains unclear how everyday objects instantiate an interface which is not even needed in everyday interaction.

3. Bridging the Gap

Ishii and Ullmer present in (Ishii & Ullmer, 1997) a number of projects that implement tangible interfaces to some extent. From their analysis they hint on metaphors apt for digital representation display. From their research they found metaphors especially fitting to bridge the real and the virtual world and to integrate seamlessly into real space. Optical metaphors in general have been found to do so quite nicely.
One of these metaphors can be found in the metaDesk project (Ishii & Ullmer, 1997). MetaDesk combines large scale maps on a desk with movable computer displays. These displays function as magic active lenses and show three dimensional views of the position on hand. The see-through metaphor as magical lens has been presented by Bier et al. as a concept (Bier et al., 1993; Stone et al., 1994) and is used in metaDesk in combination with real environments.
Another option of using a visual metaphor is the idea of digital shadows (Ishii & Ullmer, 1997). Here real objects cast virtual shadows showing their digital information using real world constraints. They are fitting their display nicely into the real world by mimicking real object properties.
Of course these shadows can either be projected onto the surface or shown virtually by a magical lens. Either way, the objects need additional hardware to implement this functionality to convey their digital information.

Figure 4. Digital light metaphor on a Microsoft Surface. (Courtesy of Microsoft Corporation)

A closely related imaging solution is the digital light metaphor. Instead of casting shadows, real objects emit virtual light in this case. This metaphor is implemented in the new Microsoft Surface project for example (see Fig. 4). Here objects can be put on a table whose surface is a large display. This way, real objects can be annotated with digital information quite easily (Microsoft Surface, 2008). The digital representation and operations can be shown in an orb surrounding the object, combining the digital light metaphor with Fitzmaurice's idea of a graspable interface in the ActiveDesk project (Fitzmaurice et al., 1995).

The projects briefly presented so far have all one thing in common: they need proper preparation of the environment in order to facilitate interfaces for real objects. All projects need intelligent rooms or need to be at least permanently installed. Nevertheless, even the early projects such as metaDesk demonstrate the benefit of mobile devices: The mobility and the position and configuration in real-space turn even the early devices into useful tools.

The enhancement of mixed reality rooms with mobile devices as described above is the first step towards a seamless integration of real world objects with smart devices like Personal Digital Assistants or Smart Phones. However, a real seamless and integration demands the ubiquity of the virtual information and its display wherever the need and wherever the location. A further development towards this view of ubiquity is presented by Butz and Krüger (Butz & Krüger, 2006). They present a concept of intelligent rooms which are interconnected with each other. They thereby extend the space digital objects work in and provide the basis to investigate interacting with digitally enhanced objects across the borders of single rooms. For visualisation of digital information and invocation of digital functions they make use of the peephole metaphor (Yee, 2003). The peephole metaphor is similar to the toolglass or magic lens metaphor by Bier et al. (Bier et al., 1993) as mentioned above. Both provide additional information relative to a certain real or virtual position. But where the magic lens metaphor displays more or special information to an object at the coordinates, a peephole display returns only the contents of the virtual layer at that point. This is not necessarily linked to the real world and the objects in it. But with the integration in mixed reality rooms and the connection with objects they become magic lenses or tool glasses.

3.1 Small Devices

With the rise of small devices such as Personal Digital Assistants (PDA) and Smart Phones we nowadays have the possibility of bringing computing power everywhere. The devices are conveniently small and portable. However, these two factors introduce new problems for interaction and interface design. The displays are limited in size due to the dimensions of the device; they have lower resolution and often fewer colours. The aspect ratios differ a lot and there is a great diversity in hardware setup considering onboard memory, computing power, graphical capabilities and energy supply. The interaction possibilities range from touchpads to small keyspads. Constant development reduces these problems but is has to be stated that some of the limitations cannot be eliminated as Chittaro points out (Chittaro, 2006):

The permanent use everywhere and every time introduces the problem of different and even changing surroundings. The size of a PDA or smart phone always causes small displays and interaction with a small device demands for different approaches apt for small devices and usage in motion.

All these points need investigation and demand for new approaches. Pascoe et al. describe the drawbacks of using mobile devices in the field (Pascoe et al., 2000). They especially focus on the environment and environment interaction. The context of use limits the interface in many ways. The difference in lighting is clearly a factor for mobile interfaces and their use of colour and contrast. Even more important is the simple act of moving introduces problems in device handling and especially reduces the mental capacities free for interaction as other tasks interfere.

3.2 Peephole Displays

The peephole metaphor (Yee, 2003) is a solution especially designed for small devices reducing the drawback of the small display. It combines nicely the interaction possibilities of a small device with the idea of expanding the display. Instead of the actual display and its limited size, it brings together movement as input with clipping, resulting in a much larger virtual screen.

This concept can be seen as an extension of Fitzmaurice idea of an extensional workspace using spatially aware palmtop computers (Fitzmaurice, 1993). An example for this paradigm is the active map application. Here moving a small device to a certain position in front of a wall map results in the display of additional information for this location. The static 2D map is enhanced with up to date dynamic information. Beside the very intuitive example Fitzmaurice presents other scenarios for interactive libraries offices and living rooms. The data presented ranges from completely virtual information like calendar data and stock market prices to virtual 3D views of certain locations.

The concept of peephole displays is an extension to Fitzmaurice' work as it combines the large virtual display with interaction on the displayed data. Yee uses today's input techniques like pen interaction and hand writing recognition for data manipulation. Interaction here is not only used to move the virtual layer, bringing up intended information, but also to manipulate this information in place Fig. 5 shows a peephole display being used in a calendar application.

Clearly, the peephole metaphor is a step towards ubiquitous computing as it opens windows to the virtual world. Notably, the introduction of the interaction concept makes known interfaces and application available on the move, making the limitation of small screen disappear. Unlike Fitzmaurice's principle this extension allows for porting desktop application onto palmtops. The integration into the environment is no integral part of this metaphor. In fact, it leaves this option untouched and open.

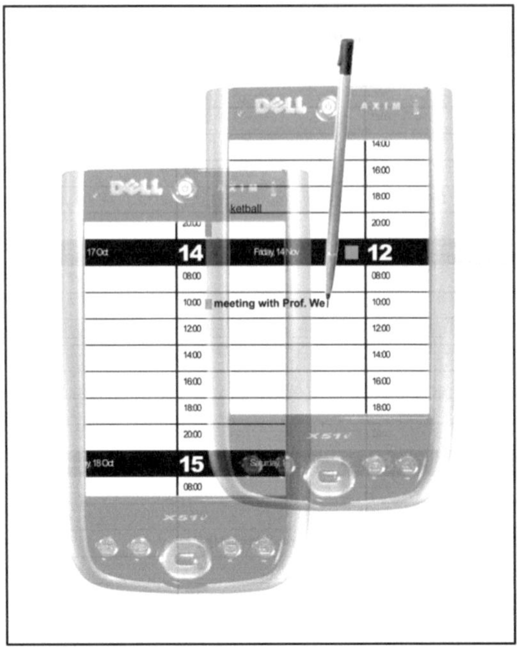

Figure 5. Writing on a Peephole Display. Moving the device allows for viewing different parts of the virtual document while simultaneous editing is possible. (Yee, 2003)

The usage of the peephole metaphor is restricted to bringing virtual content into the real world. But it can also be used the other way around. A nice example for bringing the mobility and spatial awareness of a device to the virtual world is presented by Hachet et al. (Hachet et al., 2005). They use a mobile device capable of displaying 3D graphic to interact with the objects in the virtual world. The mobile device in this case acts as a window in the virtual world. The movements of special objects in the real world and the movements of the small device itself affect the configuration of the virtual world.

3.3 Mobile Augmented Reality

Augmented Reality solutions are getting more and more common (Schmalstieg et al., 2002; Looser et al., 2004) and some even use mobile devices (Butz & Krüger, 2006) but today's mobile devices have the computational power to generate and render 3D scenes in real-time themselves. The devices are capable of virtual reality rendering enabling rich virtual worlds and new interaction techniques induced by the mobile devices (Hachet et al., 2005; Hwang et al., 2006; Çapın et al., 2006).

Bringing virtual reality techniques together with real world images and videos make way for the superimposition of digital information into real world views, following closely the Magic Lense paradigm in the domain of 3D imaging (Bier et al., 1993; Viega et al., 1996).

First concepts for virtual windows range back to Gaver et al. (Gaver et al., 1993) who describe a system which turns a monitor into a virtual window bringing together real-world

interaction with camera display. Clearly this project is not yet an Augmented Reality system as it does not use superimposition but it already describes and masters the problem of bringing together real world perspective view and a virtual model.
Henrysson et al. show an example for a classical AR application ported to a mobile device, making use of the interaction possibilities offered by a smart phone (Henrysson et al., 2005). The phone equipped with a camera is enabled to track markers, thus being able to track the position relative to the enhanced room. According to that, virtual objects can be placed in the natural environment. The difference to classical AR applications lies in the limited interaction possibilities of the small device on which special attention is posed on here. Though the obvious drawback of the limited keyboard the mobile device provides a six degree of freedom (6 DOF) mouse.
Its mobility can be used for augmented world interaction similar to the peephole example presented above. Nevertheless, this solution focuses on interaction with virtual world objects. The superimposition is not dependant on the special location. The marker system set up is only needed to enable tracking in 6 DOF interactions.
The full capabilities of mobile device application in augmented reality are shown by Wagner et al. in the invisible train system (Wagner et al., 2005). Here a virtual toy train can be steered by interaction with a small device.
In contrast to the just described system by Henrysson, the invisible train system makes massive use of real world interaction. The virtual train runs on real wooden railroad tracks generating an immersive environment with nicely fitting metaphors. The user takes the role of a signalman keeping the train on the right track. There are real crossings for which the junctions have to be operated. This can be done on the device using pen interaction (see Fig. 6).

Figure 6. The Invisible Train application. (Courtesy of Vienna University of Technology)

The invisible train application can even be played as a game with up to four players. All of them have constant and simultaneous access to all invisible train elements. They all can set junctions and prevent trains from crashing; they all get the same view of the current situation only differing in perspective depending on their viewpoint.

The interesting point here is not the fact that this application is multi user capable, but the degree of immersion being achieved. The virtual objects and interfaces integrate smoothly into a real environment. They react as if they were real, imitating their real prototypes, providing a suitable interface metaphor and implementing their functionalities.

Together with the heavy use of real objects as reference points not only with markers for tracking but especially with the wooden rails to get across the mental model, this application allows for a very high degree of immersion. The seamless integration of virtual objects into a real environment allows for true augmented reality and follows the vision of a physical world interwoven with virtual reality.

A drawback of most of the existing augmented reality applications is their dependency on an environment especially prepared for tracking purposes. As a result most of the environments are plastered with tags, patterns easily recognized by the tracking hardware. Thus, furthermost careful preparation of the spot is needed and often calibrations have to be conducted, a problem that has to be solved for ubiquitous computing to become reality.

3.4 Context Aware Mobile Computing

The increasing density of sensory equipment present in our surrounding together with the increasing sensory repository of today's mobile devices make way for context adaptable systems. The strong linkage between context and ubiquitous computing, its important role for seamless device integration and proactive system behaviour is recognized and researched by a whole research community. Especially the notion and comprehension of context and its diversity is subject of research.

Abstractly, context can be defined as the attributions of an entity depending on its surrounding, where an entity can be a device or a human being and the surrounding a situation or environment. Here, different kinds of surrounding can be determined:

At first and most notable, the real surrounding can be understood as context. This physical context can for example be a location of a real entity, its orientation but also environmental attributes like brightness, lighting or temperature.

Second, the social context or the situation a user is in at a certain location can be taken into account. Interaction with people in general belongs to this section. For instance, cultural constraints have to be met, certain behaviour may be inappropriate in a certain social situation or it may just be right under those circumstances only.

Third, the condition the user is in can be taken in account. His emotional state may be interesting for certain applications, notifications or distractions should be kept to a minimum, according to the user's state (Pascoe et al., 1999; Want et al., 1999; Pascoe et al. 2000; Schmidt, 2002; Messeter et al. 2004; Ho & Intille, 2005).

With mobile devices, another most notable point is added to this diversion. As Messeter et al. point out, mobile devices enables the user to detach from his context as they allow for applications to become mobile and reachable whenever and wherever desired (Messeter et al. 2004). The user therefore takes a virtual context with him, carried by the smart device rather than interacting with the context at hand.

Figure 7. A context aware application using Halo circles to show off screen locations (Mahler et al. 2007)

Clearly, context awareness as well as mobility allow for new adaptive systems. Depending on the application a special notion of context is used and implemented. Yet, new possibilities pose new challenges for device interaction and interfaces. Context can not only be used for the application itself but also to enable new ways of interaction or, depending on the application, use additional sensory information for data visualization.

Ho and Intille for instance present a way of how to reduce the perceived interruption burden in mobile device usage. They analyse the user's condition and the degree of his activity and concentration. By that they can shift distractive messages to times when the user shifts tasks in order to reduce the degree of distraction (Ho & Intille, 2005). The notion of user attention and its importance for the interface is found to be a very important and valuable resource in mobile computing by other researchers as well (see Pascoe et al., 2000). However, for ubiquitous computing to seamlessly integrate into the real world it is crucial to seamlessly recognize context and to integrate existing sensory information (Pascoe et al., 1999).

An example for seamless integration of context in a mobile application, especially its visualization, and its reduction of the user's burden is shown by Mahler et al. (Mahler et al. 2007). For a pedestrian navigation system different visualization techniques were analysed and evaluated with special regard to the cognitive load. The application makes use of physical context, especially location and orientation. According to the current attribution a map sector is shown (see Fig. 7). This introduces the problem that some points of interest (POIs) for the task at hands are located outside the part of the map currently shown. By only adapting the user interface in using a special visualization method, it could be shown that the user's burden is reduced significantly. The visualization in use, the Halo circle metaphor by Baudisch and Rosenholtz proposes to draw circles around off screen POIs. The on screen

circle segments then allow the user to easily estimate the location of each off screen POI (Baudisch & Rosenholtz, 2003).
This example shows the possibilities made available by context usage. Additionally, the important role of a suitable interface for mobile device interaction is illustrated. The integration of context for interface control and its combination with apt visualization techniques leads to new and improved interfaces as shown above. These steps together with the integration and location of context information are necessary to make the vision of ubiquitous computing and its benefits come true.

3.5 Mobile Devices and Tangible Interfaces

From our point of view the seamless integration of the ideas described above is the goal. Intelligent environments offer opportunities, we are only at the very beginning to understand or being able to implement. Nevertheless, the sensory equipment needed along with the computational power, cannot be implemented and reach everywhere. There will still be places that cannot provide the needed equipment for full mixed reality and complete transparency.
A possible solution to this is to take the computing power with us to these spaces. Of course there are some drawbacks in this case as we can only use what we bring with us and we do not intend to install huge environments. We rather think that the key lies in the seamless integration of mobile devices in the vision of intelligent environments, ubiquitous computing and tangible interfaces. This does not seem to be too farfetched as we can observe a rapid increase in both the computing power and the sensory capabilities of mobile devices.

Figure 8. The two components of the Tangible Reminder: On the left, the ambient display subsystem with tangible personal objects in different states of urgency coded by colour. On the right the original input solution consisting of a tablet PC with touch screen and the coding plate

Furthermore we do not think that the goal of these new paradigms should be to replace existing solutions but rather to integrate them into the existing environment to enrich our world and carefully replace where better solutions are provided. Mobile devices have the potential to pave an evolutionary road towards truly pervasive ubiquitous computing. Bødker formulates similar goals for what she calls third wave challenges (Bødker, 2006).
In our institute we are working on different projects tackling the field of ubiquitous computing. The example we want to present here focuses especially on the convergence of tangible interaction and ambient displays.

We have included a brief overview of the Tangible Reminder in the following, for further reading a detailed description can be found in (Hermann et al., 2007). The goal of the Tangible Reminder was to create an easy to use and comprehensible physical installation to deal with appointments and deadlines. The first version of this system consists of two parts, an ambient display subsystem which is capable of holding tangible objects and showing the states of their digital representative and an input subsystem to connect and change digital information associated with an object (see Fig. 8).

The display part integrates in everyday life smoothly as it makes use of ambient technology to deliver the status of an object at a glance and stays in the background otherwise. To convey the urgency state of an appointment the Tangible Reminder maps the urgency level onto three colours following cultural constraints. The colours used are green for far away deadlines, yellow for approaching ones and red for urgent deadlines. Additionally the light starts flashing when an appointment is due. This way the display is no more ambient but pressing and draws the user's attention when needed.

The Tangible Reminder's display subsystem has a tangible interface and is operated by actions with graspable objects. The objects used can be chosen freely. As stated earlier this supports the strong mental linkage between an object and its digital representation.

To associate an appointment with an object the input subsystem is used. By placing the object in question on the programming plate an interaction mask appears on the tablet PC. Here the properties of an appointment can be defined or changed. The input subsystem can also be used as a viewer to display associations between task and objects.

Clearly, the use of the Tangible Reminder detaches appointments from the computer, a way of keeping track of deadlines today. It gives the deadline a physical representation and allows for appointment management. It provides a solution that works through interaction of personal objects with an ambient display system. The Tangible Reminder stays in the background providing information at a glance and additionally comes forward and warns of due deadlines when necessary.

Although the Tangible Reminder is already a convenient system for appointment management it falls short when it comes to appointment linkage. The use of a tablet PC with handwriting as input method is a step into the right direction, but it clearly is still a rather computerized solution. Still a computer interface has to be used for the coupling of appointment and object.

This is true for simple appointments. But we have already taken steps to push the computer further to the background. By distinguishing three different kinds of appointments we can get rid of the regular programming for every appointment. The usual appointment has one deadline, which can be specified by an absolute date. In contrast to that relative deadlines allow for simple programming by action. The simple act of putting an object linked to a relative deadline programs the Tangible Reminder, it is programmed by implied action. A nice example that conveys this idea is the tea cup - the Tangible Reminder can help to prevent that the tea is brewed too long. Simply by putting the cup into the Reminder the relative deadline gets programmed and thus the system will remind us in say three minutes. Similar to the relative deadline and an extension to it is the multiple deadline approach. Here a multitude of appointments can be bound to one object. These objects can remind us on different deadlines with just one object. This is very neat if we think of a medication box. Put into a Reminder tray the box itself will remind us on the times to take medicine.

These examples clearly show the urge to get rid of the computer. However, the problem of how these objects get linked in the first place remains unclear. Furthermore the objects lack an interface for reflection purpose.

To tackle this circumstance we turned our attention to the intertwining of ubiquitous computing and mobile devices, Personal Digital Assistants (PDA) in this case. A PDA capable of recognizing a personal digitally enhanced object can fill in for the input subsystem used in the first version of the Tangible Reminder. Clearly, this is not a seamless way of enhancing the physical environment. It rather follows the idea of bringing together new ways of interaction with known and approved technology. For implementation purpose we decided to follow the digital lens metaphor. The PDA thus embodies a window to the digital world (Bier et al., 1994; Viega et al., 1996; Looser et al., 2004), representing all information associated with the close by physical object. It therefore embodies an extension of an existing real object into the digital realm.

The use of the PDA as mobile interface acts as a tool glass offering virtual information for the close by real object. It presents its linked virtual information and allows for editing. We chose this approach to be independent of a special room and extensive preparation. Instead we focus on the seamless integration of the virtual tool glass and rather accept minor inaccuracies in rendering compared to a fully equipped mobile AR system. Even the use of conventional mobile interfaces is an option in this application as it is completely consistent with the magic lens (Bier et al., 1993) or the peephole metaphor (Yee, 2003). Clearly this approach needs further investigation, nevertheless it is a promising approach to combine tangible interfaces and ubiquitous computing, lending real objects a mobile interface.

4. Conclusion

In a world of constant intertwining of virtuality and reality a consistent way of discovering links between the real and the virtual world is needed. Clearly, the interaction with real world objects offers new possibilities for interfaces to reduce task complexity and to embed virtual tasks into the real world. However, this leads to problems in device use. Ready-mades in our everyday environment already have a function, expressed in its physical form. To link such objects with additional virtual options leads to the question of how such a linkage can be made comprehensible.

The construction of reactive environments and intelligent rooms with huge amounts of sensing equipment is a well witnessed direct result. And within these interface metaphors are developed, that allow for the seamless integration of real and virtual objects. Where these intelligent environments come close to Weisers' vision of transparency, they fall short in behave of ubiquity. In this situation mobile devices can fill in. While our environment is not fully equipped with sensors, mobile devices can extend local installations by taking the computational power and the sensory equipment with the user. Acting as magic lenses, they can provide everyday objects with the interfaces needed for device usage. They can display the functions an object provides; they can help in setting up linkages and even help with reconfiguration.

At the same time, the mobile devices, acting as virtual tool glasses, can provide an interface only when needed, reflecting the dynamic role an object can play depending on the context the object is used in. Thus, the mobile device, giving real word objects an interface, can be used as tool to scale virtuality to the extend needed.

From our point of view the great challenge ahead is the seamless integration of the many different promising ideas described above. Living in intelligent environments, interacting in natural ways is the great goal. Nevertheless, these solutions require a considerable amount of ubiquitous and omnipresent hardware, sensors, actuators and computing power. Even if we manage to accomplish this tremendous effort for our living environments or work spaces, there will be still spaces we cannot equip with the required systems. That is where mobile devices can fill in.

5. References

Azuma, R. (1997). A Survey of Augmented Reality. *Presence: Teleoperators and Virtual Environments,* Vol. 6, No. 4, (August 1997), pp. 355-385, 10547460.

Baudisch, P. & Rosenholtz, R. (2003). Halo: a technique for visualizing off-screen objects. *Proceedings of the SIGCHI Conference on Human Factors in Computing Systems,* pp. 481-488, 1581136307, Ft. Lauderdale, April 2003, ACM, New York.

Beigl, M., Gellersen, H. & Schmidt, A. (2001). Mediacups: experience with design and use of computer-augmented everyday artefacts. *Computer Networks: The International Journal of Computer and Telecommunications Networking,* Vol. 35, No. 4, March 2001, pp. 401-409, 13891286.

Bier, E., Stone, M., Pier, K., Buxton, W. & DeRose, T. (1993). Toolglass and magic lenses: the see-through interface, *Proceedings of the 20th Annual Conference on Computer Graphics and interactive Techniques SIGGRAPH '93,* 0897916018, pp. 73-80, ACM, New York.

Bier, E., Stone, M., Fishkin, Buxton, W. & Baudel, T. (1994). A taxonomy of see-through tools. *Proceedings of the SIGCHI Conference on Human Factors in Computing Systems: Celebrating interdependence,* pp. 358-364, 0897916506, Boston, April 1994, ACM, New York.

Bødker, S. (2006). When second wave HCI meets third wave challenges. *Proceedings of the 4th Nordic Conference on Human-Computer interaction: Changing Roles,* pp. 1-8, 1595933255, Oslo, October 2006, ACM Press, New York.

Bolter, J. & Gromala, D. (2004). Transparency and Reflectivity: Digital Art and the Aesthetics of Interface Design, In: *Aesthetic computing,* Fishwick, P. (Ed.), pp. 369-382, MIT Press, 0-262-06250-X.

Butz, A. & Krüger, A. (2006). Applying the Peephole Metaphor in a Mixed-Reality Room. *IEEE Computer Graphics and Applications* ,Vol. 26, No. 1, January/February 2006, pp. 56-63, 02721716.

Çapın, T., Haro, A., Setlur, V. & Wilkinson, S. (2006). Camera-Based Virtual Environment Interaction on Mobile Devices, *Lecture Notes in Computer Science,* Vol. 4263/2006, October 2006, pp. 765-773, Springer, 9783540472421, Berlin.

Chalmers, M. (2004). Coupling and Heterogeneity in Ubiquitous Computing, ACM CHI 2004 Workshop Reflective HCI: Towards a Critical Technical Practice.

Chittaro, L. (2006). Visualizing Information on Mobile Devices, *Computer* , Vol. 39, No. 3, March 2006, pp. 40-45, 00189162.

Cohen, P. (1992). The Role of Natural Language in a Multimodal Interface, *Proceedings of the 5th annual ACM symposium on User interface software and technology,* pp. 143-149, 0897915496, Monteray, California, November 1992, ACM, New York.

Fitzmaurice, G. W. (1993). Situated information spaces and spatially aware palmtop computers. *Communications of the ACM,* Vol. 36, No. 7, July 1993, pp. 39-49, 00010782.

Fitzmaurice, G., Ishii, H. & Buxton, W. (1995). Bricks: laying the foundations for graspable user interfaces, *Proceedings of the SIGCHI Conference on Human Factors in Computing Systems,* pp. 442-449, 0201847051, Denver, May 1995, ACM Press/Addison-Wesley Publishing Co., New York.

Gaver, W., Smets, G. & Overbeeke, K. (1995). A Virtual Window on media space. *Proceedings of the SIGCHI Conference on Human Factors in Computing Systems,* pp. 257-264, 0201847051, Denver, May 1995, ACM Press/Addison-Wesley Publishing Co., New York.

Hachet, M., Pouderoux, J. & Guitton, P. (2005). A camera-based interface for interaction with mobile handheld computers. *Proceedings of the 2005 Symposium on interactive 3D Graphics and Games,* pp. 65-72, 1595930132, Washington, April 2005, ACM, New York.

Hermann, M., Mahler, T., Melo, de G. & Weber, M. (2007). The tangible reminder. *Proceedings of 3rd IET International Conference on Intelligent Environments,* pp. 144-151, 9780863418532, Ulm, September 2007.

Heidegger, M. (1927). Sein und Zeit, In: *Jahrbuch für Phänomenologie und phänomenologische Forschung,* Vol. 8, Husserl, E. (Ed.).

Henrysson, A., Ollila, M. & Billinghurst, M. (2005). Mobile phone based AR scene assembly. *Proceedings of the 4th international Conference on Mobile and Ubiquitous Multimedia,* pp. 95-102, 0473106582, Christchurch (New Zealand), December 2005, ACM, New York.

Ho, J. & Intille, S. (2005). Using context-aware computing to reduce the perceived burden of interruptions from mobile devices. *Proceedings of the SIGCHI Conference on Human Factors in Computing Systems,* pp. 909-918, 1581139985, Portland, April 2005, ACM, New York.

Holmquist, L.; Schmidt, A. & Ullmer, B. (2004). Tangible Interfaces in Perspective, *Personal Ubiquitous Computing,* Vol. 8, No. 5, September 2004, pp. 291-293, 16174909.

Hornecker, E. & Buur, J. (2006). Getting a grip on tangible interaction: a framework on physical space and social interaction, *Proceedings of the SIGCHI conference on Human Factors in computing systems,* pp. 437-446, 1595933727, Montréal, April 2006, ACM, New York.

Hoven, E. van den & Eggen, J. (2004). Tangible Computing in Everyday Life: Extending Current Frameworks for Tangible User Interfaces with Personal Objects, *Lecture Notes in Computer Science,* Vol. 3295/2004, October 2004, pp. 230-242, Springer, 03029743, Berlin.

Hoven, E. van den & Eggen, J. (2005). Personal souvenirs as Ambient Intelligent objects, *Proceedings of the 2005 Joint Conference on Smart Objects and Ambient intelligence: innovative Context-Aware Services: Usages and Technologies,* pp. 123-128, 1595933042, Grenoble, October 2005. ACM Press, New York.

Hwang, J., Jung, J. & Kim, G. (2006). Hand-held virtual reality: a feasibility study. *Proceedings of the ACM Symposium on Virtual Reality Software and Technology,* pp. 356-363, 1595933212, Limassol (Cyprus), November 2006, ACM, New York.

Ishii, H. & Ullmer, B. (1997). Tangible Bits: Towards Seamless Interfaces Between People Bits and Atoms, *Proceedings of the SIGCHI conference on Human factors in computing systems*, pp. 234-241, 0897918029, Atlanta, March 1997, ACM, New York.

Looser, J., Billinghurst, M. & Cockburn, A. (2004). Through the looking glass: the use of lenses as an interface tool for Augmented Reality interfaces. *Proceedings of the 2nd international Conference on Computer Graphics and interactive Techniques in Australasia and South East Asia,* pp. 204-211, 1581138830, Singapore, June 2004, ACM, New York.

Mahler, T., Reuff, M. & Weber, M. (2007). Pedestrian Navigation System Implications on Visualization, *Lecture Notes in Computer Science*, Vol. 4555/2007, August 2007, pp. 470-478, Springer, 9783540732808, Berlin.

Messeter, J., Brandt, E., Halse, J. & Johansson, M. (2004). Contextualizing mobile IT. *Proceedings of the 5th Conference on Designing interactive Systems: Processes, Practices, Methods, and Techniques*, pp. 27-36, 1581137877, Cambridge, August 2004, ACM, New York.

Microsoft Surface. http://www.microsoft.com/surface/, visited July 19th, 2008.

Milgram, P. & Kishino, F. (1994). A Taxonomy of Mixed Reality Visual Displays, *IEICE Transactions on Information Systems*, Vol. E77-D, No. 12, December 1994, pp. 1321-1329.

Norman, D. (1988). *The Psychology of Everyday Things*, Basic Books, 0465067093, New York.

Norman, D. (1998). *The Invisible Computer: Why Good Products Can Fail, the Personal Computer Is So Complex, and Information Appliances Are the Solution*, The MIT Press, 0262640414, Cambridge.

Pascoe, J., Ryan, N. & Morse, D. (1999). Issues in Developing Context-Aware Computing. *Proceedings of the 1st international Symposium on Handheld and Ubiquitous Computing*, pp. 208-221, Karlsruhe, September 1999, Springer-Verlag, London.

Pascoe, J., Ryan, N. & Morse, D. (2000). Using while moving: HCI issues in fieldwork environments. *ACM Transactions on Computer-Human Interaction,* Vol. 7, No. 3, September 2000, pp. 417-437, 10730516.

Rath, M. & Rocchesso, D. (2005). Continuous Sonic Feedback from a Rolling Ball, *IEEE MultiMedia*, Vol. 12, No. 2, April 2005, pp. 60-69, 1070986X.

Schmalstieg, D., Fuhrmann, A., Hesina, G., Szalavári, Z., Encarnação, L. M., Gervautz, M. & Purgathofer, W. (2002). The studierstube augmented reality project. *Presence: Teleoperators and Virtual Environments,* Vol. 11, No. 1, February 2002, pp. 33-54 10547460.

Schmidt, A. (2002). Ubiquitous Computing - Computing in Context, *Ph.D. Thesis*, November 2002, Lancaster University.

Shimoga, K. (1992). A Survey of Perceptual Feedback Issues in Dexterous Telemanipulation: Part I—Finger Force Feedback, *Proceedings of VRAIS 93*, IEEE Press, Piscataway, N.J., 1993, pp. 263-270.

Shimoga, K. (1992). A Survey of Perceptual Feedback Issues in Dexterous Telemanipulation: Part II—Finger Touch Feedback, *Proceedings of VRAIS 93*, IEEE Press, Piscataway, N.J., 1993, pp. 271-279.

Stone, M., Fishkin, K. & Bier, E. (1994). The movable filter as a user interface tool. *Proceedings of the SIGCHI Conference on Human Factors in Computing Systems: Celebrating interdependence,* pp. 306-312, 0897916506, Boston, April 1994, ACM, New York.

Ullmer, B. & Ishii, H. (2000). Emerging Frameworks for Tangible User Interfaces, *IBM Systems Journal*, Vol. 39, No. 3-4, 2000, pp. 915-931.

Ullmer, B. & Ishii, H. (2001). Emerging Frameworks for Tangible User Interfaces, In: *Human-Computer Interaction in the New Millenium*, Carroll, J. (Ed.), pp. 579-601, Addison-Wesley, 0201704471.

Viega, J., Conway, M., Williams, G. & Pausch, R. (1996). 3D magic lenses. *Proceedings of the 9th Annual ACM Symposium on User interface Software and Technology*, pp. 51-58, 0897917987, Seattle, November 1996, ACM, New York.

Wagner, D., Pintaric, T. & Schmalstieg, D. (2004). The invisible train: a collaborative handheld augmented reality demonstrator. In *ACM SIGGRAPH 2004 Emerging Technologies*, Elliott-Famularo, H. (Ed.), p. 6, ACM, 1595938962, New York.

Wagner, D., Pintaric, T., Ledermann, F. & Schmalstieg, D. (2005). Towards Massively Multi-user Augmented Reality on Handheld Devices, *Lecture Notes in Computer Science*, Vol. 3468/2005, May 2005, pp. 208-219, Springer, 03029743, Berlin.

Want, R., Fishkin, K., Gujar, A. & Harrison, B. (1999). Bridging physical and virtual worlds with electronic tags. *Proceedings of the SIGCHI Conference on Human Factors in Computing Systems: the CHI Is the Limit*, pp. 370-377, 0201485591, Pittsburgh, May 1999, ACM, New York.

Weber, M. & Hermann, M. (2008). Advanced Hands and Eyes Interaction, In: *Handbook of Research on Ubiquitous Computing Technology for Real Time Enterprises*, Mühlhäuser, M. & Gurevych, I. (Eds.), pp. 445-469, Information Science Reference, 9781599048321, Hershey.

Weiser, M. (1991). The Computer for the 21st century, *Scientific American*, Vol. 265, No. 3, September 1991, pp. 94-105.

Yee, K. (2003). Peephole displays: pen interaction on spatially aware handheld computers. *Proceedings of the SIGCHI Conference on Human Factors in Computing Systems*, pp. 1-8, 1581136307, Ft. Lauderdale, April 2003. ACM, New York.

20

Integrating Software Engineering and Usability Engineering

Karsten Nebe[1], Dirk Zimmermann and Volker Paelke[2]
[1]University of Paderborn (C-LAB), [2]Leibniz University of Hannover (IGK)
Germany

1. Introduction

The usability of products gains in importance not only for the users of a system but also for manufacturing organizations. According to Jokela, the advantages for users are far-reaching and include increased productivity, improved quality of work, and increased user satisfaction. Manufacturers also profit significantly through a reduction of support and training costs (Jokela, 2001). The quality of products ranks among the most important aspects for manufacturers in competitive markets and the software industry is no exception to this. One of the central quality attributes for interactive systems is their usability (Bevan, 1999) and the main standardization organizations (IEEE 98, ISO 91) have addressed this parameter for a long time (Granollers, 2002). In recent years more and more software manufacturer consider the usability of their products as a strategic goal due to market pressures. Consequently, an increasing number of software manufacturer are pursuing the goal of integrating usability practices into their software engineering processes (Juristo et al., 2001). While usability is already regarded as an essential part of software quality (Juristo et al., 2001) the practical implementation often turns out to be a challenge. One key difficulty is usually the integration of methods, activities and artefacts from usability engineering into the existing structures of an organization, which typically already embody an established process model for product development and implementation. Uncoordinated usability activities that arise frequently in practice have only a small influence on the usability of a product. In practice the activities, processes and models applied during development are usually those proposed by software engineering (Granollers et al., 2002). A systematic and sustainable approach for the integration of usability activities into existing processes is required.

In order to align the activities from both software engineering (SE) and usability engineering (UE) it is necessary to identify appropriate interfaces by which the activities and artefacts can be integrated smoothly into a coherent development process. The central goal of such integration is to combine the quality benefits of usability engineering with the systematic and planable proceedings of software engineering. This chapter provides a starting point for such integration. We begin with a discussion of the similarities and differences between both disciplines and review the connection between models, standards and the operational processes. We then introduce integration strategies at three levels of abstractions: the level of

standards in SE and UE, the level of process models, as well as the level of operational processes.
On the most abstract level of standards we have analyzed and compared the software engineering standard ISO/IEC 12207 with the usability engineering standard DIN EN ISO 13407 and identified 'common activities'. These define the overarching framework for the next level of process models.
Based on this, we have analyzed different SE process models at the next level of abstraction. In order to quantify the ability of SE process models to create usable products, a criteria catalogue with demands from usability engineering was defined and used to assess common SE models. The results provide an overview about the degree of compliance of existing SE models with UE demands. This overview not only highlights weaknesses of SE process models with regards to usability engineering, but also serves to identify opportunities for improved integration between SE and UE activities.
These opportunities can form the foundation for the most concrete implementation of an integrated development approach at the operational process level. We present recommendations based on the results of the analysis.

2. Software Engineering

Software engineering (SE) is a discipline that adopts various engineering approaches to address all phases of software production, from the early stages of system specification up to the maintenance phase after the release of the system (Patel & Wang, 2000; Sommerville, 2004). SE tries to provide a systematic and planable approach for software development. To achieve this, it provides comprehensive, systematic and manageable procedures, in terms of SE process models (SE models).
SE models usually define detailed activities, the sequence in which these activities have to be performed and the resulting deliverables. The goal in using SE models is a controlled, solid and repeatable process in which the project results do not depend on individual efforts of particular people or fortunate circumstances (Glinz, 1999). Hence, SE models partially map to process properties and process elements, adding concrete procedures.
Existing SE models vary with regards to specific properties (such as type and number of iterations, level of detail in the description or definition of procedures or activities, etc.) and each model has specific advantages and disadvantages, concerning predictability, risk management, coverage of complexity, generation of fast deliverables and outcomes, etc.
Examples of such SE models are the Linear Sequential Model (also called Classic Life Cycle Model or Waterfall Model) (Royce, 1970), Evolutionary Software Development (McCracken, & Jackson, 1982), the Spiral Model by Boehm (Boehm, 1988), or the V-Model (KBST, 1997).
SE standards define a framework for SE models on a higher abstraction level. They define rules and guidelines as well as properties of process elements as recommendations for the development of software. Thereby, standards support consistency, compatibility and exchangeability, and cover the improvement of quality and communication.
The ISO/IEC 12207 provides such a general process framework for the development and management of software. 'The framework covers the life cycle of software from the conceptualization of ideas through retirement and consists of processes for acquiring and supplying software products and services.' (ISO/IEC, 2002). It defines processes, activities and tasks and provides descriptions about how to perform these items on an abstract level.

In order to fulfil the conditions of SE standards (and the associated claim of ensuring quality) SE models should comply with these conditions. In general, standards as well as SE models cannot be directly applied. They have to be adapted and/or tailored to the specific organizational conditions. The resulting instantiation of a SE model, fitted to the organizational aspects, is called software development process, which can then be used and put to practice. Thus, the resulting operational process is an instance of the underlying SE model and the implementation of activities within the organization.
This creates a hierarchy of different levels of abstractions for SE: standards that define the overarching framework, process models that describe systematic and traceable approaches and the operational level in which the models are tailored to fit the specifics of an organization (Figure 1).

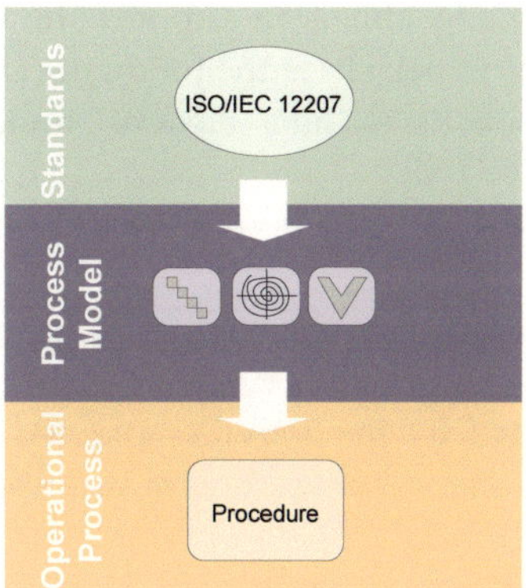

Figure 1. Hierarchy of standards, process models and operational processes in SE

3. Usability Engineering

Usability Engineering (UE) is a discipline that is concerned with the question of how to design software that is easy to use (usable). UE is 'an approach to the development of software and systems which involves user participation from the outset and guarantees the efficacy of the product through the use of a usability specification and metrics.' (Faulkner, 2002a)
UE provides a wide range of methods and systematic approaches for the support of development. These approaches are called Usability Engineering Models (UE Models) or Usability Lifecycles. Examples include Goal-Directed-Design (Cooper & Reimann, 2003), the UE Lifecycle (Mayhew, 1999) or the User-Centred Design-Process Model of IBM (IBM, 1996). All of them have much in common since they describe an idealized approach that ensures the development of usable software, but they differ in their specifics, in the applied methods and the general description of the procedure (e.g. phases, dependencies, goals, responsibilities, etc.) (Woletz, 2006). UE Models usually define activities and their resulting deliverables as well as the order in which specific tasks or activities have to be performed. The goal of UE models is to provide tools and methods for the implementation of the user's needs and to guarantee the efficiency, effectiveness and users' satisfaction of the solution.
Thus, UE and SE address different needs in the development of software. SE aims at systematic, controllable and manageable approaches to software development, whereas UE focuses on the realization of usable and user-friendly solutions.

The consequence is that there are different views between the two disciplines during system development, which sometimes can lead to conflicts, e.g. when SE focuses on system requirements and the implementation of system concepts and designs, whereas UE focuses on the implementation of user requirements, interaction concepts and designs. For successful designs both views need to be considered and careful trade-offs are required.
UE provides standards similar to the way SE does. These are also intended to serve as frameworks to ensure consistency, compatibility, exchangeability, and quality, which is in line with the idea of SE standards. However, UE standards focus on the users and the construction of usable solutions. Examples for such standards are the DIN EN ISO 13407 (1999) and the ISO/PAS 18152 (2003).
The DIN EN ISO 13407 introduces a process framework for the human-centred design of interactive systems. Its overarching aim is to support the definition and management of human-centred design activities, which share the following characteristics:

- The active involvement of users and a clear understanding of user and task requirements ('context of use')
- An appropriate allocation of function between users and technology ('user requirements')
- The iteration of design solutions ('produce design solutions')
- Multi-disciplinary design ('evaluation of use')

These characteristics are reflected by the activities (named in brackets), which define the process framework of the human-centred design process, and have to be performed iteratively.
The ISO/PAS 18152 is partly based on the DIN EN ISO 13407, and describes a reference model to measure the maturity of an organization in performing processes that make usable, healthy and safe systems. It describes processes and activities that address human-system issues and the outcomes of these processes. It provides details on the tasks and artefacts associated with the outcomes of each process and activity.
There is a sub-process called human-centred design that describes the activities that are commonly associated with a user centred design process. These activities are 'context of use', 'user requirements', 'produce design solutions' and 'evaluation of use', which are in line with the DIN EN ISO 13407. They are, however, more specific in terms of defining lists of activities (so called base practices) that describe how the purpose of each activity can be achieved (e.g. what needs to be done to gather the user requirements in the right way). Thus, the ISO/PAS 18152 enhances the DIN EN ISO 13407 in terms of the level of detail and contains more precise guidelines.
In order to ensure the claims of the overarching standards, UE models need to adhere to the demands of the corresponding framework. Thus, a connection between the standards and the UE models exists, which is similar to the one identified for SE above. Similar to SE, there is also a hierarchy of standards and subsequent process models.
Additionally, there are similarities on the level of operational processes. The selected UE model needs to be adjusted to the organizational guidelines. Therefore, a similar hierarchy of the different abstraction levels exists for SE and for UE (Figure 2). Standards define the overarching framework, models describe systematic and traceable approaches and on the operational level, the SE models are adjusted and put into practice.

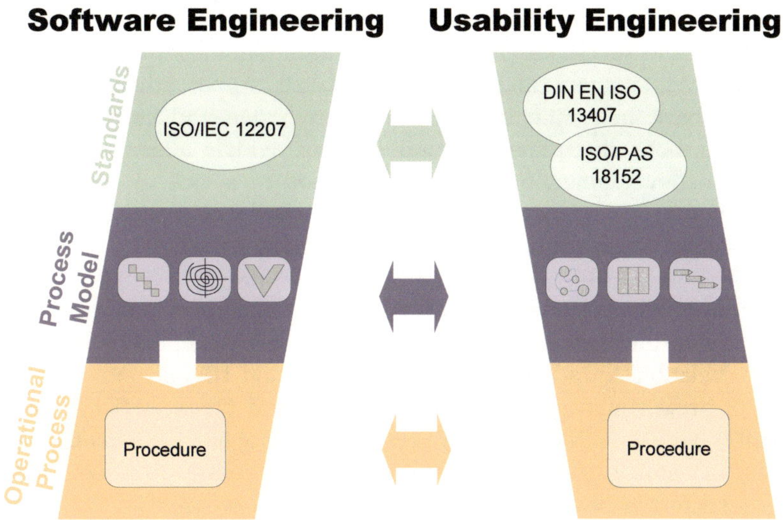

Figure 2. Similar hierarchies in the two disciplines SE and UE: standards, process models and operational processes

4. State of the Art: Integration of Standards, Models and Operational Processes

In general, standards and models are seldom applied directly, neither in SE nor in UE. Standards merely define a framework to ensure compatibility and consistency and to set quality standards. For practical usage, models are being adapted and tailored to organizational conditions and constraints, such as existing processes, organizational or project goals, legal policies, etc. Thus models are refined by the selection and definition of activities, tasks, methods, roles, deliverables, etc. as well as the responsibilities and relationships in between. The derived instantiation of a model, fitted to the organizational aspects, is called software development process (for SE models) or usability lifecycle (for UE models). The resulting operational processes can be viewed as instances of the underlying model. This applies to both SE and UE.

In order to achieve sufficient alignment between the two disciplines, all three levels of abstraction must be considered to ensure that the integration points and suggestions for collaboration meet the objectives of both sides and the intentions behind a standard, model or operational implementation is not lost.

The integration of SE and UE leads to structural, organisational and implementation challenges, caused by 'differences relating to historical evolution, training, professional orientation, and technical focus, as well as in methods, tools, models, and techniques' (Constantine et al., 2003).

As discussed in sections 2 and 3, SE and UE have evolved with different objectives. SE's main goal is the design of software, covering the process of construction, architecture, reliable functioning and design for utility (Sutcliffe, 2005). Historically, UE has been considered in contrast to this system-driven philosophy of SE (Norman & Draper, 1986) and focuses on social, cognitive and interactive phenomena (Sutcliffe, 2005). This conceptual difference between the two disciplines highlights the challenges for integration in practice.

A lack of mutual understanding between practitioners of both disciplines is common. As reported by Jerome and Kazmann (2005) there is substantial incomprehension of the other field between software engineers and usability specialists. Apparently, scientific insights on design processes have had little impact on the exchange and communication so far. Practitioners from both disciplines commonly hold widely disparate views of their respective roles in development processes. This leads to a lack of communication and collaboration. Often cooperation is deferred to late stages of the development lifecycle where it is usually too late to address fundamental usability problems.

Hakiel (1997) identifies additional areas where understanding is lacking. A central problem is the perception of many project managers that the activities and results of UE are irreproducible and result from unstructured activities. This perception is in part caused by the missing interrelation/links between activities of SE and UE and indicates the need for the education of project management about UE goals and practices (Faulkner & Culwin, 2000b; Venturi & Troost, 2004). This is a prerequisite to achieve adequate executive and managerial support and to consider UE in the project planning from the outset (staffing, organisational structure, scheduling of activities) (Radle & Young 2001).

Many of the mentioned problems are caused by the act of changing established processes by adding and adapting UE activities. Particularly there, where formal SE process models are applied UE activities are rarely considered as a priority. Granollers et al. (2002) summarize this in their study: „the development models used by the software industry in the production of solutions are still those proposed by SE. SE is the driving force and the UE needs to adapt to this in order to survive'. While so called UE models, which address the complete development from the usability perspective, have been proposed (e.g. Mayhew, 1999, Cooper & Reimann 2001), a complete replacement of SE engineering processes by these is often infeasible. Rather, it seems necessary to gather knowledge about the fundamental concepts, the methodologies and techniques of UE in a form that is accessible to all stakeholders in a development process and to incorporate this knowledge and the corresponding activities into existing software development processes (Aikio, 2006). Early on Rideout (1989) have identified the use of effective interdisciplinary design teams, the creation and dissemination of company and industry standards and guidelines, and the extension of existing processes to encompass UE concerns as keys to the acceptance and success of UE. Most existing approaches have tried to achieve unification at specific levels of abstraction. While this can lead to successful results, it fails to provide a continuous strategy for integration that considers the structural, organizational and operational aspects on equal footing and is adaptable to a variety of established and evolving SE practices. This has been illustrated by the advent of so called agile development approaches that have become popular in recent years, resulting in the need for newly adapted strategies for UE integration. In the following sections we introduce a systematic approach that covers the three levels of abstraction from standards over process models to operational processes to address this challenge in a systematic way.

5. Integration on three Levels of Abstraction

In order to identify integration points between the two disciplines examination and analysis has to be performed on each level of the abstraction hierarchy: On the most abstract level of standards it has to be shown that the central aspects of SE and UE can coexist and can be integrated. On the level of process models it has to be analyzed how UE aspects can be incorporated into SE models. And on the operational level concrete recommendations for activities have to be formulated to enable effective collaboration with reasonable organizational and operational efforts. In previous work the authors have addressed individual aspects of this integration approach (Nebe & Zimmermann, 2007a; Nebe & Zimmermann, 2007b; Nebe et al., 2007c), which are now composed into a coherent system.

5.1 Common Framework on the Level of Standards

To figure out whether SE and UE have similarities on the level of standards, the standards' detailed descriptions of processes, activities and tasks, output artefacts, etc. have been analyzed and compared. For this the SE standard ISO/IEC 12207 was chosen for comparison with the UE standard DIN EN ISO 13407.

The ISO/IEC 12207 defines the process of software development as a set of 11 activities: Requirements Elicitation, System Requirements Analysis, Software Requirements Analysis, System Architecture Design, Software Design, Software Construction, Software Integration, Software Testing, System Integration, System Testing and Software Installation. It also defines specific development tasks and details on the generated output to provide guidance for the implementation of the process.

The DIN EN ISO 13407 defines four activities of human-centred design that should take place during system development. These activities are labelled 'context of use', 'user requirements', 'produce design solutions' und 'evaluation of use'. DIN EN ISO 13407 also describes in detail the kind of output to be generated and how to achieve it.

On a high level, when examining the descriptions of each activity, by relating tasks and outputs with each other, similarities can be identified in terms of the characteristics, objectives and proceedings of activities. Based on these similarities single activities were consolidated as groups of activities (so called, 'common activities'). These 'common activities' are part of both disciplines SE and UE on the highest level of standards. An example of such a common activity is the Requirement Analysis. From a SE point of view (represented by the ISO/IEC 12207) the underlying activity is the Requirement Elicitation. From the UE standpoint, specifically the DIN EN ISO 13407, the underlying activities are the 'context of use' and 'user requirements', which are grouped together. Another example is the Software Specification, which is represented by the two SE activities System Requirements Analysis and Software Requirements Analysis, as well as by 'produce design solutions' from a UE perspective.

The result is a compilation of five 'common activities': Requirement Analysis, Software Specification, Software Design and Implementation, Software Validation, Evaluation that represent the process of development from both, a SE and a UE point of view (Table 1).

These initial similarities between the two disciplines lead to the assumption of existing integration points on this overarching level of standards. Based on this, the authors used these five 'common activities' as a general framework for the next level in the hierarchy, the level of process models.

However, the identification of these similar activities does not mean that one activity is performed in similar ways in SE and UE practice. They may have similar goals on the abstract level of standards but typically differ significantly in the execution, at least on the operational level. Thus, Requirement Analysis in SE focuses mainly on system-based requirements whereas UE requirements describe the users' needs and workflows. The activity of gathering requirements is identical but the view on the results is different.

Another example is the Evaluation. SE evaluation aims at functional correctness and correctness of code whereas UE focuses on the completeness of users' workflows and the fulfilment of users' needs.

ISO/IEC 12207 Sub- Process: Development	Common Activities	DIN EN ISO 13407
Requirements Elicitation	Requirement Analysis	Context of Use User Requirements
System Requirements Analysis Software Requirements Analysis	Software Specification	Produce Design Solutions
System Architecture Design Software Design Software Construction Software Integration	Software Design and Implementation	n/a
Software Testing System Integration	Software Validation	Evaluation of Use
System Testing Software Installation	Evaluation	Evaluation of Use

Table 1. Comparison of SE and UE activities on the level of standards and the identified similarities (Common Activities)

Consequently, it is important to consider these different facets of SE and UE likewise. And as usability becomes an important quality aspect in SE, the 'common activities' not only have to be incorporated in SE models from a SE point of view, but also from the UE point of view. Some SE models already adhere to this, but obviously not all of them. To identify whether UE aspects of the 'common activities' are already implemented in SE models, the authors performed a gap-analysis with selected SE models. The overall goal of this study was to identify integration points on the level of process models.
Therefore a deep understanding about the selected SE models and an accurate specification of the requirements that specify demands from an UE perspective was required.

5.2 Ability of SE models to Create Usable Products

In order to assess the ability of SE models to create usable products, criteria are needed to define the degree of UE coverage in SE models. These criteria must contain the UE demands and should be used for evaluation later on.
To obtain detailed knowledge about UE activities, methods, deliverables and their regarding quality aspects, the authors analyzed the DIN EN ISO 13407 and the ISO/PAS 18152.
As mentioned above the DIN EN ISO 13407 defines a process framework with the four activities 'context of use', 'user requirements', 'produce design solutions' and 'evaluation of use'. The reference model of the ISO/PAS 18152 represents an extension to parts of the DIN EN ISO 13407. Particularly the module Human-centred design of the ISO/PAS 18152 defines base practices for the four activities of the framework. These base practices describe in detail how the purpose of each activity is achieved. Thus, it is an extension on the operational process level. Since the ISO/PAS 18152 is aimed at process assessments, its base practices describe the established steps. Therefore they can be used as UE requirements that

need to be applied by the SE models to ensure to create usable products. For the following analysis they form the basic requirements against which each activity is evaluated. As an example table 2 shows the base practices of the activity 'user requirements'.

HS.3.2 User Requirements	
BP1	Set and agree the expected behaviour and performance of the system with respect to the user.
BP2	Develop an explicit statement of the user requirements for the system.
BP3	Analyse the user requirements.
BP4	Generate and agree on measurable criteria for the system in its intended context of use.
BP5	Present these requirements to project stakeholders for use in the development and operation of the system.

Table 2. Base practices of the module HS.3.2 User Requirements given in the ISO/PAS 18152.

Based on these requirements (base practices) the authors evaluated the selected SE models. The comparison was based on the description of the SE models in the standard documents and official documentation. For each requirement the authors determined whether the model complied with it or not. An overview of the results for each model is shown in table 3. The quantity of fulfilled requirements for each activity of the framework provides some indication of the level of compliance of the SE model with the UE requirements. According to the results, statements about the ability of SE models to create usable products were made. Table 4 shows the condensed result of the gap-analysis.

The compilation of findings shows, that for none of the SE models all base practices of ISO/PAS 18152 can be seen as fulfilled. However, there is also a large variability in the coverage rate between the SE models. For example, the V-Model shows a very good coverage for all modules except for smaller fulfilment of 'produce design solutions' HS 3.3 criteria, whereas the Linear Sequential Model only fulfils a few of the 'evaluation of use' (HS 3.4) criteria and none of the other modules.

Evolutionary Design and the Spiral Model share a similar pattern, where they show only little coverage for 'context of use', medium to good coverage of 'user requirements', limited coverage for Produce Design Solution and good support for 'evaluation of use' activities.

Modul	Activity	LSM	ED	SM	VM
HS 3.1	**Context of use**				
1	Define the scope of the context of use for the system.	-	-	+	+
2	Analyse the tasks and worksystem.	-	-	-	+
3	Describe the characteristics of the users.	-	-	-	+
4	Describe the cultural environment/organizational/management regime.	-	-	-	+

5	Describe the characteristics of any equipment external to the system and the working environment.	-	-	-	+
6	Describe the location, workplace equipment and ambient conditions.	-	-	-	+
7	Analyse the implications of the context of use.	-	-	-	+
8	Present these issues to project stakeholders for use in the development or operation of the system.	-	+	-	-
HS 3.2	**User Requirements**				
1	Set and agree the expected behaviour and performance of the system with respect to the user.	-	-	+	+
2	Develop an explicit statement of the user requirements for the system.	-	+	+	+
3	Analyse the user requirements.	-	+	+	+
4	Generate and agree on measurable criteria for the system in its intended context of use.	-	-	+	+
5	Present these requirements to project stakeholders for use in the development and operation of the system.	-	-	-	-
HS 3.3	**Produce design solutions**				
1	Distribute functions between the human, machine and organizational elements of the system best able to fulfil each function.	-	-	-	-
2	Develop a practical model of the user's work from the requirements, context of use, allocation of function and design constraints for the system.	-	-	-	-
3	Produce designs for the user-related elements of the system that take account of the user requirements, context of use and HF data.	-	-	-	-
4	Produce a description of how the system will be used.	-	+	+	+
5	Revise design and safety features using feedback from evaluations.	-	+	+	+
HS 3.4	**Evaluation of use**				
1	Plan the evaluation.	-	+	+	+
2	Identify and analyse the conditions under which a system is to be tested or otherwise evaluated.	-	-	+	+
3	Check that the system is fit for evaluation.	+	+	+	+
4	Carry out and analyse the evaluation according to the evaluation plan.	+	+	+	+
5	Understand and act on the results of the evaluation.	+	+	+	+

Table 3. Results of the gap-analysis: Coverage of the base practices for the Linear Sequential Model (LSM), Evolutionary Development (ED), Spiral Model (SM) and V-Model (VM)

	Context of Use	User Requirements	Produce Design Solutions	Evaluation of Use	Across Activities
Linear Sequential Model	0 %	0 %	0 %	60 %	13 %
Evolutionary Development	13 %	40 %	40 %	80 %	39 %
Spiral Model	13 %	80%	40 %	100 %	52 %
V-Modell	88 %	80 %	40 %	100 %	78 %
Across Models	28 %	50 %	30 %	85 %	

Table 4. Results of the gap-analysis, showing the level of sufficiency of SE models covering the requirements of UE

The summary of results (Table 4) and a comparison of the percentage of fulfilled requirements for each SE model, shows that the V-Model performs better than the other models and can be regarded as basically being able to produce usable products. With a percentage of 78% it is far ahead of the remaining three SE models. In the comparison, the Linear Sequential Model falls short at only 13%, followed by Evolutionary Development (39%) and the Spiral Model (52%).

If one takes both the average values of fulfilled requirements and the specific base practices for each UE activity into account, this analysis shows that the emphasis for all SE models is laid on evaluation ('evaluation of use'), especially comparing the remaining activities. The lowest overall coverage could be found in the 'context of use' and Produce Design Solution, indicating that three of the four SE models don't consider the relevant contextual factors of system usage sufficiently, and also don't include (user focused) concept and prototype work to an extent that can be deemed appropriate from a UCD perspective.

The relatively small compliance values for the 'context of use' (28%), 'user requirements' (50%) and 'produce design solutions' (30%) activities across all SE models, can be interpreted as an indicator that there is only a loose integration between UE and SE. There are few overlaps between the disciplines regarding these activities and therefore it is necessary to provide suitable interfaces to create a foundation for integration.

This approach does not only highlight weaknesses of SE models regarding the UE requirements and corresponding activities, it also pinpoints the potential for integration between SE and UE: Where requirements are currently considered as not fulfilled, recommendations for better integration can be derived.

The underlying base practices and the corresponding detailed descriptions provide indicatory on what needs to be considered on the level of process models.

As an example, initial high-level recommendations e.g. for the Linear Sequential Model could be as followed: In addition to phases likes System Requirements and Software Requirements there needs to be a separate phase for gathering user requirements and analysis of the context of use. As the model is document driven and completed documents are post-conditions for the next phase it has to be ensured that usability results are part of this documentation.

The approach can be applied in a similar way to any SE model, to establish the current level of integration and to identify areas for improved integration. This can be used a foundation for implementing the operational process level and will improve the interplay of SE and UE in practice.

The results confirmed the expectations of the authors, indicating deficiencies in the level of integration between both disciplines on the level of the overarching process models. Thus, there is a clear need to compile more specific and detailed criteria for the assessment of the SE models. The analysis also showed that the base practices currently leave too much leeway for interpretations. In addition, it turned out that a dichotomous assessment scale (in terms of 'not fulfilled' or 'fulfilled') is not sufficient. A finer rating is necessary to evaluate process models adequately. Thus, the documentation analysis of the SE models produced first insights but it turned out that the documentation is not comprehensive enough to ensure the validity of recommendations derived from this analysis alone.

6. Detailed Criteria of Usability: Quality aspects in UE

In order to gather more specific and detailed criteria for the assessment of SE models and the derivation of recommendations a further analysis had to be performed.

The authors believe that there is such thing as a 'common understanding' in terms of what experts think of when they talk about UE and this is certainly represented by the definition of the human-centred-design process in the DIN EN ISO 13407. Although the definitions of base practices defined in the ISO/PAS 18152 are not considered as invalid they leave leeway for interpretation as shown in section 5.

However, while this 'common understanding' seems true on a very abstract level, strong differences in how to implement these in practice can be expected. The key question therefore is not only what should be done, but rather how it can be assured that everything needed is being performed (or guaranteed) in order to gain a certain quality of a result, an activity or the process itself. In addition, the completeness and correctness of the base practices and human-centred design activities as defined in the ISO/PAS 18152 itself needs to be verified.

For a more detailed analysis, based on current real-world work practices, the authors performed semi-structured interviews and questionnaires with six experts in the field of UE. These experts are well grounded in theoretical terms, i.e. standards and process models, as well as in usability practice. As a result, overarching process- and quality characteristics were derived that led to statements about the relevance, the application and need of usability activities, methods and artefacts to be implemented in SE.

The following results highlight initial insights, especially with regards to the quality characteristics/aspects of UE activities.

A substantial part of the interviews referred explicitly to quality characteristics/aspects of the four human-centred design activities of the DIN EN ISO 13407: 'context of use', 'user requirements', 'produce design solutions' and 'evaluation of use'. The goal was to identify what constitutes the quality of a certain activity from the experts' point of view and what kind of success and quality criteria exist that are relevant on a process level and subsequently for the implementation in practice.

In summary, it can be said that the quality of the four activities essentially depends on the production and subsequent treatment of the result generated by each activity. From the quality perspective it is less important how something is accomplished, but rather to guarantee the quality of the results. In order to answer the question what constitutes this quality, the analyzed statements of the experts regarding each activity are discussed in the following paragraphs. The core characteristic (essence) of each activity is described, followed by requirements regarding the generation and treatment of content, a summary of (measurable) quality criteria and success characteristics, as well as a list of operational measures that can be used for the implementation in practice.

6.1 Context of Use

There is a common agreement of all experts involved in the study in that the fundamental goal of the activity is the formation of a deep understanding of the users, their goals, needs and the actual work context. This then forms the base for the derivation of requirements as well as for validating user requirements of the solution. The focus of the context analysis should therefore be on the original tasks and workflows, independent of concrete solutions and/or any supporting systems.

Apart from a documentation or rather communication of the analyzed knowledge it is crucial to anchor the activity within the overall process model. The context analysis provides a base for the entire process of development, in particular for deriving requirements, which provide the link to the next process step/sub-process. It generally applies that an output is only as valuable as it serves as input for a following sub-process. Thus, the context analysis must start at an early stage, preferably before any comprehensive specification is being created. This could be in a pre-study phase of the project, where neither technical platform nor details about the implementation have been determined. The quality of the context analysis and its results also depends on organisational conditions. A sufficient time schedule and the allocation of adequate resources is required in order to be able to accomplish the context analysis in an appropriate way. The support by the management and the organization is crucial in this case.

As mentioned before, the results are the most significant factor for the quality. In their comments, most experts focused on the documentation of the results, but it turned out that this is not a necessity. The important aspect is not the documentation itself. Rather, the results must exist in an adequate form so that all people involved can access or read it, and that it is comprehensible for anyone involved. With regard to the description (respectively the communication) of context information two major points have been identified that need to be considered and distinguished: First, the context information must be formulated in an appropriate way so that even people who were not involved in the process of analysis can comprehensibly understand its content. And second, the information must be unambiguous, consistent and complete. That is, only reasonable and context-relevant data is gathered and completeness (pertaining to the systems that are essential for the accomplishment of the tasks) is assured.

One major quality aspect of a successful context analysis is the ability to identify so called 'implied needs' based on the context information. Implied needs are 'those needs, which are often hidden or implied in circumstances in which requirements engineers must sharpen their understanding of the customer's preferred behavior' (ProContext, 2008). Hence, the context information must contain all details needed to derive the user requirements.

All experts agreed on the fact that the quality of the results strongly depends on the experience and qualification of the analysts. The abilities to focus on the substantial and to focus on facts (rather that interpretation) are crucial for this activity. Additionally, the experiences of the users are important as well. Their representativeness, ability to express themselves and the validity of their statements are a prerequisite for good results.

A measureable quality criterion is the amount of predictable user requirements derived based on the context information. One example: If five comparable skilled experts are asked to derive all user requirements based on the given context information independently, and if all experts finally compile a similar set of requirements in terms of quantity and meaning, then the context information could be rated as high quality. This implies that the entire user requirements could be derived based on the context information.

A success criterion for the analysis and its context information is the ability to identify coherent patterns, e.g. similar workflows, similar habits, the usage of similar tools, etc. Accordingly, the identification of non-similar workflows might imply the need for further analysis. Another success factor is the feedback obtained from presenting the results not only to the users of the system but also to the customers. Good feedback from the users implies a good solution and in combination with good customer feedback it indicates a good balance between user and business goals.

The success of a context analysis activity itself can often only be estimated/evaluated afterwards, then when the users have not found any major gaps or critical errors in the concept of the solution. Summative evaluation is a suitable method to measure this.

An additional, but difficult to quantify, quality criterion is the acceptance and the utility of the results (context information) for the process and for the organization. If the context information enables the derivation of user requirements and if it is useful to create concepts and designs out of it than it has been obviously good.

A central characteristic of good context information is that all questions that appear during the design process can be answered from it.

An important measure for ensuring the quality is the training of the analysts in applying the methodologies and methods. The qualification of the analysts determines the result's quality. Qualification means not only to know (theoretically learned), but rather to perform (practically experienced). The context analysis is the corner stone for the user-centred development and it is crucial for the success of a solution. In order to ensure its quality, it requires the integration of the activities and regarding results (deliverables) into the overall process, the supply of sufficient and qualified resources as well as appropriate time for the execution of an entire analysis within the project plan. Therefore, the support by the management and the organization is necessary.

6.2 User Requirements

The main goal of the activity 'user requirements' is to work out a deep understanding about the organisational and technical requirements, the users' workflows and the users' needs and goals of the future system. This results in a valid basis for system specifications. From the UE perspective it is crucial that this is not purely technically driven perception (as often in SE processes) but extents to a utilization- and situational-view.

The majority of the experts described the core of this activity as the specification and documentation of requirements in coordination with development, users and customers. However, the result does not always have to be defined in the way of fine-granular requirements and extensive specifications. More important is to transfer this knowledge successfully into the development process. Similar to the activity of context analysis, both the experience and skills of the analysts are essential for the success and for the quality of the results, as well as the users' representativeness, ability to express themselves and the validity of their statements.

According to statements of the experts, a set of quality criteria can be defined, both at the execution of the activity, and at the result. User requirements should have a certain formulation quality (legibility, comprehensibility, consistency, etc.) and should be formulated system-neutrally. Requirements should be based on demands (prerequisite for something that should be accomplished), which guaranteed the validity. This can be important for the argumentation when trade-offs in the development process are required. User requirements must be adequate and precisely formulated on level of the tasks. A negative example would be: „The system must be usable' - this requirement is not embodied at a task level, it is just an abstract goal. Good user requirements are not interpretable per se. The solution itself derived from the requirements is interpretable of course, but the requirements are not.

In particular the consideration of user goals and requirements and the trade-off with business goals is seen as an important success criterion. Further success criteria are the comprehensibility and utility of the results (requirements) in the further process.

In order to achieve this quality the experts recommended several measures, such as an iterative procedure during the collection and derivation of requirements. The involvement of all stakeholders (users, customer, management, development, etc.) at all stages of the process is inevitable. In particular the presentation of user requirements to the management is considered as an important means for arising awareness. Dedicated and qualified roles are also crucial for the success of the entire process (e.g. no developer should write the specification - this should be done by someone qualified and skilled).

6.3 Produce Design Solution

The design activity Produce Solution covers the creative process of transferring user requirements and knowledge about the user domain and the business perspective into design concepts for new solutions. For this, different ideas have to be produced, investigated and critiqued. As most design activities, this is an open-ended problem solving process without a unique solution, especially regarding the user interface. The main goal is to provide a functional system with a user interface that allows satisfactory interaction and efficient use (all information, no errors, no unnecessary steps, etc.), as described in the seven ISO dialogue design principles (DIN EN ISO 9241-Part 110, 2006).

Essential for a good design solution is that it handles all requirements collected in the specification (validity) but also (increasingly) that the user feels safe and confident in the use of the designed system and feels satisfied with the results. The form in which the design is created, communicated and documented is not the decisive factor. Representations can range from sketches over formal specifications to working prototypes. What is central is that the representation provides information at a level of detail that is deemed useful for implementation and can be successfully communicated.

As in most design disciplines it is considered good practice to consider design alternatives that are critiqued by experts and evaluated with users to guide the design process. Process support for such exploratory activities is considered useful and important. If questions from the users - but also from the development team - arise during these reviews it is often a strong indication that further analysis and review are required. The quality of the proposed solutions depends critically on the experience and knowledge of the persons involved in the design work. The experts consider a multidisciplinary qualification, but with a clear account of the assigned roles and competencies (developer, analyst, designer, etc.) as the key to the production of successful high quality design.

With regards to design, criteria for success and measurable quality criteria can be difficult to define. What can, however, be checked and measured are for example, the implementation of user requirements through the design, the design accordance with the principles of dialogue design (DIN EN ISO 9241-110, 2006) and information presentation standards (DIN EN ISO 9241-Part 12, 1998). Comparative studies of alternative designs and performance measurements can provide further information on design quality to guide further refinement or to identify problematic design choices.

Appropriate measures for quality assurance are to strengthen the links with the related process activities of 'user requirements' and the 'evaluation of use'. An established best practice is the use of iterative approaches in which alternative design proposals are examined and refined to evolve a suitable solution. To ensure a wide creative potential and a correspondingly large solution space the integration of a variety of roles and experts from different backgrounds into this activity is advisable. It is, however, vital that the leadership of this activity is assigned to a qualified user interface designer, whose role is explicitly communicated and who has the final decision power in this activity. This must be communicated to the complete team and adequately supported by the management.

6.4 Evaluation of Use

The central aim of the 'evaluation of use' activity is to collect feedback on the practical use of a system design in order to refine the design and the system. Problems in use are to be identified and subsequently corrected. The key to a successful integration of evaluation into a development process is to consider it as a continuous ongoing activity throughout the process. Of course, the methodology and applied techniques have to be adapted to the maturity of the design representations/implementation at different stages of development. Evaluation is most useful in the larger process context, as many evaluation methods identify problems, but provide no solution for the problems found. It is therefore important to not only identify problems but to feed this information back into the design process to resolve the identified issues. This should be reflected in the process. It is critical that the results of this activity are used in the ongoing process. Therefore the information must be available in a form that is understandable to the stakeholders in the development process.

The quality of the activity 'evaluation of use' is primarily defined by the results. In this activity what was previously designed (based on the preceding analysis) and implemented is now evaluated. It is crucial that mayor usability problems are identified at this stage, especially issues that are seen as disruptive from the user's perspective. Second categories of problems cover issues that are valid but do not necessarily disturb users, which are less critical. The activity can be considered completed, once no new significant problems are found. The commitment of all stakeholders, the expertise of usability experts and the ability of stakeholders to accept criticism and to act constructively on it are of central importance for the success of the evaluation activity. Measurable quality criteria can be derived from the selection and use of established evaluation methods (Freymann, M. 2007).

Decisive measures for quality assurance include the qualification of key stakeholders in evaluation techniques and process, the explication of the evaluation as an essential activity in the process and the allocation of sufficient time for multiple iterations of design-evaluation cycles in the process plan.

7. Summary & Outlook

Today, the usability of a software product is no longer only a crucial quality criterion for the users but also for the organizations. It can be seen as unique selling point in the competitive market. However, the various differences in each organisation's structure, its process model, development process and the organizational conditions makes it difficult to transfer the knowledge about usability methodologies, methods and techniques into practice. There are many different approaches to integrate usability engineering and software engineering but each focuses on different measures. Some are very specific, e.g. to an organization or to a development process, while others are very abstract, e.g. to process models. However, each of them has its authority and each leads to the regarding results in detail on a specific level of abstraction. However, there are fewer approaches that combine approaches on all levels of abstractions. The presented approach identifies integration points between software engineering and usability engineering on three different levels of abstractions. The authors showed that standards define an overarching framework for both disciplines. Process models describe systematic and planable approaches for the implementation and the operational process in which the process models are tailored to fit the specifics of an organization.

On the first level ('level of standards') the authors analyzed, compared and contrasted the software engineering standard ISO/IEC 12207 with the usability engineering standard DIN EN ISO 13407 and identified a set of 'common activities' as part of both disciplines. These activities define the overarching framework for the next level, the 'level of process models'.

In order to identify the maturity of software engineering process models' ability to create usable products, the authors used a two-step approach to synthesize the demands of usability engineering and performed an assessment of selected software engineering models.

To obtain detailed knowledge about usability engineering activities, methods, deliverables and their regarding quality aspects, the authors analyzed the two usability engineering standards DIN EN ISO 13407 and the ISO/PAS 18152. The ISO/PAS 18152 defines detailed base practices that specify the tasks for creating usable products. These base practices have been used as a foundation to derive requirements that represent the 'common activities'' usability engineering perspective. The quantity of fulfilled requirements for each activity of the framework informs about the level of compliance of the software engineering model satisfying the base practices and therewith the usability perspective of activities.

The results of the assessment provide an overview about the degree of compliance of the selected models with usability engineering demands. It turned out that there is a relatively small compliance to the usability engineering activities across all selected software engineering models. This is an indicator that only little integration between usability engineering and software engineering exists. There are less overlaps between the disciplines regarding these activities and therefore it is necessary to provide suitable interfaces to create a foundation for the integration.

The analysis of software engineering models also showed that more detailed and adequate criteria for the assessment are necessary by which objective and reliable statements about process models and their ability to create usable software could be made. Therefore the authors performed a second analysis and conducted expert interviews and questionnaires to elicit appropriate criteria for the evaluation of software engineering models. A substantial part of the questions referred explicitly to quality characteristics/aspects of the four human-centred design activities of the DIN EN ISO 13407: 'context of use', 'user requirements', 'produce design solutions' and 'evaluation of use'. The goal was to identify, what constitutes the quality of a certain activity from the experts' point of view and what kind of success and quality criteria exist that are relevant on a process level and subsequently for the implementation in practice.

The results highlight first insights especially regarding quality aspects of usability engineering activities. Even if these could not be generalized, the results reflect the experts' fundamental tendencies and opinions.

Beyond this, it could have been proved that there is such thing as 'common mind' in terms of what experts think of when they talk about user centred design and this is certainly represented by the definition of the human-centred-design process in the DIN EN ISO 13407. However, even if the experts' opinions sometimes differ on how to implement these activities (e.g. in using methodologies, methods, tools, etc.), they follow the same goal: to ensure a specific quality of these activities. Thus, there is no generic answer of how an activity has to be performed in detail - the question is how to assure that everything needed is being performed in order to gain a certain quality of a result, an activity or the process itself. This article shows first results on this important question.

The presented approach does not only highlight weaknesses of software engineering process models, it additionally identifies opportunities for the integration between software engineering and usability engineering. These can be used as a foundation to implement the operational process level and will help to guarantee the interplay of software engineering and usability engineering in practice, which is part of the authors' future work.

The gathered knowledge about the quality aspects of usability engineering can serve as a basis for a successful integration with software engineering and leads to high quality results and activities.

In the future, the authors expect to derive specific recommendations to enrich software engineering models by adding or adapting usability engineering activities, phases, artefacts, etc. By doing this, the development of usable software on the level of process models will be guaranteed. Furthermore, the authors will present further results based on the questionnaires and will work out a guideline/checklist of usability engineering demands that account for the integration of usability engineering into software engineering models.

8. Acknowledgement

We would like to express our sincere appreciation to all those who have contributed, directly or indirectly, to this work in form of technical or other support. In particular we would like to thank Markus Düchting for his assistance. A special thank to Lennart Grötzbach always helping us to find the right words. We would like to thank Thomas Geis and Jan Gulliksen for the fruitful and intensive discussions and the helpful input. We also like to thank the remaining interview partners for their help and efforts.

9. References

Boehm, B. (1988). A Spiral Model of Software Development and Enhancement. *IEEE Computer*, Vol. 21, pp. 61-72

Constantine, L., Biddle, R. and Noble, J. (2003). Usage-centered design and software engineering. Models for integration, In: *IFIP Working Group 2.7/13.4*, ICSE 2003 Workshop on Bridging the Gap Between Software Engineering and Human-Computer Interaction, Portland, Oregon

Cooper, A. & Reimann, R. (2003). *About Face 2.0.*, Wiley, Indianapolis, IN

DIN EN ISO 13407 (1999). Human-centered design processes for interactive systems, CEN - European Committee for Standardization, Brussels

DIN EN ISO 9241-12 (1998) Ergonomic requirements for office work with visual display terminals (VDTs) - Part 12: Presentation of information, ISO Copyright Office, Geneva, Switzerland

DIN EN ISO 9241-110 (2006), Ergonomics of human-system interaction - Part 110: Dialogue principles, ISO Copyright Office, Geneva, Switzerland

Faulkner, X. (2000a). *Usability Engineering*, pp. 10-12, PALGARVE, New York, USA

Faulkner, X. & Culwin, F. (2000b). Enter the Usability Engineer: Integrating HCI and Software Engineering. *Proceedings of ITicSE 2000 7/00*, ACM Press, Helsinki, Finnland.

Freymann, M. (2007). Klassifikation nutzerzentrierter Evaluationsmethoden im User Centered Design Prozess, *Diploma Thesis*, University of Paderborn, Germany

Glinz, M. (1999). Eine geführte Tour durch die Landschaft der Software-Prozesse und - Prozessverbesserung, *Informatik – Informatique*, Vol. 6/1999, pp. 7-15

Granollers, T., Lorès, J. & Perdrix, F. (2002). Usability Engineering Process Model. Integration with Software Engineering, *Proceedings of HCI International 2003*, Crete, Greece, June 22-27-2003, Lawrence Erlbaum Associates, New Jersey, USA

Hakiel, S. (1997). Delivering ease of use, In: *Computing & Control Engineering Journal*, Vol. 8, Issue 2, 04/97, p. 81-87

IBM (2004). Ease of Use Model. Retrieved from http://www-3.ibm.com/ibm/easy /eou_ext.nsf/ publish/1996, (11/2004)

ISO/IEC 12207 (2002). Information technology - Software life cycle processes, Amendment 1, 2002-05-01, ISO copyright office, Switzerland

ISO/PAS 18152 (2003). Ergonomics of human-system interaction – Specification for the process assessment of human-system issues, First Edition, 2003-10-01, ISO copyright office, Switzerland

Jerome, B. & Kazman R. (2005). Surveying the Solitudes. An Investigation into the relationships between Human Computer Interaction and Software Engineering in Practice, *In: Human-Centered Software Engineering – Integrating Usability in the Software Development Lifecycle*, Ahmed Seffah, Jan Gulliksen and Michel C. Desmarais, 59-70, Springer Netherlands, 978-1-4020-4027-6, Dordrecht, Netherlands

Jokela, T. (2001). An Assessment Approach for User-Centred Design Processes. In: *Proceedings of EuroSPI 2001*, Limerick Institute of Technology Press, Limerick

Juristo, N., Windl, H., Constantaine, L. (2001). Special Issue on Usability Engineering in Software Development, In: *IEEE Software*, Vol. 18, no. 1

KBST (2006). V-Modell 97. Retrieved from: http://www.kbst.bund.de , 05/2006

Mayhew, D. J. (1999). *The Usablility Engineering Lifecycle*, Morgan Kaufmann, San Francisco

McCracken, D.D., Jackson M.A. (1982). Life-Cycle Concept Considered Harm-ful. *ACM Software Engineering Notes*, 4/1982, pp. 29-32

Nebe, K. & Zimmermann, D. (2007a). Suitability of Software Engineering Models for the Production of Usable Software, *Proceedings of the Engineering Interactive Systems 2007*, Lecture Notes In Computer Science (LNCS), Salamanca, Spain (in print)

Nebe, K. & Zimmermann, D. (2007b). Aspects of Integrating User Centered Design to Software Engineering Processes, *Human-Computer Interaction. Interaction Design and Usability*, Vol. 4550/2007, pp. 194-203, Beijing, P.R. China

Nebe, K., Düchting, M., Zimmermann, D. & Paelke, V. (2007c). Qualitätsaspekte bei der Integration von User Centred Design Aktivitäten in Softwareentwicklungsprozesse, *Proceedings of Mensch & Computer 2008*, Lübeck, Germany (in print)

Norman, D.A. & Draper, S.W. (1986). Eds. User Centered System Design. Laurence Erlbaum

Patel, D., Wang, Y (eds.) (2000). Comparative software engineering. Review and perspectives, In: *Annals of Software Engineering*, Vol. 10, pp. 1-10, Springer, Netherlands

ProContext (2008). retrieved from: http://www.procontext.com/en/methods/context-scenario/implied-needs.html, 07/2008

Radle, K. & Young, S. (2001). Partnering Usability with Development. How Three Organizations Succeeded, In: *IEEE Software*, January/February 2001.

Rideout, T., Uyeda, K. & Williams, E. (1989). Evolving The Software Usability Engineering Process at Hewlett-Packard, *Proceedings of Systems, Man and Cybernetics 1989*, Vol. 1, pp. 229-234

Royce, Winston W. (1970). Managing the Development of Large Software Systems: Concepts and Techniques. In: *Technical Papers of Western Electronic Show and Convention (WesCon)*, pp. 328-338, August 25-28, Los Angeles, USA

Sommerville, I. (2004). *Software Engineering*, 7th ed, Pearson Education Limited, Essex, GB

Sutcliffe, A. (2005). Convergence or competition between software engineering and human computer interaction, In: *Human-Centered Software Engineering – Integrating Usability in the Software Development Lifecycle*, Ahmed Seffah, Jan Gulliksen and Michel C. Desmarais, 71-84, Springer Netherlands, 978-1-4020-4027-6, Dordrecht, Netherlands

Woletz, N. (2006). Evaluation eines User-Centred Design-Prozessassessments - Empirische Untersuchung der Qualität und Gebrauchstauglichkeit im praktischen Einsatz. *Doctoral Thesis*, 4/2006, University of Paderborn, Paderborn, Germany

Venturi, G. & Troost, J. (2004). Survey on the UCD integration in the industry. *Proceedings of NordiCHI '04*, pp. 449-452, Tampere, Finland, October 23-27, 2004, ACM Press, New York, USA

21

Automated Methods for Webpage Usability & Accessibility Evaluations

Hidehiko Okada[1] and Ryosuke Fujioka[2]
[1] *Kyoto Sangyo University,* [2] *Kobe Sogo Sokki Co. Ltd.*
Japan

1. Introduction

Because of the rapid growth of the web and its users, web usability and accessibility become more and more important. This chapter describes two automated methods for evaluating usability/accessibility of webpages. The first method, for usability evaluation, is based on interaction logging and analyses, and the second method, for accessibility evaluation, is based on machine learning. In the following Sections 2 and 3, the two methods are described respectively.

Several methods have been proposed and developed for usability evaluation based on user interaction logs. Interaction logs can be recorded by computer logging programs (automated logging) or by human evaluators (observational logging). Analysis methods and tools for the former type of logs are well summarized by Ivory (Ivory & Hearst, 2001; Ivory, 2003), and those for the latter type of logs have also been developed (for example, by Qiang (Qiang et al., 2005)). Our method is for analyzing former type of logs. In the survey by Ivory, analysis methods for automatically captured log files for WIMP (Window, Icon, Menu and Pointing device) applications and web applications are categorized in terms of their approaches including metric-based, pattern-based, task-based and inferential ones. Some of the methods with the task-based approach compare user interaction logs for a test task with desired (expected) interaction sequences for the task and detect inconsistencies between the user logs and the desired sequences (Kishi, 1995; Uehling & Wolf, 1995; Okada & Asahi, 1996; Al-Qaimari & Mcrostie, 1999; Helfrich & Landay, 1999; Zettlemoyer et al., 1999). The inconsistencies are useful cues for finding usability problems: for example, an evaluator can find that users selected some unexpected link on a webpage when another link on the page was expected for the test task and that the link selected by the users may have some usability problem in its design (labeling, layout, etc.).

The existing methods require widget-level logs for the comparisons. For example, the method proposed by Okada (Okada & Asahi, 1996) requires interaction logs to include data of widget properties such as widget label, widget type, title of parent window, etc. This requirement degrades independency and completeness of the methods in logging user interactions with systems under evaluation. Section 2 in this chapter describes our method that detects inconsistencies between user logs and desired sequences based on logs of *clicked points ((x, y) coordinate values)*. Coordinate values of clicked points can be easily and fully logged independently of what widgets are clicked on. Several existing methods have also utilized the logs of mouse clicked points (for example, "Mousemap" that visualizes mouse moves (Gellner & Forbrig, 2003)), but the methods do not achieve the detection of inconsistencies. The authors have developed a computer tool for logging and analyzing user interactions and desired sequences by our method. The tool is applied to experimental usability evaluations of websites. Effectiveness of the method in usability testing of webpages is evaluated based on the application result.

Besides, to make webpages more accessible to people with disabilities, <table> tags should not be used as a means to visually layout document content: layouting contents by <table> tags may present problems when rendering to non-visual media (W3C, 1999ab). It is reported that the number of tables on pages doubled from 7 in 2000 to 14 in 2003, with most tables being used to control page layouts (Ivory & Megraw, 2005). Therefore, to evaluate the accessibility of webpages, it should be checked whether the pages include layout-purpose <table> tags. Several methods and tools have been proposed and developed for web accessibility (Cooper, 1999; Scapin et al., 2000; Ivory, 2003; Ivory et al., 2003; Abascal et al., 2004; Brajnik, 2004; Beirekdar et al., 2005; Vanderdonckt & Beirekdar, 2005). Accessibility tools are listed in (W3C, 2006; Perlman, 2008) and compared in (Brinck et al., 2002). Some tools detect deeply nested <table> tags that are likely to be layout-purpose ones. Still, a method for automated detection of layout-purpose <table> tags in HTML sources is a challenge: it requires further than simply checking whether specific tags and/or attributes of the tags are included in the sources. Section 3 describes our method for the detection that is based on machine learning. The proposed method derives a <table> tag classifier that classifies the purpose of the tag: the classifier deduces whether a <table> tag is a layout-purpose one or a table-purpose one. The section describes our system that implements the proposed method and report a result of experiment for evaluating classification accuracy.

2. Automated Method for Webpage Usability Evaluation

2.1 Method for analyzing mouse click logs

2.1.1 User logs and desired logs

A user log can be collected by logging mouse clicks while a user (who does not know the desired sequence of a test task) performs the test task in user testing. In our research, a log file is collected for a test user and a test task: if the number of users is N and the number of tasks is M then the number of user log files is N*M (where all the N users completes all the M tasks). A "desired" log is collected by logging mouse clicks while a user (who knows well the desired sequence of a test task) performs the test task. For a test task, one desired log file is usually collected. If two or more different interaction sequences are acceptable as desired ones for a test task, two or more desired log files can be collected (and used in the comparison described later).

2.1.2 Method for detecting inconsistencies in user/desired logs

Our method models two successive clicks as a vector and thus a sequence of operation in a user/desired log as a sequence of vectors. A vector is from the ith clicked point to the (i+1)th clicked point in the screen. To detect inconsistencies in a user log and a desired log, each vector from the user log is compared with each vector from the desired log. If the distance of the two vectors ($\mathbf{v}_u$ from the user log and $\mathbf{v}_d$ from the desired log) is smaller than a threshold, $\mathbf{v}_u$ and $\mathbf{v}_d$ are judged as being matched: the user operation modeled by $\mathbf{v}_u$ is supposed to be the same operation modeled by $\mathbf{v_d}$. The method defines the distance $D(\mathbf{v_u}, \mathbf{v_d})$ as a weighted sum of D_p and D_v (Fig. 1).

$$D_p = (w_x(x_{u1}-x_{d1})^2 + w_y(y_{u1}-y_{d1})^2)^{0.5} \quad (1)$$

$$D_v = (w_x(x_{u2}-(x_{u1}-x_{d1})-x_{d2})^2 + w_y(y_{u2}-(y_{u1}-y_{d1})-y_{d2})^2)^{0.5} \quad (2)$$

$$D(\mathbf{v_u}, \mathbf{v_d}) = w_pD_p + w_vD_v \quad (3)$$

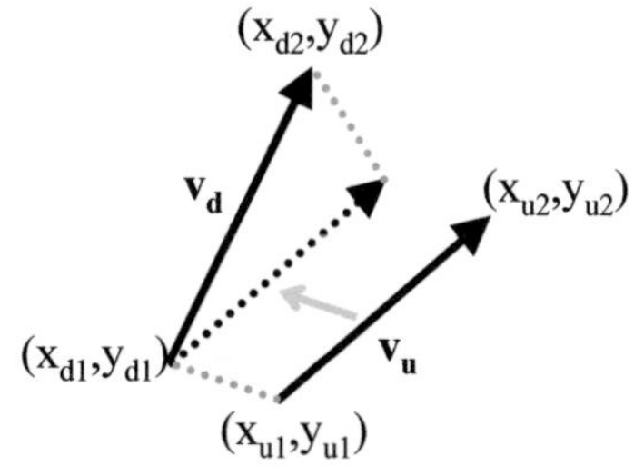

Figure 1. Two vectors $\mathbf{v_u}$, $\mathbf{v_d}$ and their distance

The role of weight factors w_x and w_y used in the calculations of D_p and D_v is as follows. Users click on links in webpages under evaluation to perform their tasks. The width of a link is usually larger than the height of the link, especially of a text link. Therefore, the differences of clicked points for clicking on the same link are likely to become larger for the horizontal axis (the x coordinate values) than for the vertical axis (the y coordinate values). To deal with this, weights w_x and w_y are used so that the horizontal differences can be counted smaller than the vertical differences.

User operations to scroll webpages by using mouse wheels should also be taken into account: scrolls by mouse wheels changes widget (e.g., link) positions in the screen so that the clicked positions may not be the same even for the same widget. Our method records the amount of wheel scrolls while logging interactions. By using the logs of wheel scrolls, coordinate values of clicked points are adjusted. Fig. 2 shows this adjustment. Suppose a user clicked on the point (x_i, y_i) in the screen (Fig. 2(a)) and then clicked on the point (x_{i+1}, y_{i+1}) (Fig. 2(b)). In this case, the vector derived from the two clicks is the one shown in Fig. 2(c). As another case, suppose a user scrolled down a webpage along the y axis by using the mouse wheel between the two clicks and the amount of the scroll was S pixels. In this case, the vector derived from the two clicks is the one in Fig. 2(d).

2.1.3 Two types of inconsistencies as cues of usability problems

As cues of usability problems, the proposed method detects two types of inconsistencies between user interactions and desired sequences. The authors refer to them as "unnecessary" operations and "missed" operations. Fig. 3 illustrates these kinds of operations.

Unnecessary operations are user operations judged as not included in the desired sequences, i.e., unnecessary operations are operations in a user log for which any operation in desired logs is not judged as the same one in the comparison of the user/desired logs. Our method supposes such user operations as unnecessary because the operations may not be necessary for completing the test task. Unnecessary operations can be cues for human evaluators to find usability problems that users clicked on a confusing link when another link is desired (expected) to be clicked on for the task.

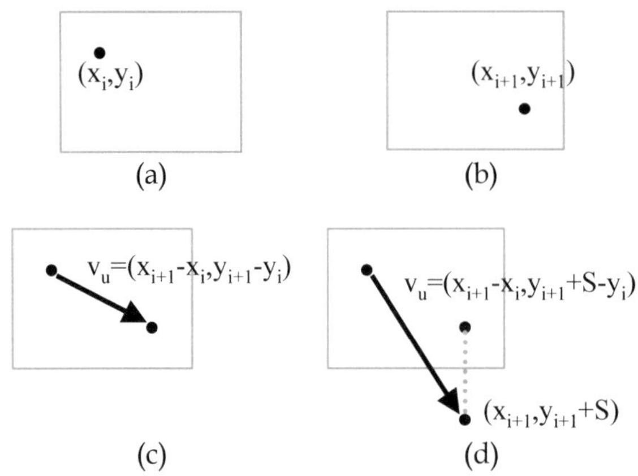

Figure 2. Adjustment of clicked point for mouse wheel scroll

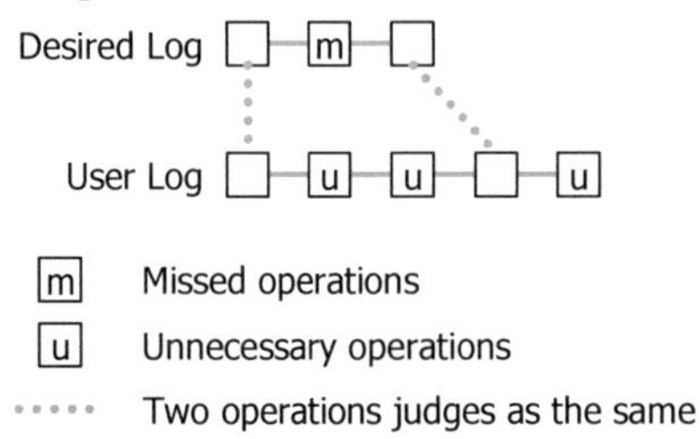

Figure 3. Unnecessary operations and missed operations

Missed operations are desired operations judged as not included in the user interaction sequences, i.e., missed operations are operations in desired logs for which any operation in a user log is not judged as the same one. Our method supposes such user operations as missed because the operations may be necessary for completing the test task but the user finished the task without performing the operations. Missed operations can be cues for human evaluators to find usability problems that a link is not clear enough or not easy to find for users. Our method models an operation in a user/desired log by a vector derived from clicked point logs, so the method detects unnecessary/missed operations as unnecessary/missed vectors.

Suppose two or more successive operations are unnecessary ones in a user log. In this case, the first operation is likely to be the best cue in the successive unnecessary operations. This is because the user might deviate from the desired sequence by the first operation (i.e., the expected operation is not clear enough for the user) and had performed additional operations irrelevant to the test task until the user returned to the desired sequence. Our method can extract the first operations in the successive unnecessary operations and show them to human evaluators so that the evaluators can efficiently analyze usability problem cues (unnecessary operations in this case).

The idea of analyzing unnecessary/missed operations in user interaction logs (inconsistencies in user/desired logs) is not novel (e.g., Okada & Asahi, 1996), but our method described in this section is unique in that it extracts those inconsistent operations from logs of clicked points (logs of (x, y) coordinate values), not widget-level logs.

2.1.4 Unnecessary/missed operations common to users

Unnecessary/missed operations common in many of test users are useful cues for finding problems less independently of individual differences among the users. Our method analyzes how many users performed the same unnecessary/missed operation.

The analysis of the user ratio for the same missed operation is simple: for each missed operation, the number of user logs that do not include the desired operation is counted. To analyze the user ratio for the same unnecessary operation, the method compares unnecessary operations extracted from all user logs of the test task. This comparison is achieved by the same way as operations (vectors) in user/desired logs are compared. By this comparison, unnecessary operations common among multiple users can be extracted (Fig. 4).

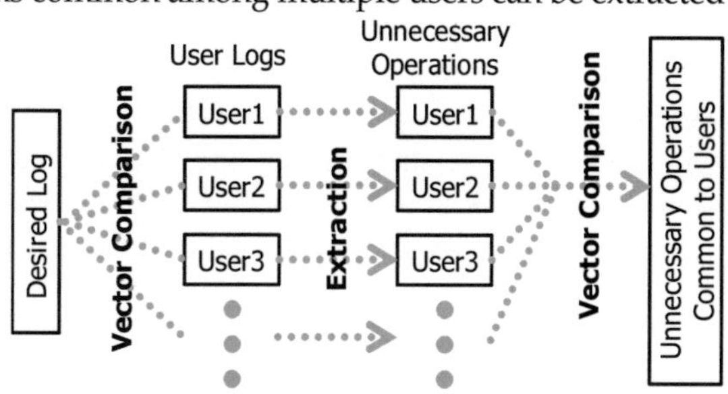

Figure 4. Extraction of unnecessary operations common to users

2.2 Evaluating effectiveness based on case study

2.2.1 Design of experiment

Ten websites of business/public organizations were selected. For each site, a test task was designed. The average number of clicks in the designed sequences for the ten test tasks was 3.9. Five university students participated in this experiment as test users. Each test user was asked to perform the task on each site. They had enough knowledge and experience in using webpages with a PC web browser but they used the websites for the first time. The desired sequences of the test tasks were not told to the test users. Thus, if the desired sequences are not clear enough for the test users, the users are likely to deviate from the desired sequences and unnecessary and/or missed operations are observed. The interaction of each user for each test task was logged into a user log file. To avoid fatigue affecting the results, the time of experiment for each user was limited to 60+ minutes: each test user was asked to perform a test task within five or ten minutes depending on the task size.

Fifty user logs (five users * ten tasks) and ten desired logs (a log per test task) were collected. For each task, our tool implementing the proposed method analyzed the logs and extracted possible cues of usability problems (i.e., unnecessary/missed operations). An evaluator tried to find usability problems based on the extracted cues.

2.2.2 Weight factors and thresholds for vector distance

Our method requires us to determine the values of weight factors w_x, w_y, w_p and w_v and the threshold value of vector distance (see 2.1.2). To determine these values, a pre-experiment was conducted with another test user. Based on the analysis of the log files collected by the pre-experiment, appropriate values were determined that led an accurate result in detecting unnecessary/missed operations. Values in the row labeled as "Original" in Table 1 show the obtained values.

	w_x	w_y	w_p	w_v	Threshold (pixel)
Original	0.4	1.0	0.5	1.0	100
Variation A	0.4	1.0	0.0	1.0	67
Variation B	0.4	1.0	1.0	0.0	34

Table 1. Values of weight factors and threshold for vector distance

In our method, distance of two operations (vectors) is defined by Eqs. (1)-(3). In the case where $w_v = 0$ and $w_p = 1$, $D(\mathbf{v_u}, \mathbf{v_d}) = D_p$ so that two operations are not compared on the basis of two successive clicks (i.e., on the basis of vectors) but compared on the basis of a single click. In this case, a click in a user log and a click in a desired log are judged as the same operation if the clicked points are near. Similarly, in the case where $w_p = 0$ and $w_v = 1$, $D(\mathbf{v_u}, \mathbf{v_d}) = D_v$ so that two operations are compared by the size of vector difference only (i.e., the absolute position on which the click is performed in the screen is not considered). These two variations of the method were also evaluated in addition to the original one. Variations A/B in Table 1 denote them in which $(w_p, w_v) = (0.0, 1.0)$ and $(1.0, 0.0)$, respectively.

2.2.3 Number of problems found

To evaluate the effectiveness of our method in finding usability problems, the number of problems found by the method were compared with the number by a method based on manual observation of user interactions. In addition to record click logs in user interaction sessions, PC screen image had been captured to movie files (a screen recorder program was used in the PC). A human evaluator observed user interactions with the replay of the captured screen movies and tried to find usability problems. This manual method is expected to require much time for the interaction observation but contribute to find problems thoroughly. In this experiment, the evaluator who tried to find problems by the proposed method and the evaluator who tried to find problems by the manual method were different so that the result with a method did not bias the result with another method.

Table 2 shows the number of problems found by each of the methods. The values in the table are the sum for the ten test tasks (sites). Eleven problems were shared in the four sets of the problems, i.e., the proposed (original) method contributed to find 61% (=11/18) of the problems found by the manual method. Although the number of problems found by the proposed method was smaller than the manual method, the time for a human evaluator to find the problems by the proposed method was much less than the time by the manual method. In the case of the manual method, an evaluator had to investigate all clicks by the users because user clicks that would be possible problem cues were not automatically extracted. In the case of the proposed method, an evaluator required to investigate smaller number of clicks extracted as possible problem cues by the method. In this experiment, the number of clicks to be investigated in the case of the proposed method was 10-20% of the number in the case of the manual method.

This result of case study indicates that the proposed method will

- contribute to find usability problems to a certain extent in terms of the number of problems, and
- be much efficient in terms of the time required.

Method	#Problems
Manual	18
Original	15
Variation A	14
Variation B	13

Table 2. Number of problems found by each method

2.2.4 Unnecessary/missed operations contributing to finding problems

Not all unnecessary/missed operations extracted by the proposed method may contribute to finding usability problems. As the number of unnecessary/missed operations that contribute to finding problems is larger, the problems can be found more efficiently. The contribution ratio was investigated for the proposed method and its variations (Table 3). Values in the "Counts (first)" column are the counts of unnecessary operations that were the first in two or more successive unnecessary operations (see 2.1.3). For example, the original method extracted four missed operations in total from log files of the ten test tasks, and 25.0% (one) of the four operations contributed to finding a problem. Similarly, the original method extracted 375 unnecessary operations in total, and 7.5% (28) of the 375 operations contributed to finding problems.

	Missed Operations		Unnecessary Operations			
Method	Counts	Ratio	Counts (all)	Ratio	Counts (first)	Ratio
Original	4	25.0%	375	7.5%	51	49.0%
Variation A	8	37.5%	422	5.7%	58	39.7%
Variation B	1	0.0%	299	9.4%	72	37.5%

Table 3. Number of unnecessary and missed operations found by each method and the ratio of contribution in finding problems

Findings from the result in Table 3 are as follows.

- In the three methods, the ratios were larger for unnecessary operations (first) than those for unnecessary operations (all). This result supports our idea that an evaluator can find usability problems more efficiently by analyzing the first operations only in successive unnecessary operations.
- In the result of unnecessary operations (first), the ratio for the original method was larger than either of the two variations. In the result of missed operations, the ratio for the original method was larger than that for the variation B but smaller than that for the variation A. This indicates that both the original method and its variation A are promising ones.

See Section 4 for the conclusion of this research on the log-based usability evaluation method.

3. Automated Method for Webpage Accessibility Evaluation

3.1 Basic idea

<Table> tags are used for (a) expressing data tables as the tags are originally designed for or (b) adjusting the layout of document contents. In the case where a <table> tag is used for the

table-purpose, the data in the same row or column are semantically related with each other (e.g., values of the same property for several data items, or values of several properties for the same data item) and the relation can be expressed by row/column headers. On the contrary, in the case where a <table> tag is used for the layout-purpose, the data in the same row or column may not be semantically related. Thus, to deduce the purpose of a <table> tag in a fundamental approach, it should be analyzed whether or not the data in the same row/column of the table are the semantically related ones. To make the analyses automated by a computer program requires a method for semantic analyses of table contents, but the automated semantic analyses with enough precision and independency for any kinds of webpages is hard to achieve.

Our basic idea focuses on machine-readable design attributes of a table instead of analyzing semantics of data in a table. If some common design pattern is found in some attribute values of layout-purpose <table> tags and another common design pattern is found in the attribute values of table-purpose <table> tags, the two purposes can be discriminated by denoting classification rules based on the design patterns. However, it is unknown whether we can find such design patterns, and even if we can, it will be hard for us to manually investigate common patterns by analyzing design attribute values in a large number of <table> tag instances and denote sufficient rules to precisely classify the tags. In our research, the authors manually investigate design attributes only: to automatically derive classification rules, a machine learning method is utilized.

Among several kinds of machine learning methods available, ID3 (Quinlan, 1986), a method for deriving a decision tree from a set of data instances, is utilized. An advantage of a decision tree as a classifier over other forms of classifiers (e.g., a multi-layered neural network) is that classification rules are obtained as tree-formed explicit if-then rules and thus easy to read for human users of the method.

3.2 <Table> tag design attributes for classification rules

The authors first collected and investigated <table> tag instances (webpage HTML sources in which <table> tags were included) and extracted design attributes of <table> tags that were likely to contribute to the classification. Webpages were collected from various categories in Yahoo webpage directory so that the pages were not biased from the viewpoint of page categories. The authors manually judged purposes of the <table> tag instances in the collected pages. By this way, 200 <table> tags were collected, a half of which were layout-purpose ones and the others table-purpose ones. The authors then extracted common design patterns for each set of <table> tags. Findings were as follows.

Common design patterns in layout-purpose <table> tags

- <Table> tags are nested.
- Some cell(s) in the table include(s) image(s).
- The number of HTML tags that appear before the <table> tag in the source is small.
- Some cells in the table are spanned.
- The width and/or height are/is specified.

Common design patterns in table-purpose <table> tags

- The table has visible border lines.
- The table includes many rows.
- <Th> tags for row/column headers are included.
- Table titles are specified.

By denoting classification rules based on these common design patterns, it will be possible to deduce the purposes of <table> tags to a certain extent. To derive the rules in a form of decision tree by ID3, 10 attributes in Table 4 were determined.

- Binary values for the eight attributes of "border"-"width" mean whether or not the table has visible borders, captions, etc. For example, if the border attribute is specified for the <table> tag and the attribute value is 1 or more then border = Y (Yes), else border = N (No).
- A value of the attribute "num_tag" is the number of HTML tags that appear before the <table> tags in the source. In counting the tags, those in the header part are not counted.
- A value of the attribute "num_tr" is the number of rows (<tr> tags) in the table.

Name	Meaning	Values
border	Whether the table has visible border lines.	Binary
caption	Whether the table has a caption.	
height	Whether the table height is specified.	
img	Whether a cell in the table includes an item of image data.	
nest	Whether the table includes a nested table in itself.	
span	Whether some cells are spanned.	
th	Whether a row/column has a title header for the data in the row/column.	
width	Whether the table width is specified.	
num_tag	The number of HTML tags that appear before the <table> tags in the source.	Positive integer
num_tr	The number of rows in the table.	

Table 4. Attributes for decision tree

3.3 System configuration for the proposed method

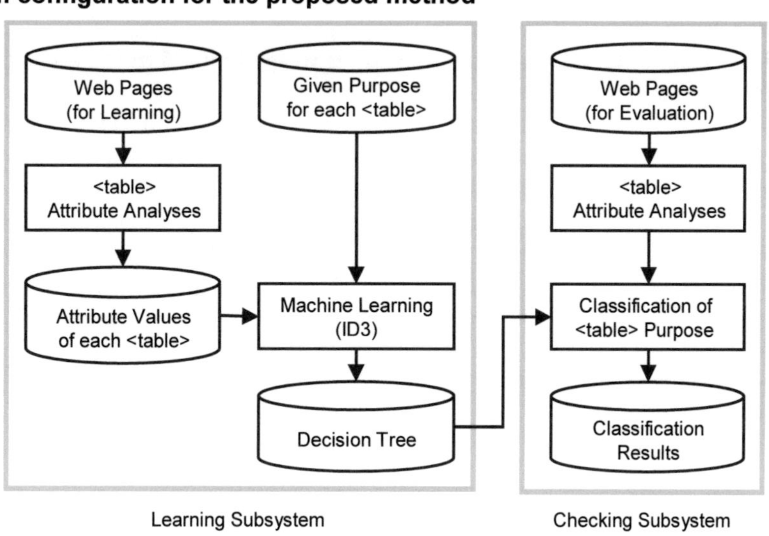

Figure 5. System configuration for the proposed method

Fig. 5 shows the system configuration for our method. In the learning phase, the method derives rules for classifying <table> tags from a set of webpages in which layout/table-purpose <table> tags are included. First, for each <table> tag in the learning data, attribute values are obtained by analyzing the webpage HTML source in which the tag is included. The purpose of each tag in the learning data is given by manual judgments in collecting the learning data. From these data of attribute values and given purposes, classification rules are derived by a machine learning method. In the case where ID3 is applied as the learning method, the rules are obtained as a decision tree (i.e., tree-formed if-then rules). In the checking phase, <table> tags (of which the purpose is unknown) are classified by the rules obtained in the learning phase. Attribute values of each <table> tag for the classification are obtained by the same way as in the learning phase (the <table> attribute analyses module in Fig. 5 is shared by the learning and checking subsystems). The obtained attribute values are applied to if parts of the rules, and the purpose of each <table> is deduced by the rule of which the if part is satisfied.

3.4 Evaluation of the proposed method

3.4.1 Evaluation method

To evaluate the effectiveness of our method, the authors investigated the classification accuracy by 10-fold cross validation (CV) with the 200 <table> tags collected (see 3.2). The 200 tags were randomly divided into 10 groups (G1, G2, ..., G10). A decision tree was derived by ID3 applying to 180 <table> tags in 9 groups excluding Gi, and the classification accuracy was checked with 20 <table> tags in Gi (i=1,2,...,10). The accuracy rate was calculated as follows.

$$\text{Accuracy Rate} = (\text{Number of <table> tags correctly classified})/20 \qquad (4)$$

Ten values of the accuracy rate were obtained by a trial of 10-fold CV. The authors tested the 10-fold CV three times and statistically investigated the accuracy rates.

3.4.2 Decision trees obtained by ID3

By the three trials of 10-fold CVs, 30 decision trees were obtained in total. Examples of the decision trees are shown in Tables 5-7 (only the nodes in the depth 3 are shown). Values in the "No." column are the serial numbers of the nodes where the #0 node is the root node. Tables 5-7 denote parent-child node relationships by indents in the "Rule Element" column. For example, in Table 5, the #1 and #8 nodes are child nodes of the #0 node and the #2 and #5 nodes are child nodes of the #1 node. Values in the "Rule Element" column are the conditions in if-parts of rules. Conditions that appear in a path from the root node to a leaf node are connected with AND. Values in the "Table" and "Layout" columns are the numbers of table/layout-purpose <table> tags in the learning data included in the node. For example, Table 5 shows the followings.

- The root node includes 89 table-purpose tags and 91 layout-purpose tags (see #0 node).
- Of the 180 <table> tags in the root node,
  - those with border=N are 86. Nine tags are table-purpose ones and the other 77 tags are layout-purpose ones (see #1 node), and
  - those with border=Y are 94. Eighty tags are table-purpose ones and the other 14 tags are layout-purpose ones (see #8 node).
- Leaf nodes are those of which the value in the "Table" column or the "Layout" column

is 0. A leaf node corresponds to an if-then rule. For example, the #3 node denotes that all tags that meet the condition:

(border = N) and (num_tr <= 7) and (num_tag <= 12)

are layout-purpose ones. Thus, the following rule is obtained from the #3 node.

"If (border = N) and (num_tr <= 7) and (num_tag <= 12) then the tag is a layout-purpose one."

The examples of decision trees shown in Tables 5-7 are typical ones in the 30 trees obtained. The other trees had similar structures from the root node to nodes in depth 3 as either of the three examples. The 30 trees reveal that the attributes border, num_tr, num_tag and nest is likely to appear in the upper layers of the tree, i.e., these attributes well contribute to the classification.

No.	Rule Element	Table	Layout	Total
0	(root)	89	91	180
1	border = N	9	77	86
2	num_tr <= 7	1	71	72
3	num_tag <= 12	0	66	66
4	num_tag > 12	1	5	6
5	num_tr > 7	8	6	14
6	nest = N	8	1	9
7	nest = Y	0	5	5
8	border = Y	80	14	94
9	nest = N	78	5	83
10	img = N	59	2	61
11	img = Y	19	3	22
12	nest = Y	2	9	11
13	height = N	0	5	5
14	height = Y	2	4	6

Table 5. Example (1) of decision trees obtained in the experiment

No.	Rule Element	Table	Layout	Total
0	(root)	89	91	180
1	num_tr <= 6	15	82	97
2	border = N	3	69	72
3	img = N	3	18	21
4	img = Y	0	51	51
5	border = Y	12	13	25
6	nest = N	12	5	17
7	nest = Y	0	8	8
8	num_tr > 6	74	9	83
9	nest = N	72	1	73
10	border = N	9	1	10
11	border = Y	63	0	63
12	nest = Y	2	8	10
13	num_tag <= 7	0	8	8
14	num_tag > 7	2	0	2

Table 6. Example (2) of decision trees obtained in the experiment

No.	Rule Element	Table	Layout	Total
0	(root)	86	94	180
1	num_tr <= 6	15	84	99
2	num_tag <= 12	3	76	79
3	img = N	3	20	23
4	img = Y	0	56	56
5	num_tag > 12	12	8	20
6	nest = N	12	4	16
7	nest = Y	0	4	4
8	num_tr > 6	71	10	81
9	nest = N	69	1	70
10	border = N	10	1	11
11	border = Y	59	0	59
12	nest = Y	2	9	11
13	border = N	0	8	8
14	border = Y	2	1	3

Table 7. Example (3) of decision trees obtained in the experiment

3.4.3 Evaluation of classification accuracy

Accuracy rates obtained by the three trials of the 10-fold CVs are shown in Table 8. Ten values of the accuracy rates are obtained by a single trial of CV, and the values in Table 8 are the minimum, maximum, mean and SD values of the ten accuracy rates for each trial. In all of the three trials, the maximum rate was 100% so that all checking <table> tags were correctly classified. The mean values were around 90% and the SD values were small, which supports the effectiveness of our method. Improvements for better values of the minimum accuracy rates are the further research challenges.

4. Conclusions

In this chapter, Section2 described our method that extracts cues for finding usability problems from user/desired logs of clicked points. To detect inconsistencies between user and desired logs, the method compares operations in the logs. The method compares user/desired operations by modeling each operation as a vector derived from coordinate values of the clicked points and checking the distance between two vectors. The distance was defined as a weighted sum of distance between start points and size of difference for the two vectors. The method extracts two types of inconsistencies: unnecessary and missed operations. Effectiveness of the proposed method was evaluated based on a case study. Each of the two human evaluators tried to find usability problems for ten websites by the proposed method and the manual method respectively. The proposed method contributed to find 61% of the usability problems found by the manual method in much smaller amount of time: the number of clicks analyzed by an evaluator with the proposed method was only 10-20% of that with the manual method. This result indicates that the method will help evaluators to quickly and roughly focus their attentions to problems cues in user interactions. In our future work, additional case studies are necessary for further evaluations and improvements of the method.

	1st CV	2nd CV	3rd CV
Min.	85	80	80
Max.	100	100	100
Mean	92	89	94
SD	6.0	7.5	6.7

Table 8. Classification accuracy rates (%)

Section 3 described our method for detecting layout-purpose <table> tags in webpage HTML sources. A machine learning method was utilized for deriving <table> tag classifiers. A system was developed that utilized ID3 as the machine learning method. The system derives a decision tree as the classifier from a set of <table> tag data for learning. Classification accuracy was evaluated by 10-fold CVs with 200 webpages collected from the web. It was found that the purposes could roughly be discriminated with attributes of border, num_tr, num_tag and nest shown in Table 4: these attributes were likely to appear in upper layers in decision trees. In the experiment with the 200 <table> tags collected, mean accuracy rates were around 90%. In our future work, it will be investigated whether machine learning methods other than ID3 (e.g., C4.5, multi-layered neural network, support vector machine) can improve the accuracy. These methods will be utilized in our system and classification accuracy rates will be compared within the methods.

5. References

Abascal, J.; Arrue, M.; Fajardo I.; Garay, N. & Tomas, J. (2004). Use of guidelines to automatically verify web accessibility, *Universal Access in the Information Society*, Vol.3, No.1, pp.71-79.

Al-Qaimari, G. & Mcrostie, D. (1999). KALDI: a computer-aided usability engineering tool for supporting testing and analysis of human computer interaction, *Proc. of the Third Int. Conf. on Computer-Aided Design of User Interfaces*, pp.337-355.

Beirekdar, A.; Keita, M.; Noirhomme, M.; Randolet, F.; Vanderdonckt, J. & Mariage, C. (2005). Flexible reporting for automated usability and accessibility evaluation of web sites, *Lecture Notes in Computer Science, Vol.3585 (Proc. of 10th IFIP TC 13 Int. Conf. on Human-Computer Interaction (INTERACT2005))*, pp.281-294.

Brajnik, G. (2004). Comparing accessibility evaluation tools: a method for tool effectiveness, *Universal Access in the Information Society*, Vol.3, Nos.3-4, pp.252-263.

Brinck, T.; Hermann, D.; Minnebo, B. & Hakim, A. (2002). AccessEnable: a tool for evaluating compliance with accessibility standards, *CHI'2002 Workshop on Automatically Evaluating the Usability of Web Sites*, available at http://simplytom.com/research/AccessEnable_workshop_paper.pdf.

Cooper, M. (1999). Evaluating accessibility and usability of web sites, *Proc. of 3rd Int. Conf. on Computer-Aided Design of User Interfaces (CADUI'99)*, pp.33-42.

Gellner, M. & Forbrig, P. (2003). ObSys - a tool for visualizing usability evaluation patterns with Mousemaps, *Proc. of the Tenth Int. Conf. on Human-Computer Interaction*, pp.469-473.

Helfrich B. & Landay, J. A. (1999). QUIP: quantitative user interface profiling, available at http://www.helcorp.com/bhelfrich/helfrich99quip.pdf.

Ivory, M. Y. (2003). *Automated web site evaluation: researchers' and practitioners' perspectives*, Kluwer Academic Publishers.

Ivory, M. Y. & Hearst, M. A. (2001). The state of the art in automated usability evaluation of user interfaces, *ACM Computing Surveys*, Vol.33, No.4, pp.1-47.

Ivory, M. Y.; Mankoff, J. & Le, A. (2003). Using automated tools to improve web site usage by users with diverse abilities, *IT&Society*, Vol.1, No.3, pp.195-236. available at http://www.stanford.edu/group/siqss/itandsociety/v01i03/v01i03a11.pdf.

Ivory, M. Y. & Megraw, R. (2005). Evolution of web site design patterns, *ACM Trans. on Information Systems*, Vol.23, No. 4, pp.463-497.

Kishi, N. (1995). Analysis tool for skill acquisition with graphical user interfaces based on operation logging, *Proc. of the 6th Int. Conf. on Human-Computer Interaction*, pp.161-166.

Okada, H. & Asahi, T. (1996). GUITESTER: a log-based usability testing tool for graphical user interfaces, *IEICE Transaction on Information and Systems*, Vol.E82-D, No.6, pp.1030-1041.

Perlman, G. (2008). Accessibility links - tools, *HCI Bibliography*, available at http://www.hcibib.org/accessibility/#TOOLS.

Qiang, Y.; Suzuki, T.; Sakuragawa, S.; Tamura, H. & Kurosu, M. (2005). The development of OBSERVANT EYE to effective implement observation records for usability testing, *Proc. of the 11th Int. Conf. on Human-Computer Interaction*, CD-ROM.

Quinlan, J. R. (1986). Induction of decision trees, *Machine Learning*, Vol.1, pp.81-106.

Scapin, D.; Leulier, C.; Vanderdonckt, J.; Mariage, C.; Bastien, C.; Farenc, C.; Palanque, P. & Bastide, R. (2000). A Framework for organizing web usability guidelines, *Proc. of the 6th Conf. on Human Factors & the Web*, available at http://www.isys.ucl.ac.be/bchi/publications/2000/Scapin-HFWeb2000.htm.

Uehling, D. L. & Wolf, K. (1995). User action graphing effort (UsAGE), *Proc. of the Conf. on Human Factors in Computing Systems*, pp.290-291.

Vanderdonckt, J. & Beirekdar, A. (2005). Automated web evaluation by guideline review, *Journal of Web Engineering*, Vol.4, No.2, pp.102-117.

W3C. (1999a). HTML 4.01 specification, available at http://www.w3.org/TR/html4/.

W3C. (1999b). Web content accessibility guidelines 1.0, available at http://www.w3.org/TR/WCAG10/.

W3C. (2006). Complete list of web accessibility evaluation tools, available at http://www.w3.org/WAI/ER/tools/complete.

Zettlemoyer, L. S.; St.Amant, R. S. & Dulberg, M. S. (1999). IBOTS: Agent control through the user interface, *Proc. of the Int. Conf. on Intelligent User Interfaces*, pp.31-37.

22

Emotion Recognition via Continuous Mandarin Speech

Tsang-Long Pao, Jun-Heng Yeh and Yu-Te Chen
Tatung University
Taiwan, R.O.C.

1. Introduction

Emotion plays a significant role in cognitive psychology, behavioural sciences and humanoid robot design. The continuing improvements in speech recognition technology have led to many new and fascinating applications in human-computer interaction, context aware computing and computer mediated communication. A growing number of research studies in emotion recognition via an isolated short sentence are available to shed some light on the implementation of human-computer interface. However, to the best of our knowledge, no work has focused on automatic emotion tracking from continuous Mandarin speech. In this chapter, we will elaborate an emotion recognition method in continuous Mandarin speech, by dividing the utterance into independent segments, each of which contains a single emotional category.

In the growing range of interactive interfaces, the research of emotional voice is still at an early stage, not to mention a paucity of literatures on real applications. The crucial difficulty of this subject is how to blend the knowledge of interdisciplinary, especially in speech processing, applied psychology and human-computer interface. To date, no clear direction has emerged to suggest how such considerations translate into practical interface design. The crux of this problem is that the emotion recognition in continuous speech has not yet been much explored.

From the viewpoint of communication, it is natural for human beings to communicate with others in continuous dialogue. Even though, most proposed methods of emotion recognition via voice can only be provided with a fragmented sentence (i.e. a manual and deliberate cutting sentence). To ensure the practicability, the purpose of this chapter attempts to address these areas by processing speech signals rather than interpreting the lexicons of speaking. Moreover, the benefit from the outlook of processing speech signals can also tack the violent change of emotional expression in dialogue. In light of these concerns, this chapter has three purposes: (a) to report on trends in published research in the major journals of emotion recognition; (b) to provide a method in recognition of emotion from continuous Mandarin speech; and (c) to recommend promising research paradigms for recognition of emotion via continuous speech.

This chapter is organized as follows. In section 2, related works are presented. In section 3, the testing corpus is introduced. In section 4, the proposed speech recognition method is presented in detail. In section 5, the experimental results are shown and commented. The chapter concludes in section 6 showing directions for future research and conclusions.

2. Emotions and Speech

Research on understanding and modelling human emotions, a topic that has been predominantly dealt with in the fields of psychology and linguistics, is attracting increasing attention within the engineering community. A major motivation comes from the need to improve both the naturalness and efficiency of spoken language human-machine interfaces. Researching emotions, however, is extremely challenging for several reasons. One of the main difficulties results from the fact that it is difficult to define what emotion means in a precise way. Various explanations of emotions given by scholars are summarized in [Kleinginna & Kleinginna, 2005]. Research on the cognitive component focuses on understanding the environmental and attended situations that give rise to emotions; research on the physical components emphasizes the physiological response that co-occurs with an emotion or immediately follows it. In short, emotions can be considered as communication with oneself and others [Kleinginna & Kleinginna, 2005].
For research related to continuous speech signal, most works are found on the continuous speech recognition. Also, most of the emotion recognition researches are based on short sentences. However, human beings speak continuously. People will change emotions when they are triggered by some incidents in the course of speaking. The short-sentence emotion recognition system may not be able to detect the emotional state correctly because there may have several emotions in a long conversation. One objective of this chapter is to find a proper segmentation algorithm to segment the continuous speech and to develop a method to recognize emotion of each segment correctly so we can track emotion changes of the speaker.

2.1 Emotional Categories

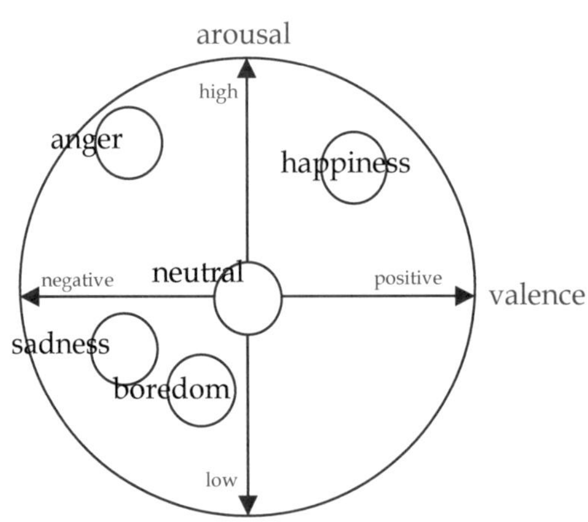

Figure 1. Graphic representation of the arousal-valence dimension of emotions [Osgood et al., 1967]

Traditionally, emotions are classified into two main categories: primary (basic) and secondary (derived) emotions [Murray & Arnott, 1993]. Primary or basic emotions generally can be experienced by all social mammals (e.g., humans, monkeys, dogs and whales) and have particular manifestations associated with them (e.g., vocal/facial expressions, behavioral tendencies and physiological patterns). Secondary or derived emotions are combinations of or derivations from primary emotions.

Emotional dimensionality is a simplified description of the basic properties of emotional states. According to the theory developed by Osgood, Suci and Tannenbaum [Osgood et al., 1967] and in subsequent psychological research [Mehrabian & Russel, 1974], the computing of emotions is conceptualized as three major dimensions of connotative meaning: arousal, valence and domaniance. In general, the arousal and valence dimensions can be used to distinguish most basic emotions. The locations of emotions in the arousal-valence space are shown in Figure 1, which provides a representation that is both simple and capable of conforming to a wide range of emotional applications.

2.2 Speech Features of Emotional Expressions

Speech communication is one of the basic and most essential capabilities possessed by human beings. Emotions play an important role in human-to-human communication and interaction, allowing people to express themselves beyond the verbal domain. Interactions between people not merely transmit through the speech, but also include behaviours, emotion language, heart, and spirit [Sebe et al., 2005]. Detecting emotions in speech is a topic that has been predominantly dealt with in psychology and linguistics. It is attracting the attention of engineering community also. To recognize emotions, we need to know not only what information a user conveys but also how it is being conveyed.

Numerous previous reports indicated that emotions could be detected by psychological cues [Busso & Narayanan, 2007, Cowie et al., 2000, Ekman, 1999, Holzapfel et al., 2002, Inanoglu & Caneel, 2005, Kleinginna & Kleinginna, 1981, Kwon et al., 2003, Murray & Arnott, 1993, Nwe et al., 2003, Park et al., 2002, Park & Sim, 2003, Pasechke & Sendlmeier, 2000, Picard, 1997, Ramamohan, & Dandapa, 2006, Schröder, 2006, Tao et al., 2006, Ververidis et al., 2004]. Vocal cues are among the fundamental expressions of emotions, on a par with facial expressions [Busso & Narayanan, 2007, Cowie et al., 2000, Ekman, 1999, Holzapfel et al., 2002, Kleinginna & Kleinginna, 1981, Murray & Arnott, 1993, Nwe et al., 2003, Park et al., 2002, Park & Sim, 2003, Pasechke & Sendlmeier, 2000, Ververidis et al., 2004]. All mammals can convey emotions by means of vocal cues. Humans are especially capable of expressing their feelings by crying, laughing, shouting and more subtle characteristics of speech.

Determining emotion features is a crucial issue in emotion recognizer design. All selected features have to carry sufficient information about transmitted emotions. However, they also need to fit the chosen model by means of classification algorithms. Important research was done by Murray and Arnott [Murray & Arnott, 1993], whose results particularized several notable acoustic attributes for detecting primary emotions. Table 1 summarizes the vocal effects most commonly associated with the five primary emotions [Murray & Arnott, 1993]. Classification of emotional states based on prosody and voice quality requires classifying the connections between acoustic features in speech and emotions. Specifically, we need to find suitable features that can be extracted and modelled for use in recognition. This also implies that the human voice carries abundant information about the emotional states of a speaker.

	Anger	Happiness	Sadness	Fear	Disgust
Speech Rate	Slightly faster	Faster or slower	Slightly slower	Much faster	Very much faster
Pitch Average	Very much higher	Much higher	Slightly lower	Very much higher	Very much lower
Pitch Range	Much wider	Much wider	Slightly narrower	Much wider	Slightly wider
Intensity	Higher	Higher	Lower	Normal	Lower
Voice Quality	Breathy, chest	Breathy, blaring tone	Resonant	Irregular voicing	Grumble chest tone
Pitch changes	Abrupt on stressed	Smooth, upward inflections	Downward inflections	Normal	Wide, downward terminal inflects
Articulation	Tense	Normal	Slurring	Precise	Normal

Table 1. Emotions and speech relations [Murray & Arnott, 1993]

A variety of acoustic features have also been explored. For example, Schuller et al. chose 20 pitch and energy related features [Schuller et al., 2003]. A speech corpus consisting of acted and spontaneous emotion utterances in German and English was described in detail. The accuracy in recognizing 7 discrete emotions (anger, disgust, fear, surprise, joy, neutral and sad) exceeded 77.8%. Park et al. used pitch, formant, intensity, speech rate and energy related features to classify neutral, anger, laugh and surprise [Park et al., 2002]. The recognition rate was about 40% for a 40-sentence corpus. Yacoub et al. extracted 37 fundamental frequency, energy and audible duration features for recognizing sadness, boredom, happiness and anger in a corpus recorded by eight professional actors [Yacoub et al., 2003]. The overall accuracy was only about 50%, but these features successfully separated hot anger from other basic emotions. Tato et al. extracted prosodic features, derived from pitch, loudness, duration and quality features [Tato et al., 2002], from a 400-utterance database. The significant results of emotion recognition were the speaker-independent case and three clusters (high = anger/happy, neutral, low = sad/bored). However, the accuracy in recognizing five emotions was only 42.6%. Kwon et al. selected pitch, log energy, formant, band energies and Mel frequency spectral coefficients (MFCC) as base features, and added velocity/acceleration of pitch to form feature streams [Kwon et al., 2003]. The average classification accuracy achieved was 40.8% in a SONY AIBO database. Nwe et al. adopted the short time log frequency power coefficients (LFPC) along with MFCC as emotion speech features to recognize 6 emotions in a 60-utterance corpus produced by 12 speakers [Nwe et al., 2003]. Results showed that the proposed system yielded an average accuracy of 78%. In [Le et al., 2004], the authors proposed a method using MFCC coefficients and a simple but efficient classifying method, Vector Quantization (VQ), for performing speaker-dependent emotion recognition. Various speech features, namely, energy, pitch, zero crossing, phonetic rate, linear predictive coding (LPC) and their derivatives, were also tested and combined with MFCC coefficients. The average recognition accuracy achieved was about 70%. In [Chuang et al. 2004], Chuang and Wu presented an approach to emotion recognition from speech signals and textual content using the principal component analysis (PCA) and the support vector machine (SVM), and achieved 81.49% average accuracy using an extra corpus collected from the same broadcast drama.

According to the experimental results stated above, some simple prosodic features, such as duration and loudness, can not consistently distinguish all primary emotions. Furthermore, the prosodic features of females and males are obviously intrinsic in speech. The simple speech energy feature calculation method is also unconformable to human auricular perception.

3. The Testing Corpora

An emotional speech database, Corpus I, was specifically designed and set up for emotion recognition studies. The database includes short sentences portraying the five primary emotions, including anger, boredom, happiness, neutral and sadness. In the course of selecting emotional sentences, two aspects were taken into account. First, the sentences did not have any emotional tendency. Second, the sentences could involve all kinds of emotions. Non-professional speakers were selected to avoid exaggerated expression. Twelve native Mandarin speakers (7 females and 5 males) were asked to generate the emotional utterances. The recording format is mono channel pulse-code modulation (PCM) with sampling rate of 44.1 kHz and 16-bit resolution.

Emotion \ Sex	Female	Male	Total
Anger	75	76	151
Boredom	37	46	83
Happiness	56	40	96
Neutral	58	58	116
Sadness	54	58	112
Total	280	278	558

Table 2. Corpus I

Combining emotions	Combined sentences
Angry-Happy (AH)	35
Angry-Sad (AS)	37
Angry-Bored (AB)	25
Angry-Neutral (AN)	34
Happy-Sad (HS)	27
Happy-Bored (HB)	24
Happy-Neutral (HN)	26
Sad-Bored (SB)	22
Sad-Neutral (SN)	29
Bored-Neutral (BN)	20
Total sentences	279

Table 3. Corpus II

All of the native speakers were asked to speak each sentence with the five chosen emotions, resulting in 1,200 sentences. We first eliminated sentences that suffered from excessive noise. Then a subjective assessment of the emotion speech corpus by human audiences was carried out. The purpose of the subjective classification was to eliminate ambiguous emotion utterances. Finally, 558 utterances with over 80% human judgment accuracy were selected and are summarized in Table 2. In this study, utterances in Mandarin were used due to the immediate availability of native speakers of the language. It is easier for speakers to express emotions in their native language than in a foreign language.

The continuous emotional corpus, Corpus II, used in the experiment is obtained by combining the short emotional sentences in the corpus database. There are ten kinds of combination of emotion as shown in Table 3. Each combined utterance is from the same speaker. Every combined utterance consists more than five short sentences. There are 277 combined semntences for the experiments.

Sentences can be divided into two sets: one set for training and one set for testing. In this way, several different models, all trained with the training set, can be compared based on the test set. This is the basic form of cross-validation. A better method, which is intended to avoid possible bias introduced by relying on any one particular division into test and train components, is to partition the original set in several different ways and then compute an average score over the different partitions. An extreme variant of this is to split the p patterns into a training set of size p-1 and a test of size 1, and average the squared error on the left-out pattern over the p possible ways of obtaining such a partition. This is called leave-one-out (LOO) cross-validation. The advantage here is that all the data can be used for training; none have to be held back in a separate test set.

4. Speech Processing of Emotion Recognition

In this section, we present an emotion tracking system, by dividing the utterance into several independent segments, each of which contains a single emotional category. Figure 2 shows the block diagram of the emotion recognition from continuous Mandarin speech signal.

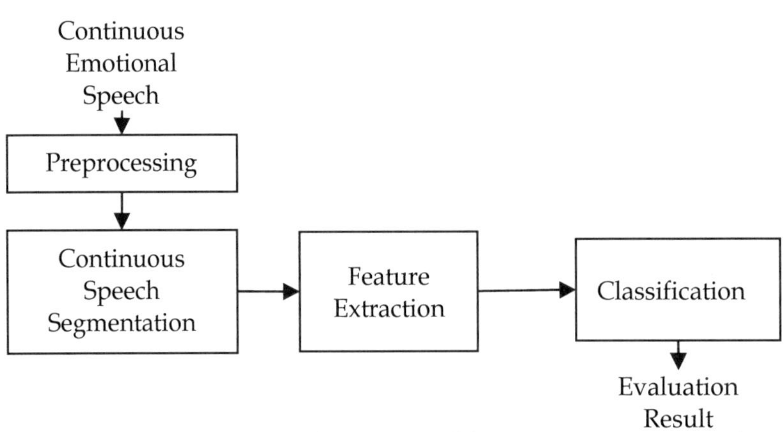

Figure 2. The block diagram of the block diagram of the emotion recognition from continuous mandarin speech signal

4.1 Pre-Processing

The signal from the microphone is an analogy signal. It is essential to transform the analogy signal into digital form so the computer can be used to process the signal. Before the emotion recognition can be done, the input speech signal has to go through some pre-processing. To deal with the discrete-time signal $x(n)$, framing is used to divide the speech signal into sections. In this study, the speech frame is partitioned into frames consisting of 256 samples each. Each frame overlaps with the adjacent frames by 128 samples. The next step is to apply the Hamming window as shown in Eq. (1) to each individual frame to minimize the signal discontinuities at the beginning and end of each frame. Each windowed speech frame is then converted into several types of parametric representations for further analysis and recognition. Figure 3 depicts the result of frame partition.

$$w(n) = \begin{cases} 0.54 - 0.46\cos(\frac{2n\pi}{N-1}), & 0 \le n \le N-1 \\ 0 & \text{, otherwise.} \end{cases} \quad (1)$$

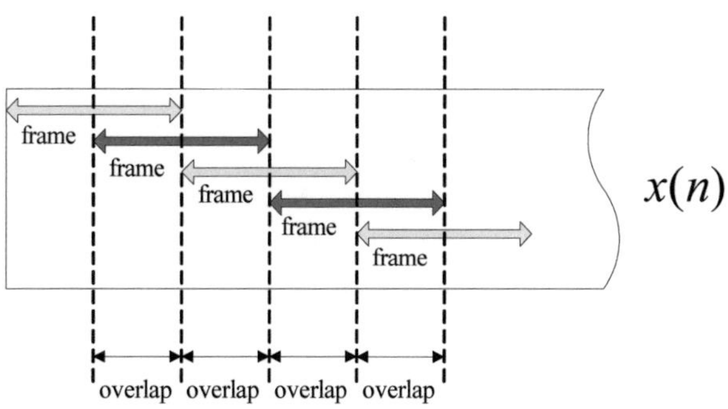

Figure 3. Frame partition of a sequence $x(n)$

4.2 Feature Selection

In order to find a suitable combination of extracted features, we used the regression selection method to determine beneficial features from among more than 100 speech features. The feature vector of each frame of a sentence from Corpus I was calculated.

The recognition rate in each step was calculated using the LOO cross-validation method with the K-Nearest Neighbour (KNN) decision rule (K=3) classifier. Finally, 10 candidates were selected: LPC, linear prediction cepstral coefficient (LPCC), MFCC, Delta-MFCC (dMFCC), Delta-Delta-MFCC (ddMFCC), perceptual linear prediction (PLP), RelAtive SpecTrAl PLP (RastaPLP), LFPC, pitch and formants (F1, F2 and F3).

The feature selection is to reduce the dimensions of feature set. And the forward feature selection (FFS) and backward feature selection (BFS) are used to decrease the computational complexity. FFS and BFS correspond to growing and shrinking feature one at a time, respectively. The FFS starts from an empty set and sequentially adds features, whereas BFS starts from the full set and sequentially removes features. In FFS, the starting set is empty. It then chooses a best single one and adds it to the set. The next step is to choose the second best one. The step repeated until the criteria are full fill. In BFS, the starting set is all the features. It removes the worst one remaining in the set step by step. Figure 4 shows the feature ranking of these 10 speech features by FFS and BFS using KNN.

Without loss of generality, the collected speech samples are split into t data elements $X_1, \cdots, X_t$. The space of all possible data elements is defined as the input space X. The elements of the input space are mapped into points in a feature space F. In our work, a feature space is a real vector space with dimension n, Γ^n. Accordingly, each point f_i in F is represented by an n-dimensional feature vector:

$$f_i = (MFCC_{i1}, \cdots, MFCC_{im}, \cdots, LPCC_{i1}, \cdots, LPCC_{iq}), \tag{2}$$

where m, q are the dimension of MFCC and LPCC respectively, and

$$n = m + q. \tag{3}$$

Finally, MFCC and LPCC are individually obtained from FFS and BFS as the most important features. In the field of speech recognition, LPCC and MFCC are the popular choices as features representing the phonetic content of speech. For each speech frame, 12 LPCC components and 20 MFCC components are used in this study.

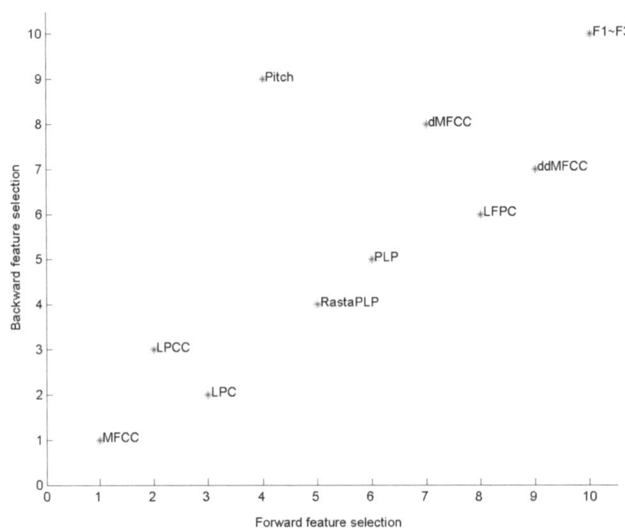

Figure 4. Feature ranking of 10 speech features

4.3 Classifier

A feature map is defined as a function that takes an element in the input space and maps it to a point in the feature space. We use ϕ to define a feature map, that is

$$\phi : X \rightarrow F. \tag{4}$$

Being simple, elegant and straightforward, many researchers often adopt KNN as the classifier for their applications. It is an instance-based learning algorithm and classifies unlabeled data based on the similarities with data in the training set. When a new test data x arrives, KNN finds the k neighbours nearest to the unlabeled data from the training space based on a suitable distance measure. In this study, the Euclidean distance is used. That is, given two samples in the input space x_1 and x_2, the Euclidean distance between them in the feature space is defined as

$$\begin{aligned} & d(x_1,x_2) \\ & =|\phi(x_1)-\phi(x_2)| \\ & =|f_1-f_2| \\ & =\sqrt{(MFCC_{1m}-MFCC_{2m})^2+\cdots+(LPCC_{1q}-LPCC_{2q})^2}. \end{aligned} \tag{5}$$

Assume that we want to classify the data into one of the l classes and let the k prototypes nearest to x be $N_k(x)$ and $c(y)$ be the class label of y. Then the subset of nearest neighbours within class $j \in \{1,\cdots,l\}$ is

$$N_k^j(x)=\{y \in N_k((y):c(y)=j)\}. \tag{6}$$

The classification result $j^* \in \{1,...,l\}$ is then defined as a majority vote:

$$j^* = \arg\ \max_{j=1,\cdots,l} |\mathrm{N}_{\mathrm{k,i}}^{\mathrm{j}}(x)| . \tag{7}$$

Modified-KNN (M-KNN) is a technique based on the KNN [Pao et al., 2008]. It is based on the comparison of similarity among samples in each class. An unknown sample can be viewed as a point in the n-dimensional feature space, then the k nearest points of the training samples in each class are found by using Euclidean distance as similarity measure. The distance between unknown sample and the ith nearest point in class j is defined as d_j^i.

Then, the classification result $j^* \in \{1,\cdots,l\}$ is obtained by summing up the distance values in each class and picking up the smallest one, that is

$$j^* = \arg\ \min_{j=1,\cdots,l} \sum_1^k d_i^j. \tag{8}$$

In this study, we use a weighted D-KNN to improve the performance of M-KNN. M-KNN assigns equal weight to each neighbour. This may cause confusion when there are some irrelevant data in the training set. One obvious refinement to M-KNN is to weight the contribution of each of the k neighbours in each class. The purpose of weighting is to find a vector of real-valued weights that would optimize classification accuracy of the classification or recognition system by assigning lower weights to less relevant features and higher weights to features that provide more reliable information. Let $x_i^j, i=1,\cdots,z_j$, be the training samples of class j, where z_j is the number of samples belonging to class j. The total number t of training samples is

$$t=\sum_{j=1}^{l} z_j \tag{9}$$

When a test sample x and Euclidean distance measure d_j^i are given, we obtain the k nearest neighbours belonging to class j, $M_j^k(x)$, which is defined as

$$\forall x_i^j \in M_k^j(x), x_p^j \notin M_k^j(x) \Rightarrow d_i^j < d_p^j, \tag{10}$$

$$d_i^j = d\left(x_i^j, x\right), \tag{11}$$

$$d_p^j = d\left(x_p^j, x\right), \tag{12}$$

where the cardinality of the set $\left|M_k^j(x)\right|$ is k. Among the k nearest neighbours in class j, the following relationship is established:

$$d_1^j \le d_2^j \le \cdots \le d_k^j, \tag{13}$$

Let w_i be the weight of the ith nearest samples. From above, we can know that the one have the smallest distance value d_1^j is the most important. Consequently, we set a constraint $w_1 \ge w_2 \ge \cdots \ge w_k$ to conform the idea of weighting. Then, the classification result $j^* \in \{1, \cdots, l\}$is defined as

$$j^* = \arg\ \min_{j=1,\cdots,l} \sum_{i=1}^{k} w_i d_i^j \tag{14}$$

4.4 Segmentation of Emotional Expressions from Continuous Mandarin Speech

In previous studies, the methods to segment continuous speech signal are usually applied in the speech recognition system. To recognize the emotion from continuous emotional speech, the first step is to segment the sentence by finding out the changing points. And emotion of each segment is recognized individually.

People may pause for a while when they turn one emotion to the other emotion. In [Lu et al., 2006], two thresholds are defined to preliminarily quantize the energy envelope into three levels instead of binaries. Therefore, it will generate a larger number of potential partition boundaries whenever either threshold is crossed in the energy envelope. This method is applied in this study. The thresholds, T_L and T_U, are defined as

$$T_L = \mu_E - 0.5\sigma_E. \tag{15}$$

$$T_U = \mu_E + 0.5\sigma_E. \tag{16}$$

where μ_E is the mean energy of partition, and σ_E is the standard deviation of the energy of that partition. Then, the points of the energy contour crossing T_L and T_U are checked every two frames. It will place a partition between two points. The partition energy is represented as

$$E_x(m) = \sum_{n=m-N+1}^{m} \left|f_x(n;m)\right|^2 . \tag{17}$$

The feeling of the sound intensity perceived by human ears is not linear but rather logarithmic. Thus, it is better to express the energy function in logarithmic form.

$$E_x(m) = 10 \times \log[\,|\sum_{n=m-N+1}^{m} |f_x(n;m)|^2\,|\,]\,. \tag{18}$$

The μ_E and σ_E are defined as

$$\mu_E = \frac{1}{N_f}\sum_{l=1}^{N_f} E_{x,f}, \tag{19}$$

and

$$\sigma_E^{\ 2} = \frac{1}{N_f}\sum_{l=1}^{N_f}(E_f - \mu_E)^2, \tag{20}$$

where f is the frame index and N_f is the number of frames.

The mean energy between two intersection points will be calculated. In order to determine the silence, the energy of the partition and T_L are compared after obtaining the intersection points. When the energy of the partition is greater than T_L, the adjacent partitions will be merged. If the merged duration L_i is less than a threshold, the adjacent partitions will be combined again. The threshold T is set as the average of the duration

$$T = \frac{1}{N_L}\sum_{i=1}^{N_L} L_i, \tag{21}$$

where N_L is the number of the merged duration. After this processing step, the segmented partitions are recognized separately.

4.5 Segmentation with Endpoint Detection

In the real-time processing, it is important for the system to be able to detect the endpoints of an utterance so that an assessment can be constructed immediately. There exist some noises in the beginning and the end of the sound. The purpose of endpoint detection is to find the start and the end of meaningful partitions. A simple method to obtain endpoints is to calculate the energy contour and zero-crossing rate contour. The energy is calculated according to Equation (18).

There is a zero line on the speech signal. When a zero-crossing occurred, the amplitude is either from the positive to negative or from the negative to positive. The number of zero-crossing of the speech signal in a predetermined time interval, which is counted as the number of times when adjacent sample points have different signs, approximately corresponds to the frequency of the major spectral component. The calculating of the number of zero-crossing in a partition gives the zero-crossing rate. The equation is defined as

$$Z_x(m) = \sum_{n=m-N+1}^{m} \frac{1}{2}\left|\ \mathrm{sgn}\left[x(n)\right] - \mathrm{sgn}\left[x(n-1)\right]\right|, \tag{22}$$

where sgn[.] is defined as

$$\mathrm{sgn}[y] = \begin{cases} 1, & y \geq 0 \\ -1, & y < 0 \end{cases}. \tag{23}$$

The absolute value of sgn[x(n)]-sgn[x(n-1)] will be 2 when x(n) and x(n-1) are different in sign, and is 0 otherwise.
The equations for the two energy thresholds and one zero-crossing rate threshold is defined as follows

$$T_L = \mu_E + \alpha_1 \sigma_E, \tag{25}$$

$$T_U = \mu_E + \alpha_2 \sigma_E, \ \alpha_1 < \alpha_2, \tag{26}$$

$$T_Z = \mu_Z + \alpha_3 \sigma_Z. \tag{27}$$

The α_1, α_2, and α_3 are parameters, which are obtained by experiments.
In the sequence of partitions, the first partition with energy greater than T_L is labelled as N_B. If the energies of the next B successive frames are greater than T_L, N_B may be regarded as the beginning of a sound. On the other hand, if the energy of one of the B frames is less than T_L, it is not the beginning of the sound. In this case N_B will be neglected.
After locating the N_B, the next step is to check the zero-crossing rate of all the B frames to see if their zero-crossing rate is greater than T_Z. Now the frame is regarded as the true beginning of the sound, and is labelled as N_S. The frame after N_S with energy greater than T_L means that the sound exists. The first frame after N_S with energy less than T_L is the end of the sound, and is labelled as N_E. As a result, the region of the sound is from N_B to N_E or from N_S to N_E.
After the endpoint detection processing step, the number of the segmented partitions are still too large to process. So, it is necessary to reduce the numbers of partitions. The way is to combine adjacent partitions if they have similar characteristics or too short in length. The mean of the lengths between the beginning and end of all the merged segments are calculated individually as the threshold for the corresponding segment. If the length of the frame is less than the threshold, it will be merged with adjacent frames. The threshold is obtained by experiments.

4.6 Emotion Evaluation

The values used in the evaluation are calculated as follows

$$Eva_j = [(\sum_{i=1}^{k} w_i d_j^i)^{-1}]^2. \tag{28}$$

Equation (28) is used to get the scores of the test sample corresponding to each emotion. Five values are obtained with respect to five emotion categories. The five values indicate emotion components of the test sample correspond to each emotional state. The five evaluation values represent the scores for each emotional state. The value of the score is normalized so it is between 0 and 1.

5. Emotion Recognition from Continuous Mandarin Speech

In this section, the method of emotion recognition is presented. And several experimental results are discussed.

5.1 Experimental Results of Segmentation with Silence

In this method, two thresholds are utilized to locate the intersection points between energy contour and thresholds. In this experiment, it is checked every two frames. In Fig. 5, the top figure shows the result of the intersection points between energy contour and the two thresholds. The bottom figure shows the mean energy in every segmented partition. The short horizontal line is the mean energy in every partition, and the long horizontal line is the threshold T_L. Application of the procedure will result a lot of partitions which is not easy to process. Therefore, it needs some post processings. First, the mean energy is calculated in every partition. If the values of the mean energy in adjacent partitions are all smaller or all greater than T_L, these partitions are merged.

Figure 6 is the enlarged plot from the marked rectangle in Fig. 5. Figure 7 shows the merged results. The top one shows the result of the intersection points between energy contour and the two thresholds. The bottom one shows the merged results for partition with similar mean energy. The horizontal line indicates the threshold T_L.

Figure 8 shows the result of segmentation with silence using threshold T_L. The segmentation result is still not good enough, so another threshold is needed to combine small partitions. The threshold T is set to the average of the duration of all the partitions. When the adjacent partitions all have mean energy smaller than T, they are combined together.

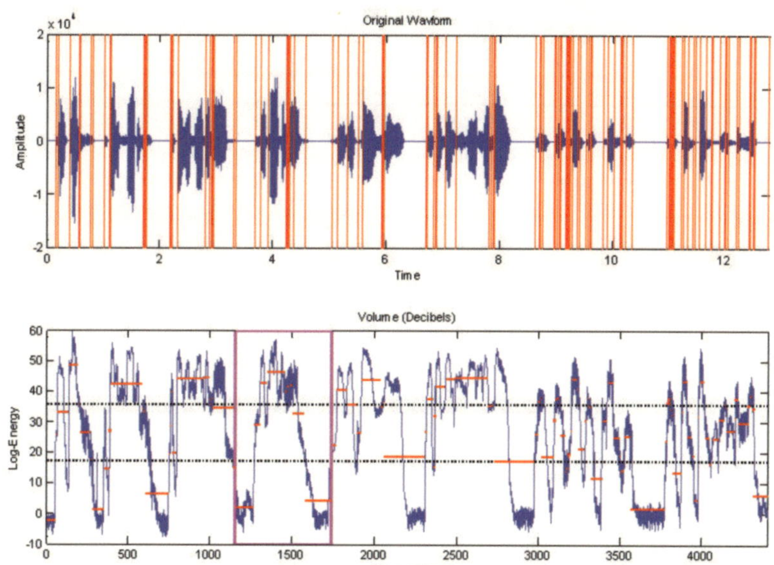

Figure 5. The intersection points between energy contour and two thresholds

Figure 9 shows the segmentation result. The score is shown in Fig. 10. When the mean energy of the segmented partition is greater than T_L, it is regarded as non-silence. Therefore its score is calculated. The short horizontal line is the mean energy for each partition, and the long horizontal line is the threshold T_L. Ten partitions are obtained after the merging operation. P1 and P2 whose emotional states are anger, P3 and P4 are happiness, P5 and P6 are sadness, and P7 and P8 are neutral. Comparing with the result shown in Fig. 10, the recognition of P6 is wrong.

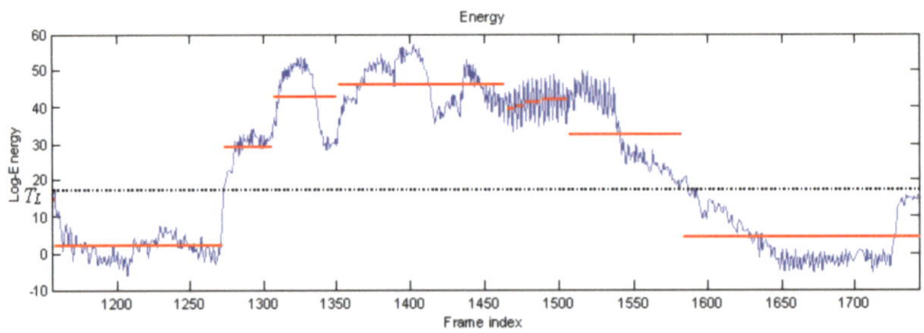

Figure 6. The enlarged plot from the marked rectangle in Fig. 5

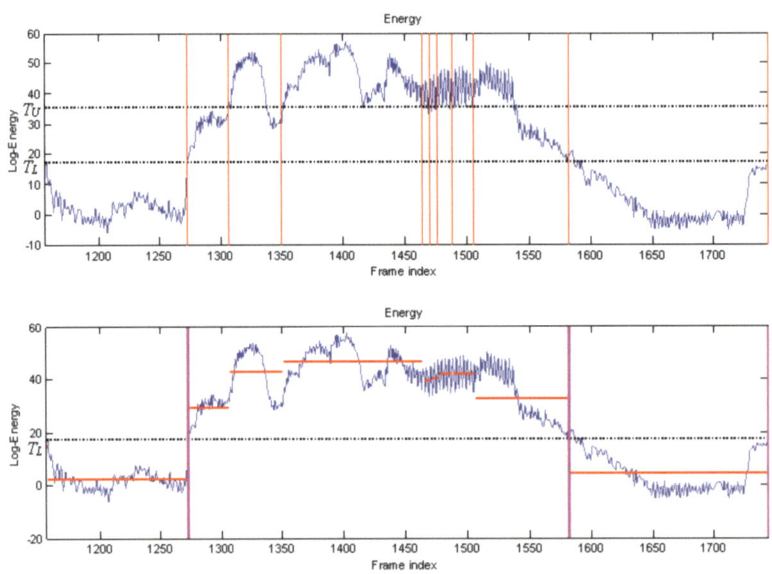

Figure 7. The merged result

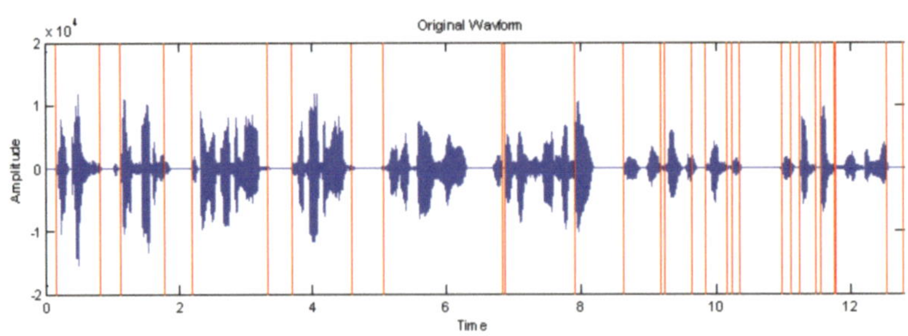

Figure 8. Result of segmentation with silence

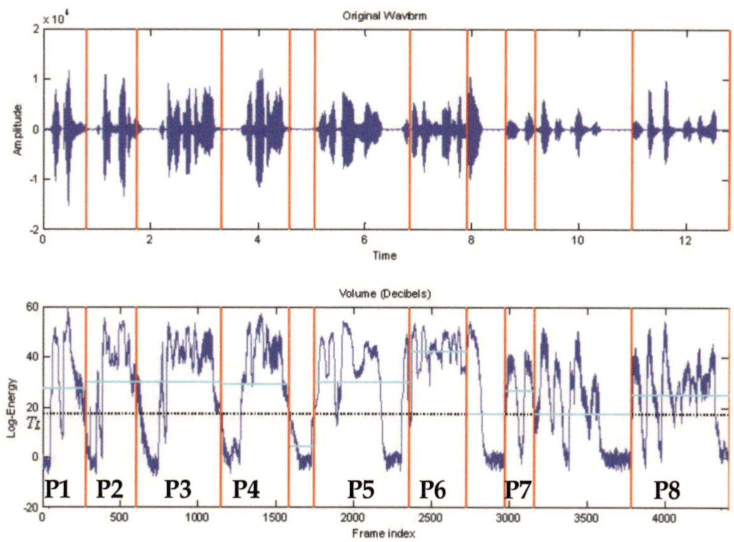

Figure 9. The final segmentation result with segmentation with silence

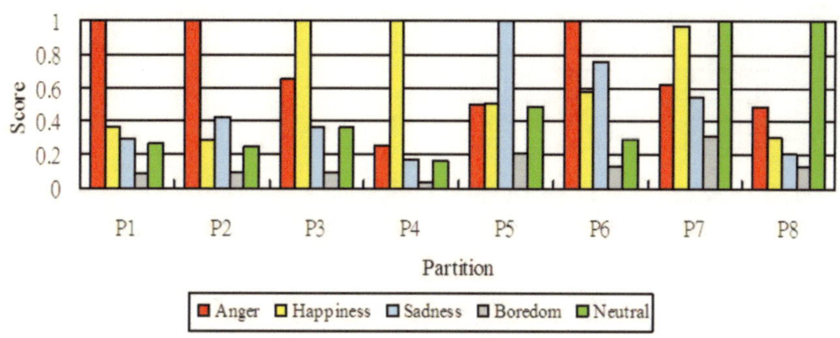

Figure 10. The score bar chart of each partition shown in Fig. 9

5.2 Experimental Results Using Segmentation with Endpoint Detection

From Equations (25)-(27), setting $\alpha_1 = -0.5$, $\alpha_2 = 0.5$, and $\alpha_3 = 0.5$, three thresholds are obtained. Figure 11 shows an example of segmentation with endpoint detection. The thick line is the beginning of the partition and the thin line is the end of the partition. In Fig. 11, we see that there are too many partitions. Thus, we need to merge partitions with similar characteristics together.

In Figure 12, the distances of the beginning and end in two adjacent endpoints are expressed as

$$D_i = B_{i+1} - E_i,\ i = 1, 2, \ldots, N \tag{29}$$

where N is the total number of the intervals, B_{i+1} and E_i correspond to the beginning point of partition i+1 and the ending point of partition, respectively. Another threshold is used to merge the partitions. The threshold is calculated as

$$T_D = \overline{D} + \alpha_D D_{STD} \tag{30}$$

where $\overline{D}$ is the average distance between two non-silence partition, and D_{STD} is the standard deviation of the distances. α_D is obtained from experiments and is set to 0.3. If D_i is less than T_D then the two intervals are combined, as shown in Fig. 13.

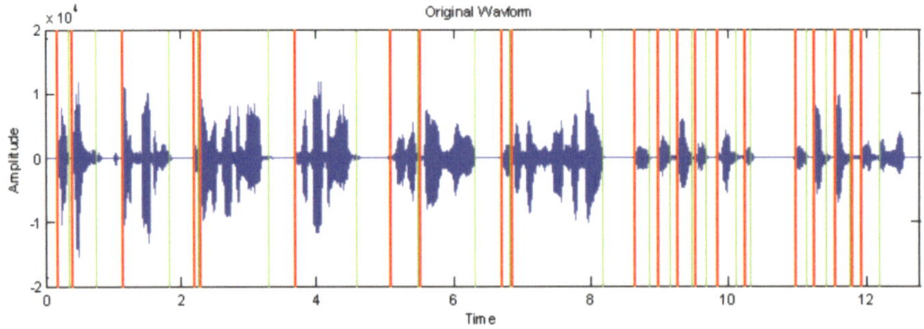

Figure 11. The initial result of endpoint detection

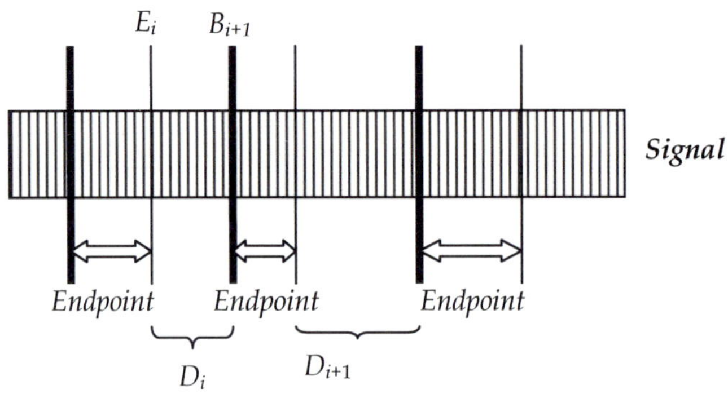

Figure 12. Distance between two adjacent partitions

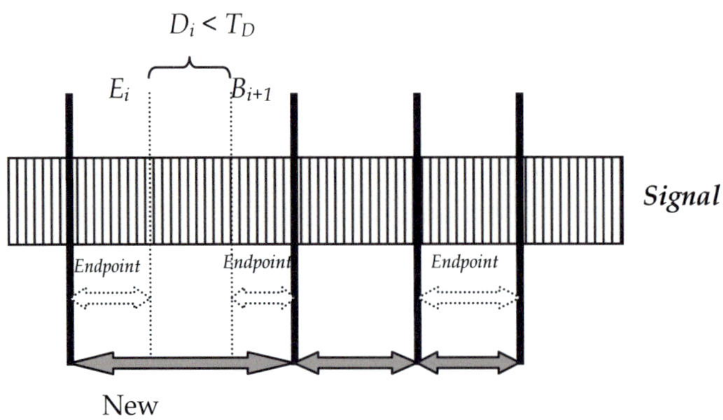

Figure 13. Two non-silence partitions are merged when the distance between them is less then T_D

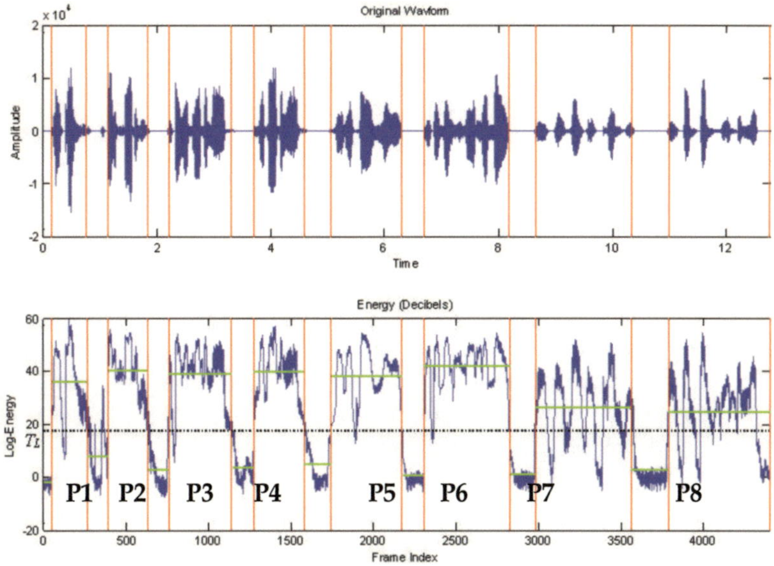

Figure 14. Partition result after merging using the threshold T_D

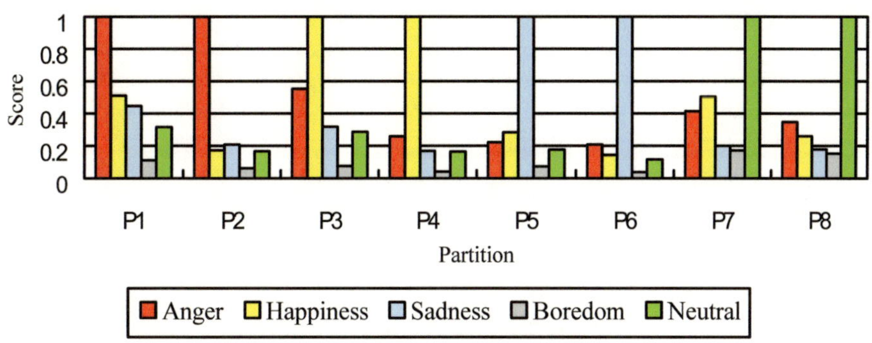

Figure 15. The score bar chart of each partition shown in Fig. 14

The result of the application of threshold T_D is shown in Fig. 14. In the bottom figure, the short horizontal line is the mean energy of each partition, and the long horizontal line is the threshold T_L. When the mean of the segmented partition is greater than T_L, it is regarded as non-silence. Eight partitions are obtained, whose original emotions are 2 anger short sentences, 2 happiness short sentences, 2 sadness short sentences, and 2 neutral short sentences, respectively. The score for each partition is shown in the Fig. 15. The classified result matches with the original emotion in the corpus. Since segmentation with endpoint will obtain better results than the other two segmentation methods, we adopt it as the segmentation method in this study.

5.3 Recognition Accuracy of Continuous Speech

Table 4 shows the recognition accuracy for all the sentences listed in Table 3. The recognition accuracy is calculated from dividing the total correct recognition by the total number of short corpora in the sentences in each category. Finally, the overall recognition accuracy is 83%.

	AH	AS	AB	AN	HS	HB	HN	SB	SN	BN	Average
Accuracy	0.91	0.89	0.72	0.84	0.89	0.80	0.80	0.86	0.78	0.81	**0.83**

Table 4. The recognition accuracy of Corpus II

6. Conclusions and Future Works

In recent years, emotion recognition is used in more and more applications. In this study, the emotion recognition from continuous speech is realized. Emotion recognition used in real world can be expected soon. The application in the call-centre can help the customer service personnel to better serve the customer. Endpoint detection is used to segment the continuous speech. The feature sets are 12 LPCCs and 20 MFCCs. The classifier is D-KNN with Fibonacci series weighting. The recognition accuracy of 83% is obtained.

It is not easy to obtain the emotional corpus, especially continuous emotional corpus. In the future, it is necessary to get more emotional speech corpora, and hope to collect them in various forms, such as recording in a noisy environment or not so perfect sound quality. In real life, speeches do not always be recorded in a quiet environment or with high quality devices. The emotion recognition from continuous speech can be used in business, such as call centre. If the real-time system is going to be realized, the performance of the program must be improved. In other words, the programming language need to be changed to that can be used not only in personal computers but also in other devices, such as personal digital assistants (PDAs) or mobile phones.

7. References

Busso C. & Narayanan S.S. (2007). Between Speech and Facial Gestures in Emotional Utterances: A Single Subject Study, *IEEE Transactions on Audio, Speech, and Language Processing*, Vol. 15, No. 8, pp. 2331-2347, ISSN: 1558-7916.

Chang, B.H. (2002). *Automated Recognition of Emotion in Mandarin*, Master thesis, National Cheng Kung University.

Cowie, R. E.; Douglas-Cowie, E., Tsapatsoulis, N., Votsis, G., Kollias, S., Fellenz, W. & Taylor, J. (2001). Emotion Recognition in Human-Computer Interaction, *IEEE Signal Processing Magazine*, Vol. 18, No. 1, pp. 32-80, ISSN: 1053-5888.

Chuang, Z.J. & Wu, C.H. (2004). Multi-Modal Emotion Recognition from Speech and Text, *International Journal of Computational Linguistics and Chinese Language Processing*, pp. 1-18, Vol. 9, No. 2, ISSN: 0349-1021.

Ekman, P. (1999), *Handbook of Cognition and Emotion*, John Wiley & Sons, ISBN-10: 0471978361, New York, USA.

Inanoglu, Z. & Caneel, R. (2005). Emotive Alert: HMM-Based Emotion Detection in Voicemail Messages, *Proceedings of Intelligent User Interfaces*, pp. 251-253, January 2005, San Diego, USA.

Kleinginna Jr., P.R. & Kleinginna, A.M. (2005). A Categorized List of Emotion Definitions with Suggestions for a Consensual Definition, *Motivation and Emotion*, Vol. 5, No. 4, pp. 345-379, ISSN: 0146-7239.

Kwon, O.W.; Chan, K., Hao, J. & Lee, T.W. (2003). Emotion Recognition by Speech Signals, *Proceedings of Eurospeech*, pp.125-128, September 2003, Geneva, Switzerland.

Le, X.H.; Quenot, G. & Castelli, E. (2004). Recognizing Emotions for the Audio-Visual Document Indexing, *Proceedings of the Ninth IEEE International Symposium on Computers and Communications*, pp.580-584, July 2004, Alexandria, Egypt.

Lu, L.; Liu, D.H. & Zhang, J. (2006). Automatic Mood Detection and Tracking of Music Audio Signals, IEEE Transactions on Audio, Speech and Language Processing, pp. 5-18, Vol. 14, ISSN: 1558-7916.

Mehrabian, A. & Russel, J. (1974). *An Approach to Environmental Psychology*, the MIT Press, ISBN-10: 0-262-63071-0, Cambridge, USA.

Murray, I. &. Arnott, J.L. (1993). Towards the Simulation of Emotion in Synthetic Speech: A Review of the Literature on Human Vocal Emotion. *Journal of the Acoustic Society of America*, Vol. 93, No. 2, pp. 1097-1108, ISSN: 0001-4966.

Nwe, T.L.; Foo, S.W. & De-Silva, L.C. (2003). Speech Emotion Recognition Using Hidden Markov Models, *Speech Communication*, Vol. 41, No. 4, pp. 603-623, ISSN: 0167-6393.

Osgood, C.E.; Suci, J.G. & Tannenbaum, P.H. (1967). *The Measurement of Meaning*, the University of Illinois Press, ISBN-10: 978-0252745393, Urbana, USA.

Pao, T.L.; Chen, Y.T. & Yeh, J.H. (2008). Emotion Recognition and Evaluation from Mandarin Speech Signals, International Journal of Innovative Computing, Information and Control (IJICIC), pp. 0-07-107, Vol. 4, No. 7, ISSN: 1349-4198.

Park, C.D. & Sim, K.B. (2003). Emotion Recognition and Acoustic Analysis from Speech Signal, *Proceedings of International Joint Conference on Neural Networks*, pp. 2594-2598, July 2003, Portland, USA.

Park, C.H.; Heo, K.S., Lee, D.W., Joo, Y.H. & Sim, K.B. (2002). Emotion Recognition based on Frequency Analysis of Speech Signal, *International Journal of Fuzzy Logic and Intelligent Systems*, Vol. 2, No.2, pp. 122-126, ISSN: 1064-1246.

Pasechke, A. & Sendlmeier, W.F. (2000). Prosodic Characteristics of Emotional Speech: Measurements of Fundamental Frequency Movements, *Proceedings of ISCA Workshop on Speech and Emotion*, pp. 75-80, September 2000, Northern Ireland.

Picard, R.W. (1997). *Affective Computing*, the MIT Press, ISBN-10: 0-262-16170-2, Cambridge, USA.

Ramamohan, S. & Dandapa, S. (2006). Sinusoidal Model-Based Analysis and Classification of Stressed Speech, *IEEE Transactions on Audio, Speech, and Language Processing*, Vol. 14, Issue. 3, pp. 737-746, ISSN: 1558-7916.

Sebe N.; Cohen, I., Gevers, T. & Huang, T.S. (2005). Multimodal Approaches for Emotion Recognition: A Survey, *Proceedings of the International Society for Optical Engineering (SPIE)*, pp. 56-67, Vol. 5670, February 2005. San Jose, CA.

Schröder, M. (2006). Expressing Degree of Activation in Synthetic Speech, *IEEE Transactions on Audio, Speech, and Language Processing*, Vol. 14, Issue. 4, pp. 1128-1136, ISSN: 1558-7916.

Schuller, B.; Rigoll, G. & Lang, M. (2003). Hidden Markov Model-based Speech Emotion Recognition, *Proceedings of International Conference on Acoustics, Speech, and Signal Processing*, pp. 401-405, April 2003, Hong Kong, China.

Tato, R.S.; Kompe, R. & Pardo, J.M. (2002). Emotional Space Improves Emotion Recognition, *Proceedings of International Conference on Spoken Language Processing*, pp. 2029-2032, September 2002, Colorado, USA.

Tao J.; Kang, Y. & Li, A. (2006). Prosody Conversion From Neutral Speech to Emotional Speech, *IEEE Transactions on Audio, Speech, and Language Processing*, Vol. 14, Issue. 4, pp. 737-746, ISSN: 1558-7916.

Ververidis, D.; Kotropoulos, C. & Pitas, I. (2004). Automatic Emotional Speech Classification, *Proceedings of International Conference on Acoustics, Speech, and Signal Processing*, pp. 593-596, May 2004, Montreal, Canada.

Yacoub, S.; Simske, S., Lin, X. & Burns, J. (2003). Recognition of Emotions in Interactive Voice Response Systems, *Proceedings of Eurospeech*, pp. 729-732, September 2003, Geneva, Switzerland.

23

Nomad Devices Adaptation for Offering Computer Accessible Services

L. Pastor-Sanz[1], M. F. Cabrera-Umpiérrez[1], J. L. Villalar[1], C. Vera-Munoz[1], M. T. Arredondo[1], A. Bekiaris[2] and C. Hipp[3]
[1]Universidad Politécnica de Madrid, [2]Hellenic Institute of Transport, [3]Fraunhofer Institute
[1]Spain, [2]Greece, [3]Germany

1. Introduction

During the last years a transition from desktop computers and fixed phones to nomad devices such as mobile phones, palmtops and mobile Personal Computers has been experienced. Their market penetration is continuously increasing, mainly because they offer to their users the possibility to stay connected with their near ones and with the world whenever and wherever possible.

The technological development of the aforementioned nomad devices provides not only the chance but the need to explore these systems in order to provide computer-based interactive applications and services accessible to the broadest possible population. At the same time, this development must also cope with diversity of the end users, the access media and devices, as well as in the contexts of use.

The adaptation of nomad devices, applications and services, for the benefit of people with disability and of the elderly is especially challenging. This is because it requires a revision of the traditionally prevailing Human Computer Interaction (HCI) assumptions, such as that of designing for a non-disabled user in a desktop environment.

ASK-IT[1] (Ambient Intelligence Systems of Agents for Knowledge Based and Integrated Services for Mobility Impaired People) is a European Integrated Project (IST-2003-511298) within the IST 6th Framework Program in the e-Inclusion area. The driving vision behind the project is to develop services based on Ambient Intelligence (AmI) and Information and Communication Technologies (ICT) that allow mobility impaired people to move independently, live a quality life, and as a result, establish and secure economic and social inclusion. These services include the provision of relevant and real-time information, primarily for travelling, but also for use at home and at work. Nomad devices allow content access at any time, at any place, and across multiple networks. These devices combined with the ASK-IT platform aim at covering a wide range of the mobility impaired users personal needs (Gardner, 2006). ASK-IT provides applications and services in five main areas:
(i) transportation, tourism and leisure; (ii) personal support; (iii) work; (iv) business and education support; and (v) social relations and community building (ASK-IT, 2004).

---

[1] http:// www.ask-it.org

This chapter describes the technological solutions adopted in the framework of the ASK-IT project in order to offer services and interfaces adapted to the special needs and demands of mobility impaired people.

2. Materials and Methods

2.1 Hardware and Software User Interface Solutions Relevant to the Platform

In this section it is considered the adopted technical approach in relation to four different aspects of the User Interface (UI) configuration: device form factors, operating system, runtime software and networking technology.

Three device form factors have been chosen for the application development and user testing, supporting the targeted scenarios (Alcaine & Salmre, 2006):

- **Smart Phone** is today's most common nomad device. Smart Phones are full-featured mobile phones with personal computer like functionality, rich displays and miniature keypads for text entry. Voice input and output capabilities are also inherent to this form factor.
- **Personal Digital Assistant (PDA)** represents a richer user input/output modality than Smart Phones, with larger touch screens, better feature sets and more powerful processors.
- **Mobile Personal Computer (PC)** has the largest display area among nomad devices and the most flexible user input mechanism, at the cost of a larger size than Smart Phone and PDA form factors. The Ultra Mobile PC (UMPC), attractive because of its portability, deserves to be highlighted here.

The choice of the selected **Operating Systems (OS)** was based on the features needed or preferred by end-users, as well as on their potential commercial exploitation. Finally, three operating **systems allowing Java development**, based on the Mobile Information Device Profile (MIDP) combined with the Connected Limited Device Configuration (CLDC), have been selected (Alcaine & Salmre, 2006):

- **Symbian OS** is a widely used operating system, available on many Smart Phones.
- **Windows Mobile OS** is a commonly used operating system for mobile devices such as PDAs.
- **Windows Tablet PC** is a version of Windows OS with specific Tablet functionality enhancements facilitating interaction with or without keyboard.

A "run-time" is a programming system that lies on top of an O.S. and aids in the development of rich software. The final implementation was based on Java Run-Time Environment (JRE).

Solutions adopted with respect to hardware and Operating Systems support some sub-set of the following networking technologies (Alcaine & Salmre, 2006):

- **GPRS/UMTS** represents data communications over mobile Wide Area Networks (WAN).
- **Wi-Fi** represents Wireless communications over Local Area Networks (LAN).
- **Bluetooth/Zigbee** provides optimized communications for Body Area Networks (BAN) and Personal Area Networks (PAN).

The specific devices used by mobility impaired users during the Project trials were, among others:

- **Smart Phones:** Nokia N95[2], Nokia E90[3]
- **PDAs:** HTC Touch Dual[4], HTC Touch Find
- **Mobile PCs:** Fujitsu FMV-U8240[5], ASUS R2H

The UI configuration of the final system takes into consideration the functional limitations of the user, the type of service that needs to be supported in each case, the context of use, and finally, the benefits offered by each one of the nomad devices (Ringbauer & Hipp, 2008).

2.2 Application Design Guidelines for Nomad Devices

This section reviews several design guidelines that have been considered for the development of applications for nomad devices (Häkkilä & Mäntyajärvi, 2006):

- **GL1. Consider the uncertainty in decision-making situations:** the designer should weight whether the user must be made aware of the uncertainties. This guideline leads the application designer to consider if the device asks the user a confirmation before executing actions.
- **GL2. Prevent from interruptions**: the designer should consider the priority order of actions and whether the user's interruptability in certain situations can be taken into account.
- **GL3. Avoid information overflow**: the device should not seek to present too much information to the user at once, and the presented information should be arranged in a meaningful and understandable manner.
- **GL4. Enable personalization:** the designer should consider using customization to meet the user's individual needs. This can be done, for instance, by implementing filtering according to the user's personal preferences.
- **GL5. Secure the user's privacy:** applications employing information sharing require special care in privacy issues. Possibility of anonymity should be provided.
- **GL6. Remember mobility**: simple and fast interaction should be favoured, as the user may interact with the device while moving or doing something else. The designer must consider how mobility affects the availability and use of the context information - for instance to the available data connections or location detection accuracy.
- **GL7. Guarantee the user control**: the user should always be able to get control over the device. In addition, the designer should consider if there is a need to drop the automation level or ask for confirmation from the user instead of executing fully automated actions.
- **GL8. Customise access to context:** sometimes it may be appropriate to provide the user with the possibility to edit context attributes and their measures. Letting the user rename locations or other context attributes can increase the intelligibility of the application.
- **GL9. Provide visibility of system status:** visibility of system status should be provided for the user to understand and keep up what the device is doing. In addition to general

[2] http://www.nokia.com/

[3] http://www.nokiausa.com/

[4] http://www.htc.com/

[5] http://www.fujitsu.com/

issues, such as showing feedback of executed actions, having logs or history information can be appropriate.

- **GL10. Enhance usefulness**: as an overall point when designing a context awareness application, attention should be paid to the utility value of the provided information and device adaptation.

2.3 User Interface Design Guidelines Applied to Nomad Devices

This section lists some of the main design guidelines that have been considered when designing UIs for nomad devices.

Half of Shneideman's eight interface design guidelines (Schneiderman, 1997) apply to nomad devices without explicit changes (Gong & Tarasewich, 2004):

- **IDGL1. Enable frequent users to use shortcuts:** the user's desire to reduce the number of interactions increases with the frequency of use.
- **IDGL2. Offer Informative feedback:** for every operator action, there should be some system feedback, substantial and understandable by the user.
- **IDGL3. Design Dialogs to yield closure:** users should be given the satisfaction of accomplishment and completion.
- **IDGL4. Support Internal Locus of Control:** systems should be designed such that users initiate actions rather than respond to them.

The remaining four guidelines require modifications and/or an increased emphasis on its use with nomad devices:

- **IDGL5. Consistency:** the designer should guarantee that applications maintain their coherence across multiple platforms and devices.
- **IDGL6. Reversal of actions:** this issue may be more challenging for mobile devices, because of the lack of available resources and computing power (Satyanarayanan, 1996).
- **IDGL7. Error prevention and simple error handling:** error management is always an important issue, but it becomes more critical in the mobile environment due to a more rapid pace of events (Gong & Tarasewich, 2004).
- **IDGL8. Reduce short term memory load:** interfaces should be designed such that very little memorization from the user side is required during the tasks performance. Using alternative interaction modes such as sound can be beneficial (Chan et al., 2002).

Additional guidelines for mobile device design are (Gong & Tarasewich, 2004):

- **IDGL9. Design for multiply and dynamic contexts:** the usability or appropriateness of an application (e.g. brightness, noise levels, weather) can change depending on location, time of day and season (Kim et al., 2002).
- **IDGL10. Design for small devices:** as technology continues to advance, mobile platforms will continue to shrink in size and include items such as bracelets, rings, earrings, buttons, and key chains.
- **IDGL11. Design for limited and split attention:** interfaces for mobile devices need to be designed to require as little attention as possible (Poupyrev et al., 2002).
- **IDGL12. Design for speed and recovery**: for mobile devices and applications, time constraints need to be taken into account in initial application availability and recovery speed.
- **IDGL13. Design for top-down interaction:** the use of multilevel or hierarchical mechanisms might be a better way of presenting information to reduce distraction, interactions, and potential information overload (Brewster, 2002).

- **IDGL14. Allow for personalization:** since nomad devices are more personal than traditional ones, it is more likely that a user of mobile applications will personalize the device and its applications to his preferences.
- **IDGL15. Design for enjoyment:** since aesthetics is also part of designing an overall enjoyable user experience with mobile devices.

2.4. User Interface Approach

Within the ASK-IT project, prior to the final integration of the UI in the ASK-IT devices, the following services' prototypes have been built: route guidance, e-commerce & e-payment, domotics, Advanced Driver Assistance Systems & In-Vehicle Information and Communication Systems (ADAS/IVICS), medical, e-working & e-learning and assistive devices (Bekiaris & Gemou, 2005).

Figure 1 shows an ASK-IT mock-up using a PDA as a nomad device. The ASK-IT services are grouped on application domain related categories: Route planning, Points of interest, Domotics, Assistance and My car.

Most of the systems reported in the literature dealing with content adaptation for small devices consist of tailoring several presentations of the same content to different kind of devices. The difficulty of such approach is that it requires a lot of human efforts in authoring and storing the different content variants.

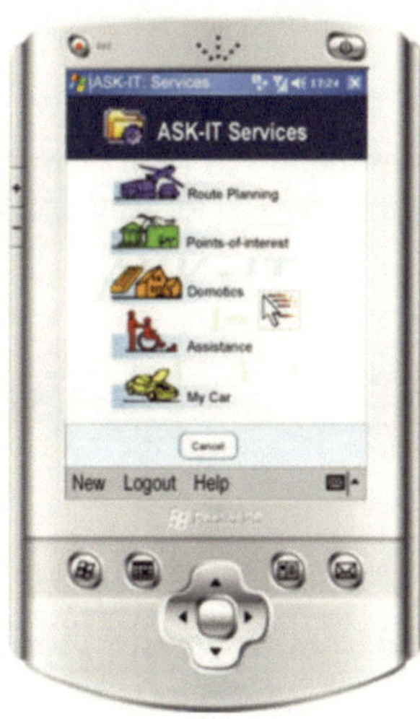

Figure 1. Mock-up illustrating the Services menu (Ringbauer, 2006)

The concept of automatic software adaptation reflects the capability of the software to adapt, during runtime, to the individual end-user, as well as to the particular context of use, by delivering the most appropriate interface solution. For the UI adaptation in ASK-IT, the Decision Making Specification Language (DMSL), which includes a method for automatic adaptation-design verification, was found to be a useful solution (Savidis & Ioannis, 2006). This solution was adopted with Mobile PCs, with satisfactory performance results. However, due to capacity device restrictions, the traditional model for content adaptation had to be used in Smart Phones and PDAs.

3. Results

This section illustrates and describes some of the implemented UIs.
Figure 2 illustrates the "Access menu" UI interface implemented for the PDA form factor. It shows the use of shortcuts (IDGL1) and the design for limited and split attention, by using icons (IDGL11).

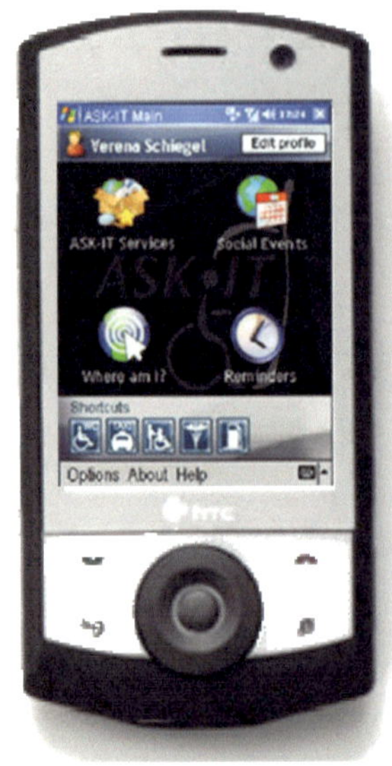

Figure 2. Screenshot of the Access menu for a PDA

Figure 3 illustrates the final "Services menu" UI for a Smart Phone. Compared with the PDA mock-up from Figure 1, only textual and basic information is presented, in accordance with guideline GL3.

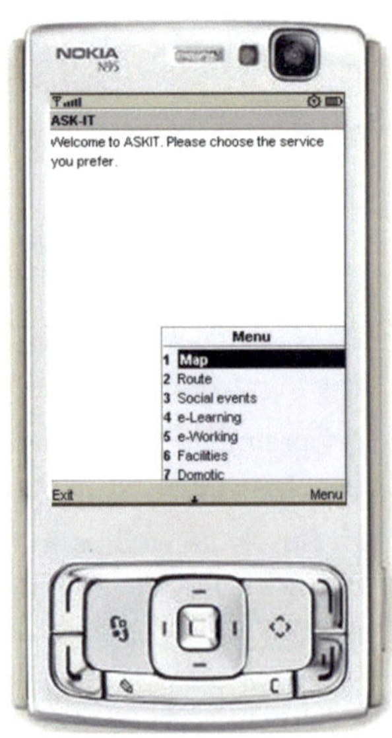

Figure 3. Screenshot of the Services menu UI for a Smart Phone

Figure 4 presents the ASK-IT UI for the domotics scenario in a Smart Phone. The image on the left shows how the user selects the room he is interested in controlling. The image on the right informs the user about the current status of the system following guideline IDGL2, as well as guideline GL4, since it is implemented in black and white, assuring adaptation to visually impaired users needs.

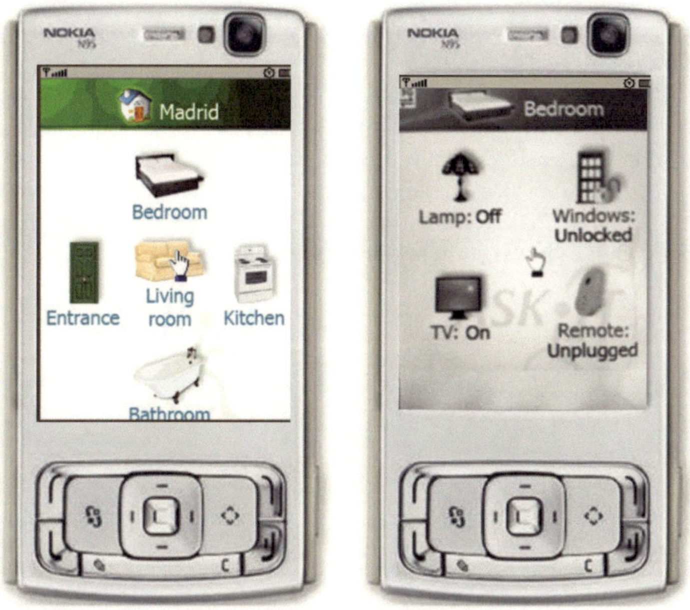

Figure 4. Domotics UI for a Smart Phone (left). UI adapted to a visually impaired user, indicating the status of several devices in the bedroom (right)

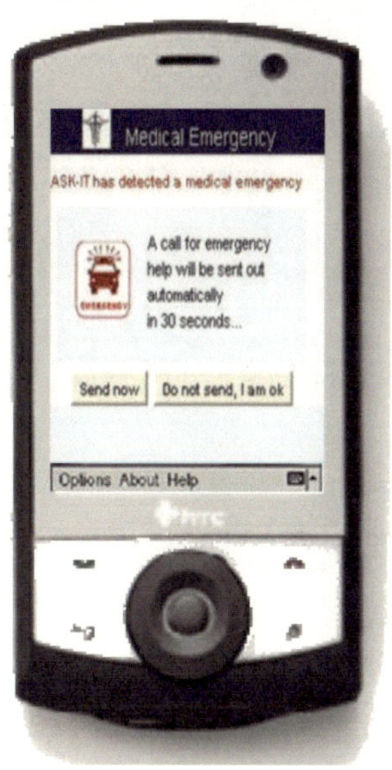

Figure 5. ASK-IT Emergency support scenario UI for a PDA

Figure 5 shows the UI developed for the emergency support scenario. It is compliant with guideline GL9, since the device informs the user about the detection of a medical emergency, and with GL7, as the system asks for user confirmation before sending an ambulance, instead of executing fully automated actions.

Figure 6 shows the final implementation of the UI providing Points of Interest (POI) search functionality, integrated with the "Guide Me" navigation service. After the user performs a POI search operation and receives results, the available POIs are displayed on a map, and if clicked, further information is given.

This specific UI illustrates some of the principles described before. It provides auditory information by clicking on the loudspeaker icon in the upper right corner, making the information available for hearing impaired users (GL4). The positive effect of sound in user interface design of mobile devices has been shown in several studies (Brewster & Cryer, 1999; Brewster & Walker, 2000). Moreover, it provides the user with the possibility to reverse his actions (IDGL6) by clicking on the "Back" button.

Figure 6. PDA screenshot illustrating POI search functionality (left). Information provided for a specific POI (right)

Figure 7 depicts the UI designed specifically to offer information about social events on a Mobile PC. Compared with the previously described ones, this device is most useful when the user is at home or at work. The screen is divided into six different areas: welcome, help and log-out buttons, at the top; navigation, to the left; shortcut buttons; system status; information, which provides the data and position of the user, at the bottom; and a content area, in the centre. It takes into account guideline GL10, since it is aiming to provide useful information to the user about social events that may improve his social relations and leisure time.

Figure 7. UI developed for the Social events service for a Mobile PC

4. Validation

This section provides the preliminary evaluation results from some stand-alone tests of the ASK-IT applications and UIs carried out during June 2008 in several locations of Spain and Greece.

Nine users, with ages ranging from 18 to 68 and with diverse disabilities, participated in the tests and subsequent evaluation.

They received a two hours training session explaining the testing objectives, the specific services and applications that have been developed and describing the tests and the evaluation process.

Feedback from the users was gathered through pre-test questionnaires, mainly designed to obtain demographic data, and post-test questionnaires to assess both the content and the tools utilized.

Figure 8, Figure 9 and Figure 10 illustrate some of the results obtained.

Generally users were satisfied with the graphical interface (GL4) of the system (see Figure 8 left), except the ones that dealt more with maps (POI Search). This is due to the fact that ASK-IT uses the original maps of each service provider and cannot modify them. The font size was thought to be small and zoom was necessary for most of the cases (Figure 8 right).

Figure 9 (left) illustrates that colour contrast was not satisfying for many participants, especially for outdoor users during the planning a trip task. Figure 9 (right) shows that 3 out of 9 participants thought it was difficult to cancel a wrong selection while planning a trip. As the complexity of the service menu increased, the more difficult it seemed to re-adjust wrong selections or to get help from the menu.

Figure 10 (left) shows that for activities such as domotic interaction, planning a trip and searching for social events, the possibility of using touch screens should be considered.

Figure 10 (right) demonstrates that 67% (N=6) of the participants thought the information provided was helpful (GL10).

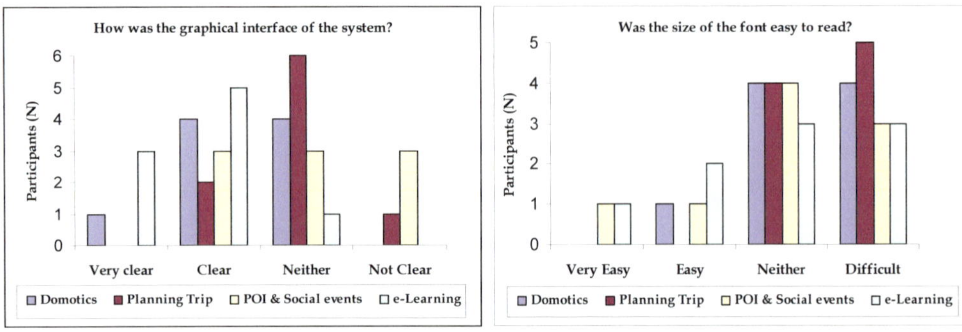

Figure 8. Evaluation results about the clarity of the UI (left). Ease of reading textual information (right)

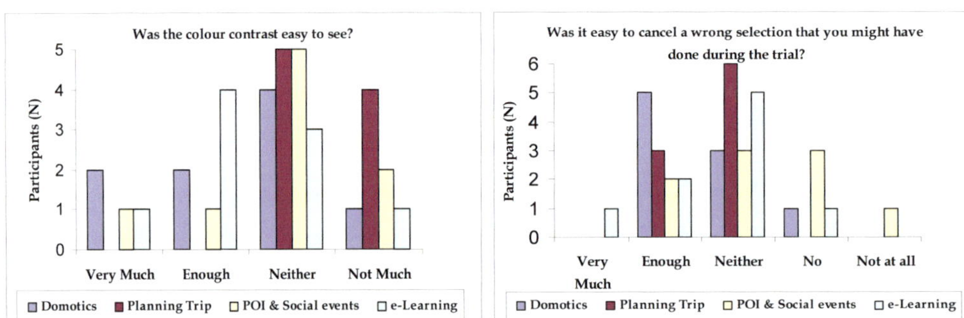

Figure 9. Evaluation results about the colour contrast (left). Ease of cancelling a wrong selection (right)

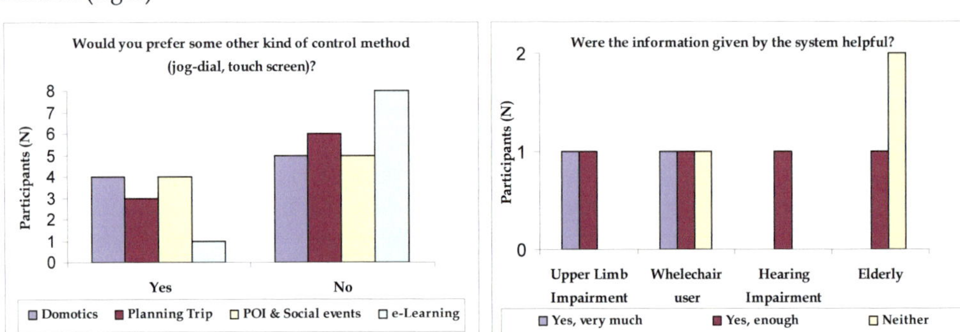

Figure 10. User satisfaction with the input/output modality (left). Usefulness of the information provided by the system (right)

Initial tests have provided useful information about the developed applications and UIs, including their adaptation to nomad devices and to the needs of disabled users and the elderly. Further integrated trials with an extended number of users are envisaged to demonstrate the feasibility and viability of the implemented solution.

6. Conclusion

This paper builds on the importance of supporting the adaptation of the User Interface to different devices and diverse user needs. This is particularly relevant in the case of nomad devices - Smart Phones, PDAs and Mobile PCs - as they allow the user to access information at any time and at any place. Several hardware and software UI design options have been described. Some of the UIs currently implemented have been presented for several scenarios, underlying their compliance with the design guidelines for UIs and applications for nomad devices, and their diverse adaptations to each user.

So far, the automatic adaptation of the UIs using the DMSL has only been possible with Mobile PCs. Future steps should include dynamic UIs adaptation using other types of nomad devices.

Current developments show UI adaptation based on the user profile and more specifically, on the user disability. Future implementations should take into account a possible adaptation based on the context and user preferences.

Results already gathered from stand-alone tests, together with results to be obtained from integrated tests will provide useful information for future improvements of the developed applications and user interfaces. They will also contribute to enhance the access to information and the quality of life of disabled users and the elderly.

7. Acknowledgements

We wish to acknowledge to the ASK-IT partially funded EU Project Consortium for their valuable contributions to this work.

8. References

Alcaine, P. & Salmre, I. (2006). *Internal Report* ASKIT-SIE-WP33-R1-V11, Target Devices Specifications. ASK-IT Project. (IST-2003-511298).

Bekiaris, E. & Gemou, M. (2005). *Internal Deliverable* ASK-IT ID3.2.1-final, Definition of Configuration Parameters. ASK-IT Project. (IST-2003-511298).

Brewster, S. (2002). Overcoming the Lack of Screen Spaces on Mobile Computers, In: *Personal and Ubiquitous Computing*, Springer (Ed.), pp. 188-205.

Chan, S.; Fang, X.; Brzezinski, J.; Zhou, Y.; Xu, S. & Lam, J. (2002). Usability For Mobile Commerce Across Multiple Form Factors, *Journal of Electronic Commerce Research*, Vol. 3, No. 3 (187-199).

Gardner, M. (2006). Nomadic devices. Toward simpler, *Standardized Integration into Vehicles Via a Nomadic Gateway*.

Gong, J. & Tarasewich, P. (2004), Guidelines for handheld mobile device interface design, *Proceedings of the 2004 DSI Annual Meeting*, Boston, MA, USA, November 2004.

Kim, H.; Kim, J.; Lee, Y.; Chae, M. & Choi, Y. (2002). An Empirical Study of the Use Contexts and Usability Problems in Mobile Internet, *Proceedings of the 35th Hawaii International Conference on System Sciences*, ISBN: 0-7695-1435-9, Big Island, Hawaii, January 2002, IEEE Computer Society, Washington, DC, USA.

Hákkilä, J. & Mäntyjärvi, J. (2006). Developing Design Guidelines for Context-Aware Mobile Applications, *Proceedings of the 3rd International Conference on Mobile Technology Applications & Systems*, Art. 24, ISBN: 1-59593-519-3, Bangkok, Thailand, October 2006, ACM, NY, USA.

Lemluma, T. & Layaïda, N. Context-aware adaptation for mobile devices, *Proceedings of the IEEE International conference on Mobile Data Management*, pp.106-111, Berkeley, CA, USA, January 2004, IEEE.

Poupyrev, I; Maruyama, S; Rekimoto, J. (2002). Ambient Touch: Designing Tactile Interfaces for Handheld Devices, *Proceedings of the 15th Annual ACM Symposium on User Interface Software and Technology*, pp. 51-60, Paris, France, 2002.

Ringbauer, B. (2005). Smart Home Control via PDA - an Example of Multi-Device User Interface Design. In: A. Sloane (Ed.), *Proceedings of the Home oriented Informatics and Telematics Conference (HOIT 2005)*, ISBN-10: 0387251782, York, UK, April 2005, Springer, London.

Ringbauer, B. (2006). Internal Deliverable ASKIT ID2.10.2_v01, Simulation and mock/up of all devices for MI. ASK-IT Project. (IST-2003-511298).

Ringbauer, B. & Hipp, C. (2008) ASK-IT Deliverable D.2.10.1. Full Set of Interfaces Concepts and Prototypes. ASK-IT Project. (IST-2003-511298).

Satyanarayanan, M. (1996). Fundamental Challenges in Mobile Computing, *Proceedings of the Fifteenth Annual ACM Symposium on Principles of Distributed Computing*, pp. 1-7, ISBN: 0-89791-800-2, Philadelphia, Pennsylvania, USA, May 1996, ACM.

Savidis, A & Lilis Ioannis, L. (2006). Internal deliverable ASK-IT-ID3.2.2, UI Configuration according to user abilities.

Schneiderman, B. (1997). *Designing the User Interface: Strategies for Effective Human Computer Interaction*, Addison-Wesley, ISBN: 0201694972, Boston, MA, USA.

Stephanidis, C. & Savidis, A. (2003). Unified User Interface Development. In: J. Jacko & A. Sears (Eds.), *The Human-Computer Interaction Handbook - Fundamentals, Evolving Technologies and Emerging Applications* (pp. 1069-1089). Mahwah, New Jersey, Lawrence Erlbaum Associates.

Annex 1- Description of Work. (2004). ASK-IT Project (IST-2003-511298).

24

Rewriting Context and Analysis: Bringing Anthropology into HCI Research

Minna Räsänen[1] and James M. Nyce[2]
[1]*Royal Institute of Technology (KTH),* [2]*Ball State University*
[1]*Sweden,* [2]*USA*

1. Introduction

The use of technology is not a given; rather, we use tools and technology to interact with each other and/or cooperate with each other in various social contexts. Human-Computer Interaction (HCI) research has for long time emphasized the importance of understanding the social context in which this interaction occurs. The concern for and importance of understanding the social context in system design is often motivated by research on immediate context in which work and system development occurs and/or where a certain technical artefact or a computer is used. Analysis within HCI tends to focus on the ongoing activity, the moment-by-moment action of individual lay actors. These events and actions are given priority and are regarded as significant in part because these can be counted. The focus of the analysis is on the particularities of the immediate situation, thus missing the larger picture of what is going on. These types of studies as they have been carried out in HCI deemphasize the study of more stable phenomena and reproduction of a series of structures that inform individual action. In conclusion, the study of moment-by-moment actions of the technology use provides us with only a partial understanding of the social context.

The role of ethnography, other than as a research methodology, within HCI has been to point out the importance of understanding the social context, the routines of users' workday, its practical management and organization. However, the use of ethnography in HCI-research and particularly in design is not unproblematic as the ongoing discussions about the role of ethnography suggests. For example, designers and developers tend to use ethnography instrumentally as a form of data collection in order to identify and solve problems. Results of ethnographic analyses are expected to feed directly into the interests and issues related to technological development. This misrepresents the role ethnography has in anthropology and in the social sciences, more generally.

The more we know about the socio-cultural and historical circumstances the users live in and act on, the better the chances that we can design technologies that support (or change) the users' everyday work. What we are suggesting here is the need for a more analytical, more inclusive way of understanding technology, its design and implementation. This, we believe, is the contribution anthropology can bring to the field of HCI community. Today in the HCI community anthropology is generally equated with ethnography. This is

unfortunate because anthropology can provide the HCI community with an interpretive agenda, one that can help strengthen traditional HCI research.
We start with an introduction to ethnography then turn to how the social context has been defined in HCI and point towards a more adequate social science approach. Thereafter we will demonstrate what this analytical "turn" can contribute to the study of technology use in the workplace.

2. Ethnography in HCI

Ethnography started to appear in HCI in the 1980's. Ethnography's original role in IT research was critical, drawing attention to the failure of conventional research methods to capture the differing perspectives on the use situation (Crabtree, 2004). It pointed to and stressed the importance of the daily routines of the users' workday, the practical management of organizational contingencies, "the taken-for-granted, shared culture of the working environment, the hurly-burly of social relations in the work place, and the locally specific skills (e.g., the 'know-how' and 'know-what'), required to perform any role or task" (Anderson, 1994: 154). The formal models and methods characteristic of HCI research at the time were found to be "incapable of rendering these dimensions visible, let alone capturing them in the detail required to ensure that systems can take advantage of them" (op. cit. 154). Ethnography was thought to be a method that could access these dimensions.
Ethnography, in its broadest sense, has been useful in several areas within design and system-development projects, such as examining work domain, workplaces, and work practices (e.g. Blomberg et al., 2003; Nardi, 1997; Pycock & Bowers, 1996), capturing the situatedness of specific skills (Normark, 2005), investigating the relationship between technology and work, evaluating the products and software systems i.e. conducting a sanity check on design (Hughes et al., 1994), or even acting as "user's champions" (Bentley et al., 1992: 129) and sometimes functioning as an user's advocate in development and design projects. Technology can also be seen as a vehicle for social research, which emerges through a socio-technical methodology, "technomethodology" (Button & Dourish 1996). The ethnographer's role in IT research, it is suggested, would be to identify researchable topics for design through workplace studies and use them to develop abstract design concepts and work up design-solutions (Crabtree & Rodden, 2002).
However, the use of ethnography in HCI-research and particularly in design is not unproblematic (e.g. Anderson, 1994; Bader & Nyce, 1998; Forsythe, 1999; Nyce & Bader, 2002; Nyce & Löwgren, 1995). Designers and developers tend to use ethnography instrumentally to identify and solve problems. It has been reduced to a realistic strategy, one that collects "things" and "answers" questions. In the design-and-development community, what a "problem" is, almost always takes an instrumental, pragmatic turn. "In particular, what a 'problem' is and how to 'solve' it get reduced to a series of practical interventions and practical outcomes" (Nyce & Bader, 2002: 35). This again reflects the legacy of ethnography within HCI, where its role is to handle event(s) and action(s) in order to "predict" outcomes. Ethnography here is reduced to a useful method for gathering and specifying end-user requirements in order to inform systems design: "Instead of focusing on its analytic aspects, designers have defined it as form of data collection. They have done this for very good, design-relevant reasons, but designers do not need ethnography to do what they wish to do" (Anderson, 1994: 151).

There is often a gap between accounts from the field and how the "information can be of practical use to system developers" (Schmidt, 2000: 141). Even if designers work closely with users and representatives of ethnography and psychology in a particular setting, "the objectives of the experiment are clearly defined and the technological options identified and bounded in advance" (op. cit. 148). "Traditional" ethnography does not necessarily fit the requirements and working practices of a design project. For example, requirement analysis is reductionist in character, which in some important ways sets it apart from ethnographical analysis (Crabtree & Rodden, 2002). There are differences between an "adequate account" for the purposes of social science and an adequate account for the purposes of design, one which is intended to contribute to the development of a particular set of occupational practices (Crabtree, 2004; Crabtree & Rodden, 2002; Räsänen & Lindquist, 2005; Shapiro, 1994).

Within HCI and related research areas, ethnomethodology (Garfinkel, 1967/2002) has been promoted as the kind of field research approach that is needed in design (Crabtree, 2004). However, the way it was applied in HCI reduced both ethnomethodology and ethnography to a kind of empirical exercise, which lessened the contributions it might have been able to make to the study of man-machine operations (Nyce & Löwgren, 1995). Whatever criticisms one has, ethnography and ethnomethodology in HCI both offered an opportunity to better specify design practice; the results in turn could improve the innovation and invention into the future (Button & Dourish, 1996; Crabtree, 2004; Crabtree & Rodden, 2002).

One strand of ethnography emphasizes interpretation, not discovery, and the analysis of our own practises as well of those of others. The approach is concerned not only with the production of the society, but also with its reproduction as series of structures (Anderson, 1994; Bader & Nyce, 1998; Chalmers, 2004; Dekker & Nyce, 2004; Dourish, 2006; Giddens 1984/2004; Nyce & Bader, 2002). Recently, the idea of informing design, a key idea in HCI, has been questioned. Dourish (2006) criticizes the politics and conditions under which ethnographic work is done in HCI. By "forcing" ethnography to work towards "implication for design," it misplaces and misconstrues the ethnographic enterprise. In short, the question of how one can get ethnography to *work* and *work well* within systems development has not yet been resolved. Dourish suggests that ethnography (that is, ethnography that goes beyond the "implications for design") has a critical role to play in system design; it provides models for analyzing settings and what is going on there. In addition, it may also uncover constraints or opportunities, in particular design practices, and therefore help to shape research strategies (Dourish, 2006; see also Räsänen, 2007; Räsänen & Nyce, 2006).

Nevertheless, social scientists such as anthropologists have long been thought to be able to contribute to the articulation of the social context of technology use. It seems appropriate to draw from that experience, especially since the social context is of importance for HCI and Computer Supported Cooperative Work (CSCW) research. When considered as much a form of analysis as a field method, ethnography can raise the question of what social context "means" in general terms and how it should be taken into account in a particular design and development project. In this chapter, we suggest an analytical position that is in line with social science traditions such as social and cultural anthropology. We suggest that this analytic frame can help the HCI community to "make sense" of the use situation. To achieve this however, it will be necessary to look more carefully at how ethnographic research has been communicated to designers/developers. If the translation of ethnographic research findings is to be successful, it may be as much attention has to be paid to knowledge, information and work requirements of designers and developers as to those who have traditionally been "targets" of ethnographic research in HCI.

3. Social Context in HCI

The interest in the social context within HCI and related research areas such as CSCW is not new. There are several reasons for this. For one, it became obvious that ICT systems fail when insufficient attention is paid to the social context where the technology is used, for example, at work (Hughes et al., 1994). Human activities involve practices and relations that become meaningful and can be understood in a particular situation, setting and context, and these need to be studied and understood (e.g. Ball & Ormerod, 2000; Blomberg et al., 2003; Blomberg et al., 1993; Dourish, 2001; Nardi, 1996; Nyce & Löwgren, 1995; Suchman, 1987/1990). New technical innovations combined with falling costs, sizes, and power requirements have opened possibilities for ICT packaged in a variety of new devices. The technology is now used for working from home, but also for leisure and other purposes (Bødker, 2006). These changes also emphasize the need and importance to understand and pay attention to the notion of context.

Within the multidisciplinary research areas of HCI and CSCW, the different disciplines involved tend to bring in their various understandings of what context means. The way in which the term is defined reflects differences in intellectual history and research paradigms as well as the different disciplinary backgrounds such as computer science, psychology, communication studies, anthropology, and others found in HCI. Some of the starting points for approaching the notion of context reflect these different research areas, focus, and positions such as learning (e.g. Chaiklin & Lave, 1993) and context-aware computing (e.g. Chalmers, 2004; Dey et al., 2001; Dourish, 2001; 2004). The development of several methods and techniques, such as contextual design (Wixon & Holtzblatt 1990), and the use of weak and strong ethnographical methods reflect the need for understanding the context in which users act (e.g. Blomberg et al., 2003; Nyce & Bader 2002; Spinuzzi, 2000).

It is difficult to precisely define the notion of context. It is an ambiguous concept "that keeps to the periphery, and slips away when one attempts to define it" (Dourish, 2004: 29). However, there have been attempts to define the term in order to handle the various needs of HCI research and practice. User's location, environment, identity, and time specifications when the application is used are aspects found in the early definitions of context (Dey et al., 2001; for one of the earliest attempts to define context within HCI see Schilit & Theimer, 1994). Definitions of context can also be found in guidelines and standards. Standard ISO 13407, for example, defines the "context of use" as "users, tasks, equipment (hardware, software and materials), and the physical and social environments in which a product is used" (ISO 9241-11:1998, definition 3.5). The context of use, it is suggested, should guide early design decisions as well as provide basis for evaluation. The term, context of use, itself draws attention to a specific situation and circumstances where technology is or will be used. Similar attempts to specify context as a term include, for example, usage context, user context, product context, and market context (Moran, 1994).

The notion of context in HCI (particularly in context-aware computing) has dual origins (Dourish, 2001; 2004). It is, first, a technical notion that offers "system developers new ways to conceptualize human action and the relationship between that action and computational systems to support it" (Dourish, 2004: 20). Second, many contemporary HCI and CSCW approaches also rest implicitly or explicitly on divergent social science traditions with analytic focus on aspects of social settings. The term context is used in the terms of social context, where the work task is performed or the technology used (e.g. Ball & Ormerod, 2000; Blomberg et al., 2003; Blomberg et al., 1993; Hughes et al., 1994). The social oriented perspective focuses on groups of individuals and their interaction and/or cooperation with each other. Various workplace studies combine an interest in technology use and work practices in various fields and work settings covering cooperative work, organizational roles as well as the uses and consequences of information and communication technology in organizations. These include, for example, an ethnographic study of air traffic controllers and how this research was used to inform the technology design (Bentley et al., 1992). Workplace studies vary both in the length of time spent in the field as well as the character of the workplace. See, for example, studies of the London Underground, collaborative work such as in the control rooms (Heath & Luff, 1992) and the operation of a train (Heath et al., 1999), a study of CSCW in a small office (Rouncefield et al., 1995), and a study of the fashion industry (Pycock & Bowers, 1996). These studies draw attention to the social context of technology use, which is also a focus of the present chapter.

3.1 Situated Action

One of the most influential social analyses of social context in HCI research is Suchman's (1987/1990) analysis of social action based on ethnomethodology, an analytic approach to social analysis developed by Garfinkel (1967/2002). Suchman focuses on the practical, everyday, ordinary achievements and actions of members of a particular society. She showed that individual's interaction with technology (in her study, a photocopier) did not follow or obey a formal model, but rather exhibited a moment-by-moment, improvised character. Suchman suggests that "however planned, purposeful actions are inevitably *situated actions*"; they are "[...] taken in the context of particular, concrete circumstances" (Suchman, 1987/1990: viii, emphasis in origin). Her work was a welcome critique and corrective of planned accounts of human social action at the time. Even today, the concern for and importance of understanding the social context in system design is often motivated by research on "situated actions." Suchman's work pointed out and made visible the need to study the social context where the technology is used. Various studies of technology use follow up on this tradition. However, we should keep in mind that Suchman's detailed and careful analytic project was concentrated on the immediate context of technology use. It looks at the situated, moment-by-moment actions between the actors, but also what occurs between the actors and the technology as well as between the actors and their immediate environments. This, we believe has had significant consequences for how social context is understood, what is included, and what is left out of such a studies in HCI.

While holding out the promise of methodological and analytical strength, the analysis of situated action has come to define what constitutes acceptable research and analysis of the context of technology use. These studies, we believe, represent a more or less a win-win situation for HCI research. They point out the importance of situation, agency, and the actor and bring them into the analysis of the social context of technology use. They also have helped legitimatize field methodology at large and as research practice in HCI. One reason for the use of the situated action models might be, we suggest, the need to investigate the detailed accounts of everyday practices for design and development purposes, where the focus is, for example, on behaviour, benefits, and evaluation of the artefact and its use. This type of inquiry is often limited by strict, short timelines. Situated action models do not deny the importance of social relations, knowledge, or values of the community or individual. Nevertheless, analysis within HCI still tends to focus on the ongoing activity, the moment-by-moment action of each lay actor. As such it either neglects or underestimates the influence of other elements present and important in social life (Chalmers, 2004; Nardi, 1996). The focus of the analysis is on the particularities of the immediate situation, thus missing the larger picture of what is going on. It is also argued that these types of studies as they have been carried out in HCI deemphasize the study of more stable and elemental phenomena (Nardi, 1996). They tend to be "[...] concerned with the production of society, [...] but much less with its reproduction as a series of structures" (Chalmers, 2004: 230). In conclusion, the study of moment-by-moment actions of the use of technology can give us only a partial understanding of the social context. However, this approach tends to define how most of us think about the social context within HCI. Analysis of the immediate use context and moment-by-moment actions can be useful for certain purposes. However this does not exhaust the possible ways in which social context can be understood.

3.2 Extending the Approach

A continuing debate within HCI revolves around how to broaden our analysis and approaches to the social context so that they can provide a more comprehensive picture, a broader and/or deeper account of technology use. Chaiklin and Lave (1993) and Dourish (2004), for example, have acknowledged the role that cultural and historical elements play in everyday practice. Dourish (2004) reminds us that there is a link between action and meaning, that these together inform what we mean by context, and that structure, history, and culture, not just individual action, constitute, inform, and influence what context means for those who both participate in and study it. The basis for understanding context lies in not just lived experience but also in the structures and resources that make this possible. Context is more than something that people do. Nor can this be reduced to "embodied practice" or "embodied interaction" (Dourish, 2001; 2004). Nyce and Löwgren (1995) discuss how fundamental categories (such as practice and change) are often taken for granted or assumed to be universal. This can neglect significant cultural as well as historical features. The authors examine the concept of participatory design tradition and point out that it rests on and reflects a Nordic tradition not just of cooperation and collaboration but of language use in the workplace (about the Nordic tradition see e.g. Bødker et al., 2000). Chalmers (2004) also refers to the historical elements of context.

Often the starting point and interest for the social context of technology use in HCI and CSCW is the particular work tasks. Consequently, to focus on other aspects of the work life can be seen as extending (broadening) the approach to the social context. This includes the daily routines and shared culture of the working environment (Anderson, 1994). Orlikowski and Hofman (1997), for example, explain how an existing organizational, team-oriented, cooperative culture allowed the staff to take advantage of the novel groupware technology for knowledge sharing (Lotus Notes). The benefits of the same technology were predicted to be much slower in another organization that rewarded individual performance. There, knowledge sharing via technology was seen as a threat to status and individual competence. This and other similar studies point towards the importance of paying attention to the organizational culture of a workplace. The organizations' structure and culture influence how, for example, groupware technology is implemented and used.

Moran and Anderson (1990) developed interest in working life beyond task performance by proposing a "Workaday World" paradigm for CSCW design. This paradigm is based on the idea of a life-world, which includes people's everyday activities, their relationships, knowledge, as well as various resources. The Workaday World paradigm includes technology, sociality, and work practice, suggesting that these aspects are not to be separated, but constitute a dialectic and are together involved in the shaping of a working day. It suggests "the richness of the settings in which technologies live--the complex, unpredictable, multiform relationships that hold among the various aspects of working life" (op. cit. 384). The Workaday World suggests that technology is not central within the working day, but rather has to be put in "proper perspective" (op. cit. 384).

3.3 Unpacking Social Context

The English noun, context, comes from Latin *contextus,* meaning connection of words, coherence, and from *contexere,* to weave together, connect (*The Oxford English Dictionary* 1989 vol. III). Context is defined as "The weaving together of words and sentences," and "The connexion or coherence between the parts of a discourse" as well as "The whole structure of a connected passage regarded in its bearing upon any of the parts which constitute it: the parts which immediately precede or follow any particular passage or 'text' and determine its meaning" (ibid.). Word context also refers to environment and setting. The notion of context implies a combination of two entities: a phenomenon and an environment within which it is embedded (Holy, 1999). Context is described as a frame, an environment, a background, a perspective, or a stage that surrounds a phenomenon or an event and provides resources for its appropriate and meaningful interpretation. What is posited as context in one study may well be the central object of study in another (ibid.).

The notion of context is an important concept in the social sciences, such as anthropology. There it works both explicitly as well as in the background, weaving together with other concepts, approaches, and models of social organizations. As far as we know, there is no single, agreed upon definition of the concept within anthropology. Nevertheless, ever since Malinowski, anthropologists have tried to place and understand social and cultural phenomena in context (Dilley, 1999). However, the notion of context draws attention to both epistemological and methodological problems in social anthropology (ibid.). It is difficult to define precisely the concept of context. Agreement on a single theoretical position or definition of the term context may not even be possible or necessary (Dilley, 1999; Goodwin & Duranti, 1992/1997; Holy, 1999). The aim here is neither to solve the problem of context, nor to propose a new definition. What follows instead is a way of unpacking the idea of the context in order to be able to discuss it (as a "whole") in relation to technology use. One way to extend the notion of context within HCI, we believe, is to pay attention to what goes on beyond the immediate use of technology itself, i.e. to turn towards the structures and conventions that constitute technology use and vice versa. This would make it possible to analyze the activities within which the use is embedded and through which it becomes meaningful. It is this kind of analysis we would like to argue for here.

We take the practices and routines of the work day as our analytical point of departure in order to start approaching the context of technology use. We pay attention to the day-to-day practices during the everyday encounters. Various technologies are often, but not always, used to help carry out these practices. This way, we hope to be able to approach and address not just the speech acts or the practices and routines of a working day, but also the social and cultural conventions that provide the "infrastructure" of daily life (Goodwin & Duranti, 1992/1997: 17) through which the daily practice gains its force as a particular kind of action. In other words, we wish to approach context so that recognizable socio-cultural conventions can be used to make sense of the technology use. As Goodwin and Duranti (1992/1997) emphasize, not only are the activity and the material environment of importance here, but also knowledge of the social dimensions that is created and negotiated through historical processes. The term infrastructure implies an idea of a "frame" (Goffman, 1974/1986) that surrounds the event and makes an appropriate interpretation possible. Context then becomes the framework within which a certain activity is embedded. Implicitly, it indicates that the activity is informed by previous history. However, it also suggests an asymmetry between an event and its "background," which would be somewhat misleading for our purposes here. While it calls attention to the event and the participants, it tends to neglect certain aspects of its surroundings and furthermore, aspects of reproduction. The challenge here is to call at least as much attention to the context as to the event (technology use) itself. The everyday practices we are interested in are, as the word indicates, everyday practices. They can be monotonous and not always reflected upon. The monotony in the practices makes these practices to a certain extent "invisible." The task here is to make visible not just what is immediate but what informs it—infrastructure, the background, or the environment. It is necessary to replace context as the focus of analysis, although this may sound paradoxical. One has to map the context, not entirely in the sense of situating the phenomena (e.g. technology use) in a context, but in the sense of mapping the context and what makes it appear logical and natural (Daryl Slack, 1996; Dilley, 1999). Articulation is a process of creating connections that can make a unity of (two) different elements under certain conditions (Daryl Slack, 1996). It is a complex, unfinished process that tends to foreground some and background other "theoretical, methodological, epistemological, political and strategic forces, interests and issues" (op. cit. 114). Articulation has to some extent come to stand for contextualization itself (Dilley, 1999). How to map context and these connections as well is the interpretative problem we want to discuss here.

This brings us to a central problem in the social sciences, how in analysis can we connect all the various elements, the "layers" such as event and context, as well as individual and social perspectives? What are the significance (conditions, forces, motives, causes, consequences, and so on) of the relationships between the individuals and society? According to Giddens, perhaps the most important contribution the social sciences can make to intellectual discourse is to rework conceptions of human action, i.e. social reproduction and social transformation (Giddens, 1984/2004). However, "micro" and "macro" levels of analysis are carried out in the social science as separate enterprises. Giddens argues that there is no necessary conflict between the two perspectives: one is not more fundamental than the other. Pitting them against each other implies that one needs to choose between them. This "unhappy division of labour" (op. cit. 139) tends to separate analysis and theoretical standpoints, which Giddens believes is unfortunate. He argues that structuration theory is a solution to this problem.

When Giddens talks about structure, he does not mean those "facts" and features of social life that define what can or cannot be done. Rather, he is concerned with what is internal to individuals. For Giddens, structure is embedded both in memory and in social practices, i.e. those "conditions of social action that are reproduced through social action" (O'Brien, 1998: 12). Social actions (or forms of conduct) are situated in and reproduced through time and space, both of which are organized independently. According to Giddens, structure is both generative and transformative. It is both the "medium and outcome of the practices they recursively organize" (Giddens, 1984/2004: 27). Everyday life consists of repetitive practices through time-space. The term structuration captures and allows us to understand the routine sense of practices as well as their continuation and justification. While the analysis of day-to-day life is essential to analysis of the reproduction of institutionalized practices, the point of departure for Giddens is the actions of knowledgeable individuals. In other words, "structure" should not in itself be objectified and explained. Rather, human action has to be explicated for social production to be understood. However, everyday activities should not be treated as the "foundation" of social life, but rather "connections should be understood in terms of an interpretation of social and system integration" (op. cit. 282). Next, we will analyse human action and practices at a workplace and make connections to the structures and ideology of that workplace and beyond. As individuals engage in everyday practices, they recreate and help maintain these practices and context itself. This Giddens makes clear helps inform, define and legitimatize the culture and society these individuals belong to.

4. Operators and Work on Display

The example that follows suggests how social context might be "expanded" in HCI research. This vignette comes from the first author's fieldwork in a Swedish call centre workplace, the Police Contact Centre. The Contact Centre is an in-house service within the police authority. The Contact Centre in Stockholm is located on three islands in the archipelago with management and headquarters on mainland. However, the Contact Centre is organized and managed as a single unit. Its primary task is to handle crime reports from the public concerning everyday crimes. The exceptions are ongoing crimes and crimes where perpetrator is known. The police handle these kinds of calls, many of which are made to the emergency telephone number 112 (in Sweden) and are handled by SOS operators. The crime reports handled by the Contact Centre, on the other hand, concern everyday delinquency, such as thefts of mobile phones, wallets and cars, as well as damage and vandalism. At the time of the fieldwork, the service goals at the Contact Centre included, for example, that 90 per cent of all telephone calls must be answered within three minutes. At worst, only 15 percent of all incoming telephone calls, ones with more than a ten second wait time, could go unanswered.

One morning in October 2002, Kerstin was sitting at a work desk next to researcher's desk. There was a telephone, a computer screen, a keyboard, and a computer mouse on her desk. There was also a notebook, pens, and papers, and a pile of damage reports of graffiti found in buses, underground trains and station areas in Stockholm. That morning Kerstin was assigned to register the reports about graffiti in a police computer application. Kerstin was doing this work one report at a time. There was a display on the telephone. Kerstin looked at the display and commented to herself on the high number of incoming telephone calls as well as the low number of persons logged in to answer them. She looked around the open-plan office and turned back to the damage reports and her computer. Now and again, she glanced at the telephone display. After a while, she put a sheet of paper on the telephone to cover the display and hide the information (the number of operators logged in, the number of incoming calls). Some time went by, and she continued to work on the damage reports. Once again, Kerstin turned to the telephone. She removed the paper and looked at the display. She sighed deeply and looked around the open-plan office. Kerstin covered the

display again and continued to work on the graffiti reports. Now and again, she lifted the sheet of paper and checked the display as she continued to enter her graffiti reports.
We will now attempt to unpack what seems to be going on here. Kerstin's actions, like those of any other actor, need to be understood in relation to time, location and setting. Following Giddens, some questions immediately come to mind. What is the moment-to-moment action here? What can the action tell us about social production? What is the structure and what does it mean to one's informants like Kerstin? Do we need history or culture, two central structural properties, to understand what is going on here? Can we infer (discover) what these are through workplace observation alone? A related question is what kind of discovery procedure, analysis, or interpretive operation, will enable us to make sense of "what's 'really' going on here?" Finally, what can we learn from this example about the design, development and implementation of work technology?

4.1 Situated Practices

The telephone is one of the most used working devices in the Contact Centre. All incoming telephone calls regarding the crime reports from the public are distributed through an automated call distribution system to a free operator regardless of where s/he is. The display on the telephone shows the total number of incoming telephone calls from the public placed in queue to the operators at the Contact Centre. It also shows the number of operators logged in on the call distribution system and ready to receive telephone calls. Login procedure has two main steps. The first command on the telephone activates only the display on the telephone. The display now shows the total number of incoming telephone calls from the general public queuing to be answered. It also shows the total number of operators logged in on the call distribution system at the Contact Centre. The next step is to type in a personal login-code; then the operator is connected to the call distribution system and the system starts handing the operator telephone calls. The display on the telephone shows the most current information on the number of telephone calls as well as the number of operators accepting calls. In a way, it represented information on the workload based on the telephone calls. It also showed how many persons were working with incoming telephone calls at that moment.
When asked, Kerstin explained it was important to keep herself up to date about the workloads of others at the Contact Centre. She did not like to do other work when the number of incoming telephone calls was high. That morning she raised the question about which work really counted. Could filing graffiti reports, she asked, really be more important than answering incoming telephone calls? Later, Kerstin and her fellow staff members explained that the checking the queue had much to do with "responsibility towards the work tasks" and that this helped insure that "the work was done."
At the Contact Centre, Kerstin was not the only person to monitor the display closely even when not expected to do so, for example, while writing or reading e-mails or being engaged in a conversation with someone else. If staff noticed that the number of incoming telephone calls increased, they would start to take telephone calls. When the number of incoming calls is high, it most likely means long waiting times and some degree of irritation for the persons calling. This, in turn, creates a stressful situation for the personnel because callers often start their conversations with complaints about how long they had to wait. For the personnel, it is not pleasant to deal with annoyed people call after call. Nevertheless, there were valid reasons for not being logged in on the call distribution system. One of them, as seen here, is

other work tasks. For a number of reasons, an employee also needed to log out of the call distribution system in order to complete a report for the police. The regular (at that time) five minutes delay set up between the telephone calls was not always enough time for employees to complete this task.

Once an operator logged out, i.e. left the call distribution system, the information regarding him/her, as a number on the display, was no longer available. For Kerstin and her fellow staff members at the same location, this was not a problem; they saw each other anyway and could keep themselves apprised of another person's whereabouts and work efforts. At the other two locations, it was not always clear what was happening with call queuing. Did an operator at a site quit working? Posted, shared information about personnel and working hours did not always answer the questions operators had at a particular moment. Several times personnel wondered what was happening at the other two sites when the number of operators was low. When this happened personnel from one site called another to ask, "What is going on [there]?" Those who received the telephone calls did not appreciate this, which caused some tension among the sites. What underlay, it seemed, these conversations was divergent understandings of work and work responsibilities. This practice of "checking" partly led the notion of "big sister" being coined at the Contact Centre. This did at times indicate the relationship with the site that was, in a way, parenting (supporting) others. While parenting is about caring for and helping those who were new to the Contact Centre, this notion of "big sister" also was a statement about hierarchy, that one site can be seen as somewhat superior to the other two.

Not knowing what was going on at the other sites, especially why the number of logged on operators was sometimes low, was an issue that came up again and again at the Contact Centre. The question was also raised at a semi-annual joint workplace meeting for all the Contact Centre staff. The topic came up when "everyday comfort/well-being, working environment, and ethics" was discussed. This discussion started in small groups and became an issue the group took up as a whole. It became clear that the issue was a sensitive one--one that raised the spectre of control and surveillance. Staff believed that the checking on each other across the sites was not appropriate. The staff concluded, "We must trust each other." They also raised a number of related work issues. The five minutes delay between the telephone calls, the staff argued, is sometimes too short for finishing up a report before the next call arrives. The telephone display, personnel added, did not always show accurate information. This points to an issue of trust and truthfulness in relationship to technology - an issue the HCI literature has not systematically explored yet. The telephone is an important tool in the Contact Centre, not only for making and receiving telephone calls. The numbers on the telephone display represent current information about the workload ahead. This information and the way it was interpreted became a kind of thermometer that said much about the climate at the workplace. The telephone became an instrument staff used to plan, make sense of, and prioritize work. Keeping an eye on the telephone display or, rather, the queue information there, was, in a way, keeping an eye on the number of general public calling in, taking action so as not to make them wait. Not making them wait is part of the service the authority wants to give the public. It is also an action to protect the Contact Centre staff from people who become irritated when they had to wait too long. It was also used for checking on, interrogating, and monitoring each other. While checking on someone has a somewhat positive meaning in this context, issues related to accountability and surveillance were there too, and not far beneath the surface. The telephone display allowed the staff to monitor each other without revealing that they actually were doing this. How an individual assessed a particular situation varied according to his/her previous understandings and his/her perception of "work load" at that particular time and place. Among Contact Centre employees, these were important, unresolved issues. They came up in discussions at a joint workplace meeting, one with a tight time schedule and agenda. This shows how important these issues were at the time.

In Contact Centre, face-to-face encounters are not always possible because of diverse work tasks, different working hours and/or geographical distances. Under such conditions, mediated interaction and mediated communication between staff become important. In every workplace, employees create ways of finding out what is going on, who is doing what, and how to indicate belonging to the same organization. When face-to-face interaction was not possible various signs—meeting minutes, Christmas cards, electronic mail, duty schedules and other indicators—constituted intermediary links across the three sites. The presence of others as well as a sense of a common workplace was distributed and communicated by low-tech and high-tech artefacts. Sending employee pictures of one other is also a way to introduce and remind staff of the existence of other personnel.

"Out of sight, out of mind" (*Syns du inte, finns du inte*) was flashed on an electronic outdoor advertisement board at in Stockholm a few years ago. The text advertised the advertisement board itself, high up on a house wall, perfectly placed for road traffic on its way in to the city. However, even small indications such as numbers on a telephone display can help us orientate ourselves in everyday life. The personnel at the Contact Centre need and create possibilities for checking on, monitoring, and supervising their working situation of which they are a part. The problem the telephone display raised for the Contact Centre employees was that their work, all their work, was made visible. In effect, their work could never be out of sight, out of mind. As a result, work, especially the work of others, could not only be inventoried. It could be assessed, questioned and challenged as well. In open-plan office, these issues, especially how to balance control and trust, are complex enough even when one can look around the office and check on the people there. They are compounded at the Contact Centre because both work and responsibility is divided between four geographically distributed sites. Contact Centre staff used their telephone displays to take the temperature not just of their own particular work environment, but also of all those they collaborate with. Given the distance and geography, sense making required even more complicated interpretative procedures than that at most workplaces. To work successfully in and across three different workplaces suggests staff had to negotiate a very complex social context.

Not all personnel experience, of course the same thing. We may react to the same information on the telephone display differently. However, workplace representations and artefacts do not necessarily include everything that is needed in order to understand any one specific action. In order to understand for example what appears on the telephone display, it is necessary to come to an understanding of how different signs and meanings have become embedded in a working day and what these signs mean. Here both use of technology and meaning are iterative. Prior use and experience feeds into the interpretations of subsequent activity, which in turn informs and affects use again. This can take artefact, use and the meaning of them both in different directions. For this reason, it is not enough to treat these elements instrumentally and sequentially. Nor is it sufficient to be content analytically with unpacking the semantic "load" they carry and acquire only in direct reference to the work itself. If we confine ourselves to this, we would miss a whole series of situated notions that we also need to unpack if we are to understand in any adequate way what is going on in work at any one site.

4.2 Work Domain to Socio-structural Context

The numbers on the telephone display lead us to the institutionalized practices of a call-centre organization. In line with the idea that (monotonous) tasks can be quantified and that efficiency aspects can easily be identified, it is common to collect statistics about work tasks in call centres. The telephone and computer technologies that are used to handle work tasks make these measurements possible (Callaghan & Thompson, 2001; Lindegren & Sederblad, 2004). With help of ICT, there are several technical possibilities management could use to follow up work tasks and to monitor staff members. The use of statistics is also common within the police authority. The degree of criminality in our society, the success of the police authority, and so on is measured, for instance, by the number of reported and resolved crimes. The ICT systems at the Contact Centre that are used to store information about criminality in Sweden can also be used to measure the work performance, a well known fact for Kerstin and others who work there. To find such a direct link between technology, crime statistics and workplace surveillance would not have surprised Foucault.

One informant described the work in the early days of Contact Centre like this; "We are very anxious about our work. We needed to fight for the work opportunities on this island." Work at the Contact Centre was often described as a kind of struggle. The Stockholm archipelago is in many ways a rural area despite its proximity to Stockholm. As such, issues like access to school and work opportunities are important for those who live there. The Contact Centre organization was established in a rural area by process best described as "push" and "pull." The establishment of the Contact Centre is a result of a labour-market project to create work opportunities in the archipelago. It is a joint effort between various actors and islanders who were interested in maintaining and creating new work opportunities in the archipelago. The Contact Centre also represents a form of work redistribution to which HCI researchers have not yet paid much attention. The Contact Centre represents a kind of relocation, a movement of capital, infrastructure, and, in a way, labour quite literally "off shore." The decision to locate this work in the archipelago as well recapitulates a long prior history of connections and businesses between the islands and the Stockholm region.

Work at the Contact Centre was taken even more "seriously" because of the need to draw new work opportunities to the archipelago and keep them there. Staff wanted to show that they were "capable" and "worked hard" to prove their worth to their employer. Some Contact Centre employees were themselves involved in the starting the Contact Centre and now worked there. This work opportunity seems to have been turned into a collective matter in the archipelago and thus become everyone's responsibility. What you fight for, you also want to preserve. Not only was there a need to bring new economic opportunities to the archipelago, but staff also believed they had to work hard to keep their jobs there. As a result, work issues were framed, not just as monitoring issues, but as issues about collective and individual (moral) responsibility. Given this, it is no wonder that the staff studied their telephone displays so carefully.

Establishment of Contact Centre can also be seen as an attempt to maintain a "living archipelago" (*levande skärgård*). The concept of a living archipelago is one often used today both on and off the archipelago. While to some extent this idealizes archipelago life and society, it also represents the modern Swedish state's commitment to improving living conditions there. Normatively, the state's intention here is to protect and preserve the archipelago's natural environment and culture. The state's commitment to a living archipelago reflects some kind of a conclusion of a long historical debate on the significance of the archipelago in Sweden. This is no longer so much a debate about a nation's boundaries or regions as it is one about how both the destiny and history of a particular locality is to be defined and negotiated within the nation. Nevertheless, the archipelago has long played an important role in negotiations about place and power in the history of Sweden. This is a debate that essentially revolves around the constitution of national and regional governments in Sweden and ultimately what determines "the order of things."

What is at work here are just the kinds of historical, socio-structural processes HCI researchers have not yet acknowledged as important nor paid much attention to. Nevertheless they have profoundly influenced work and work conditions in the archipelago at a number of levels. As we have argued, social context is not neutral. In the archipelago it reflects a series of recurring social, historical and ongoing political processes. In this way, different forms of social conduct are reproduced continuously across time and space. It would be unwise to neglect these "larger" issues, these other "layers," structures and strictures in our analyses if we wish to understand the circumstances in which our informants live and work. Further, knowledge of this order of things enables what Giddens terms mutual understanding – the epistemological basis he tells us is necessary to carry out any adequate interpretive work in the social sciences. This "know-how" while embedded in and informed by history, including that of the workplace, informants cannot directly report to us.

5. Conclusions

Is it enough to be aware of that conventions and norms that inform the hurly-burly of the organizational culture? Or do we also have to understand and interpret events that extend beyond the particular social reality we are interested in. It is one thing to acknowledge that to study events beyond a certain scale is "hard to do." However, do we really want to "stop" argument and interpretation at this point just because events are, as the HCI literature often puts it, "hard to capture"? The question is, if we "stop" here, do we without realizing it, weaken both the kind of science we can do in HCI and the kinds of practical advice we can give designers and developers?

Social science such as anthropology gives us ways to extend our analysis of technology use. In particular, what comes into view are the different layers, webs, aspects, and perspectives that inform everyday life. The same is true for those resources and structures which underlie and help determine what in everyday life is taken to be "true", "logical" and "natural." This would strengthen the understanding of action that is already the focus of (ethnographic) HCI research. By looking beyond artefact use and the artefact itself we would be able to link artefact to agency and structure. This would help HCI bridge the gap between actor and socio-structural points of views. This offers a way to understand elements and relationships that so far are either under reported or not well analysed in the HCI literature. Anthropology can provide us with the analytic terminology we need to start talking about key issues, a terminology that links individual practice to the socio-structural context in which they occur.

This would provide an opportunity to extend those objects and domains that today define HCI research. Borrowing from anthropology, would help us avoid the temptation to reify or empiricize social action. A more productive line of attack would be to try to explicate the social (re)production of action especially as this pertains to work and artefact. If the HCI community would like to strengthen the kinds of research it carries out, HCI should, we believe, extend its analytical toolbox in these directions. To make this "toolkit" suitable for the HCI, more work is required.

To mistake interaction for context, as HCI research often does, turns attention all too quickly to the individual and individual actions. This encourages us to write accounts of failure and success that implicate only individual actors. To correct for this individualistic fallacy, we need to move beyond immediate situation (workplace, organization) to the analysis of those "larger" historical, socio-structural processes and discourses which both individuals and technology participate in and are shaped by. Further, the more we can learn about the socio-structural and historical circumstances users live in and act on, the better are the chances that we can design technologies that actually support the users' everyday work. What we are arguing for here is the need for a more analytical, more inclusive way of understanding technology, its design and implementation. This, we believe, would be the contribution anthropology can bring to the HCI community.

6. Acknowledgments

We would like to thank the personnel in the Police Contact Centre for opening their workplace for our research. Minna Räsänen's fieldwork was done within project Community at a Distance that was coordinated by Centre for User Oriented IT Design (CID) at Royal Institute of Technology (KTH), and carried out together with Laboratory for Advanced Media Technology (AMT) at KTH, Arbetstagarkonsult AB and the police authority in Stockholm County. This chapter is based on corresponding argument and examples presented in Räsänen (2007) and in Räsänen & Nyce (2006). We would also like to thank reviewers for their comments on earlier drafts of this chapter.

7. References

Anderson, R. J. (1994). Representations and Requirements: The Value of Ethnography in System Design. *Human-Computer Interaction*, 9(2), 151-182

Bader, G. and J. M. Nyce (1998). When Only the Self Is Real: Theory and Practice in the Development Community. *The Journal of Computer Documentation*, 22(1), 5-10

Ball, L. J. and T. C. Ormerod (2000). Putting Ethnography to Work: The Case for a Cognitive Ethnography of Design. *International Journal of Human-Computer Studies*, 53(1), 147-168

Bentley, R., Hughes, J. A., Randall, D., Rodden, T., Sawyer, P., Shapiro, D. and I. Sommerville (1992). Ethnographically-Informed System Design for Air Traffic Control, *Proceedings of the 1992 ACM Conference on Computer-supported Cooperative Work*, pp. 123-129

Blomberg, J., Burrell, M. and G. Guest (2003). An Ethnographic Approach to Design. In: *The Human-Computer Interaction Handbook: Fundamentals, Evolving Technologies and Emerging Applications*, J. A. Jacko and A. Sears, (Eds.), 964-986, Lawrence Erlbaum Associates, New Jersey

Blomberg, J., Giacomi, J., Mosher. A. and P. Swenton-Wall (1993). Ethnographic Field Methods and Their Relation to Design. In: *Participatory Design: Principles and Practice*, D. Schuler and A. Nimioka (Eds.), 123-155, Lawrence Erlbaum, London

Button, G. and Dourish, P. (1996). Technomethodology: Paradoxes and Possibilities, *Proceedings of the 1996 Conference on Human Factors in Computing Systems*, pp. 19-26

Bødker, S. (2006). When Second Wave HCI Meets Third Wave Challenges [Keynote], *Proceedings of the Fourth Nordic Conference on Human-Computer Interaction (NordiCHI2006)*, pp. 1-8

Bødker, S., Ehn, P., Sjögren, D. and Y. Sundblad (2000). Co-operative Design: Perspectives on 20 Years with "The Scandinavian IT Design Model" [Keynote], *Proceedings of Nordic Conference on Human-Computer Interaction (NordiCHI2000)*, pp. 23-25

Callaghan, G. and P. Thompson (2001). Edwards Revisited: Technical Control and Call Centres. *Economic and Industrial Democracy: An International Journal*, Sage, London, 22(1), 13-37

Chaiklin, S. and J. Lave (1993). *Understanding Practice: Perspectives on Activity and Context*, Cambridge University Press, Cambridge

Chalmers, M. (2004). A Historical View of Context. *Computer Supported Cooperative Work*, 13 (3), 223-247

Crabtree, A. (2004). Taking Technomethodology Seriously: Hybrid Change in the Ethnomethodology-Design Relationship. *European Journal of Information Systems*, 13(3), 195-209

Crabtree, A. and T. Rodden (2002). Ethnography and Design? *Proceedings of the International Workshop on "Interpretive" Approaches to Information Systems and Computing Research*, pp. 70-74

Daryl Slack, J. (1996). The Theory and Method of Articulation in Cultural Studies. In: *Stuart Hall: Critical Dialogues in Cultural Studies*, D. Morley and K-H. Chen (Eds.), Routledge, New York

Dekker, S. W. A. and J. M. Nyce (2004). How Can Ergonomics Influence Design? Moving from Research Findings to Future Systems. *Ergonomics*, 47(15), 1624-1639

Dey, A. K., Abowd G. D. and D. Salber (2001). A Conceptual Framework and a Toolkit for Supporting the Rapid Prototyping of Context-Aware Applications. *Human-Computer Interaction*, 16, 97-166

Dilley, R. (1999). Introduction: The Problem of Context. In: *The Problem of Context*, R. Dilley (Ed.), Berghahn Books, New York

Dourish P. (2006). Implications for Design, *Proceedings of the SIGCHI Conference on Human Factors in Computing Systems (CHI2006)*, pp. 541-550

Dourish, P. (2004). What We Talk about When We Talk about Context. *Personal and Ubiquitous Computing*, 8(1), 19-30

Dourish, P. (2001). Seeking a Foundation for Context-Aware Computing. *Human-Computer Interaction*, 16, 229-241

Forsythe, D. E. (1999). It's Just a Matter of Common Sense: Ethnography as Invisible Work. *Computer Supported Cooperative Work* 8, 127-145

Garfinkel, H. (1967/2002). *Studies in Ethnomethodology*, Polity Press, Cambridge

Giddens, A. (1984/2004). *The Constitution of Society*, Polity Press, Cambridge

Goffman, E. (1974/1986). *Frame Analysis: An Essay on the Organization of Experience*, Northeastern University Press, Boston

Goodwin C. and A. Duranti (1992/1997). Rethinking Context: An Introduction. In: *Rethinking Context: Language as an Interactive Phenomenon*, A. Duranti and C. Goodwin (Eds.), Cambridge University Press, Cambridge

Heath, C., Hindmarsh, J. and P. Luff (1999). Interaction in Isolation: The Dislocated World of the London Underground Train Driver. *Sociology*, 33(3), 555-575

Heath, C. and P. Luff (1992). Collaboration and Control: Crisis Management and Multimedia Technology in London Underground Line Control Rooms. *Journal of Computer Supported Cooperative Works*, 1(1), 24-48

Holy, L. (1999). Contextualisation and Paradigm Shifts. In: *The Problem of Context*, R. Dilley (Ed.), Berghahn Books, New York

Hughes, J., King, V., Rodden T. and H. Andersen (1994). Moving out from the Control Room: Ethnography in System Design, *Proceedings of the Conference on Computer-supported Cooperative Work*, pp. 429-439

ISO 9241-11:1998, definition 3.5, "context of use". Swedish Institute for Standards (1999). ISO 13407: *European Standard for Human-centred Design Processes for Interactive Systems.* SIS Standardiseringsgruppen STG, Stockholm

Lindegren, A. and P. Sederblad (2004). Teamworking and Emotional Labour in Call Centres. In: *Learning to Be Employable: New Agendas on Work, Responsibility and Learning in a Globalizing World*, C. Garsten and K. Jacobsson (Eds.), Plagrave Macmillan, Hampshire

Moran, T. P. (1994). Introduction to This Special Issue on Context in Design. *Human-Computer Interaction*, 9, 1-2

Moran, T. P. and R. J. Anderson (1990). The Workaday World As a Paradigm for CSCW Design, *Proceedings of the 1990 ACM Conference on Computer-supported Cooperative Work*, pp. 381-393

Nardi, B. A. (1997). The Use of Ethnographic Methods in Design and Evaluation: Chapter15. In: *Handbook of Human-Computer Interaction*, M. Helander, T.K. Landauer and P. Prabhu (Eds.), 361-366, Elsevier Science B.V.

Nardi, B. A. (1996). Studying Context: A Comparison of Activity Theory, Situated Action Models, and Distributed Cognition. In: *Context and Consciousness: Activity Theory and Human-Computer Interaction*, B. A. Nardi (Ed.), MIT Press, Cambridge, MA

Normark, M. (2005). *Work and Technology Use in Centers of Coordination: Reflections on the Relationship Between Situated Practice and Artifact Design*. Doctoral thesis, The Department of Numerical Analysis and Computing Science, the Royal Institute of Technology, Stockholm

Nyce, J. M. and G. Bader (2002). On Foundational Categories in Software Development. In: *Social Thinking: Software in Practice*, C. Floyd, Y. Dittrich and R. Klischewski (Eds.), MIT Press, Cambridge

Nyce, J. M. and Löwgren, J. (1995). Toward Foundational Analysis in Human-Computer Interaction. In: *The Social and Interactional Dimensions of Human-Computer Interfaces*, Thomas, P.J. (Ed.), Cambridge University Press, New York, NY

O'Brien M. (1998). The Sociology of Anthony Giddens: An Introduction. In: *Conversations with Anthony Giddens: Making Sense of Modernity*, A. Giddens and C. Pierson (Eds.), Polity Press, Cambridge

Orlikowski, W. J. and J. D. Hofman (1997). An Improvisational Model of Change Management: The Case of Groupware Technologies. *Sloan Management Review*, 38(2), 11-22

The Oxford English Dictionary (1989). Second edition, volume III Cham-Creeky. Clarendon Press, Oxford (*context*)

Pycock, J. and J. Bowers (1996). Getting Others To Get It Right: An Ethnography of Design Work in the Fashion Industry, *Proceedings of the 1996 ACM Conference on Computer Supported Cooperative Work*, pp. 219-228

Rouncefield, M., Viller, S., Hughes, J.A. and T. Rodden (1995). Working with "Constant Interruption": CSCW and the Small Office. *The Information Society*, 11, 173-188

Räsänen, M (2007). *Islands of Togetherness: Rewriting Context Analysis*. Doctoral thesis, Royal Institute of Technology, School of Computer Science and Technology, Stockholm

Räsänen, M. and J. M. Nyce (2006). A New Role for Anthropology? Rewriting "Context" and "Analysis" in HCI Research, *Proceedings of the Fourth Nordic Conference on Human-Computer Interaction (NordiCHI2006)*, pp. 175-184

Räsänen, M. and S. Lindquist (2005). "Och du ska göra lite etno": Gestaltningar av etnografi inom MDI, *Kulturstudier i Sverige. Nationell forskarkonferens, Linköping Electronic Conference Proceedings* ecp 015

Schilit, B. N. and M. M. Theimer (1994). Disseminating Active Map Information to Mobile Hosts. *IEEE Network*, 8 (5): 22-32

Schmidt, K. (2000). The Critical Role of Workplace Studies in CSCW. In: *Workplace Studies: Recovering Work Practice and Informing System Design*, P. Luff, J. Hindmarsh and C. Heath (Eds.), Cambridge University Press, Cambridge

Shapiro, D. (1994). The Limits of Ethnography: Combining Social Sciences for CSCW, *Proceedings of the 1994 ACM Conference on Computer Supported Cooperative Work*, pp. 417-428

Spinuzzi, C. (2000). Investigating the Technology-Work Relationship: A Critical Comparison of Three Qualitative Field Methods, *Proceedings of IEEE Professional Communication Society International Professional Communication Conference*, pp. 419-432

Suchman, L. A. (1987/1990). *Plans and Situated Actions: The Problem of Human Machine Communication*, Cambridge University Press, Cambridge

Wixon, D. and K. Holtzblatt (1990). Contextual Design: An Emergent View of System Design, *Proceedings of the SIGCHI Conference on Human Factors in Computing Systems*, pp. 329-336

25

Interface Design of Location-Based Services

Chris Kuo-Wei Su and Li-Kai Chen
National Kaohsiung First University of Science and Technology
Taiwan, R. O. C.

1. Introduction

Recently, mobile networks have been widely deployed in global mobile markets and returns from telephony services had proven to be significant to specific mobile operators (Varshney, 2003). According to reports from market research studies (Canalys, 2005), the shipments of converged smart mobile devices, namely Smartphone and wireless handhelds, rose by 170% year-on-year in Europe and Middle East in the first part of 2005. Reed (2001) stated that "telecommunication companies are making huge investments and they know that Location-Based Service (LBS) technology is a key application from which they can generate revenue". For example, NTT DoCoMo reports that the number of I-mode subscribers in Japan now exceeds 38 million, which is nearly half of all cellular phone subscribers in Japan (NTT DoCoMo, 2003). Furthermore, a market overview shows that the global LBS market is already noticeable and continues to grow rapidly.

A wide range of services that rely on users' location information have been conceived although the markets are not completely mature. In the future, while mobile users access the Value Added Service (VAS), they always suffer some possible problems induced by the small physical size of the screen. In fact, the screen of Smartphone is too small to display dynamic content such as PoI (Point of Interest) of LBS information which included graphics, icons, and multimedia on the map. The display of PoI information on the map should be tailored to the needs of users, meaning display of information should be simple way to avoid overly complex information. Hence, previous research presents two different ways to display information on handhelds, both List View Display (LVD) and Map View Display (MVD) (Dunlop et al., 2004). Unfortunately, very little has been published on the evaluation of LBS on Smartphone users, and the main focus of the few available papers is not on the rigorous experimental evaluations demanded by research of mobile Human-Computer Interaction (HCI). Thus this study not only concerns issues of mobile HCI, but also of user interface (UI), that concerns cognitive and psychological aspects in process of development.

This aim of the study discusses an empirical study which is undertaken to extend the original interface and compare MVD and LVD of diversity visualization of PoI information developed for Smartphone. Two objectives of the study are the following:

1. To develop a diverse prototype of LBS interface, which displays dynamic PoI information on the map in an intuitive and clear way base on the design principles of mobile HCI.
2. To evaluate and extract the more adaptable element of visualization of display through rigid experimental evaluations, and give specific post-questionnaire for investigating and analyzing users' subjective opinions.

2. Literature Review

2.1 Local based service (LBS)

Mobile location-based commerce refers to the provision of location-based information on mobile devices as a result of a user request (Varshney, 2003). It aims to provide specific targeted information to users based on each specific user's location at any time (Benson, 2001). OGC (2003) stated that LBS is defined as a wireless-IP service that uses geographic information to serve a mobile user, or as any application service that takes advantage of the position of a mobile device.

The LBS applications include emergency and safety-related services, entertainment, navigation, directory and city guides, traffic updates, and location-specific advertising and promotion in addition to site-based purchasing with e-wallet enabled wireless devices. These services can answer questions such as, "Where can I find a Chinese restaurant," or "Where are my nearest friends?". For example, NTT DoCoMo expresses a "friend finder" service on its iMode system (Levijoki, 2000). Users can predefine which friends are allowed to know their location. Integrating the map database with the PoI database can create detailed, available digital representation of the road network and business services. To cover simple city maps, routings, business finder, etc., these services are usually combined with a digital map associated to the user location. Reichenbacher (2001) shows that LBS applications typically use information from several content databases:

- Road network (digital maps).
- Business and landmark information often referred to as Yellow Pages or PoI information.
- Dynamic data such as traffic and weather reports.

The POI information can vary from maps to maps, as the icons of how the information is presented in the map view. Colourful bitmap icons are used to represent interesting objects on the map (Dunlop et al., 2004). Neudeck (2001) also presents the first practical guidelines for screen map graphics that can be embedded in the design of mobile maps. These guidelines suggest that mobile maps should be simple and highly generalized, should be based on cartographic principles, rendered fast, graphically concise, attractive, crisp, and legible.

In addition, their content should be flexible and should be dynamically updated and linked to other information. These services must be capable of displaying PoI and landmarks, the geo-location of people, objects, and events, routes, and search results (i.e. people, objects, events). The basic functionality of solutions for mobile geographic information visualization is provided by city maps with searchable PoI like the Digital City Kyoto Guide (Ishida et al., 1999). Apart from research projects, industry solutions offer a view on the commercial state of the art in mobile geographic information visualization. These solutions are strongly influenced by solutions of navigation systems. Dunlop et al., (2004) present two types of views providing both map and list-index information access:

1. Map View Display (MVD) (Left of Fig. 1.): The main part of the MVD shows a map of a city centre with an overlay set of attractions represented by squares. Users can browse a selected set of attractions by pointing and tapping on symbols of attractions in a selected area.
2. List View Display (LVD) (Right of Fig. 1.): LVD shows a list displaying the names of attractions in a sorted order in a manner similar to an index at the end of a guidebook.

An electronic method of presentation has an advantage over paper editions in providing different sorting criteria.

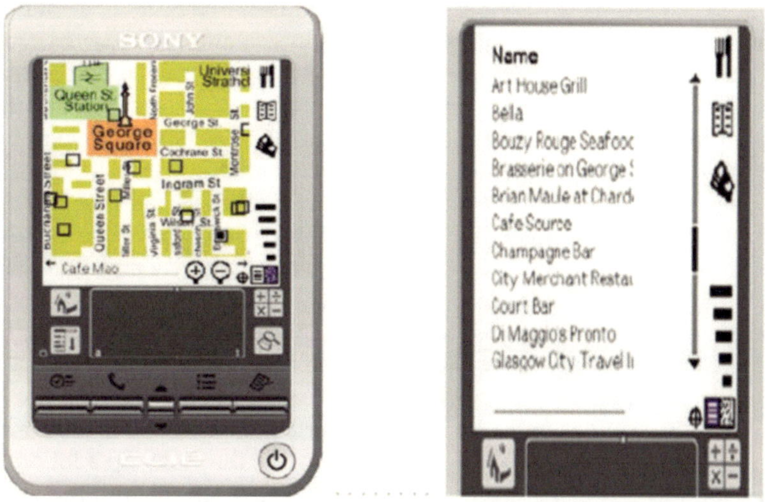

Figure 1. MVD and LVD

As mentioned above a core functionality of the Taeneb City Guide user interface (Dunlop et al., 2004) is incorporating dynamic query filters for searching and finding tourist attractions. Query filters are predefined for different types of attractions and are designed for rapid selection either as pop-up lists for single choice, or a separate view with a checklist for multiple choice selections (see Fig. 2). For example, for restaurants there is a multi-choice filter with a food type (Fig. 2) and a single choice filter with a price range (Fig. 2(b)). The results of a query are displayed as a subset of data either as a list using LVD or as a scattered plot of matching attraction-icons on a map display using MVD.

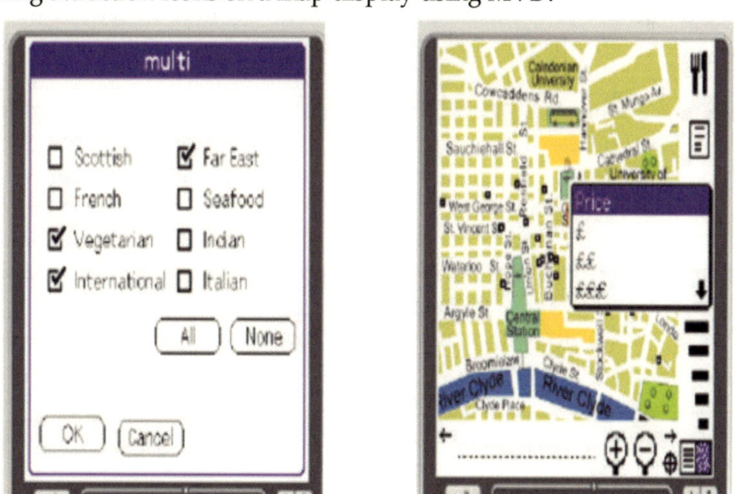

Figure 2. Restaurant query filters

2.2 Mobile human-computer interaction (M-HCI)

The mobile environment has its own characteristics. Mobile users have little patience for learning how to operate new services. The mobile users have less "mental bandwidth" capacity for absorbing and processing content than a stationary user in front of a PC (Rischplater, 2000) as the interaction with the mobile phone is often reduced to a secondary task that must not interfere with their primary task. Interactivity is a more intuitive way of working with a computer. This intuitive approach in HCI has the objective to make the use of a computer easier, faster to learn and more transparent to the user.

Interactivity is mostly used to compensate for the small displays, and not for enhancing the user experience. Thus, while small displays can interface design processes, consideration of user aspect is indispensable. Meanwhile, it is important to separate the physical or technical interactions from symbolic interactions, i.e. the surface and deep structure of interaction. Hitting a button or moving the mouse is a surface, physical or explicit interaction, while a symbolic or implicit interaction is for instance the selection of a menu option. A menu is a set of options displayed on the screen where the selection and execution of one (or more) of the options results in a change in the state of the interface (Paap and Roske-Hofstrand, 1988). In the past, one of the problems with using menus is that they take up a lot of space on the screen. A solution to this is the use of a pull-down or pop-up menu (Preece, 1995). Also, most windowing systems provide a system of menus consisting of implicit or explicit pop-up menus (Marcus, 1992).

Empirical studies prove that systems requiring too much attention or too many interactions are either not used efficiently or are not used at all. One reason for this is "information overload" from complicated interfaces. While some problems are affiliated with cognitive abilities, the main reason is that mobility increases the load of cognitive processing. The objective should be to simplify visualization to such an extent that the user is not required to think unnecessarily. For web site design, Krug (2000) coined the term "Don't Make Me Think!" Visual comprehension can be summarized as "what you see depends on what you look at and what you know". Multimedia designers can influence what users look at by controlling attention with display techniques such as using movement, highlighting, and salient icons.

However, designers should be aware that the information people assimilate from an image also depends on their internal motivation, what they want to find, and how well they know the domain (Treisman, 1988). So far, many existing location-aware systems use some kind of metaphor, very often taken from the real world, in order to illustrate their concept of interaction with location-aware information. Our mental representations of spatial knowledge include information on spatial relationships and how to navigate within our environment.(Medin, Ross, and Markman, 2001). One of these may be an interpretation of how well the user knows the map symbols and how familiar he is with using the mobile device and the map on it. It has been stated that "mobile devices are not aesthetically pleasing enough, navigation is troublesome and services are hard to use" (Olsson and Svanteson, 2001). Before further investigating this statement, it is important to explore the principles of usability and why it is so important.

Nielsen (1993) separates five attributes for usability - represented in the usability branch below:

- Learnability: The system should be easy to learn so that the user can rapidly start getting some work done with the system.

- Efficiency: The system should be efficient to use, so that once the user has learned the system, a high level of productivity is possible.
- Memorability: The system should be easy to remember, so that the casual user is able to return to the system after some period of not having used it, without having to learn everything all over again.
- Errors: The system should have a low error rate, so that users make few errors during the use of the system, and if they do make errors, they can easily recover from them.
- Satisfaction: The system should be pleasant to use so that users are subjectively satisfied when using it.

A major portion of usability engineering and thus usability testing is the Human-Computer Interaction (HCI) "the study of how people interact with computer technology and how this interaction can be made more effective" (Battleson, 2001). Usability Engineering by Faulkner (2000) has a couple of pictures in the whole book showing a user interface that discusses several methods for collecting usability data which include observation, thinking aloud, questionnaires, interviews, focus groups, logging actual use, heuristic evaluation and user feedback. Usability testing can be done either in a laboratory environment or in an authentic real-world environment. In this research, the effectiveness of maps for mobile devices was tested in the laboratory environment due to constraint of research time involved in conducting real-world testing. The laboratory environment is not a real-world situation which is a disadvantage. Karat, Campbell and Fiegel (1992) stated that usability testing was compared with individual and team walkthroughs in order to identify usability problems in two graphical user interfaces.

2.3 Mobile interface visualization

Most of the research projects described above use maps to communicate geographic information on mobile devices. There have been few studies that have dealt with map displays on mobile devices. Reichenbacher (2001) has studied the process of adaptive and dynamic generation of map visualization for mobile users. Jern (2001) states that dynamic user interfaces play a major role in enabling the user to take on a more active role in the process of visualizing and investigating data.

Compared to the PC world, mobile access is still quite restricted, especially with respect to the display of graphical representations such as images, drawings, diagrams, maps and logos. Reichenbacher (2004) expresses graphical means to put a visual emphasis or focus on several features. These graphical means are:

- highlighting the object using a signal color, e.g. pink or yellow.
- emphasizing the outline of the object.
- enhancing the contrast between the object and the background.
- focusing on the object of interest while blurring other surrounding objects (crispness).
- enhancing the LoD(Level of Detail) of the object of interest against that of other objects.
- animating the object (blinking, shaking, rotating, increasing/decreasing size).
- clicking on a graphics object to display more detailed information about that object (Jern, 2000).

By the way, in recent years the visualization of information has evolved to an important and innovative area in computer graphics. Graphical user interfaces (GUI) are on their way to becoming the most pervasive interfaces for mobile systems, at least in part because of conventional wisdom about their ease of use (Marcus et al., 1998). The GUI technologies have

tended to focus heavily on the user-input aspects of human-computer interaction, with little integration of data output and display technologies (or data visualization technologies). This will change very quickly, and a variety of "output widgets" will become as commonplace in GUIs as input widgets are today. Popular GUI such as Windows, Macintosh, Motif and OpenLook are basically more similar to each other than dissimilar. A design innovation targeted specifically at improving the mobile interface is the use of icon-based input techniques (Rohr and Keppel, 1984). A previous study has evolved a highly standardized set of metaphors for interaction with the computer based on a series of user friendly on-screen input techniques such as icons and pull-down menus. The GUIs that present information to the user in the form of icons, images representing objects, actions, and commands can typically be directly manipulated by the user (Benbasat and Todd, 1993; William Horton, 1994). Furthermore, because of the limited space on the display, the graphical indicators cannot all be displayed simultaneously. Therefore they have been prioritized so that only the most important indicators for each situation and task are displayed at a time.
Besides, in a symbolic presentation of GUI, the main rule is to ensure that the symbols are easy to recognize and understand. Hence maps use different symbols to represent the reality, and each symbol must be clearly distinguishable from other. The symbols should be based on the signs usually seen on the street and in other places and should be presented in a way familiar to people. People should easily recognize these symbols from the map on the handheld devices without much effort. Keeping this in mind, pictorial symbols are usually selected to represent points of interest; for example, a representation of a bus is used for bus stands, an icon of a person for friend finder, a fork and knife for restaurants or a stethoscope and needle for hospitals. A list of these symbols is shown in Table 1.

Feature	**Symbol**
Bus Stand	
Friends Finder	
Hotel	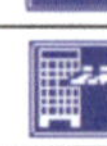
Petrol Pumps	
Restaurant	
Hospital	

Table 1. Pictorial PoI symbols

These kinds of symbols are very familiar to most people and will ease the map reading process significantly. Thus the size of the symbols should be optimally selected. These sizes are determined using legibility principles and are then tested for effectiveness by the user. The legibility of symbols is increased through the use of the tool tip option shown in Fig. 3 (Reichenbacher, 2002), which displays a description in text form as soon as the user places his/her stylus on the object.

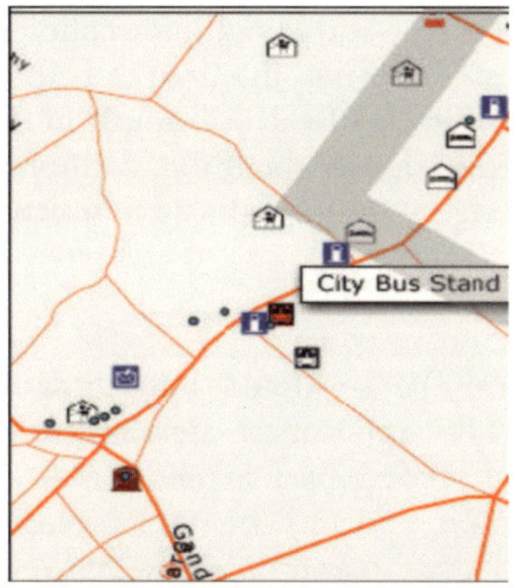

Figure 3. Text description using tool tip (Reichenbacher, 2002)

To find the proper symbol for a map, one has to execute a cartographic data analysis process. The core of this analysis process is to access the characteristics of the data to find out how it can be visualized. The data that has to be visualized will always refer to objects or phenomena in reality. The characteristics of the data are size, value, texture (grain), colour, orientation, and form (Kraak, 2001). These characteristics lead to the use of simple, easily recognizable symbols that are familiar to the users, with much of conventional map symbol association such as blue for water, green for forest, etc. To make the symbols understandable, certain possibilities used in case of web maps can be employed, for example mouse-over (shown in Fig. 4), tool tips, etc., which trigger the information in text form describing the object. One more possibility to increase the legibility of the symbol can be to increase the size of the object when the user moves his/her pointer on it, and to provide further information when it is clicked (Rajinder, 2004).

Figure 4. Mouse-over effect

Figure 5. Map with further information for identified feature

Clickable icons can be used to access additional information on specific points or areas on the map, information that is not shown all the time to help reduce the overloading of the map presentation (Gartner & Uhlirz, 2001). The example in Fig. 5 shows the use of a popup information box that gives further details about the identity of a selected geospatial object. Such informative 'boxes' compensate for the reduced information density of the map.

3. Methodology

This research methodology can be separated into three parts. The first part is the introduction of the current LBS application architecture and platform in the mobile commerce environment. The second part is undertaken to compare LVD and MVD visualizations of LBS information, and to develop a prototype interface for Smartphones based on small-screen design principles from previous research. The interface of this prototype is called LBSI. The final part is to conduct an experiment to verify the performance of LBSI for intuition and usability. After the experiment, the sampling users are given questionnaires which evaluate variations on a multiple rating scale. This scale is the five-point Likert scale, which is used to response their opinions.

3.1 Framework of current LBS system

LBS apart from the already described technology require specific infrastructure for positioning the mobile terminal. The systems offering positioning for mobile terminals in LBS are divided into three main classes: satellite positioning, network-based positioning, and local positioning (Paikannussanasto, 2002). Fig. 6 shows the conceptual model of the Smartphone solution from this study. While the Smartphone can play many roles in different domains, this study aims only at LBS. There are many related fields involved, which have been discussed in the literature review above.

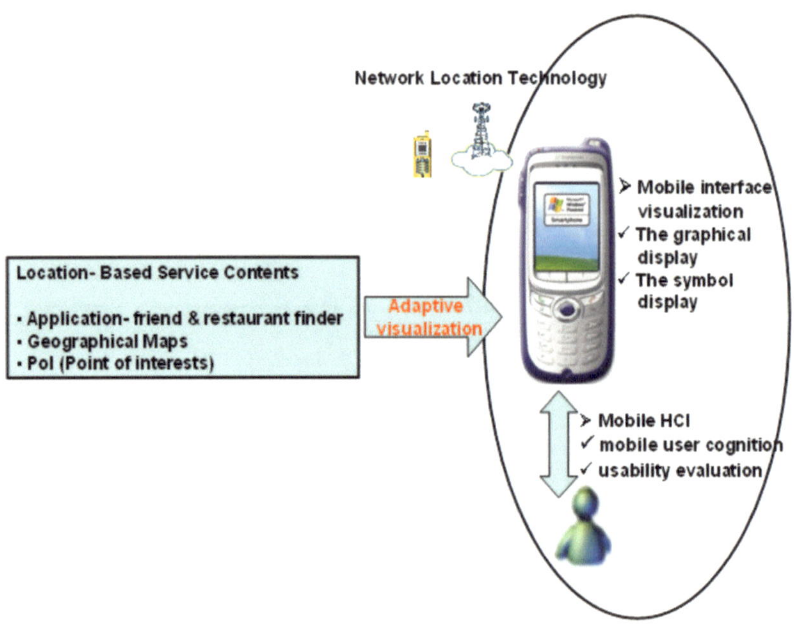

Figure 6. Conceptual model of the Smartphone solution

3.2 LBSI - A prototype of a MVD/LVD mobile visualization

As the aim of this experiment was to compare two different visualizations of LBS interfaces (LBSI) rather than its entire usability in real-life settings, it was decided that the experiment could be conducted reasonably well using a Smartphone emulator embedded in a desktop computer instead of using a much more expensive Smartphone. The participants interacted with the LBS interface using a mobile phone capable of running the Microsoft Windows Mobile™ 2003-based Smartphone Emulator, which emulator screen size was set at 6cm×5cm to simulate the users holding the device approximately 25cm from their face. The procedure of development uses the Microsoft Visuall Basic.Net program to establish a prototype of interfaces.

The inspiration for the development of LBSI is not only based on several ideas of design paradigms from NTT DoCoMo's I-mode (I-area) and refer to some web pages (http://www.phonedaily.com/、http://www.olemap.com/), but also extended by concepts of papers that have been reviewed to consider usability for the mobile domain.

3.2.1 Task of navigating LBS

There are several applications for LBS. Based on LBS usage analysis, previous studies reveal that the most popular services are tracking friends and finding restaurants (Assarf and Taly, 2003). Hence the development of interfaces in this study adopts both applications - friend finder and restaurant finder. Thus the experiment assigned tasks were based on two fictional navigational routes. Each user was exposed to two typical navigation tasks:

- Task 1: First the user adds selected friends to his friend finder list simply by adding some friends (e.g.Yuchang, Alice, Steven, Breind, Wow) in the friend list. He then uses the powerful LBS functionality (Friend Finder application) to find a randomly assigned friend who is visible on the screen of the Smartphone. Then he needs to contact the assigned person with a message.
- Task 2: How should a traveler choose a restaurant for lunch in unknown city? To assign the user to find one of several types of restaurants and a particular price level randomly. He then operates either MVD or LVD of LBSI on the Smartphone emulator and selects a restaurant in an assigned area (e.g. Shihlin, Taipei).

3.2.2 LVD / MVD - friends finder / restaurant finder scenarios

Let us assume that the Smartphone is able to use the embedded LBS function. Related persons will be located on the map (Taipei Shihlin 7(a)) as shown in Fig. 7(g). For friend finder information, the LBSI generally provides a LVD as the preferred type of view. Fig. 7 shows several sample pages accessed via LBSI. As can be seen from Fig. 7, LVD in LBSI allows the users to do the step by step from 7(a) to 7(i).

The LVD as shown procedure step by step in Fig. 7 and 8 below, they provides a rapid way to seek information of restaurant and friend by method of query filters which are predefined for different types of attractions as lists for choice. The MVD as shown procedure step by step in Fig. 9 and 10 below like LVD.

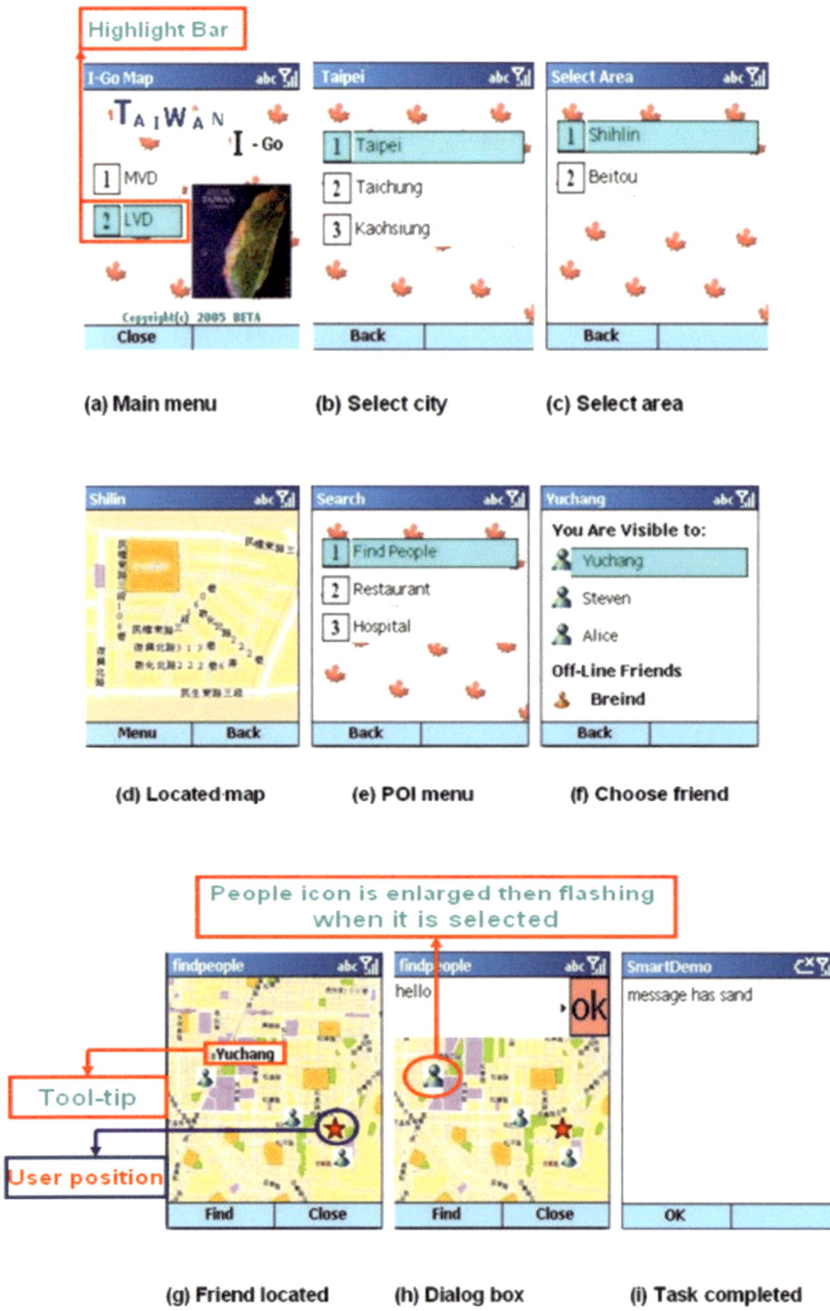

Figure 7. Interface flow of an application of friend finder (LVD)

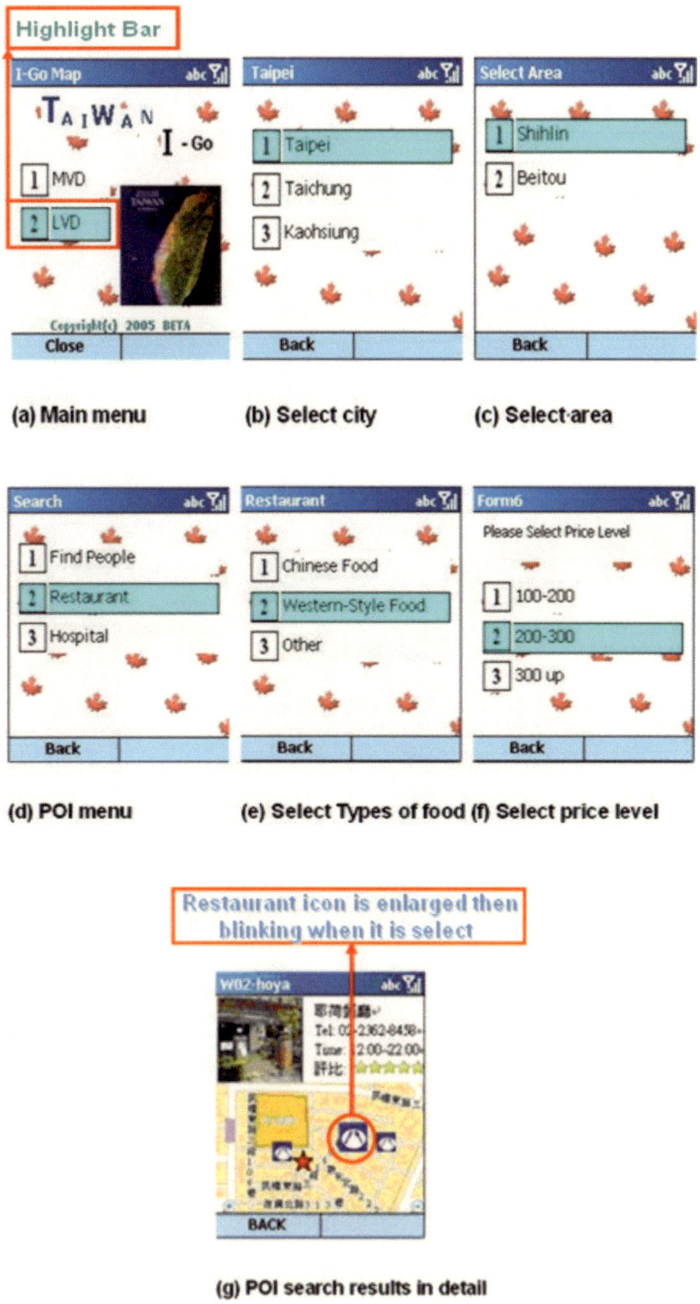

Figure 8. Interface flow of a generic restaurant finder application (LVD)

Figure 9. Interface flow of a generic friend finder application (MVD)

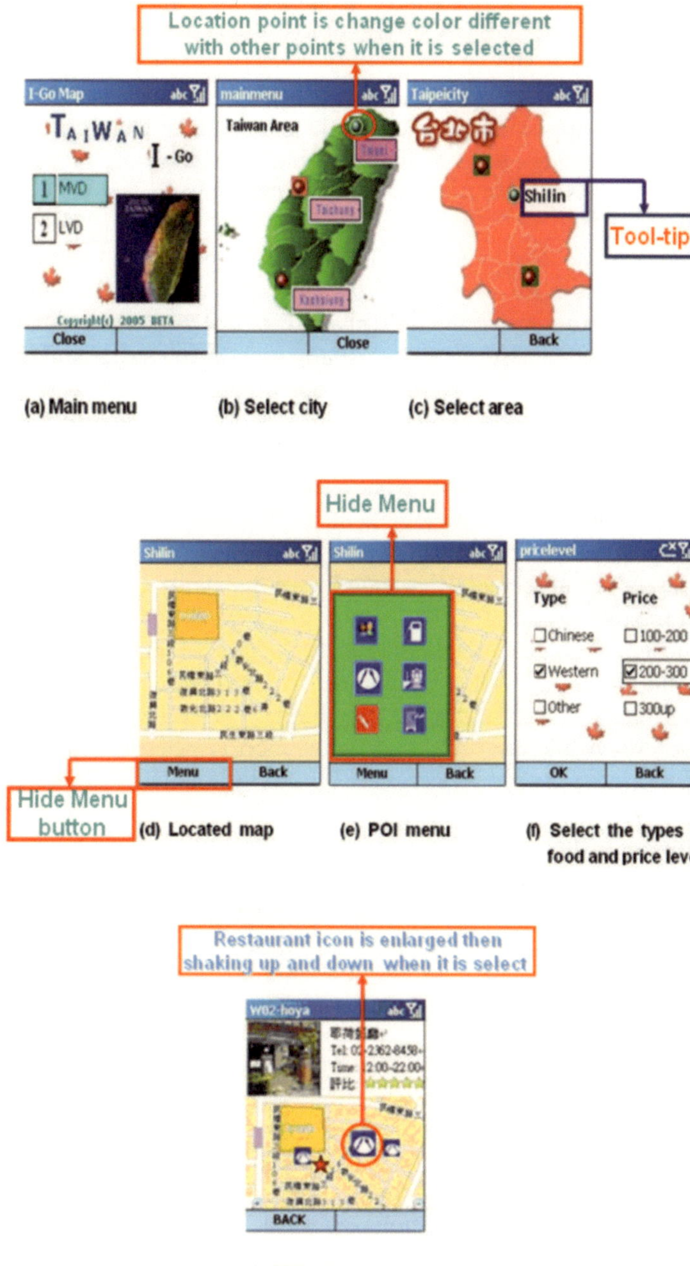

Figure 10. Interface flow of a generic restaurant finder application (MVD)

These designs of the interfaces are based on principles of small screen design and mobile HCI (Masoodian and Lane, 2003; Kraak, 2001; Nivala, 2004; Rohr and Keppel, 1984; Jern,

2000; Reichenbacher, 2004; Holmquist, 1999; Gartner and Uhlirz, 2001; Krug, 2000; Marcus, 1992; Dunlop et al., 2004). It is summarized as follows:

- Query filters are predefined for different types of attractions and designed for rapid selection as either pop-up lists for single choice, or a separate view with a checklist for multi choice selections as shown in Fig. 10(f).
- The object is highlighted using a signal color and its outline is emphasized. Graphics and icons can help support the function of the table of contents during this process. In addition to the many new tools available to highlight their functionality, they can be even more effective as guides through and around a product as shown in Fig. 7(a)-(f), Fig. 8(a)-(f) and Fig. 9(c).
- Clickable icons can be used to access additional information on specific points or areas on the map, information that is not shown all the time to help reduce the overloading of the map presentation as shown in Fig. 7(h) and Fig. 9(h).
- The symbols should be based on signs usually seen in the street and other places and should be presented in a way familiar to people. People should easily recognize these symbols from the map on the handheld devices without much effort as shown in Fig. 9(e) and Fig. 10(e).
- Multimedia designers can influence what users look at by controlling attention through display techniques such as using movement, highlighting, and salient icons as shown in Fig. 7(a)-(f), Fig. 8(a)-(f) and Fig. 9(c).
- One more possibility to increase the legibility of the symbol to increase the size of the object when the user moves his/her pointer on it, and to provide further information when it is clicked, as shown in Fig. 7(h), Fig. 8(g), Fig. 9(h) and Fig. 10(g).
- A previous study has evolved a highly standardized set of metaphors for interaction with the computer based on a series of user-friendly on-screen input techniques such as icons and pull-down menus. A design innovation targeted specifically at improving the mobile interface is the use of icon-based input techniques as shown in Fig. 9(d)(e)(f) and Fig. 10(d)(e).
- Most windowing systems provide a system of menus consisting of implicit or explicit pop-up menus as shown in Fig. 9(e)(f) and Fig. 10(e).
- The object can be animated (blinked, shaken, rotated, increased/decreased in size) as shown in Fig. 7(h), Fig. 8(g), Fig. 9(h) and Fig. 10(g).
- To increase the legibility of symbols, the tool tip option is used to display the description in the form of text as shown in Fig. 7(g), Fig. 8(b)(c)(g) and Fig. 9(b)(c).

3.3 Experiment

3.3.1 Environment and apparatus of experiment

All displays of LSBI are developed by Visual Basic.Net to simulate a scenario for the environment of a city guide. These participants used mouse buttons to navigate forward or backward through each step of LBS functions.

3.3.2 Subjects

There are twelve undergraduate students participated in the experiment and assumed that the variance of different groups were equal. Each participant was randomly assigned into one of two groups, the control group or experiment group. The control group used a LVD interface and the experimental group used a MVD interface on a Smartphone emulator to fulfill their assignment of task. None of the subjects had LBS experience from before, and while they had used mobile phones in the past, few had used Smartphone. Table 2 gives a summary of the profile of the subjects.

Average Age	22 Years	
Gender	Male (50%)	Female (50%)
Smartphone Experience	Yes (50%)	No (50%)
LBS Experience	Yes (0%)	No (100%)

Table 2. Profile of the subject

3.3.3 Experimental variables

This study used a 'within-subject' design where each participant responded to a different task within each environment. Participants were parted in two groups, with six subjects in each group. One was named group1, the other was named group2. Each group focused on two guiding tasks of PoI (restaurant, friend) directions successfully. These sets of tasks, referred to as task 1 and 2, were randomized across the two environments (see Table 3). Each ordering of the tasks and environments were replicated 6 times, requiring 12 participants in total.

Task \ Display	LVD	MVD
Task 1	Group1	Group2
Task 2	Group2	Group1

Table 3. Profile of the task

Two independent variables are involved in the study below:

- The type of display interface, i.e. MVD or LVD, and
- The type of task, i.e. friend finder and restaurant finder for accessing PoI information.

Besides, user-dependent variables were measured to characterize user efficiency and usability:

- Operating Time: time of operation for the tasks of finding their PoI (Friends or Restaurants).
- Clicks: times of clicks of assigned task performance in all procedure.
- Error of Clicks: error times of clicks of assigned task performance in all procedures (other clicks without correct route which include backward).

3.4 Experimental procedure and hypothesis proposing

Each user was first asked to familiarize themselves with the LBSI for approximately 5minutes. No LBSI manual was at hand. The experimenter stressed that it was a prototype service and that automatic location of the user's present location was not implemented. The user was asked to accomplish each task while "talking aloud". Since clarifications regarding an opinion were regarded as important, only the accuracy was considered and completion times were measured. If difficulties occurred, the user was first given a hint by the experimenter, and if this information did not suffice, the user was guided through the task before starting with the next.

Participants parted in two groups were required to fill out a background questionnaire at the end of the session. General background information such as age and gender was recorded along with users' previous travel and mobile device experience. The recorded data was categorized as:

- Objective: time taken to complete the individual questions, the number of clicks needed to be followed to complete a task (refereed to here as clicks).
- Subjective: degree of user satisfaction, user comments and suggestions.

The hypotheses were tested in the SPSS V12.0 software using the repeated measurement General Linear Model (GLM). The significance level was set to 5% and the level of multiple comparisons was an independent T-test. Our hypotheses for the experiment were:

- By operating time, usability of LVD was more effective than MVD.
- By clicking times, usability of LVD was more effective than MVD.
- By clicking times of error, usability of LVD was more effective than MVD.

4 Results and discussion

4.1 Experimental results

In this chapter, the performance of all participates was evaluated by three indicators: Operating time, Clicks, Error of clicks and post-questionnaire.

Dependent Variable	Operating Time	
Independent Variable	LVD	MVD
Mean	42.58	77.05
Standard Deviation	35.76	35.51
Sample Size	12	12
Degreeof Freedom	22	
T-value	-2.369	
P-value	0.027*	

Table 4. T-Test for average operating time of independent populations (α=0.05)

4.1.1 Operating Time

As shown in Table 4 the operating time when using LVD is significantly different from that of MVD ($p<.05$). From the sample means for the two groups, one can see the group using LVD spent significantly less training time than the MVD group.

4.1.2 Clicking times

As shown in Table 5 the click time when using LVD is significantly different from that of MVD ($p<.05$). From the sample means for the two groups, one can see the using group LVD spent significantly less clicking times than the MVD group.

Dependent Variable	Clicks Times	
Independent Variable	LVD	MVD
Mean	6.08	8.42
Standard Deviation	2.234	2.151
Sample Size	12	12
Degree of Freedom	22	
T-value	-2.606	
P-value	0.016*	

Table 5. T-Test for average clicking times of independent populations (α=0.05)

Dependent Variable	Error of Clicks Times	
Independent Variable	LVD	MVD
Mean	1.17	92
Standard Deviation	2.855	4.981
Sample Size	12	12
Degree of Freedom	22	
T-value	-1.659	
P-value	0.111	

Table 6. T-Test for error of clicking times of independent populations (α=0.05)

4.1.3 Error of Clicking Times

As shown in Table 6 there is no significant difference in error of clicking times when using LVD versus MVD visualization.

4.1.4 Result of objectivity

From the measurements of this experiment shown in table 4 and table 5 the study clearly indicates that both, the operating time and the mean number of clicks are lesser in LVD than MVD, no matter what task, task1 or task2 was selected. The result of error of clicks was not significant, which may be due to the complexity of scenario and the user sample size not being large enough to reveal the effect between the two displays in the experiment. According to Standard Deviation of MVD 4.981 reveals each user recognize symbol of MVD so divergence. Hence, the symbol of the icon is the main factor for efficiency while each user operates LVD and MVD. In a nutshell, LVD visualization was more effective than MVD visualization.

4.1.5 Post questionnaire analysis

In order to comprehend users' preference and opinion in more detail, in addition to objective evaluation, this study uses a post experiment questionnaire after experiment to collect subjective data for analysis. The second construct inside the questionnaire about some symbol items is revised from Rajinder (2004). Others designs of querying items refer to related previous studies (Reichenbacher, 2004 ; Masoodian and Lane, 2003) where content validation was appropriate within the target context. Composite reliability of questionnaire reflects the degree to which the construct is represented by the indicators. All results, as reported in table 7 almost exceed the recommended value of 0.7 for composite reliability.

Construct	# items	Composite Reliability
Interface Investigation	6	0.74
Symbol Investigation	7	0.75
Content of Display Investigation	3	0.72

Table 7. Estimates of composite reliability

Construct	Mean	S.D
Interface Investigation	4.33	0.569
Symbol Investigation	4.46	0.186
Content of Display Investigation	4.22	0.484

Table 8. Result of construct

Further, mean values of three constructs are all above 4 (see Table 8), i.e. between agree and partially agree. Although users' opinions showed that satisfaction is high in three constructs, they also present some suggestion in the questionnaires. These suggestions and comments from the users are summarized below. Although the visualization of MVD was reasonably effective in providing users with overview of some aspect of their LBS functions as well as giving them sufficient access to necessary details of events, overall it was less effective than the visualization of LVD, which made them operate intuitively and easily.

- Subjective results indicate that two-third of the users totally agreed and responded that the size of the symbols was ok, while one-third of the users only partially agreed and felt that it would be easier to recognize symbols on the Smartphone mobile map if the sizes of pictorials were bigger than the original. All users responded that they only partially agreed to the question whether the symbols were expressive enough. Most of the users commented that all the icons were not expressive enough and they were unable to relate it to the real world. For example, the icon of hotel featuring a symbol of a building and two beds led many users to misunderstand it. The post-questionnaire revealed that the Fork and Knife symbol for restaurants in table 1 was almost always recognized correctly as opposed to the icon of the hotel which was always misunderstood. When users were asked about what kind of symbols in their opinion were more expressive, they suggested using symbols that were more familiar with general standards of everyday life and could be recognized easily.

- Objective results indicate that recognizing symbol intuitively is a critical factor in operating MVD effectively. Finally, results of both subjective and objective criteria show that the symbol-based interface (MVD), which is designed to focus on user symbol cognitive level, should adopt simple and intuitive icons that are more helpful for humanize interfaces.
- Majority of the users commented that having pop-up legends would be more helpful. When users were asked about the contents of display, some users suggested that the level of information displayed should be increased for PoI and should show as much detailed information about a restaurant as possible.

5. Conclusions and future work

The main design principles to implement two diverse displays of LBSI and use Smartphone to access LBS information are guided by the display of I-mode and the current study of SSI (Dunlop et al., 2004). Subsequently, an empirical experiment conducted to investigate the effectiveness of the pictorial and textual visualizations of the prototype has shown that the list style generally outperforms the pictorial style when they are used on their own. In the other aspect, the post-questionnaire investigates users' preference of display in detail. The chosen design methodology, user interface concepts, and the technical considerations for implementation have been discussed in detail. It is expected that when both of these visualizations of the prototype are used together in real-world settings, they will provide the users with effective and intuitive access to their PoI information. It is feasible to fulfill PoI on-map presentation on smart phones with small displays. The prototype of the Smartphone offers a ubiquitous tourist guide for the inner city of Taipei. This form of access would certainly be a major improvement over the use of conventional paper-based methods for the same purpose. The mobile maps of LBSI have provided mobility, accessibility, actuality and extra information about users' preferences. Finally, the applicability of adaptation within a mobile geo-visualisation service through a prototypical implementation has been proven.

6. References

Assaf Burak , Taly Sharon, Analyzing usage of location based services, *CHI '03 extended abstracts on Human factors in computing systems*, April 05-10, 2003, Ft. Lauderdale, Florida, USA

Battleson, B., Booth, A., & Weintrop, J. (2001). Usability testing of an academic library web site: A case study. *The Journal of Academic Librarianship*, 27, 188-198.

Benson J. (2001) LBS Technology Delivers Information Where and When it is Needed, Business Geographics, http://www.geoplace.com/bg/2001/0201/0201lbs.asp

Benbasat, Izak and Todd, Peter,(1993). An experimental investigation of interface design alternatives: icon. vs. text and direct manipulationvs. menus, *International Journal of Man-Machine Studies* 38(3), pp. 369-402.

CANALYS, 2005. Changing times in the smart mobile device market. Canalys website, company press release, 29th September 2005. Available at: http://www.canalys.com/pr/2005/r2005094.htm [last accessed: 11/10/05].

Dunlop, M, Ptasinski, P., Morrison, A., McCallum, S., Riseby, C. & Stewart, F. (2004). Design and development of Taeneb City Guide - From *Paper Maps and Guidebooks to Electronic Guides*. Proc.

Faulkner, X. (2000), Usability Engineering, *Grassroots Series*, MacMillan Press.

Gartner, G. & Uhlirz, S. (2001), Cartographic Concepts for Realizing a Location Based UMTS Service: Vienna City Guide "Lol@". In: *Proceedings 20th International Cartographic Conference, Beijing, China*, August 6 - 10, 2001. WWW site 55 http://lola.ftw.at/homepage/content/a40material/Vienna_City_Guide_LoLa.pdf (accessed 20.8.04)

Gartner, G. (2003), Telecartography: Maps, Multimedia and mobile Internet. In: Peterson, M.P. (eds.), *Maps and the Internet*. Amsterdam etc.: Elsevier, Chapter 24, pp. 385 - 396.

Haack, J. (1995): Interaktivität als Kennzeichen von Multimedia und Hypermedia, in L. J. Issing and P. Klimsa (Eds.), *Information und Lernen mit Multimedia*, Weinheim: Psychologie Verlags Union, 151-166.

Heeter, C. (1989): Implications of New Interactive Technologies for Conceptualizing Communication, in S. J. L. and J. Bryant (Eds.), *Media Use in the Information Age: Emerging Patterns of Adoption and Consumer Use*, Hillsdale (NJ): Lawrence Erlbaum Associates.

Holmquist, L.E. (1999): Will Baby Faces Ever Grow Up? In: Bullinger, H.-J., Ziegler, J. (eds.): Ergonomics and User Interfaces. *HCI International Conference Proceedings*, Munich, Germany, 22-26 August, Lawrence Erlbaum Associates, Vol. 1, 706-709.

Ishida, T., Akahani, J., Hiramatsu, K., Isbister, K., Lisowski, S., Nakanishi, H., Okamoto, M., Miyazaki, Y., and Tsutsuguchi, K.: Digital City Kyoto: Towards A Social Information Infrastructure, *Cooperative Information Agents III*, pp. 23-35 (1999).

Jern M (2000). Collaborative Visual Data Navigation on the Web. Invited Keynote Lecture to INFVIZ 2000, *IEEE International Conference on Information Visualization*, London, IEEE Computer Science Press

Jern M (2001) Visual Data Navigators Collaboratories - True Interactive Visualization for the Web. Invited Speaker, *Mobile and Virtual Media International Conference 2001*

Karat, C., Campbell, R. L. & Fiegel, T. (1992). Comparison of empirical testing and walkthrough methods in user interface evaluation. In P. Bauersfield, J. Bennet & G. Lynch (Eds.), *Proceedings ACM CHI `92 Conference*, 397--404, New York. ACM.

Kraak, M. J. (2001) Settings and needs for web cartography. *In Web cartography: developments and prospects*, edited by Kraak, M. J. and Brown, A., (Taylor & Francis: London) Chapter 1, pp 1-7

Krug, S. (2000): Don't Make Me Think! *A Common Sense Approach to Web*

Levijoki, S. (2000). Privacy vs Location Awareness, Department of Computer Science, Helsinki University of Technology. 2002.

Marcus,1992: A. Marcus. *Graphic Design for Electronic Documents and User Interfaces*. ACM Press, New York, 1992.

Marcus, A., Ferrante, J., Kinnunen, T., Kuutti, K. and Sparre, E. (1998) Baby faces: user-interface design for small displays. *Proceedings of the International ACM Conference on Computer-Human Interaction (CHI '98).*

Masood Masoodian , Nicholas Lane, An empirical study of textual and graphical travel itinerary visualization using mobile phones, *Proceedings of the Fourth Australian user interface conference on User interfaces 2003*, p.11-18, February 01, 2003, Adelaide, Australia

Marcus, G.F. (2001). *The Algebraic Mind*. Cambridge, Mass.: MIT Press.

Medin, D. L., Ross, B. H. and Markman, A. B. (2001). *Cognitive Psychology*, Harcourt, Orlando.

Neudeck, S. (2001): Gestaltung topographischer Karten für die Bildschirmvisualisierung. Schriftenreihe des Studienganges Geodäsie und Geoinformation der Universität der Bundeswehr München, Neubiberg: 2001, vol. 74.

Nivala, A-M (2004), Interruptions in mobile map environments. WWW site http://www.hiit.fi/uerg/seminaari/T-121900-2004-essay-nivala.pdf (accessed 21.09.04)

Nielsen, J.(1993). *Usability Engineering*. Morgan Kaufmann, Academic press, London.

NTT Docomo (2003) Subscriber growth. NTT Docomo, accessed June 1, 2003, http://www.nttdocomo.com

Olsson, A. and Svantesson, S. User Intelligence Will Make Mobile Solutions Fly (2001).

OGC (2003): OpenGIS Location Services (OpenLS): Core Services, OGC Implementation Specification, OGC 03-006r1, *Open GIS Consortium.*

Paap, K. R. and Rosice-hofstiwnd, R. J. 1988. Design of menus. *In Handbook of Human. Computer Interaction*. Elsevier Science Publishers, Amsterdam, 205-235.

Paikannussanasto, Vocabulary of Positioning (2002). Tekniikan sanastokeskus, TSK 30, Helsinki.

Preece, J., 1995. *Human-computer Interaction*, Wokingham, England: Addison- Wesley Pub. Co.

Rajinder Singh Nagi, Cartographic visualization for mobile applications (2004). *International institute for geo-information science and earth observation enschede*, the netherlands and Indian institute of remote sensing, National Remote Sensing Agency (NRSA), department of space, dehradun, India.

Reed .C(2001). Are mobile wireless location-based services hype or reality? Business Geographics http://www.geoplace.com/bg/ 2001/0201/0201mob.asp

Reichenbacher, Tumasch (2001): Adaptive concepts for a mobile cartography (English). *Journal of Geographical Sciences*, Acta Geographica Sinica, Vol.11 Supplement 2001, Beijing. 43-53

Reichenbacher, T.: Mobile Cartography - Adaptive Visualization of Geographic Information on Mobile Devices. Dissertation submitted at the Institute of Photogrammetry und Cartography, Technical University, Munich, 2004.

Rohr, G. and Keppel, E.,(1984). Iconic Interfaces: Where to Use and How to Construct?, in Human Factors in Organizational design and Management, H.W. Kendrick and O. Borwn (eds.), New York Elsevier, pp. 269-275

Siau, K., Shen, Z. and Varshney, U. (2003) Communications and mobile services, *International Journal of Mobile Communications*, Vol. 1, Nos. 1–2, pp.3–14.

Treisman, A. (1988). Features and objects: Fourteenth Bartlett memorial lecture. *Quarterly Journal of Experimental Psychology*, 40A(2), 201-237

Varshney, U. (2003) 'Location management for wireless networks: issues and directions',*International Journal of Mobile Communications,* Vol. 1, Nos. 1–2, pp.91–118.

Varshney, U. (2003) Issues, requirements and support for location-intensive mobilecommerce applications, *International Journal of Mobile Communications*, Vol. 1, No. 3,pp.247–263.

William Horton(1994) The Icon Book: Visual Symbols for computer Systems and Documentation,John Wiley & Sons,Inc.

26

Brain-CAVE Interface Based on Steady-State Visual Evoked Potential

Hideaki Touyama
The University of Tokyo
Japan

1. Introduction

Recently, a new modality of the human-computer interface has been more and more emerging; The Brain-Computer Interface (BCI). The BCI is a communication channel, which enables us to send commands to external devices by using human brain activities (Wolpaw et al., 2002). As one of the remarkable achievements, we can see the report on invasive Brain-Machine Interface (BMI) (Hochberg et al., 2006).

Besides the technique of the invasive BMI, there are several types of non-invasive approaches for the brain signal acquisitions; for example, functional magnetic resonance imaging (fMRI), near infrared spectroscopy (NIRS), etc. Non-invasive methods have been noteworthy owing to the recent development of the signal processing method as well as acquisition apparatus. The performance of the BCI system is going to be improved and the applications has been seen; for example, the communication tool for people with disability, virtual reality games, and so on. Among them, the electroencephalography (EEG) has been investigated as one of the candidates for the low-cost and portable BCI system. It is well known that the EEG activities can be detected by the scalp recording, which are typically the order of 5-10 micro volts of potentials. The BCI system can extract the specific temporal and spatial patterns from the brain potentials, and translates them into the commands to control the machine according to the users' intent.

A variety of brain activities has been reported so far in the context of the BCI systems based on EEG signals; for instance, motor related potential (Pfurtscheller & Neuper, 1997), event related P300 evoked potential (Farwell & Donchin, 1988), visual evoked potential (VEP) (Kuroiwa & Celesia, 1981), etc. With such brain activities, many applications have been developed in laboratories such as a virtual keyboard or joystick. However, most of them were studied on the system with the simple visual feedback involving a normal computer monitor.

The purpose of this book chapter is to show the technique to realize a BCI system in virtual reality environment and to suggest the possibility of the online control of computer-generated objects. Note that the most advantage of testing the BCI system in virtual reality is that we can easily test and simulate procedures for the BCI applications in reality (Pfurtscheller et al., 2006). Our works are based on the VEP, which is expected to yield high performance BCI systems. In spite of the expected use of the VEP, the BCI system based on such EEG oscillations has never reported in immersive virtual environments.

In the next section, we briefly review the virtual reality technology including the immersive projection technology. In section 3, the previous works on a variety of BCI systems are presented. In section 4, we explain the visual stimuli in our experiments and report the performance in inferring the users' eye-gaze directions from the brain signals. We state about the results of the online controls of a stereoscopic virtual panorama. Finally, discussions and future works are followed.

2. Virtual Reality

Virtual reality is a technology with which the user can interact with a computer-generated environment; The virtual environment. There are seven concepts which are required for the virtual reality: simulation, interaction, artificiality, immersion, telepresence, full-body immersion, and network communication (Heim, 1993). In the context of the virtual reality, a variety of special devices have been newly developed; the data glove or data suit etc. The essence of these concepts may be familiar even with people who don't work with the technology.

The virtual environments are mainly provided by the visual stimuli displayed on a computer monitor, a head mounted display, or other special devices realizing stereoscopic images. However, the modality is not restricted to the visual one, owing to the recent understanding of the human perception and the development of the special 'displays'. There are several types of sensory information to obtain such virtual experiences; auditory, haptic, olfactory, and other possible sensations. For example, the force sensation is well experienced by a force display.

There are a lot of applications using the virtual reality technology: For example, the modelling and visualization of the invisible phenomena and the experiences of them in the simulations, the surgical applications sometimes involving telepresence or telexistance, the remote operations of the industrial machine, prototyping or mock up of the developing products, the educational use, the entertainments such as games, the applications for mental therapy, and so on.

There are remarkable advantages in the use of the virtual reality technology. The technology can easily provide the user with the safety and reproducibility owing to the artificially simulated environment. Furthermore, we can reduce the cost and other possible resources.

Among the technologies of the virtual reality, there is a system which provides the users with high degree of immersion: The CAVE (Computer Augmented Virtual Environment). The original CAVE was developed by the group of the University of Illinois and demonstrated at the SIGGRAPH (Cruz-Neira et al., 1993). This type of display system has been designed to perform the activities in a variety of use as mentioned above. The descendant systems have been developed all over the world based on the novel concept and technology of the CAVE. The fundamental technologies of CAVE-like display system will be briefly explained later.

The users can interact with virtual objects by using the standard input devices like a joystick, game controller or newly developed devices such as a data glove. The interaction can be in real time to reflect the input information appropriately to the system. It is sometimes realized by sensing the physical states of the user; for example, using the motion capturing system with which the position or movement of the users' head or entire body can be detected.

Recently, the BCI system has been studied with virtual reality (Bayliss, 2003; Bayliss & Ballard, 2000; Friedman et al., 2004; Friedman et al., 2007; Lalor et al., 2003; Leeb et al., 2005; Ron-Angevin et al., 2005; Scherer et al., 2007; Fujisawa et al., 2008a), which enables people to interact with the virtual environment using the human brain activities: with no standard input devices. For example, by using a head mounted display, Bayliss et al. investigated P300 evoked potential (Bayliss, 2003; Bayliss & Ballard, 2000). The group of Graz University of Technology and the UCL has been studying the 'walking from thought' in CAVE-like system using motor imagery tasks (Friedman et al., 2004; Friedman et al., 2007; Leeb et al., 2005). Most advantage of testing the BCI system in virtual reality environments is that we can easily test and simulate procedures for the BCI applications in reality (Pfurtscheller et al., 2006). However, except for the BCI system based on motor imagery tasks, such applications have never been implemented into immersive virtual reality environment. This book chapter will focus on the Brain-CAVE Interface based on the VEP.

3. Previous Works on BCI

There are two types of signal aquisition in the context of the interface based on the brain activities; The invasive and non-invasive. The invasive BCI, which is often called as BMI, has been developed for people with disability. Neurosurgery enabled a person to control an artificial hand using the Cyberkinetics Neurotechnology's BrainGate as well as the operation of a computer cursor, a variety of swithing operations of lights etc (Cyberkinetics, Inc.). In the BMI system, the electrodes are directly implanted into the brain. Therefore, high quality of the brain signals can be obtained.

The most advantage of the non-invasive approaches is that we can be blessed with the system in our ordinary life. For able-bodied people, the demand on the non-invasive BCI system will be more and more enlarged. In fact, the low-cost products of the non-invasive BCI systems have been developed today. Of course, there is no risk of neurosurgery in such systems and thus it is comparably easy to prepare for the use, while the non-invasive approaches produce poor signal resolution.

There are several types of non-invasive BCI systems; for example, functional magnetic resonance imaging (fMRI) (Buxton, 2002; Huettel et al., 2004), near infrared spectroscopy (NIRS) (Watanabe et al., 1996), etc. Remarkable achievements have been reported on these approaches in laboratories. Based on the decoding technology (Kamitani & Tong, 2005) in the fMRI study, the system could infer the shape of the users' hand (among three states of scissors, paper, and rock) with 85% of the correct rate and a seven second delay, and then could control the robot hand in online (Tech-on, 2006). The NIRS study showed the possibility to control a model train by mental arithmetic task resulting in the haemodynamic response; The optical-BCI system (Utsugi et al., 2007). However, in the present stage these measurement apparatus give high cost and no portability.

The Electroencephalography (EEG) was reported by Hans Berger in 1929. Since then, it has been the most studied method among the non-invasive measurements. The advantage of the EEG in the context of the BCI is; its high temporal resolution, ease for practical use, low-cost, and portability. The low spatial resolution may be the disadvantage. And the artefact or environmental noise tend to reduce the performance of the BCI system. However, the BCI system based on EEG is prosperous owing to the recent extensive studies on the signal processing which may cover the disadvantage.

The P300 response is the event related potential which can measure the degree of concentration of the subject on the specific stimulus. Farwell et al. investigated a P300 speller, which enabled the user to type strings only by brain activities of P300 responses (Farwell & Donchin, 1988; Krusienski et al., 2008). The 6 x 6 matrix of letters flashing randomly were presented on the computer display. The user selected 'A' by counting the number of times that the letter 'A' flashed. A variety of applications has been studied using this type of evoked potentials. Note that Bayliss showed the P300 responses could control the virtual objects (Bayliss, 2003; Bayliss & Ballard, 2000) .

The mu rhythm of somatosensory cortices was found owing to the recent development of computer-based analyses on EEG activities. Movement and even phantom movement are accompanied by a suppression of mu and beta rhythms. This suppression has been known as event-related de-synchronization (ERD). After the movements or when inactive, the idling rhythm increase call as event-related synchronization (ERS) occurs, as in the case of visual alpha rhythm during eye close in relax. It is a strong motivation for EEG-based brain computer interfacing (Pfurtscheller & Neuper, 1997).

A lot of laboratory has developed the BCI system based on the ERD/ERS modulation (Wolpaw & McFarland, 2004; Blankertz et al., 2006; Pfurtscheller et al., 2006). The group of Wolpaw demonstrated the operation of one and two dimensional cursor on a computer screen (The Wadsworth BCI) (Wolpaw & McFarland, 2004). However, prior to the experiments, the participants had to learn to control their own mu and beta rhythms. The BCI system of the group of Graz University of Technology and UCL (Pfurtscheller et al., 2006) is also based on the motor imagery. The BCI system has been implemented in immersing virtual environment (ReaCTor, which is a CAVE-like system). The walking from thought was demonstrated. The subjects participated with many runs of the BCI control in a variety of experimental environments using PC, head-mounted display, and CAVE. Note that the novel works on motor imagery and the BCI system based on it are reviewed in the report of (Wolpaw et al., 2002).

Most of the previous studies on BCI systems has been pefromed in the ideal environments. In the present stage the performance of the BCI system has been more and more improved. However, it is important to study the systems in the simulated environments in order to extract the problems in future practical use in reality. Our concern is in the simulated environment to examine the performances of the BCI system.

4. The BCI Based on SSVEP

4.1 Visual Evoked Potential

Let us see the mechanism of the BCI system based on the VEP. The VEP is an event driven response to an external visual stimulus that is observed on visual cortex (Kuroiwa & Celesia, 1981). In general, if a subject undergoes a flickering visual stimulus with the flickering frequency more than 4 or 5 Hz, the steady-state responses can be obtained; The steady-state VEP (SSVEP), which is the synchronized signals with the flickering frequency often accompanied by the harmonic ones. This type of EEG oscillations has been proven as a reliable signal for the control of a BCI system.

Vidal introduced a BCI system based on the VEP (Vidal, 1973). The system could infer the users' eye-gaze directions in order to determine the direction in which the users wished to move a cursor. Furthermore, Middendorf et al. (Middendorf et al., 2000), Cheng et al. (Cheng et al., 2002), and Trejo et al. (Trejo et al., 2006) also reported a feasibility of such systems to determine the eye-gaze directions. In these works, several checkerboard patterns or virtual buttons (more than 10 buttons in the report of (Cheng et al., 2002)) appear on a computer monitor or a LED-based display and flash at different rates. When the user gazes at an interested flickering button, the system determines the frequency of the steady-state response.

The performance of the BCI system depends both on the speed and the accuracy. In general, the VEP yields high information transfer rate (Wolpaw et al., 2002). In fact, the group of Tsinghua University reported the advantage of EEG oscillations of SSVEP (Hong, 2007). The user could input the sequence of interested phone numbers on the virtual telephone using LED-based visual stimuli. The information transfer rate reached to 55 bits/min (Cheng et al., 2002).

4.2 Immersive Virtual Environment

The design of the visual stimuli is one of the key for the reliable BCI system based on the VEP. In this study, we adopted the visual stimuli in immersive virtual environment.

One of the features of CAVE display system (Cruz-Neira et al., 1993) is its multi-screen configuration. The viewing angle of the user is remarkably enlarged, compared to normal computer monitors. The image displayed in CAVE is interactive. For instance, the user can change the views of the images in real time according to the users' viewpoint measured by the position tracker and also via input devices such as game controllers. These input data are transmitted to the graphics workstations from the input devices. Since the LCD shutter glasses are used to generate stereoscopic images, shutter timing of the glasses must be synchronized with the scanning of the screens.

We have experimented with our BCI system in an immersive virtual environment in the University of Tokyo. Figure 1 shows the external appearance of the projection system that is a cubic shape with five screens positioned at the front, the left, the right, the ceiling, and the floor. The area of each screen is 2.5m x 2.5m. By using this type of projection system, the user can feel high degree of immersion. Therefore, the immersive virtual environment is expected to be a reasonable method to evaluate a BCI system in advance before the implementation into the real world, extracting a variety of problems in practical use. Nevertheless, there has been no extensive study on the Brain-CAVE Interface but only the works on motor related potentials.

Figure 1. The external appearance of a projection system to generate an immersive virtual environment. The system has a viewpoint tracking apparatus and LCD shutter glasses for appropriate stereoscopic images to make the users feel high degree of immersion

Two flickering virtual buttons were prepared being superposed on a 3D virtual panorama in immersive virtual environment. The configuration is illustrated in Figure 2. Each button had the visual angle more than 10 degrees of both in horizontal and vertical at a view distance of 2 m. The subjects were instructed to gaze at a fixation point on either buttons. The flickering frequencies were selected between 4 and 8 Hz so as to synchronize with the refresh rate of vertical scans of the CAVE-projector. Note that this range of flickering frequency had been found to yield clear SSVEP, while the frequency more than 20 Hz resulted in unclear brain responses. The viewpoint tracking system was activated during experiments.

Note that in previous studies on the SSVEP, the visual angle for the visual stimulus was at most a few degrees, being restricted on the size of the usual computer displays. On the other hand, the CAVE system would have an advantage of large visual angles and a variety of visual stimuli would be arranged in the virtual space.

When the user gazed at one of the two flickering objects, the other stimulus was still in the visual field. This is an interesting problem related with the selective attention for the specific visual stimulus, which will be mentioned later.

Figure 2. The left and right flickering (white/black) visual stimuli with square shape superposed on a front screen and a subject sitting in immersive virtual environment. These two flickering frequencies have different rates

4.3 EEG Recordings

The healthy volunteers (s1-s4) with normal or corrected to normal vision participated in the experiments as subjects (range 22-36 years old). They were not trained for the EEG measurements with the flickering visual stimuli. During the experiments, each subject relaxed on an arm-chair facing the front screen of the immersive virtual environment, wearing LCD shutter glasses.

A modular EEG cap system was applied for scalp EEG recordings. Three-channel EEG signals were recorded from parieto-occipital and occipital; that is, PO7, PO8 and Oz according to the extended international 10/20 system (Jasper, 1958) as shown in Figure 3. A body-earth and a reference electrode were on a forehead and on a left ear lobe, respectively. The analogue EEG signals were amplified at a multi-channel bio-signal amplifier (MEG-6116, NIHON KOHDEN, Inc. Japan). A notch filter was applied to reduce the 50 Hz power line interference. The amplified signals were band-pass filtered between 1.5 and 30 Hz, and sampled at 100 Hz by using an A/D converter with a resolution of 16 bits. The digitized EEG data was stored in a standard personal computer.

There were two types of offline experimental tasks (task 1 and 2) were imposed to collect data sets for the later EEG-classification. The users were asked to gaze at and pay attention to a left visual stimulus in the task 1 and a right one in the task 2. For all subjects, one experiment consisted of 5-10 sessions for each task. Each session lasted for 30 seconds. The session of the task 1 and 2 were performed by turns. After one session, one-minute rest was imposed. For several subjects, the experiments were repeatedly performed several times over several days. During these offline measurements the virtual panorama was not controlled (with no visual feedback).

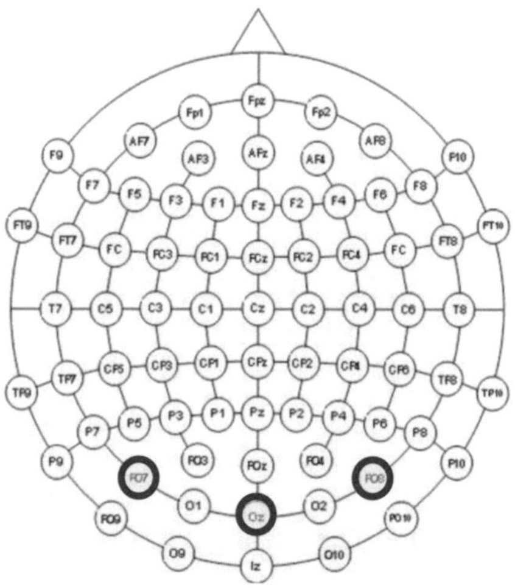

Figure 3. Location of electrodes to collect the SSVEP. Three-channel EEG signals were recorded from parieto-occipital sites (PO7 and PO8) and occipital (Oz) according to the extended international 10/20 system

4.4 Classification of EEG Oscillations

After the data acquisitions, the recorded EEG signals were at first analyzed in offline. Frequency analysis was applied to extract the expected EEG oscillations. The analyzing time period and the window function were fixed to 2 seconds and Hanning, respectively. The EEG features were extracted from the linear combination of voltage value between three electrodes [V(Oz)-{V(PO7)+V(PO8)}/2], expecting the reduction of the environmental noise or possible artefacts, where V(E) means the voltage value detected at the scalp-electrode E. The typical power spectral densities in average are shown in Figure 4. The harmonic signals of the SSVEP were observed. As for one subject s4, the SSVEP was not clear.

The SSVEP was observed at 16 and 18 Hz, which was expected to be harmonic signals induced by 8 and 6 Hz of flickering frequency, respectively. Therefore, wide range of the power spectral densities including these frequencies (range 3-25 Hz) were considered in single trial (non-average) EEG data to evaluate the classification performance discussed below. The spontaneous EEG signals of alpha rhythms (typically 8-13 Hz) were not excluded in these analyses. Note that in our previous study the alpha band contributed to three-class classification aiming the online navigations in the virtual world (Touyama & Hirose, 2007a).

The algorithm of support vector machines (SVM) (Vapnik, 2000) with linear kernel was applied to classify two states of brain activities (during gazing at left stimulus and right one, respectively). To estimate the performance, a leave-one-out method was applied, where only one data is used for testing and the others are for training.

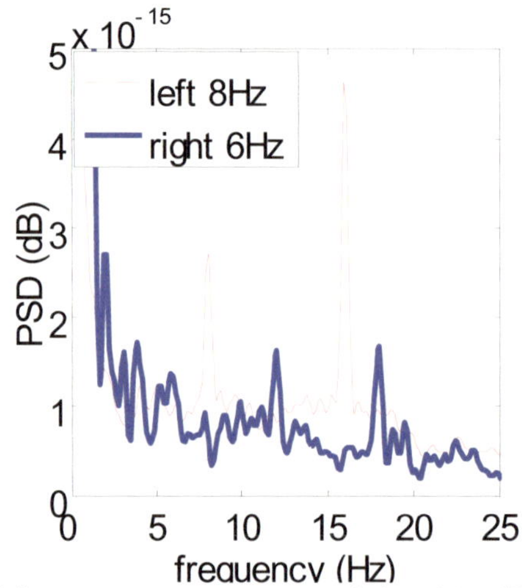

Figure 4. Typical result of the average power spectral densities (PSD). The flickering frequencies are 8 and 6 Hz for left and right visual stimulus, respectively

The results of the classification are shown in Table 1. The performances were found to be 86.6, 71.4 (80.0, 78.0), and 81.0 (82.0) % for the subjects s1, s2, and s3, respectively. The grand average of three subjects was 79.9%. The numbers in the parentheses denote the results of different experimental days.

Now the maximum information transfer rates can be estimated for three subjects with offline results above, while the rate is strongly dependent upon the application design. The rates are dependent on both speed and accuracy, and defined by the following equation (1) (Wolpaw et al., 2002). If a trial has N possible selections and each selection has the same probability of being the one that the user desires, if the probability P that the desired selection will actually be selected is always the same, and if each of the other selections has the same probability of being selected, the bit rate B can be expressed as

$$B = \log_2 N + P \log_2 P + (1-P) \log_2 [(1-P) / (N-1)]. \quad (1)$$

This equation yielded the maximum information transfer rate between 4.1 and 13.0 bits/min from our offline measurements, which amounts to the standard performances (5-25 bits/min) of BCI today.

Subjects' Name (day)	Flickering Frequency (Hz) (left, right)	Classification Performances (%)
s1(1)	(8.0, 6.0)	86.6
s2(1)	(8.0, 6.0)	71.4
s2(2)	(8.0, 6.0)	80.0
s2(3)	(6.9, 4.8)	78.0
s3(1)	(8.0, 6.0)	81.0
s3(2)	(6.9, 4.8)	82.0
Avr.	-	79.9

Table 1. Classification performances (percent corrects) for two conditions of flickering frequencies. The number with subjects' name denotes the experimental day. For example, s3(2) denotes the subject s3 on the 2nd experimental day

4.5 Binary Controls

We will show here the experimental results on the online control of a virtual panorama in the immersive virtual environment. After the data acquisition at an amplifier, the digitized EEG data was transmitted to a signal processing server through the network. At the server, the two-class classification mentioned before was performed by using latest 2 seconds of data. The results of the classification (binary control commands) from the brain activities on visual cortex (l or r corresponding to the left or right flickering stimulus, respectively) were transmitted to the workstation of the immersive virtual environment also through the network. At this workstation, both the images of panorama (a virtual city including roads, buildings, trees, sky, etc.) and the flickering stimuli for each eye were independently generated by using the library of OpenGL Performer (SILICON GRAPHICS, Inc.) to reflect on the screen. The user observed the visual feedback of stereoscopic images through the LCD shutter glasses (with visual feedback).

It is well known that there is a speed-accuracy trade off in the BCI system. There were two types of online experiments in this study to demonstrate the trade off. One is the online system with a consecutive counter (Cheng et al., 2002), and the other is without it. With this counter, the control command was set to r only if the result of the classification was more frequently recognized than l for certain time period, and the same in the case of setting l command. In this study, the time period was set to 1 second.

With the flickering frequency of 6.9 (left) and 4.8 Hz (right), the subjects participated in the online experiments. The frequency combinations were same with our previous online studies. Before the experiments, the participants had no specific training and were only instructed to gaze at and focus attention on a red-coloured fixation point on the flickering stimulus. The eye-fixation point changed its position every 10 seconds between the left and right (as shown in Figure 2). One session lasted for 90 seconds. In the online experiments, the left and right visual stimuli play a key role in controlling a virtual panorama.

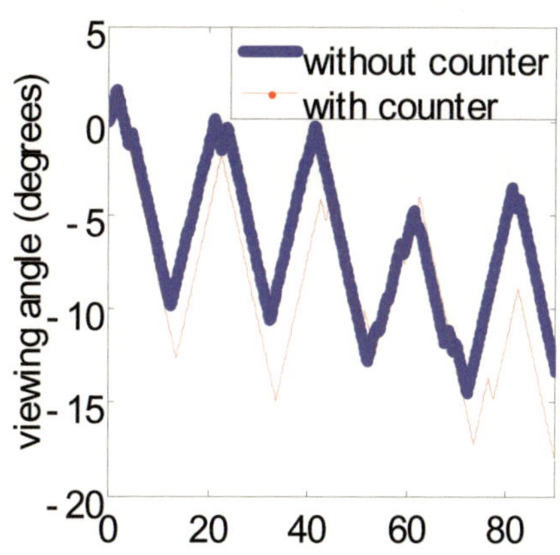

Figure 5. The typical result of the time dependence on the viewing angle of the subject in the virtual city. The flickering frequencies were 6.9 and 4.8 Hz for left and right flickering stimulus, respectively. The results with and without consecutive counter are illustrated

In Figure 5, the graphs show typical experimental results of the binary control of a virtual panorama. The plot shows the relation between the time and the viewing angle of the subject in the virtual city, which varies one after the other by the classification result from the signal processing server. Even without consecutive counter, the user could control the panorama well according to the subjects' intent. With the counter, the accuracy seems to be slightly improved, but the speed was modest, which demonstrated the trade off in the online system. In the online analyses, the average classification performance was 85%.

4.6 Discussions and Future Works

This study presented a non-invasive BCI system based on the SSVEP in immersive virtual environment. The EEG oscillations, induced by two flickering virtual buttons superposed on the computer-generated panorama, were recorded and analyzed. The flickering frequencies were selected between 4 and 8 Hz. Applying support vector machines, the single trial EEG data with 2 seconds of analyzing time yielded 85% of average classification performance in controlling the virtual panorama inferring the eye-gaze directions. The online demonstrations in immersive virtual environment showed a possibility to control the virtual objects according to the brain signals.

The previous study on BCI based on EEG in CAVE-like system investigated the walking in virtual environment using motor related potentials. The work in the report of (Pfurtscheller et al., 2006) required eight seconds of hand/foot imagery tasks to achieve two-class classification (estimated 1.5 bits/min of average information transfer rate), while non-cue based BCI system has been discussed elsewhere (Pfurtsheller et al.). On the other hand, the future advantage of our SSVEP-based BCI is in shortening of analyzing time period and sliding of the window which requires no cue for the user. It was reported that the information transfer rate reached to 55 bits/min (Cheng et al., 2002). Furthermore, the SSVEP-based BCI system requires no training for users, which is one more advantage. However, in our experiments, clear SSVEP could not be observed for one subject, which will be investigated again.

In this study, the binary classification rate was about 80% and 85% in offline and online, respectively. In our previous study, the rate was about 92% even with 1 second of analyzing time and occipital recordings, involving two virtual buttons floating in the dark virtual space (Touyama & Hirose, 2007b). Thus, the condition of the visual stimulus is thought to influence the performance to a large extent. This is an important point in developing the BCI system based on SSVEP using the flickering stimuli superposed on the real scene, because the conditions of the images is in general varied rapidly. Therefore, the conditions of the visual stimulus would be systematically investigated in our future works in order to have clear and robust brain responses. As well as the flickering frequency, spacing, and size are required to be considered.

The improvement of the classification algorithm will be in our research scopes. In the report of (Trejo et al., 2006), kernel partial least squares (KPLS) algorithm was investigated to have high recognition rate of 80-100% in multi-class classification with 1-5 seconds of latencies. With this algorithm, the moving map display based on flickering checkerboard patterns was successfully controlled in a computer monitor. In the analyses in our study, we just adopted simple FFT analyses combined with SVM for the binary classification. It would be required to use only the power spectral densities corresponding to the flickering frequencies and their harmonic signals instead of all the power spectral densities between 3 and 25 Hz. Such kind of feature selection would help the SVM to increase the classification accuracy.

It is necessary to show a useful online application using our BCI system with multi-class classification in immersive virtual environment. One of the examples is to realize the free navigation (walk-through or fly-through) by the SSVEP as well as a manipulation of virtual objects or operation of menu windows. In our preliminary studies, three-class classification has been studied in the context of the navigation. The results for a subject are shown in the Table 2. The experimental settings were similar to that in this study. There, the Fishers' linear discriminant analyses showed about 74% of an average classification performance in inferring three eye-gaze directions, that is, left, right visual stimuli, and a centre eye-fixation point (Touyama & Hirose, 2007a). The ultimate goal in such multi-class applications is that by using tiny visual stimuli arranged in the virtual space with the flickering frequencies near or more than critical one to realize more natural interaction.

	Classified into left	Classified into right	Classified into centre
Task left	68.7 [71.4]	4.0 [7.6]	27.3 [21.0]
Task right	5.3 [14.3]	69.4 [65.2]	25.3 [20.5]
Task centre	6.7 [13.8]	5.3 [6.7]	88.0 [79.5]

Table 2. The performance (percent correct) of three-class classification of EEG activities during gazing at left, right, and centre fixation point. The visual stimuli were similar to those of this study (involving two flickering stimuli superposed on the virtual panorama). Note that there was no flickering stimulus at the centre fixation point. The number out of [ ] (in [ ]) denotes the result on the 1st (2nd) experimental day

During the EEG measurements, the subjects were sitting on the luxury sofa and were instructed not to move. This gives the subjects both physical and mental fatigue. Aiming to realize free postures during EEG acquisitions, we started to analyse the SSVEP measurements during standing in the immersive projection system. The results for a subject are shown in Table 3. It was found that the SSVEP were clearly obtained and the rather high classification performance was achieved in three-class classification.

	Classified into left	Classified into right	Classified into centre
Task left	81.4 [81.4]	9.3 [1.3]	9.3 [17.3]
Task right	5.3 [1.3]	64.0 [86.7]	30.7 [12.0]
Task centre	5.3 [5.3]	16.0 [2.7]	78.7 [92.0]

Table 3. An example of the performance of three-class classification of EEG activities during standing. The subject gazed at left, right, and centre fixation point. There were two flickering stimuli floating in the dark virtual space. Note that there was no flickering stimulus at the centre fixation point. The number out of [ ] (in [ ]) denotes the result on the 1st (2nd) experimental day

There is a noteworthy topic in the context of independent BCI systems. The report of (Kelly et al., 2005) presented the data suggesting that the SSVEP can be used as a measure of visual spatial attention. This type of the independent BCI (see (Walpow et al., 2002)), which requires no eye-movement, would be one of the challenges of the EEG-based interfacing

systems. We are performing the experiment on the EEG measurements with visual-spatial attention (Fujisawa et al., 2008b).
The study of the BCI system in immersive display has not been performed extensively so far. We hope that the Brain-CAVE Interface would be one of the research paradigms in the field of virtual reality and contributes to the advances in human-computer interaction.

5. Acknowledgment

This work was partly supported by Mizuho Foundation for the Promotion of Sciences.

6. References

Bayliss, J.D. (2003). The use of the evoked potentials P3 component for control in a virtual apartment, *IEEE Transaction on Neural Systems and Rehabilitation Engineering,* 11(2).

Bayliss, J.D. & Ballard, D.H. (2000). A virtual reality testbed for brain-computer interface research, *IEEE Transactions on Rehabilitation Engineering,* 8(2), pp. 188-190.

Blankertz, B.; Dornhege, G.; Krauledat, M.; Muller, K.R.; Kunzmann, V.; Losch, F. & Curio, G. (2006). The Berlin Brain-Computer Interface: EEG-based communication without subject training, *IEEE Trans Neural Syst. Rehabil. Eng,* 14(2), Jun, pp. 147-152.

Buxton, R.B. (2002). An Introduction to Functional Magnetic Resonance Imaging: Principles and Techniques, Cambridge Univ. Press, ISBN 0-52158-113-3.

Cheng, M.; Gao, X.; Gao, S. & Xu, D. (2002). Design and Implementation of a Brain-Computer Interface With High Transfer Rates, *IEEE Transactions on Biomedical Engineering,* 49(10), pp. 1181-1186.

Cruz-Neira, C.; Sandin, D.J. & DeFanti, T.A. (1993). Surround-screen projection-based virtual reality: The design and implementation of the CAVE, *ACM SIGGRAPH'93 Proc,* pp. 135-142.

Cyberkinetics, Inc.
http://www.cyberkineticsinc.com/content/medicalproducts/braingate.jsp

Farewell, L.A. & Donchin, E. (1988). Taking off the top of your head: Toward a mental prothesis utilizing event-related brain potentials, *Electroenceph Clin Neurophysiol,* 70, pp. 510-523.

Friedman, D.A.; Slater, M.; Steed, A.; Leeb, R.; Pfurtscheller, G. & Guger, C. (2004). Using a Brain-Computer Interface in Highly-Immersive Virtual Reality, *IEEE Virtual Reality Workshop.*

Friedman, D.A.; Leeb, R.; Guger, C.; Steed, A.; Pfurtscheller, G. & Slater, M. (2007). Navigating virtual reality by thought : What is it like ? *Presence: Teleoperators and Virtual Environments,* 16(1), pp.100-110.

Fujisawa, J.; Touyama, H. & Hirose, M. (2008). EEG-based navigation of immersive virtual environments using common spatial patters, *Proc. of IEEE Virtual Reality Conference* 2008, pp.251-252.

Fujisawa, J.; Touyama, H. & Hirose, M. (2008). Extracting Alpha Band Modulation during Visual Spatial Attention without Flickering Stimuli using Common Spatial Pattern, *Proceedings of 30th Annual International Conference of the IEEE Engineering in Medicine and Biology Society (EMBC'08),* pp.620-623.

Heim, M. (1993). The Metaphysics of Virtual Reality, *Oxford University Press.*

Hochberg, L.R.; Serruya, M.D. ; Friehs, G.M. ; Mukand, J.A. ; Saleh, M.; Caplan, A.H.; Branner, A.; Chen, D.; Penn, R.D. & Donoghue, J.P. (2006). Neuronal ensemble control of prosthetic devices by a human with tetraplegia. *Nature 442*, pp. 164-171.

Hong, B. (2007). BCIs using EEG oscillations: Towards practical applications, *International Workshop on Brain-Computer Interface Technology 2007.*

Huettel, S.A.; Song, A.W. & McCarthy, G. (2004). Functional Magnetic Resonance Imaging, Sinauer Associates, ISBN 0-87893-288-7.

Jasper, H.H. (1958). The ten-twenty electrode system of the International Federation, *Electroencephalogr Clin Neurophysiol, 10*, pp. 371-375.

Kamitani, Y. & Tong, F. (2005). Decoding the visual and subjective contents of the human brain. *Nature Neuroscience*, 8, 5, pp. 679-685.

Kelly, S.P.; Lalor, E.C.; Reilly, R.B. & Foxe, J.J. (2005). Visual spatial attention tracking using high-density SSVEP data for independent brain-computer communication, *IEEE Trans Neural Syst Rehabil Eng, 13*(2), pp. 172-178.

Kuroiwa, Y. & Celesia, G.G. (1981). Visual evoked potentials with hemifield pattern stimulation, Their use in the diagnosis of retrochiasmatic lesions, *Arch. Neurol. 38,* pp. 86-90.

Krusienski, D.J.; Sellers, E.W.; McFarland, D.J.; Vaughan, T.M. & Wolpaw, J.R. (2008). Toward enhanced P300 speller performance. *J Neurosci Methods.* Jan 15; 167(1): 15-21. Epub 2007 Aug 1.

Lalor, E.; Kelly, S.P.; Finucane, C.; Burke, R.; Smith, R.; Reilly, R. & McDarby, G. (2003). Steady-state VEP-based Brain-Computer Interface control in an immersive 3-D gaming environment, *Proceedings of the EURASIP*, 2003.

Leeb, R.; Scherer, R.; Keinrath, C.; Guger, C. & Pfurtscheller, G. (2005). Exploring Virtual Environments with an EEG-based BCI through Motor Imagery, *Biomedzinishe Technik, Berlin, 52,* pp. 86-91.

Middendorf, M.; McMillan, G.; Calhoun, G. & Jones, K.S. (2000). Brain-Computer Interfaces Based on the Steady-State Visual-Evoked Response, *IEEE Transactions on Rehabilitation Engineering, 8*(2), pp. 211-214.

Pfurtscheller, G. et al. Human brain-computer interface. In: Vaadia,E., Riehle,A.(Eds.), Motor Cortex in Voluntary Movements: A Distributed System for Distributed Functions. Series: Methods and New Frontiers in Neuroscience. CRC Press, pp. 367-401.

Pfurtscheller, G.; Leeb, R.; Keinrath, C.; Friedman, D.; Neuper, C.; Guger, C. & Slater, M. (2006). Walking from thought, *Brain Research, 1071*, pp. 145-152.

Pfurtscheller, G. & Neuper, C. (1997). Motor imagery activates primary sensorimotor area in man, *Neurosci Lett, 239*, pp. 65-68.

Ron-Angevin, R.; Estrella, A.D. & Reyes-Lecuona, A. (2005). Development of a brain-Computer Interface (BCI) based on virtual reality to improve training technique, *Applied Technologies in Medicine and Neuroscience,* pp. 13-20.

Scherer, R.; Lee, F.; Schlögl, A.; Leeb, R.; Bischof, H. & Pfurtscheller, G. (2007). Towards self-paced (asynchronous) Brain-Computer Communication: *Navigation through virtual worlds, IEEE Transactions on Biomedical Engineering, 2007.*

Tech-on. (2006). To operate robot only with brain, ATR and Honda develop BMI base technology, 26 May 2006.

Touyama, H. & Hirose, M. (2007). Steady-state VEPs in CAVE for walking around the virtual world, *Proc. of 12th International Conference on Human-Computer Interaction,* LNCS 4555, pp. 715-717.

Touyama, H. & Hirose, M. (2007). Brain Computer Interface via Stereoscopic Images in CAVE, *Proc. of 12th International Conference on Human-Computer Interaction,* LNCS 4557, pp. 1004-1007.

Trejo, L.J.; Rosipal, R. &Matthews, B. (2006). Brain-computer interfaces for 1-D and 2-D cursor control: designs using volitional control of the EEG spectrum or steady-state visual evoked potentials, *IEEE Trans. Neural. Syst. Rehabil. Eng, 14*(2), Jun, pp. 225-229.

Utsugi, K.; Obata, A.; Sato, H.; Katsura, T.; Sagara, K.; Maki, A. & Koizumi, H. (2007). Development of an Optical Brain-machine Interface, Engineering in Medicine and Biology Society, 2007. EMBS 2007. 29th Annual International Conference of the IEEE Volume, Issue , 22-26 Aug. 2007 Page(s): 5338-5341.

Vapnik, V.N. (2000). The nature of statistical learning theory, *Statistics for Engineering and Information Science,* Springer-Verlag, New York.

Vidal, J.J. (1973). Towards direct brain-computer communication, *Annu. Rev. Biophys. Bioeng, 2,* pp. 157-180.

Watanabe, E., Yamashita, Y., Maki, A., Ito, Y. & Koizumi, H. (1996). Non-invasive functional mapping with multi-channel near infra-red spectroscopic topography in humans. *Neurosci Lett* 205: pp. 41-44.

Wolpaw, J.R.; Birbaumer, N.; McFarland, D.J.; Pfurtscheller, G. & Vaughan, T.M. (2002). Brain-computer interfaces for communication and control, *Clinical Neurophysiology, 113,* pp. 767-791.

Wolpaw, J.R. & McFarland, D.J. (2004). Control of a two-dimensional movement signal by a noninvasive brain-computer interface in humans, *PNAS, 101*(51), pp. 17849-17854.

Multimodal Accessibility of Documents

Georgios Kouroupetroglou and Dimitrios Tsonos
National and Kapodistrian University of Athens
Greece

1. Introduction

Traditionally a "document" was considered as a textual record. Schamber (1996) defined document as a unit *"consisting of dynamic, flexible, nonlinear content, represented as a set of linked information items, stored in one or more physical media or networked sited; created and used by one or more individuals in the facilitation of some process or project"*. Buckland (1997) tries to answer the question "what is a document?" through a discussion on how far the meaning of "document" can be pushed and which are the limits of "documentation".

The evolution of Computer Science and Information Technology created a new perspective for the word "document". The concept "electronic documents" can be differentiated from the "printed documents" having specific characteristics (Schamber, 1996): easily manipulabable, internally and externally linkable, readily transformable, inherently searchable, instantly transportable and infinitely replicable.

The term document used in this chapter refers to all kind of printed or electronic documentation the content of which is most text, like newspapers, books, journals, magazines, educational material, letters, brochures, leaflets, etc.

A document contains elements that arrange content in the page or even in the document itself. For example, the title of a chapter can be recognized by placing it on the top of the page and in larger font size than the body of text. Also, page indexing at the end of a document links the reader to specific part of the document.

The document functionality can be distinguished into browsing, searching, navigation and reading (Doermann et al., 1998). Additional concepts related to document's functionality are legibility, readability and aesthetics.

Legibility is a measure of easiness to distinguish one letter from another in a particular typeface and readability is a gauge of how easily words, phrases and blocks of copy can be read. These two measures were introduced as a comparison between printed and electronic documents on a computer screen (Mills & Weldon, 1987). Readability and legibility are closely related to typographic elements, typeface design and font/background color combinations (Hill & Scharff, 1997; Richard & Patrick, 2004; Eglin & Bres, 2003). Readability is more related to the overall and layout structure of a document (Holmqvist & Wartenberg, 2005; Holmberg, 2004; Kupper, 1989; Wartenberg & Holmqvist, 2005; Axner et al., 1997). Aesthetics of a document play a significant role during the reading process as well as reader's preferences (Porat et al., 2007; Harrington et al., 2004; Laarni, 2003).

"Dynamic" concepts like navigation and browsing are related to the interaction process with the reader. Navigation in electronic documents is a set of instructions to create an appropriate flow of a document for each type of devices (W3C, 2008a). The traditional way for navigation is by simply scrolling the window that presents the electronic document (like browsing in printed). By digitizing any printed document and transforming it into electronic format, new techniques derive that lead to a more sufficient and versatile navigation process combining navigation and browsing (W3C, 2008b; Czyzowicz, 2005; Cockburn et al., 2006). Thus, the functionality of a document can be distinguished into two tasks (Tsonos et al., 2007a):

- **Presentation task**, as an output; e.g. presenting the content and the information to the reader.
- **Navigation task**, as an input; e.g. performing actions by the reader, like searching or browsing for specific information.

Print disabilities prevent people from reading standard printed documents. They can be due to a visual, perceptual or physical disability which may be the result of vision impairment (blindness, low vision or dyschromatopsia), a learning disability (including dyslexia) or a disability (such as loss of dexterity) that prevents the physical holding of a book. Print-disabled are referred also as print-handicapped or read-disabled. Demographics for the print-disabled varied from 10% of the general population in Canada (IELA, 2008) to 17.5% in Australia (RPH, 2008).

People with print disabilities require printed documents in alternative formats, such as Braille, audio, large print or electronic text. They may also require assistive technology to meet their information needs. Braille displays provide in real-time text information into haptic modality. Screen magnifiers are software applications that help people with either low vision or dyschromatopsia to read documents. Text-to-Speech (TtS) is a common software technology that converts in real-time any electronic text into speech (Fellbaum & Kouroupetroglou, 2008). In most cases the text on a Graphical User Interface is detected by a software application named screen reader, which feeds actually the TtS system. TtS can be applied not only in Personal Computers, but also in Smart Mobile Phones and Personal Digital Assistants (PDAs). Automated Reading Devices (ARDs) are stand-alone machines that can convert printed or electronic text to audible speech using Text-to-Speech. They do not require to be connected to any other device, like a computer. ARDs have been designed for use by individuals who are print-disabled. Depending on the type of the source material, there are two main classes of ARDs (Freitas & Kouroupetroglou, 2008):

- Printed-Text (PT) ARDs,
- Electronic-Text (ET) ARDs.

Most of the current Text-to-Speech systems do not include effective provision of the semantics and the cognitive aspects of the visual (such as font and typesettings) and non-visual document elements. Recently, there was an effort towards Document-to-Audio (DtA) synthesis, which essentially constitutes the next generation of the Text-to-Speech systems, supporting the extraction of the semantics of document metadata (Fourli-Kartsouni et al., 2007) and the efficient acoustic representation of both text formatting (Xydas & Kouroupetroglou, 2001a; 2001b; Xydas et al., 2003; 2005) and tables (Spiliotopoulos et al., 2005a; 2005b) through modelling the parameters of the synthesised speech signal.

According to Stephanidis (2001), **accessibility** concerns the provision and maintenance of access by disabled and elderly people to encoded information and interpersonal communication, through appropriate interaction with computer-based applications and telematic services. W3C (2008e) determines Web Accessibility as means that people with disabilities can perceive, understand, navigate, and interact with the Web and its content.

The last two decades there were many efforts in the domain of the accessibility of documents. Some of them deal with the web content accessibility for visually impaired users (Kouroupetroglou et al., 2007; Harper & Yesilada, 2007; Chen et al., 2006; Rosmaita, 2006). Bigham et al. (2006) studied how images can be accessible and Saito et al. (2006) proposes a method to transform existing Flash content into XML structures. Edwards et al. (2006) tried to create mathematics accessible to blind students and Francioni & Smith (2002) proposed a framework for the accessibility of computer science lessons for visually impaired students. Tsonos & Kouroupetroglou (2008) proposed recently a Design-for-All approach for accessible documents on the board and during the presentations in the classroom.

Multimodal interaction with documents is considered the execution of the presentation and navigation tasks according to reader's preferences in one of three modalities, visual, acoustic and haptic or in any preferable combination. Guillon et al. (2004) proposed an integrated publishing procedure for accessible multimodal documents based on DAISY 3.0 (DAISY, 2008). World Wide Web Consortium (W3C, 2008c) proposes guidelines for the multimodal interaction (W3C, 2008b). Multimodal Accessibility should support any device: thin clients (devices with little processing power or capabilities that can be used to capture user input - microphone, touch display, stylus, etc. - as well as nonuser input, such as GPS), thick clients (devices such as a PDA or notebook) and medium clients (devices with some degree of interpretation) (Mikhalenko, 2008). Besides the above efforts, there is still a challenging question for both the navigation and the presentation tasks: "Are documents accessible by anyone?"

In this chapter we first present an integrated architecture on how a document is structured. Then, the existing international standards and guidelines for creating accessible documents are given. Based on these, we propose in the following section a novel holistic XML-based system for the real time production, presentation and navigation of multimodal accessible documents.

2. Document Architecture

The way a document is composed and presented either on paper or on screen, refers to the term "document architecture" (Peels et al., 1985). In Figure 1 we propose a general document architecture, which constitutes an extension of the basic ITU/ISO model (ITU, 1993; ISO, 1989). One can identify two different but complementary views of a specific document:

- *Logical view*: associates content with architectural elements such as headings, titles /subtitles, chapters, paragraphs, tables, lists, footnotes and appendices.
- *Layout view*: associates content with architectural elements relating to the arrangement on pages and areas within pages, such as columns and margins.

Typography essentially includes font (type, size, color, background color, etc.) and typesetting (such as bold, italics, underline). It can be applied to both the logical and the layout view of a document. For example, the title of a chapter (Logical view) can be in bold or in larger font size than the body of the text. The vertical space in a text block, called leading (Layout view) can be affected by the font type. Furthermore, typography can be applied to the body of the text directly, e.g. a word in bold is used to indicate either emphasis or the introduction of a new term. "Typography exists to honour content" (Bringhurst, 1996).

There is an analogy of the above terminology with the classification of document elements proposed by Tsonos et al. (2007a):

- Text Formatting ↔ Typography

- Text Structure ↔ Logical View
- Text Layout ↔ Layout View

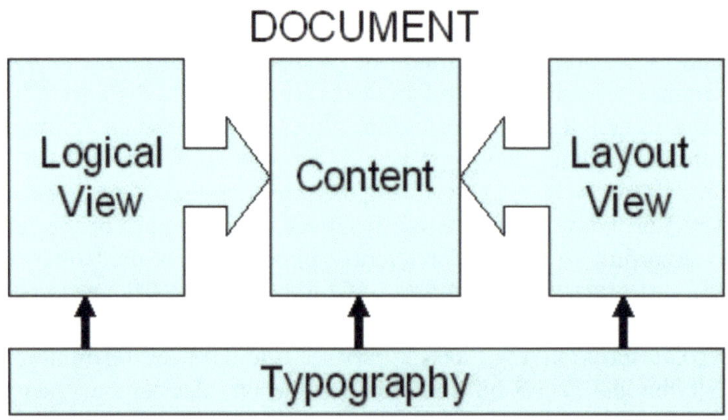

Figure 1. The general model of the document architecture

According to Tsonos et al. (2007a) the content of a document includes also non-textual elements, such as figures, drawing etc.

The document elements described above affect the readability, the legibility, as well as the aesthetics of a document. Axner et al. (1997) found that the three-column text format is easier to be read than single-column. Hall & Hanna (2004) examined the impact of text-background color combinations on readability and aesthetics providing the following results:

- colors with greater contrast ratio lead to greater readability,
- preferred colors (e.g. blues and chromatic colors) lead to higher ratings of aesthetic quality.

Laarni (2003) investigated the effects of color, font type and typesetting on user preferences. He concluded that: i) the most readable combinations are: i.1) plain Times New Roman black color font on white background, i.2) italized Arial white font on blue background and i.3) plain Arial white font on black background and ii) the less readable are the combinations of red font on green background. Also he examined their impact of color on document aesthetics (e.g. combinations of red font on green background were rated as the most unpleasant and black on white were considered the least arousing).

3. Standards and Guidelines of Accessible Documents

This section is intended to give a brief overview of the available guidelines and standards that are direct related with the accessibility of documents.

3.1 Web Accessibility Guidelines

Web Content Accessibility Guidelines (W3C, 2008d) are part of Web Accessibility Guidelines provided by Web Accessibility Initiative (W3C, 2008e). The scope of these guidelines is to create accessible web content to people with disabilities.

The guidelines concern all the Web content developers (page authors and site designers) as well as the developers of authoring tools. Following these guidelines the Web content becomes device / software independent, thus it makes it accessible in any of three modalities. The guidelines address not only people with permentant impairements but also those with temporal or transient disabilities (e.g., a person that uses a mobile device and drives a vehicle in a noisy environment).

These guidelines help people to access the Web more quickly. Also, the developers are encouraged to use multimedia content (like images, videos, sounds etc.) but in a manner that is properly accessible.

The content of a web page can be presented by a *text* or *non-text equivalent*. These two terms are comprehensible using the following examples:

1. Suppose there is an image in a web page. A non-sighted user is unable to view the image. A description (*text equivalent*) of the image can make the image accessible to the user. The description can differ according to author's intentions, by simply describing the image that is supplementary to the main content-text of the web page or to guide the user to click the image for navigation purposes. Thus, two users with different needs can access the image using the same kind of web browser, sighted user can view the image and non-sighted can hear the description using synthesized speech through a Text-to-Speech or "read" the description through a Braille display.
2. Other multimedia features in web page are the pre-recorded speech (e.g. a welcome message in a site). A deaf user is unable to hear the welcome message. A text equivalent of the audio file can be accessed by the user and read the welcome message.
3. In the previous example, a deaf user can alternatively "hear" the description or the message using a video stream or a virtual agent that translates the description into sign language. This is the *non-textual* equivalents of text.

The WAI guidelines address two general goals: ensuring graceful transformation and making content understandable and navigable (W3C, 2008d). Web Content Accessibility Guidelines:

- Provide equivalent alternatives to auditory and visual content.
- Don't rely on color alone.
- Use markup and style sheets and do so properly.
- Clarify natural language usage.
- Create tables that transform gracefully.
- Ensure that pages featuring new technologies transform gracefully.
- Ensure user control of time-sensitive content changes.
- Ensure direct accessibility of embedded user interfaces.
- Design for device-independence.
- Use interims solutions.
- Use W3C technologies and guidelines.
- Provide context and orientation information.
- Provide clear navigation mechanisms.
- Ensure that documents are clear and simple.

3.2 Open Document Format Accessibility

The OpenDocument Format (ODF) is an open XML-based document file format for office applications to be used for documents containing text, spreadsheets, charts, and graphical elements. The file format makes transformations to other formats simple by leveraging and reusing existing standards wherever possible (ODF, 2008a, OASIS, 2008). The creation and support of this standard imposes the possibility for the implementation of new applications and the backward compatibility of the traditional office applications.

The ODF schema provides high-level information suitable for editing documents. It defines suitable XML structures for office documents and is friendly to transformations using XSLT or similar XML-based tools.

Under the guidelines and support of ODF, the Open Document specification for accessibility has been created. The specification intends to discover and improve accessibility issues and enhance the creation, reading and editing process of office documents for people with disabilities (ODF, 2008b). The Open Document Format comprises much structural and semantic information that is needed for the proper access to this information by people with disabilities.

Open Document accessibility subcommittee categorizes accessibility into three types of access: direct access, mediated access and indirect access (ODF, 2008b).

Combining the use of computer - assistive technologies and Open Document Accessibility specifications, a disabled user can have direct access to the content of a document.

The types of disabilities supported by ODF – Accessibility are:

- Minor vision impairments.
- Major vision impairments.
- Near or total blindness.
- Minor physical impairments.
- Major physical impairments without speech recognition.
- Major physical impairments with speech recognition.
- Hearing impairments.
- Cognitive impairments.

3.3 Math Markup Language

W3C through MathML (W3C, 2008f) proposes recomendations for the production and representation of mathematics in XML. Traditionally, the representation of mathematical expressions and scientific notation in electronic documents were implemented using pictures and images and the caption of the image as a description of the image (even in HTML). But, these figures are not accessible by, e.g. a blind student. This is because, a screen reader is not able to "read" the image but only the description provided by the caption or any metadata accompanying the image.

MathML is a low-level specification for describing mathematics as a basis for machine to machine communication. It provides a much needed foundation for the inclusion of mathematical expressions in Web pages (W3C, 2008f)

MathML has been designed with the following goals (W3C, 2008g):

- Encode mathematical material suitable for teaching and scientific communication at all educational levels.
- Encode both mathematical notation and mathematical meaning.
- Facilitate conversion to and from other mathematical formats, both presentational and semantic. Output formats should support: graphical displays, speech synthesizers, input for computer algebra systems, other mathematics typesetting languages, such as TEX, plain text displays, e.g. VT100 emulators, print media, including Braille.

It is recognized that conversion to and from other notational systems or media may involve loss of information (W3C, 2008g).

MathML combines not only visual representation tasks but also the meaning - semantics (like "divide", "times", "power of") of mathematical notations. For example, embedded mathematical expression using MathML in web pages can be viewed as normal web pages (visual representation task). Blind individuals can use a screen reader along with a Text-to-Speech system to hear the description of the same mathematic expression using MathML (semantic representation).

An application, basically for the acoustic rendering of the scientific notations using MathML, is the free available MathPlayer plugin (Soiffer, 2005; MathPlayer, 2008) for the web browsers.

3.4 Braille Markup Language

A new and promising standard for haptic representation of documents' content in Braille is the Markup Language (BrailleML). BrailleML is an effort towards the standardization of Braille documents. Masanori et al., (2007) proposes the automated conversion of ODF documents into Braille Documents using the BrailleML, which is an XML language described in the XML Schema.

3.5 Scalar Vector Graphics

Scalar Vector Graphics (SVG) is a language for describing two-dimensional graphics and graphical applications in XML (SVG, 2008). SVGs offer a number of features to make graphics on the Web more accessible, to a wider group of users. Users who benefit include; those with low vision, color blind or blind users, and users of assistive technologies. A number of these SVG features can also increase usability of content for many users without disabilities, such as users of PDAs, mobile phones or other non-traditional Web access devices (SVG, 2000).

Disabled users are provided with many accessibility features by the SVG specification. SVG images are scalable - they can be zoomed and resized by the reader as needed. Scaling can help users with low vision and users of some assistive technologies (e.g., tactile graphic devices, which typically have low resolution).

3.6 Ink Markup Language

InkML is an XML data format for representing digital ink data that is input with an electronic pen or stylus as part of a multimodal system. Ink markup provides a format for:

- transferring digital ink data between devices and software components,
- storing hand-input traces for: Handwriting recognition (including text, mathematics, chemistry), Signature verification, Gesture interpretation.

The InkML specification is designed by the ink subgroup of the Multimodal Interaction Working Group of the W3C (InkML, 2006). The InkML requirements can be divided into two categories (InkML, 2003):

- primitive elements, which represent low-level information about digital ink (like device and screen context characteristics and pen traces),
- application-specific elements, which characterize meta-information about the ink (a group of traces that belong to a field in a form).

3.7 DAISY/NISO standard

The DAISY Consortium (DAISY, 2008) is the official non-profit maintenance agency for the DAISY/NISO standard (officially known as ANSI/NISO Z39.86) (ANSI/NISO, 2008) provided by the National Information Standards Organization NISO. This standard defines the format and the content of the electronic file set that comprises a digital talking book (DTB) and establishes a limited set of requirements for DTB playback devices. This standard specifies the guidelines for the production and presentation of Digital Talking Books (DTBs) for print-disabled readers (blind, visually impaired, physically disabled and those with learning disabilities).

DAISY/NISO standard provides specifications for the format of DTB files (production of DTBs) and also sets the specifications for the DTB playback devices:

- Player performance related to file requirements.
- Player behaviour in areas defined in user requirements.

A Digital Talking Book (DTB) is: a collection of electronic files arranged to present information to the target population via alternative media, namely, human or synthetic speech, refreshable Braille, or visual display, e.g., large print (ANSI/NISO, 2008).

The files that comprise a DTB can be divided into the following ten categories:

- Package File.
- Textual Content File.
- Audio Files.
- Image Files.
- Synchronization Files.
- Navigation Control File.
- Bookmark/Highlight File.
- Resource File.
- Distribution Information File.
- Presentation Styles.

The merge of these files' functionalities and the creation of a DTB according to DAISY/NISO standard incorporates many features for either Navigation or Presentation tasks during the reading process. A few features are:

- In Navigation task: rapid - flexible navigation, bookmarking – highlighting, keyword searching.
- In Presentation task: user control over the presentation of selected items (e.g., footnotes, page numbers, etc.).

The navigation features provided by DTB include: Fast Forward and Fast Reverse, Reading at Variable Speed, Notes, Cross Reference Access, Index Navigation, Bookmarks, Highlighting, Excerpt Capability, Searching, Spell-Out Capability, Text Attributes and Punctuation, Tables, Nested Lists, Text Elements, Skipping User-Selected Text Elements, Location Information, Summary and Reporting Information, Science and Mathematics.

These features enable the presentation and navigation in DTB either in visual, acoustic or haptic modality. According to reader's disabilities and needs, the document can be presented and accessed in multiple ways and combinations of the three modalities.

Following this standard one can implement a DTB player with a variety of capabilities and functionalities. A DTB player can vary from a portable device, which simply "reads" to the user the content of the book using synthetic speech supporting basic navigation features like fast forward and reverse, reading at variable speed, to a more efficient PC-based player, supporting all modalities and all navigation features provided by the standard.

4. An XML-based system for Multimodal Accessibility of Documents

The discussion on accessibility of documents imposes questions on how the documents can be accessed either in visual, acoustic or haptic modality. Studies, such as (Edwards et al., 2006; Raman, 1992; Xydas & Kouroupetroglou, 2001b), are trying to create accessible documents in the acoustic modality using speech synthesis or by combining earcons (Kramer, 1994; Brewster et al. 1996; Mynatt, 1994), auditory icons (Gorny, 2000) and 3D sounds (Djennane, 2003) for the auditory. Recently a rather ad-hoc approach for multimodal accessibility of mainly TEX formatted technical documents was introduced by Power (2008). In this section we present a novel integrated XML-based system for the real-time production, presentation and navigation of multimodal accessible documents by conforming to the guidelines and standards discussed in section 3. This approach includes a unified methodology for the multimodal rendering of text formatting, text structure, text layout and non-textual elements.

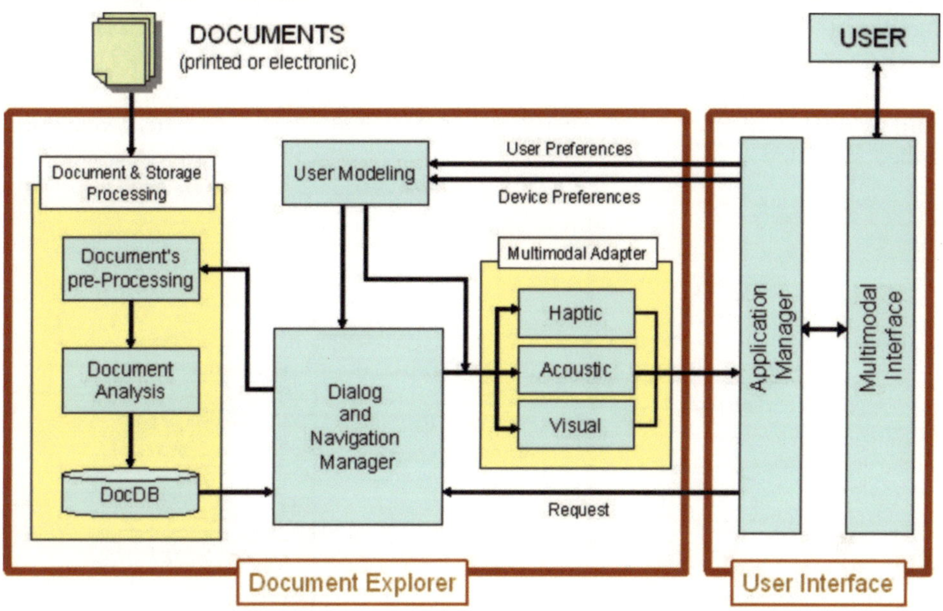

Figure 2. The XML-based system for multimodal accessibility of documents

The overall proposed architecture consists of two main parts (Figure 2): the *User Interface* and the *Document Explorer*. The later is responsible for document analysis during the production process and the exploration in the documents (in the navigation task). User Interface is responsible for the multimodal interaction with the documents. It collects the user preferences and the device requests, as well as the navigation commands, and executes the presentation task. These parts are implemented by two different modules following the Client - Server model. The Document Explorer can be hosted on a powerful server machine due to the resource demanding tasks that performs. In contradiction, the User Interface can be hosted on any common computer (e.g. a personal computer, a PDA, mobile smart phone). This kind of implementation fulfills the Web Content Accessibility Guidelines, in order to be device and software independent. The implementation and the communication between the modules are XML-based.

The presentation that follows is given according to the:

- Production task,
- Navigation task,
- Presentation task.

4.1 Production of Multimodal Accessible Documents

The *Documents' Processing and Storage* module is responsible for the production of accessible documents. It parses a document and then creates the output according to DAISY/NISO standard. The output is stored in a database (DocDB), so the Dialog and Navigation Manager module can have quick access to the content.

Document pre-processing

Figure 3 illustrates the document's pre-processing module. It can handle either printed or electronic documents. The *printed* documents are scanned and pass an Optical Character Recognition (OCR) software application. The Markup Normalization Module parses the digitized or the electronic documents in order the file format conforms to the DAISY/NISO specification. The output file (namely the Document-ML) includes: the content of the document, text formatting, text structural, text layout and non-textual elements (as described in section 2).

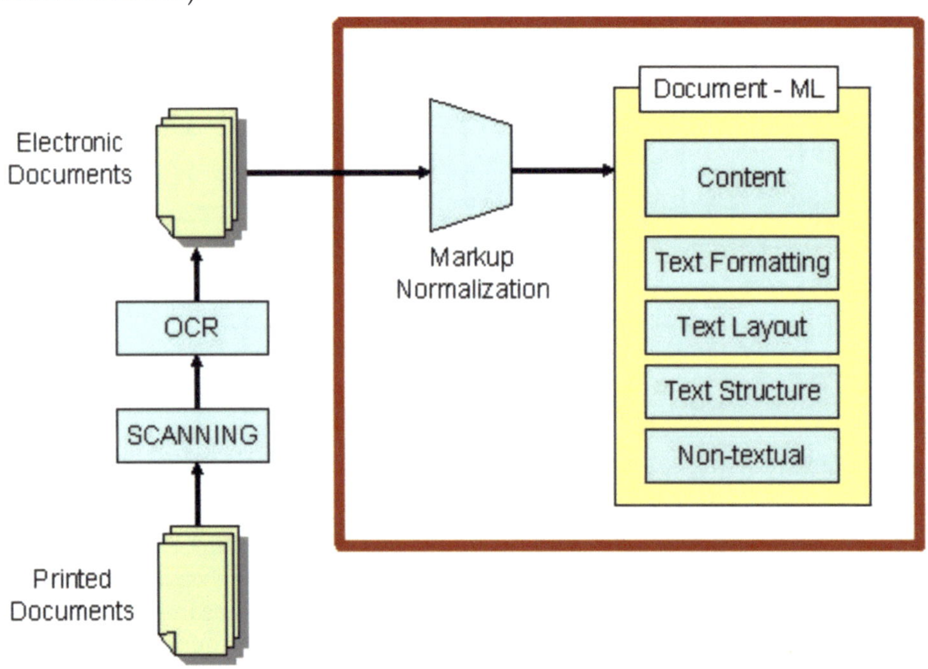

Figure 3. Documents' Pre-processing Module

To serve the multimodal accessibility requirements, the architecture tags the document at the:

- *Semantic* layer,
- *Emotional* layer.

Both these layers are free of presentation details. The Semantic layer aims to record the reader's understanding of the document. The later layer encodes the emotional state of the reader during the reading process. The output data of these two layers can be transformed to any modality. In the following paragraphs we present the way the original visual stimulus affects the multimodal presentation, via these layers, emphasizing the acoustic modality.

Semantic layer

Recently there was an attempt to produce an automatic extraction system of semantic information based only on the document layout, without the use of natural language processing (Fourli-Kartsouni et al, 2007). However, there are several studies on the automatic identification of logical structure of documents e.g. (Conway, 1993; Yamashita et al., 1991; Derrien-Peden, 1991; Krishnamoorthy et al., 1993). Most traditional approaches in this field have employed deterministic methods (decision trees, formal grammars) (Mao et al., 2003; Tsujimoto & Asada, 1990; Derrien-Peden, 1991), which may suffer from poor performance due to noise and uncertainty. In addition, such approaches create models which are not flexible to domain changes and cannot easily evolve in the presence of new evidence. In order to overcome such limitations, Fourli-Kartsouni et al. (2007) employed a probabilistic approach based on Bayesian networks trained on a series of labelled documents. Bayesian networks offer a significant tolerance to noise and uncertainty, they can capture the underlying class structure residing in the data and they can be trained on examples, thus adapting to existing and future evidence. It can learn the mapping between text's formatting, structure, layout and logic elements. The mapping rules (which in some cases is 1:N) can be derived from a series of experiments, (e.g. bold can be mapped as emphasis but also as strong emphasis).

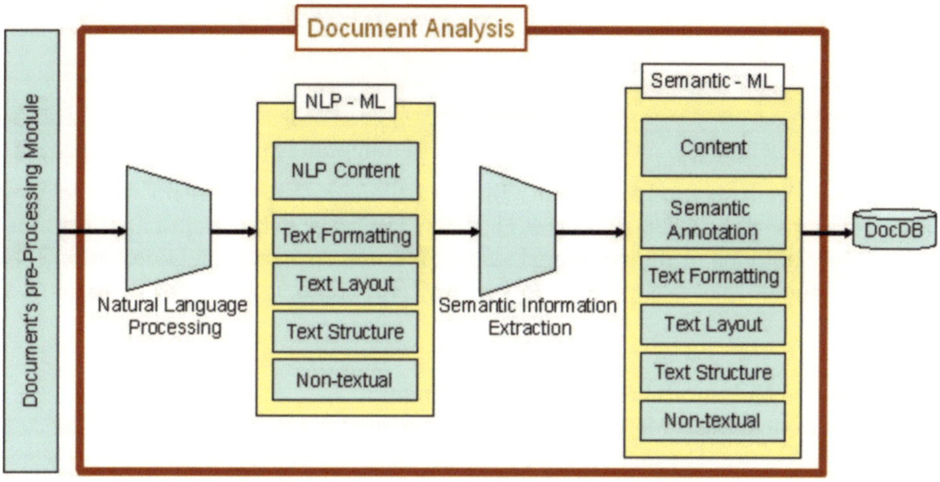

Figure 4. Document Analysis module: The Semantic Information Extraction approach

The Document Analysis Module (Figure 4) adds semantic annotation tags to documents using the methodology proposed by Fourli-Kartsouni et al. (2007). The module produces an XML-file (Semantic-ML) including all the document elements described in section 2 and stores the output on the database (DocDB).

Emotional layer

Many studies in the field of Human Computer Interaction focus on the user's emotional response during the interaction (Kärkkäinen & Laarni, 2002; Humaine Portal, 2008;

Dormann, 2003). The document elements affect directly the reader's emotions, emotional state and the readability of the document. Multiple combinations of colors (Birren, 1984), font size, type and style in a document affects the emotional state (Laarni, 2003; Sánchez et al., 2005; Sánchez et al., 2006; Tsonos et al., 2008) and the readability of the document (Laarni, 2003; Saari et al., 2004) not only in printed but also in electronic documents (Larson, 2007).

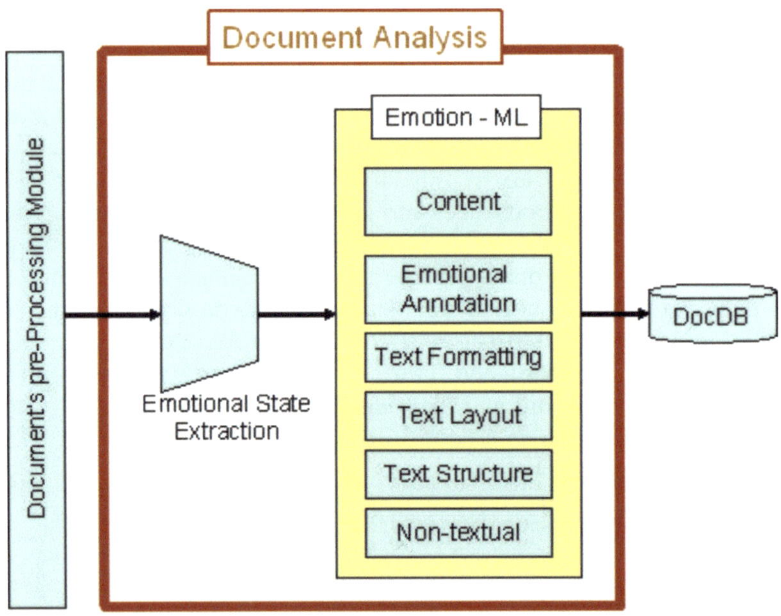

Figure 5. Document analysis module: The Reader's Emotional State Extraction approach

The Document Analysis module (Figure 5), using the automated readers' emotional state extraction (Tsonos et al., 2007b, Tsonos et al., 2008), implements the mapping of document's elements into variations of the emotional states Pleasure, Arousal and Dominance (P.A.D.) or specific emotions. The module produces an XML file (Emotion-ML) with emotional state annotation.

4.2 Navigation in Multimodal Accessible Documents

The Dialog and Navigation Manager handles the navigation tasks and forwards the content to Multimodal Adapter. The manager supports all the navigational functionalities suggested by the DAISY/NISO standard using the Navigation Control File (this file describes the hierarchy of the document).

For the implementation of the manager it is optimum to use an adaptive, agent-based dialog system as proposed in (Frink, 1999; Hjalmarsson, 2005) to support:

- System Use, taking over parts of routine tasks, adapting the interface, giving advice of system use, controlling a dialogue,
- Information Acquisition, helping users to find information, tailoring information presentation.

Such an agent-based dialog system allows every module to interact and is capable of reasoning. It is a flexible allowing the user to have full control of the dialog (McTear, 2002) and supports multimodal dialog input (Turunen et al., 2005).

User preferences and device requests are processed by the User Modeling module and are handled by the Dialog and Navigation Manager. *User Modeling* module creates the user's profile according to her/his interaction and device requests. As an example, the user is able to select the desired modality for the presentation of document's content according to her/his needs or the way a command is given to the system, along with the requirements of the user's device. The user profile is a collection of actions and preferences acquired by the interaction with the Application Manager. Such can be the user's needs, the interaction modality, the navigational factors, environmental factors etc. The produced XML file (User-ML) is forwaded to the Dialog and Navigation Manager. Thus, depending on the user preferences, the dialog manager handles the way the content will be treated and delivered in each modality (acoustic, visual, haptic) through the Acoustic Adapter or/and the Visual Adapter and/or the Haptic Adapter.

4.3 Presentation of Multimodal Accessible Documents

User Interface includes two parts: the *Multimodal Interface* and the *Application Manager* (Figure 2). Multimodal Interface is responsible for the user's interaction with the documents supporting the three interaction modalities visual, acoustic and haptic. The User Interface supports the:

- input tasks (operation or navigation commands): accomplished by using either input devices (e.g. keyboard, mouse, buttons) or input applications (e.g. Automatic Speech Recognition),
- output tasks: The user receives the requested content or system prompts in sequential and hierarchical navigation.

The functionality of the above tasks can be changed according to user's preferences.

The Application Manager collects and handles the device requests and the user preferences provided by the Multimodal Interface. The output of the Application Manager is used by the: a) User Modeling module and b) Dialog and Navigation Manager (navigation or application commands).

The Dialog and Navigation Manager feeds the Multimodal Adapter with the document that should be presented in Semantic-ML or Emotion-ML. The corresponding adapter is triggered and produces an output data according to the user preferences and the device requests. The output is handled by the User Interface for the content presentation in visual, acoustic or haptic modality.

Focusing on the acoustic modality the mapping is obtained using a Document-to-Audio (DtA) platform (Xydas & Kouroupetroglou, 2001b). In the acoustic adapter, the Adaptation module (Figure 6) combines information about user preferences (User Modeling) and the rules for the acoustic mapping (CAD script) so the result can be used by the e-TSA Composer. The Cluster Auditory Definition (CAD) scripts provide the mapping rules to DtA platform. The rules, that are used to describe the relation of document's elements and acoustic representation, depend on the methodology that is followed, using the semantic (Xydas et al., 2003, Spiliotopoulos et al., 2005) or the emotional approach utilizing Expressive Speech Synthesis (Campbell et al., 2006; Pitrelli et al., 2006; Schröder, 2006).

The DtA platform offers greater priority to user preferences than the default CAD rules. For example, the user might need to hear faster the content of the book, but some elements should be read slower. The Adaptation Module will give higher priority to the rules provided by User Modelling. Using the DtA platform, documents are mapped into specific acoustic elements which are realised by the auditory synthesizer (the output format can be e.g. MPEG4, SMIL or WAV).

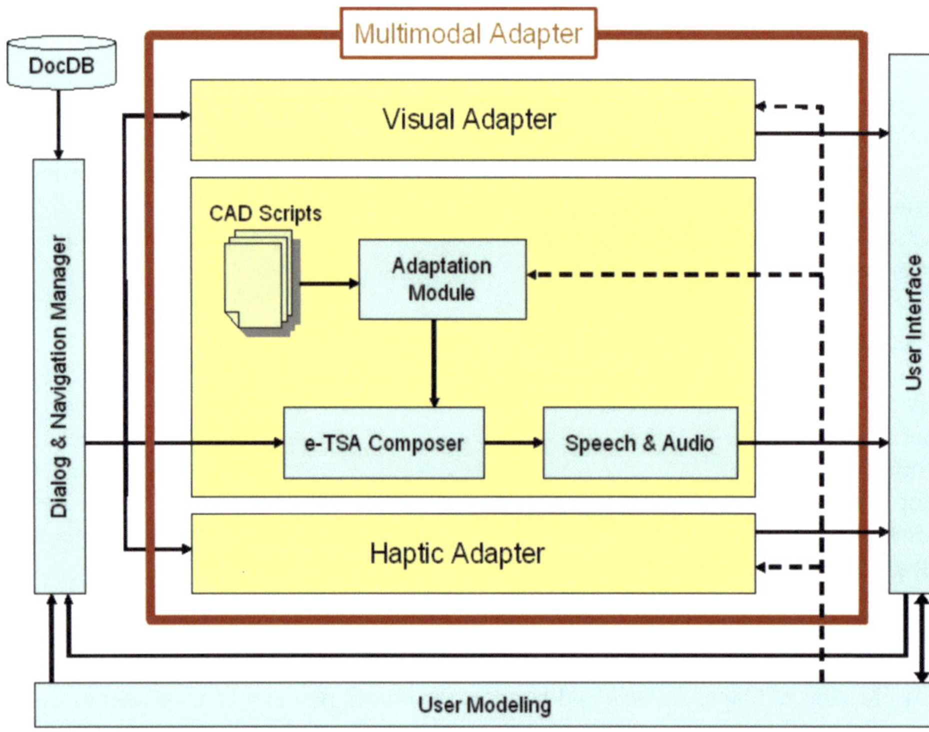

Figure 6. Multimodal Representation

5. Conclusions

To ensure that people with print disability are able equally to participate in society, it is crucial to develop more effective ways for the accessibility of both printed and electronic documents.

In this chapter we have first presented an integrated architecture on how a document is structured. Then, the existing international standards and guidelines for creating accessible documents were briefly analyzed. Based on these, we have proposed a novel holistic XML-based system for the real time production, presentation and navigation of multimodal accessible documents.

6. Acknowledgements

The work described in this chapter has been funded by the European Social Fund and Hellenic National Resources under the HOMER project of the Programme PENED, Greek General Secretariat of Research and Technology.

7. References

ANSI/NISO (2008). National Information Standards Organization, The DAISY standard, *http://www.niso.org/workrooms/daisy/*

Axner, E.; Strom B.; Linde-Forsberg, C.; Dyson, M. C. & Kipping, G. J. (1997). The legibility of screen formats: Are three columns better than one? *Computers & Graphics*, Vol. 21, No. 6, December 1997, pp. 703-712, ISSN: 0097-8493

Bigham, J. P.; Kaminsky, R. S.; Ladner, R. E.; Danielsson, O. M. & Hempton, G. L. (2006). WebInSight: making web images accessible, *Proceedings of the 8th international ACM SIGACCESS Conference on Computers and Accessibility (ASSETS '06)*, pp. 181-188, ISBN: 1-59593-290-9, Portland, Oregon, USA, 23-25 October 2006, ACM, New York

Birren, F. (1984). *Color & Human Response: Aspects of Light and Color. Bearing on the Reactions of Living Things and the Welfare of Human Beings*, J. Wiley & Sons Inc, ISBN: 978-0-471-28864-0, New York

Brewster, S. A.; Räty, V. & Kortekangas, A. (1996). Earcons as a Method of Providing Navigational Cues in a Menu Hierarchy, *Proceedings of HCI on People and Computers XI*, pp. 169-183, ISBN: 3-540-76069-5, M. A. Sasse, J. Cunningham, and R. L. Winder, Eds. Springer-Verlag, London

Bringhurst, R. (1996). *The elements of typographic style*, 2d ed. Hartley and Marks, ISBN: 0881791326, Vancouver

Buckland, M. K. (1997). What is a "document"? *Journal of the American Society for Information Science*, Vol. 48, No. 9, September 1997, pp. 804-809, ISSN: 0002-8231

Campbell, N.; Hamza, W.; Hoge, H.; Tao, J. & Bailly, E. (2006). Special Section on Expressive Speech Synthesis. *IEEE Transactions on Audio, Speech and Language Processing*, Vol. 14, No. 4, July 2006, pp. 1097-1098, ISSN: 1558-7916

Chen, X.; Tremaine, M.; Lutz, R.; Chung, J. & Lacsina, P. (2006). AudioBrowser: a mobile browsable information access for the visually impaired. *Universal Access in the Information Society*, Vol. 5, No. 1, June 2006, pp. 4-22, ISSN: 1615-5297

Cockburn, A.; Gutwin, C. & Alexander, J. (2006). Faster document navigation with space-filling thumbnails, *Proceedings of the SIGCHI Conference on Human Factors in Computing Systems (CHI '06)*, pp. 1-10, ISBN: 1-59593-372-7, Montréal, Québec, Canada, 22-17 April 2006, ACM, New York

Conway, A. (1993). Page grammars and page parsing: a syntactic approach to document layout recognition, *Proceedings of the Second International Conference on Document Analysis and Recognition*, pp. 761-764, ISBN: 0-8186-4960-7, Tsukuba Science City, Japan, 20 – 22 October 1993

Czyzowicz, M. (2005). Intelligent Navigation in Documents Sets Comparative Study, *Proceedings of the International Intelligent Information Processing and Web Mining Conference (IIPWM' 05)*, pp. 421-425, ISBN: 978-3-540-25056-2, Gdansk, Poland, 13-16 June 2005, Springer, New York

DAISY Consortium (2008), *www.daisy.org*

Derrien-Peden, D. (1991). Frame-based system for macro-typographical structure analysis in scientific papers, *Proceedings of International Conference on Document Analysis and Recognition (ICDAR91)*, pp. 311-319, Saint-Malo, France, September 1991

Djennane, S. (2003). 3D-Audio News Presentation Modeling. *Lecture Notes in Computer Science (LNCS)*, Vol. 4556, pp. 280-286, ISBN: 978-3-540-00855-2

Doermann, D. S.; Rivlin, E. & Rosenfeld, A. (1998). The function of documents. *Image Vision Computing*, Vol. 16, No. 11, 1 August 1998, pp. 799-814, ISSN: 0262-8856

Dormann, C. (2003). Affective experiences in the home: measuring emotions, *International Conference on Home Oriented Informatics and Telematics (HOIT2003)*, California, U.S.A., 6-8 April 2003

Edwards, A. D.; McCartney, H. & Fogarolo, F. (2006). Lambda: a multimodal approach to making mathematics accessible to blind students, *Proceedings of the 8th international ACM SIGACCESS Conference on Computers and Accessibility (ASSETS '06)*, pp. 48-54, ISBN:1-59593-290-9, Portland, Oregon, USA, 23-25 October 2006, ACM, New York

Eglin, V. & Bres, S., (2003). Document page similarity based on layout visual saliency: Application to query by example and document classification, *Proceedings of the Seventh International Conference on Document Analysis and Recognition (ICDAR)*, Vol. 2, pp. 1208, ISBN: 0-7695-1960-1, Washington DC, 3–6 August 2003, IEEE Computer Society

Fellbaum, K. & Kouroupetroglou, G. (2008). Principles of Electronic Speech Processing with Applications for People with Disabilities. *Technology and Disability*, Vol. 20, No. 2, pp. 55-85, ISSN: 1055-4181

Fink, J.; Kobsa, A. & Nill, A. (1999). Adaptable and Adaptive Information Provision for All Users, Including Disabled and Elderly People. *New Review of Hypermedia and Multimedia*, Vol. 4, pp. 163-188, ISSN: 1361-4568

Fourli-Kartsouni, F. ; Slavakis, K. ; Kouroupetroglou, G. & Theodoridis S. (2007). A Bayesian Network Approach to Semantic Labelling of Text Formatting in XML Corpora of Documents. *Lecture Notes in Computer Science (LNCS)*, Vol. 4556, pp. 299-308, ISBN: 978-3-540-73282-2

Francioni, J. M. & Smith, A. C. (2002). Computer science accessibility for students with visual disabilities, *Proceedings of the 33rd SIGCSE Technical Symposium on Computer Science Education (SIGCSE '02)*, pp. 91-95, ISBN: 1-58113-473-8, Cincinnati, Kentucky, 27 February – 3 March 2002, ACM, New York

Freitas, D. & Kouroupetroglou, G. (2008). Speech Technologies for Blind and Low Vision Persons. *Technology and Disability*, Vol. 20, No. 2, pp. 135-156, ISSN: 1055-4181

Gorny, P. (2000). Typographic semantics of Webpages Accessible for Visual Impaired Users, Mapping Layout and Interaction Objects to an Auditory Interaction Space, *Proceedings of 7th International Conference on Computer Helping with Special Needs*, pp. 17-21, ISBN: 3-85403-145-9, Karlsruhe, Germany, 17-21 July 2000

Guillon B.; Monteiro J. L.; Checoury C.; Archambault D. & Burger D. (2004). Towards an Integrated Publishing Chain for Accessible Multimodal Documents. *Lecture Notes in Computer Science (LNCS)*, Vol. 3118, pp. 514-521, ISBN: 978-3-540-22334-4

Hall, R. H. & Hanna, P. (2004). The impact of web page text-background colour combinations on readability, retention, aesthetics and behavioural intention. *Behaviour & Information Technology*, Vol. 23, No. 3, May 2004, pp. 183-195, ISSN: 1362-3001

Harper, S. & Yesilada, Y. (2007). Web Authoring for Accessibility (WAfA). *Web Semantics: Science, Services and Agents on the World Wide Web*, Vol. 5, No. 3, pp. 175-179, ISSN:1570-8268

Harrington, S. J.; Naveda, J. F.; Jones, R. P.; Roetling, P.; & Thakkar, N. (2004). Aesthetic measures for automated document layout, *Proceedings of the 2004 ACM Symposium on Document Engineering (DocEng '04)*, pp. 109-111, ISBN: 1-58113-938-1, Milwaukee, Wisconsin, USA, 28-30 October 2004, ACM, New York

Hill, A. & Scharff, L. V. (1997). Readability of screen displays with various foreground/background color combinations, font styles, and font types, *Proceedings of the Eleventh National Conference on Undergraduate Research (NCUR-97)*, Vol. 2, pp. 742-746, Austin, Texas U.S.A., 24-26 April 1997

Hjalmarsson, A., (2005). Adaptive Spoken Dialog Systems. In *GSLT, Speech Technology 1 Closing Seminar*

Holmberg, N. (2004). *Eye movement patterns and newspaper design factors. An experimental approach*, Master Thesis, Lund University Cognitive Science, Lund: LUCS, ISSN: 1101-8453, Sweden

Holmqvist, K. & Wartenberg, C. (2005). *The role of local design factors for newspaper reading behaviour – an eye-tracking respective*, Lund University Cognitive Studies, No. 127, Lund: LUCS, ISSN: 1101-8453, Sweden

Humaine Portal (2008), *http://emotion-research.net/*

IELA (2008). Initiative for Equitable Library Access, *http://www.lac-bac.gc.ca/iela/*

InkML, (2003). Ink Markup Language, Requirements for Ink Markup Language, *http://www.w3.org/TR/inkreqs/*

InkML, (2006). Ink Markup Language, *http://www.w3.org/2002/mmi/ink/*

ISO, (1989). Information processing -- Text and office systems -- Office Document Architecture (ODA) and interchange format, *http://www.iso.org/iso/iso_catalogue/catalogue_ics/catalogue_detail_ics.htm?csnumber=15926/*

ITU, (1993). ITU-T T.412, Open document architecture (ODA) and Interchange format - document structures, *Telecommunication (03/93) Standardization Sector of ITU Information Technology*

Kärkkäinen, L. & Laarni, J., (2002). Designing for small display screens, *Proceedings of the Second Nordic Conference on Human-Computer interaction,* Vol. 31, pp. 227-230, ISBN: 1-58113-616-1, Aarhus, Denmark, 19–23 October 2002, NordiCHI '02, ACM, New York

Kouroupetroglou, C.; Salampasis, M. & Manitsaris, A. (2007). Browsing shortcuts as a means to improve information seeking of blind people in the WWW. *Universal Access in the Information Society*, Vol. 6, No. 3, pp. 273-283, November 2007, ISSN: 1615-5289

Kramer, G., (Ed) (1994). *Auditory Display: Sonification, Audification, and Auditory Interfaces*, Addison-Wesley Longman Publishing Co., Inc., ISBN: 0201626039, Boston, MA, USA

Krishnamoorthy, M.; Nagy, G.; Seth, S. & Viswanathan, M. (1993). Syntactic segmentation and labeling of digitized pages from technical journals. *IEEE Transactions on Pattern Analysis and Machine Intelligence*, Vol. 15, No. 7, July 1993, pp. 737-747, ISSN: 0162-8828

Kupper, N. (1989). Recording of Visual Reading Activity: Research into Newspaper Reading Behaviour, *(Available as pdf from http://calendardesign.de/leseforschung/ /eyetrackstudy.pdf)*

Laarni, J. (2003). Effects of color, font type and font style on user preferences, *Adjunct Proceedings of HCI International 2003*, C. Stephanidis (Ed.), pp. 31-32, Heraklion, Greece, ISBN: 960-524-166-8, Crete University Press

Larson, K. (2007). The Technology of Text. *IEEE Spectrum*, Vol. 44, No. 5, May 2007, pp 26-31, ISSN: 0018-9235

Mao, S; Rosenfeld, A. & Kanungo, T. (2003). Document structure analysis algorithms: a literature survey. *Proceedings of SPIE Electronic Imaging*, Vol. 5010, pp. 197-207, January 2003, ISBN 0-8194-4810-9

Masanori, K.; Takeshi, M.; Eizen, K. & Kazuhito, U. (2007). Proposal of BrailleML as an XML for Japanese Braille: Conversion from ODF to BrailleML. *IEIC Technical Report,* Vol. 106, No. 485, pp. 31-36, ISSN: 0913-5685

MathPlayer (2008). MathPlayer, Design Science, *http://www.dessci.com/en/products/mathplayer/*

McTear, M. F. (2002). Spoken dialogue technology: enabling the conversational user interface. *ACM Computing Surveys (CSUR),* Vol. 34, No. 1, March 2002, pp. 90-169, ISSN: 0360-0300

Mills, C. B. & Weldon, L. J. (1987). Reading Text from computer screens. *ACM Computing Surveys (CSUR)*, Vol. 19, No. 4, December 1987, pp. 329–357, ISSN: 0360-0300

Mikhalenko, P. V. (2008), Multimodal interaction promises device integration, accessibility, and enhanced communication services, *http://articles.techrepublic.com.com/5100-10878_11-5090322.html*

Mynatt, E. D. (1994) Designing with auditory icons: how well do we identify auditory cues? *Conference Companion on Human Factors in Computing Systems,* pp. 269-270, ISBN: 0-89791-651-4, Boston, Massachusetts, USA, 24-28April 1994, C. Plaisant, Ed., CHI '94, ACM Press, New York

ODF (2008a). Open Document Format, *http://www.oasis-open.org/committees/tc_home.php?wg_abbrev=office*

ODF (2008b). Open Document - Accessibility, *http://www.oasis-open.org/committees/ /tc_home.php?wg_abbrev=office-accessibility*

OASIS (2008). Organization for the Advancement of Structured Information Standards, *www.oasis-open.org/home/index.php*

Peels, A. J.; Janssen, N. J. & Nawijn, W. (1985). Document architecture and text formatting. *ACM Transactions on Information Systems (TOIS),* Vol. 3, No. 4, October 1985, pp. 347-369, ISSN: 1046-8188

Porat, T.; Liss, R. & Tractinsky, N. (2007). E-Stores Design: The Influence of E-Store Design and Product Type on Consumers' Emotions and Attitudes. *Lecture Notes in Computer Science (LNCS)*, Vol. 4553, pp. 712-721, ISBN: 978-3-540-73109-2

Power, C. D. (2008). Multi-Modal Exploration, PhD *thesis*, University of Western Ontario

Pitrelli, J. F.; Bakis, R.; Eide, E. M.; Fernandez, R.; Hamza, W. & Picheny, M. A. (2006). The IBM expressive Text-to-Speech synthesis system for American English. *IEEE Transactions on Audio, Speech and Language Processing*, Vol. 14, No. 4, July 2006, pp. 1099-1108, ISSN: 1558-7916

Raman, T. V. (1992). An Audio view of (LA)TEX Documents, *Proceedings of the Annual Meeting TUGboat*, Vol. 13, No. 3, pp. 65–70, ISBN: 0896-3207, Portland, Oregon, October 1992, TEX Users Group, USA

Richard, H. & Patrick, H. (2004). The Impact of Web Page Text-Background Colour Combinations on Readability, Retention, Aesthetics and Behavioural Intention. *Behaviour and Information Technology*, Vol. 23, No. 3, May-June 2004, pp.183-195, ISSN-0144-929X

Rosmaita, B. J. (2006). Accessibility first!: a new approach to web design, *Proceedings of the 37th SIGCSE Technical Symposium on Computer Science Education (SIGCSE '06)*, pp. 270-274, ISBN: 1-59593-259-3, Houston, Texas, USA, 3-5 March 2006, ACM, New York

RPH (2008). Radio for the Print Handicapped, *http://www.rph.org.au/*

Saari, T.; Turpeinen, M.; Laarni, J.; Ravaja N. & Kallinen, K. (2004). Emotionally Loaded Mobile Multimedia Messaging. *Lecture Notes in Computer Science (LNCS),* Vol. 3166, pp. 476-486, ISBN: 978-3-540-22947-6

Saito, S.; Takagi, H., & Asakawa, C. (2006). Transforming flash to XML for accessibility evaluations, *Proceedings of the 8th international ACM SIGACCESS Conference on Computers and Accessibility (ASSETS '06)*, pp. 157-164, ISBN: 1-59593-290-9, Portland, Oregon, USA, 23-25 October 2006, ACM, New York

Sánchez, J. A.; Kirschning, I.; Palacio, J. C. & Ostróvskaya, Y. (2005). Towards mood-oriented interfaces for synchronous interaction, *Proceedings of the 2005 Latin American Conference on Human-Computer interaction*, Vol. 124, pp. 1-7, ISBN:1-59593-224-0, Cuernavaca, Mexico, 23-26 October 2005, CLIHC '05, ACM, New York

Sánchez, J. A.; Hernández, N. P.; Penagos J. C. & Ostróvskaya, Y. (2006). Conveying mood and emotion in instant messaging by using a two-dimensional model for affective states, *Proceedings of the Symposium on Human Factors in Computer Systems IHC 2006*, pp. 66-72, ISBN: 1-59593-432-4, Brazil, 2006, ACM, New York

Schamber, L., (1996). What is document? Rethinking the concept in uneasy times. *Journal of the American Society for Information Science*, Special issue: Electronic Publishing, Vol. 47, No. 9, pp. 669–671, ISSN: 0002-8231

Schröder, M. (2006). Expressing degree of activation in synthetic speech. *IEEE Transactions on Audio, Speech and Language Processing*, Vol. 14, No. 4, July 2006, pp. 1128-1136, ISSN: 1558-7916

Soiffer, N., (2005), MathPlayer: Web-based Math Accessibility, *Proceedings of the 7th international ACM SIGACCESS Conference on Computers and Accessibility (ASSETS '05)*, pp. 204-205, ISBN: 1-59593-159-7, Baltimore, MD, USA, 9-12 October 2005, ACM, New York

Spiliotopoulos, D.; Xydas, G.; Kouroupetroglou, G. & Argyropoulos, V. (2005a). Experimentation on Spoken Format of Tables in Auditory User Interfaces, *Proceedings of the 11th International Conference on Human-Computer Interaction (HCII2005)*, pp. 361-370, ISBN: 0-8058-5807-5, Las Vegas, Nevada, USA, 22-27 July 2005, Lawrence Erlbaum Associates, Inc

Spiliotopoulos, D.; Xydas, G. & Kouroupetroglou, G. (2005b). Diction Based Prosody Modeling in Table-to-Speech Synthesis. *Lecture Notes in Artificial Inteligence (LNAI)* Vol. 3658, September 2005, pp. 294–301, ISBN: 978-3-540-28789-6

Stephanidis, C. (2001). *User Interfaces for All. Concepts, Methods, and Tools.* Lawrence Erlbaum Associates, Inc., Publishers, ISBN: 0-8058-2967-9, USA

SVG (2000), Scalar Vector Graphics, Accessibility Features of SVG, *http://www.w3.org/TR/SVG-access/*

SVG (2008), Scalar Vector Graphics, XML Graphics for the Web, *http://www.w3.org/Graphics/SVG/*

Tsonos, D.; Xydas, G. & Kouroupetroglou G. (2007a). Auditory Accessibility of Metadata in Books: A Design for All Approach. *Lecture Notes in Computer Science (LNCS)*, Vol. 4556, pp. 436 - 445, ISBN: 978-3-540-73282-2

Tsonos, D.; Xydas, G. & Kouroupetroglou, G. (2007b). A Methodology for Reader's Emotional State Extraction to Augment Expressions in Speech Synthesis, *Proceedings of 19th IEEE International Conference on Tools with Artificial Intelligence (ICTAI 2007)*, Vol. 2, pp. 218-225, ISBN: 0-7695-3015-X, Patras, Greece, 29-31 October 2007

Tsonos, D. & Kouroupetroglou, G. (2008). Accessibility of Board and Presentations in the Classroom: a Design-for-All Approach, *IASTED International Conference on Assistive Technologies (AT 2008)*, pp. 13-18, ISBN: 978-0-88986-739-0, Baltimore, Maryland, USA, 16-18 April 2008

Tsonos, D.; Ikospentaki, K. & Kouroupetrglou, G. (2008). Towards Modeling of Readers' Emotional State Response for the Automated Annotation of Documents, *IEEE World Congress on Computational Intelligence (WCCI 2008)*, pp. 3252 - 3259, ISSN: 978-1-4244-1821-3, Hong Kong, 1–6 June 2008

Tsujimoto, S. & Asada, H. (1990). Understanding multi-articled document, *Proceedings of 10th International Conference on Pattern Recognition*, Vol. 1, pp. 551-556, ISBN: 0-8186- 2062-5, Atlantic City, NJ, USA, 16-21 June 1990

Turunen, M.; Hakulinen, J.; Räihä, K.; Salonen, E.; Kainulainen, A. & Prusi, P. (2005). An architecture and applications for speech-based accessibility systems. *IBM Systems Journal*, Vol. 44, No. 3, August 2005, pp. 485-504, ISSN: 0018-8670

W3C (2008a). XML Document Navigation Language, *http://www.w3.org/TR/xdnl/*

W3C (2008b). Multimodal Interaction Activity, *http://www.w3.org/2002/mmi/*

W3C (2008c). World Wide Web Consortium, *www.w3.org*

W3C (2008d). Web Content Accessibility Guidelines 1.0 (WCAG 1.0), *http://www.w3.org/TR/WCAG10/*

W3C (2008e). Web Accessibility Initiative (WAI), *http://www.w3.org/WAI/*

W3C (2008f). W3C Math Home, *http://www.w3.org/Math/*

W3C (2008g). Mathematical Markup Language (MathML) Version 2.0 (Second Edition), Introduction, *http://www.w3.org/TR/2003/REC-MathML2-20031021/chapter1.html*

Wartenberg, C. & Holmqvist, K. (2005). *Daily Newspaper Layout - Designers' Predictions of Readers' Visual Behaviour - A Case Study*, Lund University Cognitive Studies, No. 126, Lund: LUCS, ISSN: 1101-8453, Sweden

Xydas, G. & Kouroupetroglou, G. (2001a). Text-to-Speech Scripting Interface for Appropriate Vocalisation of e-Texts. *Proceedings of EUROSPEECH 2001*, pp. 2247–2250, ISBN: 87-90834-09-7, Aalborg, Denmark, 3-7 September 2001, International Speech Communication Association

Xydas, G. & Kouroupetroglou, G. (2001b). Augmented Auditory Representation of e-Texts for Text-to-Speech Systems. *Lecture Notes in Artificial Intelligence (LNAI)*, Vol. 2166, pp. 134-141, ISBN: 978-3-540-42557-1

Xydas, G.; Spiliotopoulos, D. & Kouroupetroglou, G. (2003). Modelling Emphatic Events from Non-Speech Aware Documents in Speech Based User Interfaces, *Proceedings of HCI International 2003 - The 10th International Conference on Human-Computer Interaction*, pp. 806–810, ISBN: 0805849319, Crete, Greece, 22-27 June 2003, C. Stephanidis and J. Jacko, eds,. Lawrence Erlbaum Associates, Inc., Mahwah, NJ

Xydas, G.; Argyropoulos, V.; Karakosta, T. & Kouroupetroglou, G. (2005). An Experimental Approach in Recognizing Synthesized Auditory Components in a Non-Visual Interaction with Documents, *Proceedings of the 11th Int. Conference on Human-Computer Interaction*, Vol. 3, pp. 411-420, ISBN: 0-8058-5807-5, Las Vegas, Nevada, USA, 22-27 July 2005, Lawrence Erlbaum Associates, Inc

Yamashita, A.; Amano, T.; Takahashi, I. & Toyokawa, K. (1991). A model based layout understanding method for the document recognition system, *Proceedings of International Conference on Document Analysis and Recognition*, pp. 130-138, Saint Malo, France, September 1991

28

The Method of Interactive Reduction of Threat of Isolation in the Contemporary Human Environment

Teresa Musioł and Katarzyna Ujma-Wąsowicz
Silesian University of Technology
Poland

1. What is the place of a man in an organization?

In the work process human activity contains rational and irrational elements. Irrational ones are purposes of the activity, whereas ways of achieving them are rational. Irrationality of these purposes lies in constant escalation of improvement a degree of consumerism, i.e. material needs. On the other hand non-material needs are given a role of a derivative, according to modern theories of management in market economy: i.e. first a profit and later the rest. An organization as a group of human individualities cannot constitute a monolith of rational actions. Irrational purposes of an organization are first of all time factors, it means the future determined by consciousness of members of an organization.

The success of an organization is conditioned not only by technical and economic or marketing factors but also by the factors which create favourable conditions for a sense of personal safety of a member of the organization, such as: health, an accident-free job and satisfaction from the activity. In order to make it possible, there must be the atmosphere favourable to basic activities promoting safety. It means that the climate of organizational culture must be a characteristics of a particular organization. Risk and safety are the values which are considered in a particular way in every organization. The attitude of the members of the organization to these values depends on such factors as:

- Kinds and the area of threats and possibility to reduce them;
- The degree of compliance of the conducted business activity with legal requirements, determining the possibility of functioning of the organization in a particular social and legal system;
- The number and seriousness of accidents at work and related material losses of the organization.

The above factors determine the level of culture of safety within the organization, without which functioning in the social environment is not possible (Musioł, 2002).

Every organization as a system, that is a group of elements and relations between them, is subjected to actions of powers of endo- and egzogenic characteristics. In order to realize its purposes, an organization needs to aim at balance between these powers, it means at a state of safety of an organization. The state of organization's safety is understood here as its ability to protect internal values from external threats, however it may be also the vice versa. It is related to a kind of these threats and their attribution in two aspects: objective and

subjective. Risks existing in an organization are every event or a process undesirable from a point of view of undisturbed system operation. We can't talk about an isolated human or a situation. There is only a relation between a human and the environment - the relation which can be well defined by a word THREAT (Musioł & Ujma-Wąsowicz, 2007).
With such defining of the term 'threat', any form of disruption of the state of safety within the organization is subjected to assessment and evaluation of measurable and immeasurable threats. They step into the area of "soft organizational culture", which fundamental characteristics is style of management and coordination of activities in the work process, it means orienting the work process towards argumentation, not power. Careful observation of all events inside and outside the organization enables to identify a kind of a threat and to evaluate it correctly. It is very important because the threat may contribute to the organization's success as well as its failure (Musioł, 2007).
The work process, as every process, is subjected to static - dynamic quantification (Musioł & Ligarski, 2004), where there is specific feedback between technical and economic conditions and a man operating and controlling this process. The information flow, particularly its quality and kind, message codes, the size of a stream and the level of the information flow is an indispensible condition to achieve the balance between a sender and a receiver in the process of communication. The level of balance is determined by the function of the state of communication in its area, i.e. entropy (Fig. 1). It depends mainly on self-consciousness of people who communicate with each other and being together in the communication process. The lack of balance between basic kinds of verbal and non-verbal communication leads to disruptions in exogenous as well as endogenous environment of human life. Therefore, a man in his ontological dimension must all his life broaden the knowledge about ontology of work and ontology of culture and consequently, develop consciousness of such civilization threats as: exploitation, unemployment, famine, devastation of natural environment, violence, terrorism, racism, lack of tolerance, and first of all isolation.

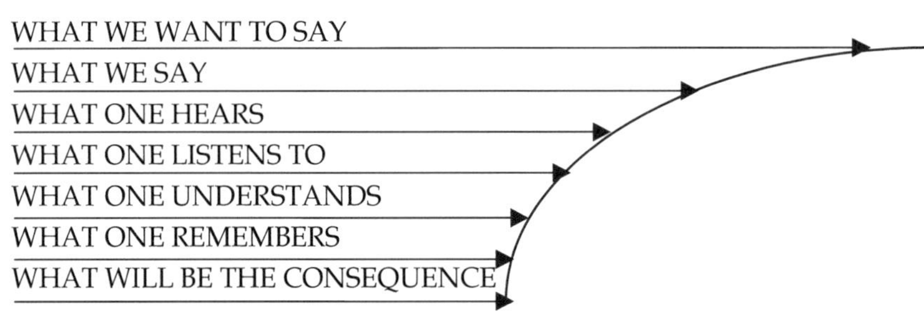

Figure 1. Graphic representation of communication entropy

2. What is consciousness?

The problem of consciousness can be approached from different points of view.
The neurobiologist A. R. Damasio in his book "The Feeling of What Happens: Body and Emotion in the Making of Consciousness" writes: "... the theory of consciousness should not be only the theory describing how the brain turns attention to the image of a particular object. In my opinion, the natural attention on low level precedes consciousness in development, whereas the controlled attention appears after consciousness comes into being. Attention is equally indispensable for consciousness as images. However, it is not sufficient to create consciousness and it is not identical with consciousness. Eventually, the

theory of consciousness should not be only the theory describing how the brain creates integrated and unified mental scenes, although creating these scenes is an important aspect of consciousness - especially its highest levels. Consciousness does not happen publicly but inside the organism. Nonetheless, it is connected with a number of external symptoms. Those manifestations do not describe an internal process in the same direct way as a sentence expresses a thought but there are some observable signs of presence of consciousness. Relying on what we know about "personal" human brains and what we can observe in human behaviour, we can create three-cornered relationship between:

1. Some external indications, e.g. vigil, emotion, attention or specific behaviour;
2. Corresponding internal manifestations described by the same human being in whom we find the above external indications;
3. Internal manifestations, which we as observers can verify in ourselves, when we are in the circumstances similar to these in which the observed person is found.

This three-cornered relationship entitles us to make considerably motivated conclusions about personal states of a human, on the basis of his external behaviours. Therefore, consciousness is the key to the knowledge about life for good and bad, our first pass to understand famine, desire, sex, tears, laugh, kicks, punches, streams of images called thoughts, feelings, words, history, opinions, music and poetry, happiness and delight. The basic, elementary role of consciousness is making it possible to discern irresistible need for staying alive and development of caring for oneself. However, the most complex and sophisticated task is making it possible to develop care for other people and perfecting the way of life" (Damasio, 1999).

Another approach to the problem of consciousness is represented by the Danish existentialist S. Kiergegaard.

In his book "The Sickness Unto Death" he writes that consciousness does not exist as a separate function, having a structure and a location in a brain. It is not anything either internal or external. It is given, so it meets the requirements of a phenomenon. Consciousness is self-knowledge, which decides about an attitude of a human to himself. The more consciousness, the more personality and will. A man who does not have will, doesn't have personality and self-knowledge. Lack of consciousness is always a reason of evil. And in human activity it creates a base for destructive processes in every organized sphere of life, especially in an organization. The human activity in work process without the ergonomic consciousness will be always the reason of destructive activities and it proves the lack of safety consciousness of all work process participant. (Kiergegaard, 1995). Why? His psychological and emotional process determined the satisfaction while capturing needs of self-knowledge through understanding needs of surrounding external world by empathy (Stein, 1988).

And here the following questions appear. How to find relationships between neurobiological, philosophical and behavioural conception of consciousness and self-consciousness and can these relationships be evaluated in a clear way? This is a difficult problem because a human as an individual is a phenomenon, in whom internal conceptual area is not always compatible with external perceptual area, conditioned by a particular situation (Fig. 2) (Musioł, 2003).

The imperative of recognition for behaviours consciousness are exogenous and endogenous factors that change human work and therefore the state changes for safety of the environment. Continuing the question it may be worth to ask how large is the evil, which is the result of consciousness missing in every society that the safety is an element of the cultures in their psychological dimension. It is also everyday and basic obligation of the ethical duty not only in relation to oneself but also to other people. So it is necessary to change in the thinking process basing on the "Newton's paradigm", which is going into the thinking basing on the "paradigm of the imagination".

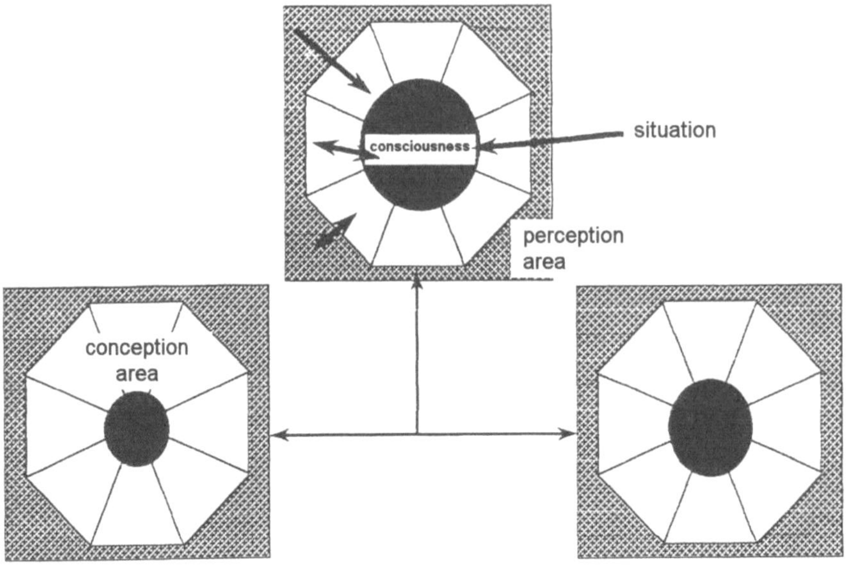

Figure 2. The relations between the consciousness and the behaviour

And there is a question: why? The answer this question is: because a human as a unique individual is a phenomenon, in which the psychophysical and emotional processes determine the satisfaction of the need of capturing a self-knowledge about itself and surrounding external world by category as like empathy, in other words of understanding situation of another human. (Stein, 1998)

Because the area of the culture represents the collection of skilled phenomena it means that the culture is not transmitted throughout the genes activity but throughout the learning process. The learning may be the result of the imitation (benchmarking) or the active training. As it was mentioned above the essence of learning process of the ergonomics cognitive is the growth of ergonomic consciousness. It means capturing the theoretical and practical information about manners of the behaviour in many kinds of situations related to many different phenomena. A result of a lack of these of information is a conflict focus between the conceptional and perceptual assessment of the given situation and it is the primitive threats. These threats have an exogenous character and they are the reason of destructive behaviours.

In the age of globalization and computerization, communication between people without meetings and verbal conversations is becoming a standard. Young people prefer to shut themselves away in the world of the Internet and computer games rather than to go for example for a walk and play with friends in the open space (often considering such activities as a waste of time). Case studies of reasons of suicides, increase in aggression or becoming depressed among young people indicate necessity of monitoring threats caused by these facts. Regarding this, the following thesis was proposed in the elaboration: "Isolation caused by coexistence with information technology devices of different kinds is a threat for psychological environment of not only an individual human, but also any social and professional groups".

The purpose of research, which result is this report, was an answer for a question if there is a problem of isolation caused by work with a computer and if a person subjected to 'the research' is aware of it. Furthermore, if such isolation exists, is its reduction in Polish society possible by active recreation and practicing sport in groups?
In the industrial period an assembly line was a place of creation economic value of an organization. Today interpersonal communication with transmission of information about different values but first of all about global trade offer attracting consumer's attention is becoming such a place (Musioł, 2007).

3. Case Study – how to make an evaluation of the state of consciousness? (Musioł, 2005)

The essence of the process of learning the ergonomics cognitive is the growth of the ergonomics consciousness degree related to the environment of human life and work. For this purpose the knowledge about all threats around us and methods of their identification helps us first of all. It is influenced by the ergonomic cognitive, which stands (treats)a human as a subject in his environment and it is natural cognitive act performed in the relation to the environment.
Correct identification of threats in environment of our life, according to their attribution, is a necessary condition of preventive actions as well as actions correcting results of these threats for an individual as well as the rest of society. Monitoring of the state of consciousness concerning the reasons but also results of threats seems purposeful in aspect of ergonomic knowledge.
During a period from June 2004 to January 2005 after an ergonomics lecture research of individual assessment of a state of consciousness within a group of 265 persons was carried out. Research was carried out during classes of part-time studies and post-graduate studies.
All questionnaires in number of 265 items were verified by the author. The results of the verification were :

- 61 questionnaires were filled in incorrectly;
- 26 persons filling in questionnaires were unemployed;
- 81 employed persons had secondary education (s.ed.);
- 97 employed persons had higher education (h.ed.);
- the range of age of participants was: from 21 to 60 years;

For meritoric analysis of answers there were chosen at random:

- 45 questionnaires of employed participants with secondary education (s.ed.)
- 45 questionnaires of employed participants with higher education (h.ed.).

Both groups are in the age range from 25 to 40 years, so in a period of intensive gaining of work experience.
Research was conducted by means of a questionnaire of individual assessment of ergonomic consciousness. The essence of the questionnaire was a following description of a case:
"A housewife is having an accident after having used an electric bread slicer. The result is cutting a fingertip of an index finger of a right hand. Give reasons of this accident in aspect of ergonomic requirements. Choose an answer separately for every reason, giving one mark in a scale 1-3 (1-the lowest mark, 3-the highest mark)."
The questionnaire was constructed in matrix system in the following way: vertically there were 7 reasons of an accident, horizontally there were 3 states of consciousness concerning these reasons.

Horizontally – 3 states of consciousness concerning reasons of an accident

- I am sure;
- it seems to me;
- I must have more information.

Vertically – 7 reasons of an accident

- incorrect work area;
- lack of protective equipment;
- technical reasons;
- lack of knowledge about threats;
- excessive static-dynamic load;
- incorrect material environment;
- psychophysical state.

Meritoric analysis of answers was conducted by means of indexes of attribution of ergonomic consciousness as arithmetical average and weighted average of a given attribute. Attribute of a reason of an accident $\overline{c}_{a_r}$ and attribute of a state of an ergonomic consciousness $\overline{c}_{a_c}$ were calculated by means of arithmetical average sum of marks from 45 measures chosen at random.

The attributes of a state of consciousness during a choice of reasons of an accident were calculated by means of weighted average $\overline{c}_{w_{r1-7}}$ i $\overline{c}_{w_{c1-3}}$ (1)(2).

$$\overline{c}_{wr_j} = \frac{1}{i}\sum_{i=1}^{3} \overline{c}_{w_{c_i}} \tag{1}$$

where:

$\overline{c}_{w_{r_j}}$ - weighted average for one reason of an accident, from 1 to 7

$\overline{c}_{w_{c_i}}$ - arithmetical averages of three states of consciousness concerning one reason of an accident

i = 3 - maximum number of points for assessment of one reason

$$\overline{c}_{wc_i} = \frac{1}{j}\sum_{j=1}^{7} \overline{c}_{a_{r_j}} \tag{2}$$

where:

$\overline{c}_{w_{c_i}}$ - weighted average for one state of consciousness from 1 to 3

$\overline{c}_{a_{r_j}}$ - arithmetical averages for seven reasons of an accident

j = 7 - maximum number of points for assessment of one state of consciousness

Table 1 refers to answers of participants with secondary education and Table 2 refers to answers of participants with higher education.

Reason of accident $\overline{c}_{a_{r_{1-7}}}$		I am sure $\overline{c}_{a_{c_1}}$	It seems to me $\overline{c}_{a_{c_2}}$	I must have more information $\overline{c}_{a_{c_3}}$	$\overline{c}_{w_{r_{1-7}}}$
$\overline{c}_{a_{r_1}}$	Incorrect work area	1,24	0,64	0,40	0,76
$\overline{c}_{a_{r_2}}$	Lack of protective equipment	1,44	0,40	0,33	0,72
$\overline{c}_{a_{r_3}}$	Technical reasons	0,60	0,78	0,47	0,61
$\overline{c}_{a_{r_4}}$	Lack of knowledge about threats	1,71	0,67	0,07	0,81
$\overline{c}_{a_{r_5}}$	Excessive static-dynamic load	0,62	0,73	0,35	0,57
$\overline{c}_{a_{r_6}}$	Incorrect material environment	0,55	0,73	0,62	0,63
$\overline{c}_{a_{r_7}}$	Psychophysical state	1,84	1,09	0,44	1,12
$\overline{c}_{w_{c_{1-3}}}$		0,38	0,24	0,13	

Table 1. Value of indexes of attribution of ergonomic consciousness - persons with secondary education (s.ed.)

Reason of accident $\overline{c}_{a_{r_{1-7}}}$		I am sure $\overline{c}_{a_{c_1}}$	It seems to me $\overline{c}_{a_{c_2}}$	I must have more information $\overline{c}_{a_{c_3}}$	$\overline{c}_{w_{r_{1-7}}}$
$\overline{c}_{a_{r_1}}$	Incorrect work area	0,51	0,51	1,00	0,67
$\overline{c}_{a_{r_2}}$	Lack of protective equipment	1,20	0,42	0,31	0,64
$\overline{c}_{a_{r_3}}$	Technical reasons	0,66	0,60	0,78	0,68
$\overline{c}_{a_{r_4}}$	Lack of knowledge about threats	1,70	0,60	0,13	0,81
$\overline{c}_{a_{r_5}}$	Excessive static-dynamic load	0,48	0,44	0,67	0,53
$\overline{c}_{a_{r_6}}$	Incorrect material environment	0,40	0,26	0,95	0,54
$\overline{c}_{a_{r_7}}$	Psychophysical state	1,29	0,64	0,47	0,80
$\overline{c}_{w_{c_{1-3}}}$		0,30	0,16	0,20	

Table 2. Value of indexes of attribution of ergonomic consciousness– persons with higher education (h.ed.)

Graphs 3 and 4 show graphic representation of research results.

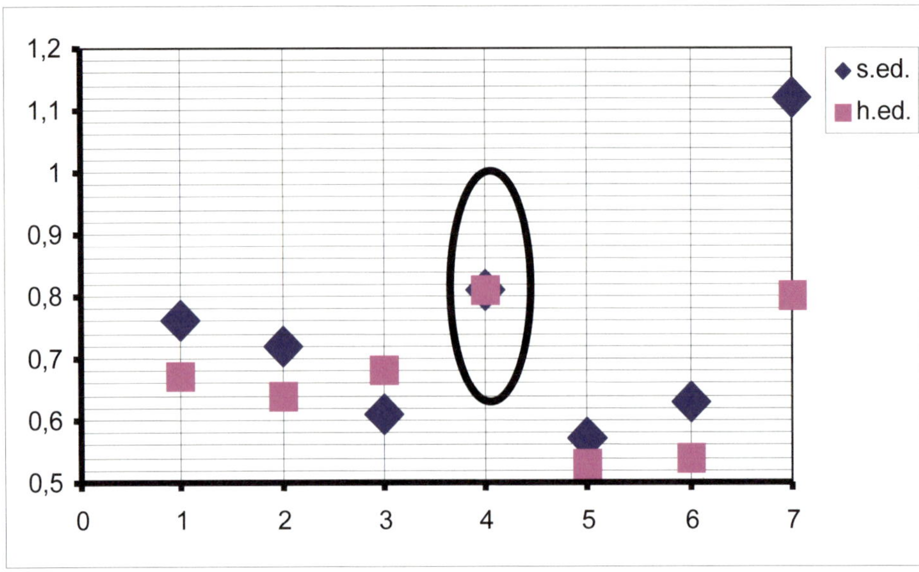

Figure 3. Graphic representation of indexes of attribution of ergonomic consciousness in configuration reason –states

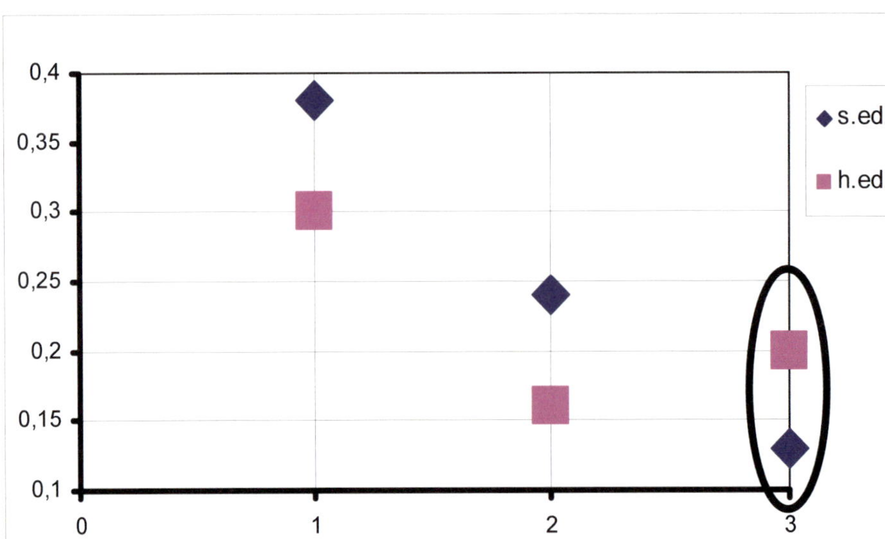

Figure 4. Graphic representation of indexes of attribution of ergonomic consciousness in configuration state – reasons

While analyzing the results the conclusions are following:

- Analysis of research results shows that the lack of knowledge about threats regardless of a level of education is a basic reason of an accident. Index 0,81 for persons with higher education as well as for these with secondary education confirms this conclusion.

- Interpreting a kind of states of ergonomic consciousness depending on a reason of an accident (graph 2) one must notice that persons with higher education must have more information about a threat to make a decision than persons with secondary education (index 0,20 and 0,13)
- Persons with secondary education as well as persons with higher education indicate a psychophysical state as a main reason of an accident - index 1,84 and 1,29. In case of participants with higher education this index is consirably high (lack of immunity to stress).

4. Can the lack of face-to-face communication be a threat?

As it was mentioned before (point 1.), entropy of the state of communication is communication space depends first of all on its kind, message codes, intensity of information flow between a sender and a receiver, as it was presented in Fig. 5

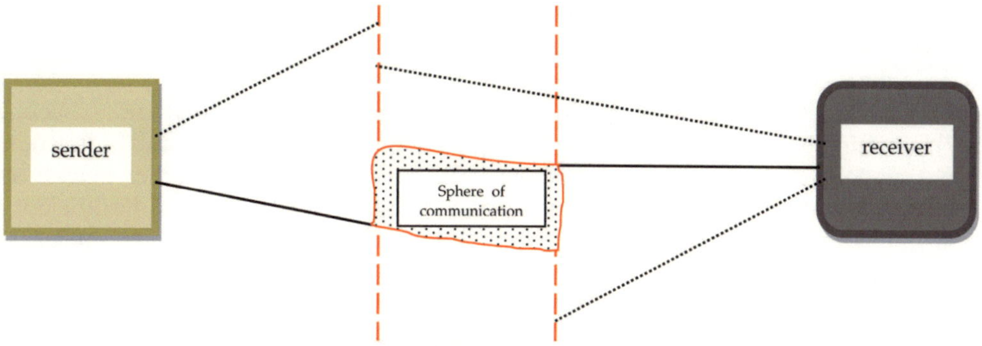

Figure 5. Ideogram of communication process

It is important if the communication is verbal or non-verbal. Functioning of the rational brain is manifested by words, whereas emotions are manifested by non-verbal behaviours. Actually, when words of a person do not correspond with pitch of the voice or other non-verbal signals, not what is said but how it is said indicates his or her real emotions. In the research on communication it was found that 90% or more of conveyed emotions are sent by non-verbal canals. Messages such as anxiety heard in someone's voice, irritation indicated by fast gestures are almost always received unconsciously, without putting particular attention to a character of a message, with a silent assumption that real content enables good or bad reception of such messages. It proves that directing emotions towards a useful purpose is a masterly skill. Regardless of the fact, if it is represented by constant controlling of impulses or temporary putting off fulfilments for later, mood should be controlled in such a way, so that it simplified our life, and didn't make it more difficult. (Goleman, 1997).

Apart from energy, we also need empathy to communicate. The term 'empathy' was used for the first time in the 20s by the American psychologist E. B. Tichener (Goleman, 1997). This meaning differs slightly from the Greek word *emathea* "emphasizing" adopted earlier, previously used by theorists of aesthetics to describe the ability to perceive subjective sensations of another individual. According to Ticherer's theory, empathy derives from a certain kind of physical imitating of worry or depression of another person, which would semantically differ from the term "sympathy" meaning what we feel towards another person, not experiencing to any extent the same feeling which she or he does. Empathy grows from self-consciousness - the more we are open on our own emotions, the more and better we perceive emotions of other people. Edith Stein in her doctoral thesis "About Empathy Problem" proved that empathy is a phenomenological category because a human is an individuality and a phenomenon in his physiological-psychological and emotional dimension (Stein, 1988). Some empathy researchers, e.g. Martin Hoffman (Goleman, 1997) formulate a hypothesis that apart from direct relation between empathy and altruism in personal relationships, empathy, it means putting oneself on the place of another person, induces us to obey some moral rules and observing the natural development of empathy from the early childhood to adolescence. Empathy underlies different aspects of evaluation and moral activities. One of such aspects is empathic anger, which John S. Mill (Goleman, 1997) describes as a natural feeling of retaliation triggered off by intellect and sympathy related to injustice, which hurts us because it hurts others. Mill described this feeling as "guard of justice". Another case in which empathy leads to undertaking moral action is a situation when an outside observer protects a victim. The research proves that the more empathy the observer feels towards the victim, the higher is the probability of his intervention. The is also evidence proving that the level of empathy can tinge our moral evaluations (Goleman, 1997).Summing up, some people while feeling empathy must make particular (dependent on a situation) effort meaning identifying with emotional effort of other people and experiencing their emotions. Their emotional intelligence happens to be insufficient in some situations. Thus, the escape into the state of isolation with one-sided communication, related to anonymity.

5. What is the isolation and can it be a threat?

Isolation is a basic risk in the area of communication in process of every kind of work. Isolation, as it is defined by Norbert Sillamy is a protective mechanism which aims at weakening perception by breaking it away from a context and its emotional basis'. It means that we deal here with emotional effort with a different degree of intensity, which depending on results of human actions, will have a sign 'plus' or 'minus'. According to Ruben Gallego a bad system of organization, no matter what it concerns, dooms a human to isolation of any kind The author states that isolation is misfortune and he even claims that every kind of isolation is a curse. It's difficult to disagree with this because a man is a social being and contrary to appearances emotional effort in communication with another person is essential, such as dynamic effort is indispensable for keeping correct figure. Isolation should not be confused with loneliness, particularly chosen one, because isolation is also a result of rational actions undertaken by natural, social and family environment on an isolated person (Musioł & Ujma-Wąsowicz, 2007).
The World Health Organization (WHO) examined young people in 41 countries in Europe and Northern America. In Poland five and half thousand teenagers, aged 11, 13 and 15, were subjected to examination. The children were asked how they feel, what they eat, if they have friends, how their relationships in the family look like, if they like school, drink alcohol, smoke cigarettes and take drugs. Generally, the received answers indicate that Polish teenagers do not differ considerably from their peers from other countries, taking into

account the threat of pathologies. However, there are some symptoms which may worry. It turns out that a Polish teenager uses stimulants more frequently than young people from other countries. What also worries is the fact that Polish teenagers have less friends and instead of meeting them they prefer playing computer games. The reasons for this phenomenon are sought in mentality and the style of bringing up in a Polish family - being mistrustful of the outer world, i.e. isolating oneself and on the other hand lack of a sufficient number of educational programmes improving self-esteem, developing communication skills and work in a group (Karwowska, 2008).

Another worth mentioning reason for isolation is professional burnout. More and more people suffer from psychosomatic diseases. There is an increasing number of strokes, heart attacks because of overwork, exhaustion, stress and too many duties at work. The syndrome of burnout may strike down everyone but first of all it applies to people who are very ambitious and extremely involved in their work. They are usually people with low self-esteem whose opinion about themselves is dependent on opinion of others. Also perfectionists who feel responsible for everything and want to do everything the best are prone to burnout. There are few employees who have courage to assure their employers that this problem does not apply to them - mainly because they are afraid to lose their job.

Ian Harvey, an independent English journalist is a great supporter of digital technology. He talks about his passion of discovering intelligent gadgets. He is fascinated that every day some novelty enters his everyday life. He is fully conscious that the borderline between his job, fun and family life is fading away. However, he claims that his digital likings are as important as a proverbial cup of morning tea.

Cyberspace - the topic which arouses emotions and controversies. We all live in the real world, which is a symbol of the truth and tangibility. Cyberspace can move us to the virtual world, which is a personification of subjectivism.

In the recent years in the world dominated by Virtual Reality (VR) or similar technologies, the attempts of connecting the virtual reality Immersed Virtual Environment (IVE) and the real world - Augmented Reality (AR) are becoming more and more popular. These technologies are present in the areas of:

- interactive games: Motion capture system - "Half-Life2", Mixed Reality MR - „AquaGauntlet";
- film: Motion capture system - "Shrek", MR-Space Odyssey - "Matrix", Seeing Through, Inside Out - "Power Rangers";
- advertising;
- trade: Clear and Present Car;
- tourism: Archeoguide, Vilars Augmented Reality, Seeing Through, Inside Out;
- military forces: GRIDS, BARS, Landwarrior, SignPost - Mobile AR Navigation System (Ujma - Wąsowicz & Gil, 2005).

Cyberspace can be treated as a response to existence of so called mental reception of space. The mental model of space ruled by three types of processes: Enactive Mentality (enables navigation in space), Iconic Mentality (the ability of identification and comparison of mental images and objects in the real world) and Symbolic Mentality (the ability of abstract thinking) allows to create relationships with external environment, remember and find information. Supporters of cyberspace recognise as a drawback a fact that mental reception of space is available only for a single user and the received information is not only a subject to interpretation but also when it is not used and not updated, it is deleted. In the contemporary world of cyberspace available via the Internet, chat-rooms, online public spaces these drawbacks do not exist. They are vibrant with human activity and thanks to imagination supported by technology they have become the space of social interaction, taking different forms. An example of such environment is the domain MUD (Multi Users Domain) called Active World. This world has got hundreds of thousands of users called *avatars* and a similar number of virtual objects. It functions in a form of real communities with their authorities, ordinary citizens, public and private spaces and even politics. In this world a user can exchange views and is offered different ways of spending free time. Everyone can become a citizen of the domain, the only restriction is access to the Internet.

Another form of using cyberspace are so called colaboratories, which are used as a tool for exchanging experiences by professionals specialising in different fields and which are becoming better and better functioning work centres. Interaction of their users is realised mostly via the Internet. Different forms of cooperation are possible: from asynchronous of e-mail type to synchronous of MUD type. One of factors determining the quality and comfort of cooperation is the user interface, evolving from a graphic to multimodal form. The future cooperation can be imagined as meetings of avatars in a selected cybernetic space (Zalewski, 2007).

Threat created as a result of computerization of every sphere of life – also free time, is first of all isolation of personal space. A man is assigned to NIPs, PINs, kodes, so he is identified by numbers. With help of his fingers he communicates with another person in the cybersphere, more and more controlled by other suitable and unsuitable people.

A man, who selectively receives information (limit of amount of information received per second), is not able to receive and process all information he would like to. Selecting requires decisions, i.e. a psychological act, and performing it requires a meaningful emotional effort. An examined man wants to be on his own and he thinks that he can't deal with this effort, and by some thought abbreviations he reduces not so much emotional, but rather intellectual effort. This is a simple way for limiting dialogue with another man, justifying pseudo individuality and negating group work. According to this, a man transmits more and receives less information. He starts to create his internal world, which characteristics obstructs reception of reality. It's simply better to dream than accept 'real' facts (are there any others?). It is a danger leading to all kinds of psychic disorders, because it influences lack of self-acceptance and in consequence to self-destruction in every form. All the more so because very often life in virtual reality deflates self-criticism and there follows subjective favourisation.

It is worth emphasizing that the problem does not lie in development of digital technology, it is quite the opposite. The possibilities to use it in order to obtain information, keep in touch with family and friends, navigate in the area or document memories are all benefits of the 21st century. The problem is that for many people the digital world replaces a friend, deprives them of their free time, limits independent thinking or even deteriorates their functioning in the society. In such circumstances it is easy to imagine a situation in which people on a large scale close in their virtual worlds and isolated from reality lead digital life.

6. The method of measurement and evaluation of the threat of isolation caused by computer among Polish students and school teenagers.

The measurement of a level of isolation was carried out with sociometric measure type 'Rating Scale Questionnaire' (Charlton, 2002), constructed according to the following rules.

The measure contained:

- 10 open questions, a respondent was to answer them by choosing only one option,
- 5 possible answers for
    - each of 10 questions,
    - which were assessed in the
    - scale from –2 to +2

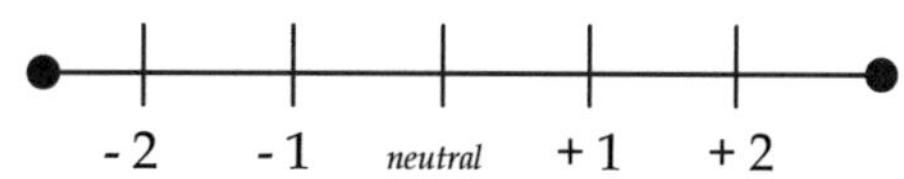

- the sixth answer – other comments – which was assigned to a proper scale;
- information gaps, such as age, course mode, date of measurement.

The interpretation of results of measurement of isolation was carried out by assessing every chosen answer for 10 questions in the scale from –2 to +2.

The questions included such areas as:

- Ways of spending free time the most frequently and the most willingly;
- Amount and quality of free time spent in front of a computer monitor;
- Consciousness of risks related to work with a computer or with other;
- Active recreation and participation in team games as a method of reducing risks related to life in cyberspace.;

The presentation of results of isolation measurement lied in confirming or negating isolation during work with a computer in free time, coming out of a difference of positive (P_+) and negative (P_-) points in the examined sample and. The answers described in the scale as 'neutral' (P_N) are considered as 'standard' behavior and are not taken into account . Commenting on positive answers would be necessary if the difference between (P_+) and (P_-) accured to be "negative". The answers described in the questionnaire as positive represented the methods of reducing the threat of isolation. First of all they included active recreation, participation in team games and social meetings in a group.

6.1 The first phase of research - students (Musioł & Ujma-Wąsowicz, 2007).

Three hundred twelve students of full-time and extension courses were subjected to research. The measurement of isolation was taken during semester classes (thanks to this students had direct contact with the researchers) in the period from 3rd to 27th January 2007. The students represented three faculties of the Silesian University of Technology: Faculty of Organization and Management, Faculty of Architecture and Faculty of Mechanical Engineering as well as Silesian College of Economics and Administration in Bytom (Table 3)

A1	**Examined sample**	Full-time course not working	Aged 19-25	110 questionnaires
B1	**Comparative sample**	Extension course working	Aged 19-33	110 questionnaires

Table 3. The kind of the sample accepted for measurement of isolation caused by using computers in free time.

Results of measurement of a level of isolation among students are presented in Table 4 .

Scale of Questions −2, −1, neutral, +1, +2		
A 1 Full time course, not working		
$P_{A1\_}$ number of negative points	**- 2**	**- 1**
	number of answers 176 x (-2) = **- 352**	number of answers 289 x (-1) = **- 289**
P_{NA1} number of neutral points	number of answers 266 = **neutral**	
P_{A1+} number of positive points	**+ 1**	**+ 2**
	number of answers 205 x (+1) = **+ 205**	number of answers 168 x (+2) = **+ 336**
B 1 Extension course, working		
$P_{B1\_}$ number of negative points	**- 2**	**- 1**
	number of answers 161 x (-2) = **- 322**	number of answers 269 x (-1) = **- 269**
P_{NB1} number of neutral points	number of answers 304 = **neutral**	
P_{B1+} number of positive points	**+ 1**	**+ 2**
	number of answers 237 x (+1) = **+ 237**	number of answers 145 x (+2) = **+ 290**

Table 4. Results of measurement of a level of isolation among students caused by using computers in free time

Interpretation of results:

Level of isolation Δp_i was calculated as a difference between a number of points from answers to questions contained in positive scale and a number of points from answers to questions contained in negative scale in relation to: full-time course **A1** - examined sample according to formula (3) (Fig. 6) and extension course **B1** - comparative sample according to formula (4) (Fig. 7).

$$\Delta \mathbf{p}_{\mathbf{i\,A1}} = P_{A1+} - P_{A1\_} \tag{3}$$

$$\Delta \mathbf{p}_{\mathbf{i\,A1}} = \{(+205) + (+336)\} - \{(-289) + (-352)\} = 541 - 641 = -\mathbf{100}$$

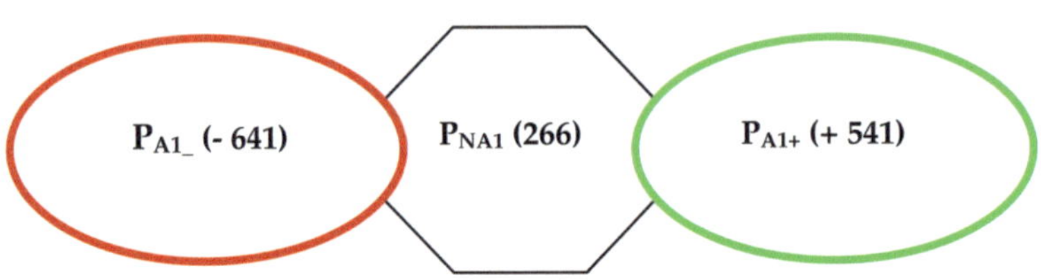

Figure 6. Graphic presentation of the results for full-time course, not working students (A1)

where:

$\Delta p_{i\,A1}$ - level of isolation for full-time course, not working students,

$P_{A1+} = P_{A1(+1)} + P_{A1(+2)}$ – summary number of positive points from answers.

$P_{A1\_} = P_{A1(-1)} + P_{A1(-2)}$ – summary number of negative points from answers

P_{NA1} – number of neutral points

$$\Delta \mathbf{p}_{\mathbf{i\,B1}} = P_{B1+} - P_{B1\_} \tag{4}$$

$$\Delta p_{i\,B1} = \{(+237) + (+290)\} - \{(-269) + (-322)\} = 527 - 591 = \mathbf{-64}$$

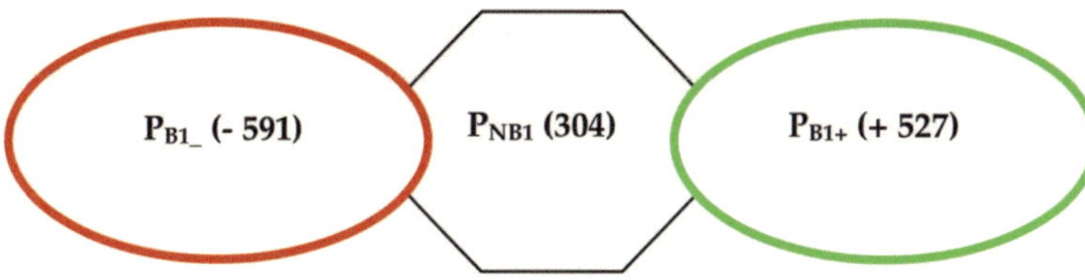

Figure 7. Graphic presentation of the results for working students (B1)

where:
$\Delta p_{i\,B1}$ - level of isolation for extension, working students,
$P_{B1+} = P_{B1(+1)} + P_{B1(+2)}$ – summary number of positive points from answers.
$P_{B1\_} = P_{B1(-1)} + P_{B1(-2)}$ – summary number of negative points from answers
P_{NB1} – number of neutral points
Summary:
looking at the above data we come to a conclusion that the level of isolation of full-time students $\Delta p_{i\,A1} = -100$ is higher than the level of isolation of extension students $\Delta p_{i\,B1} = -64$. While analyzing the reasons of isolation, number of points for answers in the negative scale and in the positive scale of full-time and extension students were taken into account. The conclusions are following:

1. The full-time students are not as aware of risk of isolation as the extension students;
2. The full-time students prefer active recreation and team games to a larger extent than the extension students
3. The extension students are more aware of risks caused by work with a computer and they can reduce them better than full-time students For this reason they are in favor of family and social contacts ;
4. The research confirmed the thesis that users of the computers are not aware of this risk. However, instinctively they feel that active recreation and team games are the methods which help not only to relax but also to reduce the effect of isolation.

6.2 Second phase of research – school teenagers (Ujma-Wąsowicz & Musioł 2008).

In June 2008 the research including two phases was conducted. The subject of the research were school teenagers aged from 15 to 19. The young people attend three middle schools and two secondary schools in Gliwice. The teenagers subjected to the research attend 3 sport classes and 5 general education classes (Table 5).

Age	Sports activity	Number of questionnaires
15 - 19	Young people practising sport in a sport class or a sport club	135
	Young people not practicing any sport discipline	89
	TOTAL	224

Table 5. The structure of the sample accepted for measurement of isolation among school teenagers caused by using computers in free time

Thirty-five questionnaires were completed incorrectly. From the remaining 190 questionnaires 136 were chosen according to the following rules:
For the sample A2 representing young people practising sport in a sport class or a sport club 68 questionnaires were chosen at random out of 121 correctly completed questionnaires and for the sample B2 representing young people not practicing any sport discipline all 68 correctly completed questionnaires were accepted.

A2	**Examined sample**	Young people practising sport in a sport class or a sport club	Aged 15 - 19	110 questionnaires
B2	**Comparative sample**	Young people not practicing any sport discipline		110 questionnaires

Table 6. The kind of the sample accepted for measurement of isolation caused by caused by computer and digital devices in free time

Results of measurement of a level of isolation among school teenagers are presented in Table 7.

Scale of Questions −2, −1, neutral, +1, +2		
A 2 Young people practising sport in a sport class or a sport club		
	- 2	**- 1**
P_{A2-} number of negative points	number of answers 40 x (-2) = **- 80**	number of answers 54 x (-1) = **- 54**
P_{NA2} number of neutral points	number of answers 126 = **neutral**	
	+ 1	**+ 2**
P_{A2+} number of positive points	number of answers 51 x (+1) = **+ 51**	number of answers 143 x (+2) = **+ 286**
B 2 Young people not practising any sport discipline		
	- 2	**- 1**
P_{B2-} number of negative points	number of answers 43 x (-2) = **- 86**	number of answers 74 x (-1) = **- 74**
P_{NB2} number of neutral points	number of answers 304 = **neutral**	
	+ 1	**+ 2**
P_{B2+} number of positive points	number of answers 66 x (+1) = **+ 66**	number of answers 88 x (+2) = **+ 176**

Table 7. Results of measurement of a level of isolation among school teenagers caused by computer and digital devices in free time

Interpretation of results:

Level of isolation Δp_i was calculated using the same rule as in the first measurement a difference between a number of points from answers to questions contained in positive scale and a number of points from answers to questions contained in negative scale in relation to young people practising sport in a sport class or a sport club: **A2** - examined sample according to formula (5) (Fig. 8) and young people not practising any sport discipline **B2** - comparative sample according to formula (6) (Fig. 9).

$$\Delta p_{i\,A2} = P_{A2+} - P_{A2\_} \qquad (5)$$

$$\Delta p_{i\,A2} = \{(+51) + (+286)\} - \{(-80) + (-54)\} = 337 - 134 = +\mathbf{203}$$

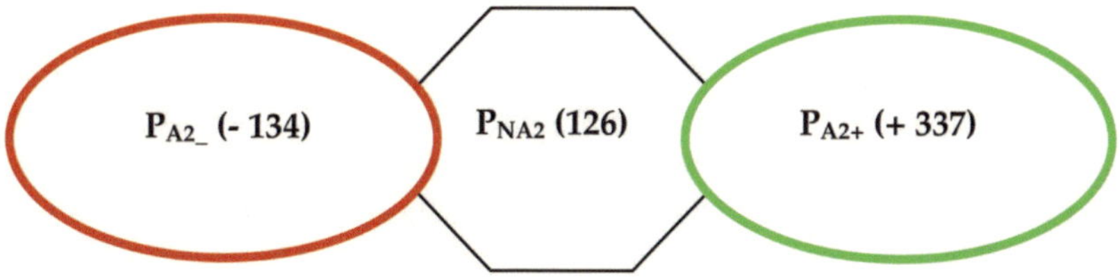

Figure 8. Graphic presentation of the results for school teenagers practising sport in a sport class or a sport club

where:

$\Delta p_{i\,A2}$ - level of isolation for school teenagers practising sport in a sport class or a sport club

$P_{A2+} = P_{A2(+1)} + P_{A2(+2)}$ – summary number of positive points from answers

$P_{A2\_} = P_{A2(-1)} + P_{A2(-2)}$ – summary number of negative points from answers

P_{NA2} – number of neutral points.

$$\Delta p_{i\,B2} = P_{B2+} - P_{B2\_} \qquad (6)$$

$$\Delta p_{i\,B2} = \{(+66) + (+176)\} - \{(-86) + (-74)\} = 242 - 160 = +\mathbf{82}$$

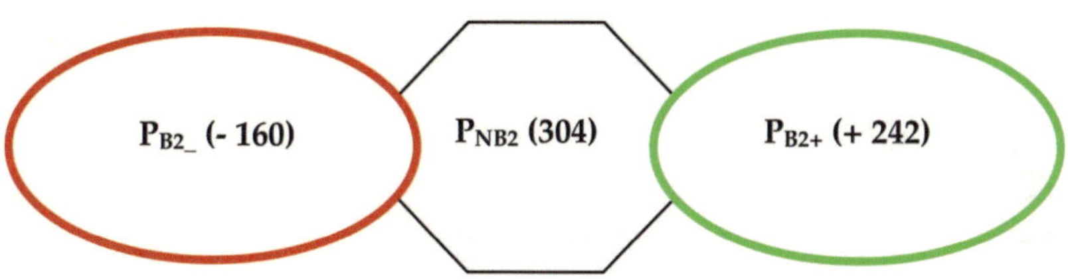

Figure 9. Graphic presentation of the results for school teenagers not practising any sport discipline

where:

$\Delta p_{i\,B2}$ - level of isolation for , school teenagers not practising any sport discipline

$P_{B2+} = P_{B2(+1)} + P_{B2(+2)}$ – summary number of positive points from answers

$P_{B2\_} = P_{B2(-1)} + P_{B2(-2)}$ – summary number of negative points from answers

P_{NB2} – number of neutral points.

Summary:

Looking at the above data we come to a conclusion that isolation among school teenagers was not identified.

While analyzing the reasons of isolation the conclusions are following:

1. Young people practising sport value the possibility of active recreation in a group more than young people who do not practise any sport discipline

2. Young people practising and not practising sport are unconscious of threats caused by isolation while using a computer and other mobile digital devices. However, in a natural way they intuitively avoid the mentioned dangers reducing them to a smaller or greater degree by group or individual sports activity .
3. For the teenagers who train sport is the most interesting form of spending free time, whereas such a form is perceived as marginal by young people who do not practise sport.
4. In spite of the fact that isolation was not affirmed among school children, the difference of the way of spending free time by teenagers who practise sport and those who do not train was observed. The hypothesis is formulated that the differences result from behavioural consciousness formed during the pedagogical process.

7. Can the development of outdoor sports contribute to reduction of the threat of isolation?

In the 90s the research was conducted in the European counties, which revealed that in Poland (like in other counties of Eastern Europe) on average 15 % of adult society regularly practices sport. This phenomenon is amazing, especially in comparison to Western Europe, where this proportion reaches almost 70 % (Ujma-Wąsowicz, 2007). Since then not much has changed in Poland and a lot of circumstances indicate that the forthcoming future will look similarly.

It is easy to observe that the tendency of sports absence among adult people does not only remain on the same level but increases. Two factors create favorable conditions for deepening these incorrect habits: on the one hand spending long hours in front of a computer monitor by children and teenagers, in perspective adult people, and on the other hand the shortage of commonly available sports infrastructure taking advantage of the technical potential of 21st century and expectations of users. That is why it seems that "environment sport" should offer young people a new and attractive formula of spending free time by means of commonly accessible and safe infrastructure, adjusted to the needs of varied users. Otherwise, the process of lack of interest in active recreation among currently young people and adults in future will be deepened.

Outdoor sport and recreation areas are a considerable percentage of public and semi-public spaces in Polish towns and cities. The serious problem connected with these previously well-kept and today degraded areas e.g. school sports areas and also sports facilities previously belonging to dynamically developing sports clubs, started in the period of our country's political transformation. The related changes caused among others such effects as lack of institutional interest of local authorities in the problem of renovation of sports areas or giving up supporting such complexes by their previous owners e.g. mines or steelworks.

Another condition that was an encouragement to begin the research is absence of the disabled in outdoor sports life The disabled are often perceived as the people of the second category. The mentality of able-bodied people does not allow such persons to function normally. These people are not aware that the disabled have the same needs and aspirations as the rest of the society, however their ability to realize them is limited. They do not expect from the society sympathy but support and partnership in aiming at normal functioning in all spheres of life, also in realizing their sports aspirations (Ujma-Wąsowicz, 2007)

7.1 Urban, physical and mental health and social behaviors context

In Poland, particularly in post-industrial towns and cities, the process of degradation of existing sports areas, constituting the considerable percentage of outdoor areas in towns is intensifying. On the other hand, there is a shortage of commonly accessible sport and recreation areas, equipped with suitable infrastructure, i.e. complying with the 21st century standards and, which is the most important, situated in the proximity of the place of residence that encourages different age groups to everyday, spontaneous, active recreation. The existing outdoor sport areas in cities, easily accessible and affordable, such as football pitches by school or housing estates, are in most cases neglected and developed in old-fashioned way. By contrast, the possibility of using attractively organized outdoor sport areas is connected with the necessity of travelling and often fees. They are mostly commercial facilities. The additional problem in Polish cities is lack of commonly accessible sports infrastructure, adjusted to the expectations of the disabled, giving them opportunity to practice sports which are popular among them.

The changes worth aiming at in the context of open sports areas should be understood as:

- realization of the city spatial policy related to balanced development principles;
- restoration of city landscape advantages;
- enliving city public spaces;
- making sports areas available to a broader social group like the disabled or the ones not interested in traditional sports;
- creating new workplaces for everyday supervision and equipment care.

In the era of globalization the characteristic of labour processes is first of all fast information flow. It is based primarily on mobile cybernetic technologies and quality and efficiency of communicating of different cultures in all the world. Therefore, the cyberspace area leads to the future, simultaneously quantifying the past. The side effect of these processes are all kinds of civilization diseases and the syndrome of burnout. To maintain a balance between professional and personal life it is good to invest time in physical, emotional and spiritual development. It can be realized by participation in active practicing uninstitutioned sport, which is a factor reducing health risks. In the same time the awareness of ergonomics and safety of an individual as well as a team is being increased.

Taking into consideration this sphere of human life enables to influence the development of such personality features as:

- physical condition;
- internal motivation to work on oneself;
- resistance to stress;
- ability to work in a group and to solve problems.

On the other hand, the quality of social behaviors of city inhabitants is permanently worsening, particularly of young people, which results in the phenomenon of isolation, aggression and becoming addicted. One of the reasons of such behaviors is lack of alternative forms of spending free time, adequate to the needs of the contemporary man.

To what extend practicing amateur outdoor sport influences our personality?

- it shapes the abilities of spontaneous team work organization;
- it enables organization of active spending free time according to individual needs without necessary "top-down" timetables;
- it creates favorable conditions for integration and co-participation of the disabled in outdoor sports life;
- participation in non-toxic competition. (Ujma-Wąsowicz, 2007b)

8. The method of measurement and evaluation of the reduction of isolation among Polish school teenagers

Considering the specifics of the undertaken problem, it was assumed that the young people were potential external clients of the future facilities. Accordingly, the tools of Total Quality Mangement (TQM) were applied. In order to obtain information which enables to describe the examined reality, by means of number indexes of a single phenomenon as well as showing its specifics, sociological standarized and non-standarized techniques are used – for example: a survey form, a questionnaire or an free interview (Bonstingl, 1999). In the presented research non-standarized techniques, i.e. a questionnaire having characteristics of a free interview was applied, constructed on the basis of the authors' set of issues.

The purpose of the research was to diagnose the attitude of young people to pro-sport behaviours in everyday life and then to describe the directions of transformations of existing sports areas in a Polish city (Ujma-Wąsowicz & Musioł, 2008).

The questionnaire was constructed according to the following principles.

The young people were asked to present their attitude to 5 issues (I_i):

I_1 - attitude to television sports programmers;

I_2 - the types of facilities that should be built in the surroundings;

I_3 - frequency of practicing outdoor sports;

I_4 - a way of practicing sport (sports class, sports club);

I_5 - the attitude to Physical Education lessons at school.

Each issue was given 3 options of choice (C_j):

C_1 - the first one negated the sense of sport existence;

C_2 - the second one described it as an important element of human life;

C_3 - the third one described sport as the greatest enjoyment in life.

The respondents were to choose one option C_j, which obtained 1 point.

The analysis of the results was carried out according to the following formula (7):

$$P_i = \frac{I_i\, C_j}{R} \tag{7}$$

where:

P_i - point value of a chosen option C_j of a particular issue, where i = 1 – 5;

I_i - a number of responses for an issue, where i = 1 – 5;

C_j - 1 point for the chosen option, where j = 1 – 3;

R - number or verified questionnaires; R = 125.

The results of the research are presented in Table 8.

Point value $P_{i\,(1\text{-}5)}$	Option of choice C_j		
	C_1	C_2	C_3
P_1	**0,04**	**0,83**	**0,13**
P_2	**0,15**	**0,30**	**0,55**
P_3	**0,02**	**0,80**	**0,18**
P_4	**0,48**	**0,08**	**0,44**
P_5	**0,14**	**0,60**	**0,26**

Table 8. Determining the proportion of teenagers to individual issues P_i

Then point values for the chosen option C_j were summed up, determining tendencies of pro-sport behaviours (8)

$$T_j = \sum_{i=1}^{5} P_i \tag{8}$$

where:
T_j - point value of the tendency for the option C_j, where j = 1 - 3
P_1, P_2, P_3, P_4, P_5 - point values of issues for the chosen option C_j
The is presented in Table 9.

Point value of the tendency T_j of pro-sport behaviors'		
T_1	T_2	T_3
0,83	**2,61**	**1,56**

Table 9. Determining the tendency of everyday pro-sport behaviours of young people T_j

Summary:
The value T_2 = 2,60 indicates that active recreation is an essential element of a young man's life, proving its quality. In spite of long hours spent in front of a computer monitor young people instinctively feel that sport is the method for reduction of isolation , improving physical condition and enjoying time in a group.

9. Programmes and implementations referring to outdoor sports (Ujma-Wąsowicz & Musioł, 2008)

The state of possessed knowledge enables the authors to present examples of programmes intended for popularization of outdoor amateur sport in Poland and abroad as well as modern solutions of outdoor sports areas in urbanized spaces.
The programmes: "A Pitch Nearby" building multifuntional sports pitches commonly accessible to children and teenagers and "Orlik 2012", a very new one are realized in Poland by the Ministry of Sport and Tourism of the Republic of Poland (the difference between them lies in the method of funding). The analysis of these programmes shows that the driving force behind these activities is the good will of investors submitting offers for building complexes of this type. It means that single implementations are realized in new locations in the country, which are not subjected to system activities in the city and district scale.
An extremely interesting foreign example is Millenium Programme "Changing Places" presented at Royal Society of Arts in London in March 1995. The programme is destined for landscape regeneration of 21 sites degradated by industry in England and Wales. The primary principle of "Changing Places" is framing directions of changes on the basis of cooperation of many authorities, particularly local ones (government and non-governmental organizations and the private sector). The programme in every location covers several hectares of land and involves unurbanized areas.
In Poland in urbanized areas the illustration of modern solutions can be "Krakowski Square" in Gliwice, the city where the Silesian University of Technology is located. In 2000 in the centre of the city the multifuntional outdoor complex, covering 800 m^2 was built. The

area belongs to the local government's assets and till 1990s it had been undeveloped and neglected. The implemented project is the place willingly visited by the inhabitants. It comprises varied funtional zones, such as a square with a scene and a stand destined for organizing different kinds of events e.g. every year the street basketball competition is organized here, in which on average 80 teams, mostly from the Silesia, participate (a), a skatepark (b), an alley with a playground for small children (c) and a fountain. Also additional facilities like public toilets, benches and a bus stop, were skillfully integrated into the project (Photo 1).

Photo 1. Krakowski Square, Gliwice, Poland (a, b, c)

Another sport and recreation area, having some features of a city square is "Westblaak Skatepark" in Rotterdam in the Netherlands, the project implemented in 2005. It was built in the centre of the city, on a former street. The area is a very popular place. It gathers great numbers of sportsmen and spectators because of its localization and the function it fulfils .

10. The threat of isolation in a selected professional group

The professional group of architects was selected for evaluation of the threat of isolation. Presently, designing facilities destined for interactive reduction of the threat of isolation requires application of different kinds of system IT tools. Thus, there is a feedback human – computer and consequently, all results of disruption of this relation. One of secondary effects of this relation is the threat of isolation.

The work of architect - creating the space for a man, requires spatial imagination, knowledge and experience. The architect must coordinate four basic elements: the function of the designed area and its form (aesthetics), construction and economically justified costs of the investment. It means that taking into account such extensive spectrum of issues, only professionals, at least theoretically, should undertake architectural designing. Beginning from submitting an offer for performing a design, through proposing solutions, carrying out a construction and detailed design and finishing with building a facility and putting it into operation, an architect's activity is a subject to constant verification, on side of an investor as well as a user. From their point of view the subject of evaluation are:

- functionality of the whole facility;
- adapting the created space to its limitations;

- guaranteeing its biological and psychological comfort among others, by an appropriate selection of microclimatic conditions, lighting, colours;
- form and aesthetics of the whole facility;
- the way in which a designer communicates and informs about proposed solutions in other words striving to understand expectations of a user and skilful justifying designing decisions).

According to G. Schmitt, our architectural space will develop in three basic trends: *Pure Physical Architecture* - space conditioned culturally or by specifics of existing, external conditions; *Virtual Architecrure* - in many respects alternative to physical architecture, understood as virtual environment used for development of social activity and *"Bit and Bricks"Architecture* - physical structure of buildings is enriched with electronic tools, which create a new environment - monitored, controlled and protected by computers (Zalewski, 2007).

The possibility of creation the virtual world with a real user would make it possible to create a user-friendly space and also to improve communication of a designer with an investor. In this case a designer would be still treated, as it is now, as the only creator of a particular place.

Previous recognition of demand related to potential users, scenarios of behaviour of a larger number of people in a particular situation has fundamental meaning for the correct solution of building's functions. Introducing such tools to work of architect as a programme which recognises designing errors, which make free moving of a man in a designed space difficult, would fulfil a role of "a reviewer" of an architectural functional conception. The possibility of 3D designing with participation of virtual, moving users - "avatars" - 3D models, created on the basis of ergonomic research would be extremely useful.

However, there is another available, although not common, option of designing based on using augmented reality as a basic tool for better communication of an architect, an investor and a user. Software developed on this basis can enable active participation of a recipient in the process of facility creation. Systems of AR or IVR type allow a user to have an impression of being in a designed space, matching VR projection to real user's movements. The well-known software solution of this type is JCAD-VR, developed by a group of scientists from the University Strathclyde in Glasgow. A model of a designed building can be freely scaled, according to users' needs (Fig. 10) (Ujma-Wąsowicz & Gil, 2005).

Figure 10. Augmented reality: the possibilities of scaling and "emerging" of a user in a facility with examples of similar solutions from other spheres of human life

Digital space supports physical environment not only by its constant control and customization. It enables for example, by means of the idea of programmable structure of a building called Hyperbody, to change a shape of this environment and its information content in real time. Such a space is an active structure, controlled by data flow, which changes a shape, volume and information content in real time. A user is not only an observer of the skin - coating, but he is emerged in it. He can "manage" it - alter it using Internet data or doing it from the structure's inside, having direct contact with it. According to the intention of its designers, Hyperbody should be compatible with premises of the new architectural triad, which is not any more: Function - Construction - Form, but Game - Set - Match. Game means that architecture is becoming a game, played in the space of Hyperbody. Set derives from setting the space parameters by users, which is the result of the game, and Match - matching to new conditions. It means that the designed space is fully programmable to systematically meet requirements and needs of a user (Zalewski, 2007).

Thanks to these new technologies the future of architectural designing may present in the following way. Computer - a creator, thanks to entering suitable data, e.g. area of a facility, cubature, functions, a number and "kind" of users, construction materials, roof inclinations, type of elevation, maximum costs etc. it will design in a virtual way and will present a ready, objectively correct project to an investor. It may imply that the role of an architect will be limited to collecting documents and signing them.

Common application of programmes based on information technology as an environment and a tool used for validation of correctness of functional, ergonomic and aesthetic solutions in architectural designing is, as it seems, a question of the near future. Visualization of a facility before it is erected is particularly interesting for persons who lack spatial imagination or who do not want to learn the details of a technical drawing. Such future is also fascinating from the point of view of conceptual work - the programmes will enable a designer and future users to test a non-existent building in conditions very similar to real ones and they will also favour creative reinterpretation of the observed model and probably lead to unexpected discoveries.

Architectural software for work in virtual reality may also develop in two directions. The first one is desired by designers. It would support avoiding errors which cause user's discomfort, and on the other hand, it would enable to present solutions to an investor in the way understandable for him. Another direction is less optimistic for a designer. However, it is justified to think that in the near future an investor will be able, by means of a suitable computer programme, to generate a building meeting his requirements, not asking an architect for his opinion (Ujma-Wąsowicz & Gil, 2005).

11. Can a disabled person be protected from isolation?

Earlier the only directions of activities in the area of improvement of quality of life of disabled people was elimination of architectural barriers. This process with better or worse results is carried out in required by law architectural and construction documents as well as in the phase of activities correcting the existing state (Ujma-Wąsowicz, 1996). It turns out that limiting oneself only to making architectural space available is insufficient. A greater challenge is eliminating psychological barriers, which have exogenous or endogenous background.

How can a disabled person get out of proverbial 'four walls'? Communication of the disabled with the outer world is a task which is often difficult to realize. Fortunately, in the

era of the Internet it does not have to mean the necessity of getting out of a flat. It is just the strength of the Internet. It is enough to express one's reflections on the computer monitor and they will trigger off discussions. It is not a problem that during a discussion for example about literature a person expressing very interesting opinions does not walk or hear. In the same way as in the real world, also on the Web it is important not to limit oneself to four walls. It is the fact that the Internet is ideal for supporting different abilities of members of the Internet community. Contacting the disabled with other users of the Web encourages to take up new challenges and turns attention to some issues they would not care about otherwise. The possibility of sharing their, often exceptional knowledge with others is equally important for disabled people, they create their own Internet sites, blogs or participate in different Internet forums (Kowalczyk, 2006).
Paradoxically, from one isolation being often nobody's fault they move to so called secondary isolation, which is the subject of these reflections. The problem requires undertaking research concerning reasons for existence of this phenomenon in the mentioned environment as well as the methods of its active reduction. Obviously, it is dependent on a kind of a disability and orders given by doctors and physiotherapists.

Photo 2. Extreme sports practised by the disabled

People who suffer from irreversible changes of some organs, but whose other organs function correctly, can be helped by intensive training, which can contribute to improvement of activity of the healthy organs and compensate for the lost functions. In order to achieve the best possible physical fitness of healthy organs it is essential to practise a properly selected sport discipline, even on the competitive level. Among the disciplines which improve physical fitness swimming should be mentioned on the first place. For people with dysfunctions of lower limbs but whose upper limbs function correctly, who use a wheelchair to move, among others the following sport disciplines are recommended: discus throw, putting the shot, javelin throw, archery, basketball (in a sitting position on a wheelchair) and others. Running and jumping are sport disciplines advised for people with dysfunction of upper limbs, whose lower limbs function correctly. Practising canoeing and sailing is available and recommended for people with different dysfunctions of motor

organs, even with amputated upper limbs, thanks to using appropriate prostheses. These sports activities develop general physical fitness and are very beneficial for the psychological condition, giving a lot of satisfaction and pleasure. For the blind or for people with hearing disorders it is possible to practise a lot of sport disciplines with properly adapted rules. Winter sports, such as skiing and ice skating are advisable for people with preserved, different fitness of upper and lower limbs (Milanowska, 1997). Also practising extreme sports is popular, independently of a degree of disability (Photo 2.) (Ujma-Wąsowicz, 2007a).
It is possible to state, that interactive reduction of the threat of isolation caused by using electronic devices e.g. a computer, enters the area of active rehabilitation. Better fitness and physical condition achieved by the disabled is very beneficial for their psyche and social behaviours. It gives them self-esteem, encourages to take up a job, a professional training or to change a profession. These factors are essential because they positively influence social integration of the disabled in their environment.

12. Final remarks

- Growing meaning of knowledge and new economy of global society requires access to information and we can't withdraw from using more and more advanced information technologies, computer technics and electronic tools.
- The research of isolation risk among students caused by using computers digital devices in free time confirmed the thesis that users of computers, iPAQs or DVD devices are not aware of this risk. However, instinctively they feel that active recreation and team games are the methods which help not only to relax but also to reduce the effect of isolation.
- The subsequent conducted research proved that the problem of isolation among school children does not exist. It is natural for them to spend time in a group. In the same time, being asked a question concerning the possibility of practising sport disciplines with the disabled, 90% of young people are for integration, which may take different forms;
- The comparison of conducted research allows to confirm the thesis that isolation starts to be a threat when a man takes on particular social roles and has to decide about his life and many a time about life of other people
- In spite of rich sports base, a problem is a limited inclination of students for regular and also spontaneous practicing sport. One of essential reasons of such a situation is neglect in the period of bringing up a young man, because in this time follows a process of transformation exuberant willingness to spend free time in active way into a habit. The habit, which later appears to be very desirable.
- Widening educational market in Poland will require a transition from learning methods 'face-to-face' to methods 'e-learning', in which isolation will be not only a threat but also a social problem. While reducing intellectual effort and treating work with a computer as a reduction of emotional effort, such a situation may be a reason of degeneration of interpersonal communication, indispensable for team work.
- The research concerning a threat of isolation caused by work with a computer in free time, confirmed assumptions of the authors that students cannot manage health risk, connected with hygiene of studying and of working.

- It is necessary to work out new planning and design giudelines for implementation of outdoor sports facilities in urbanized environment, matching the expectations of different groups of users and current technological development. These facilities, because of their locations and realized functions, are important elements of composition of urban space. Therefore, the state policy should be oriented on investing in commonly accessible outdoor sport areas, according to the latest trends.
- The authors of the article are academic teachers and have opportunities to encourage for discussion on these issues the student environment, which also includes disabled persons. The discussions prove the usefulness of the begun research and indicate the need of its expansion into the environments of the disabled, working people and senior citizens, it means creating a map of isolation and methods of its reduction for particular environment and professional groups.

13. References

Bonstingl J.J. (1999). *Quality School. Introduction to Total Quality Management in Education.* Pub.: CODN (Centralny Ośrodek Doskonalenia Nauczycieli), ISBN 83-85910-23-9, Warsaw, Poland

Charlton S.G. (2002). Questioner Techniques for Test and Evaluation, In: *Handbook of Human Factor Testing and Evaluation.* Charlton, S.G. & O'Brien T.G., pp. 225-231, Lawrence Erlbaum Associates Publishers, ISBN 0-8058-3290-4 - ISBN 0-8058-3291-2 Mahwah, New Jersey, London

Damasio A.R. (2000). *The Feeling of What Happens.* Pub.: Dom Wydawniczy Rebis, ISBN 83-73-01-001-7, Poznań, Poland

Goleman D. (1997). *Emotional Intelligence.* Pub. Media Rodzina of Poznań, ISBN 83-85594-46-9, Poznań, Poland

Kiergegaard S. (1995): *The Sickness unto Death (Sygdommen til doden).* Pub. Zysk i S-ka Wydawnictwo s.c., ISBN 83-86530-87-1, Poznań, Poland

Karwowska A. (2008). *Zakompleksieni i nieufni,* Daily News METRO

Kondziela J.J. (1986): *A Person in Community. Social ethic, economic and international problems.* Pub.: Księgarnia św. Jacka, Imprimatur, Janusz Zimniak, Bp VI-1637/86, Katowice, Poland

Kowalczyk A. (2006): Wyjść z czterech ścian. *Journal Integration. Magazyn dla niepełnosprawnych, ich rodzin i przyjaciół.* (1/2006) 54-55, ISSN 1232-8510

Milanowska K. (1997): The importance of increased loco motor activity for disabled people as a compensating factor of their psychophysical efficiency. *Sport - Chance for Disabled,* pp. 259-260, ISBN 83-87252-0304, Pub. Polish Association of Disabled People Central Committee in Cracow, Poland

Musioł T. (2003): The State Ergonomics Consciousness Employed a Like Index the Quality Safety of Organisation. *Proceedings of Human-Computer-Interaction,* pp.1401-1405, ISBN 0-8058-49-31-9, Crete, Greece, June 2003. Lawrence Erlbaum Associates, Publishers, Mahwah, New Jersey, London

Musioł T. & Ligarski M. (2004): A didactic measure of quality of work safety management classes - case study. *Proceedings of Dilemmas and Issues of Modern Ergonomics and Work Safety Education and Researches* pp. 209-214, ISBN 83-906191-4-8, Poznań, 2004, Pub. By Poznan University of Technology, Poznań, Poland

Musioł T. (2004). Organization as a Phenomenon. *Proceedings of Czy dwie kultury?*, pp. 267-270, ISBN 83-913835-5-5, Joint The Society for Development of Polish Science, Zabrze, Poland

Musioł T. (2005a) Ergonomical aspect of disabled people education at Faculty of Organisation and Management of Silesian University of Technology. *Zastosowania Ergonomii,* Vol. No 1-3. 2005, pp. 181-188, ISSN 1232-7573

Musioł T. (2005b). The State of Ergonomics Consciousness of Participants of Didactic Process in Individual Assessment. *Proceedings of Human-Computer-Interaction,* Vol. No 8, ISSN 1044-7318/ online ISSN 1532-7590, Las Vegas USA, June 2005r. ,Mira Digital Publishing

Musioł T. (2007). Próba identyfikacji zagrożeń organizacji w warunkach globalizacji. *Proceedings of Rozwój i funkcjonowanie przedsiębiorstw w warunkach globalnej gospodarki światowej* pp. 101-106. ISBN 978-83-87296-23-0, Pub. Agencja Artystyczna PARA, Katowice

Musioł T. & Ujma-Wąsowicz K. (2007) Identification of Threat of Isolation as a Result of Work with a Computer In Free Time, *Proceedings of Human-Computer-Interaction,* pp.707-715, ISBN 978-3-540-73282-2, Springer Pub., Heilderberg, Gemany

Stein, E. (1998). *About empathy problem.* Doctorate dissertation

Ujma-Wąsowicz, K. (1996). Gliwice Przyjazne Osobom Niepełnosprawnym. The programme of adaptation the city of Gliwice for disabled people. *The Report prepared by K. Ujma-Wąsowicz, M. Węgrzyn, S. Zemła.* Silesian University of Technology, Gliwice, Poland

Ujma-Wąsowicz, K. (2005). Outdoor Sport in the City. Development Trends. *Czasopismo Techniczne, series of Architecture part 2,* Vol. No 9-A/2005, pp. 312, ISSN 0011-4561

Ujma-Wąsowicz K, Gil A.: (2005) Ergonomics and Architecture. Designing in Virtual Reality. Future or Choice?, *Proceedings of Human-Computer-Interaction,* Vol. Posters ISSN 1044-7318/ online ISSN 1532-7590, Las Vegas USA, June 2005r. ,Mira Digital Publishing

Ujma-Wąsowicz K. (2007a): Ergonomiczne czynniki jakości środowiska aktywnej rekreacji. *Zastosowania Ergonomii,* Vol. No 1-2. pp. 235-244, ISSN 1232-7573

Ujma-Wąsowicz K. (2007b): Outdoor places of active recreationin urbanized areas. Development targets and directions. *Czasopismo Techniczne, series of Architecture* Vol. No 1-A/2007 pp. 169-174, ISSN 0011-4561, ISSN 18976271

Ujma-Wąsowicz K., Musioł T. (2008) Outdoor sport in the city of the future: planning and designing issues, *Proc. of the 5th Int. Conf. on The Sustainable City,* pp. 13-22, eds. C.A. Brebbia, A. Gospodini & E. Tiezzi, WIT Press, Southampton, UK,

Zalewski K. (2007). Cybrids: Hybrids of Psyhical Space and Cyberspace. *Cyberspace, Architecture & Urban serie 1/2007,* pp.23-30, Published with permission of the President of the Silesian University of Technology, Gliwice

29

Physical Selection as Tangible User Interface

Pasi Välkkynen
VTT Technical Research Centre of Finland
Finland

1. Abstract

Physical browsing is an interaction paradigm that allows associating digital information with physical objects. In physical browsing, the interaction happens via a mobile terminal - such as a mobile phone or a Personal Digital Assistant (PDA). The links are implemented as tags that can be read with the terminal. They can be, for example, Radio Frequency Identifier (RFID) tags that are read with a mobile phone augmented with an RFID reader. The basis of physical browsing is physical selection - the interaction task with which the user tells the mobile terminal which link the user is interested in and wants to activate. After the selection, an action occurs, for example, if the tag contains a web address, the mobile phone may display the associated web page in the browser. Physical selection is thus a mobile terminal and tag based interaction technique, which is intended for interacting with the physical world and its entities.

In ubiquitous computing, the physical environment is augmented with devices offering digital information and services. Ubiquitous computing can be divided into two broad categories: distributed, in which widgets with user interfaces are embedded into the environment, and mobile terminal centred, in which the user interacts with the devices with a mediator device. In both cases, an important issue in ubiquitous computing is how to interact with the devices embedded into the environment. Physical selection is a direct selection technique for choosing a target in the mobile terminal centred approach.

Computer-augmented environment is a concept very similar to ubiquitous computing. The concept grew from the combination of ubiquitous computing and augmented reality, but common to both approaches is the emphasis on the physical world and the tools that enhance our everyday activities. Another concept close to ubiquitous computing and computer-augmented environments is physically based user interfaces, in which the interaction is based on computationally augmented physical artefacts. Tangible user interfaces are based on tangible or graspable physical objects and are thus closely related to physically based user interfaces.

2. Introduction

Physical browsing is an interaction paradigm that allows associating digital information with physical objects. It can be seen analogous to browsing the World Wide Web: the physical environment contains links to digital information and by selecting these physical hyperlinks, various services can be activated.

In physical browsing, the interaction happens via a mobile terminal - such as a mobile phone or a Personal Digital Assistant (PDA). The links are implemented as tags that can be read with the terminal, for example Radio Frequency Identifier (RFID) tags that are read with a mobile phone augmented with an RFID reader. The basis of physical browsing is physical selection - the interaction task with which the user tells the mobile terminal which link the user is interested in and wants to activate. After the selection an action occurs, for example, if the tag contains a Universal Resource Identifier (URI, "web address"), the mobile phone may display the associated web page in the browser. Optimally, the displayed information is somehow related to the physical object itself, creating an association between the object and its digital counterpart. This user interaction paradigm is best illustrated with a simple scenario (Välkkynen et al., 2006):

Joe has just arrived on a bus stop on his way home. He touches the bus stop sign with his mobile phone and the phone loads and displays him a web page that tells him the expected waiting times for the next buses so he can best decide which one to use and how long he must wait for it. While he is waiting for the next bus, he notices a poster advertising a new interesting movie. Joe points his mobile phone at a link in the poster and his mobile phone displays the web page of the movie. He decides to go see it in the premiere and "clicks" another link in the poster, leading him to the ticket reservation service of a local movie theatre.

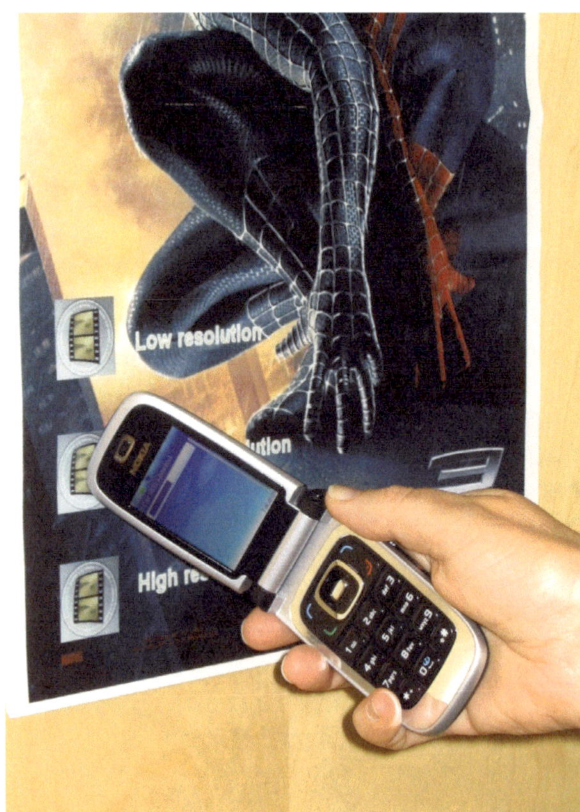

Figure 1. User selecting a link in a movie poster

To better illustrate the evolution of physical selection, the road of digital information from the purely digital form in desktop computers to mobile terminal readable physical containers and tokens is traced through a few well-known and interesting example systems. The beginnings of the desktop metaphor are first described briefly, and then how computing was brought from the virtual desktop to the real desktop, and to the physical world through concepts such as tangible user interfaces and computer-augmented environments. Eventually, these ideas led to bridging the physical and virtual worlds by identifying physical objects, and with mobile computing, also to the concept of physical browsing.

3. Dynabook

Kay and Goldberg (1977) presented the idea of Dynabook - a general-purpose notebook-sized computer, which could be used by anyone from educators and business people to poets and children. In the vision of Kay and Goldberg, each person has their own Dynabook. They envisioned a device as small and portable as possible, which could both take and give out information in quantities approaching that of human sensory systems. One of the metaphors they used when designing such a system was that of a musical instrument, such as a flute, which the user of the flute owns. The flute responds instantly and consistently to the wishes of the owner, and each user has an own flute instead of time-sharing a common flute.

As a step towards their vision, Kay and Goldberg designed an interim desktop version of the Dynabook. The Dynabook vision led eventually to building the Xerox Star (Smith et al., 1982) with graphical user interface and to the desktop metaphor of the Star. On the other hand, the original vision of Dynabook was an early idea of a mobile terminal, making the Dynabook vision even more significant in the evolution of physical browsing.

4. The Star User Interface and the Desktop Metaphor

The desktop metaphor refers to a user interface metaphor in which the UI is designed to resemble the physical desktop with familiar office objects. The beginning of the desktop metaphor was Xerox Star (Smith et al., 1982), a personal computer designed for offices. The designers of Xerox Star hoped that with the similarity of the graphical desktop user interface and the physical office, the users would find the user interface familiar and intuitive.

Wellner (1993) stated that the electronic world of the workstation and the physical world of the desk are separate, but each "has advantages and constraints that lead us to choose one or the other for particular task" and that the desktop metaphor is an approach to solving the problem of choosing between these two alternatives.

Like the interim Dynabook, the Star user interface hardware architecture included a bit mapped display screen and a mouse (English et al., 1967). Smith et al. (1982) claim that pointing with the mouse is as quick and easy as pointing with the tip of the finger. However, the mouse is not a direct manipulation device (Wellner, 1993); the movements of the mouse on a horizontal plane are transformed into cursor movement on a typically vertical plane some distance away from the mouse itself.

5. From Desktop Metaphor to the metaDESK

The physical desk led to the desktop metaphor, taking advantage of the strengths of the digital world, but at the same time ignoring the skills the users had already developed for interacting with the real world, and separating the information in digital form from the physical counterparts of the same information. It is also easy to see that the desktop metaphor suits best office tasks and not for example mobile computing. These shortcomings have led to two directions in bridging the physical and virtual worlds:

1. Integrating the physical objects back into the user interface, as is done in the tangible user interfaces approach;
2. Augmenting physical objects with digital information and accessing that information with a computational device, such as a mobile terminal.

In the next subsections, the first of the aforementioned approaches - integrating physical objects with the user interface - is explored through a few example systems that illustrate well the ideas of bridging the gap between the physical and virtual worlds. The DigitalDesk (Wellner, 1993) is an early system for merging the physical and digital worlds in an office desktop setting. It is also one of the pioneering augmented reality systems. Although Wellner's focus was on office systems, his ideas of combining the physical and digital worlds, while taking advantages from each, are still valid in the ubiquitous computing environments. Bricks (Fitzmaurice et al., 1995) and Active Desk is another physical desktop-based system in which physical and digital objects are connected.

5.1 DigitalDesk

Wellner (1993) states that we interact with documents in two separate worlds: the electronic world of workstation (using the desktop metaphor), and the physical world of the desk. Both worlds have advantages and constraints that lead us to choose one or the other for particular tasks in the office setting. Although activities on the two desks are often related, the two are unfortunately isolated from each other. Wellner suggests that "instead of putting the user in the virtual world of the computer, we could do the opposite: add computer to the real world of the user." Following this thought, instead of making the electronic workstation more like the physical desk, the DigitalDesk makes the desk more like a workstation and supports computer-based interaction with paper documents. According to Wellner, the difference between integrating the world into computers and integrating computers into the world lies in our perspective: "do we think of ourselves working primarily in the computer but with access to physical world functionality, or do we think of ourselves as working primarily in the physical world but with access to computer functionality?"

The DigitalDesk system (Wellner, 1993) is based on a real physical desk, which is enhanced to provide the user some computational capabilities. The desk includes a camera that projects the computer display onto the desk, and video cameras that track the actions of the user and can read physical documents on the desk. The interaction style in DigitalDesk is more tactile than the non-direct manipulation with a mouse. The user does not need any special input devices in addition to the camera: pointing and selecting with just fingers or a pen tip is sufficient. The projected images can be purely digital documents, user interface components, and images and text that are superimposed onto paper documents with the existing contents of the paper.

5.2 Bricks

Fitzmaurice et al. (1995) took another step towards integrating the physical and virtual worlds with Graspable User Interfaces, a new user interaction paradigm. They described their concept: "the Graspable UIs allow direct control of electronic or virtual objects through physical artefacts which act as handles for control." Graspable UIs are a blend of virtual and physical artefacts, each offering affordances in their respective instantiation. A graspable object in the context of graspable UIs is an object that is composed of both a physical handle, and a corresponding virtual object.

The prototype system in Bricks (Fitzmaurice et al., 1995) consists of Active Desk, the Bricks (roughly one inch sized cubes) and a simple drawing application. As in DigitalDesk (Wellner, 1993), the Active Desk uses a video projector to display the graphical user interface parts on the surface of the desk. Instead of tracking the fingers of the user or a pen tip with a camera, the Bricks system uses six-degrees-of-freedom sensors and wireless transmitters inside the Bricks. The location and orientation data is transmitted to the workstation that controls the application and the display. Although it offers a new user interaction paradigm, Bricks still builds upon the conventions of the graphical user interface in a desktop setting.

5.3 The metaDESK and Tangible Geospace

The metaDESK (Ullmer and Ishii, 1997) is an example of a tangible user interface (TUI, further explored in the next subsection), which brings familiar metaphorical objects from the computer desktop back to the physical world. The metaDESK is an augmented physical desktop on which phicons - physical icons - can be manipulated. The use of physical objects as interfaces to digital information forms the basis for TUIs. The metaDESK was built to instantiate physically the graphical user interface metaphor. The desktop metaphor drew itself from the physical desktop and in a manner of speaking, metaDESK again realised physically the GUI components. In metaDESK, the interface elements from the GUI paradigm are instantiated physically: windows, icons, handles, menus and controls each are given a physical form. For example, the menus and handles from GUI are instantiated as "trays" and "physical handles" in TUI.

Tangible Geospace (Ullmer and Ishii, 1997) is a prototype application built on the metaDESK platform. In Tangible Geospace, a set of objects was designed to physically resemble different buildings appearing on a digital map of the MIT campus. By placing a model of a building on the display surface, the user could bring up the relevant portion of the map. Manipulating the building on the metaDESK surface controlled the position and rotation of the map. The physical form of the objects would serve as a cognitive aid for the user in finding the right part of the map to display. For example a model of a familiar landmark such as the Great Dome of the MIT is easy to recognise on the metaDESK surface. The model thus acts as a container for the digital information and as a handle for manipulating the map. Adding a second phicon on the map rotates and scales the map so that both phicons are over correct locations on the digital map. Now the user has two physical handles for rotating and scaling the map by moving one or both objects with respect to each other, which is very similar to interaction with Bricks.

The Tangible Geospace application already resembles the basic idea of physical browsing. Although the "terminal" is a desk surface and instead of physically manipulating the terminal, the user manipulates tagged objects. The tagged objects act as links to digital information and bringing the "terminal" and the tagged objects together, the digital information can be displayed to the user.

6. Tangible Bits Vision

According to Ishii and Ullmer (1997), the GUI approach falls short in many respects, particularly in embracing the rich interface modalities between people and the physical environments. Their approach to this problem is a tangible user interface (TUI), part of which was demonstrated earlier with graspable user interfaces and the metaDESK platform. TUIs are user interfaces employing real physical objects, instruments, surfaces, and spaces as physical interfaces to digital information, and the user can physically interact with digital information through the manipulation of physical objects. The use of tangible objects - "real physical entities which can be touched and grasped" - as interfaces to digital information forms the basis for TUIs. This use of physical objects as containers for digital information makes tangible user interfaces important to physical browsing.

As a part of their work with tangible user interfaces, Ishii and Ullmer introduced the Tangible Bits vision (Ullmer and Ishii, 1997). The Tangible Bits vision includes three platforms: metaDESK, transBOARD and ambientROOM. Together these three platforms explore graspable physical objects and ambient environmental displays. In the Tangible Bits vision, people, digital information and the physical environment are seamlessly coupled - an idea very similar to the physical browsing systems of Want et al. (1999) and to the Cooltown (Kindberg et al., 2002). An important topic in their work is exploring the use of physical affordances within TUI design. The ambientROOM explores ambient, peripheral media and is outside the scope of this Chapter.

The transBOARD (Ishii and Ullmer, 1997) is an interactive surface in spirit of both the vision of Tangible Bits and Weiser's vision of boards as one class of ubiquitous computing devices. This kind of interactive surface absorbs information from the physical world and transforms it into digital information what can be distributed to other computers in the network. The transBOARD uses hyperCARDS, which are paper cards with barcodes to identify and store the strokes on the physical board as digital strokes. The cards can be attached onto the transBOARD and the when the strokes are recorded and stored, the barcode of the card is associated with the location of the stored data. The board contents can this way be saved, taken to other computers and replayed when the card is introduced to a suitably equipped computer again. Whereas the metaDESK is an interactive surface, which can also alter its contents, the transBOARD is a simple recording device. The interesting idea here from the point of view of physical browsing is "saving the contents of the board into a card", making the card a container for or a link to the information.

7. Closely Coupling Physical Objects with Digital Information

In their further work, Ullmer and Ishii (2001) re-defined tangible user interfaces to have no distinction between input and output. According to their definition, physical objects act both as physical representations and controls for digital information. With the new definition, tangible interfaces give physical form to digital information instead of just associating physical objects and digital information, employing physical artefacts both as representation and controls for computational media. The important distinction between tangible user interfaces and traditional input devices that have physical form - such as keyboards and mice - lies in that the traditional input devices hold little representational significance. In graphical user interfaces the information representation is separated to displays.

In physical selection, the control and representation (input and output) are not integrated as tightly as in this model for tangible user interfaces. This definition of tangible user interfaces separates TUIs somewhat from physical browsing. In physical browsing, the links are rarely controls, and the physical objects with tags only represent the information, but do not dynamically display it. The physical object acts only as an input token to the mobile terminal.

7.1 mediaBlocks

MediaBlocks (Ullmer et al., 1998) are small, electronically tagged wooden blocks that serve as phicons (physical icons) for the containment, transport and manipulation of offline media. They allow digital media to be rapidly stored into them from a media source such as a camera or a whiteboard and accessed later with a media display such as a printer or a projector. MediaBlocks thus allow "physical copy and paste" functionality. MediaBlocks do not store the media internally but instead they are augmented with tags that identify them, and the online information is accessed by referencing to it with a URL. MediaBlocks function as containers for online content and they can be understood as a physically embodied online media. Ullmer et al. see mediaBlocks as filling the user interface gap between physical devices, digital media and online content. They intended mediaBlocks as an interface for the exchange and manipulation of online content between diverse media devices and people.

Several tangible user interfaces described earlier have influenced the design of the mediaBlocks (Ullmer et al., 1998). Bricks (Fitzmaurice et al., 1995) were among the first phicons, although Bricks were not containers for digital content but instead were used to manipulate digital objects inside a single area, the Active Desk. In metaDESK (Ullmer and Ishii, 1997), phicons were used, not only as short cuts to digital information, but also as physical controls - for example rotating a phicon on the metaDESK rotated the displayed map. The functionality of mediaBlocks as storage devices for whiteboards draws from the transBOARD (Ishii and Ullmer, 1997), but instead of barcodes, electronic tags are used to link to the contents of the board. Ullmer and Ishii (1997) see RFID tags as a promising technology for realising the physical/digital bindings.

The contents of mediaBlocks remain online and that makes mediaBlock seem to have unlimited data storage capacity and rapid transfer speed when the block itself is moved around or the contents are copied just by copying the link to the online content (Ullmer et al., 1998). MediaBlocks can also contain streaming media. One role of the mediaBlocks is to support simple physical transport of media between different devices. Copying and pasting information is a commonly used function in graphical user interfaces and mediaBlocks are intended to provide the same functionality to physical media. Ullmer et al. have built slots for mediaBlocks in different devices such as whiteboards and printers but also on desktop computers.

In addition to adding mediaBlock interfaces to various existing devices, Ullmer et al. (1998) have built special devices for mediaBlocks. The media browser is used to navigate sequences of media elements stored in mediaBlocks. The media sequencer allows sequencing media by arranging mediaBlocks on its racks. This extended functionality is beyond the scope of this Chapter.

7.2 Other Removable Media Devices

In addition to mediaBlocks, other removable media devices exist, from floppy disks to more current DVDs and USB sticks, which were not ubiquitous technologies at the time of the development of mediaBlocks. Ullmer et al. (1998) claim that an important difference between these technologies and mediaBlocks is that mediaBlocks store only a link to the online media instead of recording the actual content onto the storage device.

However, nothing prevents us from storing links to online media on the other removable storage media, even onto floppy disks if we so desire. This way any storage device can support almost infinite space and varying bandwidths, just as Ullmer et al. (1998) describe MediaBlocks. They claim that other media transport devices are accessed indirectly through graphical or textual interaction. But what prevents us from "auto playing" for example video files from a USB stick when it is inserted into a projector? Ullmer et al. also mention the lack of disk drives on the different media sources and targets, but neither are there mediaBlock slots on commercial devices. Granted, it is not feasible to have for example DVD drives on many devices simply because of the physical dimensions and power requirements. However, many current media devices have USB ports and can record content to USB disks and read from them. Additionally, the devices Ullmer et al. augmented with mediaBlock slots, had only one such slot and only their custom-built browsers and sequencers took advantage of the possibility to contain many blocks at the same time. So, looking briefly, it seems that the mediaBlock concept would not be valid any more.

Still, mediaBlocks have a property that is extremely useful for physical interaction. They contained electronic tags that are small and cheap compared to current storage devices, allowing the use of one block for one link, thus making it possible to physically sort the blocks and extend the manipulation and sorting of digital content into the physical world just as Ullmer et al. (1998) intended. This is a powerful interaction paradigm and the mediaBlocks demonstrate it well.

8. Token-Based Access to Digital Information

Token-based access to digital information means accessing virtual data through a physical object. The paper of Holmquist et al. (1999) is among the first systematic analyses of systems that link physical objects with digital information. They defined token-based access to digital information as follows:

> *"A system where a physical object (token) is used to access some digital information that is stored outside the object, and where the physical representation in some way reflects the nature of the digital information it is associated with."*

Holmquist et al. (1999) enumerate the two components in a token-based interaction system: tokens and information faucets. Tokens are physical objects, which are used as representation of some digital information. In physical selection, the tokens correspond to the tagged physical objects and provide links to digital information related to the objects. Information faucets or displays are access points for the digital information associated with tokens. In physical selection, the faucet corresponds to the mobile terminal, but in theory, it can be any device capable of reading the tag and presenting the information it links to.

The physical objects (tokens in previous paragraph) are further classified into containers, tokens and tools (Holmquist et al., 1999). Tools are physical objects that are used to actively manipulate digital information. They usually represent some computational function. For example, in the Bricks system (Fitzmaurice et al., 1995), the physical bricks could be used as tools by attaching them onto virtual handles on a drawing application. The lenses in the metaDESK system (Ishii and Ullmer, 1997; Ullmer and Ishii, 1997) also correspond to tools. Tools do not have a direct counterpart in physical selection.

Containers are generic objects that can be associated with any type of digital information (Holmquist et al., 1999). They can be used to move information between different devices or platforms. The physical properties of a container do not reflect the nature of the digital information associated with it. For example, mediaBlocks (Ullmer et al., 1998) are containers, because by merely examining the physical form of a mediaBlock, it cannot be known what kind of media it contains.

Tokens are objects that physically resemble in some way the digital information they are associated with (Holmquist et al., 1999). That way the token is more closely tied to the information in represents than a container is. The models of buildings in Tangible GeoSpace (Ishii and Ullmer, 1997; Ullmer and Ishii, 1997) are an example of tokens.

In physical selection, it does not matter (technologically) whether the object is a container or token. In an ideal case the information and the object are connected, but nothing prevents a user from sticking completely unconnected tags and objects together.

The two most important interactions in a token-based system are access and association (Holmquist et al., 1999). The user has to be able to access the information contained in the token by presenting the token to an information faucet. Association means creating a link to the digital information and storing that link in the tag of the token so that it can be accessed later. Holmquist et al. note that it may be useful to allow associating more than one piece of information to a single token and they call this method overloading. When the token is brought to a faucet, the information presented to the user may then vary according to the context, or the user may get a list of the pieces of information stored in the token. This may present problems to the physical hyperlink visualisation, as is shown later.

Holmquist et al. (1999) note that it is important to design the tokens in a way that clearly displays what they represent and what can be done with them. This refers to taking into account the existing affordances of the existing physical object in question when linking it to some digital information, but it can also be applied if a specific "link container" is designed for a link.

Later, Ullmer and Ishii (2001) chose to describe the physical elements of tangible user interfaces in terms of tokens and reference frames. They consider a token a physically manipulatable element of a tangible interface, such as a metaDESK phicon (Ullmer and Ishii, 1997; Ishii and Ullmer, 1997). A reference frame is a physical interaction space in which these objects are used, such as the metaDESK surface. Ullmer and Ishii (2001) accept the term container for a symbolic token that contains some media (again, as in mediaBlocks (Ullmer et al., 1998)) and the term tool for a token that is used to represent digital operations or function. Considering physical selection, we are mostly interested in the terms container and token, which take approximately the same meaning as defined by Holmquist et al. (1999).

9. A Taxonomy for Tangible Interfaces

9.1 Definitions for Tangible User Interfaces

The term "tangible user interface" surfaced in Tangible Bits, in which Ishii and Ullmer (1997) defined it as a user interface that "augments the real physical world by coupling digital information to everyday physical objects and environments". In Emerging Frameworks for Tangible User Interfaces, Ullmer and Ishii (2001) re-defined tangible interfaces as a user interface that eliminates the distinction between input and output devices. However, they were willing to relax the definition to highlight some interaction methods.

Fishkin (2004) describes the basic paradigm of tangible user interfaces as follows: "a user uses their hands to manipulate some physical object(s) via physical gestures; a computer system detects this, alters its state, and gives feedback accordingly". According with his definition, Fishkin created a script that characterises TUIs:

1. Some input event occurs, typically a manipulation on some physical object by the user, and most often it is moving the object.
2. A computer senses the event and alters its state.
3. An output event occurs via a change in the physical nature of the object.

Fishkin (2004) describes how the script applies to metaDESK (Ullmer and Ishii, 1997). The user moves a physical model of a building on the surface of the metaDESK. The system senses the movement of the model and alters its internal state of the map. As output, it projects the new state of the map onto the display surface. Another of the examples Fishkin gives, is the photo cube by Want et al. (1999). Bringing the cube a specific face down onto the RFID reader is the input event. The computer reads the tag on the cube in the second phase of the script and in the third phase, displays the associated WWW page as an output event. The output event in Fishkin's script does not thus happen in the physical object that contains the tag, but it can occur in another object, the display terminal in the photo cube case.

Similarly, we can see that physical selection is a user interaction method in a tangible user interface. In the first phase of the script, the user manipulates the mobile terminal for example by bringing it close to a tag. The tag reader in the terminal reads ("senses") the tag and alters its state according to what it is programmed to do when the tag in question is read. In the output phase, an action linked to the tag is activated and the action is visible on the screen of the phone (for example a WWW page) or can be sensed in the environment (for example an electronic lock has opened).

As Fishkin (2004) himself notes, any input device can fit into this script. Even a keyboard in a desktop computer is a physical object. Manipulating it causes an input event to occur and the computer senses the event, altering its state and produces an output event on the computer screen. Therefore Fishkin does not characterise an interface as "tangible" or "not tangible", but introduces varying degrees of "tangibility".

9.2 The Taxonomy

Fishkin proposes a two-dimensional taxonomy for tangible interfaces. The axes of the taxonomy are embodiment and metaphor. Embodiment describes to what extent the user thinks of the state of computation as being inside the physical object, that is, how closely the input and output are tied together. Fishkin presents four levels of embodiment:

1. Full: the output device is the input device and the state of the device is fully embodied in the device. For example, in clay sculpting, any manipulation of the clay is immediately present in the clay itself.
2. Nearby: the output takes place near the input object. Fishkin mentions the Bricks (Fitzmaurice et al., 1995), metaDESK (Ullmer and Ishii, 1997) and photo cube (Want et al., 1999) as examples of this level.
3. Environmental: the output is around the user. For example, ambient media (Ishii and Ullmer, 1997) corresponds to environmental embodiment.
4. Distant: the output is away from the user, for example on another screen or in another room. Fishkin mentions a TV remote control as an example of this level.

Physical selection typically has embodiment levels from Full to Environmental. Often the output occurs in the mobile terminal itself (Full), but if the output device is rather seen to be the object the user selects with the terminal, the embodiment level is then Nearby. Physical selection can also cause actions around the user, in the environment. As the photo cube (Want et al., 1999) is very closely related to physical selection, we should probably take Fishkin's classification of the photo cube to correspond to the classification of physical selection, making therefore it Nearby.

Fishkin defines the second axis, metaphor, as "is the system effect of a user action analogous to the real-world effect of similar actions?" Fishkin divides his metaphor axis to two components: the metaphors of noun and verb. Thus, there are five levels of metaphor:

1. No Metaphor: the shape and manipulation of the object in TUI does not resemble an object in the real world. Fishkin mentions the command line interface as an example of this level.
2. Noun: the shape of input object in TUI is similar to an object in a real world. The tagged objects Want et al. (1999) developed correspond to this level of metaphor. For example, their augmented bookmarks resemble real bookmarks.
3. Verb: the input object in TUI acts like the object in the real world. The shapes of the objects are irrelevant.
4. Noun and Verb: the object looks and acts like the real world object, but they are still different objects. In traditional HCI, an example of this level is the drag and drop operation in the desktop metaphor.
5. Full: the virtual system is the physical system.

Physical selection can be seen to correspond roughly to the Noun metaphor. Again, we can safely assume Fishkin's classification of Want et al.'s examples as guidelines.

Advancing on the metaphor scale means less cognitive overhead as the object itself contains in its shape and function information about how it can be used in a tangible interface. However, decreasing the level of metaphor makes the object more generic and re-usable. Therefore, the level of metaphor should, if possible, be designed consciously to suit the task (Fishkin, 2004). For example, among the strengths of Bricks (Fitzmaurice et al., 1995) and transient WebStickers (Ljungstrand and Holmquist, 1999; Ljungstrand et al.,

2000) are the possibilities to contain any information, and to act as operators to any virtual functions.

9.3 Comparison to Containers, Tokens and Tools

Fishkin (2004) compares the containers, tokens and tools of Holmquist et al. (1999) taxonomy to his own. Containers are fully embodied in the Fishkin taxonomy and use the verb metaphor. The information is considered to be inside the container and moving the container moves the information. As long as a container does not employ the noun metaphor (the shape does not resemble the data), the container retains its generic and flexible nature and can contain any information.

Tokens are objects that physically resemble the data they contain and thus correspond to the noun metaphor (Fishkin, 2004; Holmquist et al., 1999). Like containers, they can also be used to move information around and therefore also correspond to the verb metaphor, making them span the metaphor scale from Noun and Verb to Full.

As physical selection is mostly about containers and tokens, it can be seen as having the embodiment of any level, but particularly from Full to Environmental, as noted earlier. The metaphor level of containers and tokens and thus tagged objects is something between only Noun or Verb, and Full. Fishkin's own analysis of how the taxonomy of Holmquist et al. maps to his taxonomy seems to be slightly ambiguous. Perhaps we can say that even the steps in Fishkin scales are not binary but different tangible interfaces can be seen as having different degrees of "Noun-ness" or "Nearbyness".

10. Conclusion

In this chapter, physical selection, an interaction task for mobile terminal based ubiquitous computing, has been discussed. Physical selection allows the user to select a tag-augmented physical entity for further interaction, combining digital information and services with real-world objects. This close coupling between physical and digital worlds resembles tangible user interfaces and in this chapter, physical selection has been examined as a form of TUI. Physical selection can be seen as one kind of tangible user interface, with different levels of embodiment and metaphor. The tagged physical objects map to tokens and containers in a taxonomy for token-based tangible user interfaces. Examining this interaction paradigm in this way allows us to better understand the tag and mobile terminal based interactions in the light of the previous work in tangible user interfaces.

11. References

English, W. K.; Engelbart, D., C. & Berman, M.L. (1967). Display-selection techniques for text manipulation. *IEEE Transactions on Human Factors in Electronics*, Vol. 8, No. 1, 5–15, ISSN: 0096-249X

Fishkin, K.P. (2004). A taxonomy for and analysis of tangible interfaces. *Personal and Ubiquitous Computing*, Vol. 8, No. 5, 347–358, ISSN: 1617-4909

Fitzmaurice, G.W.; Ishii, H. & Buxton, W. (1995). Bricks: Laying the foundations for graspable user interfaces, *Proceedings of CHI'95*, pp. 442–449, ISBN: 0-201-84705-1, Denver, Colorado, United States, May 1995, ACM Press/Addison-Wesley Publishing Co., New York

Holmquist, L. E.; Redström, J. & Ljungstrand, P. (1999). Token-based access to digital information, *Proceedings of the 1st International Symposium on Handheld and Ubiquitous Computing*, pp. 234–245, ISBN: 978-3-540-66550-2, Karlsruhe, Germany, September 1999, Springer-Verlag, Berlin

Ishii, H. & Ullmer, B. (1997). Tangible bits: towards seamless interfaces between people, bits and atoms, *Proceedings of the SIGCHI Conference on Human Factors in Computing Systems*, pp. 234–241, ISBN: 0-89791-802-9, Atlanta, Georgia, United States, March 1997, ACM Press, New York

Kay, A. & Goldberg, A. (1977). Personal dynamic media. *Computer*, Vol. 10, No. 3, 31–41, ISSN: 0018-9162

Kindberg, T.; Barton, J.; Morgan, J.; Becker, G.; Caswell, D.; Debaty, P.; Gopal, G.; Frid, M.; Krishnan, V.; Morris, H.; Schettino, J.; Serra, B. & Spasojevic, M. (2002). People, places, things. *Mobile Networks and Applications*, Vol. 7, No. 5, 365–376, ISSN: 1383-469X

Ljungstrand, P. & Holmquist, L. E. (1999). WebStickers: using physical objects as WWW bookmarks, *Proceedings of the CHI'99 Extended Abstracts on Human Factors in Computing Systems*, pp. 332–333, ISBN: 1-58113-158-5, Pitssburgh, Pennsylvania, United States, May 1999, ACM Press, New York

Ljungstrand, P., Redström, J. & Holmquist, L. E. (2000). WebStickers: using physical tokens to access, manage and share bookmarks to the web, *Proceedings of DARE 2000 on Designing Augmented Reality Environments*, pp. 23–31, Elsinore, Denmark, ACM Press, New York

Smith, D.; Irby, C.; Kimball, R.; Verplank, B. & Harslem, E. (1982). Designing the Star user interface, *Byte* 4/1982, 242–282, ISSN: 0360-5280

Ullmer, B. & Ishii, H. (1997). The metaDESK: models and prototypes for tangible user interfaces, *Proceedings of the 10th Annual ACM Symposium on User Interface Software and Technology*, pp. 223–232, ISBN: 0-89791-881-9, Banff, Alberta, Canada, October 1997, ACM Press, New York

Ullmer, B.; Ishii, H. & Glas, D. (1998) mediaBlocks: physical containers, transports and controls for online media, *Proceedings of the 25th Annual Conference on Computer Graphics and Interactive Techniques*, pp. 379–386, ISBN: 0-89791-999-8, ACM Press, New York

Ullmer, B. & Ishii, H. (2001). Emerging frameworks for tangible user interfaces, In: *Human-Computer Interaction in the New Millennium*, Carroll, J. M. (Ed.), 579–601, Addison–Wesley, ISBN: 978-0201704471, Boston

Välkkynen, P.; Pohjanheimo, L. & Ailisto, H. (2006). Physical browsing, In: *Ambient Intelligence, Wireless Networking, and Ubiquitous Computing*, Vasilakos, T. & Pedrycz W (Ed.), 61-81, Artech House, ISBN: 978-1580539630, Boston

Want, R.; Fishkin, K. P.; Gujar, A. & Harrison, B. L. (1999). Bridging physical and virtual worlds with electronic tags, *Proceedings of the SIGCHI Conference on Human factors in Computing Systems,* pp. 370–377, ISBN: 0-201-48559-1, Pitssburgh, Pennsylvania, United States, May 1999, ACM Press, New York

Wellner, P. Interacting with paper on the DigitalDesk, *Communications of the ACM,* Vol. 36, No. 7, 87–96, ISSN: 0001-0782

30

Geometry Issues of Gaze Estimation

Arantxa Villanueva, Juan J. Cerrolaza and Rafael Cabeza
Public University of Navarra
Spain

1. Introduction

Video-oculography (VOG) is a non-intrusive method used to estimate gaze. The method is based on a remote camera(s) that provides images of the eyes that are processed by a computer to estimate the point at which the subject is gazing in the area of interest. Normally, infrared (IR) light-emitting diodes (LEDs) are used in the system, as this light is not visible to humans. The objective of the light source is to increase the quality of the image and to produce reflections on the cornea. These reflections can be observed in the acquired images (see Figure 1) and represent useful features for gaze estimation.

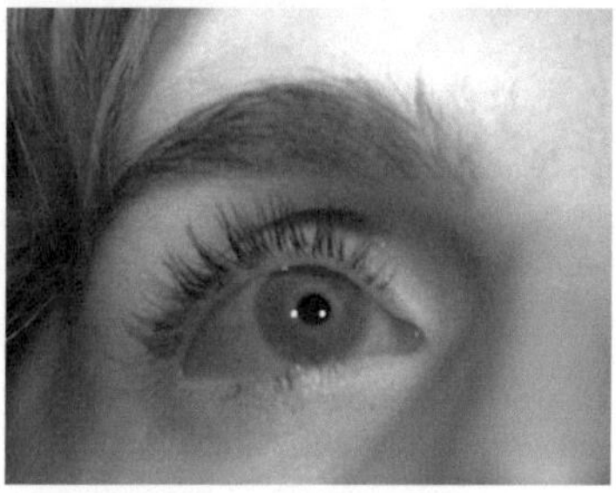

Figure 1. Image of the eye captured by the camera. The corneal reflections are the bright dots in the image

During the last several decades, gaze tracking systems based on VOG have been employed in two main fields: interactive applications and diagnostic applications. Interactive applications permit users to control the position of the mouse on the screen and the activation of items by their gaze, thus allowing highly impaired users with controlled eye movement to interact with the computer and their environment. Diagnostic applications are devoted to eye movement analysis when executing tasks such as web page browsing or reading, which have interesting applications in the fields of psychology and market research. However, gaze tracking technologies are still not useful for a large part of society. New commercial applications, such as in video games and the automotive industry, would attract more companies and general interest in these systems, but several technical obstacles still need to be overcome. For instance, the image processing task is still problematic in outdoor scenarios, in which rapid light variations can occur. In addition, the head position constraints of these systems considerably reduce the potential applications of this technology. The accuracy of gaze tracking systems is, to a large extent, compromised by head position since any head movement requires the system to readjust to preserve accuracy; i.e., gaze estimation accuracy can vary as the head moves.

Gaze estimation is defined as the function of converting the image processing results (image features) into gaze (gaze direction/gazed point) using a mathematical equation. The usual procedure in any gaze tracking session is to first perform a calibration of the user. The calibration consists of asking the user to fixate on a set of known points on the screen. Calibration adapts the gaze estimation function to the user's position and system configuration. The mathematical method (gaze estimation function) used determines the dependence of the system accuracy on head position, i.e. how the accuracy varies as the head moves.

This work is focused on exploring the connection between the image of the eye and gaze, and it constructs a mathematical model for the gaze estimation problem.

A more detailed description of the problem and a review of relevant works on gaze estimation are presented in Section 2. Section 3 presents the 3-D eyeball model to be used in the rest of the chapter and establishes relevant terms, variables, and definitions. Section 4 introduces some of the most relevant features of the eye image, such as glint(s), pupil centre, and pupil shape. Alternative models are constructed and evaluated based on these image features. The proposed gaze estimation model is described in Section 5. Section 6 introduces the experimental results of the model. Conclusions and future research are described Sections 7 and 8, respectively.

2. State of the art

The 3-D direction of gaze is defined as the line of sight (LoS). The point of regard (PoR) is determined as the 2-D intersection between the LoS and the area of interest, e.g. the screen. A visual fixation is defined as a stable position of the LoS (visual axis) that presents a visual angular dispersion below 1°. Hence, most gaze-tracking system designers try to achieve gaze estimation errors below 1° (see Figure 2).

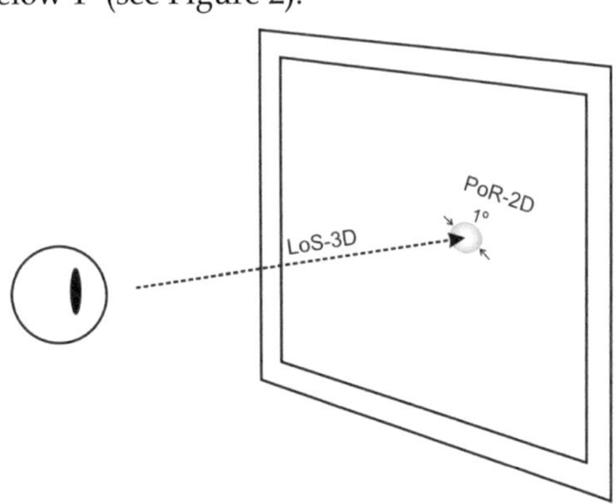

Figure 2. The LoS denotes gaze direction in 3-D space. PoR is the gazed point in 2-D. A fixation is defined as a quasi-stable position of LoS with an angular dispersion below 1°

Gaze estimation methods can be divided into two main groups: interpolation methods and geometry-based methods. Interpolation methods use general-purpose polynomial expressions, such as linear or quadratic expressions, to describe the connection between image features and gaze. These functions are based on unknown coefficients to be

determined by calibration. Although simplicity is the primary advantage of interpolation methods, the lack of control over system behaviour and system errors is a significant disadvantage. Furthermore, system accuracy can decrease as result of subject's movement from the calibration position (Cerrolaza et al., 2008) (Morimoto & Mimica, 2005).
Enhancing gaze estimation, in terms of accuracy and head movement tolerance, is one of the most sought-after objectives in gaze-estimation technology. Geometry-based methods investigate gaze estimation models that allow for free head movement, and they are based on mathematical and geometric principles. These methods provide relevant information about the systems, such as the minimal hardware required, the minimal image features and the minimal user calibration for gaze estimation purposes (hereafter, calibration refers to user calibration unless otherwise stated). Recently, remarkable studies have been published in this area. One of the most relevant (Shih & Liu, 2004) is based on a stereo system and one calibration point. (Hennessey et al., 2006) and (Guestrin & Eizenman, 2006) demonstrate geometric gaze estimation methods using a single camera and four and nine calibration points, respectively. More recent studies have been presented by (Villanueva & Cabeza, 2007) and (Guestrin & Eizenman, 2008). The aforementioned methods employ 3-D eye models and calibrated scenarios (calibrated camera, light sources, and camera positions) to estimate LoS. Interesting approaches have been carried out in non-calibrated scenarios using projective plane properties for PoR estimation as shown in (Hansen & Pece, 2005) and (Yoo & Chung, 2005).
The current work focuses on 3-D (LoS) gaze estimation models based on system geometry. Alternative models for gaze (LoS) estimation are constructed, and their properties are evaluated, including hardware used, image features, head pose constraints, and calibration requirements. This work seeks to develop a gaze estimation method with minimal hardware, allowing free head movement and minimal calibration requirements.

3. Eye Model

Figure 3 depicts the schematic system, which is composed of a subject's eye, one camera, and one infrared light source. Of all the elements of the system, the eye is the most complex one. Geometry-based gaze estimation methods employ eye models that are highly simplified to reduce the complexity introduced by consideration of physiology and eyeball kinematics. Although variations exist between the models proposed by researchers and there is no unified model, some fundamental aspects of the eyeball geometry have been agreed upon during the last few years. This model is detailed in Figure 3.
The cornea is considered a sphere with its centre at C and a corneal radius of r_c. The pupil is a circle with radius r and centre E. The pupil centre is perpendicularly connected to C at a distance of h, and both points, together with the eyeball centre A, are contained in the optical axis of the eye. The elements of the system are referenced to the camera projection centre O. The LoS can be approximated by the visual axis of the eye, the line connecting the fovea and the nodal point (approximated by C). The fovea is a small area with a diameter of about 1.2° located in the retina, and it contains a high density of cones that are responsible for high visual detail discrimination and an individual's central vision. When looking at a particular point, the eye is oriented in such a way that the observed object projects itself onto the fovea. Due to the offset of the fovea with respect to the back pole of the eyeball, an angular offset exists between the optical and visual axes, with horizontal and vertical components β (~5°) and α (2° to 3°), respectively (Guestrin & Eizenman, 2006). Several works, including the

present one, reduce this offset to just the horizontal value, i.e. β. Optical and visual axes rotate in an imaginary plane with respect to the camera when looking at different points. Once the optical axis has been determined, the 3-D position of this plane can be calculated by using Donder's and Listing's Laws and applying the "false torsion" principle stated as:

$$\sin\alpha_o = \frac{\sin\theta_0 \sin\varphi_o}{1+\cos\theta_0 \cos\varphi_o}, \tag{1}$$

where (θ_0, φ_0) are the vertical and horizontal rotation angles performed by the optical axis and α_0 is the torsion angle around itself. In this manner, once the position of the plane is determined by (θ_0, φ_0, α_0), the visual axis position is calculated from the optical axis by applying the angular offset β. In the suggested eye model, the optical axis of the eye is calculated as the line connecting *C* and *E*.

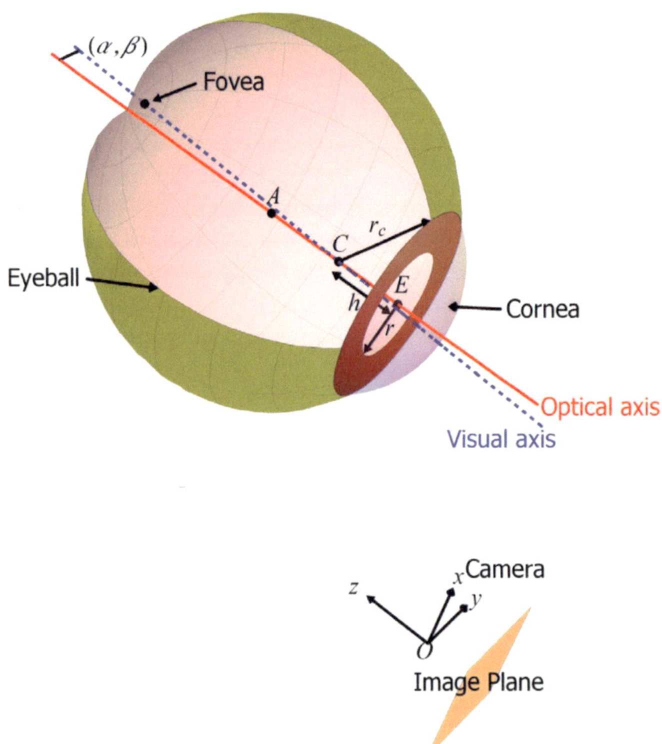

Figure 3. Eye model for gaze estimation

In the simplified model of the eyeball, the cornea is reduced to a single surface, and the aqueous humour is assumed to be homogeneous. The reflective properties of the cornea influence the position of the glint(s) in the image, while its refractive properties modify the pupil image. According to Refraction Law, corneal refraction deviates light reflected off the retina and crossing the pupil prior to reaching the VOG camera (Villanueva & Cabeza, 2008a). Figure 4 shows the 3-D pupil inside the cornea and the pupil shape after refraction. The pupil image is not the projection of the pupil but the projection of the refracted pupil.

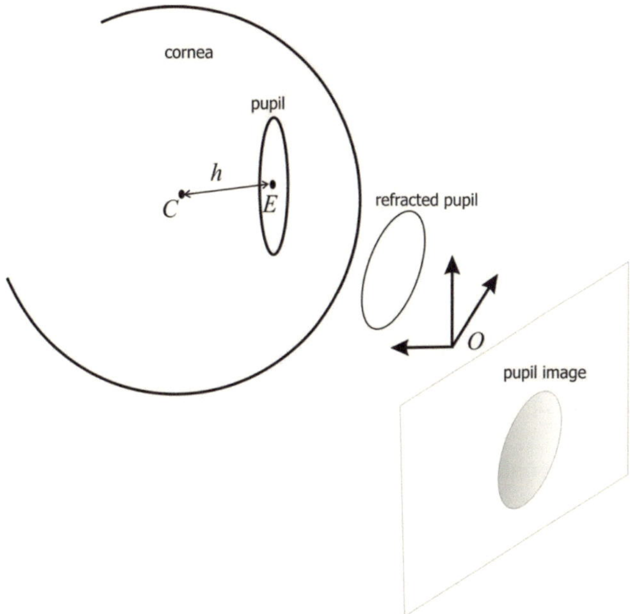

Figure 4. The pupil image is deviated due to corneal refraction when crossing the corneal sphere

Corneal refraction alters the pupil size in the image and its position with respect to the limbus, i.e. the corneal-sclera junction. Figure 5 shows the difference between the projected pupil and the real image of the pupil (refracted and projected).

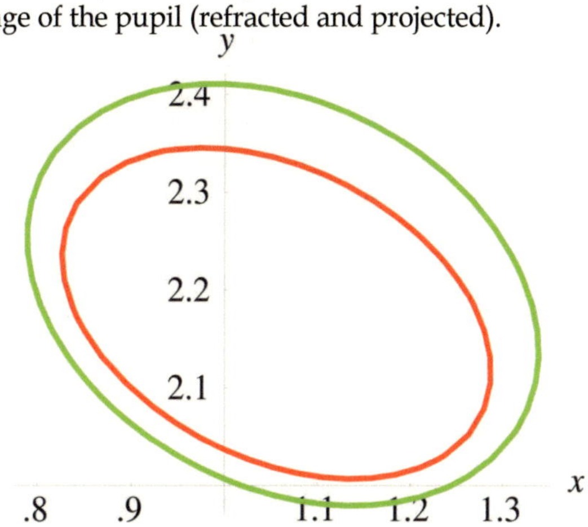

Figure 5. Comparison of the perspective projection of the pupil (smaller ellipse) and the combined refraction and projection of the pupil (larger ellipse)

4. Models for Gaze Estimation

According to the eye model described in Section 3, alternative gaze estimation methods have been proposed based on different image features. The procedure selected to accomplish the work in the simplest manner is to analyze each of the alternative features that can be extracted from the image separately. In this manner, a review of the most commonly used features employed by alternative gaze tracking systems is carried out. The constructed models can be categorized into three groups: models based on points, models based on shapes, and hybrid models combining points and shapes. The systems of the first group are based on extracting image features which consist of single points of the image and combining them in different ways. We define a point as a specific pixel described by its row and column in the image. Thus, the following models make up this group: the model based on the centre of the pupil, the model based on the glint, the model based on multiple glints, the model based on the centre of the pupil and the glint, and the model based on the centre of the pupil and multiple glints. On the other hand, the models based on shapes involve more image information; basically, these types of systems take into account the geometrical form of the pupil in the image. This group contains one model, the model based on pupil contour. The models of the third group combine both points and shapes to sketch the system. This group contains the model based on the pupil ellipse and glint, as well as the model based on the pupil ellipse and multiple glints. Figure 6 shows a classification of the constructed models.

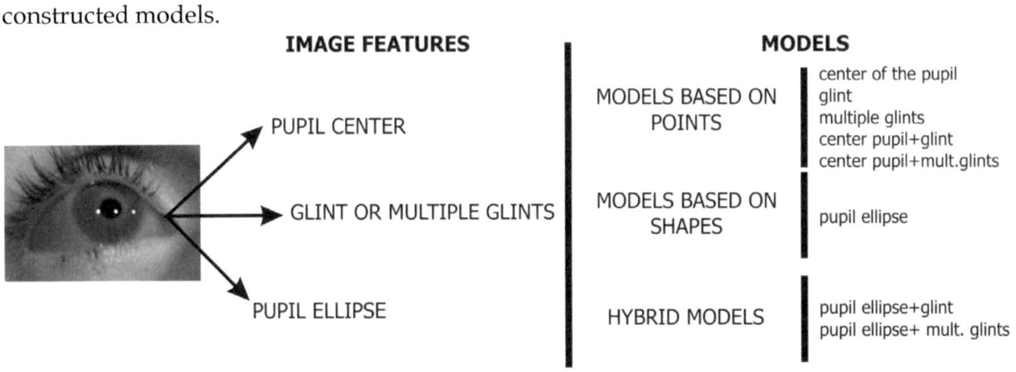

Figure 6. Model classification according to image features

Three of the most relevant features of the image of the eye are selected to be analyzed as potential features for gaze estimation models: the glint, the centre of the pupil, and the shape of the pupil.

4.1 The glint

The glint or corneal reflection in the image is denoted as G_{img} and is a consequence of the IR light reflecting off of the corneal surface and reaching the camera. According to Reflection Law, given a light source denoted as L_1, the incident ray, the reflected ray, and the normal line at the point of incidence on the corneal sphere are coplanar. Consequently, the corneal centre C, the projection centre of the camera O, the glint in the image G_{1img}, and the light source L_1 are contained in the same plane (see Figure 7a).

If an additional light source denoted as L_2 is introduced into the system, a new plane can be determined as a function of the new light source and glint, G_{2img}. The intersection between these planes is a 3-D line containing the projection centre of the camera O and the cornea centre C (see Figure 7b). Adding more light sources does not provide further information to determine the cornea centre, but rather just the aforementioned 3-D line.

In the system proposed by (Shih & Liu, 2004) an additional camera is introduced to the system. The combination of each camera with the pair of light sources results in a new 3-D line containing the new camera projection centre and C. The intersection between these lines determines the cornea centre C.

In a single camera model, point C can be obtained using two light sources if the corneal radius r_c is provided, as shown in studies (Guestrin & Eizenman, 2006) and (Villanueva & Cabeza, 2007).

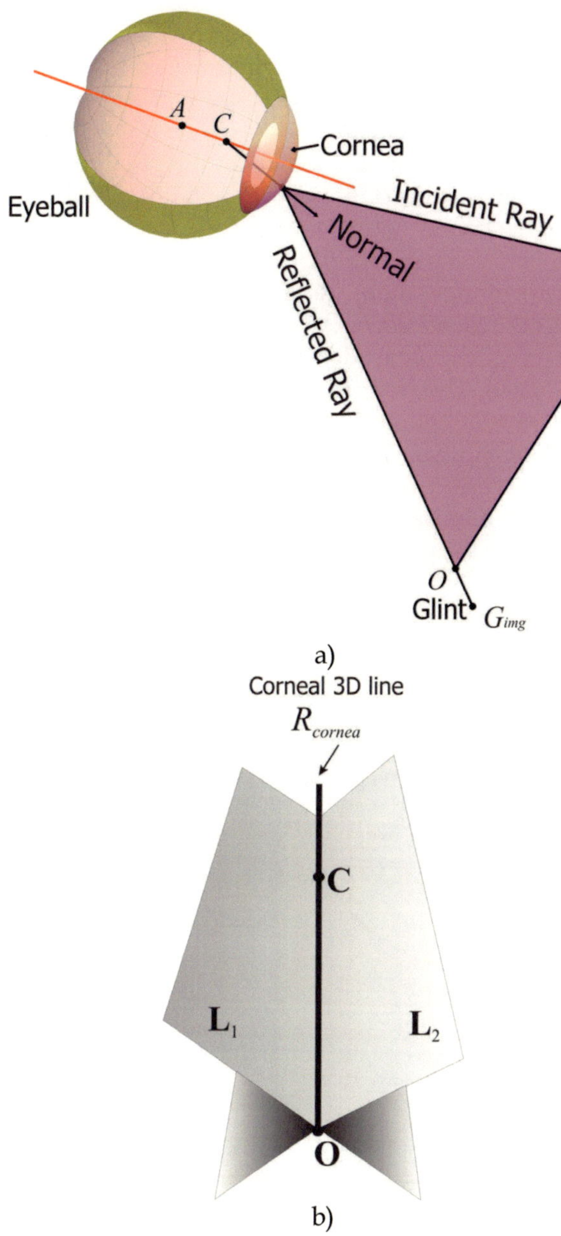

Figure 7. a) Incident ray, reflected ray, and the normal line at the point of incidence are coplanar. The light source, L_1, the cornea centre, C, and the camera projection centre, O, are contained in the plane. b) If a second light source is included, two planes are created, one for each of the light sources. The intersection of the planes determines a 3D line containing the cornea centre C and the camera projection centre, O, denoted as *Rcornea*

4.2 The centre of the pupil

Although no formal proofs about the elliptical nature of the pupil image have been provided in the literature, pupil shape is normally approximated as an ellipse. The centre of the pupil shape E_{img} is generally used as a valid feature for gaze estimation purposes. This point is normally considered to be the image of point E. According to the eye model proposed, this assumption introduces two errors into the method. First, the perspective effect of the camera produces a translation in the image between the projection of point E and the centre of the pupil shape. Second, and more importantly, as mentioned in Section 3, corneal refraction produces a translation and scaling of the pupil image with respect to its projection. It could be assumed that the centre of the pupil image is the refraction of the ray starting in E. However, refraction is not a linear process and errors are introduced. The perspective effect is negligible compared to the deviation due to refraction (errors $>1^{\circ}$ can arise depending on system configuration). Recent studies (Villanueva & Cabeza, 2008a) demonstrate that errors due to refraction can be compensated for after an adequate calibration process. However, the dependence of the accuracy on variable calibration conditions should be evaluated. The work (Guestrin & Eizenman, 2006) showed a method based on the aforementioned assumption for the centre of the pupil and calibrated using 3x3 calibration with acceptable accuracies. This model makes a previous determination of the corneal centre, C. Once C has been determined, and assuming that r_c is known, E_{img} is back-projected from the image and refracted at the corneal surface (see Figure 8). The estimated pupil centre, E', is calculated as the point contained in the refracted ray at a distance h from C.

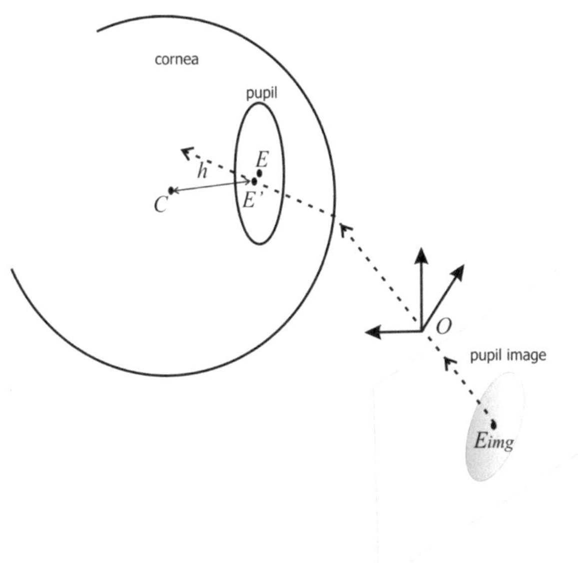

Figure 8. The approximation is based on the assumption that the pupil center is contained in the refracted line of the pupil centre in the image, i.e. $E'=E$. The error is due to the fact that corneal refraction is not linear and deviates each ray differently, hence $E' \neq E$

The system developed by (Shih & Liu, 2004) also assumes that the centre of the pupil image is the image of point E after refraction, but it uses a stereo system. According to Refraction Law, the incident ray, refracted ray, and the normal at the point of incidence are coplanar.

Consequently, if the centre of the pupil in the image E_{img} is assumed to be the projection of the ray coming from E, after refraction E (the incident ray), E_{img} (the refracted ray) and C (the normal ray) are contained in the same plane. This plane can be calculated as the plane containing C, O, and E_{img}. For each camera, a plane can be derived containing C and E (E'), the optical axis of the eye. The intersection of the two planes determines the optical axis of the eye. The method is calibrated using a single point, which makes the error due to refraction more relevant.

Regardless of the number of cameras used, both methods require a previous estimation of the corneal centre C, thus the pupil centre by itself does not provide sufficient information for optical axis estimation.

4.3 The shape of the pupil

As mentioned before, the pupil shape is the result of the refraction and projection of pupil contour. The intersection of each ray of the pupil contour with the corneal sphere suffers a deviation in its path before reaching the camera. Starting from the image, the pupil contour is sampled, and each point is back-projected from the image into 3D space. Assuming that C and r_c are known, the intersection of each ray with the corneal sphere is found, and the refracted line is calculated, using the Refraction Law equation. In this manner, we derive the distribution of pupil contour rays inside the cornea as shown in Figure 9. The pupil is contained in a plane denoted by Π that has C-E as a normal vector and is at a distance h from C. The pupil centre is calculated as the point at the centre of a circle derived from the intersections of the refracted rays with the plane Π. Alternative implementations of this method can be found in different recent works (Beymer & Flickner, 2003) (Ohno & Mukawa, 2004) (Hennesey et al., 2006) (Villanueva & Cabeza, 2007).

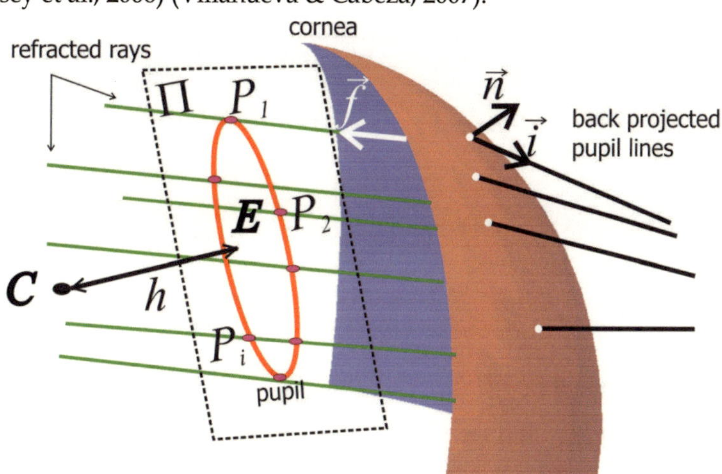

Figure 9. Cornea and pupil after refraction. E is the centre of a circumference formed by the intersections of the plane Π with the refracted lines. The plane Π is perpendicular to (C-E) and the distance between pupil and cornea centres is h

According to the proposed eye model, this method introduces corneal refraction in the method, hence no approximations are assumed, and zero error is produced. As in the previous section, to apply the model based on the shape of the pupil, knowledge about the cornea centre is required, and thus the pupil shape by itself does not permit optical axis estimation.

5. Proposed Gaze Estimation Model

Based on the above analysis, it is concluded that, models based on points and shapes do not allow for optical axis estimation. To estimate the pupil centre of the eye, *E*, a previous estimation of the corneal centre *C* is needed. Since the corneal centre information is provided by the glints and the pupil centre *E* is given by the pupil image, a hybrid model is needed for optical axis estimation in a head pose variant scenario, i.e. a model combining glints and the pupil as image features.

As shown in Section 4.1, two light sources are needed to estimate *C*. The proposed model attempts to minimise the hardware used, and although the method using the stereo system provides a geometric solution to estimate the optical axis (Shih & Liu, 2004), the proposed model focuses on a single camera system. The proposed framework uses a single calibrated camera and two light sources L_1 and L_2 with known positions with respect to the camera projection centre. According to the aforementioned analysis, the optical axis estimation is performed in two steps.

5.1 Center of the cornea estimation

According to the analysis presented in Section 4.1, the following equations can be stated:

- As shown in Figure 7a, given two light sources, L_1 and L_2, two corneal reflections will be generated in the camera, named G_{1img} and G_{2img}, respectively. Each light source, L_i, will define a plane, $\prod_{Li}$, containing the projection centre of the camera *O*. These planes can be defined as:

$$\prod_{L_1} = L_1 \times G_{1img} ; \prod_{L_2} = L_2 \times G_{2img} . \tag{2}$$

- The cornea centre C is contained in both planes, which can be stated as:

$$C \cdot \prod_{L_1} = C \cdot \prod_{L_2} = 0 . \tag{3}$$

- The Reflection Law can be applied for each one of the light sources as:

$$r_i = 2(n_i \cdot l_i)n_i - l_i \text{, } i=1,2, \tag{4}$$

where r_i is the unit vector in the G_{1img} direction, l_i is the unit vector in the (L_i - G_i) direction, and n_i is the normal vector at the point of incidence in the (G_i - C) direction. G_i denotes the incidence point at the corneal surface.

Assuming that r_c is known, G_i can be expressed as a function of C from:

$$\left| G_i - C \right| = r_c \text{, } i=1,2. \tag{5}$$

By solving equations (3) to (5), the cornea centre is determined numerically (Villanueva & Cabeza 2008b). This method requires knowledge of the corneal radius r_c to be obtained by means of calibration.

5.2 Center of the pupil estimation

Assuming that the cornea parameters C and r_c are known as calculated in previous section, the following equations can be stated:

- The pupil contour is sampled, and each point is back-projected from the image into 3-D space. The intersection of each ray with the corneal sphere is found, and the refracted line is calculated using the Refraction Law equation. Given a point k (k=1..n) of the pupil contour, the refracted ray can be calculated as:

$$f_k = \left[\frac{n_a}{n_b}\right]\left[i_k - \left((i_k \cdot n_k) + \sqrt{\left(\tfrac{n_a}{n_b}\right)^2 - 1 + (i_k \cdot n_k)^2}\right) n_k\right], k=1,..n, \tag{6}$$

  where n_a and n_b are the refractive indices of air and the aqueous humor in contact with the back surface of the cornea, f_k and i_k represent the refracted light inside the cornea and the incident light directions, respectively, and n_k is the surface normal vector at the point of incidence (see Figure 9).
- The pupil is contained in a plane Π having $(E - C)$ as the normal vector of the plane at a distance h from C. Given a 3-D point, (x, y, z), with respect to the camera, the plane Π can be formulated by:

$$\frac{(E-C)}{h} \cdot [(x,y,z) - C] + h = 0. \tag{7}$$

- After Π has been defined, the intersections of the plane with the refracted lines derive a set of points, P_k, k=1..n, that represent the contour of a circumference whose centre is E. If $|P_k - E|$ represents the distance between P_k and E, this statement can be expressed as follows:

$$|P_i - E| = |P_j - E| \quad \text{where } i \neq j, (i,j=1..n). \tag{8}$$

- The pupil centre is determined numerically by solving equation (8) to find the global optimum (Villanueva & Cabeza, 2008b). The method requires knowledge of the distance between corneal and pupil centers h to be obtained by means of calibration.

5.3 LoS estimation

Once the optical axis of the eye is determined as the line connecting C and E, gaze direction (LoS) is estimated by calculating the visual axis. Knowing the optical axis in 3-D permits calculation of the rotation angles (θ_o, φ_o) of this line with respect to the camera; thus, the additional torsion α_o is calculated by means of (1). Defining the visual axis direction (for the left eye) with respect to C as $(-\sin\beta, 0, \cos\beta)$ permits us to calculate the LoS direction with respect to the camera by means of the Euclidean coordinate transformation expressed as:

$$C + R_{\alpha_o} R_{\theta_o \varphi_o} . (-\sin\beta, 0, \cos\beta)^T, \tag{9}$$

where $R_{\theta_o\varphi_o}$ is the rotation matrix calculated as a function of the vertical and horizontal rotations of the vector $(C-E)$ with respect to the camera coordinate system, and R_{α_o} represents the rotation matrix of the torsion around the optical axis needed to deduce the final eye orientation. The computation of the PoR as the intersection of the gaze line with the screen plane can be calculated if the screen position is known. This method requires knowledge of β, which is obtained by means of calibration.

5.4 Calibration

The model just described requires specific subject's parameters to determine gaze direction. These parameters, i.e., h, r_c, and β, are obtained using calibration. The subject is asked to observe known points on the screen, and the model parameters are adjusted in order to minimise the error for the calibration points. The equations used for LoS estimation ((3) to (5) and (8)) are also used for calibration purposes. It can be theoretically demonstrated that for the proposed method, one calibration point is sufficient to obtain the necessary model parameters, i.e. h, r_c and β (Villanueva and Cabeza, 2008b).

6. Experiments

Ten users were selected to test the model. The working distance was selected as between 400 and 500 mm from the camera. The subjects had little or no experience with the system. They were asked to fixate on each test point for a period of time. Figure 10 shows the selected fixation marks uniformly distributed through the gazing area, the positions of which are known with respect to the camera. The position in mm for each point is shown.

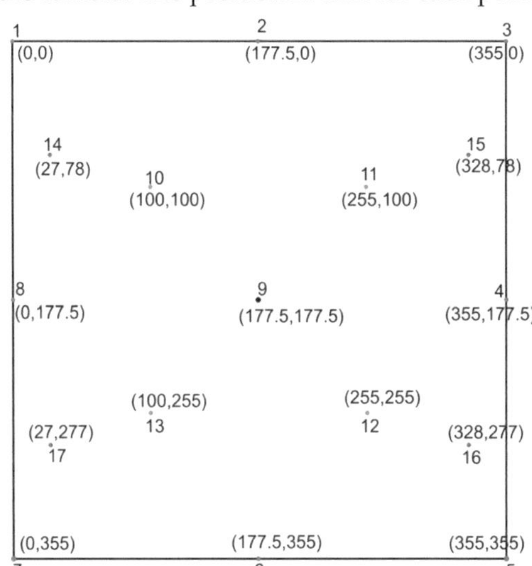

Figure 10. Test sheet

The errors obtained are compared with the limit value of 1° of the visual angle, which is a system performance indicator. The users selected the eye with which they felt more comfortable. They were allowed to move the head between fixation points and could take breaks during the experiment. However, they were asked to maintain a fixed head position during each test point (ten images). The constructed model presents the following requirements:

- The camera must be calibrated.
- Light sources and screen positions must be known with respect to the camera
- The subject eyeball parameters r_c, β, and h must be calibrated.

The images were captured with a calibrated Hamamatsu C5999 camera and digitised by a Matrox Meteor card with a resolution of 640x480 (RS-170). The LEDs used for lighting have a spectrum centred at 850 nm. The whole system is controlled by a dual processor Pentium system at 1.7 GHz with 256 MB of RAM. It has been demonstrated theoretically that system accuracy can be considerably influenced by a non-accurate glint position estimation. To reduce this effect, the number of light sources can be increased, thus compensating for the error by averaging the value of the cornea centre (Villanueva & Cabeza, 2007). Four LEDs were selected to produce the needed multiple glints. They were located in the lower part, and their positions with respect to the camera were calculated, which considerably reduced the possibility of misleading partial occlusions of the glints by eyelids when looking at different points of the screen because, in this way, the glints in the image appear in the lower half of the pupil.

6.1 Gaze Estimation

Once the hardware was defined, and in order to apply the constructed model based on the shape of the pupil and the glint positions, some individual subject eyeball characteristics needed to be calculated (r_c, β, and h). To this end, a calibration was performed. The constructed model based on multiple glints and pupil shape theoretically permits determination of these data by means of a single calibration mark and applying the model already described in Section 3. Given the PoR as the intersection of the screen and the LoS, model equations (2)-(4) and (6)-(8) can be applied to find the global optima for the parameters r_c, h, and β that minimise the difference between the model output and the real mark position. Figure 11 shows the steps for the subject calibration.

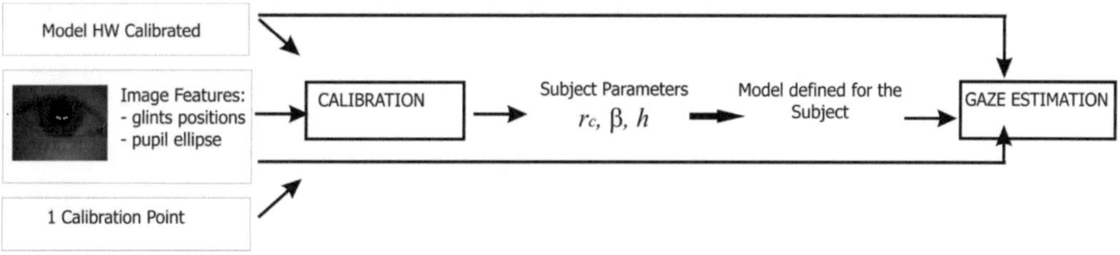

Figure 11. The individual calibration permits us to extract the physical parameters of the subject's eyeball using one calibration point, the captured image, and gaze estimation model information

In theory, one calibration point is sufficient to estimate a subject's personal parameters (Villanueva & Cabeza, 2008b). However, in practice, and to increase confidence in the obtained values, three fixations were performed for each subject, and the mean values were used for the eye parameters in the experiment. For each subject, the three points with lower variances in the extracted glint positions were selected for calibration. Each point among the three permits estimation of values for h, β, and r_c (Villanueva & Cabeza, 2007). Once the system and the subject were calibrated, the performance of the model was tested for two, three, and four LEDs. Figure 12 shows the obtained results. For each user, black dots represent the real values for the fixations. The darkest marks are the gaze points estimated using four LEDs, whereas the lighter marks represent the gaze points estimated using three LEDs. Finally, the medium grey marks are the estimations performed using two LEDs.

Corneal refraction effects are more important as eye rotation increases. In Figure 12, no significant differences can be found between the error for corner points and other points. If the model did not adequately take refraction into account, higher errors would be expected

for the corners. However, the accuracy does not depend on eye rotation, and the model is not affected by an increase in the refraction effect, since this is compensated for.
Table 1 shows a quantitative evaluation of the model competence for two, three, and four LEDs. For each subject, the average error for the 17 fixation marks was calculated in visual degrees since this is the most significant measurement of the model performance. It is clear that the model with four LEDs has the smallest errors. On average, the model with two LEDs has an error of 1.08°, the model with three LEDs 0.89°, and the model with four 0.75°. Therefore, on average, the models with three and four LEDs render acceptable accuracy values. As expected, an increase in the number of light sources results in an improvement of the system accuracy.

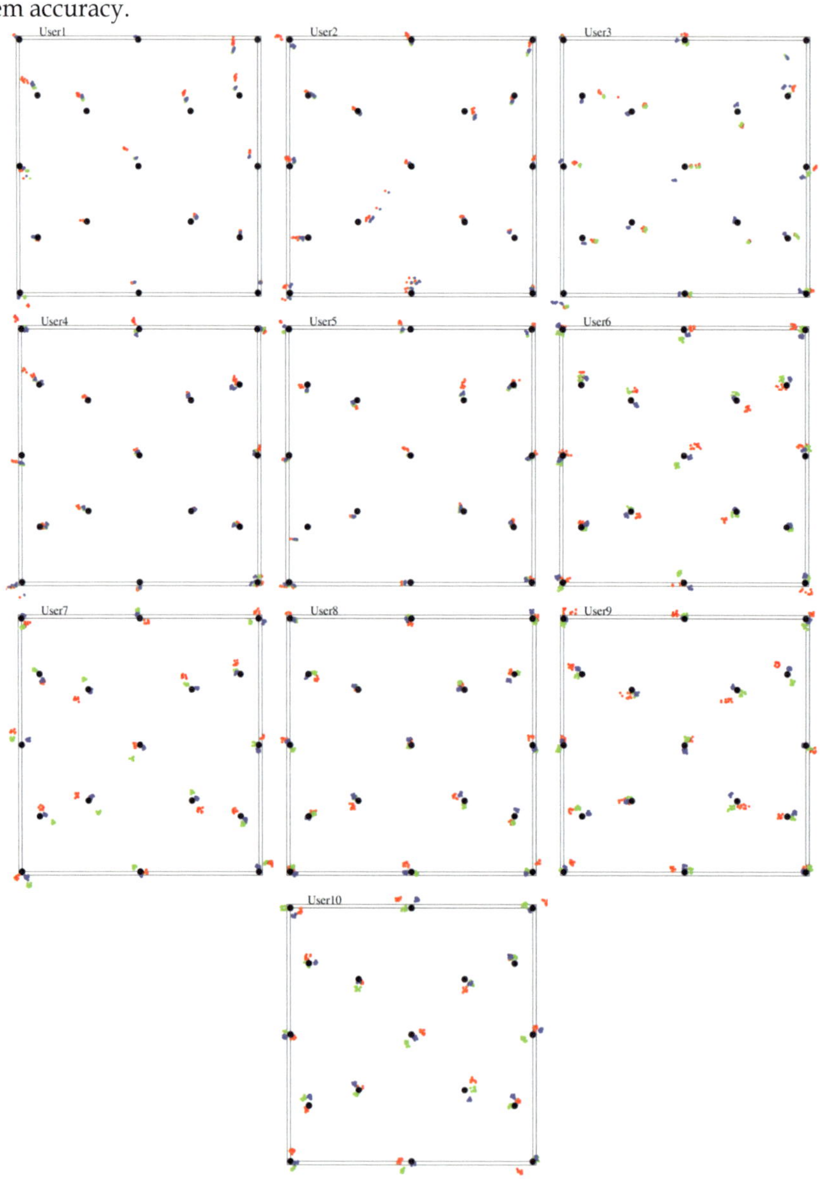

Figure 12. Results obtained by the model for users 1 to 10

Subject	1	2	3	4	5	6	7	8	9	10	Mean
2 LEDs	1.47	0.85	1.46	0.90	0.92	0.97	1.24	0.78	1.19	1.06	1.08
3 LEDs	1.06	0.80	1.35	0.58	0.75	0.78	1.20	0.79	0.74	0.86	0.89
4 LEDs	1.04	0.76	1.01	0.62	0.72	0.71	0.62	0.65	0.59	0.80	0.75

Table 1. Error quantification (degree) of the final model using 2, 3, and 4 LEDs for ten users

6.2 Image Feature Detection

The proposed gaze estimation model is based on a single camera and multiple light sources. The pupil shape and glints positions are used as working features for image data. As mentioned before, the exact determination of glints positions considerably influences system accuracy as studied in (Villanueva & Cabeza, 2008b). In the same manner, pupil contour estimation can be critical for gaze estimation. This task is frequently obviated in many gaze tracking systems devoted to gaze estimation, but we consider it important to include the following recent study in this chapter.

The acquired images (see Figure 1) are processed to extract the pupil and glints. The pupil is detected as a blob matching specific characteristics of size, grey level and compactness. These conditions depend to a large extent on the ambient light level in the room and the optics of the camera. According to the hardware configuration, it can be assumed that the glints are located in a region close to the previously estimated pupil blob. Moreover, the glints should also verify selected assumptions about size, compactness, brightness, and relative position in the image. All of these requirements permit determination of the, approximate glint and pupil position in the image. Figure 13 shows the steps used to determine pupil area. First, a rough segmentation of the glints and pupil area is carried out; second, the reduced region of interest allows for a more careful determination of the grey values in the pupil area to be used for thresholding.

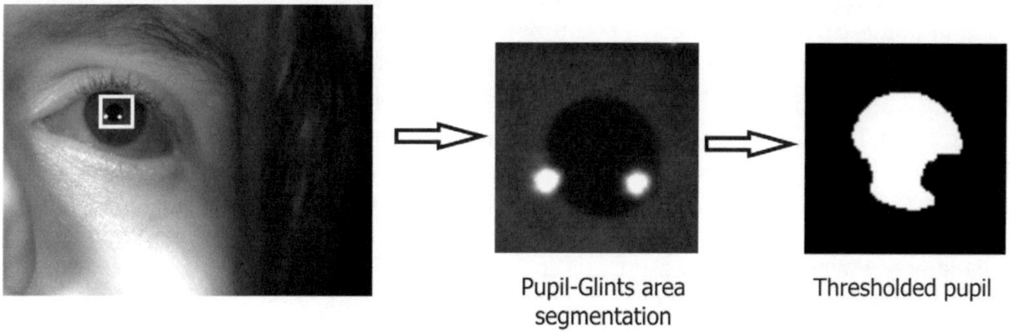

Figure 13. Pupil and glint area extraction from the image and thresholding

Once the pupil blob has been identified, two alternative methods have been compared to determine pupil contour: i) detection using grey level image and ii) ellipse detection in the thresholded image.

The first method uses a Canny edge detector. This is known to many as the optimal edge detector, and it combines Gaussian smoothing with border detection. Once the gradient is calculated, each value is analysed at each pixel by looking in the gradient direction and eliminating those pixels not belonging to the border by establishing selected threshold values. In this manner, thinner lines are obtained for image contours.

For the second method, called the Thresholding method, the binarised (black and white) pupil is used to determine the pupil contour. Once the pupil area has been thresholded, the image is sampled by rows and columns detecting the white-to-black changes. Consequently, the pupil contour points are determined.

Figure 14 shows the pupil-glint image together with the detected contour points. Box and cross shape points represent contour points calculated using the Canny and Thresholding methods, respectively. In both methods, the influence of glints is removed by removing the points of the pupil contour that are in contact with any of the glints, since the glint positions are known beforehand.

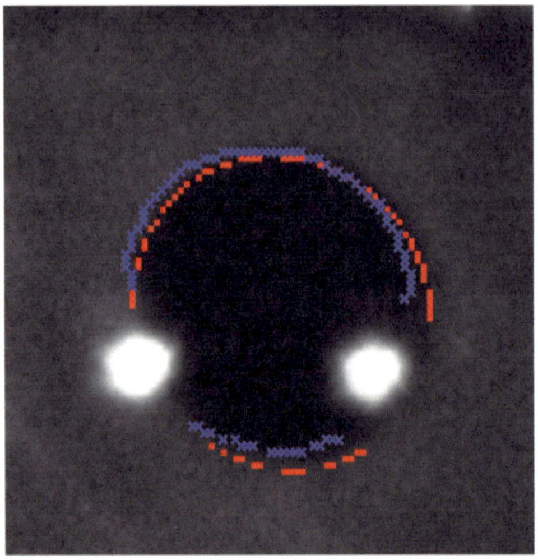

Figure 14. Comparison between Canny and Thresholding edge-detection methods for pupil contour points detection. Box shape points represent the points obtained using a Canny detector, while the cross shape points show the points obtained using the Thresholding method

As expected, the two methods present inaccuracies in the determination of contour points. Inaccurate contour detection introduces errors in gaze estimation. The objective of the analysis is first to evaluate the reliability of the two methods and second to obtain an approximate value of the existing uncertainty in detection of pupil contour points. The reliability of the methods is measured as an indicator of the goodness of fit. To this end, the processed results of images from the same gazed point are compared.

Five new subjects took part in this experiment. They were asked to observe a grid of 3x3 points on the screen. Thirty images were acquired for each one of the grid points. The estimated contours were fitted to an ellipse, and the ellipse parameters, i.e. centre, semi-axes and orientation, were calculated. Ellipse features were used as inputs of a filtering process that selected 18 images from the 30 acquired for each gazed point using the Mahalanobis Distance criteria. This process permits elimination of artifacts or outliers from the sample. In order to estimate the uncertainty of the contour detection procedure, the pupil centre of gravity is calculated as a function of the contour points by both the Canny and Thresholding methods. Thus, the statistical distribution of the centre of gravity can be calculated for each

gazed point by means of the two alternative contour detection methods. In order to compare data from different points, users, and methods, the Coefficient of Variation (CV) is calculated as the ratio between the standard deviation and the absolute value of the mean. Low CVs indicate good stability. Data from all subjects and points are evaluated, and the results show that the two methods have low CVs for pupil centre of gravity. Using the Thresholding method, a mean value of 1% is obtained for the CV, while a 2% is obtained for the Canny detector. It is concluded that both methods present and acceptable reliability. Moreover, the results show low variability regarding CV between users and screen points.
In order to evaluate the influence of contour detection errors on the calculated gaze position a previous estimation of the existing indetermination is necessary. Pupil contour can vary when looking at the same point due to alternative reasons, such as eye micro-movement, head movement or image processing algorithms errors. The objective of this study is to estimate the indetermination derived from the image processing method used. Employing the same data the difference between Thresholding and Canny methods for pupil centre of gravity is calculated for each acquired image. The obtained mean difference is ~1.1 pixels for both, x and y coordinates of the pupil centre of gravity. Consequently, a $1.1\sqrt{N}$ pixels of difference can be expected for pupil contour points, where N is the number of contour points used to calculate the pupil centre of gravity. It is assumed that this error is due to image processing algorithms inaccuracies.
Nevertheless, to evaluate the effect of image processing inaccuracies properly, gaze estimation data are needed. Forty pupil contour point positions of the pupil are corrupted in a simulated environment using Gaussian noise with alternative standard deviation values in the range of 2 to 12 pixels. Glint data are preserved with no corruption, and the effect of the pupil contour is measured on its own. For each grid point, ten noisy iterations are carried out, and the estimated gaze points are calculated. Thus, the error with respect to the real gaze point can be computed. In Figure 15, the 3x3 grid of points is represented with the estimations obtained for a standard deviation of 8 pixels.

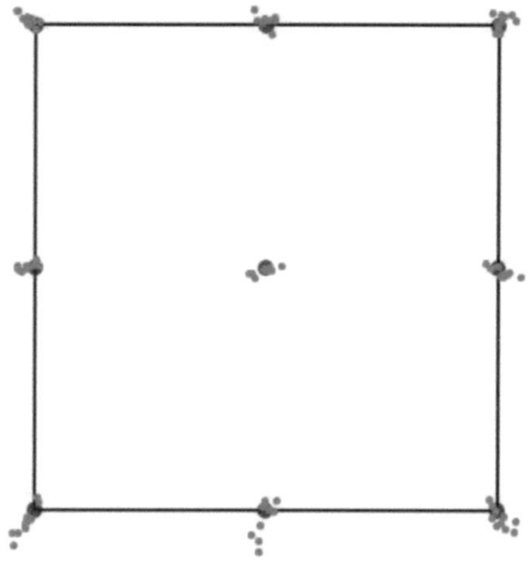

Figure 15. 3x3 grid of points and the estimated gaze positions when 8 pixels of noise is introduced

Figure 16 shows the distribution of the error for the full grid and for the different deviation values. On the horizontal axis, the error is shown in visual degrees. In addition, the threshold at 1° is also indicated, since errors below this limit are acceptable performance indicators. From the figure it is observed that 8 pixels of noise produce a mean error above the acceptable limit of 1°.

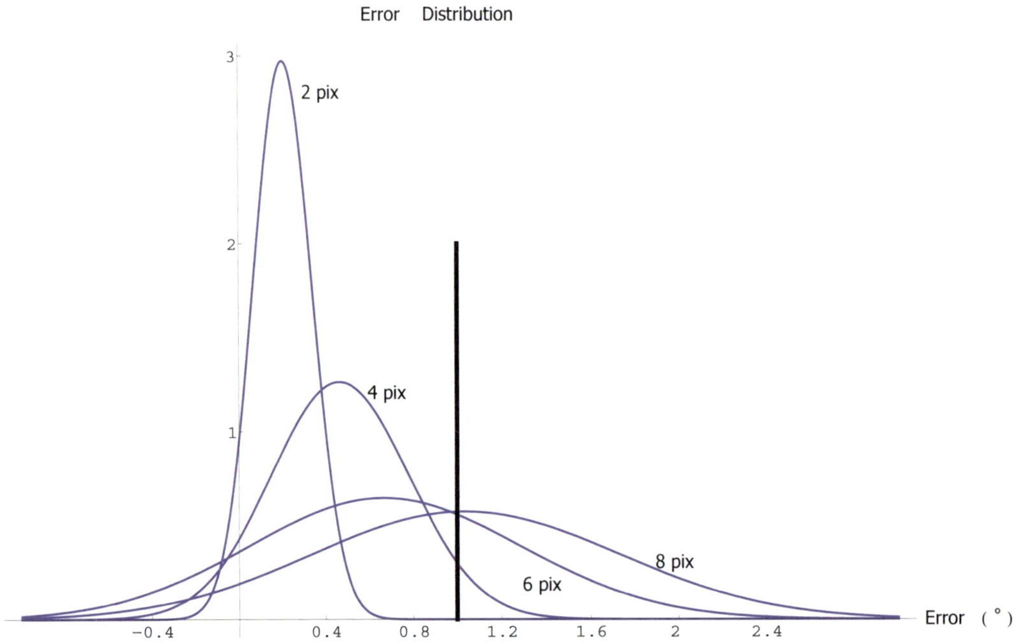

Figure 16. Error distribution for the 3x3 grid of points for different noise levels

However, the distribution can change slightly if the error is computed as the difference between the real gaze point and the averaged estimations. Figure 17 shows the same grid from Figure 15, but only shows the real gaze point and the average of the estimations. The error is clearly reduced.

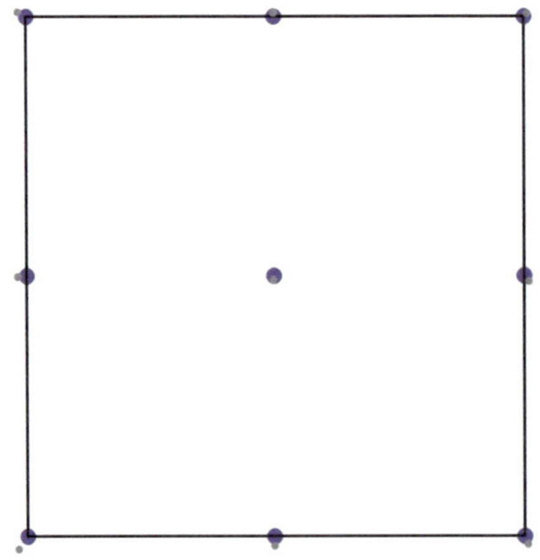

Figure 17. 3x3 grid of points and the estimated averaged gaze positions when 8 pixels of noise is introduced

In the same manner, the distribution of the error changes if this method is used, since the error is partially compensated by averaging. Thus, the average behaviour of the model is acceptable for deviations of 8 and 10 pixels (see Figure 18). Nevertheless, eye tracking system speed and our application requirements would determine the error computation method to a large extent.

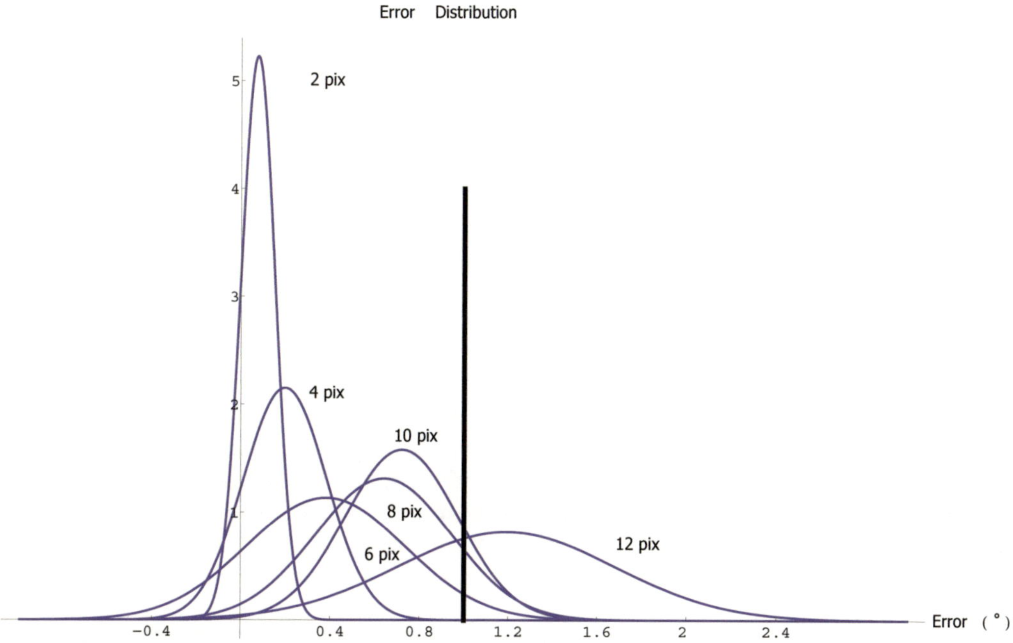

Figure 18. Error distribution for the 3x3 grid of points for different noise levels when averaged estimations are used for each point

7. Conclusions

A geometry-based model for gaze estimation has been constructed and evaluated. Alternative models have been proposed based on different image features. The results show that a hybrid model is needed for LoS estimation in a free head pose scenario, since glints and pupil separately do not provide sufficient information for optical axis estimation. Glints have been shown to be connected to the corneal centre position. Once the cornea centre has been determined, pupil shape can be used to estimate the pupil centre. The line connecting the pupil centre and the cornea centre is determined as the optical axis of the eye. Thus, the LoS is deduced using Listing's and Donder's Laws.

Cornea centre estimation is significantly sensitive to glint position inaccuracies. Hence, the number of light sources has been increased to obtain an averaged cornea centre and to compensate for the error. The obtained results show a better performance as the number of light sources is increased from two to four.

The proposed model requires the system hardware, such as the camera, light sources, and screen, to be calibrated beforehand. In addition, individual parameters such as, r_c, h, and β are required for gaze estimation. Theoretically, one calibration point is sufficient to obtain the aforementioned subject's parameters.

8. Future directions

Important obstacles need to be overcome in order to make eye tracking technology more accessible. Light variations make the image analysis more difficult, especially in outdoor settings in which light can change rapidly. New image acquisition devices, such as the silicon retina, can help solve this issue. This device produces data from those pixels for which relative brightness variations occur; however, no response is given if the overall lighting changes. Interesting attempts have been carried out using the silicon retina for eye tracking (Delbrück et al., 2008), but their production is still a difficult process and the devices that are currently available are low-resolution. Glasses and contact lenses can also introduce problems to the image processing task. Glasses can produce undesired glints in the image, while contact lenses can modify the pupil shape in the image. Most systems generally permit users to wear glasses and contact lenses; however, problems have been reported for specific subjects.

Another important area of research in the eye-gaze tracking field is gaze estimation. The connection between the image and gaze determines to a large extent the system accuracy and head movement constraints. In order to make the technology more accessible, accurate systems with head movement tolerance are needed, as head movement tolerance is a desired requirement for most eye tracking applications. Geometry-based models can provide useful information for constructing more accurate and versatile gaze tracking systems. Building models based on geometric principles results in valuable *a priori* data about possibly less accurate screen areas or system error sensitivity with respect to head movement. Geometric models can also contribute to a reduction of calibration requirements or to an increase in the effectiveness of calibration procedures. A great deal of effort has recently been put into this field, but a lot of work is still needed.

The eye model used in most of the papers devoted to gaze estimation is incomplete. Recently, a Matlab implementation for the eye model has been presented (Böhme et al., 2008) valid for gaze estimation studies. The eyeball model used in this work has been used in many works in recent years. Most researchers agree that the simplest possible eyeball model is needed and that model inaccuracies are partially compensated for during the calibration process. However, it is worth exploring additional eyeball properties, such as corneal ellipsoidal shape, and evaluating their influence in system accuracy in order to reach a proper trade-off between model complexity and accuracy. Moreover, most gaze estimation models are restricted to single-eye systems. One straightforward step would be to introduce the additional eyeball into the model. The geometrical analysis of binocular gaze estimation can considerably improve system performance and robustness.

One important issue to solve for most geometry-based gaze estimation systems is the necessity of hardware calibration. Many of these models require some extent of camera, light source, and screen position knowledge, which is not a trivial step. Although camera calibration has been widely studied, knowing the positions of light sources and the screen with respect to the camera is still a problem that needs to be solved to make this technology accessible. One possible solution is to provide the system in a closed form solution in which the camera and light sources are encapsulated together with the screen in a dedicated structure. However, the drawbacks of this solution are that it would increase the price and reduce the accessibility of the technology. Reducing hardware calibration requirements is a highly desirable task that would facilitate the employment of this technology.

Similarly, construction of eye tracking devices using off-the-shelf elements is a very interesting line of research. Thus, using webcams for eye-gaze tracking represents a goal of the field. This type of system would make eye tracking technology independent of expensive and complex hardware, but new image processing algorithms would be needed. Moreover, it is still difficult to achieve equivalent performance (resolution) with this kind of technology, since, e.g., the wider field of view of a webcam does not permit detection of the pupil with the same accuracy as a dedicated camera and optics. One possible solution to compensate for the reduction in accuracy would be to use adaptive user interfaces, such as zooming interfaces (Hansen et al., 2008).

9. References

Beymer, D. & Flickner, M. (2003). Eye gaze tracking using an active stereo head. *Proceedings of the 2003 conference on Computer Vision and Pattern Recognition*, vol. 02, p. 451, Los Alamitos, CA, USA. 2003, IEEE Computer Society.

Böhme, M., Dorr, M., Graw, M., Martinetz, M. & Barth, E. (2008). A software framework for simulating eye trackers. *Proceedings of the 2008 symposium on Eye tracking research and applications.*, pp. 251-258, Savannah, March, 2008, ACM Press, New York, NY, USA.

Cerrolaza, J.J., Villanueva, A. & Cabeza, R. (2008). Taxonomic study of polynomial regressions applied to the calibration of video-oculographic systems. *Proceedings of the 2008 symposium on Eye tracking research and applications.*, pp. 259-266, Savannah, March, 2008, ACM Press, New York, NY, USA.

Delbrück, T., Grover, D., Gisler, D., Lichtsteiner, P., Ersbøll, B. & Tureczek, A. (2008). D5.5 Silicon retina and other novel approaches for eye tracking. *Communication by Gaze Interaction* (COGAIN), IST- 2003-511598: Deliverable 5.5.

Guestrin, E. & Eizenman, M. (2006). General theory of remote gaze estimation using the pupil center and corneal reflections. *IEEE Transactions on Biomedical Engineering,* vol. 53, no. 6, pp. 1124–1133, 2006.

Guestrin, E. & Eizenman, M. (2008). Remote point-of-gaze estimation requiring a single-point. *Proceedings of the 2008 symposium on Eye tracking research and applications.*, pp. 267-274, Savannah, March, 2008, ACM Press, New York, NY, USA.

Hansen, D.W. & Pece, A.E.C. (2005). Eye tracking in the wild. *Computer Vision and Image Understanding,* vol. 98, no. 1, pp. 155–181, 2005.

Hansen, D.W., Skovsgaard, H.H., Hansen, J.P. and Møllenbach, E. (2008). Noise tolerant selection by gaze-controlled pan and zoom in 3D. *Proceedings of the 2008 symposium on Eye tracking research and applications.*, pp. 205-212, Savannah, March, 2008, ACM Press, New York, NY, USA.

Hennessey, C., Noureddin, B. & Lawrence, P. (2006). A single camera eye-gaze tracking system with free head motion *Proceedings of the 2006 symposium on Eye tracking research and applications.* pp. 87-94, San Diego, March 2006, ACM Press, New York, NY, USA.

Morimoto, C.H. & Mimica, M.R.M. (2005). Eye gaze tracking techniques applications, *Computer Vision and Image Understanding* 98 (1) (2005) pp. 4–24.

Ohno, T. & Mukawa, N. (2004). A free-head, simple calibration, gaze tracking system that enables gaze-based interaction. *Proceedings of the 2004 symposium on Eye tracking research and applications.* pp. 115-122, San Antonio (TX), March 2004, ACM Press, New York, NY, USA.

Shih, S.W. & Liu, J. (2004). A novel approach to 3-D gaze tracking using stereo cameras, *IEEE Transactions Systems Man and Cybernetics Part-B*, vol. 34, no. 1, February 2004, pp. 234–245.

Villanueva, A. & Cabeza, R. (2007). Models for gaze tracking systems. Journal on Image and Video Processing. Volume 2007, Issue 3 (November 2007) Article No. 4, 2007, ISSN:1687-5176.

Villanueva, A. & Cabeza, R. (2008a). Evaluation of Corneal Refraction in a Model of a Gaze Tracking System. *IEEE Transactions on Biomedical Engineering.* (in press). Urbana IL, USA.

Villanueva, A. & Cabeza, R. (2008b). A Novel Gaze Estimation System with One Calibration Point. *IEEE Transactions on Systems, Man and Cybernetics* Part-B, vol. 38, no. 4, August 2008, pp. 1123-1138.

Yoo, D.H. & Chung, M. J. (2005). A novel non-intrusive eye gaze estimation using cross-ratio under large head motion, *Computer Vision and Image Understanding*, vol. 98, no. 1, pp. 25–51, 2005.

31

Investigation of a Distance Presentation Method using Speech Audio Navigation for the Blind or Visually Impaired

Chikamune Wada
Graduate School of Life Science and Systems Engineering, Kyushu Institute of Technology
Japan

1. Introduction

Many navigation devices for blind or visually impaired individuals have been developed (There is a lot of researches. For example, Johnson, 2006, Velazquez, 2006). The creation of these devices requires the management of three critical research elements: first, detecting obstacles; second, measuring the present location of the blind or impaired individual for route navigation; third, method of informing the individual of direction and distance.
Regarding obstacle detection, we expect this activity to be performed using robot technology for autonomous transfer.
As for location measurement, recent studies indicate location can be determined via GPS (Global Positioning Satellite) or RFID (Radio Frequency Identification) to guide the blind or impaired person (Miyanaga, 2008, Jongwhoa, 2006, Ding, 2007). However, GPS cannot be used in underground locations or urban areas surrounded by tall buildings because of poor signal detection. In addition, many ID chips must be buried under the roads to allow the use of RFID so that location measurement using RFID is likely to be limited. To avoid these difficulties, we proposed a measurement method based on foot movement. We will detail this measurement method further in this article.
Concerning the method of presenting information to the blind and visually impaired, we believe that the device should provide the individual with necessary information about the direction and distance of obstacles/destinations. Judging from the natural human reaction to sound sources, we hypothesized that humans grasp direction based on the position of the head. Consequently, we proposed a head-centered direction display method. Our previous experimental results show that human beings can comprehend directions simply based on head position (Asonuma, Matsumoto & Wada, 2005). Incidentally, other similar systems currently use speech audio to allow the blind or impaired person to determine distance, yet difficulty still exists for the individual to accurately assess distances from speech audio. For example, this type of system notifies the person that he or she must turn right 3 meters in front of him or her if he or she wants to arrive at an entrance. However, the impaired individual may not be able to imagine a distance of 3 meters due to lack of prior physical reference. Even though there are difficulties in assessing distance using speech audio, it is thought to be a better presentation method than a tactile sensation such as vibration, at least from the standpoint of training necessity. Thus, we are attempting to examine the optimal

presentation method when speech audio is used. We investigated which speech expressions of distance were most appropriate to assess distance easily and selected the three expressions: length, number of steps and time because individuals used these expressions routinely.

To correctly utilize these three expressions, a subject's stride and position had to be accurately measured, so we developed a stride measurement device. First, we will introduce the distance measurement method based on foot movement. Then, we will explain the distance presentation method using speech audio in conjunction with our stride measurement device.

2. Distance measurement method based on foot movement

2.1 System setup

Figure 1 represents a schematic figure of our stride measurement device. During the swing phase, the foot position is calculated from the combined data of acceleration sensors and gyro sensors. To reduce error using integral calculus, the distance between both feet is measured with ultrasonic sensors during the double supporting stance phase. Pressure sensors on both the heel and toe were employed to help decide whether it was a double supporting stance phase or not. Using this measurement method, the measurement error will not increase, though the walking distance will, and foot position will be measured with no limitation of the measurement area.

To complete the measurement device, we investigated a situation using an optimal arrangement of acceleration and ultrasonic sensors, which had been placed on the foot.

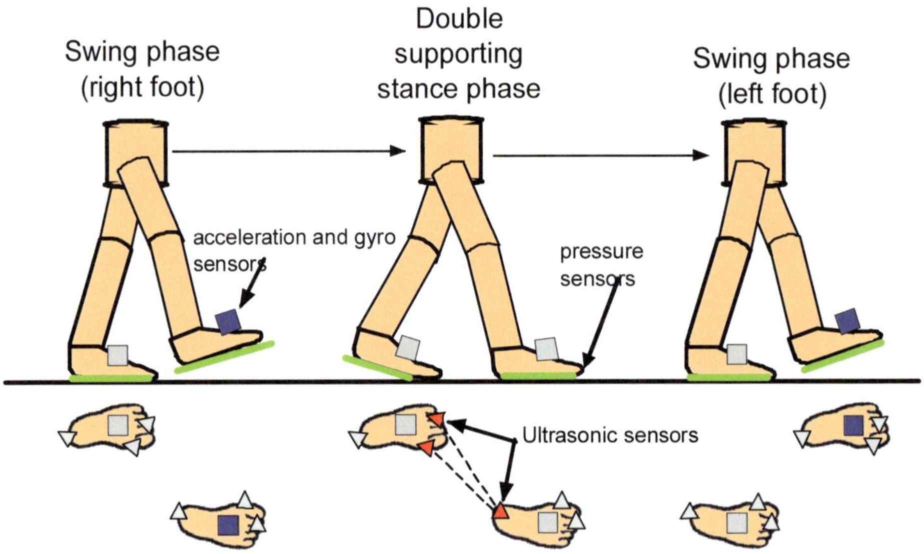

Figure 1. Stride measurement device

(a) Attaching the acceleration sensors.

First, we measured the maximum acceleration of the foot while walking to determine the necessary measurement range of the acceleration sensor. The accelerations of seven points of the foot (shown in Fig. 2) were measured with a motion capture system. The subjects were 10 young people, who were asked to walk for 10 steps and repeated the exercise three times. The theoretical maximum measurement error was 1 cm in this motion capture system. Table 1 shows the maximum and average accelerations. Data from Table 1 shows maximum acceleration was under 10G, so we decided to use an acceleration sensor that could measure up to 10G.

Next, we attempted to determine the optimal position to measure the value of the acceleration sensor. We created a measurement system consisting of a triple-axis acceleration sensor with a triple-axis gyro sensor and placed them on the seven points of the foot (shown in Fig. 2). Three subjects were then asked to walk 10 steps for 10 trials. During the experiment, the walking distance was calculated with our measurement system as well as by the motion capture system. After completion of the measurement, a distance error was established. From our results, the average distance error per step was approximately 1 cm for all points of the foot. Therefore, we concluded that the acceleration sensor should be attached to the heel.

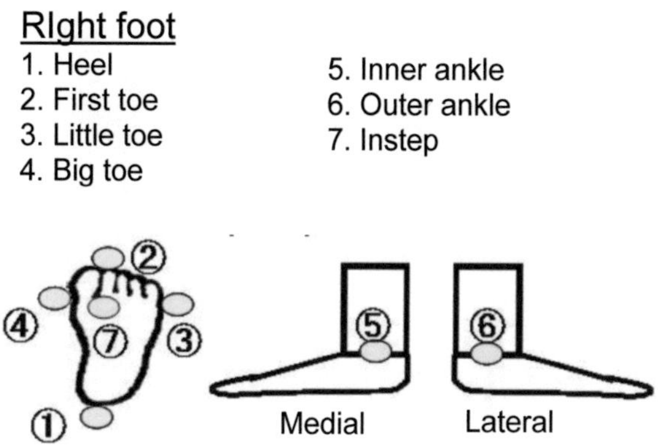

Figure 2. Acceleration measurement points

Inner ankle			Outer ankle			Instep		
Lateral	Forward	Upward	Lateral	Forward	Upward	Lateral	Forward	Upward
5.87	9.5	6.54	4.18	9.3	5.28	4.26	7.75	5.34
48.2	85.4	75.7	40.6	89.1	55.1	49	92.1	73

Table 1. Acceleration measurement points ([m/s^2])

(b) Attaching the ultrasonic sensors.

To accurately measure the distance between both feet, it was critical where we placed the ultrasonic sensors, so we simulated the sensor arrangement. As exhibited in Fig. 3, we explored which arrangement was measured correctly when the sensor position varied. Guided by our experiment results, the sensor position was chosen as shown in Fig. 4. One transmitter of the ultrasonic sensor was put on the heel and two receivers were placed on the toe. Two of the receivers were then rotated at 60 and 70 degrees toward the frontal direction of foot. Using this arrangement, the distance between both feet could be calculated correctly as the normal walking pattern of a non-disabled adult.

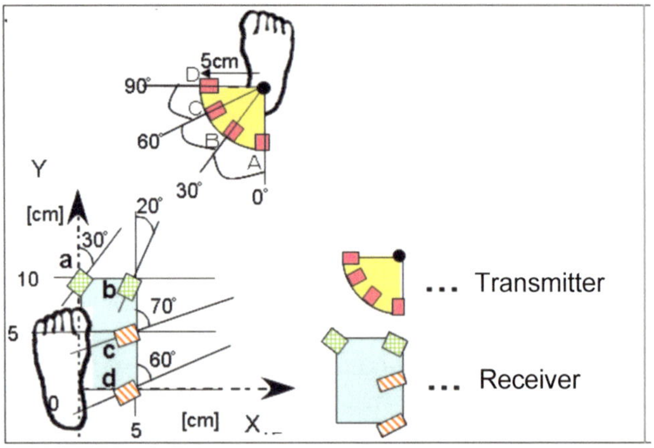

Figure 3. Ultrasonic sensor arrangement to decide optimal sensor position

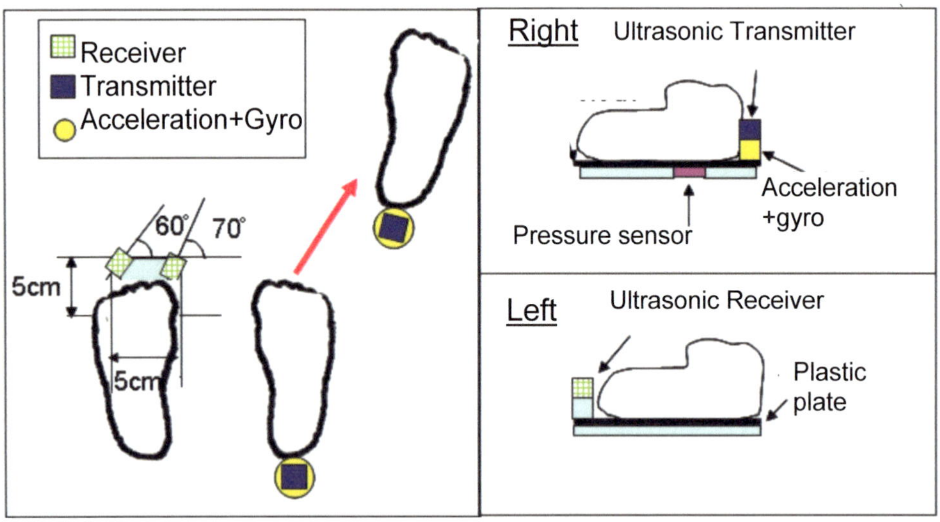

Figure 4. . Stride measurement device (sensor arrangement was shown)

Combining two triple-axis acceleration sensors, two triple-axis gyro sensors, six ultrasonic sensors and twenty-four pressure sensors, we constructed a stride measurement device (shown in Fig. 4).

2.2 System Evaluation

The subject was asked to walk while wearing our stride measurement device to evaluate its accuracy. The movements of the feet were also measured using the motion capture system and the accuracy was calculated. Three subjects walked for 10 steps and repeated this exercise for 10 trials.

Figure 5 shows a sample result of a subject during the swing phase. This figure depicts the tracks of the heel. The upper left image illustrates the tracks in a lateral direction, whereas the upper right shows the forward direction and the lower left displays the upward direction. A solid line represents the results of our device while a dotted line reveals the results of the motion capture system. According to this figure, our measurement system closely measured the track of the foot. The maximum errors for all trials were 2.8, 3.1 and 2.5 cm in the lateral, forward and upward directions, respectively.

The average errors in the walking phase varied from the swing phase to the double supporting stance phase and were 1.5 and 1.9 cm in the lateral and forward directions, respectively. These errors occurred because of the integral calculus in the calculating process of the acceleration and gyro sensors during the swing phase. However, using the measurement result of the ultrasonic sensor, those average errors decreased to 0.4 and 0.5 cm in the lateral and forward directions, respectively. Thus, our method measured feet movements correctly. Nevertheless, there is still an issue to be solved: Our method was used only on flat ground, that is, our method cannot be applied on stairs or steps.

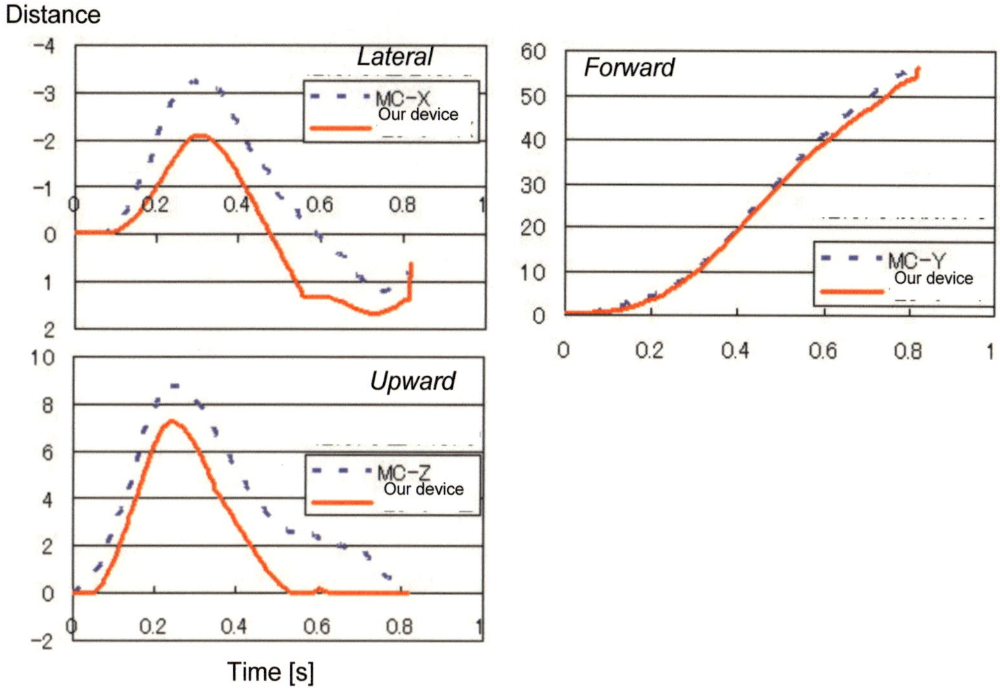

Figure 5. One result of heel tracks during swing phase

3. Distance presentation method using speech audio

3.1 Experiment setup and procedure

Next, we examined which speech expressions of distance were most appropriate in assessing distance easily. As mentioned above, we selected the three expressions: length, number of steps and time.

[Length]: When a speech expression is "3 meters" for example, the expression indicates an obstacle is 3 meters in front of the subject. Prepared expressions were 1 m, 2 m, 3 m, 4 m and 5 m for this experiment.

[Number of steps]: When a speech expression is "3 steps" for instance, the expression signifies the individual will hit an obstacle after three steps walking at the present stride. In this case, prepared expressions were 1 step, 2 steps, 3 steps, 4 steps and 5 steps.
[Time]: When a speech expression is "3 seconds" for example, the expression means the subject will hit an obstacle after three seconds of walking at the present speed, and prepared expressions were 1 second, 2 seconds, 3 seconds, 4 seconds and 5 seconds.
Figure 6 illustrates our experimental procedure. In the experiment, the subjects wore eyeshades as well as our stride measurement devices. The subjects were asked to walk toward an obstacle that was represented by a 2 m high board. When the subjects arrived at a specific point, one of the three types of expressions were presented through a speaker situated behind the subjects. After hearing the expression, the subjects were asked to obey it and perform the necessary action. For instance, if the subjects heard "3 m", they should walk as long as they felt the distance was 3 m, and if they collided with the obstacle before they intended to stop, the trial was at an end. If they did not hit the obstacle after they obeyed the expression, the distance between the subject and the obstacle was measured and the individual was asked to walk further until he or she collided with the obstacle. After the trials, the subjects were asked to indicate their sensory feeling of security at five steps using the SD method. Five non-visually disabled subjects participated in this experiment, and 10 trials were completed for each expression.

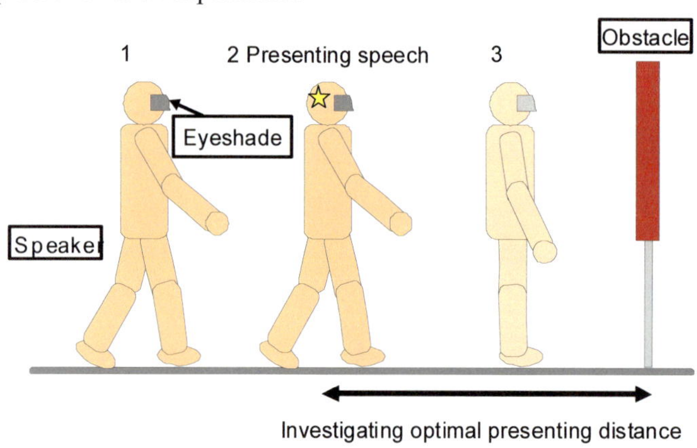

Figure 6. Experiment setup

3.2 Experiment results and discussion

Figure 7 shows our experiment results. The dark gray bar, white bar and light gray bar indicate the results of "length," "steps" and "time" expressions, respectively. The vertical axis indicates the sensory feeling of security at five steps, and value 5 shows when the subjects felt most relieved. The horizontal axis illustrates the length in meters, the number of steps and time in seconds.
As seen in this figure, relatively high evaluation score results were obtained when the expressions were 3 m, 3 steps, 3 seconds, 4 steps and 4 seconds. Furthermore, Table 2 exhibits the bumping rate of a subject into an obstacle, and according to this table, relatively low bumping rates were obtained when the expressions were 2 steps, 3 m, 3 steps, 3 seconds and 4 seconds.

From the data supplied by the bumping rate, the expression "2 steps" was optimal. However, the subjective evaluation was not as beneficial. The subjects suddenly almost stopped walking when they heard "2 steps." Then, they did not bump into the obstacle. Nevertheless, they concentrated well enough to hear the expression to stop because actually there was not enough distance margin to complete a stop action.

When expressions were "length" and "time," the bumping rates were neither substandard nor improved. Expressions of "length" and "time" were easy to comprehend, but there was a variation in subjective length and subjective time. Then, the bumping rates for "length and time" did not decrease.

From the data mentioned above, we considered the expression "3 steps" optimal to present distance in order to avoid bumping into the obstacle.

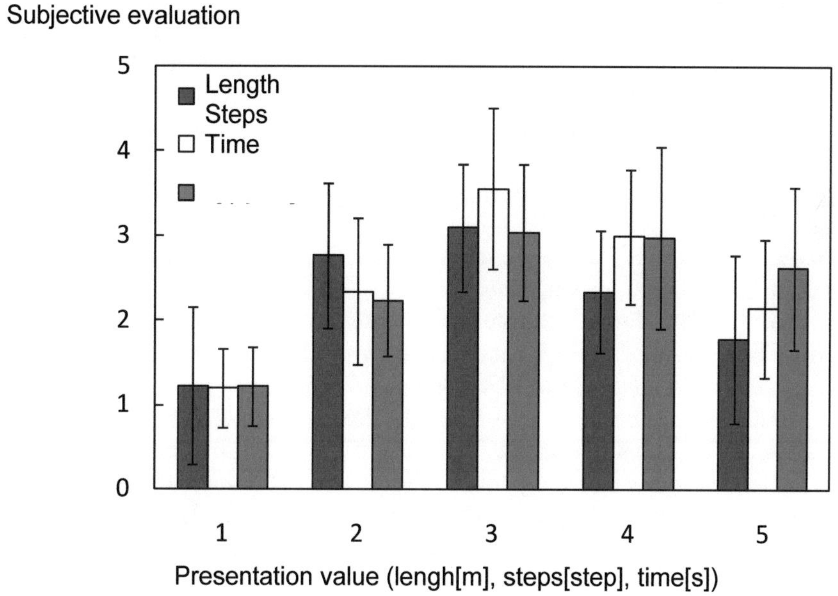

Figure 7. Experiment results

	1[m, steps, s]	2[m, steps, s]	3[m, steps, s]	4[m, steps, s]	5[m, steps, s]
Length	50%	10%	6%	14%	20%
Number of steps	28%	4%	2%	12%	24%
Time	36%	14%	8%	8%	10%

Table 2. Bumping rates

4. Conclusions and continuing research

In this article, we introduced a distance presentation method using speech audio. Although the experiment was conducted within a short walking distance inside a laboratory, we

demonstrated that the expression "3 m" was the optimal presentation method to avoid an obstacle with a sensory feeling of security.
During this experiment, our stride measurement device was connected to a computer with a wire; therefore, we were unable to execute experiments for longer walking distances. As a result, we are constructing wireless stride measurement devices. Combining our new stride measurement device, our distance presentation method, our direction display method and our obstacle detection technique, we will create an obstacle avoidance system and demonstrate the efficiency of our system in an open air environment.

5. References

Asonuma, M., Matsumoto, M. & Wada, C. (2005). Study on the use Air Stimulation as the Indicator in an Obstacle Avoidance System for the Visually Impaired, *Proceedings of the Society of Instrument and Control Engineers annual conference* 2005, MA2-14-2(CD-ROM), Japan, Oct 2005.

Ding, B., Yuan, H., Zang, X., & Jiang, L. (2007). The Research on Blind Navigation System Based on RFID, *Proceedings of International Conference on Wireless Communications, Networking and Mobile Computing*, 2007, pp. 2058-2061, Sep 2007.

Johnson, L.A. (2006). A navigation aid for the blind using tactile-visual sensory substitution, *Proceedings of Annual International Conference of the IEEE Engineering in Medicine and Biology Society*, pp. 4, Aug 2006.

Jongwhoa, Na. (2006). The blind interactive guide system using RFID-based indoor positioning system, *Proceedings of 10th International Conference of Computers Helping People with Special Needs*, pp. 1298-1305, July 2006.

Miyanaga, Y. (2008). Promotion of Free Mobility Project, *Journal of the Institute of Electrical Installation Engineers of Japan*, 28, 5, pp. 320-323 (Written in Japanese)

Velazquez, R. (2006). Walking using touch: design and preliminary prototype of a non-invasive ETA for the visually impaired, *Proceedings of 27th Annual International Conference of the IEEE Engineering in Medicine and Biology Society*, pp. 4, Aug 2005.

32

The Three-Dimensional User Interface

Hou Wenjun
Beijing University of Posts and Telecommunications
China

1. Introduction

This chapter introduced the three-dimensional user interface (3D UI). With the emergence of Virtual Environment (VE), augmented reality, pervasive computing, and other "desktop disengage" technology, 3D UI is constantly exploiting an important area. However, for most users, the 3D UI based on desktop is still a part that can not be ignored. This chapter interprets what is 3D UI, the importance of 3D UI and analyses some 3D UI application. At the same time, according to human-computer interaction strategy and research methods and conclusions of WIMP, it focus on desktop 3D UI, sums up some design principles of 3D UI.
From the principle of spatial perception of people, spatial cognition, this chapter explained the depth clues and other theoretical knowledge, and introduced Hierarchical Semantic model of "UE", Scenario-based User Behavior Model and Screen Layout for Information Minimization which can instruct the design and development of 3D UI.
This chapter focuses on basic elements of 3D Interaction Behavior: Manipulation, Navigation, and System Control. It described in 3D UI, how to use manipulate the virtual objects effectively by using Manipulation which is the most fundamental task, how to reduce the user's cognitive load and enhance the user's space knowledge in use of exploration technology by using navigation, and how to issue an order and how to request the system for the implementation of a specific function and how to change the system status or change the interactive pattern by using System Control.
Finally through the case analysis, it highlighted the experience and interactive of 3D UI. And then it analyzed elements affecting 3D UI interactive mode from the Psychology, interactive design and information show.
3D UI has come to the transition time from the technology-driven to the design-driven. This section gives the readers a basic understanding of 3D UI. It focuses on the basic concepts, advantages and limitations between different latitude UI, its applications and the studying contents.

1.1 Concept of 3D UI

1.1.1 Definition of 3D UI

With the development of computer hardware and software technology and the increased demand of application, digital terminal equipment diversification, such as cell phones, PDA (Pocket PC) terminals spread, and so on, that the time of Pervasive Computing has arrived.

Currently the shortcomings of the WIMP interface occupying the mainstream position are also increasingly reflected.
From a technical perspective, WIMP interface used "desktop" metaphor which restricted the human-computer interaction; imbalance of computer input/output bandwidth; complex operation grammar and the small-screen effect; used the ordinal dialogue mode; only supported precise and discrete input; can not handle simultaneous operation; can not use the auditory and tactile; all of these make it clear that WIMP interface is unable to adapt to pervasive computing.
Since the 1990s, researchers proposed the idea of next-generation user interface. As one of the main forms of interface, three-dimensional user interface is attaches importance for its natural, intuitive features. The increase of the dimensions brings about a qualitative change to the user interface, as shown in Fig. 1.

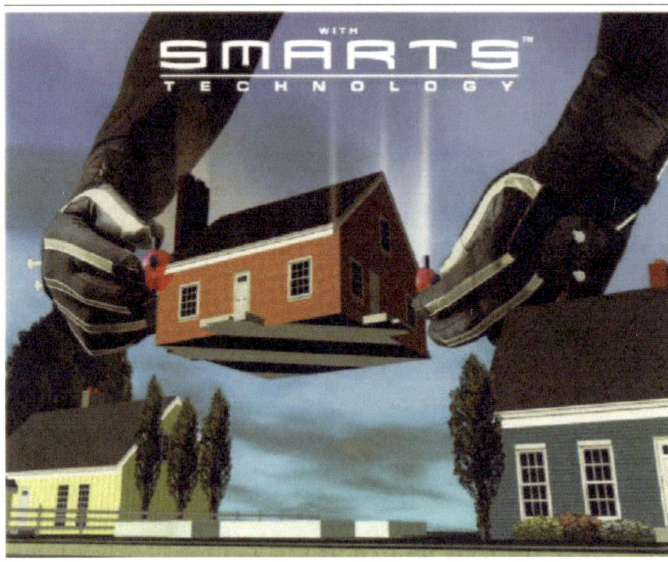

Figure 1. 3D UI

User interface can transform the user's behavior and state into an expression that computer can understand and operate, and then transform the computer's behavior and state into an expression a user can understand and operation. The three-dimensional user interface is a human-computer interaction that users can directly carry out the tasks in the 3D space. Its visual angle is like a free camera angle lens, which users can self-control the direction of visual angle.
3D virtual environment is a new human-computer interaction, using this mode the user can enter to a cyber space that virtually unlimited, and interacting with inner objects in a natural harmony way. This cyber space can describe things existing in the real world (that is, "real things to virtual"). It can also describe the things that entirely imaged or things that existing in the real word but people can not touch (that is, "virtual things to real"). It may also known as virtual reality environment.
3D virtual environment system has three features which are Immersion, Interaction and Involvement, which is called 3I characteristics.

The current 3D virtual environment system included: Desktop, Half-physical, Visual Immersion, Augment Reality, and Distributed Virtual Environment, in Fig. 2. Shown.

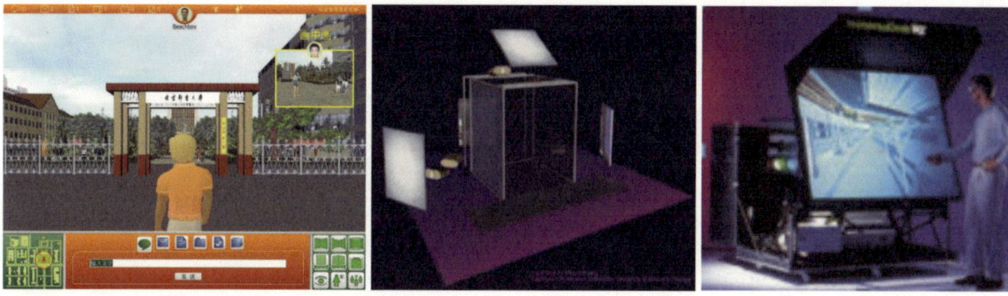

Figure 2. 3D Virtual Environments

These systems not only need the technology of viewpoint transform, but also need the system control technology of choice, move, rotate of objects. These systems can not become a mainstream application because of the immature of peripheral hardware, the naturalness of interactive technology and lower usability of these systems. The three-dimensional user interface under the desktop environment is more mature.

1.1.2 Advantages and disadvantages of 3D UI

3D UI does not replace the traditional 2D graphical user interface paradigm, but solves the poor performance of the traditional mode in interaction. Compared with the 2D interface its advantages are as follows:

- Scenario context

3D scenario enhanced the users' comprehensive capabilities of dealing with information, including awareness, perception, learning and memory.

- Information architecture and layout

3D UI provides a new space for the organizing, bearing, showing a more complex information. More importantly, with the trend of the high-capacity and high complexity of the future industrial information platform, there is an urgent need for a new interface presentation, which can not only carry information, can also performance the relationships and differences between different types of information. 3D UI shows great potential in this area.

- Information visualization

3D information visualization makes information shows more directly and more easily to understanding. In essence, graphics and representation can make the users easier to understand and identify the information.

- Interaction Experience

On one hand, 3D interaction can introduce many more natural and rich actions in the real world to traditional human-computer interaction; On the other hand it can show a more attractive new interactive way through breaking the world restrictions.

However, 3D UI also has some own shortcomings which is inevitable, such as got lost in a complex map in the 3D scenario which can bring disorientation, spending more time to learn the navigation, slow study being the cost of rich visual experience, and s unable to get the users' desired view.

- Offer new different structures

3D seems to provide the possibility for representing many dimensions of information and meta-information in a compact way and various structure (3D Navigation).

- Do something which 2D couldn't realize

3D structure / environment are helpful for certain tasks. So we have to explore the best place 3D used in.

3D UI's characteristics inherent present us with new challenges. So far, there has not been summed up a 3D fixed interface paradigm similar to WIMP. On the other hand, 3D UI related to many other subjects such as cognitive psychology, human-computer ergonomics, and so on. And the study of perception and psychological mechanism of processing is not yet mature which also limits the 3D UI research in a certain extent. Although we are living in a three-dimensional space, but in reality the rich three-dimensional objects clues such as the space layout, the human feelings, physical restraint and so on, have not been a unified expression. The existence of these problems gives many challenges to 3D UI research.

1.2 The Content of 3D UI Research

1.2.1 Related Research Fields of 3D UI

3D user interface related to cognitive psychology, human-computer ergonomics, and other disciplines of study. But the research of the perception and mechanism of psychological processing is not yet ripe, and it limited the 3D user interface research to some extent. Although we are living in a three-dimensional space, but the rich three-dimensional cues in reality, such as the objects space layout, the human body feelings, physical restraint and so on, do not have a unified expression.

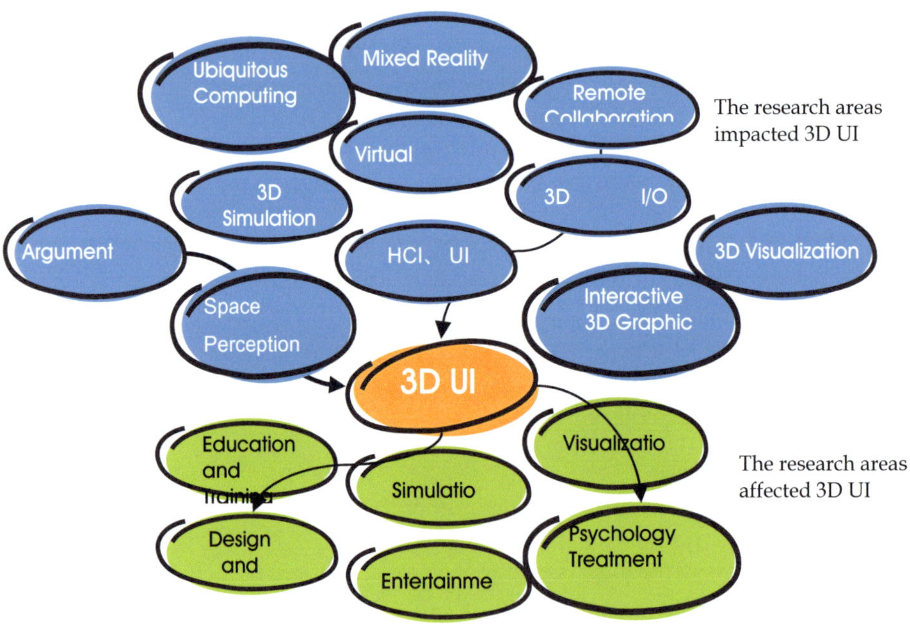

Figure 3. Related Research Fields of 3D UI

3D user interface is an intersecting research area related to multi-disciplinary, it is impacted by many research area, such as space perception, cognitive psychology. And at the same time, it also affected many research areas, such as information visualization, entertainment and education training, etc. The relationship between these parts and the related research areas can be shown by Fig. 3:

1.2.2 The content of 3D UI

3D UI can be studied from two aspects: Technology Elements of 3D UI and Design Elements of 3D UI.

(1) Technology Elements of 3D UI include: Human Factor, 3D Interaction Technique and 3D I/O Device. As shown in Fig. 4:

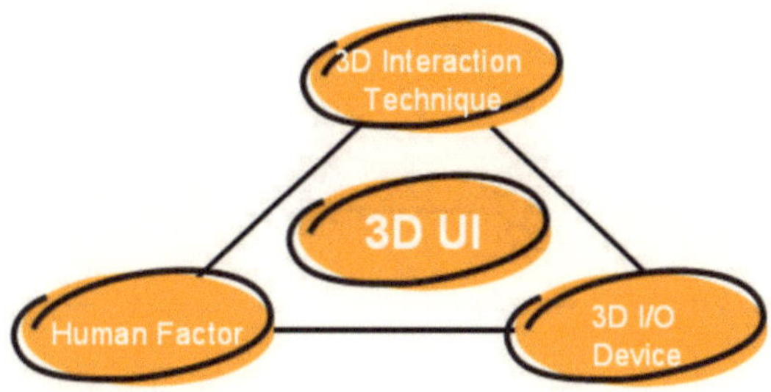

Figure 4. Technology Elements of 3D UI

Human factor mainly studied on visual perception and 3D depth cues, human spatial capabilities and the differences of individual ability, structure spatial knowledge of 3D environment, sound perception of space, manually picking and dragging characteristics, behavior cognitive planning, on-site and other aspects. Among all aspects above, on-site is a phenomenon which has been done a large number of exploration but not yet understand entirely, it was assumed that has a certain effect to the space knowledge. This means that the stronger on-site users were feeling in the virtual world, the more effective his search path done. Many factors affect the on-site feeling, such as the sense of immersion.

3D Interaction Technique mainly researched on navigation, selection and operation, system control. The navigation is mostly about on physical movement technology, driving skills, path planning, and the technology based on the destination, spatial knowledge, procedural knowledge, global knowledge, user-centered path searching and environment centered path searching. Selection and operation researched on pointing technology, virtual hand, world miniaturize technology, 3D desktop operation technique. System Control mainly include the adjusted 2D menu, 1 DOF menu, TULIP menu and 3D Widgets.

Input devices include the mechanical input devices, electronic input devices, optical input devices, voice input devices, inertial input devices and omnibus input devices. It has six aspects of usability problems: speed, accuracy, ease of learning, fatigue, cooperation, sustained and obtained of devices. Output devices include visual output devices, image output devices and mixed-output devices.

□2□Design Elements of 3D UI include 3D Scenario, 3D Widget and Interaction Devices. As shown in Fig. 5:

Relative with the traditional 2D system, 3D interface use its own three-dimensional scenes, it allows the users live in a shared virtual environment by the incarnation, it provides users the channels to understanding others, communicating and cooperating with them, and provides a context environment with different type of sharing object. 3D Widget is a conception extended meaning from 2D graphical user interface, similar to the button and icon in WIMP, the main purpose is to assist users finish complex tasks with low degree of freedom devices, user will be able to transform objects freely by indirect operating widget using mouse. 3D Widget is frequently used to data accessing of entity, such as zoom, rotate, stretch, and so on. Since the degree of freedom of one Widget is limited, so it also was known as limited manipulation technology. Excessive use of widget will occupy the screen space, and require users to remember the mapping relationship of each Widget at the same time, so it is commonly used in desktop environment of 3D interaction.

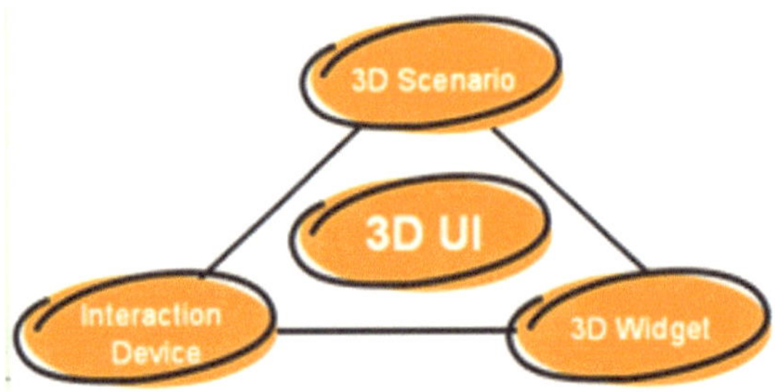

Figure 5. Design Elements of 3D UI

1.3 Application of 3D UI

Along with the improvement advance and falling price of hardware, the demand of application is increased, 3D UI gradually penetrate into lots areas of application. From the beginning of the data browsing to the interactive design, from the massive information visualization to the immersive entertainment, from military to civil parts, the extension and maturity of an increasing number of application system makes people aware the superiority and huge market potential of 3D interface. Overall, we can divide the application to several areas followed: simulation shows, real-world metaphors and 2.5D UI adapted from 2D.

(1) Simulation Shows

Figure 6. Simulation Shows

As shown in Fig. 6, the simulation shows have a typical application in simulation systems, PC games such as Sims™, prototype construction, etc. The main feature is that users have been known how to use the interface from their Day-to-day experience of life, so the time spend on interface learning is the least.

In the field of product design, the use of simulation shows is able to let the multi-designer self participate in the product design process, carry on the virtual assembly and virtual test, so it can save both time and costs.

The goal of simulation shows is to promote the intercommunions and cooperative works. Through the intercommunion, can promote the work flow, personnel arrangement, resource information optimization; provide more natural and interesting operant behavior.

(2) Real-World Metaphors

The use of real-world metaphors is shown in Fig. 7. The typical application of this area is 3D desktop management system, its main feature is that the whole area of human activity can inspire and guide the design of 3D UI.

For example, the construction and the virtual world are based on the shape and style of the arranged and organized space, thus the principles of architectural design can be transferred to the 3D UI designing. In some 3D desktop management system, some elements of architectural are used, such as the wall, desktop, they allowed users to obtain the operation knowledge quickly.

Metaphor is just a starting point, the interactive technique based on metaphor must be designed carefully, to match the application demand and the restriction of the interactive techniques.

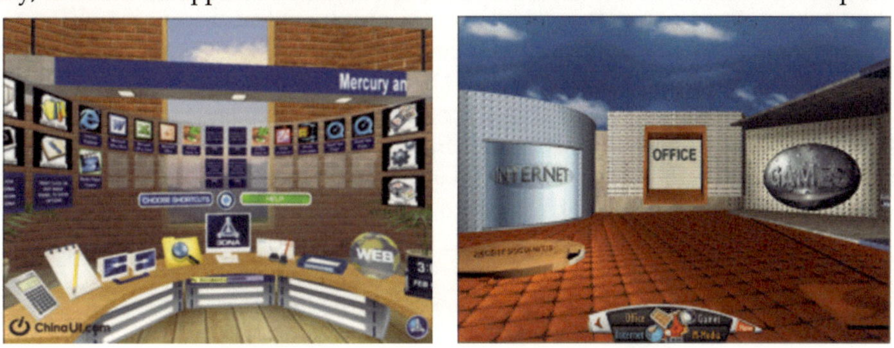

Figure 7. Real-World Metaphors

(3) 2.5D UI

2.5 D has a typical application in real-time strategy games, as shown in Fig. 8. The main feature is that the well mode of interactive had been established in 2D interface, can make the 3D interface design easier to find suitable interactive technology; learning process can also become the shortest. The interactive in 2D is obviously easier than in 3D, users just have to operate 2 degree of freedom but not 6, so 2D interactive can let users carry on some tasks with a higher accuracy (such as selection, operation).

We can apprehend the 2.5D UI as a limited 3D UI, the interface objects is three-dimensional, but they all "grow" on one plane. 2.5D user interface is a transitional stage between 2D GUI and 3D UI, it is an imitated 3D interface display mode, appeared with the progress of the game three-dimensional technique. The visual angle is no longer the overlook or side-view as traditional 2D view, but fixed the user's perspective at a certain angle in the air (it's usually the axonometric view), so it can present a virtual 3D effect. But this is only a visual on 3D, because our visual angle fixed at the certain angle, so we can just move on a plane or zoom the view range, but never see the other sides of these object on the screen. It is just like you paint a jar on canvas, but no matter it looks like a true one, you will never see the back of this jar.

Figure 8. 2.5D

2.5D UI at such a preceding position connects link 2D and 3D, it put forward an innovative integration strategy on all levels of cognitive perspective, interactive and information expression.

(4) Developing visualization information

Today there are various sophisticated methods to locate sound, but known visualizations still strongly remind of thermographic images. Acoustic shapes, unlike thermographic ones, differ from the contour of the measured object. Image overlays make it even more difficult to read and compare the results. The diploma thesis "Digital Acoustic Cartography" is an interactive experiment in mapping sonic events into a concrete visual language. Source material for the visualizations are image sequences recorded by the "acoustic camera", developed by GFaI, Berlin. Both, acoustic and photographic images are analyzed by processing. The color spectrum of the acoustic images is used as distortion matrix to warp the original picture into a three-dimensional relief. The color code is replaced by the photographic data.

NaturalHazards.info is an information-graphic elaboration of the topic of natural disasters – a java-applet. Here, place markers (cubes) of great natural disasters are arranged in space according to geographic and temporal location. They can change in colour and size according to their figures. The user can navigate in space freely, head for individual cubes and continents and get textual information. Further functions include an individual filter as well as a map of the world which can be moved in time. The result is a readable reflection of the facts changeable interactively.

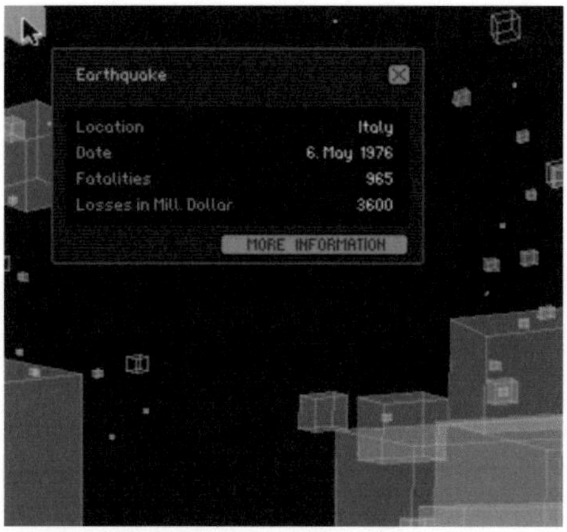

2. Theories and Principles of 3D UI Design

This section explained some theoretical knowledge such as the depth cues, and reaction time, dynamic Vision domain based on the principle of the space perception, spatial cognition and behavior. And it also introduced design concept of "Bottom—Up User Experience", and scenario-based user behavior model—GSOME. Eventually we conclude valuable principles and guidelines about screen layout, navigation, selection, feedback and etc. All of this will guide the design of 3D UI systems.

2.1 Introduction

Any of 3D UI needs export information to users through output devices. They provided information to use's one or more sensory organ through the user's perceptual system. Most of these were used to stimulate vision, auditory and tactile; a few can stimulate the sense of smell and taste. This part mainly mentioned the devices based on the Vision. How can the computer's digital content change into the information that users can understand? It mainly depends on the perception of the human eyes. Understanding of three-dimensional imaging in the human eye and static/dynamic visual characteristics contributes to the 3D UI design.

2.1.1 Depth cues

Users need to understand the structure of 3D UI scenario, particularly the visual depth. Depth information can help users interact with 3D applications, in particular to manipulation, navigation and system control in 3D system. The visual system extracts 3D information using many depth cues provided by visual devices.

Three-dimensional visual is the three-dimensional sense when observated objects, that is, the human eye has the depth perception ability of the objects. The perception about the distance and depth is called depth perception, also known as distance perception. It includes absolute distance (the distance between observers and objects) and relative distance (the distance between two objects or the distance between different parts of one object). It is very important for judging the spatial relationships between objects. Perception depth comes from the external environment extracted from the human eye and depth of the many Depth Cues extracted from internal body. In the visual, these cues can be divided into monocular and binocular clues cues.

(1) Monocular Cues

Monocular cues are the cues that are provided by only one eye. Monocular cues are mainly static, such as the environment and the physical characteristics or phenomena of objects. It also included some sportive cues of one eye. In painting, the pictures can show 3D stereo effect in the two-dimensional plane by using of static monocular cues. So Monocular Cues is also known as graphic cues.

Monocular static cues include:

Size. If the distances between the user and the objects are different, it will form different size images on the retina.

Obscured. If an object is obscured by another object, the obscuring object looks near to us, the other one looks far more.

Perspective. There are two objects having the same size. The perspective on the proportion of the object which is near to us is large, the video also big; vice versa. In railways you can see that, the two tracks near the distance between the two rails near to us are broad, far narrower.

Air Perspective. As the effect of blue-grey color air, when we look at distant objects, we will feel that, the more far from us, the less details we can see, such as more blurred and the color more light. The disintegration phenomena that appear in details, shape and color is known as the air perspective. According to such cues people can also guess the distance between the object and us.

Light and Shadow. We live in a world of light and shadow. Darkness and shadow look more far from us; but bright and high-light part look near to us. In the arts of painting, the part far from us uses dark colors, and the part near to us uses vivid color. This method can create the sense of distance and three-dimensional effect.

Relatively High. If other conditions are equal, the object relatively higher looks far more.

Texture Gradient. It means the projection size and projection density of the objects in the retina change orderly. According to texture gradient in the retina change, the small and dense objects are far from us, and large and infrequent objects are relatively close.

Monocular Movement-Produced cues:

When the observers have a relative movement of the surrounding objects, far and near objects will have a difference of velocity and direction. The mainly character is motion parallax.

Motion parallax is caused by the relative movement between the viewer and object. Such movement changes the size and location of object show on the retina, to bring a sense of depth. When the objects with different distance have different motion range on the retina at the same time, motion parallax is engendered. Once rotating head slightly, the relationship between vision and objects has changed the activities of head and body caused the changes. When we watched the scene through window on a move forward train, the poles nearby go backward rapidly, some of the remote fields, buildings moved backward more slowly. The difference of velocity among the objects in view, is an important indicator to estimate the relative distance of them.

(2) Binocular Cues

Binocular depth cues are referred to the depth cues provided by binocular vision. Although monocular cues can provide people lots of depth cues, help people to finish the operation tasks with the visual guidance. However, some depth information must be provided by both eyes.

Binocular Parallax

Since the existence of two eye space between (average being 6.5cm), the two eyes look the object from different perspective actually, the line of sight has a bit different. So for the same object, the relative position of eyes is different, which caused the binocular parallax, that is, the image in each eye is different. The binocular depth cues is changing with the distance increasing, when the distance over 1,300 m, as visual axis parallel, binocular parallax become zero, so it will not work to the distance judgement.

Oculomotor Cues

Accommodation is the eye initiative focusing action. The focus can be accurate adjustive by the crystal body. The adjustment of crystal body is realized by the muscle working, so the feedback of muscle move information helped the three-dimensional sense establishment.

Convergence is that the visual axis gathered to the regardanted object with the distance changing. Convergence is a binocular function, to get a clear video.

2.1.2 Vision and Reaction Time

(1) Vision Feature

Human beings obtained at least 80 percent of the important information of outside world by vision, such as size, brightness, color, movement, which is the most important feeling. After years of experiments, we know that the process of human visual perception has the following feature:

When we observe objects, the visual line are conditioned to the path from left to right, top to bottom and clockwise movement; eye movement in the horizontal direction priority in vertical direction, the estimated of horizontal direction size and proportion is accurate and rapid than the vertical direction.

When the observation of objects deviation from centre in the same conditions, the sequence of observation is: the left upper quadrant is optimal, and then are the right upper quadrant, the left lower quadrant, and the worst is the right lower quadrant.

There is a relationship between color contrast and the human eye capacity for differentiating colors. When people distinguish a variety of different colors from afar, the extent of how easily identifying is followed by red, green, yellow and white. The two-color match case is, black on the yellow background, white on the black, white on the blue, black on the white, and so on.

(2) Reaction time

Reaction time is the elapsed time between the presentation of a sensory stimulus and the subsequent behavioral response. First the stimulation act on sensory, aroused the excitation, then the excitation spread to the brain and processed, and next it spread through the channel to the locomotor organ, locomotor bioreactor receive nerve impulses, produce a certain reaction, this process can be measured with time that is the reaction time.

F.C.Donders had divided the reaction time into three categories, simple reaction time, choice reaction time and discriminative reaction time. Simple reaction time is usually defined as the time required for an observer to detect the presence of a stimulus. Choice reaction time tasks require distinct responses for each possible class of stimulus. Discriminative reaction time is usually stimulate more than one, but only asked for one stimulus to act a fixed response, and others didn't reaction. The factor impact on the reaction time is in four areas, respectively: stimulated sensory organ, the intensity of stimulation, the time and space characteristic of stimulation, last one is the adaptation state of organ.

2.1.3 Motion Vision

The photoreceptor cell of human eye need a course of time, to identify the signal showed on the retina since imaging. When the view point moving, the objects image show on the retina would also move with a certain angular velocity. When the objects move slowly, it can be accurately identified, but if the speed to a certain extent, people would not accurately distinguish the objects.

The visual feature have a lot of difference between the observation of moving objects and static objects, the mainly aspects is the following areas: visual acuity, visual field, space identify range. And the visual acuity is acuteness or clearness of vision, especially form vision, which is dependent on the sharpness of the retinal focus within the eye and the sensitivity of the interpretative of the interpretative faculty of the brain. The visual field is the space or range within which objects are visible to the immobile eyes at a given time. The space identify range is the ability of identification, such as the size of object, the motion state and the spatial distance. For the moving object, the shorter distance it off observer, the bigger angular velocity it got, the more difficult to distinguish it clearly. And the impact factor of motion vision concluding the relative velocity, age, the color and intensity of the target, and so on.

2.2 3D UI Interactive Principles

2.2.1 Hierarchical Semantic model of "UE"

User experience is widely affecting all aspects of the user's experience when they using a product (or a service). It refers to users' pure subjective psychological experiences. UE in 3D UI is more important than in 2D UI. The designer should meet the users' spirit needs after the psychological needs by effective design strategy. UE mainly come from the interactive process of 3D UI. The purposes of visual design about the 3D UI is to convey some information to attract users. Visual means can improve the quality of experiments. Shneiderman and Nielson, two research pioneers of HCI domain, respectively conclude design goals of interactive systems from the consideration of user interface design and usability engineering (e.g., see Table 1).

No.	Ben Shneiderman	Jakob Nielson
①	Learning Time	Learn ability
②	Executing Time	Efficiency
③	User Retention	Memo ability
④	Error Rate	Errors
⑤	Subjective Satisfaction	Satisfaction

Table 1. Interactive System Design Goal

Actually, user experience may be influenced by all these factors above. Experience is the result of interaction between human and artifact (or other creature) in specific context and accommodated by intrinsic、 psychological and individual surroundings which is composed of motivation、experience、habitude and a variety of cognitive factor. In order to measure user experience's level and compare it with different kinds of interactive system, a new concept----EQ (Enjoyment Quality) is introduced and a hierarchical semantic differential model based on EQ is established (e.g., see Fig. 9).

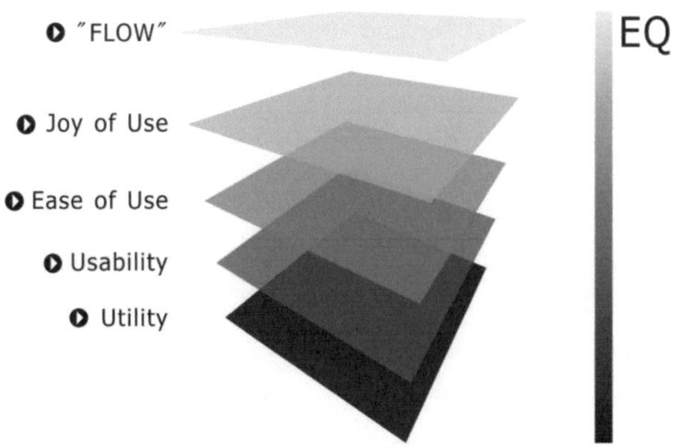

Figure 9. Semantic Differential Model for Measuring "User Experience"

In this model, we utilize five HCI glossaries "Utility", "Usability", "Ease of Use", "Joy of Use" and "the Phenomena of FLOW" to describe user experience, in which the semantic differential is able to represent different level of EQ. Although its scientificalness is yet being further proved, the model is able to indicate orientation of user experience in different systems.

With regard to "different systems", we further divide interactive systems into three groups by referring to Shneiderman's theory: key system, everyday application, and computer games .Obviously, computer games are the most representative one.

- Key system

The application of key system includes transportation control, nuclear reactor system, and military operation and so on. Their chief design goal is "Utility". In order to ensure that operators under high pressure manage to operate quickly with no errors, long time training is always necessary. In fact, adding some hedonic factors to these systems may seriously affects the system performance on its reliability and stability, so such issues are supposed to be taken into prudent consideration

- Everyday application

Everyday application includes industrial and commercial application, office application, and home application. Disordered display, complicated and stuffy operation process, incomplete function, inconsistent task sequence, and inadequate feedback information can be seen here and there [3], so "Usability" and "Ease of Use" are emphasized repeatedly.

Benefiting from the twenty years' development with usability engineering, such problems are being paid attention to and being gradually solved efficiently. The design goal of this group is moving: Usability has become an acknowledged quality aspect of a wide variety of technical products, ranging from software to washing machines. However it recently acquired a new associate, the so-called "Joy of Use". Enhances the non-entertainment system the user experience already is the information system design important idea.

2.2.2 Cognitive Scenario-based GSOMS interactional model

A group of influential theorists at Carnegie Mellon University take the views that decompose the user behavior into small acts of measurable steps to analyze layer by layer. They propose an important model: the goals, operators, methods and selection rules. The GOMS model assumes that users begin with forming the goal (edit documents) and the sub target, and then achieve each goal through methods and process (for example move the cursor to destination through a combination of the cursor key). The change of the user's mental state or the task environment should executive the operator, which includes basic sense, movement and cognition action. Selection rules select one control structure from several optional methods to achieve a goal (for example deletes repeat by the backspace key or deletes the select region by delete button).

Figure 10. Cognitive-Based Interaction Model

3D UI adopt mission analysis to describe users' behavior of each step, including identifying task, cognizing scenario, executing action, perceiving feedback, evaluating result. User's cognitive scenario decides the users' behavior. Obviously, this is where the GSOMS come out, although the original GOMS brought up by Card was once considered as the most successful user behavior model. However, if this model is applied in a tri-dimensional environment, for example, because one feature of tri-dimensional environment is "Scenario", some demerits will appear in the 3D computer games. According to Norman, "The basic challenge which people in different areas faced is the output of knowledge, rather than reproduction (copy) knowledge."Scenario is the extremely effective channel for user to form comprehensive cognition of environment, so scenario-based user interface could help user perform exact, reasonable, habitual operation. And the non-entertainment system is out of scenario and convey with symbols. It values the knowledge that is far away from the real situation, which brings difficulties to cognitive. Recently the cognitive scenario has become a theory based on study, which provide meaningful study and promote the knowledge transform to real life. Therefore, it is very necessary to extend the GOMS model into GSOMS (the Goal, Scenarios, Operators, Methods and Selection rules) model. The interactive model of tri-dimensional information system is based on the users' scenario behavior process (e.g., see Fig. 10).

2.2.3 Screen Layout for Information Minimization

Designer should focus on the layout of the interface to consider the arrangements in the 3D UI, in order to achieve information minimization. We will analyze it from psychology, interactive design, information display and other aspects. In the tri-dimensional environment, users' task is very complicate, from objects accurate movement to the overall situation control. The system offers highly effective resolution, including user behavior process, the design metaphors of the task, information minimization and immediate feedback effect.

3D UI, as a complex system, consists of numerous elements. And more and more information and data user needed to be dealt with appears. Therefore, interactive design should adopt a screen layout with compact and distinct information classification (e.g., see Fig. 11).

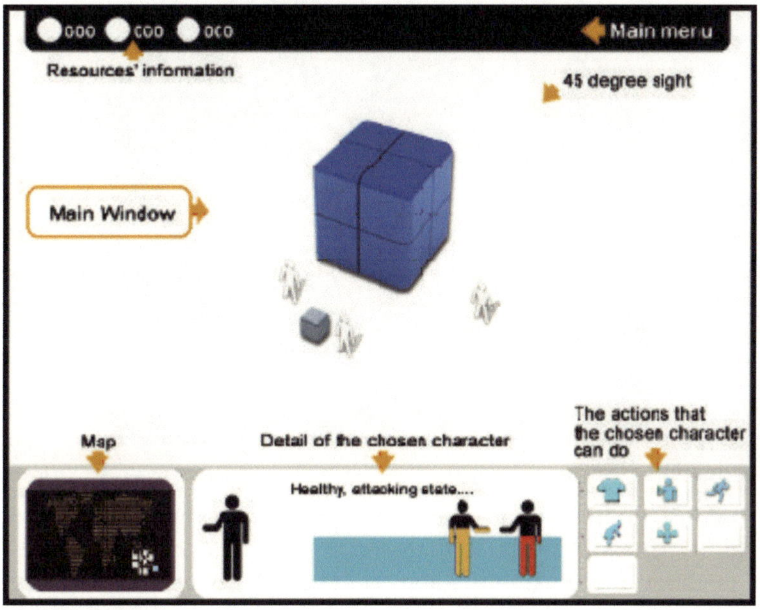

Figure 11. Screen Layout

The screen consists of three parts that are always visible: "Top", "Main Window", and "Bottom".

- Top

The top tool bar includes the scene property of the users, time icon, and so on. Here to provide users for the state and the information directly, so that users can gain the information in need during the shortest time.

- Main Window

The main window shows the detail information with maximum screen. It always shows as god view, and the objects show as rich-information (form, size, shadow, texture, lights and so on).It is called Isometric Projection.

- Bottom

The bottom is the navigation area, including the map navigation, the movement navigation and so on. The narrow sense navigation information was refers to the geography object the positional information, the generalized navigation also should include other function readout which the system provided. In the large-scale 3D scene, Navigation is very significant, by which users know their location and the way to arrive the target area. There is a navigation map of a 3D game, as shown in Fig. 12. On the one hand it distinguish different camps and terrain information through different colors, on the other hand, it reflect the important events through graphical animation. These embody the landmark knowledge, road knowledge and overall knowledge, and the combination of overall navigation and process navigation is another strategy of human-computer interaction.

Figure 12. Navigation Map

Different is in the 3D contact surface needs to unify the concrete mission requirement with the traditional 2D contact surface to carry on the dynamic operation, and to pays the territory the attention to be extremely intense. When basis operation the field of vision region gaze spatial frequency distribution, the gaze the duration, the gaze assigns target and so on sequence, level and vertical glance path scope and number of times examines the appraisal, this kind of three surface layout reasonable has manifested the dynamic sight/attention territory assignment, and is advantageous for the operation.

3. 3D UI interactive technical analysis

This part discussed the interactive technology which is used in most common 3D interactive task. It clearly expounded the basic elements of 3D UI: Manipulation, Navigation and System Control, and the following is arranged in accordance with the user's interactive mission analysis.

3.1 Summarization of 3D UI Interactive Technology

Interactive technology is the manner that performs a specific interactive task by using interactive devices. Users can use the same type of interactive devices, and use different interactive techniques to perform an interactive task. The change of interactive devices, implement methods and algorithms produced a wide range of interactive technology which served interactive services ultimately. Bowman first sorted the existing interactive technology from the three levels which are task, sub-task, and implement technology and proposed this design method based on this classification. As shown in Fig. 13.

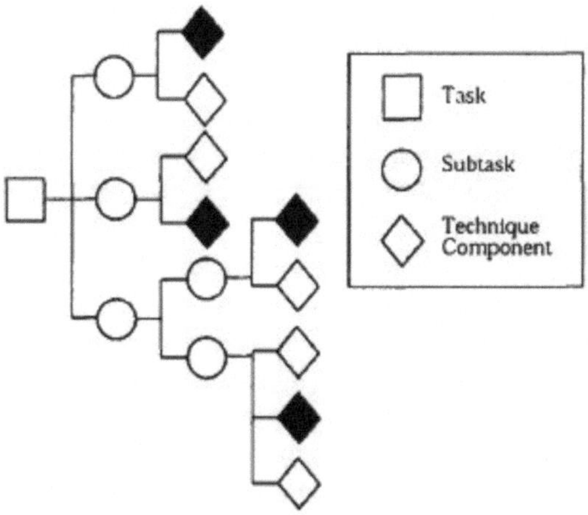

Figure 13. Classification of Bowman

Based on this classification, an interactive task is firstly divided into several sub-tasks, and each sub-task continues to be divided into smaller sub-tasks until there is an interactive technology that can complete this sub-task. These classifications mean can not only discover the affecting variables of interactive technology, but also can guide to design interactive technology. Through the combination the realization technology of different tasks we can easily find new interactive technology. Although it can not guarantee that each combination can get satisfied users' performance, it provides designers a more comprehensive design space. This method is particularly effective when interactive technology options of each sub-task are limited.

3.2 Manipulation

Choice and manipulation are one of the most fundamental tasks not only in the physical environment but also the virtual. If a user can not manipulate and choose the virtual objects effectively, many of the specific application tasks can not be implemented. People's hand is a remarkable device. It allows us to spend less intuitive sense to operate physical objects fast and accurately. The goal of studying manipulation Interface is to enhance the users' capability and comfort, and gradually narrow the impact caused by human inherent habits and hardware restrictions.

3.2.1 Introduction of the concept

Manipulation in reality usually refers to the action that people bring to the objects. In the 3D UI we restricted this action to the rigid objects, that is, the shape of the object does not change in the course of operation, and only the status of objects is changed. This restriction is the same to the 2D UI. However, even such restrictions, technical manipulation can still have a lot of changes, such as the application goals, the size and the shape of the targets, the distance between the user and the objects, the surrounding environment and so on.

3.2.2 Task analysis

A manipulation can change the location or direction of the objects, or change the appearance (such as deformation, material changes). It is impossible to fully consider the impact of these factors in the process of designing interactive technology. We can only aim at a representative task to design. The basic assumptions of any task is that, under any case all the human needs are composed by the same basic tasks, and these basic tasks composed a more complex interaction scenes. With 3D operation decomposed into a set of basic tasks, we can make interactive technology design only for those small tasks.

According to the task subdivision of two-dimensional graphical interface, manipulation task can be divided into three sub-tasks, Selection, Positioning and Rotation. The interactive technologies of each task are restricted by a number of factors which directly affect the capability and availability of technology. For example, when selected, the choice strategy is not only decided by the size of the target, the distance between the object and the uses, but also decided by the intensity of the surrounding objects. The impact of these factors has led to further refinement of manipulation task, such as the manipulation task is divided into two sub-tasks, the range within the arm can catch up and without it. The existence of these variables constitutes a design space of interactive technology. Poupyrev called these variables task parameters, Table 2 are given the task of those parameters.

Task	Parameters
Selection	Distance and direction to target, target size, density of objects around the target, number of targets to be selected, target occlusion
Positioning	Distance and direction to initial position, Distance and direction to target position, translation distance, required precision
Rotation	Distance to target, initial orientation, amount of rotation, required precision

Table 2. Sub-Tasks and Parameters

3.2.3 Manipulation Classification

There are many relationships between 3D manipulation technologies, and they have public properties. Classification of interactive technology based on the general characteristics can help us understand the relationship between the different technologies and understand the design space of the manipulation technologies macroscopically.

Any manipulation technology can be divided into smaller technology components (Bowman 1999), such as in the choice technology, the first step is to show chosen object, and then issue to confirm instructions, finally provide the feedback when chosen, such as highlights, color changed and so on. Fig. 14 classification is based on this method. Based on this method, we can design new interactive technologies through the combination of different technology components, and it provides a good foundation for the variables of the assessment.

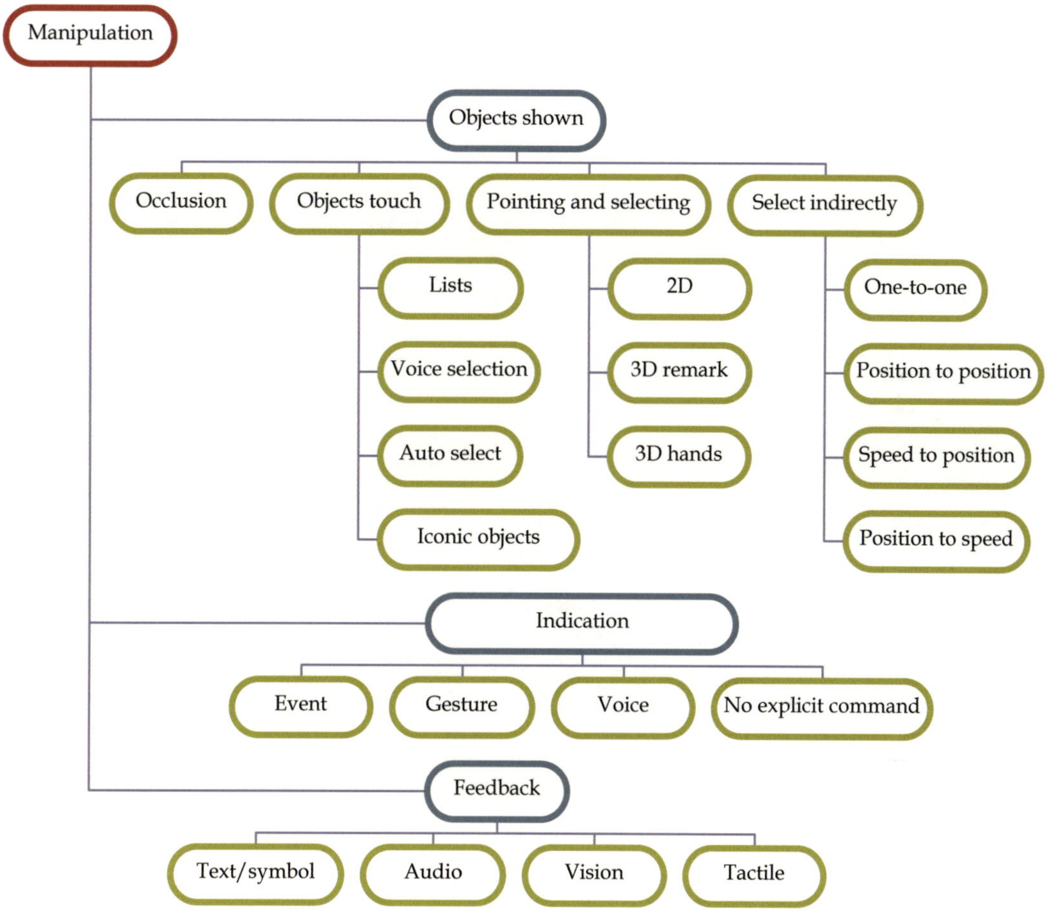

Figure 14 . Classification Based on Task Decomposition

This method based on task decomposition has the advantage that we can make the design space of interactive technology structured. The new interactive technologies are constructed by selecting the appropriate components and assembly together.

Most of manipulation technologies in the virtual environment are archived by several basic interactive metaphors or the combination of these metaphors. Each of metaphors forms a basis mental model. Using of such technology users understand what they can do and what can not do. Specific technology could be regarded as the different realization of the basic metaphors.

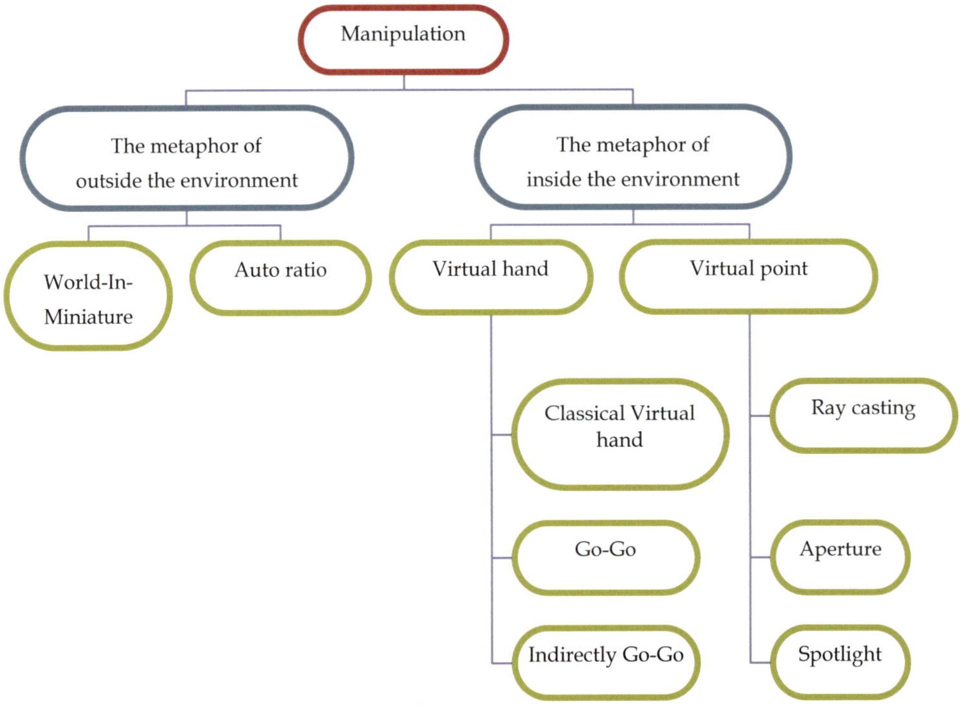

Figure 15. Classification Based on Metaphor

Fig. 15 gives a possible classification of 3D manipulation based on the metaphor in immersion virtual environment. These technologies firstly are divided into two sorts, inside and outside the environment.

Classification based on the metaphor provides a readily understandable way to organize interactive technology. For the virtual hand metaphor as an example, the user touch objects through the virtual hand.

3.3 Navigation

Navigation, which is also a basic human task, is an activity in and the surrounding the environment.

3.3.1 Introduction of the concept

Navigation included exploration and path-finding.

Roaming is a bottom activity that the users control location and direction of viewpoint. In the real world, Roaming is a more natural navigation task, such as the movement of feet, rotating steering wheel. In the virtual world, roaming allows users to move or rotate the viewpoint and change the speed.

Path- finding is an up activity that refers to high-level thinking, planning and decision-making about users' movement. It includes space understanding and planning tasks, such as identified the current location in 3D system, determination the path from the current location to the target location, the establishment of environmental maps. In the real world, path- finding is mainly by map, direction remarks, path signs and so on. In the virtual world, these elements can also help us find the path.

3.3.2 Task analysis

(1) Roaming

Understanding the different types of Roaming task is very important because the availability of a particular technology often relies on the implemented task. The sub-tasks of roaming are defined as: exploration, search and examination.

In the exploration task, the user does not have clear objectives. He just wants to have a general impression of the whole scene. The process can be assisted to users establish awareness of space. This technology provides the greatest degree of freedom to users. User can change the viewpoint direction and roaming speed at any time, can start and stop roaming at any time.

In the search task, users want to achieve a specific goal in the scene. It means that in this task, users know where he wants to go. But it is not sure whether the user knows how to achieve the goal.

In examination tasks, users should position perspective accurately in a limited area, and implement a small but precise specific task. The roaming technology based on this task allowed very precise movement, such as the head's physical movement. It is efficient, accurate and natural.

task	goal
exploration	Browser environment, get location information, establishment of space knowledge
search	Goal-oriented, roam to a specific location
examination	In the local area, involving small and precise tasks

Table 3. Sub-Tasks of Roaming and Goals of Them

(2) Path-Finding

Path-Finding is a cognitive process, which defines a path through the environment and uses natural or artificial cues, achieves and uses space knowledge. We introduce three types of Path-Finding tasks which similar to roaming sub-tasks.

In the exploration task, there is no specific target in use's mind. It helps users build cognitive map, which makes exploration more effective.

In the search task, users need not only achieve space knowledge, but also use it. The searches of known and unknown objects are all search tasks based on the objectives. The difference between them is whether users know the exact location of the objectives.

The examination task, users need to implement many small-scale movements, such as identifying a landmark from a particular perspective, or finding a very small target.

task	goal
exploration	Construction of cognitive map in the browsing process
search	Get and use space knowledge
examination	As the sub-task of search

Table 4. Sub-Tasks of Path-Finding and Goals of Them

3.3.3 Navigation Classification

(1) Classification based on the task decomposition

Like manipulation technologies, the method based on the task decomposition is a classification method which is the most detailed and affects the most variables. Navigation can be divided into three sub-tasks: Perspective direction or control roaming objectives, control roaming speed and acceleration, control the input conditions. Based on this method, we can decompose roaming technology into the form of Fig. 16. Each task can be implemented in different interactive technology. Now most of the roaming technology can find realization technology of its sub-task from the map. We can also find combination of different technologies.

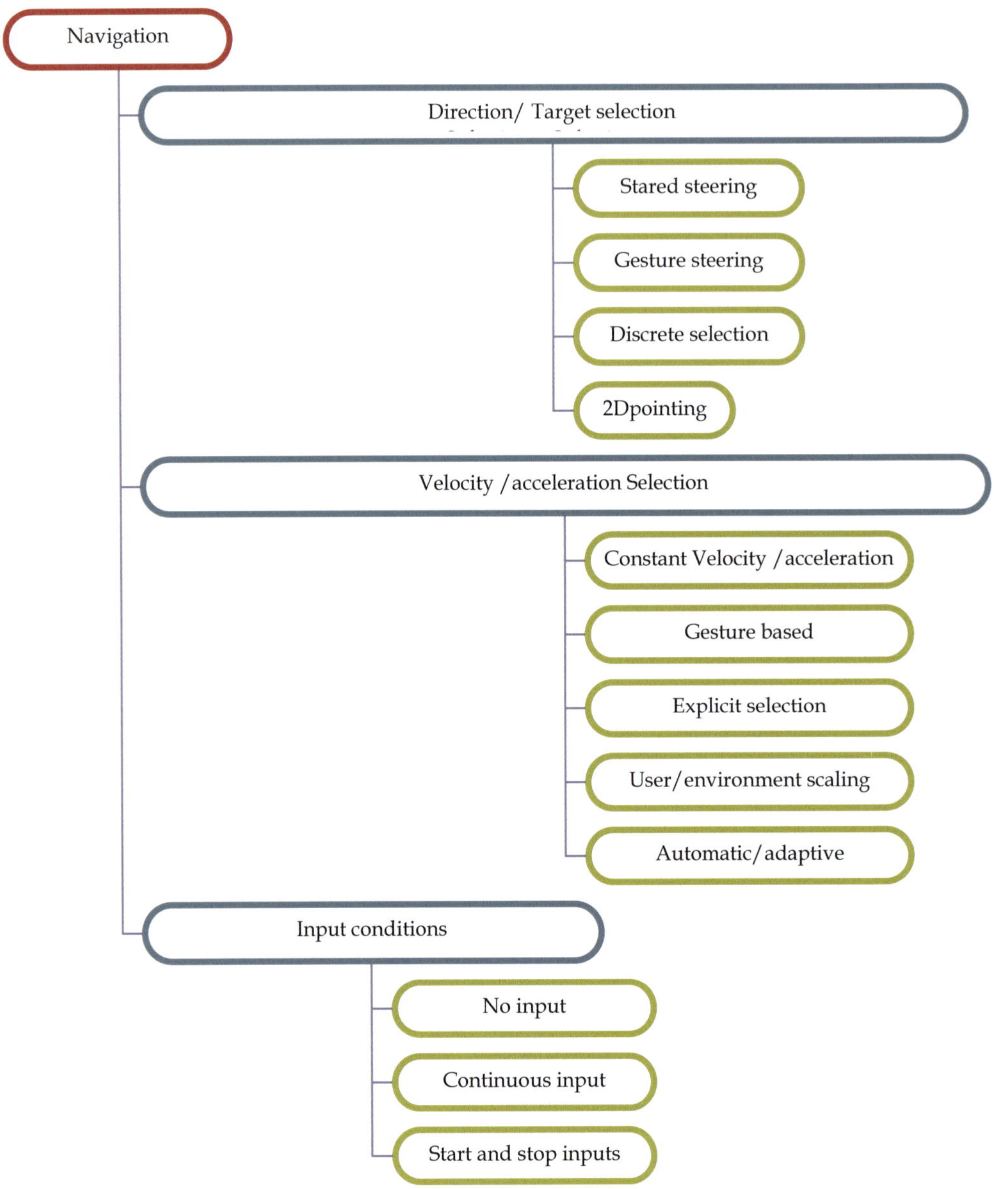

Figure 16. Classification Based on Task Decomposition

Direction or goal choice is the main sub-tasks, where users specify how or where to move. Speed or acceleration descriptions that how users control their speed. Input conditions is that how the navigation to initialize, and to terminate.

(2) Classification based on metaphor

Classification of navigation based on metaphor is easy to understand for users. For instance, if someone told you that there is a special navigation technology used "Flying blanket" as metaphor, you might infer it will allow you to move in three dimensions, and you can use of your hand's movement to drive it. Classification based on metaphor is a useful way of the design space using interactive technology. As shown in Fig. 17, navigation technology is organized through six common metaphors.

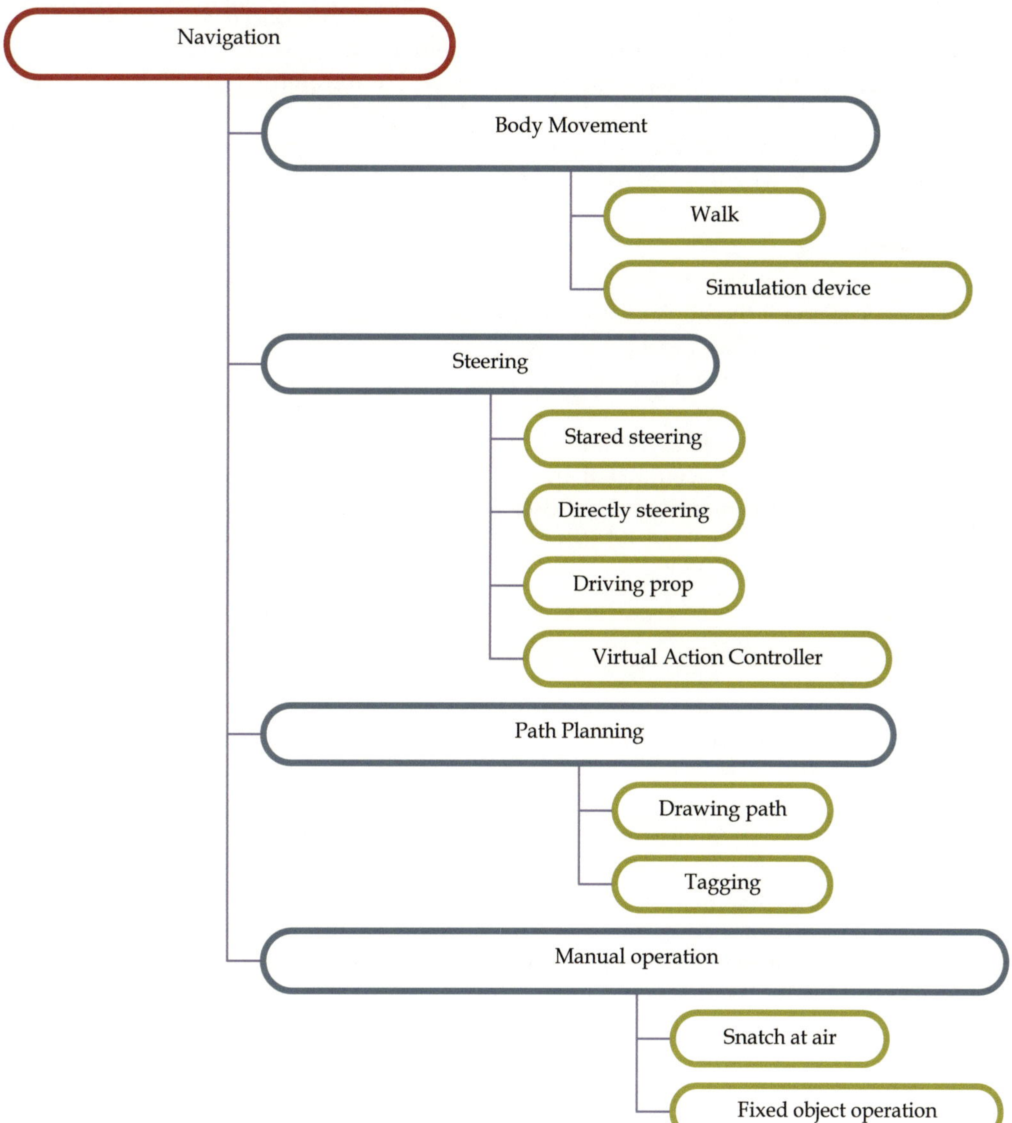

Figure 17. Classification Based on Metaphor

3.4 System Control

In 2D interface, UI elements can be seen everywhere, such as pull-up menus, toolbox, color panels, buoys, radio button and check box. All of these interface elements belong to system control, which allows us to send a command to system, or a mode change, or modify a parameter. Simple imitation 2D desktop devices are not the final solution, so we discuss 3D UI system control.

3.4.1 Introduction of the concept

Although most work in computer application makes up of choice, manipulation and symbols input, system control is still very crucial. When writing in word-processing software, the main symbol interactive input is through the keyboard to complete. These interactions interludes in many small tasks of system control, such as saving the current document through the button to, make the text underline through the shortcut key and so on.

Issued an order is an important way to access to any computer system function, and system control is a user task, which issued an order to complete certain tasks.

3.4.2 Task analysis

Control system is a user task, which issued an order to complete the following tasks:

Request system for the implementation of a specific task.

Change the mode of interaction.

Change the state of the system.

In the manipulation and navigation tasks, users usually not only designate what to do, but also how to do. In the system control, users usually only need to designate what to do, and the realization of details is completed by the system. In the first task, the system has a complete independent feature, such as if user wants the text bold, he just need simply click on the text bold button. The second task is to choose a new tool from a toolbox, such as changing the pencil model for the pen mode. The third task is a click of a button that makes a window the smallest.

3.4.3 System Control Classification

Although the system control technology of 3D user interface is various, but most still use a few basic metaphor or the combination of them, the Fig. 18 is a category based on the metaphor of a control system:

The menu of 3D UI is similar with 2D. 2D menu is rewarded by success in the desktop UI system control, users are known much about it, so the 3D UI could be able to do a attempt. Its biggest advantage is that users are familiar with the style of interaction, almost every user can identify those elements of the menu immediately, and know how to use it. But on the other hand, this type of menu could be shielded by the environment, shielded the realization of users, it may trouble users when they are doing the menu search with the selection technique of 3D. For prevent the menu to shield the 3D environment, it can be designed as a semi-transparent.

The problem of voice commands can be carried out by the simple voice recognition or spoken dialogue system and means of achieving. Speech recognition is a typical application with the simple order which users sent to the system; and the spoken dialogue system concern to improve the session between users and system.

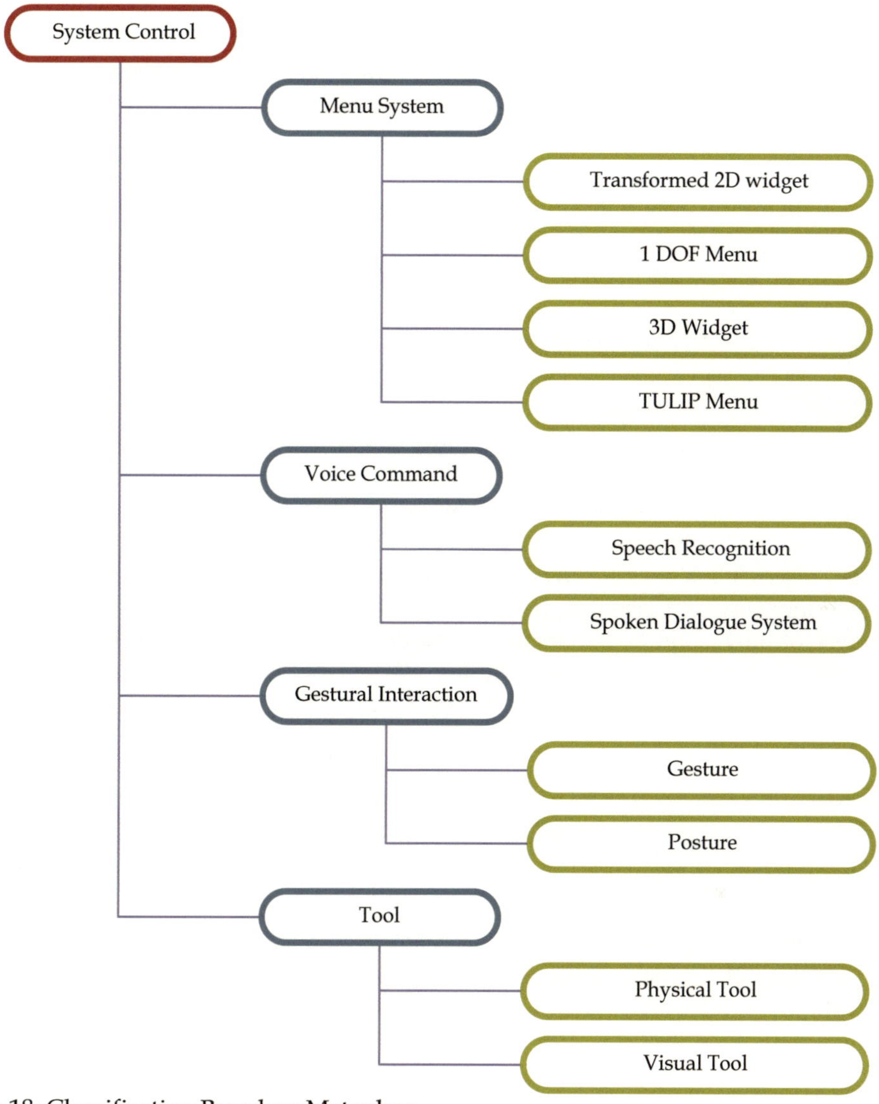

Figure 18. Classification Based on Metaphor

Gestural interaction can be divided into two categories, gesture and posture. Gesture is referred to the shape of hands, and posture is a movement of hand. For example, place the finger into a V-shaped is gesture, and the movement belongs the posture.

In many 3D applications, using familiar device to make 3D interactive can improve the usability, these devices become tools, they can provide a direct interaction.

4. Case Analysis

4.1 The Analysis of Software - Rhinoceros

A special category of 3D interactive technology is the manipulation in the 2D input environment. Next part is the analysis of a 3D modeling software – Rhinoceros, the feature

of this software is mapping the manipulation of 2D mouse to the 6 degree of freedom of 3D object.
The analysis of Rhinoceros will divide to 3 parts: the system control region on top, manipulation region of left part, and the intermediate zone of information display region.

4.1.1 System Control Region

As 3D modeling software is still a software application system, it also uses the menu mode of 2D user interface. Almost all users can identify these menu elements immediately, and also understand how to use them. Fig. 19 is the menu part of rhinoceros.

Figure 19. Menu

When in the 3D virtual environment the most simple way to ascertain the position and direction of 3D object is to ask the users, let them input the coordinate of object's position and the angle degree of direction directly. This approach is usually used in the 3D modeling softwares and CAD softwares which need the accurate position and orientation of the designated object. It's a very effictive technique, as it can adjest the location and direction precise and incremental. Users communicate with system by text typing, such as to defining the distance of movement or the angle of rotation precisely. As show in Fig. 20, it allows users to easily input the related command in order to complete the task want to achieve. A sketchy operating could be able to carry out by a direct technique, but the last value needed to enter.

Figure 20 Input Bar

If you want to implement the control of the entire three-dimensional scenes, such as new create, save the file etc, can be convenient realized by clicking the icon on the panel as shown in the Fig. 21. The icon design intuitive understanding to meet the operational needs of users. The icons in this software are very similar with ordinary 2D software interface, so it can reduce the user's learning difficulty. In addition, there are some in common used operating icons, such as movement, rotation and zoom, all these orders have their corresponding shortcuts, which can improve the work efficiency of expert users.

Figure 21 System Control

4.1.2 Manipulation Region :

In the 3D modeling software, some in commonly use operation orders are usually placed in the left of the screen, such as loft, extrude, and other specific orders. It is classified by the way to arrange the operating buttons with common attribute as a group, For example, the similar orders to generate a plane same - surface from 3 or 4 corner points, surface from 2,3 or 4 edge curves and others are in the same group. It's not only simplified the interface, but also made the system have more level.

Figure 22. Modeling Operate Order

4.1.3 Information Display Region

Rhinoceros used the method of separate the orthogonal view, in each view, users can control 2 degree of freedom at the same time. And in each view in addition, user can specify the manipulation by using the mouse directly to interactive, such as zoom in, zoom out or rotate, and so on. It set up multiple perspectives on the screen, and each perspective shows the same object or scene from a different point of view. Its usually includes a vertical view, front view, side view and perspective

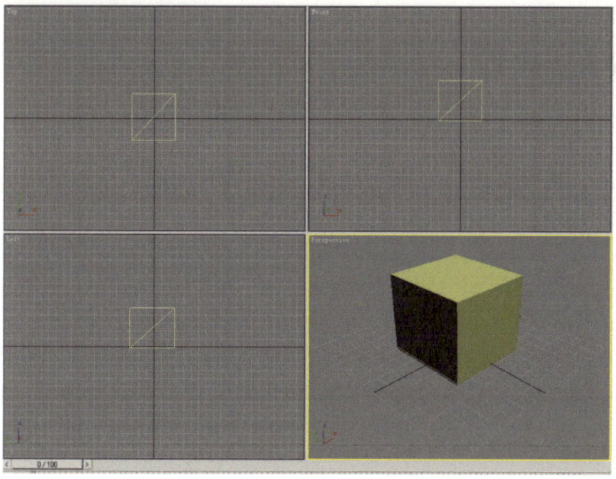

Figure 23. The Orthogonal View

The grid provides a scenario of virtual floor and walls, each axes has a baseline grid, which helps users to locate direction. When the camera view has a freedom motion, the grid will show the particularly use. And the pole is usually playing a role with the grid. When users choose a target object, there will appear a vertical line from the center and extended to the grid. When user moved the object, the pole moves followed, but always plumbs the grid. Users can understand the position of the object they moved in 3D space, by observing the movement starting point of the pole in the grid (x-axis and y-axis), as well as the distance and direction to the grid (z axis)

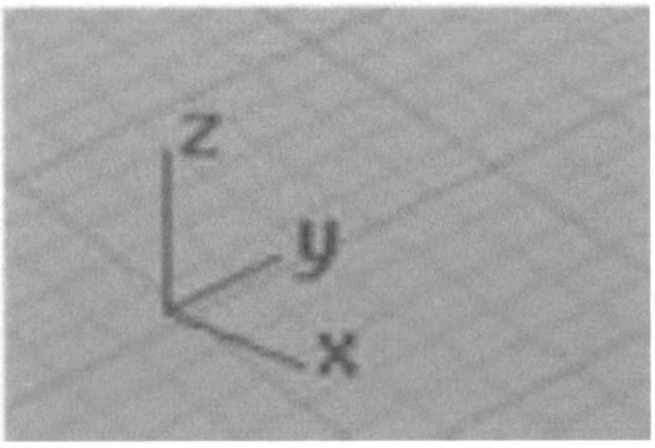

Figure 24. Grid and Poles in Rhinoceros

In the main display area, users can choose the display usage of object, as shown in Figure 1-21 is the wire-frame mode, it solved the problem of objects visualization, while show the internal structure of objects with a faster speed.

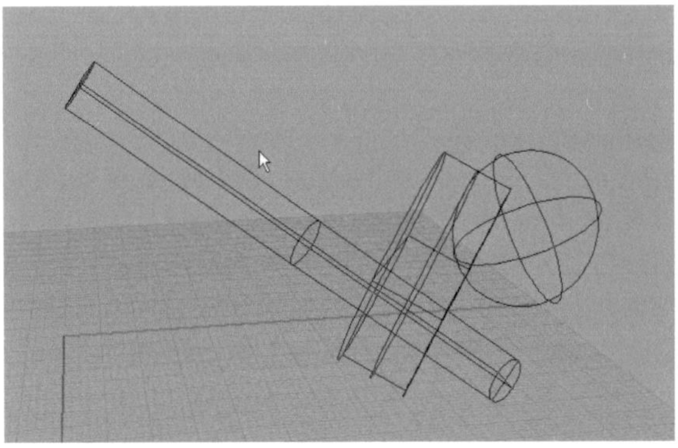

Figure 25. The Wire-frame mode in Rhinoceros

1.4.2 Personal Comupter Games

For a long while, computer games attract millions of people. Besides the how games effect he player's ethical behavior, just for user interface, PC game is the summit of civilian sectors at all times. Along whit the upgrade of both software and hardware, PC game also comes through the process of 2D, 2.5D, 3D. Nowadays, 3D computer games became more and more popular all over the world. The naturalness and interaction are attracting hundreds of thousands of players. The important reason of game's success is the advanced design conception, focus on creating the user's experience. As the game can bring people rich experience, when it has a large number of users, and following rich profit, it makes the developers put more and more energy and financial to the interaction research.

As a restricted 3D UI, we would talk about 2.5D UI as the product in the previous development. And the most typical and the most successful applications are computer games. So we will talk about the user interface in 2.5D, with a real-time strategy game Starcraft ™.

The game used the view, this 45 ° angle could make user control the overall situation, and do a orientation from a high level.

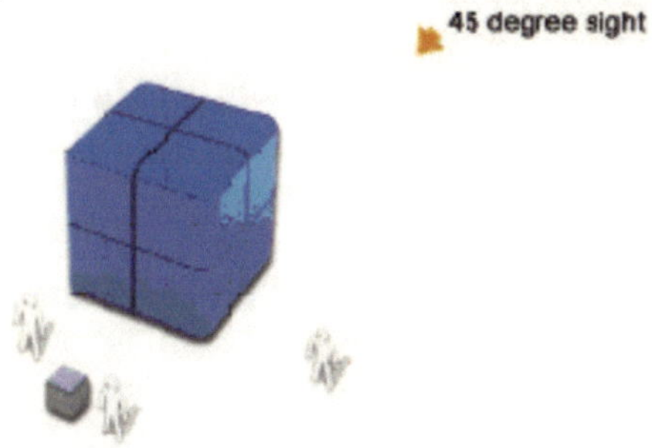

Figure 26. 45 Degree sight

The Screen is mainly divided to 2 parts: The main window and the bottom.

Figure 27. Starcraft ™

4.2.1 Main Window

The main window concludes two aspects of information:

①The resources information, are displayed on top of the detailed view and give feedback on the status of your resources. In process control the resources available are usually not critical parameters. It could be replaced with vital information for a specific process. It might be interesting to give the freedom to the operator to set for instance five most important parameters.

Figure 28. The Resources Information

②It shows a terrain with available resources on which your and your opponent's buildings and troops are situated via 45degree sight (god sight). All these objects have their own animations. Objects can be selected (multi-select possible) and when selected a bar pops up underneath the object that indicates the amount of damage of the object. Moving the cursor towards the border moves the view in that direction. First, the process components can be animated and directly indicate a certain state (e.g. running, on or off or damaged). Second, the multi-select could give an overview of a free selection of process components that are critical at a particular time. The data will be displayed in the properties frame. Third, a bar underneath the process components can indicate the amount of time passed in a process in time.

Cursor is unknown, but plays an important role in the game, such as the choice of location, operation, and other tips. Through the design of the cursor it can be feedback the user's operation effective at the first time. In the Fig. 29 are part of the cursors' difference appearance in Starcraft ™, appeared in different cases. These not only give the information feedback through the icons, but also help users to achieve accurate selection! They play a decisive role in the real-time strategy games to achieve accurate selection, and the rapid response of current operation.

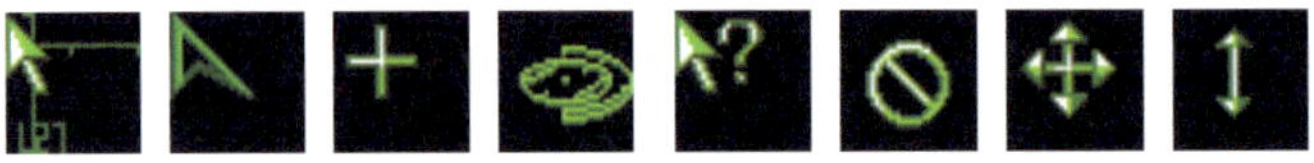

Figure 29. The Cursors

In Starcraft™, when an object is selected, a green circle emerge immediately, and the cursor changes at the same time as shown in picture. And at the same time, the group, single selection, multi-selection, formation and distribute the different colors to different nation, and so on, will help users do more convenient and efficient select operation of the keyboard and search the targets quickly and make orientation.

Figure 30. Selection State

Selection is an important manipulation behavior in both 2D GUI and 3D UI. In traditional 2D interface, all the components are located on a planar window, so it's pretty easy to realize the accurate selection. However, due to the existence of the depth of focus in 3D environment, it became difficult for user to select the objects accurately, especially the ones in the distance. This is one of the most important problem make the user often feels confused. Actually although the objects of RTSG are located on a plane, the objects themselves are 3D isometric projection. And the operator needs to move in a large scale. In the disordered game space, the player still could easily realize the accurate selection.

4.2.2 Navigation and Order Region

The navigation and order region is on the bottom of screen, it include 3 parts:

①A small overview map, is what we usually called navigation map. A white rectangle shows what portion of the total map is displayed in the detailed view. Clicking in this overview changes the position of the white rectangle accordingly and updates the detailed overview. All buildings and troops are displayed as small dots, a different color for each player. In case troops outside the detailed view are attacked, an animated red cross and some audio feedback indicate where to look. A green cross that works similarly is used to indicate that a process (e.g. building of a new unit) is finished.

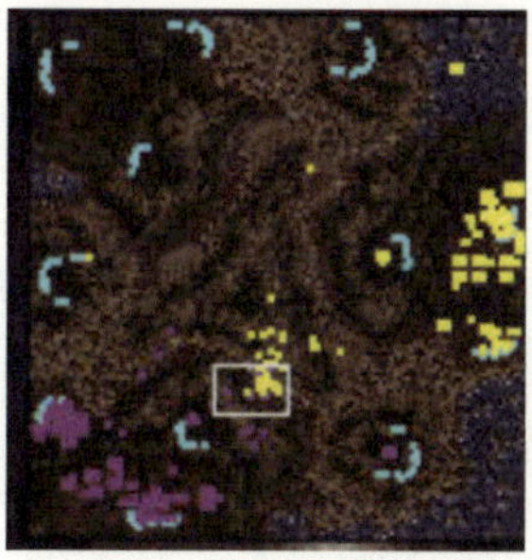

Figure 31. Overview Map

A simplified dynamic overview of the process could inform the operator about that part of the process that is not visible in the detailed overview. By simply clicking in the overview the operator can navigate to a desired part of the process. The color coding within the map could be useful to indicate the state of a component ('failure' or 'no failure'). Since at a certain time many processes can be disturbed, it will probably be a cacophony of sounds and visuals if each disturbance is animated with audio feedback, although it might be interesting to prioritize these disturbances and only animate the most important ones.

②The properties frame in the middle of the bottom part on screen. It displays the current selected object in wire frame with damage indication. Object dependent data is displayed. A small video-screen displays the commander of the object. In case troops are being built within the selected object or a new technology is investigated, a progress bar appears. This progress bar is qualitative.

A properties view could be used to show the parameters that are important for each component. Here also time related information can be displayed (e.g. time passed in shutdown sequence). If necessary a visual could indicate exactly where a failure occurred within the component (to support the service staff). The video screen could display an image of a camera stationed at the component or perhaps even a direct video- and communication link with the service staff at the site. Service staff can also be integrated into the system as objects. A local or global positioning system could update their position in the factory. Simply clicking on them could establish a communication link. In this way, the staff that is nearest to the component that needs service, can be selected by the operator.

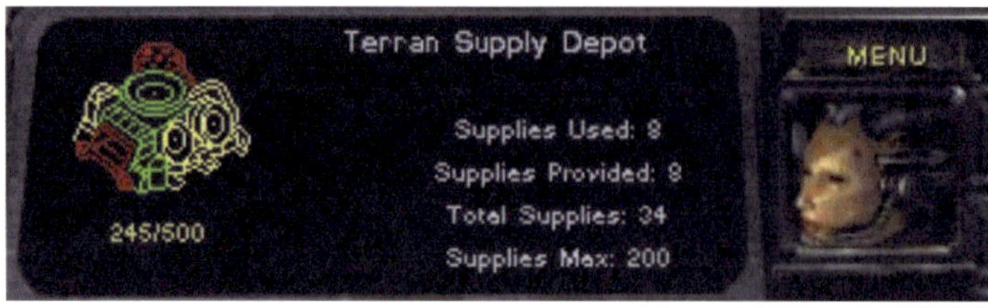

Figure 32. Properties Frame

③The action frame, it displays icons that represent the possible actions that can be done with the current object. The icons have a tooltip-text that appears when the cursor is moved over it, and all actions have shortcut keys. Some actions have one sentence of extra information. In case of place-depended actions (e.g. walk to ...) the detailed overview is used to specify them.

Figure 33. Action Frame

This frame could display the actions that are available for each component (e.g. start-up, toggle on or off, shut-down). Icon representation can be used along with tooltip-text to indicate the possible actions at a time; the set of possible actions can be updated dynamically. In case service staff is also supported by the system as objects, the staff could be directed to a particular place. The instructions could for example be sending to a pager.

5. References

Ben Shneiderman. (2004). Designing the user interface-Strategies for effective Human-Computer Interaction Third Edition (Chinese Language Version), Publishing House of Electronics Industry, ISBN: 9787505393325, Beijing China

Donald Hearn.; M. Pauline Baker. (2003). Computer Graphics with OpenGL (3rd Edition), Prentice Hall, ISBN: 9780130153906, NJ USA

Doug A. Bowman.; Ernst Kruijff.; Joseph J. LaViola. & Jr. Ivan Poupyrev. (2004). 3D User Interfaces-Theory and Practice, Addison-Wesley Professional, ISBN-10: 0201758679, USA

Fu Yonggang.; Dai Guozhong. (2005). Research on Three-dimensional User Interfaces and Three-dimensional Interaction Techniques, Institute of Software, Graduate University of Chinese Academy of Sciences, CNKI:CDMD:1.2005.075006

Ruan Baoxiang.; Jun Xianghua. (2005). Industrial Design Ergonomics, China Machine Press, ISBN: 9787111160496, Beijing China

User Needs for Mobility Improvement for people with Functional Limitations

Marion Wiethoff[1], Sascha Sommer[2], Sari Valjakka[3], Karel Van Isacker[4], Dionisis Kehagias[5] and Dimitrios Tzovaras[5]
[1]*Delft University of Technology*
[2]*Johanniter-Hospital Radevormwald, Geriatrics / Neuropsychology*
[3] *Project manager within ASK-IT, PhoenixKM BVBA*
[4]*National Research and Development Centre for Welfare and Health*
[5]*Centre for Research and Technology Hellas / Informatics and Telematics Institute*
[1] *The Netherlands,* [2] *Germany,* [3] *Belgium,* [4] *Finland,* [5] *Greece*

1. Introduction

According to the Eurostat statistics, 25.3% of the European Union (15 countries) population are "severely hampered" (9.3%) or "hampered to some extent" (16.0%). More specifically, these figures refer to "hampered in daily activities by any physical or mental health problem, illness or disability" (Simoes and Gomez, 2005; United Nations, 2003). Their quality of life would improve substantially if they could participate more actively in the society, while society itself could benefit from this contribution. The transdisciplinary project ASK-IT aims to support this and is developing an ambient intelligence system that provides information to people with functional limitations.[1] This addresses one of the main aims of the European Commission: increasing the participation of all members of the society (e-Inclusion). The idea is that people with functional limitations can benefit substantially from information on the accessibility of all types of services and infrastructure in our society (United Nations, 2003). For instance, a wheelchair user who has information on the accessibility of local meeting places can choose an accessible café to meet people. A visually impaired person who receives timely relevant information on actual arriving times of a tram can decide to take it. Important is that applications presented to the users are personalised, self-configurable, intuitive and context-related. ASK-It aims at supplying useful and timely information about mobility barriers and suitable offerings to overcome them on a mobile phone or a PDA-like device. Users will receive accessibility information tailored to their personal user profile. The information needs for every goal-directed action depend generally on the complex interaction between, on the one hand, the individual (physical abilities, psycho physiological capacities, cognitive resources etc.) and, on the other hand, relevant factors of the environment (objects in a scene, available tools, implicit and explicit

---

[1] ASK-IT: Ambient intelligence system of agents for knowledge based and integrated services for users with functional limitations. Integrated project co-funded by the Information Society Technologies programme of the European Commission. Project number IST 511298; duration 2004 - 2008).

context rules etc.). Riva suggested accordingly to focus on relevant user activities when analysing requirements for ambient intelligence environments (Riva, 2005). The psychological frameworks Action theory and Activity theory are approaches to conceptualize goal-directed human behaviour. Action theory enables the division of complex actions into smaller behavioural units (Frese and Zapf, 1994). Activity theory stresses, moreover, the social context of human behaviour (Kuuti, 1993).

In order to develop these services, the user requirements need first to be established. This paper concerns this first stage: the route from an activity-centred specification of service content requirements to the translation of the identified requirements into a machine-readable format. The methodology for defining user requirements is presented briefly and applied to developing a communication platform to support social relations and communities of people with functional limitations. The methodology is built upon the definition of user groups together with the elaboration and implementation of relevant action and activity theory principles.

2. Methodology

2.1 The content areas and the user groups

The following areas are defined for which ASK-IT develops services for the users with functional limitations: "Transportation" to identify detailed transportation-related data content requirements, e.g. what barriers might exist across different transport modes, what effect uncertainties (such as delays), "Tourism and leisure" to identify everything related to what a tourist who visits the specific area or city would need to know (e.g. hotels, museums, interesting places, embassies etcetera), and leisure content addresses all sectors that are used in every day's life not only by tourists but by residents also. "Personal support services": finding and booking a (local) personal assistant for traveling or special care. "Work and education": Accessibility to schools and working environments and distance learning and -working. "Social contacts and community building": any content to enable making contacts with other people and with people with similar functional limitations, access to meeting places and access to virtual communities.

The user groups are classified on the basis of *functional* limitations. The ICF codes are applied that take into consideration the interaction between health conditions and contextual factors, and provide an adequate basis for the definition of user groups that has been proven to be appropriate in previous projects (Telscan, 1997; WHO, 1991). User groups were defined accordingly in two stages: first a main group classification, and second a nested sub group classification of different levels of severity. The one exception is the wheelchair user group which is classified as a separate main user group, because their functional requirements differ considerably from other users with lower limb limitations. The resulting user group classification has the following main groups: (1) lower limb impairment, (2) wheelchair users, (3) upper limb impairment, (4) upper body impairment, (5) physiological impairment, (6) psychological impairment, (7) cognitive impairment, (8) vision impairment, (9) hearing impairment, (10) communication production/receiving impairment.

2.2 Implementation of Action Theory and Activity Theory into the process of user requirements definition

Sommer et al. (2006) and Wiethoff et al (2007) described in detail the methodological approach for defining the user requirements, based on Action theory and Activity theory.

The central issue in the methodology is the analysis of various types of goal-directed human behaviour (Riva, 2005) in hierachical-sequential action patterns and being organized by higher levels of action regulation.
Activity Theory (Engeström , 1987 and Kuuti, 1995) considers, in particular, organisational issues and the social cultural environment to be very important. In the theory 'activity' is defined as the 'minimal meaningful context for understanding individual actions' (Kuuti, 1993). The activity entails: tool, subject, object, rules, community and division of labour. The object is the entity (or goal) that actors manipulate. The actors interact on the object with the help of artefacts (tools), within a context of roles, and under a set of community rules. This definition of an 'activity' is used in the current project to define the elements that need to be incorporated in our scenarios (see further). For the sake of the present focus on mobile work, the space- time setting is added to define the context of mobile work, i.e. synchronous vs. asynchronous, same vs. different location, mediated by what type of tool, under which rules, and who participates.

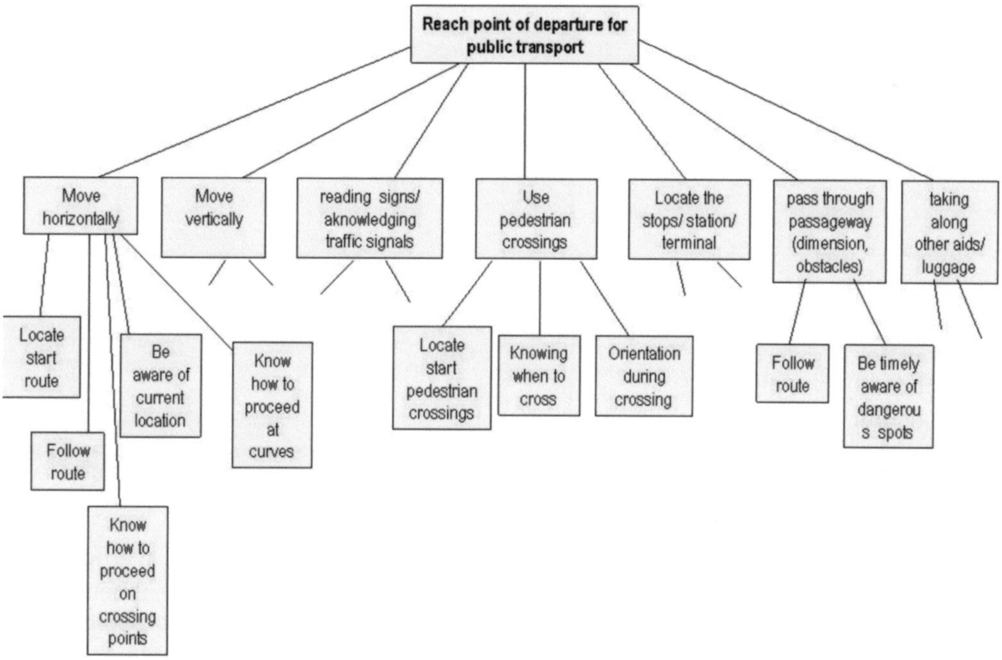

Figure 1. Example of a hierarchical-sequential action process: A severely visually impaired pedestrian finding the station or leaving the station

Figure 1 shows, as an example for a hierarchical-sequential action process, the flow of actions and operations of a visually impaired pedestrian to reach a station for public transport or leaving a station. Decomposing complex goal-directed actions in this manner enables, with sufficient detail, to identify specific support needs of users with different types of functional limitations. For the transport context, it would involve the specific types of information a visual impaired pedestrian needs to be able to navigate and walk safely, what aids people usually have (stick), or may have (dog), and what requirements this involves for the environment. For the social contacts context, it would involve knowledge about the specific patient communities or peer groups available for your user group, or specific communication opportunities if your communication options are limited (speech impairments, hearing or visual impairments).

Information need	Information element	Conditions / Attribute	Value/ type	Value limit	Priority
Find accessibility information	Accessible dedicated mailing list	Name	Text		2
		Description	Text	W3C guidelines	2
	Accessible supporting document repository	Name	Text		2
		Description	Text	W3C guidelines	2
	………				
Add location specific information through a storage unit	Voice driven Recording equipment	Available	Yes/N o		1

Table 1. An extract of the Enabling social contacts and community building Matrix 3 for the visually impaired users. Priorization level 1: nice to have; 2: important; 3: essential

Then, the hierarchical sequential action process is transformed into a set of matrices. The first matrix (Matrix 1) involves the *preparation* of activities (e.g. planning a trip at home). The second matrix (Matrix 2) involves the *execution* of activities (e.g. reaching a destination by public transport). The ASK-IT service is aimed to provide assistance at both these two stages. Each row in the matrices corresponds to a specific activity, action or operation. The columns of these matrices specify for each user group separately the information requirements, specifically for that activity, action or operation. For instance, for "use pedestrian crossings", information elements contain for the severely visually impaired people: "locate exactly the start of the crossing", "knowing when to cross", "orientation during the crossing". The attributes describe in a structured way the environmental factors, which make / do not make accessible operations possible. To each action a set of user group specific attributes can be mapped, e.g. accessible steps to a meeting place.

Then, Matrix 3 is produced. This matrix defines for each information element the characteristics of the attribute (type of variable, e.g. a value, a description), and the prioritisation (essential, important, nice, neutral) of the attribute. Table 1 shows the translation of the action process "Find accessibility information" and "add location specific information at the location through a storage unit" into required information elements for the visually impaired people: Matrix 3.

3. Content modelling procedure

The goal of the content modelling procedure is to provide a formal description of user information needs in a computer understandable and interoperable format, based on the content requirements as presented in table format (see Table 1). The outcome of the modeling procedure is a set of computer-interpretable models that represent the user information needs. These models describe the pieces of information that should be exchanged between the user and different data sources or heterogeneous applications. By imposing a set of constraints on data, a common delivery format is dictated. Thus, when a user with a functional limitation requests a new service, the common data format, which acts as an information filtering facility, guarantees that the user gets access only to valid data values. XML was chosen for representing models, because it is by far the most supported content representation language today. An XML-schema is a definition of the structure of an XML document. Given an XML document and a schema, a schema processor can check for validity, i.e. that the document conforms to the schema requirements.

The procedure for moving from the content requirement matrices to the XML schemes involves the transformation of the matrices into a *tree* structure, consistent with the notation of an XML schema. Each concept related to a specific user information need is encoded as an information element composed of several attributes, related to values of information that the user desires to know in order to be able to read. In Table 2, an example of one *information element* and its *attributes* are shown: this example is for supporting reading for the visually impaired. The full description of the content modelling procedure is presented in (Sommer et al, 2006).

Information Element	**Attributes**
Reading	Screenreaders
	Visual aids
	Audio signals
	Sound volume control for the use of a product with voice output (in a public area)
	Etc.

Table 2. Division of information elements into attributes and their description

The next step is to create the corresponding XML-Schema document. The latter is actually a representation of a collection of elements as the one described in Table 2. A graphical representation of an arbitrary information element comprised of three attributes, is illustrated in Figure 2. This tree-like graphical representation is provided by the XMLSpy authoring tool, which supports automatic generation of XML code by knowledge engineers, without requiring a deep knowledge of XML. The corresponding XML-Schema document that describes the element of Fig. 2 is given in the code segment of Figure 3. The author creates the tree, which is illustrated in Figure 2 using a set of an appropriate graphical user interface, while the authoring tool automatically generates the code shown in Figure 3.

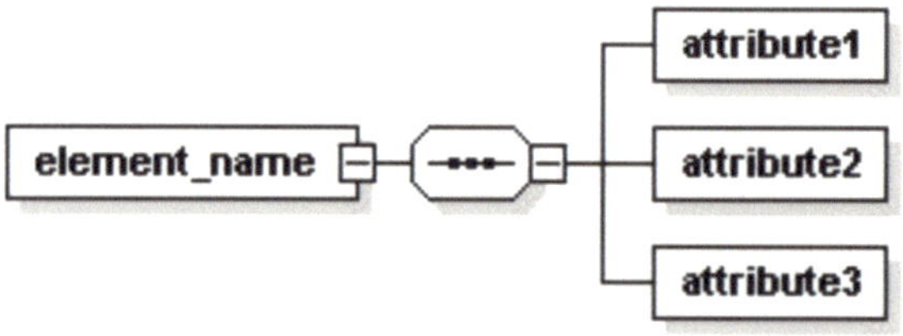

Figure 2. A XMLSpy-generated graphical representation of an element with three nested elements as attributes

```
<xs:element name="element_name">
 <xs:complexType>
  <xs:sequence>
   <xs:element name="attribute1"/>
   <xs:element name="attribute2"/>
   <xs:element name="attribute3"/>
  </xs:sequence>
 </xs:complexType>
</xs:element>
```

Figure 3. An element with attributes in XML-Schema

In the example shown in Table 2 each element is specified by the xs:element identifier. Since the element 'element_name' consists of three elements (i.e. more than one other element), it is a complex data type. This is specified by the identifier xs:complexType. The xs:sequence literal represents an ordered collection of elements that describe the list of three attributes that constitute the 'element_name' in Fig. 3. Primitive XML data types can also be encoded in any schema in order to describe simple data values of the various structural elements. For example, in order to represent temperature in Celsius degrees, the xs:decimal type, which is suitable for representing decimal numbers, would be used. The application of the transformation of the content requirements into the XML tree-like structures will eventually result in tree representations.

4. Application of the methodology to route navigation for visually impaired

Within the ASK-IT project, in collaboration with The Hague City council, a research and development subproject in the field of supporting route navigation is performed. The aim of the subproject is to increase the mobility of severely visually impaired visitors and inhabitants of the Hague. The subproject focuses on the subgroups 8b and 8d (Table 3).

8a. Light or moderate limitations (visual acuity, slow accommodation, etc)	Difficulties in reading, identifying symbols, alternating between displays and road environment
8b. Reduced field of vision	Difficulties in seeing approaching traffic, crossing streets, etc
8c. Limited night and colour vision	Difficulties in darkness or understanding codes or maps, etc
8d. Severe limitations, blindness	No reading or looking for specific locations, etc

Table 3. Subgroups visual limitations

For the groups 8b abd 8d, walking on the street without any aids or an accompanying person is virtually impossible. In general, all the people in this user group make use of a white stick, to warn the other traffic participants, and to feel where to walk and where there are obstructions on the path. In railway stations in the Netherlands, there are guide lines, and in some isolated parts of the cities, and some buildings too. Some people have a guide dog. Guide dogs warn the pedestrian for unsafe parts and obstructions, but they behave very differently concerning the use of guide lines. There are international guidelines for the shape of the lines on the tiles and paving of the tiles on the ground. Table 4 shows an extract of Matrix 3 concerning the guidelines.

Information element	Conditions / Attribute	Value	Value limit	Priority
Special guide surfaces should exist on all pedestrian routes, helping people with vision impairments move regularly and avoid possible obstacles (trees, etc.)	Minimum passage width stick user	mm	750mm	2
	Minimum obstacle free footway width	mm	1500mm	3
	Unobstructed height above footways	mm	2300mm	2
	Minimum width of guideline	mm	See W3C guidelines	3
	Minimum width of the separation of the lines on the guideline	mm	See W3C guidelines	3

Table 4. Extract of the Matrix 3 for visually impaired pedestrians. Priorization level 1: nice to have; 2: important; 3: essential

The following usage scenario illustrates how ASK-IT will support the navigation of a visually impaired person.

Josephine (45) lives in The Hague, the Netherlands and is completely blind. Her eyesight began to diminish only ten years ago, and she is now completely blind.
She is a highly educated specialist in information technology, and has happily been able to continue her work since her vision problems started. She lives on walking distance of her office and knows the route well.
Josephine is very keen on her independence and mobility, and likes to walk into the city, to visit friends, to meet in cafes and restaurants. However, she does not live in the city centre, but near a peripheral railway station. Therefore, it is very important for her to be able to make use of public transport, in particular trains and trams.
Happily, the City of the Hague has provided information on accessibility of public transport, tram stations and various public buildings. Furthermore, from the Central Railway station she can make use of the guideline for the blind, with additional information on her mobile telephone on various important destinations in the vicinity. All she has to do, as soon as she leaves the train, is to activate ASK-IT system on her mobile phone and attach the external loudspeaker on her shoulder, to keep her hands free. ASK-IT guides her from the train platform towards the streets where the cafes and shops are she wants to visit, the library, the Town Hall and the City Hall. Whenever she approaches the tram platforms, she hears which tram platforms host which trams. Whenever she approaches a crossing, she is warned beforehand by ASK-IT. Her stick helps her to feel the guideline on the ground and the obstructions nearby. When she goes through a passageway and along the exit of a parking garage, she is warned beforehand.

Figure 4. A visually impaired pedestrian explores the different routes on the crossing point of the guideline during the test

Currently The City of The Hague is installing and testing a guideline with additional information (Molenschot et al., 2006, 2008, Wiethoff et al, 2006, 2008). The guideline is produced by TG Lining and the information module by Connex-IP - RouteOnline in cooperation with ASK-IT. The guideline runs from Central Station to a few main public buildings in the vicinity, and will be extended up to the Dutch Parliament.

Figure 5. An example of a Smartphone to use ASK-IT to guide visually impaired pedestrians in The Hague

5. Pilot test

Wiethoff et al (2008) presents the first part of the pilot study currently carried out to test the guideline with ASK-IT information module to navigate and to be aware of the environment. The second part of the test will be carried out in the fall of 2008. IN this chapter, only the opinion of users is presented on what the ASK-IT module could mean for them.

In how far was the collection of user needs and the translation of the user needs into a concept for increasing the mobility of the visual impaired user successful? Sixteen subjects, all heavily visually impaired have thus far participated in an empirical study and replied.

In the study, they all walked several tracks with use of the guideline, and in one condition with and in one other condition without the additional ASK-IT information. In Figure 4, one of the participants is using the guideline, exploring a possible detour to go to the entrance of a public building. In this part of the test, participants have to keep the smartphone with the ASK-IT module in their hand.

At the end of the test, they are interviewed. On the question:

"Do you think ASK-IT could help improve:

- (a) accessibility at home,
- (b) planning a trip,
- (c)route guidance,
- (d) leisure and tourism,
- (e) work- and learning,
- (f) support abroad,
- (g) communities abroad? (more answers possible)"

Participants were particularly positive in their expectations of trip planning, route guidance and leisure and tourism and work and learning. (Fig. 6).

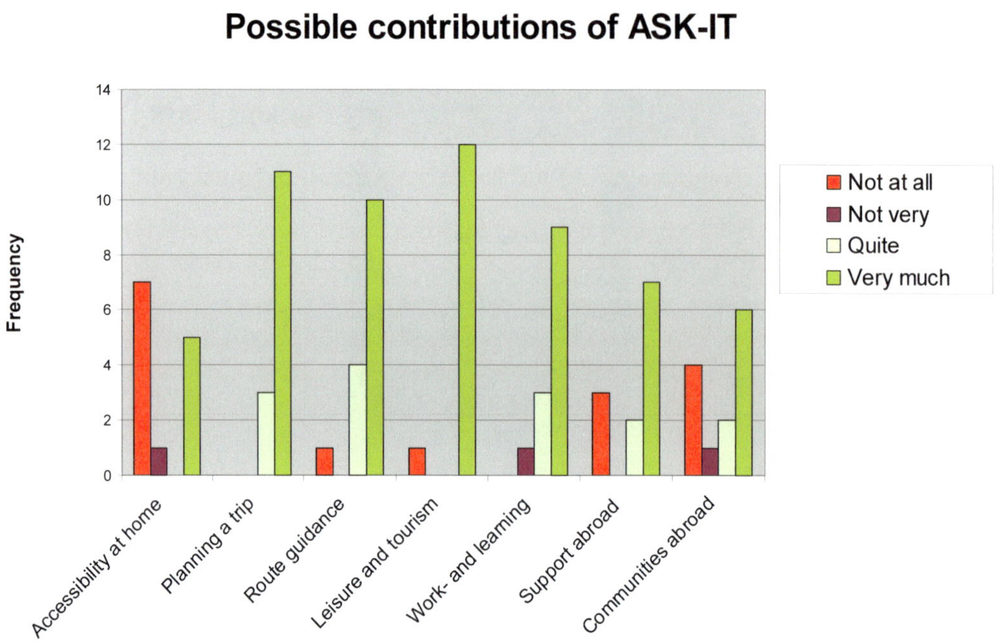

Apparently, the user requirements that were defined beforehand, concerning planning a trip, route guidance and receiving appropriate information on various types of buildings, and possibly also shops and horeca are useful. Furthermore, the accessibility information of buildings is considered of value for work and learning. Many of the severely visually impaired people, however, are currently out of work. Possibilities for re-integration into work is mentioned as very desirable. If ASK-IT can support inclusion of mobility impaired people back into work, then ASK-IT is certainly doing a fine job. A full report of the pilot study will be provided in Wiethoff et al (2009).

6. Discussion and conclusions

The above described content definition and modelling procedure has been successfully applied in the framework of the ASK-IT project. The matrix structure based on action and activity theory principles facilitated the systematic and extensive content requirements specification. Comprehensive content requirement matrices were produced. The tables include user group specific attributes for all identified actions and activities. For some domains, the domain of tourism and leisure, and the domain of transportation, there was the difficulty of the sheer extent of the activities and types of transport, and hence the huge quantity of information needs related to their performance by people with various types of functional limitations (Sommer et al, 2006). This was not so much the case for the social contacts and community building domain, or the personal services domain or the e-work and e-education domain. The lists of content requirements for all domains were evaluated and prioritised by representatives of different user groups.

Morganti and Riva emphasised recently that the focus of Ambient Intelligence for rehabilitation should be the support of the users' activities and interactions with the environment (Morganti and Riva, 2005, p. 285). The integration of action and activity theory principles has indeed proven to be a suitable theoretical framework for the specification of content requirements for a mobile communication platform to support social relations and communities of people with functional limitations. The content requirements matrices provide, for each user group, a structured representation of information elements in the form of classes with attributes and limit values. This approach facilitates the subsequent creation of XML schemes, because the input for the content modelling procedure is immediately available in a format that can be converted into a machine-readable language without difficulties. The subsequent translation of the user needs in design of the ASK-IT components is, at least to some degree successful.

7. References

Engeström, Y. (1987) *Learning by expanding*. Helsinki: Orienta-Konsultit (1987)

Frese, M., Zapf, D. (1994) Action as the Core of Work Psychology: A German Approach. In: Dunnetee M. D. et al. (eds.): *Handbook of Industrial and Organizational Psychology*, Vol. 4, 271 - 340, Consulting Psychologists Press Palo Alto

Heijden, V., Molenschot, T., Wiethoff, M. t, T, (2006) The Hague Smartline: support fort he visually impaired. *ASK-IT International Conference, Mobility for All* - The Use of Ambient Intelligence in Addressing the Mobility Needs of People with Impairments: The Case of ASK-IT

Kuutti, K. (1993) Activity theory as a potential framework for human computer interaction research. In: Nielsen, J. (eds.): *Usability Engineering*, Academic Press London (1993)

Kuuti, K. (1995) Work processes: scenarios as preliminary vocabulary. In: Carroll JM (ed) *Scenario-based design: Envisioning work and technology in system development.* John Wiley & Sons, New York (1995)

Molenschot, T., (2008) The Hague Smartline. Support for the visually impaired. Paper for the *ASK-IT Conference*, Nuremberg June 2008.

Morganti, F., Riva, R.: (2005) Ambient Intelligence for Rehabilitation. In: Riva, G., Vatalaro, F., Davide, F., Alcaniz, M. (eds.): *Ambient Intelligence*, 283 - 295, IOS Press Amsterdam (2005)

Otis, Nancy & Graeme Johanson (2004), *Community Building And Information And Communications Technologies: Current Knowledge*, Nancy Otis & Graeme Johanson, April / 2004

Riva, R. (2005) The Psychology of Ambient Intelligence: Activity, Situation and Presence. In: Riva, G. , Vatalaro, F., Davide, F., Alcaniz, M. (eds.): *Ambient Intelligence*, 17 - 33, IOS Press Amsterdam

Simoes, A. and A. Gomez (2005) User groups classification and Potential demography of MI in Europe. *ASK-It Deliverable D1.1.*(511298)

Sommer, S.M., Wiethoff, M., Valjakka, S., Kehagias, D. & Tzovaras, D. (2006) Development of a Mobile Tourist Information System for People with Functional Limitations: User Behaviour Concept and Specification of Content Requirements. In: Miesenberger, K., Klaus, J., Zagler, W. & Karshmer, A. (Eds.) *Computers Helping People with Special Needs.* Lecture Notes in Computer Science (2006) 4061, 305 - 313.

TELSCAN project (1997) Inventory of ATT System Requirements for Elderly and Disabled Drivers and Travellers, *Deliverable 3.1*

United Nations (2003) *Barrier-Free Tourism for People with Disabilities in the Asian and Pacific Region.* United Nations Publications, New York

Wellman, B (2004)The Global Village: Internet and Community. Idea&s - *The Arts & Science Review,* University of Toronto, (2004); 1(1): 26-30.

Wiethoff, M., S.M. Sommer, S. Valjakka, K. Van Isacker , D. Kehagias and F. Beenkens (2006) Development of a mobile communication platform to support social relations and communities of people with functional limitations.. *ASK-IT International Conference, Mobility for All* – The Use of Ambient Intelligence in Addressing the Mobility Needs of People with Impairments: The Case of ASK-IT

Wiethoff, M., S.M. Sommer, S. Valjakka, K. van Isacker, D. Kehagias, E. Bekiaris (2007) Specification of Information Needs for the Development of a Mobile Communication Platform to Support Mobility of People with Functional Limitations. *HCI 2007,* Springer publication

Wiethoff, M., Harmsen, E., Molenschot, T., van der Heijden, V., de Kloe, R. (2008) A test for Accessibility for the visually impaired of the Hague Smartline. Paper for the *ASK-IT Conference*, Nuremberg June 2008.

Wiethoff, M., E. Harmsen, T. Molenschot, R. de Kloe, H. Brons (2009) *Effectivity of the Hague ASK-IT Smartline.* (in prep.)

World Health Organization*: International Classification of Functioning, Disability and Health* (2001)

34

Recognizing Facial Expressions Using Model-based Image Interpretation

Matthias Wimmer, Zahid Riaz, Christoph Mayer and Bernd Radig
Department of Informatics, Technische Universität München
Germany

1. Abstract

Even if electronic devices widely occupy our daily lives, human-machine interaction still lacks intuition. Researchers intend to resolve these shortcomings by augmenting traditional systems with aspects of human-human interaction and consider human emotion, behavior, and intention. This publication focuses on one aspect of the challenge: recognizing facial expressions. Our approach achieves real-time performance and provides robustness for real-world applicability. This computer vision task comprises of various phases for which it exploits model-based techniques that accurately localize facial features, seamlessly track them through image sequences, and finally infer facial expressions visible. We specifically adapt state-of-the-art techniques to each of these challenging phases. Our system has been successfully presented to industrial, political, and scientific audience in various events.

2. Introduction

Nowadays, computers are capable of quickly solving mathematical problems and memorizing an enormous amount of information, but machine interfaces still miss intuition. This aspect is even more important to interaction with humanoids, because people expect them to behave similar to real humans. A non-humanoid manner of the robot could generate confusions for the interacting person. Therefore, researchers augment traditional systems with human-like interaction capabilities. Widespread applicability and the comprehensive benefit motivate research on this topic. Natural language recognition has already been successfully deployed in commercial systems since a few years. However, to construct convenient interaction mechanisms robots must integrate further knowledge, e.g. about human behavior, intention, and emotion interpretation. For example in computer-assisted learning, a computer acts as the teacher by explaining the content of the lesson and questioning the user afterwards.

Awareness of human emotions will significantly rise the quality and success of these lessons. For a comprehensive overview on applications in emotion recognition, we refer to [16]. Today, dedicated hardware often facilitates this challenge [14, 26, 24]. These systems derive the emotional state from blood pressure, perspiration, brain waves, heart rate, skin temperature, etc.

In contrast, humans interpret emotion via visual and auditory information only. As an advantage, this information is acquired without interfering with people. Furthermore, computers are able to easily acquire this information with general purpose hardware. However, precisely deriving human emotion from this vast amount of sensor data poses great challenges.

Figure 1. Interpreting facial expressions with a deformable face model

To tackle this challenge our goal ist to create a system that estimates facial expressions in real-time and that could robustly run in real-world environments. We develop it using model-based image interpretation techniques, which have proven its great potential to fulfill current and future requests on real-world image understanding. We take a three-step approach that robustly localizes facial features, tracks them through image sequences, and finally infers the facial expression. As explained in Section 4, some components require to be improved over the state-of-the-art, others are specifically adapted to the face interpretation scenario. Our experimental evaluation is conducted on a publicly available image database and is therefore well comparable to related approaches. Our demonstrator has been successfully applied to various real-world scenarios and it has been presented to the public and to industrial and political audience on various trade fairs.

This paper continues as follows. Section 3 explains the state-of-the-art of facial expression recognition covering both psychological theory and state-of-the-art algorithms. Section 4 describes the various components of our model-based approach. Section 5 experimentally evaluates our approach on a publicly available image database and draws a comparison to related approaches. Section 6 summarizes our achievement and points out future work.

3. Facial Action Recognition: State-of-the-art

This section elaborates on psychological aspects of facial expression recognition and indicates the state-of-the-art of current techniques.

3.1 Universal Facial Expressions and the Facial Action Coding System (FACS)

Ekman and Friesen [7] find six universal facial expressions that are expressed and interpreted in the same way by humans of any origin all over the world. They do not depend on the cultural background or the country of origin. As an example, Figure 1 shows how our technique distinguishes between the different facial expressions using a model-based approach.

The Facial Action Coding System (FACS) [8] precisely describes the muscle activities within a human face when facial expressions are displayed. Action Units (AUs) denote the motion of particular facial parts and state the facial muscles involved. Facial expressions are generated by the combinations of AUs. Extended systems like the Emotional FACS [12] specify the relation between facial expressions and emotions.

3.2 Benchmark DB

The Cohn-Kanade-Facial-Expression database (CKFE-DB) contains 488 short image sequences of 97 different persons performing the six universal facial expressions [15]. It provides researchers with a large dataset for experimenting and benchmarking purpose. Each sequence shows a neutral face at the beginning and then develops into the peak expression. Furthermore, a set of AUs has been manually specified by licensed FACS-experts for each sequence. Note that this database does not contain natural facial expressions, but volunteers were asked to act. Furthermore, the image sequences are taken in a laboratory environment with predefined illumination conditions, solid background and frontal face views. Algorithms that perform well with these image sequences are not immediately appropriate for real-world scenes.

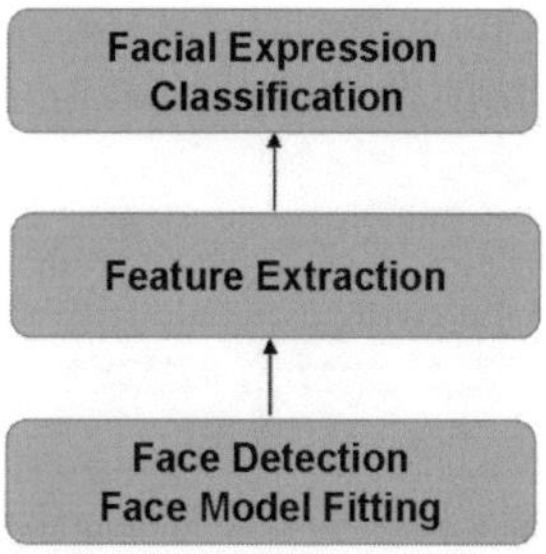

Figure 2. The common three-phase procedure for recognizing facial expressions, see [19]

3.3 The Common Three-phase Procedure

According to the survey of Pantic et al. [19], the computational task of facial expression recognition is usually subdivided into three subordinate challenges: face detection, feature extraction, and facial expression classification as shown in Figure 2. Chibelushi et al. [1] added a pre- and a post-processing step. This section presents several state-of-the-art approaches, which accomplish the involved steps in different ways. For a more detailed overview we refer to Chibelushi et al.

Phase 1, the human face and the facial components have to be accurately located within the image. This is often accomplished by computing a bounding box that roughly specifies the location and the extent of the entire face. More elaborate approaches make use of a fine grain face model, which has to be fitted precisely to the contours of the visible face. As an advantage, the model-based approach provides information about the relative location of the different facial components and their deformation, which turns out to be useful for the subsequent phases.

On the one hand, automatic algorithms compute the location of the visible face as in [18, 10, 4]. On the other hand, humans specify this information by hand, because the researchers rather focus on the subsequent interpretation task itself, as in [23, 2, 22, 25].

Phase 2, knowing the exact position of the face, features that are descriptive for facial expressions are extracted from the image data. Facial expressions consist of two important aspects: the muscle activity while the expression is developping and the shape of the peak expression. Algorithms focus on extracting features that represent these aspects.

Michel et al. [18] extract the location of 22 feature points within the face and determine their motion between an image of the neutral face and an image of the peak expression. They use feature points that are mostly located around the eyes and around the mouth. The very similar approach of Cohn et al. [3] uses hierarchical optical flow in order to determine the motion of 30 feature points. They term their approach feature point tracking. Littlewort et al. [17] utilize a bank of 40 Gabor wavelet filters at different scales and orientations to extract features directly from the image. They perform convolution and obtain a vector of magnitudes of complex valued responses.

Phase 3, the facial expression is derived from the previously extracted features. Mostly a classifier is learned from a comprehensive training set of annotated examples. Some approaches first compute the visible AUs and then infer the facial expression by rules stated by Ekman and Friesen [9]. Michel et al. [18] train a Support Vector Machine (SVM) that determines the visible facial expression within the video sequences of the CKFE-DB by comparing the first frame with the neutral expression to the last frame with the peak expression. Schweiger and Bayerl [22] compute the optical flow within 6 predefined regions of a human face in order to extract the facial features. Their classification is based on supervised neural network learning.

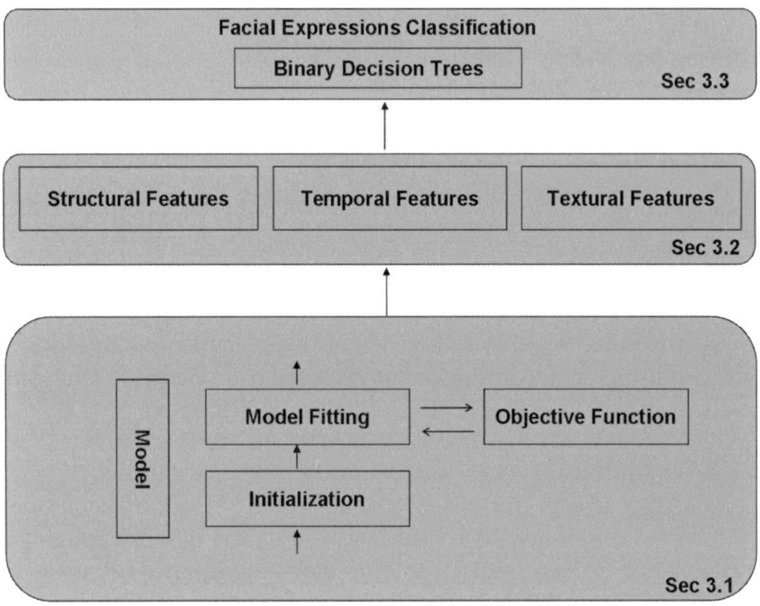

Figure 3. The three-phase procedure with our concrete implementation. Our work especially focuses on Phase 1, where we use model-based techniques. This approach splits the challenge of image interpretation into four computationally independent modules: the model, initialization, model fitting, and the objective function. Our work contributes to designing robust objective functions

4. Facial Expressions Recognition via Model-Based Techniques

Our approach makes use of model-based techniques, which exploit a priori knowledge about objects, such as their shape or texture, see Figure 3. Reducing the large amount of image data to a small set of model parameters facilitates and accelerates the entire process of facial expression interpretation. Our approach sticks to the three phases stated by Pantic et al. [19]. In Section 4.1. we consider fitting a face model to the camera image. Section 4.2

describes the extraction of meaningful features and Section 4.3 shows how we derive the facial expressions visible from these features.

4.1 Model-based Image Interpretation

Model-based techniques consist of four components: the model, the initialization algorithm, the objective function, and the fitting algorithm [28], see Figure 4.

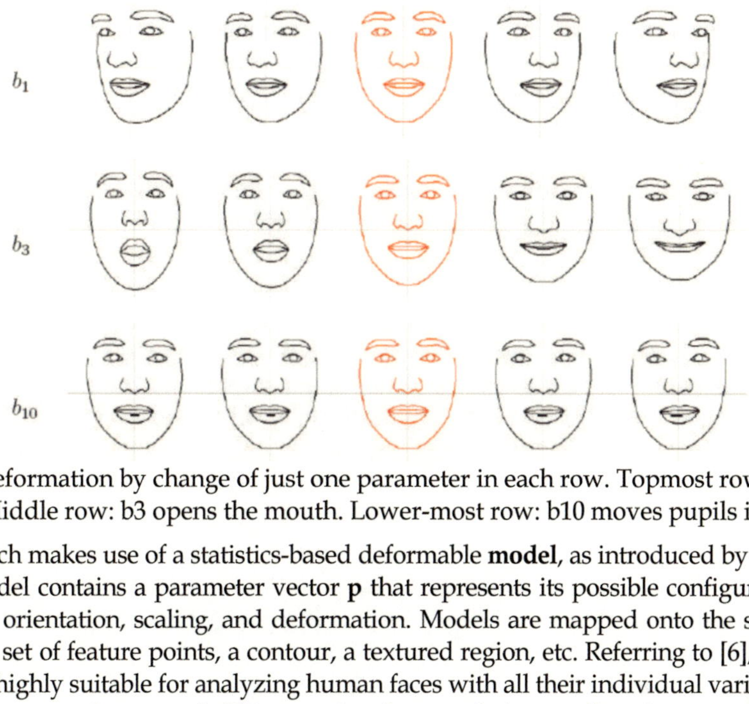

Figure 4. Deformation by change of just one parameter in each row. Topmost row: b1 rotates the head. Middle row: b3 opens the mouth. Lower-most row: b10 moves pupils in parallel

Our approach makes use of a statistics-based deformable **model**, as introduced by Cootes et al. [5]. The model contains a parameter vector **p** that represents its possible configurations, such as position, orientation, scaling, and deformation. Models are mapped onto the surface of an image via a set of feature points, a contour, a textured region, etc. Referring to [6], deformable models are highly suitable for analyzing human faces with all their individual variations.

Its parameters $p = (tx, ty, s, \theta, b)^T$ comprise the translation, scaling factor, rotation, and a vector of deformation parameters $b = (b_1, . . . , b_m)^T$. The latter component describes the configuration of the face, such as the opening of the mouth, roundness of the eyes, raising of the eye brows, see Figure 4.

The **initialization algorithm** automatically starts the interpretation process by roughly localizing the object to interpret, see Figure 5. It computes an initial estimate of the model parameters that needs to be further refined by the subsequent fitting algorithm. Our system integrates the approach of Viola and Jones [27], which is able to detect the affine transformation parameters (tx, ty, s, and θ) of frontal faces.

Figure 5. Localizing face and eyes using Viola and Jones' boosting algorithm

In order to obtain higher accuracy, we apply a second iteration of the Viola and Jones object detector to the previously determined image region of the face. In this iteration the algorithm is utilized to localize facial components, such as eyes and mouth. This extension allows to roughly estimate the deformation parameters b as well. The algorithm has been trained on positiv and negativ training examples. In the case of the eyes, our positive training examples contain the images of eyes, whereas the negative examples consist of image patches in the vicinity of the eyes, such as the cheek, the nose, or the brows. Note that the resulting eye detector is not able to robustly localize the eyes in a complex image, because it usually contains a lot of information that was not part of the training data. However, it is highly appropriate to determine the location of the eyes within a pure face image or within the face region of a complex image.

The **objective function** f(I, p) yields a comparable value that specifies how accurately a parameterized model p describes the content of an image I. It is also known as the likelihood, similarity, energy, cost, goodness, or quality function. Without losing generality, we consider lower values to denote a better model fit. Traditionally, objective functions are manually specified by first selecting a small number of simple image features, such as edges or corners, and then formulating mathematical calculation rules. Afterwards, the appropriateness is subjectively determined by inspecting the result on example images and example model parameterizations. If the result is not satisfactory the function is tuned or redesigned from scratch. This heuristic approach relies on the designer's intuition about a good measure of fitness. Our earlier works [29, 30] show that this methodology is erroneous and tedious. This traditional approach is depicted to the left in Figure 6.

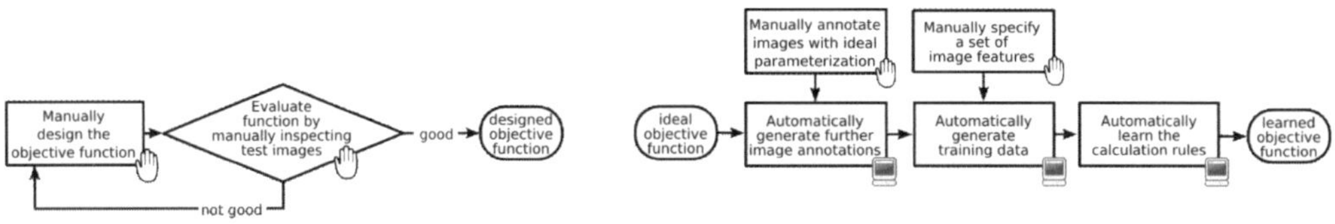

Figure 6. The traditional procedure for designing objective functions (left), and the proposed method for learning objective functions (right)

To avoid these drawbacks, we recently proposed an approach that learns the objective function from annotated example images [29]. It splits up the generation of the objective function into several partly automated tasks. This provides several benefits: firstly, automated steps replace the labor-intensive design of the objective function. Secondly, this approach is less error prone, because giving examples of good fit is much easier than explicitly specifying rules that need to cover all examples. Thirdly, this approach does not rely on expert knowledge and therefore it is generally applicable and not domain-dependent. The bottom line is that this approach yields more robust and accurate objective functions, which greatly facilitate the task of the fitting algorithm. For a detailed description of our approach, we refer to [29].

The **fitting algorithm** searches for the model that best describes the face visible in the image. Therefore, it aims at finding the model parameters that minimize the objective function. Fitting algorithms have been the subject of intensive research and evaluation, e.g. Simulated Annealing, Genetic Algorithms, Particle Filtering, RANSAC, CONDENSATION, and CCD, see [13] for a recent overview and categorization. We propose to adapt the objective function rather than the fitting algorithm to the specifics of our application. Therefore, we are able to use any of these standard fitting algorithms, the characteristics of which are well-known, such as termination criteria, runtime, and accuracy. Due to real-time requirements, our experiments in Section 5 have been conducted with a quick hill climbing algorithm. Note that the reasonable specification of the objective function makes this local optimization strategy nearly as accurate as a global optimization strategy, such as Genetic Algorithms.

4.2 Extraction of Structural, Temporal and Textural Features

Two aspects generally characterize facial expressions i.e. their structural contribution and temporal behavior: they turn the face into a distinctive state [17] and the involved muscles show a distinctive motion [22, 18]. Our approach considers both aspects by extracting structural and temporal features. Furthermore, Textural features represent context knowledge about the person, such as the general face shape, age or gender. This large amount of feature information provides a profound basis for the subsequent classification step, which therefore achieves great accuracy.

Structural features: The deformation parameters b describe the constitution of the visible face. The examples in Figure 4 illustrate the relation between the facial expression and the value of b. Therefore, we consider b to provide high-level information to the interpretation process. These features are assembled in a feature vector. In contrast, the transformation parameters tx, ty, s, and θ are not related to the facial expression and therefore, we do not consider them as features.

$$t_0 = (b_1, \ldots\ldots, b_m)^T$$

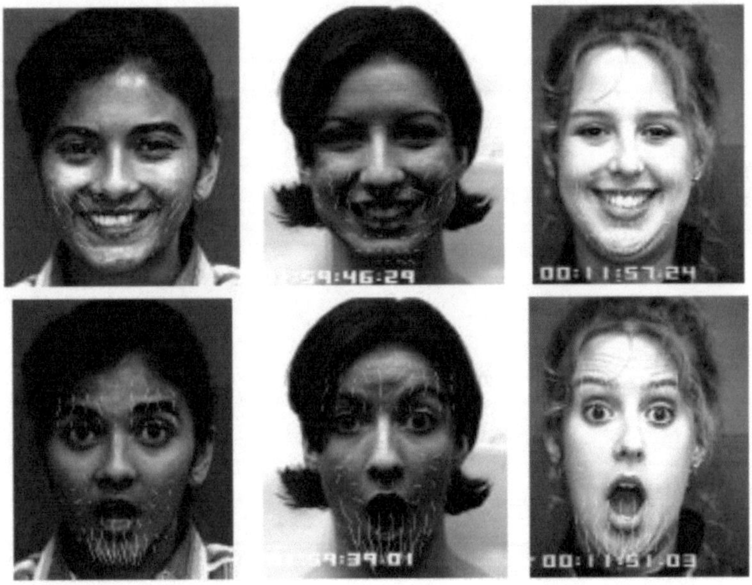

Figure 7. Fitting a deformable face model to images and inferring different facial expressions by taking structural and temporal image features into account

Temporal features: Since facial expressions emerge from muscle activity, the motion of particular feature points within the face gives evidence about the facial expression. Real-time capability is important, and therefore, a small number of feature points is considered only. The relative location of these points is connected to the structure of the face model. Note that we do not specify these locations manually, because this assumes a good experience of the designer in analyzing facial expressions. In contrast, we automatically generate G feature points that are uniformly distributed. We expect these points to move descriptively and predictably in the case of a particular facial expression. We sum up the motion $g_{x,i}$ and $g_{y,i}$ of each point $1 \leq i \leq G$ during a short time period. We set this period to 2 sec to cover slowly expressed emotions as well. The motion of the feature points is normalized by the affine transformation of the entire face (tx, ty, s, and θ) in order to separate the facial motion from the rigid head motion.

In order to determine robust descriptors, Principal Component Analysis (PCA) determines the H most relevant motion patterns (principal components) visible within the set of training sequences. A linear combination of these motion patterns describes each observation approximately correct. This reduces the number of descriptors (H ≤ 2G) by enforcing robustness towards outliers as well. As a compromise between accuracy and runtime performance, we set the number of feature points to G = 140 and the number of motion patterns to H = 14. Figure 7 visualizes the obtained motion of the feature points for some example facial expressions.

The feature vector **t** is assembled from the m structural and the H temporal features as mentioned in equation below. This vector represents the basis for facial expression classification.

$$t_1 = (b_1, \ldots\ldots, b_m, h_1, \ldots\ldots h_H)^T$$

Textural features are obtained by applying PCA on extracted texture from face images. These texture examples cover the full face boundary excluding the forehead, hair and the ears. In contrast to shape deformations, that are caused by facial expression changes and varying head poses, texture variations arise mainly due to illumination changes. Therefore, various training images of the same person consider different types of texture variations. However, shape parameters have to be estimated first before recording the texture parameters. Figure 8 demonstrates the warping of the texture extracted from an example image onto the reference shape.

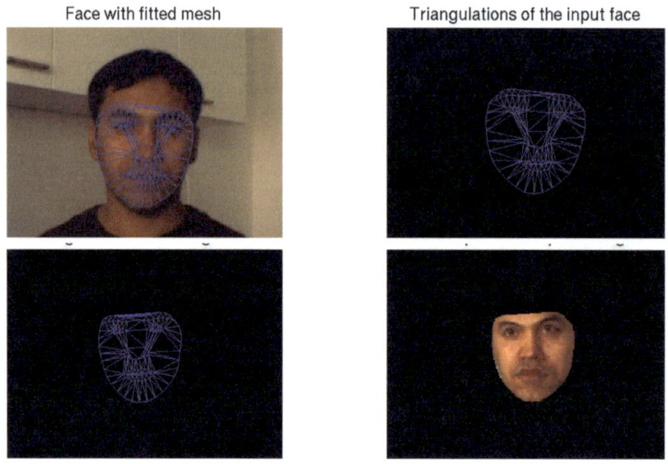

Figure 8. Face with fitted Model (Top Left) , Model of the input image (Top Right) , Reference shape (Bottom Left) ,Texture warping results on the reference shape (Bottom Right)

Ground truth	Classified as by t_0						Recognition rate
	Surprise	Happiness	Anger	Disgust	Sadness	Fear	
Surprise	61	0	0	1	3	17	85.9%
Happiness	1	57	2	3	0	**11**	77.0%
Anger	0	0	11	5	12	7	31.4%
Disgust	2	7	8	9	3	7	25.0%
Sadness	8	0	10	5	27	9	45.8%
Fear	5	**17**	2	9	8	17	29.8%
Average recognition rate							**49.1%**
Ground truth	Classified as by t_1						Recognition rate
	Surprise	Happiness	Anger	Disgust	Sadness	Fear	
Surprise	28	1	1	0	0	0	93.3%
Happiness	1	26	2	2	3	**4**	70.3%
Anger	1	1	14	2	2	1	66.7%
Disgust	0	2	1	10	3	1	58.8%
Sadness	1	2	2	2	22	1	73.3%
Fear	1	**5**	1	0	2	13	59.1%
Average recognition rate							**70.3%**
Ground truth	Classified as by t_2						Recognition rate
	Surprise	Happiness	Anger	Disgust	Sadness	Fear	
Surprise	64	0	1	2	3	1	90.1%
Happiness	1	59	0	1	0	**13**	79.7%
Anger	0	0	14	5	10	6	40.0%
Disgust	3	3	5	13	6	6	36.1%
Sadness	2	0	9	4	35	9	59.3%
Fear	4	**15**	0	8	1	30	51.7%
Average recognition rate							**59.5%**

Table 1. Confusion matrix and recognition rate of our approach

Given a set of shape points x of the input example image and x_{ref} of the reference image, we compute the relative position in the example image to every pixel position in the reference shape and sample the texture values to gain the texture vector l_{text}. The texture vector is normalized to remove global lighting effects. Piecewise affine transform is used to warp the texture of the example image on the reference shape [35]. From the warped texture and the PCA data the textural features are estimated. Texture's parameters variations cause changes in the appearance of the faces similar to the eigenfaces approach [36]. The combination of shape and texture parameters is well-known Active Appearance Model (AAM) introduced by Cootes et al [37]. Since this approach utilizes both, shape and texture information its feature vector contains shape parameters b as well as the textural features l.

$$t_2 = (b_1, \ldots\ldots, b_m, l_1, \ldots\ldots l_L)^T$$

4.3 Classification of Facial Expressions Using Decision Trees

With the knowledge of the feature vector **t**, a classifier infers the correct facial expression. We learn a Binary Decision Tree [20], which is a robust and quick classifier. However, any other multi-class classifier that is able to derive the class membership from real valued features can be integrated as well, such as a k-Nearest-Neighbor classifier. We take 67% of the image sequences of the CKFE-DB as the training set and the remainder as test set, the evaluation on which is shown in the next section.

5. Experimental Evaluation

In order to evaluate the accuracy of our approach, we apply it to the previously unseen fraction of the CKFE-DB. Table 1 shows the recognition rate and confusion matrix of each facial expression. The facial expressions happiness and fear are confused most often. The reason for this confusion is the similar muscle activity around the mouth. This coincidence is also reflected by FACS.

Facial expression	Our results t_0	Our results t_1	Our results t_2	Appraoch of Michel et al. [18]	Approach of Schweiger et al. [22]
Anger	31.4%	66.7%	40.0%	66.7%	75.6%
Disgust	25.0%	58.8%	36.1%	58.8%	30.0%
Fear	29.3%	59.1%	51.7%	66.7%	0.0%
Happiness	77.0%	70.3%	79.7%	91.7%	79.2%
Sadness	45.8%	73.3%	59.3%	62.5%	60.5%
Surprise	85.9%	93.3%	90.1%	83.3%	89.8%
Average	49.1%	70.3%	59.5%	71.8%	55.9%

Table 2. Recognition rate of our approach compared to the results of different algorithms

The accuracy of our approach is comparable to the one of Schweiger et al. [22] who also conduct their evaluation on the CKFE-DB, see Table 2. For classification, they also favor motion from different facial parts and determine principal components from these features.

However, Schweiger et al. manually specify the region of the visible face whereas our approach performs an automatic localization via model-based image interpretation. Michel et al. [18] also focus on facial motion by manually specifying 22 feature points that are predominantly located around the mouth and around the eyes. They utilize a support vector machine (SVM) for determining one of the six facial expressions.

In order to account for local variation and to fulfill the lack of ground truths, an appearance model based approach is used to train a classifier. This improves the results further.

6. Summary and Outlook

Automatic recognition of human facial gestures has recently attained a significant place in multimodal human-machine interfaces and further applications. This paper presents our proof-of concept for Facial Expression Interpretation, which is real-time capable and robust enough to be deployed to real-world scenarios.

We exploit model-based techniques and adapt them specifically to facial expression recognition. First, we extract informative features about faces from the image data that describes skin color and lip color regions. Furthermore, we learn the objective function for model fitting from example images as opposed to constructing it manually.

The obtained system shows promising referring to its recognition results and we have successfully conducted live demonstrations that were attended by industrial and political audience, such as in [11].

In future work, we aim at integrating multi-modal feature sets, for which we have already preliminary results [21]. Furthermore, we will present structural, motion and textural features to the classifier. We will apply Early Sensor Fusion in order to keep all knowledge for the final decision process and to exploit the ability of a combined feature-space optimization.

7. References

C. C. Chibelushi and F. Bourel. Facial expression recognition: A brief tutorial overview. In *CVonline: On-Line Compendium of Computer Vision*, editor Robert Fisher, January 2003. [1]

Isaac Cohen, Nicu Sebe, L. Chen, A. Garg, and T. Huang. Facial expression recognition from video sequences: Temporal and static modeling. *Computer Vision and Image Understanding (CVIU) special issue on face recognition*, 91(1-2):160–187, 2003.[2]

Jeffrey Cohn, Adena Zlochower, Jenn-Jier James Lien, and Takeo Kanade. Feature-point tracking by optical flow discriminates subtle differences in facial expression. In *Proceedings of the 3rd IEEE International Conference on Automatic Face and Gesture Recognition*, pages 396 - 401, April 1998. [3]

Jeffrey Cohn, Adena Zlochower, Jenn-Jier James Lien, and Takeo Kanade. Automated face analysis by feature point tracking has high concurrent validity with manual facs coding. *Psychophysiology*, 36:35 - 43, 1999 [4]

Tim F. Cootes and Chris J. Taylor. Active shape models - smart snakes. In *Proceedings of the 3rd British Machine VisionConference*, pages 266 - 275. Springer Verlag, 1992. [5]

G. J. Edwards, Tim F. Cootes, and Chris J. Taylor. Face recognition using active appearance models. In H. Burkhardt and Bernd Neumann, editors, *5th European Conference on Computer Vision*, volume LNCS-Series 1406-1607, pages 581-595,Freiburg, Germany, 1998. Springer-Verlag. [6]

Paul Ekman. Universals and cultural differences in facial expressions of emotion. In J. Cole, editor, *Nebraska Symposium on Motivation* 1971, volume 19, pages 207-283, Lincoln, NE, 1972. University of Nebraska Press. [7]

Paul Ekman. Facial expressions. In T. Dalgleish and M. Power, editors, *Handbook of Cognition and Emotion*, New York,1999. John Wiley & Sons Ltd. [8]

Paul Ekman and Wallace Friesen. The Facial Action Coding System: A Technique for the Measurement of Facial Movement. *Consulting Psychologists Press*, San Francisco, 1978. [9]

Irfan A. Essa and Alex P. Pentland. Coding, analysis, interpretation, and recognition of facial expressions. *IEEE Transactions on Pattern Analysis and Machine Intelligence*, 19(7):757-763, 1997. [10]

Stefan Fischer, Sven Döring, Matthias Wimmer, and Antonia Krummheuer. Experiences with an emotional sales agent. In Elisabeth Andr´e, Laila Dybkjær, Wolfgang Minker, and Paul Heisterkamp, editors, *Affective Dialogue Systems*, volume3068 of Lecture Notes in Computer Science, pages 309-312, Kloster Irsee, Germany, June 2004. Springer. [11]

Wallace V. Friesen and Paul Ekman. *Emotional Facial Action Coding System*. Unpublished manuscript, University of California at San Francisco, 1983. [12]

Robert Hanek. Fitting Parametric Curve Models to Images Using Local Self-adapting Seperation Criteria. *PhD thesis*, Department of Informatics, Technische Universität München, 2004. [13]

Curtis S. Ikehara, David N. Chin, and Martha E. Crosby. A model for integrating an adaptive information filter utilizing biosensor data to assess cognitive load. In *User Modeling*, volume 2702/2003, pages 208-212. Springer Berlin / Heidelberg, 2003. [14]

Takeo Kanade, John F. Cohn, and Yingli Tian. Comprehensive database for facial expression analysis. In *International Conference on Automatic Face and Gesture Recognition*, pages 46-53, France, March 2000. [15]

Christine L. Lisetti and Diane J. Schiano. Automatic facial expression interpretation: Where human interaction, articial intelligence and cognitive science intersect. Pragmatics and Cognition, *Special Issue on Facial Information Processing and Multidisciplinary Perspective*, 1999. [16]

Gwen Littlewort, Ian Fasel, Marian Stewart Bartlett, and Javier R. Movellan. Fully automatic coding of basic expressions from video. *Technical report*, March 2002. [17]

P. Michel and R. El Kaliouby. Real time facial expression recognition in video using support vector machines. In *Fifth International Conference on Multimodal Interfaces*, pages 258-264, Vancouver, 2003. [18]

Maja Pantic and Leon J. M. Rothkrantz. Automatic analysis of facial expressions: The state of the art. *IEEE Transactions on Pattern Analysis and Machine Intelligence*, 22(12):1424-1445, 2000. [19]

Ross Quinlan. *C4.5: Programs for Machine Learning*. Morgan Kaufmann, San Mateo, California, 1993. [20]

Björn Schuller, Matthias Wimmer, Dejan Arsic, Gerhard Rigoll, and Bernd Radig. Audiovisual behavior modeling by combined feature spaces. In *IEEE International Conference on Acoustics, Speech, and Signal Processing* (ICASSP), volume 2, pages 733-736, Honolulu, Hawaii, USA, April 2007. [21]

R. Schweiger, P. Bayerl, and Heiko Neumann. Neural architecture for temporal emotion classification. In *Affective Dialogue Systems* 2004, LNAI 3068, pages 49-52, Kloster Irsee, June 2004. Elisabeth Andre et al (Hrsg.). [22]

Nicu Sebe, Michael S. Lew, Ira Cohen, Ashutosh Garg, and Thomas S. Huang. Emotion recognition using a cauchy naïve bayes classifier. *In Proceedings of the 16th International Conference on Pattern Recognition,* volume 1, pages 17-20, Washington, DC, USA, 2002. IEEE Computer Society. [23]

Elizabeth Marie Sheldon. Virtual agent interactions. *PhD thesis,* 2001. Major Professor-Linda Malone. [24]

Ying-Li Tian, Takeo Kanade, and Jeffrey F. Cohn. Recognizing action units for facial expression analysis. *IEEE Transactions on Pattern Analysis and Machine Intelligence,* 23(2):97-115, February 2001. [25]

Rita M. Vick and Curtis S. Ikehara. Methodological issues of real time data acquisition from multiple sources of physiological data. In *Proceedings of the 36th Annual Hawaii International Conference on System Sciences,* page 129.1, Washington, DC, USA, 2003. IEEE Computer Society. [26]

Paul Viola and Michael Jones. Rapid object detection using a boosted cascade of simple features. In *Computer Vision and Pattern Recognition,* volume 1, pages 511-518, Kauai, Hawaii, 2001. [27]

Matthias Wimmer. Model-based Image Interpretation with Application to Facial Expression Recognition. *PhD thesis,* Technische Universitat M¨unchen, Institute for Informatics, December 2007. [28]

Matthias Wimmer, Freek Stulp, Sylvia Pietzsch, and Bernd Radig. Learning local objective functions for robust face model fitting. *IEEE Transactions on Pattern Analysis and Machine Intelligence* (PAMI), 30(8), 2008. to appear. [29]

Matthias Wimmer, Freek Stulp, Stephan Tschechne, and Bernd Radig. Learning robust objective functions for model fitting in image understanding applications. In Michael J. Chantler, Emanuel Trucco, and Robert B. Fisher, editors, *Proceedings of the 17th British Machine Vision Conference* (BMVC), volume 3, pages 1159-1168, Edinburgh, UK, September 2006. BMVA. [30]

Okabe, A.; Boots, B. ; and Sugihara, K. *Spatial Tessellations: Concepts and Applications of Voronoi Diagrams*, New York: Wiley, 1992 [31]

Gil Zigelman , Ron Kimmel, and Nahum Kiryati, Texture mapping using Surface Flattening via Multidimensional Scaling, *IEEE Transactions on Visualization and Computer Graphics*, vol. 8, No. 2, April-June 2002 [32]

Volker Blanz , Thomas Vetter, A morphable model for the synthesis of 3D faces, *Proceedings of the 26th annual conference on Computer graphics and interactive techniques*, p.187-194, July 1999 [33]

Stan Z. L, Anil K. J. *Handbook of Face Recognition*, Springer, 2004. [34]

Stegmann M.B., Active Appearance Models: Theory Extensions and Cases, *Master Thesis*, Technical University of Denmark, 2000. [35]

Turk M. A., Pentland A.P., Eigenfaces for Recognition, *Journal of Cognitive Neuroscience* **3** (1): 1991, pp 71-86. [36]

Cootes T.F., Edwards G.J., Taylor C.J., Active Appearance Models, *Proc. European Conference on Computer Vision* Vol. 2, pp. 484-498, Springer 1998. [37]